DATE DUE

# Prelude to Tragedy

The Negotiation and Breakdown
of the Tripartite Convention
of London, October 31, 1861

# Prelude to Tragedy

The Negotiation and Breakdown
of the Tripartite Convention
of London, October 31, 1861

By Carl H. Bock

Philadelphia
University of Pennsylvania Press

Published in Great Britain, India, and Pakistan
by the Oxford University Press
London, Bombay, and Karachi

Library of Congress Catalogue Card Number : 64–24499

7467
Printed in the United States of America

# Preface

THE TRAGEDY OF MAXIMILIAN'S REIGN IN MEXICO HAS ALWAYS interested both professional historians and the general reading public. Before World War I the persons connected in one way or another with Maximilian published many diaries, memoirs, and reminiscences. Usually these works began with Maximilian's departure for Mexico. The outlines of the background of the "adventure," as one historian has labelled the affair, could be found in documents published by the Powers concerned. Many documents were published by the Spanish Government. A few historical accounts, based on these documents, were written, notably by Leonardon. The British Government published a very large number of documents, made readily available in the "blue books." These sources formed the basis of several important studies, perhaps the most extensive by Burke. The French "yellow books" contained very few documents, edited with a view to veiling French motives. The Austrian Government maintained even a greater secrecy. Although the published diplomatic correspondence of the United States and Mexico was more extensive, there was very little that could furnish an authoritative background of Maximilian's candidacy. All these published sources constituted the

5

bases of the "standard" histories of Maximilian. In this connection,, deserving of special mention are La Gorce, Ollivier,
and Delord.

After World War I the Austrian republic permitted scholars
to view the documents kept secret by the Austrian imperial
regime. The result was an authoritative and scholarly study of
Maximilian, written in biography form, by Corti. Corti's
research was largely duplicated by Dawson, who tried to place
Maximilian's candidacy within a framework of the diplomacy
of the European Powers. Although Dawson supplemented his
research in the *Haus-Hof-und Staatsarchiv* in Vienna with
some research in the Public Record Office in London, Dawson
relied primarily on printed documents for the Mexican policies
of the Powers for the critical period of 1861–1862. The
archives of Vienna furnished materials for other scholars to
write special, but important, histories. Salomon wrote a biographical and diplomatic study of Metternich, the Austrian
Ambassador to Paris who was utilized as the medium between
Maximilian and Napoleon III. Countess Reinach Foussemagne
wrote an "official" biography of Charlotte, Maximilian's wife.
These scholarly works were popularized in the writings of
Sencourt, Guedalla, and Hyde.

The negotiation of the Tripartite Convention of London in
1861 by Great Britain, France, and Spain was a diplomatic
prelude to the establishment of Maximilian in Mexico. Osten-
sibly negotiated for the purpose of obtaining satisfaction from
Mexico for claims of British, French, and Spanish subjects, the
Convention of London was the diplomatic means by which
Napoleon III attempted to prepare the way for Maximilian's
throne in Mexico. I have attempted to trace the background,
the negotiation, and the breakdown of the Convention of
London in order to supplement the findings of the scholars
who have contributed so much to a knowledge of the origins
of Maximilian's candidacy by research in the *Haus-Hof-und*

*Staatsarchiv*. I have utilized the documents in the Public Record Office in London and in the *Archives du ministère des affaires étrangères* in Paris.

Although the Tripartite Convention of London is the subject of an article based on research in the Public Record Office, Robertson was primarily interested in the Embassy Archives of Lord Cowley, the British Ambassador to Paris. The draft instructions to Cowley, often with marginal notations and more than one version, have enabled me, I believe, to obtain more detailed information than was found by Robertson, who read the final versions of instructions sent to Cowley. Although Robertson discovered a British draft convention, there were others, filed in a volume of miscellaneous documents. As with other important documents, I have made copies of the British draft conventions and placed them in appendices. In addition to the British official diplomatic correspondence with France, my research in the Public Record Office involved the diplomatic correspondence with Spain, Austria, Mexico, and the United States. Although many of these documents have been published in the "blue books," many confidential documents were never published. For the military aspects of the British intervention in Mexico in cooperation with Spain and France, provided for by the Convention of London, I have found the correspondence between the British Foreign Office and the British Admiralty useful. Special sources consulted were the Russell Papers and the Cowley Papers in the Public Record Office. The former were made available to scholars in 1927, the latter in 1948 and 1952. The wealth of information contained in these private letter collections is invaluable. There are many private letters other than those exchanged by Lord Cowley and Lord Russell, the British Secretary for Foreign Affairs. I have also utilized the private collections of Palmerston Papers in the British Museum and in the possession of the Mountbatten family. A critical outline of the primary sources, both archive and printed, and works cited is contained in my "Sources Consulted." To avoid confusion, I have placed the details of the British, French, and Spanish claims against Mexico in explanatory appendices.

An account of the negotiation of the Convention of London, based on sources in the *Archives du ministère des affairs ètrangères* in Paris, has been written by Schefer, who has summarized the French draft convention. Unfortunately Shefer's study is almost completely devoid of footnote references to the documents he used. I have utilized the same documents forming the basis of Schefer's *La Grande Pensée,* but I have given complete references. The French draft convention is included in my appendices of documents.

I have attempted to place the origins of Maximilian's candidacy within a framework of the Mexican policies of the European Powers from 1861, when the Convention of London was negotiated, until 1862, when that convention was suspended. For the Mexican policy of Austria I have incorporated the findings of Corti and Dawson. For the Mexican policy of the United States, invited to join the European Powers in the intervention in Mexico, I am indebted to Callahan, Rippy, Owsley, and Perkins, whose pioneer works were based largely on the documents of the archives of the State Department of the United States. For the Mexican policy of the Confederacy I have found useful the works of Hendrick, Adams, Sears, and Owsley. My conclusions about the Mexican policy of Spain are tentative, because I have not done any research in the Spanish archives. Such research would form the basis of a study independent of, and yet supplementary to, the present one. Important studies of the Mexican policy of Spain, based on published Spanish documents, have been written by Leonardon. I have consulted the same documents and the speeches in the Cortes for 1861–1862, translations of which were made by the staff of the British Ambassador to Madrid. The reports of the British and French diplomatic representatives in Spain, moreover, permit a reconstruction of the Mexican policy of Spain as it was made known to the British and French Governments. The reports of the four British and French military and diplomatic commissioners in Mexico in 1862 during the allied intervention form the basis of what the British and French Governments knew about the actions and opinions of General Prim, the Spanish representative in Mexico during allied operations in Mexico in 1862.

The main emphasis of the present study is on the Mexican policies of Great Britain and France. In particular this study is concerned with the motives of Lord Palmerston and his Foreign Secretary, Lord Russell, on the British side, and on the motives of Napoleon III, Eugenie, and their Minster of Foreign Affairs, Thouvenel, on the French side. Such a narrow scope can be justified, because Napoleon and Eugenie adopted policies and continued to implement them even when French public opinion, as shown by an excellent study by Professor Case, opposed imperial policy. Palmerston and Russell, on the other hand, seldom consulted their fellow cabinet members, and the result was that the Mexican policy of Great Britain in 1861–1862 was almost entirely the result of the exchange of ideas between Palmerston and Russell. Palmerston, Russell, Napoleon III, Eugenie, and Thouvenel did not formulate Mexican policies in a vacuum. The present study is an attempt to discover just what information was available upon which high policy was based. In addition to the reports from diplomatic representatives in Mexico and the official exchange of correspondence among European Powers, there were groups with vested interests that supplied information and put pressure on the European Powers. Foremost among these vested interests were the Mexican *émigrés* and exiles, who tried to encourage a European intervention in Mexico for the establishment of a monarchy. Other groups that affected the Mexican policies of the European Powers were holders of various Mexican bonds and other claimants demanding redress of grievances from Mexico. I have attempted to evaluate the influence of these various pressure groups. I have neither intended to evaluate the influence of public opinion in general, nor to delve into the complexities of the internal affairs of the Powers that intervened in Mexico. When a particular article of a newspaper or a specific issue of internal affairs was mentioned in the diplomatic correspondence, however, I have tried to determine the importance of such factors on diplomacy.

Chapter I serves as an introduction to the Mexican policies of the European Powers and the United States before 1861. The next chapter describes the crisis in Mexico in 1861 that led to the negotiation of the Convention of London. The chapter is divided into sections, each describing how particular diplomatic representatives accredited to the Mexican Government viewed that crisis and what recommendations they made. The negotiation of the Convention of London is covered in Chapter III. Chapter IV describes the way the signatories of the Convention of London intended to carry out the terms of that convention and how the allied expeditionary forces arrived in Mexico. The next chapter describes the first difficulties, both in Mexico and in Europe. Chapter VI relates how the Convention of London was suspended, first in Mexico and then in Europe. Chapter VII contains conclusions.

I am indebted to numerous individuals and institutions for their encouragement and assistance. Professor Lynn M. Case of the University of Pennsylvania first interested me in Napoleon III. I am especially indebted to Professor Fritz Wagner, of Philipps-Universität in Marburg/Lahn, Germany. It was under his direction and with his encouragement that I have prepared this study. His advice and patience have been the primary reasons that I have been able to complete the present study. Further assistance was given me by Professor

Wolfgang Abendroth, also of Philipps-Universität. Special mention must also be made of my wife, who assisted with stylistic suggestions. The staffs of the following archives and libraries were also helpful : Bibliothèque Nationale, the Public Record Office in London, the *Archives du ministère des affaires étrangères* in Paris, the British Museum in London, the private archives of the Mountbatten family, and the libraries of the University of Pennsylvania and of Philipps-Universität. Unpublished Crown-copyright material in the Public Record Office, London, has been reproduced by the kind permission of the Controller of H.M. Stationery Office

# Contents

Preface      5

Abbreviations      17

I.   Mexico, the United States, and Europe, 1821–1860    25
    1. Monarchist Intrigue, 1821–1857    25
    2. The United States and the Mexican Civil War, 1857–1860    32
    3. Europe and the Mexican Civil War, 1857–1860    38

II.   The Diplomatic Crisis in Mexico in 1861    64
    1. Mathew and Wyke in Mexico in 1861    64
    2. Saligny in Mexico in 1861    94
    3. Corwin and Pickett in Mexico in 1861    115

III.   The Negotiation of the Tripartite Convention of London    122
    1. The Immediate Background: the Mexican Policies of the European Powers, January–August 1861    122
    2. The Negotiation of the Tripartite Convention of London, Part I, September 1861    140
    3. The Negotiation of the Tripartite Convention of London, Part II, October 1861    169

13

IV.   The Beginnings of the European Intervention in
        Mexico                                                    216
        1. The Instructions of the Allies to Their Diplo-
           matic Representatives and Commanders-
           in-Chief                                               216
        2. The Arrival of the European Expeditionary
           Forces in Mexico: European and American
           reactions                                              254
        3. The Intrigues of the Mexican Exiles, Octo-
           ber–December 1861                                      280

V.    The First Disagreements Among the European
        Powers After the Arrival of the Allied Expe-
        ditionary Forces in Mexico                                293
        1. The Negotiations of the European Repre-
           sentatives in Mexico, January–February
           1862                                                   293
        2. Maximilian and Negotiations Among the
           European Powers, December 1861–Febru-
           ary 1862                                               336
        3. The Reactions of the European Powers to the
           Initial Negotiations of their Representa-
           tives in Mexico                                        365

VI.   The Breakdown of the Convention of London          404
        1. The Breakdown of the Convention of London
           in Mexico                                              404
        2. The Breakdown of the Convention of Lon-
           don in Europe                                          430

VII.  Conclusions                                                 443

Explanatory Appendices
    Appendix A: The British Convention Bondholders,
        1842–1861                                                 453
    Appendix B: The London Bondholders, 1823–1861     458
    Appendix C: Morny, Saligny, and the Jecker Bonds   475
        1847–1861                                                 485
    Appendix D: Spanish Claims against Mexico,

Appendices of Documents

Appendix E : Saligny–Zarco Convention, 26 March 1861 (Never ratified) 491

Appendix F : Napoleon III to Count Flahault, Palais de Compiègne, (9) October 1861 495

Appendix G : (First) British Draft Convention, undated, communicated to Thouvenel by Cowley, 15 October 1861 498

Appendix H : Note by the Lord Chancellor on the (First) British Draft Convention, 17 October 1861, marked "For the cabinet" and marginal note by Lord Russell 502

Appendix I : First Version of (Second) British Draft Convention, undated, with marginal alterations indicated, and notes by Palmerston, Hammond, and Russell indicating the originators of these alterations 505

Appendix J : Final Version of (Second) British Draft Convention, 21 October 1861, communicated to Flahault by Russell, 22 October 1861 510

Appendix K : French Counter Proposal (to First British Draft Convention), undated, communicated to Russell by Flahault, 22 October 1861 514

Appendix L : Convention between Her Majesty (the Queen of the Kingdom of Great Britain and Ireland), the Queen of Spain and the Emperor of the French relative to Combined Operations Against Mexico, signed at London, 31 October 1861 (Ratifications exchanged at London, 15 November 1861) 517

Appendix M : Thouvenel's Confidential Instructions to Admiral Jurien de La Gravière, Paris, 11 November 1861 521

Appendix N : Collantes' Instructions to General Juan Prim, 17 November 1861 525

Appendix O : Convention between Her Britannic Majesty and the Republic of Mexico for the Settlement of Various Questions now pending between the Two Governments, signed at

Mexico City, 21 November 1861 (Never rati-
fied)                                                    532

Appendix P: Proclamation of the Allied Commissioners to the Mexican People, Vera Cruz, 10
January 1862                                             537

Appendix Q: Dubois de Saligny's Proposed Ultimatum, Vera Cruz, 10 January 1862                       539

Appendix R: Preliminaries of La Soledad, 19 February 1862                                              543

Appendix S: Protocol of the Twelfth Conference
of the Allied Commissioners, Vera Cruz, 19
February 1862                                           545

Appendix T: Protocol of the Final Conference of
the Allied Commissioners, Orizaba, 9 April 1862    555

Appendix U: J(uan) H(idalgo) to F(rancisco) de
A(rrangoiz), Paris, 18 April 1862                       571

Appendix V: The Intercepted Jecker Correspondence                                                579

Notes                                                   599

Index                                                   793

# Abbreviations

ABBOTT — James S. C. Abbott: *The History of Napoleon III, Emperor of the French, Including a brief narrative of all the most important events which have occurred in Europe Since the fall of Napoleon I Until the present time. Boston,* 1869.

AD — *Archives Diplomatiques: Recueil De Diplomatie et D'Histoire.* Published under the auspices of the French Ministry of Foreign Affairs. Paris, 1861 ff.

AKM — Archiv Kaiser Max.

ALBE — Duc d'Albe, ed.: *Lettres Familières de L'Impératrice Eugénie Conservées dans Les Archives du Palais de Liria.* 2 v., Paris, 1935.

BAILEY — Thomas A. Bailey: *A Diplomatic History of the American People.* 4th ed., New York, 1950.

BANCROFT — Hubert Howe Bancroft: *History of Mexico.* 6 v., San Francisco, 1883–1889.

BEYENS — Baron Napoléon Beyens: *Le Second Empire vu par un Diplomate Belge.* 2 v., Paris, 1925.

BSP — "Correspondence Respecting the Affairs of Mexico: Presented to both Houses of Parliament by Command of Her Majesty, 1862," *British Sessional Papers,* 1862, LXIV. (University of Pennsylvania microfilms.)

BURKE — Ulick Ralph Burke : *A Life of Benito Juarez, Constitutional President of Mexico.* London and Sydney, 1894.

CASE — "The Case of the Holders of Bonds of the National Debt contracted by Mexico in London," 22 Nov., 1861, encl. of Committee of Mexican Bondholders to Russell, 10 Basinghall St., London, 23 (r. 26) Nov. 1861, London, Public Record Office, F. O. 97/289.

CORTI — Count Egon Caesar Corti : *Maximilian and Charlotte of Mexico,* trans. Catherine Alison Phillips, 2 v., New York, 1928.

DAWSON — Daniel Dawson : *The Mexican Adventure.* London, 1935.

DD — *Documents diplomatiques (Livres jaunes).* Published by the French Ministry of Foreign Affairs. Paris, 1861 ff.

DOMENECH — Emmanuel Domenech : *Histoire du Mexique, Juarez et Maximilien: Correspondences Inédites des Présidents, Ministres et Généraux Almonte, Santa-Anna, Gutierrez, Miramon, Marquez, Mejia, Woll, etc., etc. de Juarez, de l'Empereur Maximilien et de l'Impératrice Charlotte, par Emmanuel Domenech, Ancien Directeur de la Presse du Cabinet de l'Empereur Maximilien, ex-aumônier de l'Armée Français du Mexique.* 3 v., Paris, 1868.

DUVERNOIS — Clement Duvernois : *L'Intervention Française au Mexique, Accompagnée de Documents Inédits et d'un long Mémoire addressé par l'Empereur Maximilian á l'Empereur Napoleon et rémis à Paris par l'Impératrice Charlotte: Précedée d'une Preface de Clement Duvernois.* 2 v., Paris, 1868.

ESSLINGER — Elisabet Esslinger : *Kaiserin Eugenie und die Politik des zweiten Kaisserreichs.* Stuttgart, 1932.

F.O. — Foreign Office.

FOUSSEMAGNE — Comtesse H. Reinach Foussemagne : *Charlotte de Belgique. Impératrice du Mexique*. Paris, 1925.

GAULOT — Paul Gaulot : *La Vérité sur l'Expédition du Mexique d'après les Documents Inédits de Ernest Louet, Payeur en Chef du Corps Expeditionnaire: Rêve d'Empire, par Paul Gaulot*. Paris, 1889.

GUERARD — Albert Guerard : *Napoleon III*. Cambridge, Mass., 1943.

HAHR — *Hispanic American Historical Review*.

HALLER — Elizabeth Haller : *Aspects of American Opinion Regarding Maximilian's Empire in Mexico*. M. A. Thesis presented to the Faculty of the Graduate School of the University of Pennsylvania in 1940.

HENDRICK — Burton Jesse Hendrick : *Statesmen of the Lost Cause: Jefferson Davis and His Cabinet*. Boston, 1939.

HHSA — *Haus-Hof-und Staats Archiv*.

HUBNER — Graf Joseph Alexander Von Hübner : *Neuf Ans de Souvenirs D'Un Ambassadeur D'Autriche A Paris sous Le Second Empire, 1851–1859, Publiés Par Son Fils, Le comte Alexandre de Hüber*. 2 v., Paris, 1940.

HYDE — H. Montgomery Hyde : *Mexican Empire: The History of Maximilian and Carlota of Mexico*. London, 1946.

LALLY — Frank Edward Lally : *French Opposition to the Mexican Policy of the Second Empire*. (Johns Hopkins University Studies in Historical and Political Science, Series XLIX, No. 3.) Baltimore, 1931.

MANNING — William R. Manning, ed. : *Diplomatic Correspondence of the United States: Inter-American Affairs, 1831–1860*. 12 v., Washington, 1932–1939.

MDAE : *CP* — Paris, Ministère des affaires étrangères, *correspondance politique*.

MEXICAN NATIONAL DEBT — *Mexican National Debt, Contracted in London. Decrees and Regulations Since the*

*Adjustment of October 14th/December 23rd, 1860.*
London, 1860. Copy filed in London, Public Record
Office, F. O. 5/359.

MONAGHAN— Jay Monaghan : *Diplomat in Carpet Slippers:
Abraham Lincoln Deals with Foreign Affairs.* Indianapolis and New York, 1945.

MONTLUC— Armand de Montluc : *Correspondance de Juarez
et de Montluc, Ancien Consul General du Mexique,
Accompagnée de Nombreuses Lettres de Personnages
Politiques Relative a L'Expedition Du Mexique,* ed.
Leon de Montluc. Paris, 1885.

MOORE— John Bassett Moore, ed. : *A Digest of International
Law, as embodied in Diplomatic Discussions, Treaties
and Other International Agreements, International
Awards, The Decisions of Municipal Courts, and the
Writings of Jurists, and especially in Documents, Pub-
lished and Unpublished, Issues of Presidents and
Secretaries of State of the United States, the Opinions
of the Attorneys-General, and the Decisions of Courts,
Federal and State.* 8 v., Washington, 1906.

MUSSER— John Musser : *The Establishment of Maximilian's
Empire in Mexico: A Thesis Presented to the Faculty
of the Graduate School of the University of Pennsylvania in Partial Fulfillment of the Requirements for
the Degree of Doctor of Philosophy.* Menasha, 1918.

OLLIVIER— Emile Ollivier : *L'Empire Libéral: Etudes, Récits,
Souvenirs.* 18 v., Paris, 1895–1912.

OWSLEY— Frank Lawrence Owsley : *King Cotton Diplomacy:
Foreign Relations of the Confederate States of America.*
Chicago, 1931.

PALEOLOGUE— Maurice Paléologue : *The Tragic Empress:
Intimate Conversations with the Empress Eugenie,
1901 to 1911,* trans. Hamish Miles, London, n.d.

PERKINS—Dexter Perkins: *The Monroe Doctrine, 1826–1867*. Baltimore, 1933.

PRIM—H. Leonardon: *Prim*. Paris, 1901.

Prim—Senate—9 Dec. 1862;

Prim—Senate—9 Dec. 1862; Prim—Senate—10 Dec. 1862; Prim—Senate—11 Dec. 1862

Prim's speeches before Senate of the Cortes, 9–11 Dec. 1862, trans., into English from *Diario de las Sesiones de Cortes*, encl. 2 of Crampton to Russell, Madrid, No. 417, 27 (r. 31) Dec. 1862, London, Public Record Office, F.O. 72/1040.

PRO—London, Public Record Office.

REPORT—*Report of the Commission of Public Credit of the Mexican Chamber of Deputies on the Adjustment of the English Debt. Dated April 1st, 1850*. Translated from the Spanish. London, 1850. Copy filed in PRO, F.O. 97/273.

ROBERTSON—David Robertson: *The "Mexican Bondholders." Letters of Messrs. McCalmont, Brothers, & Co., and Reply thereto, by David Robertson, Esq., M.P., Honorary Chairman*. London, 1861. Copy filed in PRO, F.O. 97/280.

ROMERO—Mathias Romero, ed.: *Correspondencia de la Legacion Mexicana en Washington Durante La Intervencion Extranjera, 1860–1868: Collection de Documentos Para Formar La Historia de la Intervencion*. 10 v., Mexico City, 1870–1892.

SALOMON—Henry Salomon: *L'Ambassade de Richard De Metternich A Paris*. Paris, 1931.

SCHEFER—Christian Schefer: *La Grande Pensée de Napoleon III: Les Origines de l'Expedition du Mexique (1858–1862)*. Paris, 1939.

SENIOR—Nassau Senior: *Conversations with Distinguished Persons During the Second Empire from 1860 to 1863 by the Late Nassau Senior,* ed. M.C.M. Simpson, 2 v., London, 1880.

STERN — Alfred Stern : *Geschichte Europas von 1848 bis 1871.* 10 v., Stuttgart and Berlin, 1894–1924.

THOUVENEL — L. Thouvenel, ed. : *Le secret de l'Empereur. Correspondance confidentielle et inédite exchangée entre M. Thouvenel, Le Duc de Gramont et le General Comte de Flahault, 1860–1862.* 2 v., Paris, 1889.

VERDUIN — Arnold Robert Verduin : *Modern Spanish Constitutions (1808–1931): A dissertation submitted in partial fulfillment of the requirements for the degree of Doctor of Philosophy in the University of Michigan.* Typescript, University of Michigan, 1934.

WEST — W. Reed West : *Contemporary French Opinion on the American Civil War.* (Johns Hopkins University Studies in Historical and Political Science, Series XLII, No. 1.) Baltimore, 1924.

WHITE MEMORANDUM — Memorandum, Mexico City, 22 May, 1862, prepared by Mr. White, encl. of Wyke to Russell, Mexico City, No. 71, 22 May (r. 28 Jul) 1862, PRO, F.O. 97/280.

# Prelude to Tragedy

### The Negotiation and Breakdown of the Tripartite Convention of London, October 31, 1861

# I
# Mexico, the United States, and Europe, 1821 - 1857

## 1. MONARCHIST INTRIGUE, 1821–1857

THE ARCHTYPE OF A MEXICAN EXILE SEEKING A EUROPEAN TO place on a throne to be erected in Mexico was Don Jose Maria Gutierrez de Estrada. In 1821, the very year that Mexico obtained independence from Spain,[1] he was a member of a delegation that offered the crown of Mexico to the Archduke Charles of Austria.[2] This offer, however, was contrary to Metternich's conceptions of "Legitimacy."[3] At any rate, the Archduke declined, and Estrada returned to Mexico. His interest in politics continued, and he became Senator in 1833 and Minister of Foreign Affairs in 1834.[4] He did not approve of a change of government in 1836 and left Mexico for Europe.[5] Returning in 1840, he was ". . . struck by the terrible changes that those four years had produced." For Estrada it seemed that wealth, cultivation, "almost civilisation, had disappeared." The Americans had been driving the Mexicans out of Texas without serious resistance from the "successive ephemeral governments." Estrada became convinced of Mexico's "utter unfitness for republican government." He published an open letter to President Bustamante, urging Mexi-

25

cans to return to monarchy, "the only government under which, bad as our monarchy had been, we had enjoyed anything resembling prosperity or tranquility."[6] This monarchist proposal forced Estrada into exile. He spent a year in Cuba and then went to Europe,[7] a perpetual exile, passionately clinging with blind devotion to his dream of a Mexican monarchy. His ideas and arguments never changed after 1840. Monarchy would put a stop to revolutions and anarchy by the establishment of order and stability. Without monarchy, Mexico would pass into barbarism, and all civilization would end. A monarchy, moreover, would prevent American absorption of all Mexico. This was the core of Estrada's creed, and he remained inflexible, refusing to believe that "ideas contrary to his own" made progress in Mexico.[8]

Shortly after his arrival in Europe, in 1842, Estrada urged Lord Aberdeen, the British Secretary of Foreign Affairs, to undertake the establishment of a Mexican monarchy. In this way, Estrada urged, British possessions in Central America would be safeguarded from annexation by the United States, and Great Britain would contribute to the "regeneration" of Mexico. According to the Mexican exile, he was able to "count on the sympathies of Lord Aberdeen."[9]

In January 1846 Estrada obtained an interview with Metternich and gained the impression that Austria would furnish Mexico with a monarch.[10] In March Estrada wrote the Austrian Chancellor that Mexico needed stable government to maintain its independence from ". . . the ambitious Republic of North America." Embroidering his argument, Estrada declared that such a government would stimulate Austrian trade with Mexico and represent the extension of European principles of conservatism to Mexico[11] A few weeks later Estrada again wrote Metternich, as "the great protector of order and religion," to rescue a Mexico slipping into anarchy.[12] In April Estrada secured another interview with Metternich but was unable to obtain any definite pledge.[13] Sixteen years later Estrada asserted that with the acquiescence of Metternich the Mexican throne was proposed to Archduke Frederick, who was willing to accept it.[14] Supposedly Louis Philippe himself "embraced the plan cordially—almost eagerly."[15] In all probability, however, the passing years had played tricks with Estrada's memory, and he mistook sympathy for proffered aid[16] But he did recall that Lord Clarendon was unwilling to move.

> He also approved of my plans, but urged the importance of avoiding raising the jealousy of the United States. The Monroe Doctrine was then in vigour, and he would do nothing which might be construed as an attack on it.[17]

Estrada blamed the failure of his efforts in 1846 on the affair of the Spanish marriages, which destroyed the alliance between France and Great Britain and put an end to any hope of allied action by them.[18] More important, however, was French[19] and British[20] unwillingness to risk war with a United States that had just reaffirmed the Monroe Doctrine.[21]

Several times between 1846 and 1851 Estrada approached Lord Palmerston, then British Foreign Secretary. Recalling these visits in 1861, Palmerston lumped the proposals of "people from Mexico" (not named) with those of Estrada, who came to him "repeatedly." Finding the Duke of Cambridge among the candidates, Palmerston said the Duke was out of the question. When Palmerston asked about the practicability of the scheme, "it came out that they required a Prince of a reigning European family, many millions sterling, and 20,000 European troops to give any chance of success."[22]

Estrada's contribution to the monarchist cause in 1847 was a pamphlet imploring Europe to take steps to save Mexico.[23] Copies were sent to prominent persons, including Louis Philippe and Lord Palmerston.[24] But then came the Revolutions of 1848, and "Europe was too agitated for any one to care" about Mexico and American affairs.[25]

In 1850 Estrada, while in Rome, met Jose Manuel Hidalgo

y Esnaurrizar, Secretary of the Mexican Legation at the Papal Court.[26] They struck up a friendship, and soon Hidalgo was an ardent supporter of Mexican monarchy. Hidalgo was of pure Spanish blood and closely related to aristocratic families in Spain. He was popular in diplomatic and court circles of Europe.[27] Already, or soon after meeting Estrada, Hidalgo was able to frequent the house of the Teba family, where he met the Countess of Montijo, whose daughter Eugenie was to become Empress of the French in 1853.[28]

Santa Anna became President of Mexico for the sixth time in April 1853.[29] Fears of the United States led him to make diplomatic feelers in Europe with a view to obtaining alliances.[30] Approaches were made to the British[31] and French[32] Ministers to Mexico, and treaties of alliance proposed. It was made known that Santa Anna favored a Mexican monarchy, guaranteed by Europe. Great Britain flatly refused,[33] and France would not go beyond offering "good offices."[34] An attempt to secure Prussian military aid was likewise fruitless.[35] Finally, the attempt to obtain a Spanish alliance was without result.[36]

Estrada's activities in Europe had come to the attention of Santa Anna, who now declared his "confidence in the patriotism, the merits, and the devotion" of Estrada and granted him full powers" that he may enter into negotiations with the courts of Paris, Vienna, London, and Madrid, to make . . . overtures . . . for . . . the establishment of a monarchy derived from one of the dynastic houses of these Powers."[37] Now Estrada was an official roving ambassador, not just a refugee. He chose Hidalgo as his assistant.[38] Together they went to Spain in 1854, where the name of the Enfant Don Juan was put forward.[39] According to a statement made by Estrada seven years later, the Spanish Ministry was on the point of adopting his plan, when it was suddenly overthrown by a revolution.[40] Hidalgo, however, did not return to Rome, but obtained a transfer of diplomatic duties to Madrid.[41] He was soon on terms of close friendship with Countess de Montijo, Empress Eugenie's mother.[42]

In August 1855, another revolution in Mexico caused Santa
Anna himself to become an exile, and the conservative interests
supporting monarchy were replaced by liberal groupings.
Estrada was a private person again. The orientation of Mexican foreign affairs was now towards the United States, rather
than to the Old World.[43] The exiles, however, continued to
advocate monarchy.

In early 1856 Tomas Murphy, a former Mexican Minister
to London, attempted to enlist the cooperation of France for
a plan to establish a monarchy under the joint guarantee
of France, Great Britain, and Spain. In February he wrote a
memorandum to the French Ministry of Foreign Affairs,
urging that the combined efforts of France and Great Britain
could put an end to the Monroe Doctrine.[44] In March he was
writing Napoleon III that Mexico could be saved from the
disorder that put it at the mercy of the United States by
establishing a monarchy placed under the joint guarantee of
France, Great Britain, and Spain. The sovereign should be,
if possible, Spanish, or at least Catholic.[45]

In late 1856 the French Minister to Mexico, the Comte de
Gabriac, in cooperation with a self-exile from the Napoleon
Regime, the Marquis de Radepont,[46] put in motion a scheme
to place the Duc D'Aumale on a Mexican throne with the aid
to be supplied by Great Britain and France. In September De
Gabriac wrote his Foreign Office to recommend French intervention in Mexico to establish a monarchy. France had checked
Russian ambitions in Asia and should put a check to demagogic
passions in the United States.[47]

On 15 September 1856 De Gabriac paid a visit to Mr.
Lettsom, the British Minister to Mexico. Mr. Lettsom was told
that the Mexicans could not rule themselves, and this would
lead to Mexico's falling to the ambitions of the United States.
A monarchy in Mexico would prevent it. Furthermore, the
great majority of Mexicans would cordially welcome the
change. The only problem was finding a prince. De Gabriac
could think of no one with the qualifications of religion, char-

acter, age, and rank except the Duc D'Aumale, the son of
former King Louis Philippe. The only question was whether
he would consent, for no great amount of material aid would
be necessary to establish him in Mexico. This aid could be supplied by Great Britain and France. The United States might be
offended, but it would be presented with a *fait accompli*. A
few days later, in answer to an inquiry from Mr. Lettsom
whether the plan was approved by the French Government,
De Gabriac replied that he had "not heard from his Government" and had "only entered upon the subject because he was
convinced of its supreme importance."[48]

In October 1856 De Gabriac's emissary, the Marquis de
Radepont, arrived in Paris. He saw Count Walewski, the
French Minister of Foreign Affairs, and left him a written
plan. The future monarchy would be "constitutional." The
sovereign would be designated by Napoleon III, and France
and Great Britain would lend their "moral force," nothing
more. Verbally Radepont asked for an audience with
Napoleon III.[49]

Mr. Lettsom's report of De Gabriac's proposals reached the
British Foreign Office on 15 November 1856.[50] Three days
later Lord Clarendon answered Lettsom to make clear that
Great Britain could be no party to any such plan.[51] About a
week later Lord Cowley, the British Ambassador to Paris,
introduced the subject in a conversation with Count Walewski,
who claimed the candidacy of the Duc D'Aumale had no
official French backing.[52]

In early December Radepont went to London, but he
received a blunt refusal of support for the plan from Lord
Clarendon.[53] Radepont returned to Paris and secured an interview with Napoleon III. Lord Cowley reported that Napoleon
expressed sympathy with Radepont's cause, but the Emperor
was careful not to promise material aid. If the Duc D'Aumale
"liked to try his chances," Napoleon said he had no objection
and would hear of the Duke's success "with satisfaction."
Radepont was authorized to say as much to the Duc D'Aumale.

Zuloaga Government for the cession of territory." Failing in his negotiations,[18] Forsyth attempted to justify the seizure of Mexican territory as compensation for claims of American citizens[19] against Mexico. The American Minister reasoned that Mexico actually would benefit:

> You want Sonora? The American blood spilled near its line would justify you in seizing it . . . . You want other territory? Send me the power to make an ultimate demand for the several millions Mexico owes our people for spoliations and personal wrongs . . . . You want the Tehuantepec transit? Say to Mexico, "Nature has placed that shortest highway between two oceans, so necessary to the commerce of the world, in your keeping. You will not open it yourself nor allow others to open it to the wants of mankind. You cannot be permitted to act the dog in the manger . . . . Give us what we ask for in return for the manifest benefits we propose to confer upon you for it, or we will take it."[20]

Forsyth's hostility to the Zuloaga Government increased to such an extent that, when a tax was imposed on capital in May 1858, he broke diplomatic relations with Mexico on his own initiative.[21] In September he received instructions ratifying his action and directing him to return to the United States.[22]

Before a resumption of diplomatic relations with Mexico was attempted, rumors became prevalent in Mexico that Spain intended an expedition against Mexico.[23] Secretary of State Cass even received reports that Spain sought to acquire "political ascendancy" in Mexico.[24] In the past such war scares had not been entirely groundless. In 1856 the Spanish fleet had demonstrated before Vera Cruz to put pressure on Mexico to recognize debts to Spain.[25] In 1857 Spain had demanded an indemnity for several murdered Spaniards and, when this was not forthcoming, had severed diplomatic relations with Mexico.[26] The disputed questions were still pending in 1858.[27] Cass was worried enough that he instructed the American Minister to Madrid to bring the Monroe Doctrine to the attention of the Spanish Minister of Foreign Relations. He was

Radepont at once left for Spain, where the Duke was residing.[54] In February 1857 Cowley reported that Radepont had seen the Duc D'Aumale and had "received such assurances from His Royal Highness as led him to believe that the Duke would not refuse to become King of Mexico if the throne was (*sic*) offered to him by the country." Radepont then returned to Mexico with every hope of success,[55] but the plot miscarried. At Compiègne, in the fall of 1858, Napoleon III told Hidalgo that the Duc D'Aumale had refused the offer.[56]

Radepont's departure did not leave the Mexican monarchists unrepresented in Europe. Estrada became active again. He feared the severing of diplomatic relations between Mexico and Spain would lead to war and sought French intervention to prevent Spain from destroying Mexican "nationality."[57] In April 1857 he arrived in Paris and had a conversation with Walewski. Estrada explained that, as a monarchist, he wished to ascertain the probable attitude of France, should an attempt be made to establish a monarchy in Mexico. Walewski replied that the French government could enter into no engagement whatsoever in regard to any responsibilities in Mexico without previous consultation with other Powers, particularly Great Britain.[58] Estrada went on to London, interviewed Lord Clarendon, but the Mexican exile received no greater encouragement than had Radepont.[59]

In June 1857 Estrada spoke with Napoleon III and left him a long memorandum stating the familiar arguments for European intervention in Mexico to establish a monarchy.[60] Napoleon sympathized, but he would not take the initiative without England.[61] These efforts of Estrada in 1857, which for a time "held out some promise of success," only resulted in fresh disappointment for him.[62] In search of a "friendly and powerful hand to aid Mexico," he had to admit that his efforts of 1846, 1854, and 1857, while leading him to believe himself on the verge of success, were all in vain. Estrada blamed it on "unforeseen circumstances" that "always intervened."[63]

## 2. THE UNITED STATES AND THE MEXICAN CIVIL WAR, 1857–1860

The overthrow of Santa Anna in 1855 was followed by a period of liberal reforms, aimed at reducing the powers of the Church[1] and the Executive. As a reaction to the dictatorial Santa Anna, the Constitution of February 1857 provided for a strong legislature and a weak executive.[2] Fearing that Mexico in this state of transition was too weak to resist European interference, the American Minister to Mexico, John Forsyth, determined to acquire Mexican territory so that American influence in Mexico would become so strong that Europe would not attempt to challenge the Monroe Doctrine. Not being able to gain territory at once, Forsyth did the "next best thing, which was to pave the way for the acquisition hereafter."[3] In February 1857 he completed a loan treaty with Mexico.[4] He considered it a species of floating mortgage on Mexican territory that would be foreclosed "peaceably."[5] This loan treaty, however, was not submitted to the United States Senate for ratification,[6] as Forsyth, in his eagerness, had overstepped his instructions.[7]

Defending his policy, Forsyth called upon the Monroe Doctrine, "Manifest Destiny," fears of French and British intervention, and humanitarianism as arguments in favor of assuring American hegemony in Mexico:

Whether Mexico maintains her nationality, or falls to pieces, we have a deep interest in her future, and should secure an influence in her counsels. If she cannot stand without the aid of some friendly power . . . what Power is it that should occupy the commanding position of benefactor and friend? If the United States refuse, some other must. What if it comes in the form of a French Prince, supported by ten thousand bayonets? Or of British gold, effecting that floating mortgage on her territories, which we decline? Believe me Sir, we cannot play the "dog in the manger" with our Monroe Doctrine. Mexico cannot afford to perish for the want of a Medical interventor, because we choose not to be the Physician. She must

lean on some power, shall it be Europe or the United States?
I answer unhesitatingly the United States, by every consideration of humanity, good neighborhood, and sound policy. For
if it be Europe, I can foresee a multitude of contingencies that
will make Mexico the battle ground for the maintenance of
American supremacy in America; the theater for the practical
illustration of the value and virtue of the Monroe doctrine, I
am of course a believer in what in the political nomenclature
of the day is termed "Manifest destiny." In other words I
believe in the teachings of experience and history, and that our
race, I hope our institutions,—are to spread over this continent and that the bybrid races of the West, must succumb to,
and fade away before the superior enegies of the white man.
Our chief danger is, that the national temperament will hurry
us too rapidly in the path of destiny, and that the inherited
passion for land, will break over the barriers of national honor
and national safety.[8]

These arguments were not new. President Polk had reaffirmed
the Monroe Doctrine in 1845,[9] and the term "Manifest
Destiny" dates from the same year.[10] The idea was much older,
but the Mexican War (1846–1848) gave it greater impetus.[11]
Forsyth's predecessor, James Gadsden, had already applied
these ideas to Mexico.[12]

In response to this "passion for land" the Buchanan administration sent Forsyth instructions in July 1857 to offer
$4–5 millions for Lower California and $8–10 millions for
Sonora, Chihuahua, and the right of transit across the Isthmus
of Tehuantepec.[13] Forsyth was not able to initiate negotiations
immediately, for the legislature and president provided for by
the new constitution were not yet installed.[14] Then, hardly
having assumed his presidential duties, Commonfort was overthrown by a conservative revolution that made Zuloaga President in Mexico City and suspended the Constitution of 1857.[15]
The Liberals fled Mexico City and eventually established
Benito Juarez as rival President in Vera Cruz.[16]

While the Liberals were still in flight and had not yet
organized any effective resistance to Zuloaga, Forsyth unsuc-
cessfully tried to open negotiations with the Conservative

Zuloaga Government for the cession of territory.[17] Failing in his negotiations,[18] Forsyth attempted to justify the seizure of Mexican territory as compensation for claims of American citizens[19] against Mexico. The American Minister reasoned that Mexico actually would benefit:

> You want Sonora? The American blood spilled near its line would justify you in seizing it . . . . You want other territory? Send me the power to make an ultimate demand for the several millions Mexico owes our people for spoliations and personal wrongs . . . . You want the Tehuantepec transit? Say to Mexico, "Nature has placed that shortest highway between two oceans, so necessary to the commerce of the world, in your keeping. You will not open it yourself nor allow others to open it to the wants of mankind. You cannot be permitted to act the dog in the manger . . . . Give us what we ask for in return for the manifest benefits we propose to confer upon you for it, or we will take it."[20]

Forsyth's hostility to the Zuloaga Government increased to such an extent that, when a tax was imposed on capital in May 1858, he broke diplomatic relations with Mexico on his own initiative.[21] In September he received instructions ratifying his action and directing him to return to the United States.[22]

Before a resumption of diplomatic relations with Mexico was attempted, rumors became prevalent in Mexico that Spain intended an expedition against Mexico.[23] Secretary of State Cass even received reports that Spain sought to acquire "political ascendancy" in Mexico.[24] In the past such war scares had not been entirely groundless. In 1856 the Spanish fleet had demonstrated before Vera Cruz to put pressure on Mexico to recognize debts to Spain.[25] In 1857 Spain had demanded an indemnity for several murdered Spaniards and, when this was not forthcoming, had severed diplomatic relations with Mexico.[26] The disputed questions were still pending in 1858.[27] Cass was worried enough that he instructed the American Minister to Madrid to bring the Monroe Doctrine to the attention of the Spanish Minister of Foreign Relations. He was

to be informed that, while the United States would not interfere in a war between Spain and Mexico, the United States
would not permit "the subjugation of any of the independent
states of this continent to European powers, nor to the exercise
of a protectorate over them, nor to any other direct political
influence to control their policy or institutions."[28] In reply the
Spanish Minister of Foreign Relations, Calderon Collantes,
disclaimed "interfering with the well-known policy of the
United States as expounded by Mr. Monroe."[29]

Cass' apprehensions of European interference in Mexico
were shared by President Buchanan. In his message to Congress in December 1858 he warned Europe that it was a duty
which the United States owed itself to protect Mexican territorial integrity against the hostile interference of any other
power.[30] At the same time the President urged Congress to
allow him to "assume a temporary protectorate over the
northern portions of Chihuahua and Sonora."[31]

In spite of Buchanan's aggressive proposals, Congressional
sentiment seems to have been opposed to such a policy towards
Mexico.[32] Consequently the Buchanan administration now
attempted to gain its ends through diplomacy. Robert M.
McLane was selected as Minister to Mexico. But there was a
question which government he would recognize. In January
1859 Miramon had replaced Zuloaga as head of the Conservative Government. Juarez was still maintaining the Liberal
Capital at Vera Cruz. In this situation McLane was instructed
to recognize any government in Mexico "which exercises
general authority over the country, and is likely to maintain
itself." Whether such a government existed was "not a question of right, but of fact" and in ascertaining this fact McLane
was given discretionary powers. But Cass did not hide that
"the sympathies of the United States have been strongly
enlisted in favor of the party of Juarez . . . and this government would be glad to see it successful."[33] Having reestablished
diplomatic relations, McLane was to offer $10,000,000 for
Lower California.[34]

In April 1859 McLane recognized the Juarez Government.[35] Throughout the year the Civil War continued, and American sympathies remained with Juarez. With a view to effecting the triumph of the Liberals, settling American claims, and preventing European interference in Mexico, President Buchanan proposed, in his annual message to Congress in December 1859, that the United States send a military force to Mexico. The objective would be the interior, held by Miramon, who was accused of being responsible for most of the outrages against American citizens in Mexico. The easiest way to reach the interior would be to act in concert with Juarez, pass through the territory occupied by him, and combine forces with him. This would enable the Juarez Government "to reach the City of Mexico and extend its power over the whole Republic." Then there was no reason to doubt that "the just claims of our citizens would be satisfied and adequate redress obtained." President Buchanan asked for immediate action. Otherwise the United States might have difficulties later defending the Monroe Doctrine against a European intervention in Mexico:

> . . . as a good neighbor, shall we not extend to her a helping hand to save her? If we do not, it will not be surprising should some other nation undertake the task, and thus force us to intervene at last, under circumstances of increased difficulty, for the maintenance of our established policy.[36]

McLane paved the way for American troops to pass through Mexico. On 14 December 1859 he completed a "Treaty of Transits and Commerce" with Ocampo, Juarez' Foreign Minister. The United States was granted the right of perpetual transit across Mexico by three highways. On two of these the United States might transport troops and military supplies on the same terms as the Mexican government. A commercial advantage granted the United States was duty-free shipment of goods on these highways, terminated by duty-free ports. Mexico promised to protect persons and property passing over any of the three routes. If Mexico were unable to guarantee the right of transit, it might ask the United States to act for it. But an elastic clause stated that in the "exceptional case . . . of unforeseen or imminent danger to the lives and property of citizens of the United States, the forces of said Republic are authorized to act for their protection without such consent having been previously obtained."[37] On the same day McLane signed another treaty with Ocampo "to enforce treaty stipulations and to maintain order and security." By it the United States obtained a general police power over Mexico, which was even to pay the costs of an intervention by the United States.[38]

The question arises why Juarez accepted such amazing terms that made Mexico a semi-protectorate of the United States. First of all, Juarez was urgently in need of money,[39] and the United States was going to pay $2,0000,000 for the right of transit. Secondly, the United States promised to assume $2,000,000 in claims of American citizens against Mexico.[40] With the urgency of the claims issue removed from American–Mexican relations, Juarez could count on American friendship, instead of being faced with the possibility of American punitive measures to protect American citizens, as threatened by McLane during the negotiations.[41]

It all came to nothing. The Congress of 1859–1860 was preoccupied with the slavery question and the coming Presidential election and paid little attention to Buchanan's recommendations.[42] Public opinion was opposed to the treaties.[43] Submitted to the Senate in January 1860,[44] they were defeated by partisan Republicans on 31 May 1860.[45] So ended all hope of a solution of the Mexican question by the Buchanan administration. In answer to McLane's fears in 1860 that Europe might use its claims against Mexico as a pretext for gaining political control of Mexico,[46] Cass replied that "if attempted it will be met by the armed action of the United States, should Congress adhere to the policy we have so long avowed and publicly proclaimed."[47] In December McLane had a circular to this effect transmitted to members of the diplomatic corps in Mexico.[48] By then Juarez had defeated his opponents without military aid from the United States. On 11 January 1861 he entered Mexico City in triumph.[49]

### 3. EUROPE AND THE MEXICAN CIVIL WAR, 1857–1860

The "Manifest Destiny" of the United States was partly stimulated by fears of European interference in Mexico. A series of crises in Spanish–Mexican relations in 1856–1857 concerning Spanish claims against Mexico culminated in a rupture of relations.[1] Spain, therefore, was considered the European Power most likely not only to declare war on Mexico, but also to interfere in its internal affairs.[2] Expressions of Manifest Destiny, in turn, gave rise to French and British fears that the United States would utilize a conflict between Spain and Mexico to carry out American imperialistic schemes.

"Filibustering" expeditions of small groups of adventurers, who tried to detach Sonora (and its mines) from Mexico under the guise of colonization, were neither new nor exclusively American, but they were universally unsuccessful.[3] But when William Walker, the "prince of filibusters,"[4] established himself as dictator of Nicaragua from 1855 to 1857, the Foreign Minister to Washington found evidence that Walker was the agent of the slavery interests in the United States. The British representative believed that they were conspiring to erect a slave empire embracing Central America and the West Indies.[5] The next British Minister to Washington asserted that "the adventurous classes in the United States are in high expectation of hostilities between Spain and Mexico." Then the United States might have an opportunity to annex both Mexico and Cuba. The design was "gigantic but experience forbids us to affirm that it is altogether illusory."[6] From Mexico Lord Clarendon, the British Foreign Secretary, received accounts of more American filibustering expeditions to Sonoro.[7] Lord Clarendon shared the fears of his representatives to the New World. He foresaw that the United States would take advantage of a conflict between Spain and Mexico to carry out "its own views in regard to Mexico."[8] Count Walewski, the French Minister of Foreign Affairs, predicted the United States would not recognize a Spanish blockade of the Mexican coast. War between Spain and the United States would be the result, with Spain perhaps losing its possessions in the West Indies.[9] Consequently both Great Britain[10] and France[11] urged Spain to arrive at a pacific solution of difficulties with Mexico.

A war between Mexico and Spain did not materialize. In 1858 Mexico sent a special agent to Europe with powers to effect an adjustment of disputed questions between Spain and Mexico with the aid of Anglo–French mediation. In 1859 a treaty was concluded whereby Mexico accepted Spain's demands.[12] Nevertheless, European fears of American meddling in Mexican affairs continued. In 1859 Lord Lyons, the British Minister to Washington, reported that public opinion in the United States was in favor of taking advantage of the Austro–Sardinian War in Europe to "get hold of Cuba and Mexico." Lyons observed that "no administration disregards the popular cry."[13]

The McLane–Ocampo Treaty of 1859 seemed to confirm European suspicions of American designs on Mexico. News of the treaty reached Europe early in 1860 and caused widespread indignation. Several Spanish newspapers printed articles suggesting "the expediency of opposing the ambitious projects of the United States . . . and of protecting the Latin race in America against absorption by their Anglo–Saxon neighbours."[14] The Foreign Offices of Spain,[15] France,[16] and Great Britain[17] became concerned about the threat to the independence of Mexico and the possibility that the United States might increase its trade with Mexico at European expense.

Fears that the United States might interfere in Mexico encouraged Spain and France to propose projects to counter

American influence, assist the Conservatives to defeat the Liberals fighting a Civil War in Mexico, and to end the anarchy in Mexico that was the cause of an accumulation of claims of foreigners resident in Mexico. At the same time Mexicans in Europe urged a direct intervention in Mexican internal affairs by the European Powers in order to prevent the carrying out of the reforms determined upon by the Liberals in Mexico. Great Britain, however, refused to depart from its traditional policy of non-intervention and non-interference in Mexican internal affairs. The British Foreign Office even rejected the proposals of its own Minister to Mexico to interfere in Mexican internal affairs. Napoleon III was unwilling to formulate any policy toward Mexico without British cooperation. As long as Great Britain refused to agree to an intervention in Mexico, the French Emperor told the Mexican exiles, it was "necessary to wait for better days."[18] Spain severed diplomatic relations with Mexico in 1857, but the next year Mexico sent an agent to negotiate a settlement. It was not until mid-1859, when these negotiations had not yet led to any successful result, that Spain started making proposals similar to those that France had been making from the very beginning of the Mexican Civil War in 1857. It was not Spanish and French pressure, however, that decided Great Britain to formulate a more active policy toward Mexico in 1860. It was rather the British desire to end the Civil War in Mexico. The fighting not only led to the accumulation of claims of British citizens in Mexico but also hurt British commercial relations with Mexico.

The proposal of De Gabriac, the French Minister to Mexico, of placing the Duc D'Aumale on a Mexican throne met with British opposition and came to nothing, but De Gabriac continued to maintain close relations with the Conservatives. Sometime in the late summer of 1857 Zuloaga, a Conservative army officer who was about to start a revolution to oust the Liberals and thereby initiate the Civil War in Mexico, approached De Gabriac. Zuloaga proposed that a loan, guaranteed by the goods of the Mexican Church, might furnish the money to hire five or six warships and a French corps of about 10,000. Zuloaga declared that a French general would then be placed in charge of Mexico, which had no one capable of exercising a strong authority. France sounded the British Foreign Office, but it declined to interfere in Mexican internal affairs.[19] In May, and again in August, 1858, Zuloaga, who had established himself as Conservative President in Mexico, sounded De Gabriac about the possibility of aid from France, or France and Great Britain combined. This aid would be used in the struggle against the Liberals, who had established Vera Cruz as the capital of Benito Juarez, who, they claimed, was the "Constitutional" President of Mexico.[20] But when the French Government asked the opinion of the British Secretary of Foreign Affairs in September 1858 as to the danger to Mexico of American annexation, he replied that it was "probable, and not all dangerous to European interests." Annexation would improve trade and break up the American Union. The "Yankees know this fact so well that they hesitate to touch it." British policy toward Mexico, Lord Malmesbury continued, should be to "leave it to its fate, taking care of our subjects."[21]

The special agent sent by the Conservative Government in Mexico in 1858 to effect an adjustment of disputed questions with Spain was General Juan Nepomucene Almonte. He also sought a European intervention:

> Unless we can persuade some European power to aid us in establishing some stable government, it is inevitable that the whole of Mexico must be swallowed up by the United States.

Rather than see that done, Almonte said he should "prefer to have the entire territory sunk underneath the sea."[22] In December he saw the British Foreign Secretary and suggested that "advantage might result from the joint intervention of England and France in Mexico." Lord Malmesbury, however, replied that the British Government would not interfere in the internal affairs of Mexico.[23] The Spanish Ambassador to Paris, however, seemed impressed with Almonte's proposals of mediation or intervention. In November 1858 the Spaniard talked with the French Minister of Foreign Affairs about means to employ to establish a stable government in Mexico.[24] Franco–Spanish mediation in Mexico was discussed, but the Spanish Ambassador noted, "England shows herself constrained . . . on this subject."[25] However, he added that Almonte was available for a conference with the representatives of France, Spain, and England.[26] But Collantes, the Spanish Minister of Foreign Relations, urged reserve on his ambassador and declared that moral means were sufficient.[27] Almonte's proposals, then, were rejected both by Great Britain and Spain.

By mid-1859 Collantes had changed his ideas about not using any but moral means to effect a change in Mexico. Diplomatic relations between Spain and Mexico had been severed for two years, and payments to Spanish claimants recognized by a convention in 1853 had completely ceased.[28] There had been complaints of this in the last session of the Cortes, along with demands that Mexico grant redress for the murder of several Spaniards in 1856. At that time General Prim had pointed out the awkward position of the Spanish Government :

> Anyway, to whom will you go to demand satisfaction? To the government of Juarez that is at Vera Cruz? It will answer you that in spite of its desire to give satisfaction, it can't do it, because its authority doesn't extend beyond the walls of this place. To the government of Zuloaga, that occupies the Capital? It will give you the same answer.[29]

After Prim's speech, the Civil War in Mexico had continued unabated. Miramon had replaced Zuloaga as Juarez' opponent, and no settlement of Spanish claims had been reached with General Almonte. The Cortes was in its summer recess, and the Spanish cabinet's fixed policy was to attempt nothing in domestic affairs and to maintain itself by successes in foreign affairs.[30] Collantes decided it was time to intervene in Mexico. In July 1859 he proposed to the British Foreign Office that Spain, France, and Great Britain take united action to ameliorate conditions in Mexico. Any action decided upon, Collantes believed, would not lead to any real opposition from the United States.[31] Lord Russell, who had replaced Lord Malmesbury as British Foreign Secretary, replied that an intervention was "not likely to afford a satisfactory or permanent settlement of the affairs of the Republic." Collantes answered that if Mexico were allowed to drift, the United States would annex it before long.[32]

More important than the projects of Zuloaga that De Gabriac forwarded to the French Ministry of Foreign Affairs, which referred them to the British Foreign Office, was an intrigue of Mexican exiles who had been residing in Europe for many years. Their plans gained importance when they won the serious attention of Napoleon III and Eugenie. The manner in which this happened would seem amazing if it were regarded without an appreciation of the characters and past of the French imperial pair.

In the fall of 1857 Hidalgo received orders to a new diplomatic post in Paris. He set out from Spain by way of Biarritz. By chance he crossed the path of Empress Eugenie, who was on her way to a bullfight in Bayonne. She at once recalled him as a friend of her mother and invited him to join her on her yacht the next day.[33] It was an important meeting, for thereafter Hidalgo became an intimate of Eugenie and Napoleon III, often accompanying them to St. Cloud, Fontainebleau, and Biarritz.[34]

In 1857 Hidalgo feared that the rupture of relations between Mexico and Spain that year would lead to a "War of vengeance."[35] He hoped to prevent this by persuading France to intervene so that, "both Nations being agreed, the nationality of Mexico might be saved."[36] The idea of Franco–Spanish cooperation was one that Eugenie had urged for years, so that Spain would not lose its overseas colonies to the United States and so that Spain's "credit will increase until it is treated with and counted as one of the other powers."[37] One of the standard arguments for intervention in Mexico was to thwart the ambitious United States and so to save the "nationality" of Mexico. Yet already in 1853, when it appeared that the United States might annex Cuba, the Austrian Ambassador to Paris reported:

> The ardent love which the Empress has kept for the country which gave her birth is equalled by her hatred for the nation that threatens to rob the crown of Spain of its finest jewel. "Europe," she said, "must form a league against the United States."[38]

Furthermore, Eugenie was charitable, sympathetic to suffering,[39] and a pious Catholic.[40] Though uncertainty remains, it would seem surprising if she was not influenced by exile accounts of anarchy in Mexico, represented as a Catholic country where the last vestiges of Spanish civilization were dying out.[41] In a conversation with Hidalgo at Biarritz in 1857, Eugenie said, "The establishment of a throne in Mexico has been necessary for a long time."[42] With the paucity of evidence available,[43] it must be admitted that a mystery still surrounds Hidalgo's endeavors, but it appears that the ground had been very well prepared for his ideas and proposals. By 1860 he was so much in Eugenie's confidence that she commissioned him to accompany the body of her sister, the Duchesse D'Albe, from Paris to its last resting place in Spain.[44]

Napoleon III's interest in Mexico dated from his imprisonment at Ham. In a commentary on the French expedition to Mexico in 1838–1839,[45] he bemoaned the decline of French influence afterwards and claimed the Mexicans "excluded French manufactures from their markets."[46] According to Eugenie, his first interest in Mexico stemmed from his plans for a canal through Nicaragua,[47] a map of which he made in 1845.[48] In 1847, after his escape, Napoleon published a pamphlet pointing out the political results of such a canal. Nicaragua would become a great commercial state, "powerful enough to call to life a great sentiment of nationality" and able, "by supporting Mexico, to put a stop to fresh encroachments from the North."[49] His interest in such a canal did not cease after he became Emperor.[50] Lord Cowley, who became British Ambassador to Paris in 1852, later recalled that it was "difficult to understand why the Emperor should have, ever since I have known him, evinced so much interest about such a distant country."[51]

Although Hidalgo could count on the sympathy of Eugenie and Napoleon III, the Emperor of the French refused, in Hidalgo's words, to "do something in favour of Mexico" because "Policy did not allow him to depart from his intention of action in union with England in American questions."[52] Napoleon confirmed Hidalgo's account. The French Emperor saw no pretext to intervene in Mexico and feared complications with the United States. It was "therefore necessary to wait for better days."[53]

In the fall of 1858 Empress Eugenie invited Hidalgo to Compiègne. When asked by Napoleon III what the news was from Mexico, Hidalgo replied, "The news is very bad, and the country will be ruined unless Your Majesty comes to its aid." Napoleon said he could not act without England. He had spoken about the matter with Lord Palmerston, who had been at Compiègne a few weeks ago. Napoleon had said that "an army and millions would be required for the purpose, and what is more, a prince." The Duc D'Aumale, Napoleon told Hidalgo, had refused the offer of the Mexican throne.[54] About this time, or soon afterwards, whole Mexican families fled the Civil War and settled in Paris. As Comte Fleury expressed it, the Court came to know "some of these worthy citizens personally and saw that their rights and interests had been ruthlessly trampled upon."[55] Accounts of the distress of these

Conservatives naturally tended to confirm Hidalgo's observations.

Hidalgo's efforts to convince France of the justice of the Conservative cause in Mexico were not limited to Napoleon III and Eugenie. In a conversation in March 1860 with Thouvenel, the French Minister of Foreign Affairs, Hidalgo claimed the McLane Treaty "menaces the independence and nationality of Mexico . . . adversely affects European commerce and threatens the political equilibrium in America."[56] In the following May Hidalgo sent Thouvenel a diatribe against the Liberals, who were represented as giving Mexico away to the United States. "that by race, education and political system is the irreconcilable enemy of the Latin Race and Catholicism."[57]

Hidalgo was not the only Mexican in Europe attempting to discredit the Liberals. General Almonte did not return to Mexico after negotiating a treaty to settle Spanish–Mexican difficulties in 1859. In 1860 he was nourishing intrigues in Spain and France against Juarez.[58] The General travelled between Paris and Madrid in an attempt to hasten the implementation of the British mediation proposals of that year. It was Almonte's hope that, if Juarez refused to accept the plan, "the powers . . . especially Spain and France, will adopt other more efficacious means to force the red party to listen to reason."[59]

The observations of De Gabriac, the French Minister to Mexico, reinforced the arguments of Hidalgo and Almonte. In April 1857 De Gabriac forwarded to the French Ministry of Foreign Affairs the despatch Forsyth wrote to show how he had paved the way for American annexation of Mexican territory.[60] De Gabriac claimed that in Forsyth's view monarchy was an "infraction of the laws of Monroe."[61] In his following dispatches, the French Minister continued to lament American aggressiveness and to urge French intervention in Mexico. He reported that President Buchanan's message to Congress in December 1858 was received in Mexico with "general stupor."

Now more than ever "all eyes are turned toward Europe and especially toward France."[62] McLane's recognition of the Juarez Government in April 1859 was "the application of the Monroe Doctrine in the form of defiance of Europe."[63] In April 1860, just before he returned to France from Mexico, De Gabriac reported that, if the United States continued to gain power and influence, and Europe did nothing, the French position would "become more difficult and more dangerous from day to day, until it becomes impossible."[64] The "majority" of Mexicans, De Gabriac believed, "is for us and against the North Americans as they are called here."[65]

The arguments of Hidalgo, to which those of Almonte were added directly or conveyed indirectly, and the reports of De Gabriac appear to have influenced Napoleon III to favor the Conservatives over the Liberals in Mexico. At the end of May 1860, Dubois de Saligny, appointed as De Gabriac's successor, visited Armand de Montluc, a Frenchman with may connections in Mexico and acquainted with conditions there. The newly appointed Minister to Mexico explained that he wanted to know something about "persons and things in Mexico."[66] A two hour conversation followed. Saligny defended Miramon, Zuloaga's successor as leader of the Conservatives in Mexico. Montluc gained the impression that Napoleon III also favored the Conservative President:

> The Emperor even showed personally certain sympathies for the descendant of the Miramons, this French family of old and noble race, and then because he saw in him an intrepid young leader, protected by the God of Battles, etc., etc. So true is it that M. de Gabriac and General Almonte had decried without pity the party of Juarez, and had made a demi-God of his adversary.[67]

The reports of Hidalgo, Almonte, and De Gabriac seem to have further aroused the interest that Napoleon III already had in Mexico. He speculated about extending the French Empire to the New World to obtain strategic bases to protect

French commerce. At Biarritz he had a conversation in 1860 with the famous American navigation expert, Maury, who summarized the interview:

> After having exhausted all the little information I could afford him, draining me *à sec,* and leaving me, after all, under the impression that he knew more of all the subjects on which he had examined me than I did myself, he turned with undisguised eagerness to the Mexican question. I had then just returned from Cuba and fancied I had thoroughly informed myself as to the condition of things there and in the Gulf. I was soon undeceived.
>
> He knew the very number of guns on the Morro, the sums the United States had spent on the fortifications in Florida, the exports and imports of Galverston and Matamoras, in short everything which well-informed agents could have reported to an experienced statesman, eager for information. He examined me again on Texas and its population, the disposition of the French residents, the tendencies of the German colonists, the feeling on the Mexican frontier.  Twice, I remember well, he repeated, *"La Louisiane, n'est ce pas qu'elle est Français au fond?"* At last he turned to the Colonies and then stated in round terms, *"Eh bien, il faut reconstruire L'Empire là bas."* From what I was able to gather, I was fully persuaded he proposed to seek in Mexico a compensation for the lost colonies in the West Indies, which he said, could not be recovered *"sans nous brouiller avec nos alliés."* He insisted on it that France must sooner or later have a *pied à terre* on the Florida coast for the purpose of protecting her commerce in the Gulf, for, he added, *"Nous ne voulons pas d'un autre Gibraltar de ce côté-là."*[88]

The projects of intervention in Mexico of Spain, France, and the Mexican Conservatives in Mexico and in Europe were all rejected by the British Foreign Office. It also refused to implement the proposals of Mr. Otway, the British Minister to Mexico, who wanted to include Mexico in the British Empire.

Soon after he arrived in Mexico, Mr. Otway convinced himself that the Mexicans were incapable of ruling themselves. He believed that a small Anglo-French force would be sufficient to maintain order. With stability assured, Mexico would become a veritable Utopia, prosperous and happy :

> A Foreign Intervention, or even Conquest, would be a matter of ver easy accomplishment. The great body of the Nation, including almost all the wealthy classes, is favourably inclined to such a change, and a British or Anglo-French Intervention would be preferred to any other. It would doubtless be unpalatable to our kinsmen of the North, but they could make no effective opposition, and if it were to be seriously determined on by a combination of Powers in Europe, they would attempt none beyond their favourite warfare of blustering and bullying.
>
> A native body of troops could be raised for police purposes, so that a very small European force to form a nucleus is all that is needed . . . . three or four thousand men after the first year or so would be quite sufficient. The Mexicans are a mild, easily governed people, without any of those fierce passions so fearfully displayed in India. Resources abound, and the revenue would increase annually under a honest and enlightened administration, which alone is wanting to make this country the most prosperous and happy on the face of the earth.

Mr. Otway thought England had a "*good pretext for intervention*" because about half of the Mexican public debt was British. But he advised that Spain not be included in the intervention, as the Spaniards were hated in Mexico. Furthermore it would "bother Jonathan's bile, as he covets Cuba."[69]

The argument, then, was almost identical with De Gabriac's proposals to Mr. Lettsom in 1856, except that monarchy was not specifically proposed. Mexico could not rule itself. An Anglo–French intervention, with only a limited force, would maintain order, and prosperity would follow. The United States need not be feared. It would be stymied, according to De Gabriac by a *fait accompli*, according to Otway, by a "combination of Powers in Europe." The majority of Mexicans would welcome the European intervention.

Expanding his argument, Mr. Otway depicted a Mexico

reverting to barbarism, but which was "one of the fairest and richest countries on the face of the globe" and which could be saved by ten or twelve thousand men, who *"would be welcomed."* [70] Mexicans themselves knew they were unfit for self-government, *"and the President, some of his Ministers* and many other persons" had frankly avowed this to Otway. An intervention would suppress smuggling and restore security. Commerce and industry would flourish. Then, since the resources of Mexico were "infinite," Mr. Otway considered Mexico would become a more "valuable possession than India." [71]

Mr. Otway and De Gabriac sympathized with the Conservatives and understood by the "great majority" of Mexicans the Spanish middle and upper classes, the "respectable" portion of the nation. This million, at most, in a population of about eight million, was the strata that counted. [72] The rest were "mild, easily governed people." These assumptions and conclusions were the same as those of the Mexican exiles in Europe and represented a mingling of the beliefs and propaganda of the Conservatives.

Although Otway thought Mexico was ready to give itself over to be governed by Great Britain, Lord Malmesbury wrote, in a private letter to his Ambassador to Paris in 1858, that it was not in British interests to "meddle with such a hornets' nest." As to French control of Mexico, this would not suit Great Britain "in the rear of our West India Islands and commanding the Gulf." [73] Consequently Otway was instructed that the British Government looked on the "annexation of such a dominion as Mexico, in addition to its present possessions, as an embarrassment, if not as an actual misfortune." [74]

Three months after he had written that he did not want to meddle in the "hornets' nest" of Mexico, Lord Malmesbury saw General Almonte and told him that Great Britain would not interfere in the internal affairs of Mexico. [75] Reporting this interview to Mr. Otway, however, Lord Malmesbury stated that, under certain circumstances, he was prepared to take part in an intervention in Mexico to reestablish a "stable order of things" for humanitarian and commercial reasons :

> The state of affairs in Mexico is however so deplorable, and the interests of humanity and commerce suffer so deeply, that Her Majesty's Government feel that if any measures could be taken by all the Powers who are most concerned in the reestablishment of a stable order of things, the necessity of the case might justify the Powers in resorting to them. Great Britain, France, Spain and the United States have, of all the Powers, unquestionably the greatest stake in Mexico, and if a quadruple intervention on their part could be arranged with any reasonable prospect of a satisfactory result, Her Majesty's Government, feeling that in the exceptional state of Mexico such intervention was desirable, would be ready to take part in it, and, in conjunction with other Powers, would contribute its best efforts towards establishing a settled government.[76]

In January 1859 some members of the Conservative party presented Mr. Otway with a petition to Queen Victoria, with thirty signatures. The disorders in Mexico were laid at the door of the Liberals, who received under their flag "the lowest and most degraded part of society, whose aims are the destruction of every principle of order, authority and religion, and whose acts are nothing but robbery, arson, and violence." The Zuloaga Government was unable to "repel this horde of savage murderers." The petitioners, therefore, appealed to Great Britain, France, and Spain for the assistance Mexico "so desperately needs." In coming to the aid of the Conservatives, Europe would be "defending from wicked men a holy cause; the cause of authority, of religion, and of social order."[77] Mr. Otway sent this petition, "so entirely coinciding with my own views," to Lord Malmesbury.[78] In May Otway forwarded a second petition with more signatures.[79]

Otway suggested that Great Britain open negotiations with France and the United States, inform them that Great Britain harbored no exclusive ambitions, did not even wish the intervention to be a permanent one, but felt the interests of British subjects rendered it imperative to end the anarchy and crime in Mexico. A settled government in Mexico would permit the doubling of silver production. Economic and humanitarian considerations made intervention a necessity:

> This country is not, I conceive, less important than Greece, which has had a Government given and guaranteed to it. All the Powers of Europe are now debating and negotiating about a Government for the Danubian Principalities . . . . Mexico is of more value than fifty Principalities . . . . Here we have a country almost at our very door, not hostile, but inviting us with open arms to come and take possession; a country unequalled in the whole area of the globe for riches; a country young, robust, vigorous, whose people are ignorant and superstitious it is true, but susceptible to great improvement, offering among other things a glorious field for missionary enterprise and an immediate and abundant harvest . . . .[80]

In reply to the first petition to Queen Victoria, Lord Malmesbury expressed doubt that foreign interference would benefit Mexico. It was seldom that governments whose origin was outside a country benefited it. An intervention in Mexico would have to be partisan, and all good effects would probably end when that intervention ceased. If only a foreign intervention could prevent complete disintegration in Mexico, then Her Majesty's Government, Lord Malmesbury wrote Otway, might consent to "deviate from her general policy and extend her aid toward establishing a better order of things." Even then Great Britain would not act alone but with "other Powers no less interested than herself in the preservation of Mexico as an integral member of the family of nations."[81] In June 1859, in answer to the second petition to Queen Victoria, Lord Malmesbury instructed his Minister to Mexico to "discourage the Mexicans from looking to foreign intervention as a remedy for their present ills." Lord Malmesbury's attention was now drawn to Europe. He explained to Mr. Otway, "Even if there were no other objection, the present state of Europe would render such a proposition entirely out of the question."[82]

In June 1859 the Derby Government fell, and Lord Palmerston formed a new cabinet. Lord Russell replaced Lord Malmesbury as Foreign Secretary, and Mr. Otway was recalled.[83] Otway's schemes of intervention had not been implemented, and Malmesbury had adhered to his policy of leaving Mexico "to its fate, taking care of our subjects."[84] This policy was not entirely negative, for efforts were made in 1858 and 1859 to "take care" of recognized British claimants. They were of two major categories, the "Convention Bondholders," and the "London Bondholders." The former were British subjects on whose behalf Great Britain had negotiated a series of conventions whereby redress for personal and property claims was guaranteed. The claimants were issued bonds by the Mexican Government, and a percentage of the Mexican custom receipts was promised to pay the interest on the bonds and to retire them. In 1858 Mr. Otway was able to have the interest rate raised for these Convention Bondholders, and in 1859 a higher percentage of Mexican custom receipts was reserved for them by an agreement between Captain Dunlop, the Senior British Naval Officer in the Gulf of Mexico, and the Juarez Government.[85] The "London Bondholders" held dividend-paying bonds issued by Mexico in return for loans from two British financial houses in the 1820's. Believing that their proper share of Mexican custom duties was not being turned over to them, these bondholders made a proposal to the British Foreign Office in 1858 whereby the customs due them would bypass the Mexican authorities and be transferred directly to agents appointed by the British consuls in Mexico. Lord Malmesbury approved the plan, but Mr. Otway was unable to obtain Mexican consent to the appointment of "Interventors."[86]

Mr. Mathew, who replaced Mr. Otway,[87] had no sympathy for the Conservatives. The new Chargé d'Affaires blamed all the troubles of Mexico on the "intolerance, superstition and corruption" of the Roman Catholic clergy, which had supported Zuloaga and then Miramon. In Mathew's opinion, Juarez was "genuinely striving for sound government and political freedom."[88] Consequently Mathew waited for Juarez' triumph over the Conservatives and made no such pleas for intervention as his predecessor.

In January 1860 Lord John Russell came to the conclusion that outrages committed against British subjects in Mexico could only cease with the end of the Civil War. He instructed Mathew to propose an armistice to Miramon and Juarez, during which time a national assembly, "impartially chosen . . . should make provision for the future government of the country." Great Britain did not "in any way wish to prescribe what that government should be, but it should be one that would give some prospect of stability and order." Yet Russell did suggest that the executive have a "character of permanence" and that a general amnesty ought to be proclaimed. Furthermore religious and civil tolerance ought to be declared, "for unless some mercy is shown by opposing parties there can be no hope of internal peace."[89] At the end of February, France was asked to support these proposals.[90] In answer to a French inquiry whether the United States were going to be asked to cooperate with Great Britain and France, Lord Russell replied that since the McLane Treaty had not yet been ratified by the United States Senate, it would be best to wait. If the treaty were not ratified, American cooperation could be invited. Then, if it were refused, France and Great Britain could always take action without the United States, "always provided that no force is used."[91] Seemingly Russell made no request that Spain support the plan. He placed the highest value on Mexico's proclaiming religious freedom[92] and may have feared Spain would not agree.[93] Furthermore, Spain had not yet formally reestablished diplomatic relations with Mexico.[94]

Mr. Mathew submitted Russell's proposals to Miramon and Juarez. While Miramon refused to agree,[95] he did accept the good offices of Great Britain[96] and France.[97] Juarez insisted that his was the legal government of Mexico. Peace would be more secure if the "insurgents" united with "the Government created by law, then if this Government should cast aside its titles."[98] Less than the reestablishment of the constitution of 1857 would be an "abandonment of all principle and a submission to the wrong and violence that overthrew the constitution and government of the Republic in 1857."[99] Mr. Mathew's opinion was that, even if Miramon and Juarez had accepted the plan, "they never would have agreed upon the mode of calling a national assembly."[100]

Collantes, the Spanish minister of foreign relations, learned of Russell's mediation proposal through the Spanish Ambassador to Paris. He reported that the French Ministry of Foreign Affairs believed the best way to end anarchy in Mexico was by the "convocation of a constituent assembly, which would determine a definite and stable form of government."[101] Collantes' reaction was to propose to Great Britain and France that they and Spain, with or without the United States, intervene to end the Civil War in Mexico. To substantiate the urgency of the proposal, Collantes pointed to the McLane Treaty:

> No people, and Spain no less than any other, can consent to the absorption, or even the protectorate or exclusive preponderance of any nation whatever over the vast and rich continent discovered and civilized by our ancestors.[102]

The reply from London was that Great Britain wanted "to cooperate with France and Spain, if force is not used."[103] Thouvenel, the French Minister of Foreign Affairs, answered in the sense of Russell's qualification about the McLane Treaty and observed that nothing could be done until the United States Senate approved or rejected the treaty. When this happened, "the English and French Governments, counting on Spain, will take into consideration the policy to follow in the affairs of Mexico."[104]

European policy toward Mexico as envisioned by Collantes was to assure the establishment of a Conservative government and to prevent American designs on Mexico before it was too late. In May a Conservative constitution to be imposed on Mexico was forwarded to Great Britain for approval.[105] As to the McLane Treaty, Collantes sought Anglo-French cooperation to protest instead of waiting on events:

> If France, England, and Spain show a firm resolution to stand together and protest, the United States will be forced to withdraw her intention of not dealing with European nations in affairs dealing with the New World. If the economic interests of some English subjects find in the triumph of this party (i.e., of Juarez) a momentary interest, the political interests of England would, however, suffer if the McLane-Ocampo Treaty is ratified. This treaty, if ratified, will produce complications which will affect not only Spain but all the commercial nations.[106]

The McLane Treaty was not without effect on Lord Russell and Thouvenel. For Lord Russell the treaty would entail "the absorption of all the commerce of Mexico with Great Britain, the United States monopolizing to her profit alone the maritime, commercial and industrial relations of Europe."[107] Hidalgo made the same observation in a conversation with Thouvenel and claimed the United States threatened the independence of Mexico.[108] President Buchanan's message to Congress of the previous December, asking for an armed intervention in Mexico, was brought to Thouvenel's attention by a "Note for the Minister," prepared by the Ministry of Foreign Affairs.[109] Thouvenel concluded that Miramon was preferable to Juarez, because the Conservative President safeguarded the independence of Mexico.[110]

Great Britain continued to occupy the key position in the formulation of European policy toward Mexico. France followed the British lead, and Spanish proposals for a vigorous policy toward Mexico were not implemented. Instead Europe waited for the action of the United States Senate on the

McLane Treaty. It was rejected on 31 May 1860.[111] Lord Russell then arranged that France and Spain join Great Britain in asking the United States to join in the mediation proposal to Mexico.[112] The British Minister to Washington invited the United States to join in addressing a collective note to Miramon and Juarez, advising them to call a national assembly to settle their domestic difficulties.[113] The United States, however, had recognized the Juarez Government and was unwilling to take a step which would appear to discredit the Liberals or put them on the same level as their opponents.[114] The British offer, therefore, was declined. Furthermore, Great Britain was warned that American policy was "opposed to any interference, especially the joint interference of other powers in the domestic affairs of an independent nation."[115] A similar warning was given France, with the proviso that "the United States did not call in question the right of France to compel the Government of Mexico, by force if necessary, to do it justice."[116] Spain was urged to submit its differences with Juarez to the arbitration of some friendly power.[117]

The rejection of Russell's mediation offer both by the United States and the contending parties in Mexico did not influence the British Foreign Secretary to abandon his proposal altogether. He still hoped that the Liberals and Conservatives might at least agree to a truce in Mexico. Moreover, as long as France and Spain could be held to a mediation policy, they would be unable to intervene on behalf of the Conservatives, for whom Russell had no sympathy.

At the end of August 1860 Russell concluded that redress for outrages against British subjects in Mexico could not be expected from the Miramon Government. The British Secretary, therefore, instructed Mr. Mathew to suspend relations with the Conservatives:

Since the representations of Her Majesty's Government are entirely disregarded, Her Majesty's Government have had to consider whether it is fitting that it should continue to hold relations with a Government under which such things are tolerated, and after anxious consideration it has come to the conclusion that it will best consult its own dignity and the rights of British subjects by withdrawing Her Majesty's Legation from the capital of the Republic . . . .[118]

Upon receipt of these instructions, Mr. Mathew withdrew to Jalapa and waited on events.[119]

In September a summary of Mathew's instructions to retire to Jalapa was sent to the French Ministry of Foreign Affairs, together with a proposal that France and Spain join in asking the parties in Mexico to consent to a truce for one year. The suggestion should be accompanied by a "distinct declaration that the three Powers will take no part in the Civil War, whether their mediation is accepted or rejected." During the truce, Great Britain would acknowledge neither Juarez nor Miramon as President, but only as "de facto rulers of the places occupied by them."[120]

These British proposals were analyzed at length by a French memorandum for Thouvenel.[121] Nothing new was found in the British plan. An Anglo–French accord for the establishment of a single power in Mexico already existed, and the French Minister to Mexico had instructions to do his best in cooperation with his Spanish and British colleagues. If it was only desired to give Mexico a short breathing spell, the proposal had little to recommend it. Even if Miramon and Juarez agreed, they probably would not prevent the "commanders under their orders from continuing to act on their own account." The British plan, therefore, was viewed as an attempt "to engage us indirectly to break with the . . . Government in Mexico City." The English cabinet, unknown perhaps even to itself, was falling under the influence of Mr. Mathew and blamed Miramon for all grievances for which redress was sought. But rather than act against Miramon and save Juarez, the French Government found itself "in a quite different situation." Its legation in Mexico blamed Juarez for most of the wrongs done French subjects. As to the declaration of the three Powers not to interfere in the internal dissensions of Mexico, France and Spain had already declared "spontaneously" that proceedings would have to maintain an "altogether official nature." These precautions ought not to be directed against France and Spain, "but rather against the United States." The French memorandum concluded that the British Foreign Office had no precise ideas of a remedy of the Mexican question. The instructions to the French Minister to Mexico "already satisfied, in as far it was possible, what the Cabinet of London wanted." The British communication, therefore, was merely sent to France's representative to Mexico under the heading of information.

In the midst of the mediation proposal of 1860, France changed its representative to Mexico. In May De Gabriac left Mexico for France,[122] and it was only in the following November that his successor arrived in Mexico.[123] He was Dubois de Saligny, an obscure diplomat in an unassigned status for almost ten years.[124] Thouvenel's initial instructions to Saligny in May 1860 stated that the parties in Mexico were "equally contestable," at least for the moment. But sympathies were with Miramon, because he protected Mexican independence. Saligny's rôle would be to cooperate with his Spanish and British colleagues in Mexico to obtain a truce and the calling of a constituent assembly.[125] Saligny asked to be given instructions identical with those of the British representative to Mexico, since they were going to cooperate, and that they both be given the right of initiative in case of unforeseen events, because things moved so quickly in Mexico. These suggestions were forwarded to the British Foreign Office, found reasonable,[126] and Thouvenel penned supplementary instructions in July granting Saligny the right of initiative.[127] At the end of August, when Saligny still had not left for Mexico, Thouvenel sent him a second set of supplementary instructions. Saligny was to have full latitude to determine the legitimacy of French claims against Mexico and to treat with both governments, so that neither could put an obstacle in the way of an accord signed with the other.[128] The sums owed recognized French claims were slight,[129] but many claims for compensation were unrecognized and uninvestigated.

Before leaving for Mexico Saligny interested himself in a claim that was not really French at all, the Jecker bonds. In October 1859[130] Miramon and the Swiss[131] financial house of J. B. Jecker and Co. had entered into an arrangement whereby Jecker obtained $15,000,000 in Mexican Treasury bonds in return for less than ten per cent of that figure.[132] The speculators expected to make a tenfold profit by using the bonds, as permitted by the agreement, in partial payment of Mexican custom duties and taxes.[133] In May 1860 Jecker went bankrupt.[134] The interested parties brought the Jecker bonds to the attention of De Gabriac,[135] and he was in communication with Xavier Elsesser, Jecker's brother-in-law residing in Switzerland.[136] It was this same Xavier Elsesser whom Saligny saw before leaving for Mexico. The French Minister believed that, since the bonds were issued by a Government recognized by France and Great Britain and in the hands of their nationals in large quantities, the Liberals probably would not be able to set them aside. Saligny told Elsesser :

> . . . the affected governments and even the United States would support them (i.e., the bonds), in view of the advantages that would devolve on their nationals who thus pay the high custom duties with the paper bought cheaply . . . .[137]

Saligny also approached one of Jecker's chief creditors and asked his opinion of the bankrupt Swiss financier.[138] Seemingly Saligny was particularly interested in the Jecker bonds, a circumstance that will be dwelt on in more detail in another connection.[139]

While Saligny was still in France, the Civil War in Mexico was drawing to a close. Both the Liberals and the Conservatives needed money for the last battles, and they did not hesitate to take it from foreigners. On 9 September 1860 General Degollado seized a conducta of specie of over $1,000,000 at Laguna Seca. He explained that he was acting under Juarez's orders to "protect" the conducta. Mr. Mathew despatched Mr. Glennie, the British consul at Mexico City, to recover $400,000, estimated to belong to Englishmen. Glennis obtained this amount from Degollado and conveyed it to Tampico, where the local governor attached it on the ground that other foreigners had an interest in the restored money. The upshot was that approximately one-third of it, or less than ten per cent of the original conducta, was turned over to a committee of merchants for distribution to all the rightful owners.[140] The Miramon Government resorted to a similar expedient to raise money. In November General Marquez demanded $200,000 from Mr. Whitehead, the representative of the London Bond-holders in Mexico. When this was refused, the British Legation was broken into by force on 17 November, and the $660,000 stored there for the London Bondholders seized.[141]

Saligny arrived at Vera Cruz at the end of November[142] and reached Mexico City in the middle of December.[143] His letters accredited him to Miramon, but Juarez was bringing the Civil War to an end and was about to enter Mexico City. Mediation, therefore, was no longer necessary.[144] Saligny was to act with Mathew, but the British Chargé d'Affaires was still at Jalapa. He did not want Great Britain to cooperate with France. Earlier that year he had warned Lord Russell that France "might greatly wish to *draw England into concerted measures* with her for the alleged pacification of Mexico in the very hope that ill will, and possibly hostilities, might ensue with America."[145] Whereas Mr. Mathew favored the Liberals, Saligny defended Miramon. Before he ever saw Saligny personally, the British representative had an aversion to him:

I am sorry too to believe that Monsieur de Saligny, whose forte is intrigue, according to European reports, does not seem to further the tranquil settlement of affairs.[146]

Cooperation between the British and French representatives was, therefore, unlikely. The recently arrived representative of Spain, however, had views similar to those of Saligny. The Spaniard had renewed diplomatic relations with Mexico by recognizing the Miramon Government just before Juarez defeated it.[147] Juarez revenged himself soon after entering Mexico City in January 1861 by expelling the Spanish diplomat from Mexico.[148] Spain was again unrepresented in Mexico, and Saligny and Mathew represented the major Powers of Europe in Mexico in early 1861.

All the projects of intervention and mediation during the Mexican Civil War accomplished nothing for the British bondholders. They held mortgages on Mexican custom duties, but payments to retire the bonds were withheld by Juarez, who was in possession of the most important custom houses on the Gulf of Mexico. The position of the bondholders was precarious, because Great Britain did not recognize the Juarez Government. Captain Dunlop's agreement with the Juarez Government in 1859 was not, therefore, technically a convention. But provision was made that the agreement would form the basis of a convention if Juarez were recognized by the Powers. The reason this stipulation was inserted was that a diplomatic convention was an instrument recognized by international law, which would bind Mexico legally.[119] Such had been Lord Malmesbury's policy of "taking care" of British subjects. Lord Russell continued the policy. In December 1860 Captain Aldham, the British Senior Naval Officer in the Gulf of Mexico and Captain Dunlop's successor, arrived at an agreement with the Juarez Government by an exchange of notes. The mortgage on Mexican custom duties of the Convention Bondholders was increased to make up the funds "occupied" by Juarez that year. At the same time Juarez promised to adhere to the Dunlop agreement, which stipulated that the London Bondholders would receive the share of custom duties provided for by private transactions between them and Mexico. Hitherto Great Britain had only supported the claims of the London Bondholders semi-officially, as they were private transactions. If the Dunlop and Aldham agreements were converted into conventions, the claims of the London Bondholders would be recognized by international instruments and would have the official backing of Great Britain. If Juarez abided by his promises and these agreements, he was bound to hand over 29 per cent of Mexican import duties to the Convention Bondholders and 30 per cent to the London Bondholders.[150] Whether he was willing or able to do so at the very time that Mexico was entering a period of reconstruction after the Civil War was something that would be seen in 1861. Then the British interests that had suffered from the Laguna Seca Conducta seizure and the British Legation robbery would certainly also demand redress.

With all his sympathy for Juarez and the Liberals. Mr. Mathew was not optimistic enough to believe that the bondholders would receive their proper share of Mexican custom duties. Mathew foresaw that things would be different if a foreign power administered the custom houses instead of Mexico. With a typical English prejudice against high tariffs, the British representative commented :

> An occupation and administration of the Maritime Custom Houses of Mexico, at a low tariff, by any other nation (i.e., than the United States) would free the country from debt in six years : so great are its natural resources.[151]

Captain Aldham considered the same possibility in December 1860, but he concluded that the Mexican Government would withdraw to Jalapa and there prevent any merchandise from reaching the interior.[152] In 1861, however, Aldham convinced himself of the necessity of a custom house intervention in Mexico and presented a detailed outline of such a plan to Mr. Mathew's successor, Sir Charles Wyke, who forwarded the scheme to Lord Russell.[153]

# II
# The Diplomatic Crisis in Mexico in 1861

## 1. MATHEW AND WYKE IN MEXICO IN 1861

On 11 January 1861 Juarez entered Mexico City and was soon recognized by the United States and Prussia.[1] Mr. Mathew, however, remained at Jalapa so that, by standing aloof, he could give greater weight to his demands.[2] After waiting a month, he sent his conditions for British recognition to Francisco Zarco, Juarez' Minister of Foreign Relations. Mathew demanded prompt repayment of the $660,000 taken from the British Legation, reparation, within four months, for the Laguna Seca Conducta, and appropriate apologies.[3] Without waiting for a reply, Mathew went to Mexico City, arriving on 16 February.[4] Three days later he accepted[5] a Mexican pledge acknowledging his conditions.[6] What Mathew failed to see was that Zarco did not admit responsibility for the robbery of the British Legation by the Conservatives. The matter was referred to the Mexican courts, and the Juarez Government only promised to negotiate further if the money were not recovered from the actual robbers:

> . . . the Government have already come to the determination to bring the guilty to judgement, having furnished the Tribun-

64

als with all the data that have been found, and given orders
for the embargo of the property of the responsible parties, by
which they have shown their determination to ensure prompt
administration of justice, and moreover they sincerely desire
that due reparation be made, and are ready to treat of this
matter, and to arrange in a satisfactory manner, conformable
to justice and equity, the repayment of the money seized, in
case it should not be covered by the property of the responsible
parties, in which number, neither the Nation nor its Government can in any way be comprehended.[7]

Mathew thought the arrangement was equitable, taking into
consideration the distressed conditions of the country.[8] He was
also convinced of the sincerity of the Mexican Government
to pay British claims.[9] Nor did Lord Russell see anything
objectionable in the Mexican pledge: he approved Mathew's
negotiation.[10] But when Mathew requested information about
the settlement of the Legation Robbery just before the arrival
of his successor,[11] Zarco's reply was to quote from his February
promises and to state that the legal investigation was proceeding.[12] Sir Charles Wyke, Mathew's replacement, claimed that
Mathew was deceived by "an over confidence in the good
faith of a Party he had all along befriended, for up to the last
moment he conceived that their assertion of non-responsibility
was to be taken in a moral and not a literal sense."[13]

After making his original conditions, Mathew received
Russell's instructions to recognize the Juarez regime if it agreed
to prosecute those connected with the robbery of the $660,000
and also promised to admit the just claims of British subjects
for that and other spoilations and violence they had suffered.[14]
Zarco readily accepted Russell's stipulations and told Mathew
that Juarez and the cabinet desired recognition at a reception
at the National Palace in order to restore public confidence.[15]
Mathew consented and recognized Juarez on 26 February.[16]

In March Zarco told Mathew that the Mexican Government wanted to meet legitimate British demands "in any manner that the deplorable financial condition of Mexico would
admit."[17] It was agreed that Mathew send Zarco a brief note[18]

on this subject, so that definite proposals and views could be forwarded to Russell.[19] The Mexican answer proposed that unrecognized claims be settled by a mixed commission. Zarco promised to assign to the payment of British claims "that part of the National revenues that can be disposed of reserving only what is absolutely necessary for covering the estimated expenditure." He assured Mathew that every economy "compatible with the existence" of the government had already commenced. The Mexican Minister foresaw that, when peace was consolidated, his government could give more attention to public administration. Then revenue would increase, and greater assignments could be made to pay British claims.[20]

On 29 March Mathew received Russell's instructions to draw up a statement of British claims and to require the Mexican Government to take measures "at the earliest moment for their settlement."[21] Mathew had already directed the British consular agents to send claims to Mr. Glennie, the British consul at Mexico City.[22] Within the next month he arrived at a tentative total of eighty-four claims, amounting to $18,583,187.[23] The murder of Mr. Bodmer, the British vice consul at Tasco, was a claim that attracted the special attention of Mr. Mathew and Lord Russell.[24] In spite of all his efforts, Mathew never obtained more than Zarco's assurances to take steps to apprehend the murderers.[25]

The $18,000,000 were in addition to bondholder claims. Through a downward revision of the Mexican tariff Mathew saw the means of increasing Mexican revenues and imports of British goods. Automatically assignments to British bondholders would also increase. Mathew believed that the tariff imposed unfair duties on cotton and woolen goods, the main British imports, "with the erroneous object of protecting a few local manufactures, whose hands would be more remuneratively employed in mines or agriculture." The result was smuggling in these articles and a reduction of duties at the caprice of local authorities to tempt the entry and unloading of vessels. The effect was a heavy loss of revenue.[26] Mathew urged tariff reform on the Mexican Government,[27] which appointed a committee to study the problem[28] and promised to recommend Congress to make changes.[29]

Shortly before returning to England, Mathew sent Russell a long confidential report analyzing Mexican conditions and proposing means by which "this fine country" might be spared "anarchy and ruin." The mortgage of Mexican import duties to foreigners, Mathew believed, left Mexico with less than half of the revenue needed for expenditures. The nationalized church property was only partially realized.[30] To this lack of resources Mathew attributed the continued existence and increase of guerrilla bands. Saligny was another disturbing factor. He was "actively engaged in the support of an intolerant clergy." If the Jecker speculation were recognized, there would be a serious injury to better claims, and "such a precedent would be fruitful in revolutions and civil wars." Mathew did not lose faith in Juarez. However faulty and weak his government was, there was law and order in comparison with Miramon's regime. Juarez had laid down "a wise basis of civil and religious liberty." Peace alone was needed for the "development of constitutional principles, and for the gradual enlightenment of the people." Peace would also permit the economic development of Mexico. Mathew believed there were undiscovered silver mines and that cotton could be grown on the Mexican coasts. A labor force might be obtained from China for the Pacific coast. Mathew's proposals were more in the nature of musings than specific plans. The bondholders "might perhaps save their capital by submitting to a temporary suspension of interest." The establishment of a more equitable tariff "may lay down a better future basis of revenue." Without foreign "interposition" convulsions would continue, "to the heavy injury of British interests and commerce, and to the disgrace of humanity." The United States or Great Britain might uphold Juarez or his principles of government "by a protecting alliance or by the declaration that no revolutionary movements would be permitted in any of the sea ports." Great Britain,

Mathew insisted, had to judge how far its political and commercial interests were:

> . . . involved in the continuance of Mexican nationality, and it may thus be deemed right to consider, whether some *timely* plan, similar to some extent to that adopted in the case of Greece, by a controlling aid, and by financial supervision, this fine country may not be saved from anarchy and ruin.[31]

Lord Russell's policy was one of non-intervention in Mexican internal affairs. Mr. Mathew, however, took sides and favored the Liberals, reversing Mr. Otway's policy of encouraging the Conservatives. Moreover Mathew had accepted the post of Chargé d'Affaires in Mexico, he informed Russell, as "the avowed stepping stone to a European mission."[32] By the end of 1860 Mathew was homesick to see his family and complained that "few Charges D'Affaires have had a more trying or less agreeable sphere of duty."[33] He felt his apprenticeship had been served and was happy to be relieved by Sir Charles Wyke, who was raised to the rank of Minister after ten years of duty in Central America.[34] Lord Russell had already given Mathew hopes of advancement by assuring him that he was "on the road to diplomatic employment as Minister."[35] Wyke was therefore a replacement for a representative whose views did not coincide with those of the Foreign Office and who was eager to leave Mexico. Furthermore, Wyke's ideas were in harmony with those of Lord Palmerston, who trusted the new Minister to Mexico enough to send him on a confidential mission to Napoleon III before leaving for Mexico.[36]

During the seven years in Guatemala before his appointment to Mexico, Wyke often expressed his belief "both to Lord Palmerston and to the Emperor Napoleon" that South and Central America were "ripe for monarchical institutions." But nothing could be accomplished, Wyke believed, without the aid of the moderates, with whose leaders he always tried to maintain friendly relations. Between January 1861, when he was appointed to the Mexican post, and April, when he left

Europe to assume his duties, Wyke was sent by Lord Palmerston to see Napoleon III. In the course of several confidential conversations, Napoleon said that, if Juarez refused to recognize the just claims of the three European maritime powers, war would be declared. Then the way would be paved for a Mexican monarchy. The candidature of Archduke Maximilian was already being considered, and Lord Palmerston agreed on condition that nothing be revealed before the capture of Mexico City and without the approval of the Liberals.[37]

Wyke's general instructions on proceeding to Mexico[38] were that he use his discretion about when to present his credentials if Mathew had not obtained an acknowledgment of liability for wrongs to the lives and property of British subjects.[39] After establishing diplomatic relations, Wyke's first duty was to obtain reparation. Bondholders' claims, the Legation Robbery, and the Laguna Seca Conducta were specified and defended by Russell. Whereas the British Government never acted officially for those who lent their money to foreign governments, by the Dunlop and Aldham arrangements the claims of the London Bondholders "acquired the character of international obligations." Wyke was to insist on "punctual fulfilment" of obligations thus contracted on behalf of the London and Convention Bondholders. The money stolen from the British Legation was to be returned, and Wyke was not to accept as an excuse that the Miramon Government was responsible. The entire Republic, not just the party administering the government, was responsible. Russell did not expect a "determined refusal," but if Wyke met any resistance he was to say he was authorized to call upon British naval forces to support and even enforce reparation. Russell foresaw no difficulties in obtaining reparation for the Laguna Seca Conducta, because General Degollado acted under orders from the Juarez Government. Wyke was granted full powers[40] to negotiate a convention for the liquidation of recognized and unrecognized claims that proved to be legitimate.[41] Impoverishment resulting from years of troubles, Russell admitted, might prevent immediate payment. But Wyke was warned to be careful that "temporary forebearance" not be taken for "indifference." Every opportunity should be taken to point out the necessity of developing the resources of the country to meet the expenses of the civil government and to satisfy international claims. Should money be raised from Mexican church property, British claimants should have the "benefit" and obtain an early settlement. In the eventuality of difficulties, Wyke was authorized to refer "quietly" to British naval forces on the Mexican coasts and "leave the Mexican Government to infer that those ships are available for your support if your just demands should be rejected, or if the engagements entered into with you should be disregarded." Thus Wyke was authorized to threaten but was not specifically given the power to use force. Russell viewed even threats as almost a last resort. He urged Wyke to use "tact and forebearance" and remember the "peculiarities of the Spanish character" that was "influenced by moderate language and considerate demeanour" but resisted and defied ". . . attempts to intimidate or coerce."

Throughout Wyke's instructions there were disclaimers of interfering in the internal affairs of Mexico or obtaining exclusive advantages. If the Juarez Government showed a willingness to grant redress, Wyke was to state "without hesitation" that British policy toward Mexico:

> . . . is a policy of nonintervention, and that the British Government desire to see Mexico free and independent and in a position to regulate the civil administration of the country, to maintain internal peace and to discharge its international duties without the active intervention of any Foreign Power whatsoever.

Such assurances, Russell believed, would induce the Mexican Government to rely on the disinterestedness of any advice Wyke might offer. He was not, however, to take part in political questions that might arise between contending parties nor to enter into a contest with representatives of other Powers for exclusive influence or commercial advantage. British influence should rather be employed for the ". . . promotion of general peace and the development of commercial industry." The only unsolicited advice on Mexican internal policies that Russell felt warranted to give was to urge freedom of religious worship. It would remove the barrier that prevented Christians of different sects from settling in Mexico and contributing to improve the resources of the country. Wyke was to try to prevent an open rupture between Mexico and foreign Powers, but he was warned to be careful "not to assume . . . any responsibility" and to avoid "any uncalled-for assumption of mediation."

Aside from claims, Russell urged Wyke to investigate two "political" differences between Mexico and Great Britain. Wyke was to ascertain Mexican views regarding the boundary between Mexico and British Honduras. After Wyke's departure, however, Russell decided to leave the boundary dispute in the *status quo* upon the recommendation of the Colonial Office.[42] The second issue was a difference of interpretation of a convention of 1826 exempting British subjects from forced loans.[43] If he thought Mexico would agree, Wyke was instructed to draw up an additional act to the convention to exempt British subjects from all extraordinary exactions and to refer it to Russell for consideration.[44]

Russell's instructions conformed to the standard British non-intervention policy toward Mexico. Mathew's proposal of a custom house intervention was ignored. Strict injunctions to "keep aloof from the factions" were an indirect condemnation of Mathew's partiality in favor of the Liberals. Yet Russell believed that Wyke would always be looked upon with respect "as the Representative of a country possessing liberal institutions and therefore desiring to see other nations enjoying the same blessing." Mediation was regarded with suspicion after its failure in 1860. Redress for personal and property damages, as well as compliance with conventions, was grounded in International Law. The American Secretary of State, Lewis

Cass, had stated the year before that the United States had no argument against such legitimate claims and would not challenge the use of force to obtain redress for them. Wyke's instructions were sent to the French Ministry of Foreign Affairs,[45] and so the emphasis on non-intervention and non-interference in Mexican internal affairs served as a warning. Russell may have had Spain in mind when he instructed Wyke to prevent an open rupture between Mexico and foreign Powers. The British Secretary already had information that Juarez had expelled Pacheco from Mexico in January as an "enemy" of the Republic.[46] A renewed Spanish–Mexican breach, therefore, was very likely.

Sir Charles Wyke landed at Vera Cruz on 30 April. He was sick and put in an even worse mood by a "barely civil" reception. He complained that the Mexicans had gotten "into the habit of thinking that they can do anything with impunity." In a private letter he observed that Mexico was a "wretched country, where everything seems to be going from bad to worse." Juarez could not maintain law and order. Wyke heard that Mathew was obtaining nothing but verbal promises, but that Saligny was accomplishing something by threats.[47]

On the way to Mexico City some of Wyke's furniture was ruined, and he lamented that he had to pay enormous freight charges.[48] He arrived in Mexico City on 9 May.[49] Two days later the whole cabinet resigned,[50] and Congress deprived Juarez of his extraordinary powers.[51] Everything came to a standstill, and Wyke took advantage of the interval to page through the Legation archives before relieving Mathew. When he came to Mathew's correspondence with Zarco, relating to the recognition of the Juarez Government, Wyke was struck by the unsatisfactory nature of Zarco's explanations as to the liability of the Mexican Government to repay the $660,000 robbed from the British Legation. The wording of Zarco's note of 12 February Wyke saw but as an attempt to shift responsibility to the actual culprits from the Government and to "screen themselves behind the interminable proceedings of a Mexican Court of Law." The promise to come to an arrangement, should the confiscated goods of the robbers be insufficient, Wyke noted, proposed no specific remedy and qualified it with what would be in conformity with "Right" and "Justice." Wyke asked Mathew to straighten this out with Zarco, who replied that he was no longer in office and suggested Mathew address Senor Palacio, Chargé ad interim. Palacio, however, would not enter into official communications with Mathew on the pretext that he held no official position since Wyke's arrival in Mexico City.[52] On 19 May a new cabinet was formed, with Don Leon Guzman as Minister of Foreign Relations.[53] He took the same position towards Mathew as had Palacio. So Wyke himself called on Guzman and asked for an audience with Juarez, should he be disposed to view the question of the Legation Robbery in the proper light. Guzman, while professing a willingness to render satisfaction in general terms, refused to treat officially with Wyke before he presented his credentials.[54] Wyke was skeptical but agreed to a public audience with Juarez on 25 May.[55]

Two days after presenting his credentials, Wyke wrote his Foreign Office that there was little chance of obtaining redress from the Mexican Government without the use of force. The Juarez Government had frittered away the confiscated church property and was now "without a sixpence." Reactionary chiefs were near Mexico City itself with four to six thousand troops, and Marquez had recently defeated Government troops sent out against him. Robbers and assassins swarmed the roads, even the streets of Mexico City. The Government could not maintain authority over the states, which were becoming "de facto perfectly independent." The Mexican Congress, instead of enabling the Government to put down disorders, was "occupied in disputing about vain theories of so called ultra liberal principles." Consequently, Wyke complained he was "all but powerless to obtain redress from a Government which is solely occupied in maintaining its existence from day to day, and therefore unwilling to attend to other peoples' misfortunes before their own." No redress could be expected "except by the employment of force to exact that which both persuasion and menaces have hitherto failed to obtain."[56]

In a private letter to Russell, Wyke promised to let the course of the next month show the intentions of the Mexican Government with respect to British claims before he would propose any specific measures to protect British interests. But in any eventuality, about the middle of October, when the sickly season ended, "a respectable Naval force should be concentrated at Vera Cruz which would greatly strengthen my negotiations with them."[57]

There was obviously much truth in what Wyke said, but his opinions were also formed by more than he had actually observed himself during his month's stay in Mexico. The Legation archives had convinced him that Mathew's naïve faith in the Liberals had led to nothing but worthless and fraudulent promises. Wyke had approached Saligny to put an end to the enmity between the two legations.[58] The French Minister insisted that only threats to use force accomplished anything and gave the impression that he had "full powers . . . to apply force in order to obtain redress should he consider it necessary to do so, for which purpose he has three men of war now stationed at Vera Cruz."[59] Finally, Wyke's previous experience in the Central American countries[60] had led him to the conclusion already that nothing could be expected either from Spanish American Liberals or Conservatives:

> In all these countries the Liberals, like the Conservatives, have sunk to very low levels; the scum of both parties have come to the top, and its is only among the "Moderados" that healthy elements are to be found.[61]

On 3 June a Presidential Decree appeared in the newspapers that all payments to creditors of the National Treasury were suspended for one year, with the exception of the Laguna Seca claim and the diplomatic conventions.[62] Since no exception was made for the Legation Robbery, Wyke sent

Guzman an inquiry.[63] This led to an extended exchange of notes. Guzman maintained that, since the Legation Robbery would be made good from the confiscated property of the guilty, the Mexican Treasury could not be held responsible. He implied that the actual robbers, and not the Mexican Government, were responsible and stated that orders to expedite judicial inquiries had been issued. His last word was that he was adhering to the agreement with Mathew, "without discussing whether it be good or bad, inasmuch as the opportunity of so doing has passed."[64] Wyke, in turn, appealed to International Law, and claimed Mexico was responsible, not just the perpetrators, whose property in any case would not be sufficient — all to no avail.[65]

On 11 June, the deadline for the payment of the Laguna Seca claim, Wyke sent Guzman a note to ask where the claimants could collect their money.[66] Guzman replied that the "difficulties . . . of the moment combined with the penury of the Treasury" to prevent payment. He offered compensation in the form of convents and other property formerly belonging to the Church, even the National Palace.[67] Wyke was suspicious, but referred the offer to the claimants, who demanded ready cash. At Wyke's suggestion, they accepted an offer to negotiate further with the Mexican Government.[68]

Lack of money led the Mexican Government to further expedients. Mr. Whitehead informed Wyke that custom house assignments in Vera Cruz to the London Bondholders, whom Whitehead represented, had been stopped in violation of the Dunlop and Aldham agreements. Wyke protested this as a violation of international obligations, but Guzman denied that the Dunlop and Aldham agreements bore the character of conventions. A further protest brought the answer that Wyke could not be answered officially, as Guzman had resigned, and no one had been appointed to replace him. Wyke's opinion was that the "resignation was probably so timed on purpose."[69]

The month Wyke was going to give the Mexican Government to show its intentions was now over. Just as Wyke had

predicted, the Mexican Government adhered to the letter of
its agreement with Mathew in order to put off the settlement
of the Legation Robbery. The Laguna Seca claimants were
tempted into direct negotiations with the Government, thus
taking their affairs out of the hands of the British Minister,
at least for the time being. Taking advantage of a technicality,[70]
the Mexican Government claimed assignments to the London
Bondholders were not actually based on international *conventions,* hence not grounded in International Law. So payments
to the bondholders ceased. The only satisfaction Wyke obtained
when pressing the Bodmer claim was the standard Mexican
promise to take action against those responsible for the
murder.[71]

The crux of the difficulties was that the Juarez Government
had no money, either to pay obligations to foreigners or to put
down the die-hard reactionary chiefs who ravaged the country.
Only a very small percentage of the church property was
realised, and much of this went to pay Juarez' Civil War
debts.[72] Corruption in the custom houses drained off a large
share of federal revenues.[73] The rebel leaders, however, lived
off the land, robbed, and hoped to capture Mexico City and
drive out Juarez. It was a time of troubles, and the fault of
the Juarez Government was not that it did not try to restore
order, but that it was unsuccessful. Early in June news reached
Mexico City that Marquez had seized and shot Ocampo, a
leading Liberal. Congress voted 40,000 piastres (taken from a
fund to cover French claims) to send out troops. At the same
time prices were put on the heads of Marquez, Zuloaga, and
others of the Church Party.[74] Generals Degollado and Valle
set out and were defeated and killed. Terror spread through
Mexico City, and on 25 June a hundred of Marquez' men
entered Mexico City and rescued some of their imprisoned
comrades before Government troops forced them to reteat.
Mexico City was placed in a state of siege, and martial law
was proclaimed.[75] An English newspaper, the *Mexican Extraordinary,* added to the excitement by publishing distressing

British claims resulting from the anarchy and demanding redress in "the name of humanity outraged."[76]

All the events of June went to prove to Wyke that no reliance could be put on the promises or even the formal engagements of the Juarez Government.[77] If Otway and Mathew had discredited the British Legation by "their absurd partialness in favor of one party and then another," the main cause of all difficulties was the Liberal Party. Congress was "a set of fools and knaves."[78] The Liberals were only "drifting from one vain thing to another, whilst the reins of Government are so loosened by way of courting popularity that anarchy and confusion are sure to reign triumphant."[79] While Wyke was writing one despatch, he complained that Marquez' forces were actually attacking Mexico City.[80] In what now became a monthly private letter to Russell, Wyke claimed that he never had expected much from the Liberals, but even so he was surprised :

> My past . . . experience has convinced me that nothing reasonable or good can be expected from Spanish American Liberals, and therefore I am hardly surprised at what has taken place here since that Party has been in power, but still these Mexican liberals have out Heroded Herod![81]

Nor were the Conservatives much better.[82] In one despatch Wyke mentioned that more might be expected from the "moderates," but he did not go into details.[83] But in a private letter to Lord Lyons, the British Minister to Washington, Wyke expressed his hope that the "moderates" might come forward if supported by a foreign intervention :

> The only hope one has, is that the moderate party may come forward to save this unfortunate country from the abyee into which it has fallen by the protracted struggle for power between Ultra Liberals and the high Church party. Such a party, however would I fear be all but powerless in itself, unless—supported by some foreign Power, whose interests justified an intervention in the internal affairs of the country.[84]

The proposals Wyke had promised Russell were not, however, for an intervention in Mexican internal affairs. Rather Wyke related specific military observations made by Captain Aldham with a view to a limited custom house intervention. A squadron of six to ten vessels of war would be sufficient, Aldham thought, to seize the custom houses of Vera Cruz, Tampico, Matamoras and one of those on the Pacific coast. Force would only be necessary to seize Vera Cruz and Tampico. Then two frigates and a garrison of three hundred men could hold Vera Cruz, while one or two gunboats and a few hundred men could hold Tampico. Duties on goods landed would be lowered to increase imports, and the percentage to which the British were entitled withheld. Wyke agreed that there would be little resistance and recommended Aldham's observations, but proposed that "taking one or two of those places quite sufficient." Wyke begged for prompt action so that Great Britain could act alone:

> I should be sorry to see any other nation beforehand with us in this inevitable act of justice for reasons I need not dwell on.[85]

A day later Wyke reported that he believed Corwin, the American Minister, had instructions to negotiate an offensive-defensive treaty and grant a loan of $60,000,000 to defend Mexico against the Confederacy. Wyke thought the United States was acting wisely.[86] It was not fear of intervention by the United States, but by France, that led Wyke to seek a prompt intervention. Confidentially, in a private letter to Russell, Wyke complained that, if the Jecker bonds were made good, there would be no money left to pay British claims. In addition, Saligny was pressing other questionable claims that Great Britain would have to back in acting in concert with France:

> The French have grievances also to redress, and are I have reason to believe, strongly inclined to obtain justice by force. Should they propose any joint action with Her Majesty's

Government in this sense, I think it would be inadvisable to accede to it for many reasons. Their Minister here Monsieur de Saligny is supporting the claim of a Swiss Banker . . . for $14,000,000 against this Government which if it was ever recognized would deprive them of all means of settling our claims hereafter. It appears that said Banker lent the Miramon Government $750,000 when they were in their last extremity, and they in return gave him Bonds for the immense amount above named. Monsieur de Saligny on the ground that this Government is responsible for the acts of its Predecessors claims the payment of this debt, which they refuse . . . because they have no money to pay it with, and . . . because if they had, they do not consider themselves bound to redeem the engagements of the Miramon Government. The French Minister is right in his theory but exacting the payment of such a loan under the circumstances is hardly fair or just. Besides this, they have some claim connected with a religious house and the Sisters of Charity . . . . Going hand in hand with the French Government in supporting such claims as these would only bring (unreadable word) on us and at the same time be positively injurious to our interests.[87]

The fateful month of July began with the particularly brutal murder of a British subject, Mr. Beale. The *Mexican Extraordinary* covered the story in detail and commented :

The daily events in Mexico have become so alike, that one is induced to ask, on getting up in the morning, "Who has been robbed?" "Who has been murdered?"[88]

Meanwhile Marquez continued to ravage the countryside. Stopping at Real del Monte, he forced over one hundred British miners to hand over their small savings.[89] Wyke was exasperated, because he saw no hope that the murderers of Beale would be apprehended,[90] or that Marquez would be stopped by the Government troops sent out after him.[91] In addition, Mexico was in the midst of a cabinet crisis again, and protests addressed to the Foreign Ministry usually went unanswered.[92]

Hardly appointed, Zamacona, the new Minister of Foreign

Relations,[93] found himself in the difficult position of trying to
justify a financial law passed by Congress on 17 July suspending payments to the London Bondholders[94] and foreign conventions.[95] He claimed the law did not violate international
obligations. The suspension was not a voluntary act, but was
caused by the "imperious necessity" to restore order.[96] Wyke
only became acquainted with the law through newspaper
accounts and at once protested that Mexico could not unilater-
ally suspend bilateral agreements and that he would not be
indulgent after having received no satisfaction whatsoever for
the claims he had pressed. The suspension of payments, he
charged, resulted from the squandering of a confiscated church
property by the Mexican Government. On his own initiative,
Wyke presented an ultimatum for the withdrawal of the law
and then suspended diplomatic relations on 25 July.[97]

At the end of the month Wyke prepared his despatches for
the packet to Southampton. He claimed that things had gotten
worse in the last month and pointed to the Beale murder and
Marquez' outrages at Real del Monte. The Government was
helpless, and foreigners were about to arm themselves for
mutual defense.[98] The financial law was only passed, because
"they have been treated with so much forebearance hitherto,
that they have now persuaded themselves that they can do
anything they like with impunity."[99] Their "wretched vanity
and pride," at any rate, would prevent the withdrawal of the
law.[100] In his private letter to Russell, Wyke painted an even
darker picture and predicted worse things to come if coercion
were not employed :

> This wretched Government after recklessly squandering all
> the Church property have been levying forced loans and con-
> tributions on all the respectable people in the city, and im-
> prisoning such as did not immediately pay any exorbitant sum
> that was demanded of them.
>
> .    .    .    .    .    .    .    .    .
>
> This is only a solitary instance of the many acts of cruelty and
> injustice of which these people have been guilty, whilst con-

stantly talking of liberty, toleration and the blessings of a constitutional system. I know nothing more detestable than this species of tyranny under the guise of freedom; it is like a Prostitute boasting of her virtue. Their idea of political economy seems to consist in putting their hands into other people's pockets whenever they are in want of money, whilst they take very good care never to make the least sacrifice themselves. They have squandered or pocketed all the resources of the Republick, and now make us pay for the continuance of the civil war by violating the conventions . . . . If Her Majesty's Government overlook this last outrage no Englishman's property is safe here, and they will be subjected to all sorts of exactions and annoyances.[101]

It was now that Wyke, like Otway before him, envisioned a peaceful and prosperous Mexico, "one of the richest and most prosperous countries of the world."[102] With the same interest in trade as Mathew, Wyke predicted Mexico could increase threefold her exports of silver and imports of British manufactured goods.[103] All this was impossible so long as the Liberals remained in power, and anarchy continued. Therefore it became the "interest of Great Britain to put a stop, by force if necessary, to anarchy and insist on its Government paying what is owed to British Subjects."[104] Now Wyke informed Russell for the first time of the possibility that a foreign intervention might aid the moderates. A month before Wyke had expressed the hope privately to Lord Lyons that an "intervention in the internal affairs" of Mexico might bring the moderates forward. Nothing of the sort was suggested now, for Wyke feared that "in asking too much we might obtain nothing."[105] Instead he wrote Russell that the limited custom house intervention proposed the month before might encourage the moderate party, "now cowed by the two opposing ultra factions," to "raise its head, and . . . probably establish . . . such a Government as we require."[106] The moderates, Wyke seemed convinced, would grant genuine redress and maintain law and order.

August and September drifted past without Wyke receiving

any important new instructions.[107] He busied himself with
writing a history of British claims recognized by conventions between Mexico and Great Britain. Elaborate statistical
annexes showed that the claimants, the Convention Bondholders, had received $2,304,782.18 in the last ten years but
that Mexico was $1,482,426.01 in arrears. It was for nothing,
Wyke charged, that British diplomatic efforts in the last years
had increased custom house assignments to the bondholders.
His statistics showed that Mexico had never even met the
original assignment of 12 per cent of Mexican custom duties.[108]

Wyke continued to report the usual murders of British subjects[109] and failure of a succession of Government generals
against Marquez.[110] Charges were renewed that the states were
virtually independent,[111] and that the Liberals squandered or
pocketed the resources of the nation.[112] The law of 17 July
paralyzed all trade,[113] and a decree imposing a tax of 1 per cent
on capital over $2000 was but a forced loan in another form
and the forerunner of exactions that would ruin British commerce, as Wyke had predicted.[114] A Mexican court convicted
four of those connected with the Legation Robbery of "occupying" the $660,000.[115] Wyke spelled out the results:

> This sentence will of course have the effect of absolving Mar-
> quez and all others implicated in the robbery, as it frees them
> from the danger of criminal prosecution for what is now
> designated as merely a civil misdemeanor, the only punish-
> ment for which is dismissal from offices long ago forfeited by
> all the Parties engaged in the affair.[116]

Moreover Congress publically absolved General Degollado for
his seizure of the Laguna Seca Conducta. His death was considered sufficient atonement, and Wyke insisted that it was
"so thoroughly Mexican that it needs no comment." [117] The
official and opposition parties were so balanced in Congress
that nothing could be accomplished, and Wyke believed Juarez
only obtained a small majority to counter a resolution for his
resignation by buying off some of the opposition.[118] It all went

to reaffirm Wyke's hopes in the moderates, who would be encouraged by an intervention.[119] The only alternative was that Mexico would dissolve into petty states, warring on each other until exhaustion and enacting "over again the same horrors that formerly took place in Central America."[120]

On 1 October Wyke received instructions to demand that Mexico permit the appointment of British Commissioners to Vera Cruz and Tampico. They were to be empowered to appropriate from the custom houses there the assignments due all foreign conventions and the sums taken from the Laguna Seca Conducta and the British Legation. These Commissioners would also have the right to reduce Mexican import duties up to one half. If Mexico refused to comply, Wyke was directed to withdraw his mission from Mexico.[121] Wyke foresaw that he would gain nothing by following the strict letter of Russell's demands, because Juarez could not reduce the tariff without the consent of Congress.[122] Furthermore, Wyke failed to see how the Commissioners in Vera Cruz and Tampico would be able to collect the percentage of custom duties from other ports under foreign liabilities.[123] He favored a general reduction of the Mexican tariff and did not think changes in only two ports would bring about sufficient benefits.[124] He was also loathe to act on behalf of the French convention, when France was already represented in Mexico by Saligny.[125] Wyke explained to Russell that acting in concert with Saligny would only have been possible if he had "been other than he is."[126] But the French Minister was "ever ready to bluster and bully when permitted to do so."[127] Since the amount due the French convention was a "mere trifle," Wyke urged Zamacona to grant Saligny redress for proper demands.[128] Wyke decided to act alone and hold back an ultimatum until all other means failed.[129] He thought it "much better to obtain what we want peaceably, than to allow matters to come to extremities with these people."[130]

The day after he received his instructions,[131] Wyke saw Saligny and informed him of them verbally.[132] The French

Minister gained the impression that an ultimatum calling for a pure and simple acceptance would be presented to the Mexican Government in a few days.[133] Wyke believed that Saligny scarcely was able to hide his mortification that he had not received any instructions himself.[134]

Wyke read his instructions to Zamacona. He was astonished and alarmed and asked for time to inform Juarez and the cabinet. A week later Zamacona returned, and daily unofficial negotiations started at the British Legation.[135] Saligny was piqued that he was informed of these negotiations only "in very vague terms."[136] He predicted failure so strongly that Wyke did not think it worthwhile to contradict him.[137] In public Saligny protested that Wyke was not acting in a friendly way toward him. Thereafter Wyke "neither sought nor avoided" Saligny's society.[138]

Zamacona objected to paying the $660,000 stolen from the British Legation on the ground that his Government thereby would recognize responsibility for the acts of the Miramon Government. The Mexican Minister also observed that he had no resources to meet British demands. At this juncture a "friend in need" was found in Thomas Corwin, the American Minister to Mexico. He announced that he was authorized to grant Mexico a loan. With the prospect of this financial aid, Zamacona agreed to renew the British mortgage on Mexican import duties.[139] Corwin volunteered to withhold his loan until Wyke and Zamacona reached a settlement. Wyke was pleased, for he feared that otherwise the money would have been squandered, while British claims were left unsettled. Only the hope of "obtaining these resources," Wyke wrote in a private letter, "has induced this unprincipled govt to treat with me." Under other circumstances it "would have yielded to nothing but the actual employment of force."[140]

Zamacona claimed that the Commissioners would offend the "national decorum," and Congress would reject the arrangement.[141] Wyke threatened to use force but saw there was "some degree of truth" in what Zamacona said. Wyke, therefore, proposed to put the name of Commissioners or Interventors aside and gain the same effect under another form. It was agreed that importers be required to pay the percentage of import duties due the bondholders to their agents before paying the remainder of duties to the custom house authorities.[142]

The next problem was where the money should come from to pay the Laguna Seca and Legation robberies. Wyke recalled that 20 per cent of the "majoras materiales," additional duties on imports,[143] were made over to one Don Manuel Escaudon to aid him in constructing a railroad from Vera Cruz to Mexico City. Wyke believed this project was a "chimera" and that Mexico had no right to waste its money in this way while leaving debts unpaid. So he suggested stopping payment to Don Manuel and splitting the money thus gained between the Mexican Government and the repayment of the Laguna Seca and Legation robberies. By 28 October, when Wyke summarized his negotiations in a despatch for the mail packet for England, Zamacona had agreed to the proposal. The tariff question remained, but Wyke had Zamacona's promise to use his best efforts with the Mexican Congress. Wyke was optimistic and believed that within two weeks he would be able to sign a convention.[144] His apparent success, however, did not change his old convictions:

> It is just possible that they will create some fresh difficulty when we come to draw up the Articles of the proposed Convention, and in that case, we must resort to the measures which I proposed . . . for forcing this Government to fulfil its obligations. I consider it absolutely necessary that a Naval force should soon make its appearance in the waters of Vera Cruz in order to sustain the prestige which I have obtained here by being so energetically supported by Her Majesty's Government. It is only by fear that we can hope to control (?) their evil practices.[145]

He saw no possibility of an improvement in Mexican internal confusion unless a government of moderates were formed ". . . with some material support from abroad."[146]

At the end of October Wyke saw Saligny and was "nettled" by his manner and told him "plainly" that the Mexican Government would agree to a settlement with Great Britain.[147] But Saligny believed the Mexicans were just trying to gain time.[148] He wrote Thouvenel in bitterness that Zamacona and Wyke were meeting every day to discuss "impossible" and "unbelievable" projects.[149]

In the evening of 30 October Saligny received[150] instructions[151] copied from those that Wyke had received four weeks before.[152] The next day Saligny called on Wyke, informed him of Thouvenel's instructions and proposed acting in concert.[153] What Saligny had in mind was a joint presentation of ultimatums without negotiation.[154] On 2 November he told Zamacona that Mexico had to accept French demands immediately. That evening Saligny called on Wyke again and told him that France and Great Britain were planning a joint intervention in Mexico. Since Wyke did not seem to know what was going on, Saligny proposed a meeting when he could show some pertinent documents.[155] Although Wyke had no official notification of the proposed intervention by France, Spain, and Great Britain,[156] rumors to that effect became current in Mexico at the beginning of November.[157] Wyke saw in such a tripartite intervention a step which "must inevitably upset all the advantage . . . already gained" in his negotiations with Zamacona. Wyke thought it a pity to lose the start already made and decided to go on and draw up a convention. All Great Britain required, Wyke wrote Russell, might be obtained without acting with France and Spain, "whose interests and sympathies in this country are in reality entirely opposed to our own."[158] Wyke elaborated in his monthly private letter to Russell:

> I very much regret that we do not come here alone instead of with France and Spain, as the interests we have at stake are quite sufficient to justify our doing so, and we should then be spared the odium of acting conjointly with Powers which are considered as identical with the reactionary and old Priest Party.

Although the leaders of the Liberal Party have bickered like rogues and fools since they have been in power, but there is no doubt that the principles they so badly represent have taken a deep root in the minds of the people, who would now never submit to be again governed under the old regime.

.          .          .          .          .          .          .          .

I have only adopted the line of conduct I pursued from a settled conviction that it is the only one likely to succeed with a lot of people whose prejudices and peculiarities I have had an opportunity of studying for the last ten years, during which time I have learnt that the only way . . . is . . . to make them both respect and fear you.[159]

Wyke believed that, of the three Powers, Great Britain had the greatest interest at stake, and he was determined to safeguard it by reaching an agreement with Mexico before the arrival of the allied fleet.[160] On 5 November Wyke saw Saligny but did not ask to see the documents he wanted to show. Asked about his negotiations, Wyke replied that Saligny would be informed immediately after the signing of a convention. Saligny said, if he were not informed at least a day in advance, it would be too late. Wyke departed[161] and did not see Saligny again until they both met in Vera Cruz on 26 December.[162]

When Corwin heard that England, France, and Spain were on the point of coercing Mexico to pay its foreign debt, it was only with difficulty that Wyke prevented him from at once concluding a loan convention with Mexico. Then Wyke continued negotiations with Zamacona to reduce the Mexican tariff. Without tariff reform, Wyke told Zamacona, their convention would be worthless. The Mexican Minister replied that Congress would object to any semblance of foreign interference. Wyk knew this was true, and proposed the reduction should come apparently from Congress itself, as a result of a report of the tariff committee appointed when Mathew represented Great Britain. Zamacona agreed, and the tariff committee proposed to Congress that import duties be reduced 50 per cent and that additional duties be reduced almost as much. Wyke called a meeting of British merchants to hear their

opinion. They agreed that the reduction favored trade generally, but "found half a dozen causes for grumbling."[163] Some
of them believed that Mexico was making no concession,
because it also benefited.[164] Mr. Whitehead, the agent of the
London Bondholders, observed that, if import duties were
decreased 50 per cent, imports would have to double to maintain the level of payments to the bondholders. He did not
believe this was probable so long as additional duties remained
higher than import duties. Wyke replied Mexico could not be
expected to cripple itself "for the sake of being able actually
to square the Balance-sheet of the Bondholders, or fix the exact
ticket to be placed on each separate piece of shirting that came
into the country."[165]

On 15 November the Mexican Congress passed a law authorizing the executive to reduce import duties up to 40 per
cent and additional duties up to about 42 per cent.[166] Wyke
preferred the congressional to the committee plan. He believed
that merchant and bondholder were affected almost equally.
The immense advantage was that tariff reform was taken out
of the hands of the legislature and placed under the control
of the executive. But he still feared that changes might be introduced in the future on the plea of urgent necessity. Consequently he informed Zamacona that the tariff reduction was
acceptable if accompanied by a promise to make no changes
in duties without notice six months in advance. Wyke's doubts
turned into certainty when Zamacona hesitated to make the
promise, because, he said, he believed that it implied doubt as
to the honesty of his Government. Wyke only gained the pledge
when he demanded it as a *sine non qua*. The negotiation ended
with an agreement that the tariff go into operation in four
months.[167]

Before signing their convention on 21 November,[168] Wyke
and Zamacona exchanged notes[169] to influence congressional
sentiment favorably by making it appear that the "Government had been acting from a spirit of justice, instead of being
under . . . undue pressure of menaces." At the same time Wyke

obtained an "official declaration . . . binding them to the reduction of the Tariff," which was not included in the convention.[170]

The convention provided for the payment of the Laguna Seca and Legation robberies and a resumption of custom assignments to the London and Convention Bondholders. Interventors appeared in the form of British consular agents and representatives of the bondholders, entitled to inspect the books of the custom houses. The burden of paying the bondholders was placed on the importers, in essence the proposed arrangement of the London Bondholders that Mr. Otway had failed to obtain in 1858. Instead of a mere agreement and a memorandum obtained by Captains Dunlop and Aldham, the London Bondholders had their interest guaranteed them by a formal diplomatic convention.[171]

Hopes of preventing British participation in the rumored tripartite intervention,[172] Wyke's threats to leave Mexico in accordance with his instructions, and prospects of American financial aid combined to make Zamacona give way on the Legation Robbery, the method of paying the bondholders, and the official recognition of the claims of the London Bondholders. Concessions were made only after the "studied obstinacy" of Juarez was overcome, and an obdurate Minister of Finance was replaced by another willing to permit tariff revision.[173]

In a secret session of Congress on the night of 22–23 November the Committee on Foreign Affairs, headed by a leader of the opposition, Sebastian Lerdo de Tejada, made an unfavorable report on the convention,[174] and it was rejected by more than a two-thirds majority.[175] Congressional opinion was against the articles concerning Laguna Seca, the Legation Robbery, and the powers granted British consuls.[176] Lerdo hoped to turn events to his own advantage. He made a bid to appease Wyke, reach an agreement with him, and supplant Zamacona. On 23 November Lerdo sponsored[177] and obtained the repeal of the law of 17 July, which had stopped payments to the London and Convention Bondholders.[178] Two days later Zamacona sent the convention back to Congress for reconsideration[179] and resigned when this proved futile.[180] Lerdo called on Wyke and asked him to agree to modify the articles to which Congress objected. Lerdo believed that he could obtain ratification for a modified convention and then become Minister of Foreign Relations,[181] but Wyke refused to make concessions.[182]

On 20 November a meeting of the Diplomatic Corps was called to mediate between Saligny and the Mexican Government.[183] One of the differences was what Wyke termed a "stupid dispute" with the Chief of Police.[184] Although Wyke had attended a meeting of the Diplomatic Corps in August in connection with a Mexican tax on capital,[185] he now excused himself on the ground that the meeting might end with a representation to the Mexican Government, with which he held no official communication.[186] The next day he wrote Saligny that Mexico had granted the substance of Russell's instructions in a convention just signed. Wyke added that he was sorry the efforts of the Diplomatic Corps failed and offered his own services[187] The French Minister replied that the signing of a convention confirmed what he had heard by rumor and that he believed the conditions required by France and Great Britain were the same.[188] Wyke was offended that, while thanked for his offer of services, it was neither accepted nor refused. He also believed it was "hinted far too broadly" that he had thrown Saligny "over in this business" to permit his letter to go unanswered.[189] An exchange of private notes followed that both clarified and intensified their differences. The negotiations that Saligny claimed to know by rumor, Wyke reminded him, were discussed by them both. He had yet to hear, Wyke continued, that Great Britain and France "intend any joint action on the part of their agents here." By "patience and perseverance" he had obtained all that was required, and the same course was open to Saligny, to whom the offer of services was renewed.[190] Saligny countered that he had an excellent memory. Not until 28 October, when rumor had had it for some time, did Wyke say his negotiations were serious. Previously he had said that he expected no results and that his negotiations were just to gain time. But Saligny was convinced that a joint presentation of ultimatums "would have been accepted purely and simply."[191] Wyke appealed to the French-man's "excellent memory" to recall that the language "you now put into my mouth in reality came out of your own." What actually happened, the British Minister pointed out, was that Saligny stated his conviction of failure so strongly that Wyke contented himself with saying, "It is possible, perhaps, etc., etc." On one occasion he was so angered that he told Saligny that the Mexicans were in earnest.[192] Although he had not changed his opinions of the insincerity of the Mexicans, Wyke found an exception in Zamacona.[193] He behaved in "the most straightforward and candid manner, as he proved du reste (sic) by his resigning his post when his Convention was rejected." Wyke did not believe that presenting ultimatums at the same time would have led to any good result. He founded his opinion on ten years of residence among people "who may sometimes be guided, but who never allow themselves to be driven." While he hoped to maintain the best understanding with the French Legation, it could not be expected of him to follow a policy of which he did not approve[194] and which offered no hope of success:

> In the different lines we have adopted in treating of this question you have stuck to the *letter* of your instructions, I have acted according to the *spirit* of mine, your position offered me no hope whatever of success, wheras mine ended in the most perfect success as far as I had any action in the matter and this was only marred by circumstances over which neither the Government with which I treated nor myself had any control, and on this point we differ apparently as much as North from South.[195]

Saligny maintained that he had not put words in Wyke's mouth. He had agreed about the "absolute lack of faith in the loyalty of these people." Wyke's opinions, the French Minister thought, had changed greatly. Though he didn't have ten years' experience, the eleven months Saligny had spent in Mexico "sufficed to let" him know "that these people only replied with ruse, guile, and falsehood (*mensonge*) to all the good sentiments" he showed them for a long time. He also "tried to give them advice, to guide them, but they soon forced" him "to renounce this thankless task."[196] By 25 November both Wyke[197] and Saligny[198] realized that further correspondence was unlikely to lead to any practical result, and they agreed to meet sometime in the future. Although Wyke wrote Russell that "the slight polemic between myself and my French Colleague has ended amicably,"[199] hard feelings remained. Wyke didn't call on Saligny, who had been confined to his house by illness since their last meeting on 5 November.[200] The French Minister had already felt slighted before the "polemic" that Wyke never paid him a visit, in contrast to the other diplomats, who stopped by regularly.[201]

On 25 November twenty-nine British merchants sent Wyke an address protesting that his convention made no provision for compensation for murders, robberies, and other pending claims of British subjects.[202] William Moran, the editor of the *Mexican Extraordinary,* was one of those who signed the address. He had a claim for $20,000 that later investigation proved of a "doubtful nature."[203] On 28 November an article[204] by Thomas Worrall,[205] whose claim Wyke had already found unjustified,[206] appeared in Moran's newspaper. The complaint of the "address" was renewed in more caustic terms. It was charged that Wyke did not take care of British interests and claims. His convention only provided satisfaction for two or three prominent interests. More was to be expected from Saligny, who was firm and did not negotiate. He was to be congratulated on his judgement and knowledge of people. Worrall's article ended with a recommendation that Wyke cooperate with the French Minister. Wyke replied to the merchants that his convention was just a preliminary to a settlement of further claims. He countered that he regretted they waited until just before the mail left for England, when he could only forward their address, instead of concrete proposals, to the Foreign Office.[207] Wyke sent Worrall's article to Russell and claimed Saligny had obtained nothing by acting in the letter of his instructions. In spite of the rejection of his convention, Wyke believed he could point to the abrogation of the law of 17 July and the tariff reduction as the successful results of acting in accordance with the spirit of his own instructions.[208]

The rejection of his convention by the Mexican Congress, as Wyke put it "reduces the settlement of these questions to the future employment of brute force."[209] On 24 November he sent an ultimatum,[210] based on Russell's conditions but differing somewhat from them to prevent it being known that in certain respects the convention granted more than the British Government really demanded.[211] The Mexican reply was that Zamacona had resigned and that the next Minister of Foreign Relations would reply to the ultimatum.[212] The cabinet crisis came to an end in early December, when General Manuel Doblado, the Governor of Guanajuato, arrived in Mexico City at Juarez' request and agreed to form a cabinet.[213] Not receiving an answer to his ultimatum, Wyke demanded his passports and asked for an escort to Vera Cruz.[214] Doblado sent the passports and offered to renew negotiations, because Congress had just authorized Juarez to make treaties without its consent.[215] Wyke would have accepted the offer, if he had not just received European newspapers stating that France, Spain, and Great Britain signed a convention in London on 31 December to intervene jointly in Mexico.[216] Wyke left Mexico City and arrived at Vera Cruz on Christmas Eve. He found the city in the possession of the Spanish, who arrived before the French and British components of the allied expedition. He had intended to proceed to Jamaica, but decided to remain in Vera Cruz to await the arrival of the British squadron. On 27 December the mail steamer arrived but brought no despatches for him. He did not know the stipulations of the Convention of

London, and his relations with Saligny were "naturally not of that cordial nature as to allow" Wyke "to obtain any information from him."[217] In a private letter written to Russell on New Year's Eve, Wyke revealed how bitter the estrangement was:

> It is most unfortunate that at the present juncture I have not a more suitable French colleague than Monsieur de Saligny. He is violent, imprudent, and I may say unscrupulous in his assertions, having told everybody here on his arrival that I was disgraced and recalled. He has quarrelled with everybody near him, and now wishes to do so with me, because I could not support him in the discreditable street row he lately got into in Mexico (City) with the Chief of Police. I shall endeavour to remain on civil but distant terms with him, so that our differences may not in anything prove prejudicial to any joint action we may have to take in the publick service. He has been urging the Spanish general to go out of the town and attack the Mexicans with the object of taking possession of three or four of the neighboring villages and when he hears that I have recommended exactly the reverse course to be pursued, he will doubtless consider it as a personal affront to himself. I enter into these details because he is most likely to write to Monsieur Thouvenel complaining of "la perfide Albion" and the intrigues of the British Legation etc., etc.
>
> Luckily both the Spanish General and Admiral are very different men, and show every disposition to keep things quiet until the arrival of the English and French forces.[218]

## 2. SALIGNY IN MEXICO IN 1861

In January 1861 Juarez entered Mexico City, and his rival, Miramon, fled to Cuba in the company of the Spanish Minister, Pacheco,[1] who was expelled as an "enemy" of the Republic.[2] The Mexican Government took the view that Pacheco's expulsion was merely personal and was in no way to reflect on Spain. Saligny found this distinction inadmissable[3] and feared a war between Mexico and Spain would result.[4] Rumors spread that Saligny assisted in Miramon's escape,[5] and, by his own admission, the French Minister gave General Casanova, one of Miramon's adherents, refuge in the French Legation.[6] Saligny, however, did not believe the Conservatives had a chance and that Mexico wanted to accept the Juarez Government:

> The whole country, tired of Civil War, wanted order and tranquility above all and was ready to recognize and accept the new government. The most compromised commanders and the die-hards of the Reaction only ask to leave the country.[7]

Then Pacheco's expulsion showed that the Government was a ". . . demagogic Saturnalia and the consternation of all honest men. . . ."[8] Nine days later Saligny reported that "the ideas of moderation have gained much ground recently." Interviews with Juarez and Zarco, the Minister of Foreign Relations, had changed Saligny's views. Juarez condemned the manner in which Pacheco was handled, and Saligny began to "see the possibility of avoiding a war between Mexico and Spain." Zarco's visit led him to believe that he could announce by the next mail "the friendly and satisfactory regulations of this long and so disagreeable affair of our Mexican claims."[9]

The greater part of the month of February, however, was not spent in a settlement of claims, which Saligny hoped to obtain before granting recognition to Juarez.[10] Instead, Saligny became involved in a drawn-out dispute about a Mexican search of the Convent of the Sisters of Charity. A decree of 5 February nationalized ecclesiastical property.[11] The Mexican Government believed that considerable sums of money of church organizations were hidden in the convent. By virtue of the decree of 5 February this money belonged to the state,[12] and on 15 February soldiers were sent to search the convent. The next day Saligny protested "in the name of France, under whose immediate protection the establishment of Sisters was placed in the entire world, and demanded that the Government withdraw the soldiers." Only after he protested twice more did the soldiers leave the convent. The Mexicans then asked the Mother Superior of the Sisters to accept a decree placing her under the protection of Mexico rather than under that of France, but on Saligny's advice she refused. He was so incensed that he was ready to declare "highly" that, if the Government should attempt to put its decree into operation, he would leave the country. Finally, on 21 February, Zarco called on Saligny and agreed to his proposal to leave the affair of the Sisters in the *status quo* in order to settle other differences.[13] Nevertheless, two weeks later Saligny protested the decree of 5 February on the ground that the "Government of the Emperor would never admit the validity of a decree that attacks the incontestable right of property."[14]

The Mexican Government was furious at what it considered an interference in its internal affairs. A confidential protest was sent to a member of the French Government. It was charged that Saligny was trying "to establish his prestige to the point of interrupting the course of national justice." His hostility and interference on behalf of the Sisters of Charity resulted from his listening to the "Spanish party," angry with the expulsion of Pacheco :

> . . . the interests of France and Mexico . . . could be compromised if the Imperial Government only considered the reports of Monsieur de Saligny, no doubt exact from his point of view and under the influence of the circle in which he moves, but not altogether complete, since Monsieur de Saligny has not learned and taken into consideration the reasons that the Government of Mexico has for acting within the limits of its information and its rights in the administration and politics of the country.[15]

This letter of protest was turned over to the Ministry of Foreign Affairs, which had already received Saligny's account of the affair.[16] Thouvenel instructed Saligny that France could not "officially protect in the whole world the establishments of houses founded by the congregation." A "certain circumspection" was to be exercised, and Saligny was to maintain the "status quo here."[17]

On 11 March Saligny and Zarco drew up a convention that would be made official as soon as Saligny presented his credentials to Juarez.[18] Twenty-five per cent of import duties on goods imported on French ships and eight per cent of import duties on merchandise imported on other ships were set aside. These funds were to pay recognized claims and unrecognized claims found to be legitimate by a mixed commission, which would consider claims of French origin. Every two months the funds were to be turned over to the French Legation, "which will . . . distribute them among the interested parties as it sees fit."[19] Saligny believed this convention was "the most advantageous that" France had "ever concluded with Mexico," and presented his credentials to Juarez on 16 March. Ten days later the convention was signed officially.[20] Several of the articles were only reluctantly agreed to by Zarco. He wanted to make continuous ownership a condition for the validation of claims, but Saligny refused to sign a convention that relieved French claimants of the "faculty of ceding, selling, or transporting . . . their right to a just reparation." As to the suggestion that French claims be referred to a Mexican tribunal created a few months before to investigate foreign claims, Saligny won his point that a mixed commission alone was able to offer "guarantees of impartiality." Zarco believed that the mortgage on custom duties was more than the treasury could bear and did not want to turn them over to Saligny for distribution. After "a quite lively resistance," Zarco consented when Saligny made it clear that the alternative was "a war with France." Finally, it was agreed that the convention should be submitted to Congress within a month after its opening session. Saligny only consented when he saw he was "in the presence of an express stipulation of the constitution," and Zarco assured him "it was only a simple formality."[21]

In December 1860 one hundred and fifty French, Swiss, and Belgian residents of Mexico sent Saligny a petition on behalf of the Jecker bonds. They reviewed the history of the decrees on which the bonds were based. Then they recalled a petition they had made to De Gabriac to ask whether the decrees would be observed. De Gabriac forwarded their petition to the Miramon Government, "which replied in a most categorical manner that all the articles . . . would be accomplished with a religious exactitude." The Juarez regime, however, "highly proclaims the nullity of the acts of the administration which decreed these laws." The petitioners, therefore, found themselves "dispossessed of a property legally acquired, guaranteed by the Mexican Government that solemnly bound itself toward all the Governments of the friendly nations." Commerce was "deprived of an indirect lowering of the general tariff and of direct or indirect taxes, toward the payment of which the bonds applied." Saligny, therefore, was requested to use his influence to obtain the execution of the decrees, "which by their very nature cannot be set aside." [22]

Saligny waited until 30 March to forward the petition on behalf of the Jecker bonds to Thouvenel. In his despatch written that day Saligny made his first official reference to the Jecker bonds, which he found perfectly legitimate:

> After a serious and careful examination of the question, it appeared to me that the part taken by the Imperial Legation in this affair, its intervention, more or less official, on behalf of the contract, gave the Government of the Emperor not only the right, but even a sort of moral duty, to insist on the execution of the contract. It was evident to me, on the other hand, that not only French commerce but even all foreign commerce in Mexico would have a vital interest that the arrangements concluded between the Mexican Government and M. Jecker be scrupulously observed, and that the administration itself, aside from the favorable effect that would necessarily result for the good name of Mexico and for the establishment of its credit, could indeed find immediate and very useful resources for itself in the situation of things.

Before recognizing Juarez, Saligny continued, he talked with Zarco about the bonds "loudly and firmly." After many arguments, Zarco "ended first by admitting the principle, then by saying he would arrange" with Saligny "the bases of a nature to satisfy M. Jecker." Saligny wanted to take advantage of this promise to settle the affair before presenting his credentials, but Zarco objected that certain delays were necessary. Furthermore, Juarez held the signature of the Franco–Mexican convention and Saligny's official presentation so "very important" that they "could not be put off any longer." Saligny didn't want to jeopardize his convention and agreed to postpone the settlement of the Jecker affair on condition that it was "accepted in principle."[23] Before receiving this despatch, Thouvenel had already penned an instruction to Saligny that he was to have the Jecker bonds respected. His attention, Thouvenel claimed, was brought to the matter by a "claim" signed by representatives of commercial houses.[24] On the surface it would appear that both Saligny and Thouvenel received petitions from parties interested in the Jecker bonds and that the French Minister of Foreign Affairs and his Minister to Mexico independently decided to support the bonds. Yet it was evident, as a special agent sent by Mexico to Europe told Thouvenel, that Jecker's claim was "far beyond its real value," and was, in fact, a speculation on the "chance of the triumph or the ruin . . . of the government of M. Miramon."[25] The reason France supported Jecker has been explained by a popular theory that Jecker and the Duc de Morny, Napoleon's half-brother and President of the Corps Legislatif, entered a deal in January 1861, whereby Morny was to use his influence to have the Jecker bonds respected in return for 30 per cent of the profits. This has never been conclusively proven and remains an open question.[26] Likewise, Saligny's motives in pressing the Jecker bonds remain nebulous. He had interested himself in them before he left France, but that he was a protegé of Morny and sought to have the bonds respected for the duke's personal gain is an unsubstantiated corrolary to the Jecker–Morny thesis.[27] The Jecker bonds, however, were not really a cause of the French expedition to Mexico. Napoleon saw in them merely the means of furthering his Mexican policy. He had told the

Mexican exiles that he ". . . had no pretext for intervention in Mexico. . . ."[28] In July 1861 Thouvenel told an agent of the Juarez Government that one of the reasons France had decided on a "severe coercion" was to "have the Jecker claims respected."[29] Then, once the French expedition was in Mexico, Napoleon III used the bonds as a pretext to keep it there.[30]

The day before he presented his credentials, Saligny wrote a despatch to Thouvenel that the streets of Mexico City were not safe at night. Stage coaches between Mexico City and Puebla were constantly stopped by thieves.[31] Two weeks later Saligny complained that the Mexican Treasury was empty, that expedients were used up, and that no government could maintain credit. The confiscated Church property had not been used to restore financial stability. Instead the Government had handed much of this wealth to personal friends.[32] In addition to anarchy and bankruptcy, the Mexican Government, in Saligny's view, was guilty of inhumanity in prosecuting the defeated Conservative leaders. In mid-April he took up the cause of General Casanova. The general had been given refuge in the French Legation when the Liberals captured Mexico City. After a month he left, went to the house of a friend, was captured, and on 16 April Saligny learned that Casanova would be condemned during the night and probably executed the next day. Saligny at once protested "in the name of France and humanity." The next day Saligny learned that the general would be executed about noon. then sought out Zarco, protested to him for two hours, then asked to see Juarez immediately. The execution was put off, and Saligny saw Juarez, who suspended the execution and issued an order sending Casanova before the district tribunal.[33]

Although he favored the Conservatives and acted on behalf of the Sisters of Charity and General Casanova, Saligny saw no possibility that the Conservatives could return to power. But he believed a new revolution might result from the anarchy in Mexico. Therefore, he urged that France send to the coasts of Mexico "a material force, sufficient in power no matter what happens, for the protection of our interests."[34] This was Saligny's first official reference to the necessity of a show of force, and it came at the end of April, six weeks after he recognized the Juarez Government. At the beginning of May Saligny made clear that he did not have a large scale intervention in mind. He only wanted a small naval force under his orders to make the "dignity and rights of France respected" in Mexico:

> In the state of things, it appears absolutely indispensible to me that the Government of the Emperor send without the slightest delay into the Gulf (of Mexico) forces sufficient to take care of all eventualities. Moreover, an expedition on a big scale or even a squadron will not be necessary. With three other gunboats such as the *Eclair,* which has been at Sacrificios for two months, armed with long range cannons, and a corvette as a depot for coal and munitions, I would very well make the dignity and rights of France respected. An essential point is that the commander of the boats and especially of Sacrificios be experienced, resolute, and prudent, as well as energetic and have the formal order to obey the directions of the Minister of the Emperor. Finally, it would be necessary that the Minister of His Majesty, invested with very extended powers, be authorized to act on his own personal responsibility, according to the necessities of circumstances.

He needed the discretionary powers, Saligny explained, because he had to buck each repression of rights immediately in a country where one government followed another so quickly.[35]

On 1 May Saligny met Zarco and the Minister of Finance, Mata, and they agreed on the form of a letter Saligny was to address to Zarco and the answer it would evoke. At the same time Mata promised to defend the proposed arangement before Congress.[36] The letter Saligny sent to Zarco merely requested to know the position of Mexico toward the Jecker bonds, which, if not paid, prevented France from "giving a free course to her friendly intentions toward Mexico."[37] Saligny accompanied this request with a confidential letter insisting on the "absolute right to insist upon the execution, pure and simple, of the

Jecker contract." Taking into consideration the difficulties of the Mexican Government, however, Saligny added that Jecker would probably permit certain modifications of his contract.[38] These modifications appeared to Saligny "the only means of avoiding a rupture, which would lead to the ruin of your Government and your country."[39] Zarco replied by asking Saligny to wait a few days until Congress, which would have to approve any arrangement, convened. In any eventuality Mexico would adhere to "the principles of international law."[40] Saligny thought Zarco's reply was a French diplomatic triumph in that it was the "*written* recognition of the principle that we are defending."[41]

The fate of Saligny's convention and the settlement of the Jecker bonds was now up to the Mexican Congress, which opened sessions on 9 May, the very day Wyke arrived in Mexico City. At the same time Zarco and his stopgap cabinet resigned, and Don Leon Guzman formed a new cabinet.[42] But in the first of two interpellations by Congress in May in connection with the Jecker affair, it was stated that the only legitimate government since 1857 was the Constitutional Government, which had nothing to do with "the engagements of a criminal faction." A second interpellation shelved the affair by the appointment of a commission to study the matter and report to Congress. Saligny asked for instructions in case of things "too easy to foresee." He renewed his urgings that French forces be sent to the Gulf of Mexico.[43] At the same time he reported that Sir Charles Wyke seemed to have "the same ideas . . . that one must act towards these people with energy and without losing time." The French Minister believed Wyke was "awaiting the arrival of a considerable naval force in the Gulf (of Mexico) that are to arrive shortly."[44] Saligny had hoped to be able to announce a satisfactory conclusion of the Jecker affair by the mail packet of 2 June.[45] Congress, however, rejected responsibility for Miramon's engagements with Jecker, and Saligny viewed Congress as the center of "tumult and scandal," where nothing got accomplished.[46] The Government, likewise, was doing nothing to prevent the bands of robbers from ravaging the villages and committing murders at the very gates of Mexico City. These reports of brigandage, anarchy, and the impotence of the Government and Congress were almost identical with those of Sir Charles Wyke. The two ministers both blamed the Government of "squandering" the expropriated church property. Wyke, Saligny reported, had "better spirit" than Mathew,[47] who, the French Minister believed, had tried to prevent congressional approval of the French convention.[48]

By the end of May Saligny had not obtained "the friendly and satisfactory regulation of . . . claims," which in February he had foreseen would be accomplished within a month.[49] His convention had not yet been presented to the Mexican Congress.[50] He had a written promise accepting the "principle" of the Jecker bonds by a Foreign Minister who had resigned, and Congress had rejected this principle. Although Saligny collected 10,000 piastres as an indemnity for the family of M. Rieche, the French vice consul murdered in October 1859, 11,000 piastres were still due, and Rojas, the Mexican responsible for Rieche's death, went unpunished.[51] It is not surprising, therefore, that Saligny requested naval forces to strengthen his bargaining position. In addition, he caught a touch of the plague, for which he blamed the "thoughtfulness" of the Government that permitted "each of the streets of this unfortunate city" to "become a ceter of infection from which the epidemic spreads."[52]

On 2 June news reached Mexico City that the Reactionary chief Marquez had shot Ocampo and hanged his body from a tree.[53] Two days later Guzman asked Congress for money to get troops after the bands roaming the country. The deputies voted 40,000 piastres, which were taken from a fund set aside for the French Penaud Convention of 1859. Excitement in Mexico City flamed to a fever pitch, and the mob threatened to take vengeance on the prisoners of the Reactionary Party in Mexico City. Their relatives, including Mrs. Casanova, came to the legations imploring intercession with the Government for the protection of the prisoners. Saligny called a meeting of the Diplomatic Corps and proposed a collective request be made of Juarez to prevent a massacre. Wyke and Corwin, the American Minister to Mexico, warmly approved. Baron Wagner, the Prussian Chargé, at first objected, but finally conseted. They called on Juarez, who said he had already ordered the doubling of the guard at the prisons.[54] On the same day a list of forced loans, amounting to 1,000,000 piastres was published. Foreigners were exempt, except three Spaniards, one of whom was removed from the list when Saligny protested. As to the 40,000 piastres, however, Guzman wrote Saligny, it was "imperious necessity" that forced Mexico to take this money set aside for the French Convention. Guzman promised to reinstate this sum within a week. Saligny replied that he would not write a note on the subject only on Guzman's *"engagement of honour"* to restore the money by 11 June.[55] It was also the deadline obtained by Mr. Mathew for the payment of the Laguna Seca Conducta claims.[56]

In the morning of 12 June Saligny called on Guzman, who gave his "word" that the 40,000 piastres taken from the Penaud fund would be returned by 15 June. Owing to financial difficulties, however, the Mexican Government could not immediately make good the sums still due French claimants of the Laguna Seca Conducta. Guzman proposed instead that payment be made in the form of "all the goods of the Clergy not yet disposed of" by the Government. Saligny replied this arrangement could not be accepted and that payment would have to be in specie. Then he observed that his convention provided that it be submitted to Congress within a month after its opening session, which had been on 9 May. Guzman gave assurances that the convention had been submitted to Congress a few days before and that he hoped to be able to announce a satisfactory result soon. As to the Jecker affair, Saligny insisted that Zarco's note of 4 May "fully admitted the principle invoked by France." Guzman, however, did not accept the principle, although he did not deny it. As Wyke had observed a few weeks before, the Mexican Minister "possesses in a rare degree the faculty of saying nothing in a great many words."[57] On this occasion Guzman also tried to submerge the issue in a long discourse, "full of vague and sonorous phrases, diverse reasoning, unseizable arguments with double meanings." But he did promise to resign if he did not get the Jecker affair settled. As to the Sisters of Charity and the agreement with Zarco to leave them in the *status quo,* Guzman said he found himself in difficulties to execute the laws of his country. But when Saligny demanded a yes or a no, Guzman agreed. The 11,000 piastres still owed the Riche family, he promised, would be paid in a few days. When Saligny mentioned that there were rumors that the Government would suspend payment of the foreign conventions, Guzman said that this was "completely false." The Mexican Minister, therefore, used the same tactics of procrastination that he used with Sir Charles Wyke. In reports similar to those of Wyke, Saligny wrote that the Mexican Government was "trying to gain time with the aid of a thousand ruses and to elude under all sorts of pretexts the execution of her engagements." The French Minister thought that France had to take "precautions" and added that this was also Wyke's opinion :

> Sir Charles Wyke . . . writes to Lord John Russell that the situation is intolerable, that the great Powers such as France and England can only do two things here : either give their Ministers the power and the material means necessary to make themselves respected or to recall them and not leave them exposed any longer to such indignities. I am . . . in complete agreement with Sir Charles.[58]

The Penaud funds were not returned on 15 June. Two days later Guzman resigned. During the cabinet crisis, the Chargé ad interim said he could not decide anything concerning French affairs. There was nothing to do but wait for a new Minister of Foreign Relations. Saligny got the same reply from

Juarez and found it "intolerable."[59] On 26 June Palacio, the Chargé ad interim, informed Saligny that the funds of the Penaud Convention had been restored. But when Saligny asked that the money be turned over to the Chancery of the French Legation, Palacio replied that he could not do this in the absence of a Minister of Foreign Relations. Saligny saw it all as a "bad joke that has lasted too long," and another reason that he be supplied with the "necessary means to make the interests and honour of France respected, no matter what happens."[60] Saligny then took the matter up with Juarez, who refused to give him the money "by standing on Article 8 of the Penaud Convention which formally condemns this pretension." This refusal, Saligny wrote Thouvenel, violated "engagements of honour" and further proved that "force alone can force these people to fulfill their obligations toward us."[61]

The dishonesty of the Mexican Government, Saligny believed, was matched by its "stupid system of persecution . . . against the civil and military functionaries who served under the Miramon Government."[62] He reported the defeat of the Government generals by the Reactionary chieftains in June[63] and attributed the increased activity of the bands to this persecution.[64]

On 13 July Zamacona announced himself as the new Minister of Foreign Relations to Saligny and stated a desire to "tighten the relations that exist *so fortunately* between France and Mexico."[65] This phrase was too much for Saligny, who replied :

> . . . I beg Your Excellency to be well convinced that, on my side, I will not neglect doing anything to attain the ends proposed . . . to give the relations between the two countries this character of friendliness and cordiality that until now have not depended on me and to avoid a rupture, the responsibility of which could not in any way fall on the Government of the Emperor.[66]

Saligny proudly reported to Thouvenel that this reply "appears to have produced on the new Minister the effect of a clap of thunder." On 16 July Zamacona asked to see Saligny, who declined on the ground that the "stolen" 40,000 piastres were being withheld. Nevertheless, Zamacona called on Saligny the next evening. The Mexican Minister said he wanted to respect Mexico's engagements toward France. But Saligny was not impressed and believed the men in the Government were "capable of anything to procure for themselves, at no matter what price, the resources lacking the Administration."[67]

Saligny learned of the financial law of 17 July through newspaper accounts.[68] He protested the law,[69] but refused to answer Zamacona's justifications.[70] The French Minister insisted it was ". . . one of the things that is not discussed." He presented an ultimatum that the law be annulled,[71] and severed diplomatic relations when the time limit ran out on 25 July,[72] thus taking a more drastic action than Wyke, who only suspended relations.

Saligny and Wyke saw the situation created by the law of 17 July in the same way and "acted in complete harmony." The French Minister agreed with many of the proposals Captain Aldham had made to Wyke. Unlike his British colleague, who wanted England to act alone, Saligny proposed a tripartite custom house intervention to Thouvenel. It would be easy to seize Vera Cruz and Tampico, Saligny believed, and on the first appearance of naval forces, ". . . the state of Vera Cruz will not hesitate to separate itself from the Federal Government and offer us all the reparations in its power." But in order to accomplish something durable, the occupation of Tampico, Vera Cruz, and its fortress, St. Jean d'Ulloa, had to be demanded. It would be more than sufficient if France and England each sent two steam frigates, two or three steam corvettes, and two gun-boats, all armed with long-range cannons. A few hundred men could garrison St. Jean d'Ulloa and Vera Cruz. Less than a thousand men could capture Tampico, wherethey could erect adequate defenses in twenty-four hours to stop a Mexican army. But Saligny did not expect much opposition from a Mexican army that could not even control the bandits near Mexico City. The ports on the Mexican Pacific coast would be even easier to capture, and their custom houses, from which the Federal Government received no revenues, would be "productive" in French hands. In addition to an Anglo-French "entente" with regard to Mexico, Saligny foresaw that Spain "will certainly demand nothing better than to join us."[73]

On 14 August news arrived in Mexico City that General Ortega had defeated Marquez.[74] Although Marquez only retreated, Ortega claimed a glorious victory, and his partisans made joyful demonstrations in his honor. That evening they paraded in a torchlight procession.[75] At about 8.00 P.M. Saligny took a walk after supper in the interior galleries of the French Legation. He smelled a faint oder of gunpowder and felt something touch his right arm slightly. He didn't hear a shot, but later believed that this could be explained by the noise of the bells, the cries of the population, and the music in the streets. But at the time he thought it was an accident. Two hours later, just as he was going to bed, Saligny heard a crowd in front of the Legation. There were shouts of "Death to the French!" and "Death to the French Minister!" This shouting lasted ten minutes until the crowd, which included some Mexican soldiers, moved on. The next day Saligny told Wyke and Wagner, the Prussian Chargé, about the incidents of the night before. They thought the Diplomatic Corps should be brought together, and a meeting was arranged for the next day.[76] Then it was agreed that an attempt had been made on Saligny's life,[77] and a collective note was addressed to Zamacona protesting it and the demonstration before the French Legation. The diplomats hoped that now the Mexican Government would no longer tolerate the assassination of foreigners.[78] Zamacona's answer was that it was too bad that Saligny waited so long before informing the Government, which would, however, initiate a judicial investigation. His Government, Zamacona concluded, was making a "superhuman" effort to reestablish peace and order.[79] The Diplomatic Corps replied to this standard Mexican promise to "investigate" by observing that the many attacks on foreigners led to investigations that never brought results. There were no arrests, convictions, or punishments. The seriousness of the matter was emphasized by a list of forty-five "Recent attacks on Foreigners," which was enclosed.[80] The same day a Mexican judge visited Saligny and listened to his story and examined the vicinity of the French Legation. Saligny, however, believed that "this pretended investigation . . . will not go any further."[81] Wyke shared Saligny's pessimism and reported to Lord Russell that the protests to the Mexican Government led to "no result whatever beyond specious promises of redress which are not worth the paper they are written on."[82]

On 23 August, Saligny learned of the decree published the evening before that imposed a tax of one per cent on capital over 2,000 piastres in the District of Mexico. He went to Wyke, who was equally stupified, and they called a meeting of the Diplomatic Corps. Baron Wagner was commissioned to protest in the name of the Diplomatic Corps,[83] but Zamacona gave dire necessity as an excuse.[84]

Just before the events of August Saligny proposed a tripartite custom house intervention. Now, a month later, he believed the European Powers should take Mexico under their protection :

> For a long time it has been easy to see that, if the European Powers do not decide to take this unfortunate country under their direct and effective protection, the civil wars and anarchy that have plagued it for almost half a century will bring . . . the Republic into dissolution. . . .[85]

Advantage could be taken of the troubled conditions in the United States,[86] and Mexico was taking no steps to place itself in a state of defense against British and French naval forces. The costs of the expedition, Saligny urged, should be added to the claims against Mexico.[87]

In September Saligny drew up a list of twenty-five claims

resulting from injuries suffered by French subjects in Mexico in 1861. The assassins of two Frenchmen were known, Saligny claimed, and "nothing would be easier than to arrest them."[88] The Mexican police and soldiers, however, did nothing to prevent murders,[89] and they themselves were responsible for some of the outrages.[90] It was no longer just anarchy, but "a real social decomposition."[91] Saligny became even more aroused when the Mexican investigation of the events of 14 August was published. Twenty-four pages of evidence taken from Mexicans led the Government to the conclusion that no attempt had been made on Saligny's life. He had only been frightened by a rickochet bullet.[92] But he saw it all as a "new outrage for which we will have to demand satisfaction from Mexico."[93] The Diplomatic Corps was called together again, and a collective note insisted that all the foreign diplomats had seen the bullet hole in the French Legation and that it could not have been caused by a rickochet. They further expressed their wonder that no official regret had been expressed by the Government.[94]

At the end of the month Saligny received infomation that Juarez was about to withdraw the canons from Vera Cruz and its fortress, St. Jean d'Ulloa. It was a proof for Saligny that a small European corps could march right to Mexico City:

> It is the best proof that they themselves realize the impossibility of any resistance, and, as for me, from day to day, I see less and less that could stop a corps of 4,000–5,000 European soldiers from marching right to Mexico City without encountering any resistance.[95]

Saligny's proposals became progressively more drastic. In July he proposed a custom house intervention. In August he wanted to take Mexico under European protection. In September he envisioned a march to Mexico City.

Sir Charles Wyke received instructions at the beginning of October about what demands to make.[96] Since Thouvenel copied his instructions to Saligny from those of Lord Russell, there was a delay of a few days, during which time the mail packet left for Mexico.[97] Consequently Saligny did not receive his instructions until the end of October by the next monthly mail packet.[98] While Wyke negotiated with Zamacona,[99] Saligny became more incensed against the Mexican Government. It could not pay the garrison of Mexico City and relied on forced requisitioning. The authorities put their hands on anything they could find, and acted, Saligny believed, especially against the French. The robbers were becoming so active that there were migrations to the more populated areas to seek refuge.[100] The Government troops were again defeated by the Reactionary chiefs.[101] The investigation of the affair of 14 August was republished at the end of October in brochure form. For Saligny it ". . . only aggrivates the outrage for which we will have to demand satisfaction from Mexico."[102] When an emissary of the Mexican Government promised a new investigation and the return of the Penaud funds, Saligny saw in these promises just the "same system of ruse and bad faith."[103]

In the evening of 30 October a courrier arrived in Mexico City with Thouvenel's instructions.[104] Mexico was to suspend the financial law of 17 July and permit the establishment at Vera Cruz and Tampico of commissioners designated by France. They were to distribute custom duties due the foreign conventions and other claims. If refused, Saligny was directed to leave Mexico with his legation.[105] Saligny saw Zamacona, informed him of the French demands, and gave him five days to reply.[106] Then Saligny asked how Porfirio Leon, the Chief of Police, could be entrusted with the investigation of the events of 14 August when he himself was largely responsible. Zamacona went to Juarez, and a cabinet meeting was called. Leon's dismissal was brought up, but was rejected. Leon found out about it and went through the streets of Mexico City with his friends, shouting "Death to the French!"[107] The next day Leon stopped Saligny in the street and demanded explanations. Saligny refused and saw in the incident a Mexican attempt to start a conflict "to find the occasion to get rid" of him.[108] The Government certainly was irked by Saligny. At a banquet a few days later, at which Juarez and the cabinet were present, a toast to Saligny's death was proposed, and no one protested. But the Mexican people, Saligny insisted, should not be confused with the Government:

> The population . . . in spite of all efforts made to excite it, the population, calm, indifferent when it is not secretly indignant, remains a stranger to these excesses.[109]

The time delay given Zamacona ran out without a Mexican reply to Thouvenel's demands,[110] and Saligny sent an ultimatum on 9 November threatening to leave Mexico with the Imperial Legation if he did not receive a satisfactory answer within forty-eight hours.[111] Zamacona asked Saligny to wait for congressional action on the law of 17 July,[112] but he would not wait or negotiate. His instructions stated that reports from Mexico "destroy all illusions that we would like to have" about obtaining a settlement with Mexico.[113] The same post that brought these instructions bore information that France and England were negotiating to intervene jointly in Mexico.[114] Saligny concluded that Napoleon III did not want him to negotiate with Mexico.[115] Adhering strictly to the letter of his instructions, Saligny presented a second ultimatum demanding a categorical acceptance of his demands,[116] and, when this was not forthcoming,[117] he announced that he was leaving Mexico.[118] Once the French expedition had arrived in Mexico, Saligny boasted that his "merit" was "in having divined the intention of the Emperor to intervene in Mexico and having rendered the intervention necessary."[119]

Before he left Mexico City, Saligny obtained military information from an officer in the Mexican Army that Juarez could muster 4,900 men and 30 canons against an army of invasion. Saligny did not see that these troops could offer any effective resistance:

Thus 4 to 5 thousand men that they call *Regular Troops* (and what troops!), that is all that M. Juarez could get ready for the moment if he had the expenses needed for a campaign.

The money was lacking, Saligny believed, just as were artillery, and, for the most part, horses. Furthermore, if Mexican troops went to meet the European expeditionary corps, Mexico City would be left in danger of seizure by Marquez and Zuloaga.[120] Their aid could be expected, Saligny reported, because he had information that they had met with several other Reactionary chiefs and pronounced "in favor of the Foreign Intervention." The seizure of the Gulf ports was not enough, Saligny believed, because their trade would merely shift to the Pacific ports.[121] Even seizing all Mexican custom houses would not be sufficient to stop anarchy and to protect Frenchmen in Mexico.[122]

On 6 December Saligny left Mexico City and arrived at Vera Cruz on 17 December, just as the Spanish contingent of the tripartite intervention was occupying the town without firing a shot.[123] Before Christmas Saligny was in possession of letters from Paris that the "Emperor had made the resolution and chosen his candidate." Now that Saligny knew Napoleon's intention of establishing Maximilian in Mexico, the French Minister "without compromising anything or anyone . . . began to prepare the way (*terrain*)." On Christmas Day he saw General José Uraga, the General-in-Chief of the Mexican Army of the East, at Tejeria, a small town not far from Vera Cruz. Saligny believed that Uraga would aid in the establishment of a Mexican monarchy:

After he made certain oratorical precautions, I led Uraga to recognize that republican government could not suit Mexico, and that it was the cause of these fifty years of civil wars, demoralization, and dissolution, into which this country has fallen. I said that monarchy is the only means of salvation for this country. I added that he, Robles, and Doblado had to take the initiative resolutely and declare themselves without delay. First he made some objections for the sake of appearances, then ended by showing himself half convinced. Without binding himself positively, what I could not hope for at the first meeting, he promised to write to Doblado and Robles to see about coming to an arrangement with them.[124]

Uraga's version of the interview was that Saligny offered him a Marshal's baton and the title of duke if he would disavow Juarez and undertake the formation of a new government. Saligny, Uraga asserted, "mistook the moderation and courtesy of a soldier for a tacit acquiescence."[125]

Another way Saligny tried "to prepare the way" was to urge the general in charge of the Spanish expedition to go beyond Vera Cruz and capture some of the neighboring villages.[126] Since fresh meat was becoming scarce, General Gasset was inclined to seize three villages in the vicinity to obtain cattle, but Wyke dissuaded him:

> . . . I strongly advised him not to take such a step before the arrival of the French and English forces, as by so doing he would only bring on a collision with the Mexican forces outside the town, which it was most advisable to avoid, owing to the bitter feeling still existing in this country against the Spaniards. The General most readily yielded to my wishes. . . .

The Mexicans were fortifying the mountain passes leading into the interior, and Wyke believed that "violent measures at first will spoil all, and engage us in an undertaking the difficulties of which can hardly be overrated." His hopes that an intervention would bring the "moderates" forward seemed to be on the way of being realized. General Doblado, with full powers granted by Congress, was forming a respectable government:

> He is a man of such talent and influence in the country that the Reactionary Chiefs began to lay down their arms and give in their adhesion on his appointment becoming known, and he is now engaged in forming his Cabinet from the best men he could find, irrespective of their political opinions.

Wyke wanted to give Doblado time to complete his work in

the hope that the intervention would be received in a friendly way. Then the Mexican Government could reestablish order and "take the opinion of those who alone are entitled to have a voice in the matter." These were the "men of property and intelligence" who in the past had been "completely silenced and domineered by the rabble." The "rabble" had dominated Congress and "rendered anything like good government impossible." Now, however, Doblado had adjourned Congress until April and had "full powers conferred on him by Congress, authorizing him to settle pending questions with the three Powers as he deemed best."[127]

The differences between Saligny and Wyke that had reached a climax in October and November remained. Saligny did not want to deal with the Doblado Cabinet and was not satisfied with a mere occupation of Vera Cruz. Wyke took exactly the opposite view. When he saw Saligny on 26 December for the first time since the beginning of November, they talked about insignificant things, because they could not agree about basic issues.[128]

## 3.   CORWIN AND PICKETT IN MEXICO IN 1861

Lincoln's choice of Minister to Mexico, Thomas Corwin, was ideal for the post. He was popular in Mexico for a speech he had made during the Mexican War:

> If I were a Mexican I would tell you: Have you not room in your country to bury your dead men? If you come into Mexico we will greet you with bloody hands and welcome you to hospitable graves.[1]

He was an experienced politician, having served in both houses of Congress, as Governor of Ohio, and as Secretary of the Treasury under President Fillmore.[2]

The Confederacy, seeking to stir up trouble between the North and Mexico, sent Colonel John Pickett as a special agent to Mexico.[3] He took twenty signed commissions for privateers with him.[4] But he could hardly be welcome in Mexico, for he had been a filibuster and an accomplice of Walker in Nicaragua.[5]

Seward's initial instructions to Corwin in April 1861 were that he was not to press for a settlement of claims "at the moment." Instead he was to prevent Mexican recognition of the Confederacy and combat its schemes in Mexico. Seward believed there were good reasons to believe that the Confederacy wanted to "effect either a partial dismemberment or a complete overthrow of the Mexican Government with a view to extend over it the authority of the newly projected Confederacy." Corwin was to assure the Mexican Government that "the President neither has nor can ever have any sympathy with such desires in whatever quarter they may arise or whatever character they may take on." The unselfishness of the North and the greed of the South once established, Corwin was to persuade Mexico that the existence of its sovereignty depended on the reestablishment of the American Union, because a Southern victory would be followed by a conquest of Mexico. When Mexico understood this, it would not do anything to aid the Confederacy.[6]

Corwin arrived at Mexico City on 10 May[7] and presented his credentials to Juarez on 21 May.[8] A week later, in his first despatch to Seward, Corwin reported a rumor that the Confederacy was preparing to seize Lower California and asked for instructions. He enclosed a letter from Thomas Sprague, a former United States commercial agent in Lower California, who advised that:

> . . . rather than the filibustering secessionist should get possession of the Peninsula of Lower California I think our Government quite warranted (in case no arrangement could be made for its purchase) in taking possession of it for our own protection. At least to hold it against the designs of the secessionists.[9]

Before receiving this despatch, Seward heard the same rumor

and wrote Corwin that the United States was ready to buy
Lower California "in preference to seeing it inevitably fall into
the hands of the insurrectionary party of this Country by
purchase or by conquest." The United States, Corwin was to
assure Mexico, was ready to aid Mexico militarily to prevent
the seizure of Lower California by the Confederates.[10]

At the end of June, in his second despatch, Corwin foresaw
that European Powers, as well as the Confederacy, were a
threat to Mexico. He requested permission to negotiate a treaty
with Mexico, granting it five to ten million dollars to save it
from subjugation or partition by permitting it to pay its debts
to Spain, France, and England and to put it in a state of
defense against them and the Confederacy. Security for the
loan might be the public lands of Mexico. Lower California
might also be purchased to supply Mexico with money. It was
sparcely settled and of "no value to Mexico," though indispensable to the United States and "much more valuable than
is generally supposed in mineral resources."[11]

On 6 July Pickett arrived in Mexico City.[12] His mission was
a complete failure. During the whole time he was in Mexico
he only obtained one interview with the Minister of Foreign
Relations.[13] Pickett's despatches to Confederate Secretary of
State Toombs passed through Tampico, where Don Santiago
Tapia, the Commander-in-Chief of the state of Taumalipac,
intercepted them at the request of Corwin. Then the despatches
went to Juarez. He read them and sent them to Corwin, who
forwarded them to Washington.[14] Pickett's uncomplimentary
remarks made him a *persona non grata* :

Mexicans are a race of degenerate monkeys.

This country is in the hands of robbers, assassins, blackguards
and lepers.

The government is the biggest robber of all.

Mexico City is the most disorderly city on the continent—
perhaps the globe.[15]

Corwin did not fear Confederate diplomacy, because Juarez promised him that Mexico would not recognize the Confederacy. Corwin reported to Seward that informed Mexicans realized that an independent Confederacy would be the "signal for a war of conquest with a view to establish slavery in each of the twenty-two states" of Mexico. The danger to Mexico lay in a Confederate or European conquest, which could be prevented by a loan, secured by Mexican public lands and mineral rights:

> Mexico would be willing to pledge all her public lands and mineral rights in Lower California, Chihuahua, Sonora, etc., as well as her national faith for the payment of this guarantee. This would probably end in the cession of sovereignty to us. It would be certain to end thus if the money were not promptly paid as agreed on. By such an arrangement two consequences would follow: First, all hope of extending the domination of a *separate* southern republic in this quarter or in Central America would be extinguished, and (second), any further attempt in all time to come to establish European power on this continent would cease to occupy the mind of either England or continental Europe.

If Mexico could maintain itself against "southern filibusters or European cupidity," Corwin added, he would not have made the proposal.[15] But Mexico did not appear to be able to defend itself, and the "present apparent weakness" of the United States stimulated aggression. If Mexican territory were ceded to the United States, the Mexicans would receive the benefits of Manifest Destiny:

> The United States are the only true guardians of the independence and true civilization of this continent. It is their mission, and they should fulfil it.

Mexican territory might also serve as a compensation in the eventuality of an independent Confederacy:

> England and Spain are now in possession of the best of the West Indies . . . and Mexico, a colony of England with British

power on the North of our possessions, would leave on this continent a very unimportant part for the United States—especially should the present unnatural rebellion end in the final severance from us of the eight or nine or all the slave states.[17]

The loan treaty, as Corwin envisioned it, would provide Mexico with the money to pay its European debts and prevent an intervention from that quarter. The mortgage on Mexican territory would eventually be foreclosed, thus ending Confederate and European designs on Mexico forever. Manifest Destiny would be served, and the United States would be compensated in case the Confederacy were victorious.

In accordance with his instructions, Corwin did not press for a settlement of American claims against Mexico. When a tax on capital was published in August, the Diplomatic Corps was called together. Corwin refused to join the collective protest against the tax.[18] He also declined to accept the resolution of the other diplomats to suggest to the citizens of the countries represented that they only pay the tax under pressure and after having protested.[19]

The Mexican Congress granted the United States permission to march troops across Sonora from California to Arizona.[20] When he heard that Pickett threatened that 30,000 "diplomatic agents" would cross the border into Mexico if this troop movement were permitted, Corwin urgently renewed his request for permission to negotiate a loan treaty.[21] In early September his pleas for instructions became even more insistent :

I wish to be *informed and instructed whether the United States would* agree to pay, in money, to this country, at this time any sum—say five or six or ten millions of dollars—on receiving for it stipulations of any kind from Mexico.[22]

Secretary of State Seward believed the United States Senate would oppose the advancement of so large a sum when nearly a million dollars a day was being spent on the organization of the army and navy.[23] Instead he instructed Corwin to negotiate a loan treaty with Mexico whereby the United States would pay three per cent interest on the funded debt of Mexico. Since Seward estimated that this debt was $62,000,000, the United States would lend Mexico $1,860,000 a year. The loan was to be made retroactive to 17 July 1861, when Mexico suspended payment of its funded debt. The public lands and mineral rights of Lower California, Chihuahua, Sonora, and Sinaloa would serve as a mortgage. But the treaty would only be ratified, Seward added, if England and France promised not to intervene in Mexico.[24]

During October and November Corwin declined to negotiate the loan treaty with Mexico pending Wyke's negotiation for a settlement of British claims against Mexico.[25] During this period, on the even of All Saints Day, Pickett was arrested by the Mexican authorities, in the Colonel's words, for "chastising" a citizen of the United States. Pickett protested "diplomatic immunity."[26] but he was jailed on assault and battery charges for a row with a pill vendor, Bennett, who had insulted him. Release was offered if Pickett made apologies to Bennett and paid an indemnity. The Southern agent refused and spent a month in jail. He obtained his release, he claimed, "by purchasing several hundred dollars' worth of justice." Then he left Mexico. Discovering that his despatches never reached the Confederate Secretary of State, Pickett copied them and handed them over to Dr. Riddle, the Postmaster of New Orleans. Riddle, however, was a spy for the Washington Government and forwarded the despatches to Seward, who already had the originals from Corwin.[27]

At the end of November Wyke's convention was rejected by the Mexican Congress. Since Corwin believed the terms of this convention were moderate, he did not ask for ratification of his own draft of a loan treaty. He sent the draft to Seward and requested further instructions.[28] By the time Corwin's despatch and draft treaty reached Seward, the American Secretary of State had learned that the European Powers rejected the American proposal to pay three per cent interest on Mexico's funded debt.[29] Nevertheless, Lord Lyons, the British Minister to Washington, found Seward "unwilling to abandon his own plan." He told Lyons it had the "advantage of rendering all interference on the part of the European Powers in the affairs of Mexico entirely superfluous."[30] Even after he knew that England, France, and Spain had agreed to intervene in Mexico,[31] Seward did not give up the loan scheme. He submitted the draft treaty to the Senate for previous advice. This was a procedure, he told Lyons, "in conformity with a plan occasionally adopted in important cases."[32]

# III

# The Negotiation of the Tripartite Convention of London

## 1. THE IMMEDIATE BACKGROUND: THE MEXICAN POLICIES OF THE EUROPEAN POWERS, JANUARY–AUGUST 1861

THE REPORTS OF THE MINISTERS OF THE EUROPEAN POWERS in Mexico were brought to Europe by a monthly mail packet.[1] The news from Mexico was often almost two months old when received, but reports from the United States were sometimes received more quickly. So when Lord Russell received a report from his Minister to Washington that Juarez had defeated Miramon, a copy was forwarded in January 1861 to the British Ambassador to Paris.[2] Lord Cowley then informed the French Minister of Foreign Affairs. Thouvenel commented " 'that if there really is a conqueror able to restore order, and to impose (it) by his prestige on the different parties which divide that unhappy country, it is all that the french government can desire.' "[3]

Thouvenel's instructions to Saligny through June 1861 imply a lack of interest in, or lack of time for, Mexican affairs. The instructions were short, often in reply to despatches received a month or two earlier, and largely just approved Saligny's

122

despatch that he hoped to have French claims settled soon.[4] The next day Thouvenel sent Saligny a "claim" signed by representatives of commercial houses on behalf of the Jecker bonds. Saligny was directed to have these bonds respected.[5] A few weeks later Thouvenel learned of Saligny's interference on behalf of the Sisters of Charity[6] and instructed him to maintain the *status quo* of the dispute.[7] On 30 April more important despatches arrived in Paris from Saligny. They related how he had recognized the Juarez Government, signed a claims convention and pressed the Jecker bonds.[8] The same day Thouvenel merely sent Saligny a copy of Russell's initial instructions to Wyke,[9] supplied by Cowley.[10] Thouvenel waited until 31 May to approve Saligny's efforts on behalf of the Jecker bonds.[11] At that time Thouvenel had just received Saligny's request for naval forces to support his demands and to protect French interests in view of his expectation of a revolution in Mexico.[12] Although some reader of this despatch circled this request with a red pencil, Thouvenel made no comment on the request in his instructions of 31 May. Extracts of Saligny's request for ships, however, were sent to the French Minister of Marine and Colonies.[13] No reply was received until 3 July.[14] So on 30 June, two months after receiving the claims convention signed in March, Thouvenel sent his Minister to Mexico comments on that convention.[15]

The instructions of Lord Russell in the first six months of 1861 to his representatives in Mexico were merely to obtain reparation for claims of British subjects against Mexico. The initial instructions to Sir Charles Wyke, Mathew's replacement, authorized the threat of force as a last resort, but not its actual employment, if Mexico caused difficulties with regard to British claims.[16] Wyke's first three reports from Mexico reached the British Foreign Office on 27 June.[17] They related the unwillingness of the Mexican Government to accept responsibility for the robbery of the British Legation in 1860 and Wyke's belief that no redress could be expected for this and other claims without the employment of force. In reply Russell wrote an instruction on 1 July that Wyke was to state to the Mexican Government that "Her Majesty's Government will enforce their just demands by force if necessary."[18] Wyke, therefore, was only directed to threaten.

Shortly after defeating Miramon and entering Mexico City, Juarez expelled Pacheco, the Spanish Minister who had recognized the Miramon Government several months before. At the same time the Juarez Government denied that it was bound by the Mon-Almonte Convention, signed in 1859 to settle Spanish claims. The typical pattern of Spanish Ministers departing from Mexico and disagreements about Spanish claims, therefore, continued in 1861.[19] Typically also Mexico decided to send a special agent to Europe to offer "explanations." Collantes, the Spanish Minister of Foreign Relations, decided to wait for the arrival of the Mexican agent and consider his explanations. In February Collantes told the British Minister to Spain that the Spanish Government had adopted moderation in its differences with Juarez during the Civil War when he had been established at Vera Cruz. The Spanish Government was not likely to adopt a different course now that he was in possession of the Capital. The only Mexican policy of Spain, Collantes asserted, was to promote, as far as it could, the reestablishment of peace and a settled government.[20]

The early months of 1861 went by without the arrival of the Mexican agent. It was May before he arrived in Vera Cruz to take pasage to Europe.[21] In the meantime Pacheco returned to Spain. At the beginning of May he resigned his post to Mexico. He accompanied his resignation with a declaration that it was impossible to serve a Spanish Government which compromised the honor and dignity of Spain.[22] In answer to this affront, Collantes addressed a statement to the Queen of Spain that Pacheco's declaration contained "inexact" expressions. Collantes also submitted a draft of a royal decree dismissing Pacheco (instead of accepting his resignation). Both the decree, signed by the Queen, and Collantes' statement were published in the *Gazette* of Madrid on 8 May 1861.[23] A month later Collantes spoke in the Cortes of the necessity of sending an expedition to Mexico, because there "exists in those regions a republic which threatens the Mexicans with absorption." The object of the expedition, therefore, would be "the maintenance of the integrity of the Mexican territory."[24] The Spanish Government, however, made no military preparations for such an expedition at the time.[25]

In the first six months of 1861 the Spanish, French, and British Governments agreed on the desirability of a strong and orderly government in Mexico, able to maintain internal peace and willing to grant redress of European claims. None of the three European Governments had any fixed or concrete plans to intervene in, or send expeditions to, Mexico. Saligny's request for ships to support his negotiations, it is true, was sent to the French Minister of the Marine and Colonies in June, but the Ministry of Foreign Affairs had no reply by the end of the month. There was, moreover, nothing to indicate that these ships were for any purpose other than a show of force. In reply to Wyke's observations on the necessity of using force to exert pressure on Mexico to recognize British claims, Lord Russell merely instructed his Minister to Mexico to threaten to use force. Pacheco's denunciation of his Government's passive Mexican policy only led to his formal dismissal. Furthermore, he was politely and indirectly informed that his charges were lies. Although Collantes spoke of the possibility of an expedition to Mexico in the Cortes in June, talk of such claim-collecting expeditions was nothing new in Spain,[26] and no immediate military preparations were made.

In the opening months of 1861 the Juarez Government dismissed the diplomatic representative of Miramon in Europe. Almonte and Hidalgo were left unemployed in France.[27] In their place Montluc, a Frenchman sympathizing with the Juarez Regime, was named Consul General at Paris.[28] Tomas Murphy was relieved of his post in London, and a Colonel Facio and a certain Andrade were also relieved.[29] Estrada organized them and other Conservatives, who fled a Mexico now governed by Juarez, into a committee to support the plan of converting Mexico into a monarchy.[30] Whatever influence these Mexicans had on Napoleon III and Eugenie was through Hidalgo. In October 1861 Estrada introduced Hidalgo to Maximilian's secretary as "that channel . . . by which the Mexicans communicate with the Empress Eugenie."[31]

At the end of 1860 and the beginning of 1861, Hidalgo was in Spain fulfilling his mission of accompanying the body of the Duchess D'Albe, Eugenie's sister, to its last resting place. In January Eugenie wrote her widowed brother-in-law that she hoped the entourage sent with her sister's body would take the chance to go sightseeing in Madrid and Toledo, "as it is a long voyage not often made."[32] In April Hidalgo returned and brought Eugenie a letter.[33] In May she discussed with him the possibility of sounding the Duke of Modena as a candidate for a Mexican throne. She did not allude to any French protection, as this would, in her opinion, suffice to call forth a refusal from the Duke. The Spanish General Elio, Eugenie believed, might be given command of a Mexican army to be formed by the monarchial party in Mexico.[34] Hidalgo informed Estrada, and he observed that France was only offering moral support.[35] When Hidalgo brought this remark to Eugenie's attention, she said, "If they want soldiers, that is the point at which I exclaim."[36]

Even before Hidalgo returned from Spain, apparently, Napoleon III had several conversations with Sir Charles Wyke before he sailed for Mexico as the newly appointed British Minister to Mexico. Wyke was furnished with a commission from Lord Palmerston and told Napoleon that all of South and Central America was "ripe for monarchial institutions." Wyke, however, believed that nothing could be done without the aid of the "moderates." Napoleon replied that, if Mexico refused to grant redress of grievances to France, Great Britain, and Spain, then war would be declared, and the way would be cleared for the establishment of a monarchy. Even at this time the offer of the Mexican throne to Archduke Maximilian was under consideration.[37] Whether Napoleon III was the originator of this idea is not clear.[38] Napoleon and Eugenie met Maximilian in 1856 and were impressed by his charm and compliments.[39] Two years later Napoleon III was flattered by Maximilian's present of a statuette of Napoleon I.[40] As early as 1854, when Eugenie thought the throne of Spain might soon be vacant, she mused on the possibility of establishing Maximilian there.[41] In October 1861, when Napoleon III had put his stamp of approval on Maximilian a month before, General Almonte recalled being presented to Maximilian on the occasion of his first[42] visit to Queen Victoria and Albert in 1857. Since then, Almonte claimed, he had been a fervent admirer of Maximilian.[43]

At the time of Wyke's conversations with Napoleon, Lord Palmerston "assented" to Maximilian's candidacy. The British Prime Minister ". . . stipulated however that the candidacy should not be announced before the Mexican Capital had been taken, and then only with the consent of the Liberal Party."[44] Palmerston's private letters and a memorandum he prepared on Maximilian's candidacy make it clear that the British Prime Minister was a convinced monarchist,[45] and that be believed a Mexican monarchy was both a desirable means of maintaining order in Mexico[46] and checking American agression.[47] Maximilian was "a good and unobjectionable sovereign for Mexico."[48] The means approved by Palmerston to achieve this end, however, were highly improbable of materializing, and, if they did come into being, highly respectable and acceptable to British public opinion, upon which Palmerston placed so much value.[49] The Liberals would almost certainly not accept a monarchy. Mexican monarchy schemes before 1861 were originated by, or on behalf of, the Mexican Conservatives. If the Liberals and (much more likely and by implication) Conservatives accepted a monarch, he would owe his position to the sovereign right of Mexicans to determine the form and personnel of their government.

At the end of June both Thouvenel and Lord Russell received reports from Mexico about the Jecker bonds. Mr. Mathew related a conversation with the Mexican Minister of Foreign Relations. Zarco told Mathew that Saligny claimed he had instructions to support the Jecker bonds. Zarco also stated that Saligny had threatened hostilities on their behalf.[50] Thouvenel received Saligny's despatch that he had the "*written recognition of hte principle we are defending.*"[51] Actually Zarco only promised to abide by "principles of international law,"[52] but Thouvenel was impressed and made a "Note" to this effect.[53] On 3 July Thouvenel received an answer from the French Minister of Marine and Colonies about supporting Saligny's negotiations with the French Navy.

Chasseloup-Laubat stated he had written to the Commander-in-Chief of the French Naval Division in the Pacific by the last packet. Commanding officers of ships sent to the coasts of Mexico were to be instructed to get in touch with Saligny.[54] A few days later Lord Cowley, the British Ambassador, asked Thouvenel whether Mathew's report was correct. Thouvenel replied that Jecker had made a loan to the Miramon Government. If this loan were not repaid, Jecker and two or three hundred French subjects in his employ would be ruined. French and British financial houses would also be compromised. Nothing in Saligny's despatches, Thouvenel deceitfully[55] assured Cowley, indicated that the French Minister to Mexico "had recourse to threats of any kind." Thouvenel did not mention Chasseloup-Laubat's orders, but added that Saligny was convinced that no justice could be obtained from Mexico without recourse to force. Cowley reported that Thouvenel agreed:

> France had no intention of declaring war on Mexico, but she must protect the interest of French subjects, and he (M. Thouvenel) thought that the time was come when France and England should let the Mexican Government understand that they were no longer to be trifled with.[56]

Upon reading this report from the British Ambassador to Paris, Lord Palmerston attached a note to it, stating his opinion of the Jecker claims:

> an (sic) act of robbery or injustice committed by the govt de facto of a country is a wrong from which any subsequent govt of that country is justly liable to be called upon to afford Redress; but it seems to be rather hard and not by any means Just to call upon the Juares Govt to repay a loan voluntarily made by a foreigner to Miramon to enable him more effectively to make war upon Juares.[57]

Late in July De La Fuente, the Mexican agent sent to Europe to offer explanations, was in Paris and had a conversation with Thouvenel. At this first meeting, the French Minister of Foreign Affairs "did not hide to what point we have reason to be unhappy with the obstacles" the Mexicans created and "how little confidence is permitted us."[58] The French Government, consequently, had decided to employ "the means of a severe coercion on Mexico . . . to put the Convention between Saligny and Zarco into practice and to have the Jecker claims accepted." Thouvenel added that the British Government, in connection with its money claims, would follow "the same line of conduct as France." De La Fuente replied that Mexico's failure to ratify Saligny's convention could not be a powerful enough reason to employ force. As to the Jecker claim, it was "far beyond its real value." It was a speculation based on the "chance of the triumph or the ruin . . . of the government of M. Miramon." The expectation of enormous profits was a compensation for great risks. Miramon had only represented a small party, and Mexico could not be held responsible for ". . . these absurd operations."[59]

Early in 1861 Napoleon III told Sir Charles Wyke that the European Powers would declare war on Mexico if it refused to grant redress. Still earlier Napoleon had told the Mexican exiles in Europe that he could not intervene in Mexico unless he had a pretext and the cooperation of Great Britain.[60] The

June mail packet brought Saligny's report that his ideas of using force were shared by Wyke. The British Minister, Saligny incorrectly[61] believed, was awaiting the arrival of British naval forces soon to arrive.[62] On the basis of this despatch from Saligny, Thouvenel could tell De La Fuente that the British and French Governments agreed about using force. Since Mexico refused to accept the Jecker bonds or ratify Saligny's convention, which Thouvenel himself believed an impractical convention,[63] France had a "pretext" of sorts to intervene in Mexico. If the internal difficulties of the United States worsened, they might prevent any serious opposition from that quarter.[64] There remained the last obstacle that Napoleon had foreseen, of finding a prospective monarch.[65]

On 4 July Estrada, presenting himself as the spokesman of the "Committee" of Mexicans in Europe, saw Metternich, the Austrian Ambassador to Paris. Estrada wanted to bring to the attention of the Austrian Government the desire of the "majority" of Mexicans that a European, Roman Catholic dynasty supply a Prince to establish a monarchy in Mexico. The Committee, Estrada told Metternich, wanted to approach the Austrian Government, because a Hapsburg Prince would be the most acceptable to the Mexican people.[66] Estrada also left Metternich a written statement that the internal difficulties of the United States facilitated the prospects of a Mexican monarchy esablished by an Austrian Archduke.[67] The next day Metternich forwarded Estrada's proposals to Count Rechberg, the Austrian Foreign Minister, and commented that Estrada's idea "didn't lack grandeur, but was deplorably and discouragingly impracticable."[68]

On 28 July Rechberg sent Metternich a reply to Estrada's overture. The Austrian Minister of Foreign Affairs admitted that it would "certainly be to the advantage of Austria should the monarchial principle, now so gravely endangered here in Europe, achieve a signal victory in the New World." The Austrian Government would be "happy to see so glorious a mission as that indicated by M. Gutierrez fall to the lot of a relative of the Emperor." But the plan was impracticable for two reasons, which might also be taken as conditions for the candidacy of an Austrian :

In the first place the co-operation, and indeed the active support of the two great maritime Powers of Great Britain and France is indispensable to the success of such a venture, and as yet we have no information as to the intentions of either of these countries. In the second place M. Gutierrez does not appear to be in a position to give any kind of guarantee that the Mexican nation really desires a king, and unless such a desire really exists there can be no hope of success.

With such an uncertain outlook, Austria could not "associate herself with the plan, for in a matter which involves the interests and dignity of a Prince of the Imperial House she must, before committing herself, have definite guarantees." Estrada, therefore, was to be informed that the importance of his proposal was appreciated, but "we feel that the ground is as yet insufficiently prepared." The Austrian Government did not wish to "discourage" Estrada and "to appear to repel his advances, but only to point out that the general political situation and the particular difficulties of our own position do not at present allow us to take part in an enterprise which might require the aid of foreign troops, and which could be successful only in times more favorable than the present."[69]

One Historian has regarded Rechberg's answer to "an obscure Mexican conspirator" both "remarkable" and "astonishing." Rechberg's instructions, Daniel Dawson believes, could only serve as a "strong encouragement to Gutierrez to persevere."[70] Estrada's view was that Rechberg "answered cautiously, but not unfavorably."[71] The fact that Estrada's proposal was unofficial makes Rechberg's reply less remarkable than Dawson believes. Rechberg wanted to put nothing in writing officially.[72] Since French support of an Austrian candidate to a Mexican throne was one of Rechberg's conditions, it was naturally to be feared that territorial compensation might be demanded in return. Particularly it was to be feared that Austria might be asked to cede Venetia to the newly united Italy. By refusing to deal officially with the French Government, the Austrian Government believed that such demands could be forestalled. Metternich confided to Cowley, "We have taken care that he (i.e., Napoleon III) shall have no hold upon us and I defy him to find either in his own archives or in those of Vienna one line that can be turned to our detriment." That the Austrian Government did not wish to negotiate officially is illustrated by its attitude toward hints that Napoleon III made that the Duke of Modena might go to Mexico. Napoleon made this overture to Metternich just before September 1861, the Austrian diplomat later confided to Lord Cowley. The British Ambassador passed the information to Lord Russell:

> The Prince (i.e., Metternich) thought the notion so strange and so utterly inconsistent with the general policy of his government that he refused to be the channel of any official communication upon the subject, a course which was approved by his government."

Nor did Rechberg accept Estrada as being "in a position to give any kind of guarantee" that the Mexicans really wanted a king. By making such a desire on the part of the "Mexican nation" a condition for the candidacy of an Austrian, Rechberg was cautious not to accept Estrada and his "Committee" as representing the "majority" of Mexicans, on whose behalf Estrada claimed he spoke. While one may agree with Dawson that it is remarkable that Rechberg even stated the conditions for the candidacy of an Austrian Prince," it is also true that the door was even shut on further "unofficial" negotiations until the French and British Governments and the Mexican people made their intentions known. While Rechberg politely claimed he did not want to "discourage" Estrada, Metternich told the Mexican "how inopportune the present time was to enter hazards of a tentative nature which had no chance of leading to a favorable result."[76]

When Lord Cowley mentioned the Jecker bonds to Thouvenel at the beginning of July, the French Minister of Foreign Affairs observed that it was time that the British and French Governments make it clear that they "were no longer to be trifled with." A few days before, Napoleon III himself had spoken to Cowley "of the state of Mexico . . . with great commiseration, asking whether nothing could be done to save so fine a country from ruin."[77] Lord Cowley reported these conversations to Lord Russell, but he did not comment on them, either in his official instructions or private letters to Cowley.

Late in July Napoleon went to Vichy for a cure.[78] There he met General Juan Prim, a leader of the Spanish Progressive Party. The only clue to what was discussed is contained in a letter Napoleon wrote Prim when he was in Mexico the next year as Commander-in-Chief of the Spanish portion of the Tripartite intervention:

> Your dream of Vichy is being realized; here are Spanish and French troops going to fight side by side for the same cause.[79]

Prim's "dream of Vichy" probably was not with specific reference to Mexico. A month later he was assisting in an attempt to settle differences between Spain and Mexico.[80]

While Napoleon III was at Vichy, Eugenie was the guest of Count Walewski at Château d'Etioles. During the festivities she met Metternich and spoke to him of her desire that Mexico be saved by the establishment of a monarchy.[81] He did not take the Empress seriously. Metternich believed such "Californian dreams"[82] were impractical.[83]

At the end of July the reports of Wyke[84] and Saligny[85] reached London and Paris respectively. Neither of the two Ministers to Mexico had obtained redress of grievances. Saligny's convention was unratified. A new Mexican Minister of Foreign Relations was loathe to recognize the Jecker bonds even though Saligny claimed he had "written" recognition of the "principle." Wyke found obstacles in the way of obtaining the money stolen from the London Bondholders. Indeed, custom duties assigned them were stopped on a technicality.[86] Both Saligny and Wyke reported conditions of anarchy, resulting in injury to Europeans in Mexico, and bad faith on the part of the Mexican Government in settling claims. Both Ministers suggested using force to coerce Mexico. The only alternative, Saligny and Wyke agreed, was to withdraw their missions from Mexico. Wyke preferred that Great Britain act alone. If Mexico recognized the Jecker bonds, it would have no money left over to pay the British claimants.[87] While Saligny had no detailed plan of operations, Wyke recommended seizing Mexican custom houses, lowering the tariff (to encourage trade) and appropriating custom duties to pay claims.

Throughout July Russell received a flood of resolutions, requests, and letters from Mr. Robertson, the Chairman of the London Bondholders, and Mr. Whitehead, their agent in Mexico.[88] The bondholders requested the aid of the British Government in recovering their $660,000 stolen from the British Legation by Miramon's adherents. It was also realized that technically bondholder claims to Mexican custom duties merely rested on a promise to recognize the arrangement by a diplomatic convention. Therefore Russell was asked to instruct Wyke to negotiate such a convention. While it would give the bondholders a legal claim, recognized by International Law, there was no security that Mexico would not continue to fall into dividend arrears. To prevent this the bondholders proposed that they be permitted to appoint "Interventors." These agents would collect directly from the importing merchants in Mexico the appropriate percentage of Mexican custom duties mortgaged to the bondholders. Thus any misappropriations by the Mexican Collectors of Customs would be circumvented. Russell's attention was called to the fact that Lord Malmesbury had approved the plan in 1858. Finally, as additional security, the bondholders wanted Mexican public lands and unsold nationalized church property ceded to them. The same mail packet that brought Wyke's despatches brought Russell a letter from Mr. Whitehead. He reported that all payments had been suspended to the bondholders and claimed this justified a temporary British protectorate.

Like instructions written to Wyke a month previously, those of 31 July merely authorized him to state that the British Government would use force if necessary. In this connection Russell mentioned specifically the $660,000 stolen from the London Bondholders and the technicality by which the Mexican Government escaped being bound to agreements with the London Bondholders.[89] Under the threat of force, Wyke was to "invite" the Mexican Government to "enter into a formal engagement." Russell also called Wyke's attention to the plan of "Interventors" for the London Bondholders. While the British Government would gladly see such an arrangement made, it was one to which the "free assent" of the Mexican Government had to be obtained.[90] The plan of the bondholders concerning Mexican public and church property Russell thought so impractical that he did not mention it in his instructions. Nor did he comment on the possibility of intervening in Mexico.

On 29 July, a day before receiving Saligny's bundle of despatches, Thouvenel wrote his monthly instructions. He summarized his conversation with De La Fuente earlier that month and informed Saligny that French naval forces had been notified to contact him.[91] The next day Thouvenel received the reports from Mexico but sent no comments on them to Saligny.[92] Neither the French nor the British Governments had yet decided on an intervention in Mexico. French naval forces were only to support Saligny's claims by a show of force. Although Saligny had already severed and Wyke suspended diplomatic relations with the Mexican Government, this was unknown in Europe. On 10 August De La Fuente had an audience with Napoleon III at St. Cloud, and the Emperor spoke of Juarez in friendly terms.[93]

Since Pacheco's departure from Mexico, the Spanish Government was unrepresented in Mexico. De La Fuente was in Europe to settle differences between Spain and Mexico. In August he was still trying to reach a settlement, and a Spanish representative was willing to negotiate. On 20 August a meeting took place in Paris among De La Fuente, General Prim and Camyn, an Under-Secretary of the Spanish Minister of State. Camyn said the *sine non qua* of Spanish recognition of the Juarez Government was the pure and simple acceptance by it of the Mon-Almonte Convention, the last agreement between Spain and Mexico regulating Spanish claims.[94] Once this were done, Camyn went so far to promise, claims contested by Mexico might be submitted to the examination of a commission. De La Fuente did not think the Spanish Government attached much importance to the expulsion of Pacheco and was ". . . only concerned with the convention relative to the Spanish debt."[95]

De La Fuente sent Andres Osegura, a Secretary of the Mexican Legation in Paris, to London. Osegura reported to De La Fuente that sometime in August Tomas Murphy, Miramon's representative to London dismissed earlier that year by Juarez, had two meetings with Lord Russell. According to Osegura, Murphy sounded the British Government about the possibility of putting a Spanish Bourbon on a Mexican throne.[96] Unfortunately, just whom Murphy represented is not clear.[97] From Russell's attitude before[98] and after[99] Murphy's supposed overtures in August, it seems highly improbable that the British Foreign Secretary encouraged Miramon's ex-Minister.

Shortly after the middle of August Lord Russell decided that it was "useless" to continue negotiations with Mexico and that it was necessary to "adopt more active measures to obtain redress." Stating this in a draft instruction, Russell continued that Wyke was to leave Mexico with his Legation unless the Mexican Government agreed to two demands. The first was that "Commissioners," appointed by Great Britain and France, have the power "of appropriating to the Powers having conventions with Mexico the assignments which those conventions prescribe shall be paid out of the receipts of the Maritime Customs Houses of the Republic." Also to be paid by these receipts were the $660,000 stolen from the London Bond-holders and the losses incurred by foreigners through the seizure of a "conducta" by representatives of Juarez.[100] Revising the draft instructions, Russell stated that commissioners should be appointed by Great Britain alone. The second condition was that the commissioners should have the power of reducing Mexican import duties up to one half.[101] This draft instruction to Wyke was then marked "To be sent to Paris for previous communication to French Government." Cowley brought the matter to Thouvenel's attention just before the monthly arrival of despatches from Mexico. The French Minister of Foreign Affairs admitted the legitimacy of the first demand, but seemed to doubt whether the second, concerning tariff reduction, "did not savour of too much interference in the internal concerns of another country." He added that this was not his definitive opinion. The question required more mature examination than a moment's reflection.[102] Nevertheless Russell's instruction was sent off a few days later.[103]

Before drawing up the mid-August instructions to Wyke, Russell received another request from the London Bondholders that they receive the public lands and church property of Mexico as "collateral security" for the loans[104] they had made Mexico.[105] Russell was unwilling to support such a claim. He drew up a Memorandum that "H(er) M(ajesty's) G(overnment) cannot undertake to support all the claims which the (London) Bondholders may consider themselves justified in making." The British Government "ought only to interfere when the faith of the British Crown is in some way engaged."[106] Russell's first condition in his instructions to Wyke conformed to this principle that Mexico was responsible for claims recognized by diplomatic conventions. A whole series of such conventions had been concluded between Mexico and Great Britain since 1842. Each convention recognized claims for property damage and personal injuries of British subjects, and the recognized claimants became "Convention Bondholders," who received a percentage of Mexican import duties.[107] France[108] and Spain[109] had made similar conventions with Mexico.

On 29 August the British Foreign Office received Wyke's despatches[110] relating how he had suspended diplomatic relations in protest of the Mexican law of 17 July that suspended for two years the payment of custom duties mortgaged to claims recognized by foreign conventions. Hammond, the British Under-Secretary of State, sent Russell a private letter that the ". . . Mexican news is as unsatisfactory as usual." Russell was asked whether he had any *precise* instructions."[111] Russell decided it "will be impossible for Her Majesty's Government to maintain amicable relations with Mexico in the face of such a business" as the two-year moratorium.[112] While the law of 17 July brought his patience to an end, Russell's indignation was also aroused by the particularly brutal murder of a British subject and the robbery of British miners in Mexico by Marquez, the leader of a band of conservative die-hards and bandits who eluded Juarez' soldiers. In a Minute on Wyke's despatches received on 29 August, the British Secretary observed:

In the present state of the country no efficient protection can be given to British miners. Marquez is a monster of Cruelty, and if the Church Party came into power all British subjects may expect the fate of Mr. Beale.[113]

Russell decided to use force but was not sure just how to do so. On 31 August he prepared a Memorandum, sent to Lord Palmerston:

But the practical remedy is not easy to find. If we blockade Vera Cruz and Tampico we destroy the means of repayment to the creditors. If we attempt reprisals we shall only shear the hog.
Sir C. Wyke . . . suggests that we shall take possession not

only of Vera Cruz and Tampico but of the Mexican ports on the Pacific, and collect the customs ourselves.

But if a British garrison is to occupy the fort of St. Jean de *(sic)* Ulloa in the hot season fever may make . . . havoc among them.

Perhaps the best way will be to take possession of Vera Cruz and Tampico in November, and . . . renew our offer to negotiate, declaring that if our terms are not accepted, we shall either by holding forcible possession of their forts, or by blockade take effectual means of preventing the Mexican Government from receiving any revenue of customs from their ports whether in the Atlantic or the Pacific.

The Admiralty and the Departments must be consulted on this subject before any Instructions are sent. I should be disposed to leave a large discretion as to means to Admiral Milne and the Admiral in the Pacific Station.[114]

On the same day he prepared this memorandum, Russell prepared an instruction for Wyke so that it would reach him by the next mail packet about to leave from Southampton. The suspending of diplomatic relations was approved. Further instructions would be sent by a man-of-war. In the meantime Wyke was to act on the instructions prepared in mid-August, which were sent simultaneously.[115]

On 30 August Thouvenel received Saligny's despatches[116] that he severed diplomatic relations with Mexico as a result of the law of 17 July. Unlike Wyke, who wanted Great Britain to act alone, Saligny proposed Great Britain, Spain, and France seize Tampico and Vera Cruz. According to the French Minister to Mexico, only a very small naval force and several hundred men would be sufficient. Thouvenel delayed making a decision, and the mail packet left for Mexico without instructions to Saligny.[117] De La Fuente was refused an audience by Thouvenel on 31 August.[118] The Mexican agent, however, considered the situation so grave that he sent Thouvenel a letter the same day to justify the law of 17 July.[119]

The law of 17 July was a much better "pretext" for Napoleon III to intervene in Mexico than those reasons given by Thouvenel to De La Fuente in July before the news of the Mexican moratorium reached Europe. Russell was making the transition from a policy of threats to one of military intervention. De La Fuente's negotiations at the end of August to settle differences with Spain came to nothing.[120] Whether Mexico accepted the Mon-Almonte Convention was now largely an academic question, for operation of the convention would be suspended for two years by the July moratorium. By the beginning of September 1861, therefore, it was very likely that the three European Powers with the greatest stake in Mexico would decide on an intervention.

## 2.  THE NEGOTIATION OF THE TRIPARTITE CONVENTION OF LONDON, PART I, SEPTEMBER 1861

Upon receipt of the despatches from Mexico at the end of August, Hammond, the British Under-Secretary of State, sent a letter to the British Admiralty inquiring whether it would be practical to seize Vera Cruz.[1] Then Hammond informed Russell of having taken this initiative.[2] The answer from the Admiralty was that if the Mexicans offered any "serious opposition," a ". . . great loss of life would probably be incurred and the attacking vessels greatly injured." The climate of Vera Cruz was "deadly" for Europeans until the end of September, and later in the year, when the "Northers" blew. the anchorage was unsafe. Finally, no vessels were available at the moment.[3] Lord Russell either did not read the Admiralty letter immediately or thought it of so little importance that he did not mention it in the Memorandum he drew up for Lord Palmerston on the last day of August. Therein Russell remarked that nothing could be decided upon before communicating with the Admiralty.[4]

On 3 September, when the British, French, and Spanish Governments had not yet communicated with each other about the possibility of cooperating in an intervention in Mexico, Lord Cowley reported a conversation with Thouvenel to Russell. Lord Cowley had asked whether it were true, as reported by Wyke, that Saligny had sent for French ships of war after breaking diplomatic relations with Mexico. Thouvenel replied that Saligny's severing of diplomatic relations was approved, but he had no power to declare war or give orders to Admiral Penaud. Saligny probably had just informed the Admiral what was happening in Mexico. The French Minister to Mexico could not possibly have done more, for the ". . . French squadron in those seas was not strong enough to attempt hostilities." Thouvenel added that the question of hostile measures merited consideration. He referred to Russell's instructions to Wyke and said a demand might be made for the cession of Mexican Custom Houses. Thouvenel commented that "if that demand were to be resisted, ought it not be enforced?"[5] This proposal, then, was that the first demand of the ultimatum Russell instructed Wyke to present to the Mexican Government, if refused, should be implemented by force instead of a passive withdrawal from Mexico.

Thouvenel finally granted De La Fuente an audience on 3 September,[6] but refused to listen to any justification of the Mexican law of 17 July.[7] The Mexican agent was told that Saligny's actions were approved by the French Government,[8] and that both it and the British Government were determined to use force if necessary.[9] Thouvenel had made a similar observation to De La Fuente in the previous July. At that time the French Minister of Foreign Affairs had also mentioned the need of coercing Mexico to Lord Cowley.[10] On 3 September, as in July, Thouvenel had no official indication that the British Government did indeed wish to use force against Mexico.[11]

On 4 September Cowley's report about the possibility of Anglo-French coercion envisioned by Thouvenel reached the British Foreign Office.[12] On that day, instead of making a reply to Cowley, Russell sent a request for information to the Admiralty:

First. What amount of Naval Force would be required to make an attack on the Forts of Vera Cruz with good probability of success?

Secondly. What are the facilities or difficulties of a blockade of Vera Cruz and Tampico?

Thirdly. What was the nature of the Naval operations of the French Squadron in the year 1838 under Admiral Baudin and the Prince de Joinville and what was their result?

Fourthly. Till what month could European Forces occupy San Juan de (sic) Ulloa without danger of great sickness and mortality?[13]

On 5 September Thouvenel asked Cowley whether he had any instructions from Lord Russell about Mexican affairs. Cowley had nothing to report. Then Thouvenel said he wanted to send Saligny identical instructions as those sent Sir Charles Wyke. Thouvenel also asked Cowley to inform Russell that it might be ". . . advisable to ask the association of the Spanish Government in any measures which might be taken with regard to Mexico." Should a "hostile demonstration" become necessary, "Spain possessed resources at the Havannah, which might be of great assistance to Great Britain and France."[14] Finally, Thouvenel asked Cowley to "sound" Russell how far he "would be inclined to profit from present state of affairs in Mexico, and the impossibility of any interference on the part of the United States, *to recommend* the rival parties to take unto themselves a Sovereign." If Mexico did this "of her own free choice," it was the best way of restoring it to a "creditable position among the Nations of the World." Cowley believed this proposal so delicate that he brought it to Lord Russell's attention by means of a private letter.[15] The same day that Thouvenel made these suggestions, he wrote Saligny to approve his breaking diplomatic relations with Mexico. Saligny's last reports, Thouvenel observed, "destroy all the illusions" that French claims might be settled. Saligny, therefore, was to demand the abrogation of the law of 17 July and the establishment in Vera Cruz and Tampico of commissioners having the powers specified by Lord Russell in his instructions to Wyke.

No mention, however, was made of a reduction of the Mexican tariff. If Mexico refused, Saligny was to withdraw from Mexico at once.[16]

Mon, the Spanish Ambassador to Paris, somehow gained the impression that France and Great Britain were going to cooperate militarily without Spain. On 6 September Mon telegraphed the Spanish Minister of Foreign Relations:

> France and England are going to seize the Custom Houses of Vera Cruz and Tampico in order to reimburse themselves of all the sums Mexico owes them. For this purpose, naval forces are directed towards these places. They don't seem to take us into account at all. . . . I know that the idea of a monarchy is agreeable to them; the occasion is favorable for a solution, because we are all offended, and the United States is very weak. I suggest we act without delay.[17]

Upon receipt of this telegram, but without mentioning it, Collantes telegraphed Mon to find out whether France intended to make a demonstration against Mexico.[18] That evening Collantes sent a second telegram that Spain was going to send an expedition to Tampico and Vera Cruz, but was willing to cooperate with Great Britain and France:

> Our despatches of today crossed each other. The Government has decided to act energetically. A steamer is going to leave to carry instructions to the Captain-General of Cuba that he act against Tampico and Vera Cruz with all the land and sea force which he can get together. Your Excellency is permitted to make it known to the Imperial Government. If England and France agree to act with Spain, the forces of the three powers can combine, to obtain redress of grievances as well as to establish a regular and stable order in Mexico. If they want to act without Spain, the Government of the Queen, which was waiting for an opportune time to act with vigor, without giving reason to attribute political views to it, will obtain the satisfaction which it has a right to claim by making use of the forces it has and which are superior to those necessary to accomplish an enterprize of this nature. . . .[19]

An identical despatch was sent to the Spanish Ambassador to London,[20] but he did not communicate its contents to the British Government until 23 September.[21] Four days after Collantes' telegrams to Paris, the Spanish official ministerial newspaper, *Diario Espanol,* published a statement that Spain would take action against Mexico "without considering the attitude of others, but ready to come to an understanding with whoever is disposed to . . . obtain satisfaction."[22] The next day orders to prepare a Spanish expedition to go to Mexico were issued.[23] Having waited the entire spring and summer of 1861 to arrive at a settlement of differences with Mexico,[24] the Spanish Government could not afford to permit France and Great Britain to act without Spain. The Cortes was about to start sessions after the summer recess, and it was expected that Pacheco would then attack the Government for its inactivity.[25] That such was the reason for Collantes' action of 6 September was confirmed by the Spanish Minister of State in a conversation with Crampton, the British Ambassador to Spain. Marshal O'Donnell stated that no operations could be begun before the beginning of November "on account of the prevalence of the yellow fever and the . . . hurricanes." That was the absolute deadline in view of the approaching opening of the Cortes:

> The grievances of which the Spanish Government had to complain were of long standing, and they had waited with patience for now more than six months in the vain hope of some satisfaction for them being afforded, and more especially for the indignity offered in the dismissal of the Spanish Minister from Mexico. Cortes would assemble in the course of next month; and the Spanish Government would be unable to justify themselves before that Body and the Nation if they were to defer beyond what was rendered necessary by material obstacles the vindication of its rights and dignity.[26]

Mon brought Collantes' proposals to Thouvenel's attention on 9 September. Thouvenel agreed that the three European Powers should occupy Vera Cruz and Tampico to "reimburse themselves for what Mexico owes" France, Spain, and Great Britain would also "make understood the necessity of establishing itself in a stable manner."[27] Mon mentioned orders to the Captain-General of Cuba to take action against Mexico, but that he couldn't act until the end of October. Consequently, Mon observed, there was time to negotiate.[28] Directly after speaking with Mon,[29] Thouvenel wrote a despatch to the French Ambassador to London. Flahault was to make known to Lord Russell that Saligny had been given similar instructions to those that went to Wyke about the demands to be made of the Mexican Government. (Saligny's instructions had been written, but they could not be sent for another three weeks, when the next mail packet went to Mexico.[30]) If these demands were accepted, Wyke and Saligny would reestablish diplomatic relations. It was unlikely that this would happen. Then the French Government, as in the past, desired to cooperate with the British Government. If force were used to obtain redress, it was important that the two Governments agree in advance so that identical instructions could be sent to Wyke and Saligny. Thouvenel went on to state that a political reorganization of Mexico was also desirable. He recalled the British mediation proposals of 1860[31] and proposed them as the basis of negotiations among France, Great Britain, and Spain :

> Some time ago the cabinet of London considered a general amnesty and the convocation of an extraordinary congress as the best means to obtain the participation of all political men of Mexico in the durable reconstruction of authority. The Government of the Emperor would still admit that this double proposition would serve as a point of departure for negotiations that there would be to enter upon in this connection. It would appear indispensable to me, however, that Spain be asked to cooperate with us, because we accepted its cooperation on a previous occasion. The cabinet of Madrid is placed in a position analagous to ours and has still more complaints against Mexico than we ourselves.

Since the cooperation of the United States had been invited to the proposals of 1860, Thouvenel briefly referred to this eventuality.[32] It was only mentioned to make it appear that Thouvenel was only proposing what the British Government itself had proposed the previous year. In a private letter to his Ambassador to London, Thouvenel predicted that the United States would respond to such an offer with "reserve." The Mexican expedition would be decided on "without waiting for the cooperation of the United States." It had "other fish to fry than Mexicans."[33]

On 10 September Thouvenel sent a copy of his instructions to Flahault of the previous day to Barrot, the French Ambassador to Madrid. Thouvenel commented that there would be time to negotiate, because Mon had said the Captain-General of Cuba would take no action until the end of October.[34] While the Spanish Government and Court were at San Ildefonso during the recess of the Cortes, Barrot was at Madrid. His only report concerning Mexico in September was that he had not had a chance to see Collantes.[35]

The official British answer to Thouvenel's overture of 9 September was communicated by Cowley on 24 September.[36] In the interval Lord Russell and Lord Palmerston studied the correspondence from the Admiralty and ascertained the attitude of the Spanish Government. The reports from Spain came by messenger about every two weeks, in contrast to the daily service between Paris and London. The first despatches from Crampton, reporting hte attitude of the Spanish Government in detail, arrived in London on 22 September.[37] The next day an answer was sent to Thouvenel's proposals.[38]

On 8 September the British Foreign Office received an answer from the Admiralty on the four questions sent it. No difficulties with regard to a blockade were foreseen, but operations could only be undertaken during the healthy months of September to May. No specific amount of ships necessary to capture the forts of Vera Cruz, as requested, was given. Instead it was stressed that the main fort, St. Juan d'Ulloa, had been strengthened since 1838, when the French captured it with

three heavy frigates and two "bomb vessels." The 1838 correspondence from Naval Commanders was enclosed and showed
that the fort only surrendered after the explosion of two chief
magazines. The Admiralty saw the main difficulty in that the
walls of the fort were made of coral rock. It received a "shot"
without suffering much damage. A naval force, therefore,
could not cause St. Juan d'Ulloa to surrender. A thousand
"well commanded" men would be necessary.[39] Russell sent this
information to Lord Palmerston,[40] who didn't answer until a
week later.[41]

Upon receipt of Thouvenel's proposals of 9 September,
Flahault gave Russell a copy, but the British Foreign Secretary
made no immediate answer.[42] At the same time Russell received
a despatch from Cowley, giving the substance of Collantes'
proposals as referred to Thouvenel by Mon.[43] Thouvenel, however, had led Cowley to believe that orders were underway to
the Captain-General of Cuba to take immediate possession of
Vera Cruz and Tampico.[44] If he hoped to precipitate a reply
from Lord Russell by this means, Thouvenel was mistaken.
Instead Russell sent a telegram to Crampton on 14 September
to verify this information.[45] The next day Russell had a telegraphic reply from Spain that military preparations were
underway, but nothing would be done before the end of
October ". . . in consequence of yellow fever and the equi-
noctial hurricanes." Although the Spanish Government was
determined to act, it wanted to cooperate with Great Britain
and France.[46]

Russell was reluctant to accept the cooperation offered by
the Spanish Government and recommended by Thouvenel.
On 16 September the British Foreign Secretary returned to
Flahault the copy of Thouvenel's instruction. Accompanying
it was a private letter that there were two reasons for a delayed
official reply. Palmerston had not yet commented on the
Admiralty letter detailing the difficulties of capturing St. Juan
d'Ulloa. The second difficulty was that the Spanish Government "intends the most desirable aim to be the prosecution of

Protestants." The French Government, Russell believed, " 'cannot give its sanction to such a principle,' " and the British Government " 'dreads it.' "[47] Russell was also concerned about Thouvenel's unofficial overture via Cowley about the possibility of establishing a monarchy in Mexico. In a private letter Russell replied that it "would never do for us to set up a monarchy in Mexico, though if they did it for themselves, I should think they took the wisest course."[48]

While Thouvenel stated that it was up to the Mexicans to decide by the means of a constituent assembly proposed by the British Government a year before, the Civil War was over in Mexico in 1861, even though Conservative bands roamed the land. Russell had no desire to see that "monster" Marquez, or any of the other chieftains of these bands, return to power.[49] Thouvenel's amnesty proposal, Russell feared, would "save . . . the villains who robbed and murdered our subjects."[50] Lord Palmerston saw a way out of some of these difficulties. If Great Britain did not cooperate with Spain and France, he reasoned, they might act against Mexico anyway. France and Spain, Palmerston foresaw, might try to obtain Mexican territory or set up a government of their choosing in Mexico. To prevent these possibilities, Palmerston proposed obtaining disclaimers in advance:

> This turn in Mexican affairs is curious and requires consideration. A threefold operation by England, France, and Spain has in some aspects advantages over singlehanded action by England. Indeed if we were to act alone, we ought to make known to France at all accounts our intentions, and if we did not ask their cooperation we ought as an example to her, to enter into distinct engagement towards her not to make any permanent acquisition of territory; an engagement which we could take in this case without any sacrifice on our part.
>
> If England and France were to act together we should occupy St. Jean d'Ulloa, withaut troops singly, a joint garisson would never do. If the Spaniards determine to attack the Mexicans, we might as the French cooperate with them by a naval force, and let them land troops but then we ought to

have a previous engagement by Spain that when the Mexican ports are occupied we should have officers to collect the custom duties, to make good our claims, and that the occupation would not be made the means of putting again into power either of the Political Parties who have lately so much abased power.

In this private letter of 17 September to his Foreign Secretary, Lord Palmerston also commented on the Admiralty letter sent him. Russell's request for information did "not specify what our object is, and therefore does not enable the Admiralty to propose means to an end, because the end is an unknown quantity." Russell might "ere long" request the Admiralty to have reinforcements ready for operations in Mexican waters.[51]

On 18 September Russell sent a telegram to Crampton asking whether Spain would agree "to ask (the) United States Government to act in concert with Great Britain and France in relation to the affairs of Mexico?"[52] This feeler apparently was not in connection with Thouvenel's brief mention of such a possibility in his instruction to Flahault.[53] Nor did Russell have uppermost in his mind the idea of inviting the United States in order to forestall any protests by it against a European intervention in Mexico. Although Hammond foresaw such an American attitude,[54] and Palmerston feared that Lincoln and Seward might seize Canada "to make up for ill success against the South."[55] Russell saw in the cooperation of the United States a means to frustrate supposed Spanish intolerance and Thouvenel's amnesty proposal:

> I have sent off my copy of Thouvenel's despatch too soon, and had forgotten its contents.
> But I have strongly impressed in my mind the danger of acting with France and Spain without the U.S.
> 1. They won't restore religious intolerance.
> 2. They won't save by an amnesty the villains who have robbed and murdered our subjects.

On this note that Russell wrote for Palmerston on 20 September, the British Prime Minister wrote a comment two days later : "I quite agree."[56]

Before receiving an answer from Spain about inviting the United States to cooperate with the European Powers, Lord Russell received a despatch from Lord Cowley reporting conversations on Mexico with Mon and Thouvenel. On 17 September Cowley met Mon in Thouvenel's anteroom. Mon expressed the hope that Great Britain, France, and Spain would take common action against Mexico. Lord Cowley replied that he understood Spain was going to act alone. Mon claimed such a step would only be taken if Great Britain and France refused to cooperate with Spain. He added the Spanish Government would "much rather act in concert with Great Britain and France."[57] Cowley had received a private letter from Hammond that Russell would never agree to act with Spain, because "Great Britain never can embark in a crusade against liberty of conscience."[58] Therefore Cowley observed to Mon that the British Government attached great value to religious freedom. Mon believed "questions of that nature ought to be left to the decision of the Mexican Government." At the same time he "abjured . . . on the part of Spain, all desire to impose any particular government on Mexico." Spain only wanted "a government chosen by the Mexicans, which would make itself respected and would scrupulously fulfill engagements taken with foreign Powers." At this point Thouvenel was ready to see Cowley and asked whether Russell had written about Mexico. Cowley said he had nothing to report, but Mon's recent statements "did not quite tally" with Thouvenel's that Spain had already ordered military operations against Mexico. The French Minister of Foreign Affairs then explained that he had intended only to convey that Spain was making preparations for an expedition and hoped to employ it in cooperation with France and Great Britain. He hoped, Thouvenel told Cowley, that the British Government would not refuse Spanish cooperation, for "three thousand Spanish infantry could be sent from the Havannah." The official report

Cowley sent Russell summarizing this conversation[59] was accompanied by a private letter stating that Thouvenel was "very anxious for an answer about Mexico."[60]

In the evening of 19 September the British Foreign Office received a telegram from Crampton. The Spanish Government did not object to acting with the United States but "would not consent to postpone its own action by waiting for the cooperation of the United States."[61] Three days later another telegram arrived from Crampton that the Spanish Government foresaw no difficulties provided there were no delay, but the matter of inviting the United States would be submitted to the Spanish Council.[62] The same day, 22 September, Crampton's first despatches about Mexico arrived. That Spain wished to cooperate with France and Great Britain and would have time to make the necessary arrangements before the Spanish expedition were ready at the beginning of November was nothing new.[63] Russell already knew that from Crampton's telegram and Mon's remarks made to Lord Cowley. Russell read with much greater interest[64] a report of a conversation Crampton had had with O'Donnell, the Spanish Minister of State. O'Donnell's remarks were especially important, because they could be taken as the official policy of the Spanish Government. Mon's disclaimers about not interfering in Mexican internal affairs could always have been disavowed. Furthermore, O'Donnell gave his opinion on the possibility of a Mexican throne, confidentially proposed by Thouvenel and for which the Spanish "race . . . dominate over a large portion" of North America "in order to counter balance the force of the Anglo-Saxon race."[65] O'Donnell remarked to Crampton that Spain, France, and Great Britain had all suspended diplomatic relations with Mexico. The motive was the same, "to enforce redress for the intolerable wrongs inflicted upon their respective subjects by the anarchical governments which succeeded each other" in Mexico. It was desirable, therefore, that the three European Powers agree on a common course "in enforcing upon Mexico the observance of her international duties." No matter what, Spain had to "go" to Mexico, but "not certainly with any view of conquest or exclusive advantage but for the protection of our rights." Without any instructions from his Government, Crampton made the same proposal Palmerston suggested to Russell, of mutual disclaimers about interferring in Mexican internal affairs and territorial aggrandisement. Crampton's attention had been called to these possibilities, because "a large portion of the Spanish Press has lately been advocating an intervention of this sort and the establishment of a monarchy in Mexico, and indulging in wild speculations as to the recovery by Spain of her ancient possessions in America." O'Donnell was willing that the three Powers disavow such intentions in advance and commented on "chimerical" monarchy schemes:

> I did not find Marshall O'Donnell prepared to suggest any definite plan of action on the part of the powers whose joint intervention he recommended. His Excellency remarked however that the notion, which had at different times been put forward, of establishing a Constitutional Monarchy in Mexico was in his opinion very chimerical and he seemed entirely to concur in the justice of a remark which I made in regard to this matter, viz that any engagement which should bind England, France, and Spain to a permanent intervention or tutelage of any sort in the internal affairs of a country so situated as Mexico would be liable to grave objections.[66]

On 23 September the British reply to Thouvenel's proposals was sent to Lord Cowley. The British Government was willing to cooperate with other Powers having claims against Mexico, if these claims were based on the same principles as British claims:

> 1st. The right to require security for the lives, and respect for the property of British subjects in Mexico;
> 2nd. The right to exact the fulfilment of obligations contracted towards Great Britain by the government of Mexico.

In his draft of this despatch Russell made British cooperation contingent on an invitation to the United States to cooperate with the European Powers. The United States might "decline all cooperation" or "send only a single corvette to join in an Expedition against Vera Cruz." But Russell believed "it due to the United States to have the fullest communication with Washington before joining in any combination for the purpose of coercing Mexico." Lord Palmerston crossed out this section and noted in the margin : "This is as if the French govt had objected to such communication instead of which they have themselves proposed it." Then the Prime Minister rewrote the proposal, and it replaced Russell's version in the despatch sent Cowley :

> Her Majesty's Government are glad to find by M. Thouvenel's despatch that the Government of His Imperial Majesty takes on this point (i.e., the two principles) the same view of this matter, and Har Majesty's Government will willingly enter into concert with the Government of France as to the course to be pursued. Her Majesty's Government also fully concurs with M. Thouvenel in thinking that before any active steps are taken in this matter by the European Powers, an offer of cooperation ought to be made by them to the government of the United States.

In his draft despatch, Russell claimed that nothing could be done before knowing exactly what orders had been given to the Captain-General of Cuba. Palmerston crossed this out, and Russell then revised and expanded it. Palmerston then approved the despatch, and it was sent to Cowley :

> It does not appear that the Spanish Government have as yet sent any precise orders for the immediate employment of their forces in Mexico. There is therefore time for deliberation and concert.
> With respect to the measures to be taken for the peace and tranquillity of Mexico, Her Majesty's Government are ready to discuss the subject with France, Spain and the United States. But it is evident that much must depend on the actual state of affairs at the time when our forces may be ready to

act on the shores of Mexico. The measures suggested some time ago by Her Majesty's Government appear to be inapplicable to the present state of affairs.[67]

Without any explanations, one brief sentence dismissed the suggestion made by Thouvenel to renew the British proposals of the previous year. Thereby the amnesty and the constituent assembly to establish a new government in Mexico were rejected. Both Russell and Palmerston did not want to interfere in the internal affairs of Mexico. A joint expedition might be the means of frustrating any French and Spanish attempts in this direction. By making it appear that an invitation to the United States was Thouvenel's idea, Russell and Palmerston hoped to force France to accept the cooperation of a Power, which, they foresaw, would act as a further check to any possible French and Spanish ulterior motives. If France and Spain agreed to make redress of legitimate claims the sole basis of an expedition to Mexico, Lord Palmerston would have his disclaimers. Crampton's reports received the day before indicated that Spain was willing to agree to such limited objectives. A satisfactory reply from the French Government would settle the preliminaries to a combined expedition to Mexico. Pending such a reply, Russell sent a telegram to his Ambassador to Spain to inquire whether the Spanish Government would "consent to defer their action" until France and Great Britain had "time to confer respecting concert."[68]

During the two weeks that Thouvenel waited for an answer to his proposals sent to London on 9 September, Napoleon III was at Biarritz with Eugenie and Hidalgo. There it was decided to offer the throne of Mexico to Archduke Maximilian, Emperor Franz Joseph's younger brother. While the accounts of Napoleon III,[69] Eugenie,[70] and Hidalgo[71] of how this decision was made by them are all suspect in varying degree, these accounts agree substantially. They also are in harmony with the ideas the three participants had previously.

While a guest of Napoleon III and Eugenie at Biarritz,

Hidalgo received letters that Great Britain and Spain intended to send naval expeditions to Mexico. The Mexican exile told his host and hostess. Hidalgo added that British intervention, always desired by Napoleon, was now imminent. Spain would also cooperate. Then France "will not be acting alone, which was what Your Majesty always wished to avoid." When the allied flags appeared, the "overwhelming majority" in Mexico would "annihilate the demagogues, then proclaim a monarchy." The United States was helpless in view of the Civil War there and could not hinder Mexico, which would "rise as one man" in favor of a monarchy.[72] All "men of weight, all peacefully disposed persons" in Mexico had been afraid to express their real feelings, because they feared the "attacks of the demagogic Bands." The European intervention would establish order, and these monarchists would openly declare themselves.[73]

Hidalgo's argument appealed to Eugenie. She later recalled how she was "misled" by "glowing vistas that were made to sparkle before our eyes."[74] Since she had been regent in 1859, when Napoleon was in Italy concerned with the Austro-Sardinian War, she never ceased to take a part in public affairs.[75] She felt she had a historical role to play and "would be judged with as much severity as Marie Louise."[76] What stirred Eugenie most were "the broad questions, where national interest, national prestige, were at stake."[77] She was partly Spanish and admitted a "profound . . . attachment . . . for Spain." She suffered to see it "descend to the rank of a third rate power." During the Crimean War she tried to persuade Spain to join the war "to see this flag fighting next to ours." Then Spanish "credit would increase until one treats with her and counts her as one of the other powers."[78] It could be easily done, she wrote her sister in 1860, if the Spanish Government would "give France the hand frankly."[79] A combined Spanish and French expedition to Mexico offered just such an opportunity. For Eugenie Mexico had a rich historical past.[80] It was civilized and taught the Catholic faith by Spain. Now the

Mexicans were "abandoned to demoralization" after "ceaseless
struggles." Her compassion for the "poor Mexican nation" was
added to an idealistic hope for "a new era . . . for that nation,
which only requires to be governed by a wise and firm hand to
become once more what it was."[81] Then the United States
would be prevented from annexing Mexico. Archduchess
Charlotte, Maximilian's wife, later wrote Eugenie that the
cause of Mexico was "a holy one . . . by reason of the fresh
impulse which it is bound to give to religion among a people
whose civil discords have not yet succeeded in extinguishing
the ardent Catholic faith of their ancestors."[82] Eugenie replied
that Charlotte "has defined so well . . . the bond by which all
my sympathies are attached" to Mexico. It was an enormous
task that excited the Empress' imagination: "Everything will
have to be done, both in the moral and material sphere."[83]

Napoleon, like Eugenie, believed it was a "question of
rescuing a whole continent from anarchy and misery," having
their origin in "dangerous Utopias and bloody disorders." Only
"raising the monarchist flag,"[84] Napoleon believed, "could save
the country from ruin."[85] An orderly Mexico would "form an
impassable barrier to the encroachments of North America."[86]
This barrier would protect French and Spanish "colonies in the
Antilles" and prevent an American monopoly of trade in the
New World.[87] Mexican prosperity would follow, "based upon
. . . a sincere love of progress."[88] Mexico would exploit its
natural resources and exchange them for European manufactured goods. What Napoleon especially desired was cotton.[89]
Although the large American crop of 1860 was exported[90]
before Lincoln's blockade proclamation in April 1861.[91] little
cotton could be expected from the Confederacy if the blockade
became more effective. In July Napoleon had hinted to Lord
Cowley that something might be done to aid the South, but
the British Ambassador said then that his Government would
remain neutral.[92] Napoleon did not want to aid the South unless
assisted by Great Britain.[93] An alternative way to obtain cotton
was from Mexico. Small amounts were grown there,[94] and

Napoleon hoped Mexico might "render great services to our industries by extending its cultivation of cotton."[95] A Saint Simonian faith in furthering "progress' through the economic development of Mexico was the core of Napoleon's Mexican policy.[96] He hoped to achieve this end in line with his general policy of an Anglo-French alliance.[97]

While Napoleon was little interested in religion,[98] he always had a great respect for French public opinion.[99] Extending French influence in Mexico might gain him popularity in clerical segments of French public opinion at the very time that the "Roman Question" was unsettled.[100] Such was the opinion of Baron Beyens, the shrewd Belgian Ambassador to Paris,[101] but whether Napoleon considered this possibility is unknown.[102] It is clear, however, that French public opinion, which was indifferent towards Mexico in 1861, did not force the Emperor to undertake an expedition to Mexico.[103] Opinion in France in the last half of 1861 was also uninterested in Italian affairs.[104]

Three of the most acute observers of the Emperor of the French, Baron Beyens,[105] Baron Hübner,[106] and Lord Cowley,[107] all agreed that Napoleon III conceived foreign policy as the primary means of maintaining his dynasty. An expedition to Mexico in cooperation with Spain and Great Britain, which would share part of the costs,[108] could be a French diplomatic *coup* at a time when there was peace in Europa. Eugenie was urging Napoleon to act. She admitted giving him a strong "impetus,"[109] and Lord Cowley was convinced she "governs the Emperor's decisions" on Mexico.[110] When General Fleury, Napoleon's aide-de-camp, argued that there were military and financial problems, the Emperor answered with arguments Fleury believed were furnished by Hidalgo via the Empress.[111] Persigny, Napoleon's life-long accomplice,[112] also complained that Eugenie tried to "determine" the Mexican policy of France.[113] Lord Clarendon expressed these thoughts more grossly by asking, "What on earth can have been in his head when he listened to the cock and bull stories of a refugie and believed he could . . . regenerate a nation of bandits whose normal state is anarchy."[114] While Eugenie and Hidalgo certainly did exert an influence on Napoleon, it must be added that Hidalgo's descriptions of anarchy in Mexico were to a certain extent confirmed by Saligny's despatches.[115] While Saligny's reports did not mention a monarchist party,[116] Napoleon typically preferred to carry on a personal policy outside official diplomatic channels.[117] In spite of Eugenie's urgings in the past, he waited upon events for an appropriate time to achieve his ends.[118] The time would come, Napoleon believed, when Great Britain would cooperate with France, the United States were neutralized, and when there was a "pretext" to intervene in Mexico.[119] At Biarritz, in 1861, all these conditions seemed fulfilled.[120] Only a candidate was lacking.

To Hidalgo's observations at Biarritz that the time was favorable for the establishment of a monarchy in Mexico, Napoleon replied that he had not yet received Thouvenel's despatches. If Great Britain and Spain were prepared to act, the Emperor of the French would join them. If "Mexico declares that it desires to organize itself with the support of the European powers," he would "lend a hand." The state of affairs in America was "propitious."[121]

Hidalgo then asked Napoleon whether he had a candidate for the throne of Mexico, but he claimed he had none.[122] The Mexican exile commented that it was not "judicious . . . to think of a Prince" of one of the intervening Powers in order to avoid jealousy on the part of the other two.[123] Napoleon agreed.[124] Eugenie and Hidalgo believed the candidate had to be Catholic.[125] The Dukes of Parma, Montpensier, D'Aumale were mentioned.[126] The Duke of Modena, whom Eugenie had considered earlier that year,[127] was thought of as a possible candidate.[128] Napoleon III had recently spoken about him to Metternich.[129] Hidalgo recalled the occasion and asked whether the Austrian Ambassador "did not say something, at any rate, about whether an Austrian archduke would accept this crown?" According to Hidalgo's memoirs, Eugenie then proposed Maximilian:

| | |
|---|---|
| Eugenie : | But which archduke? |
| Hidalgo : | I believe the Archduke Rainer was spoken of. |
| Eugenie : | Yes, for the Archduke Maximilian would not be willing. |
| Hidalgo : | Oh no. He would not accept. |
| Napoleon III : | Oh, no, he would not be willing. |
| Eugenie : | Well! I have a presentiment that tells me he will accept. |
| Hidalgo : | We can but try, and I might write to Gutierrez de Estrada to go to Vienna to sound His Imperial Highness.[130] |

Neither in his memoirs[131] nor in another account of the Biarritz meeting,[132] written in 1862, did Hidalgo give himself or Napoleon III credit for proposing Maximilian's candidacy. Eugenie's account was that, after various persons had been mentioned as possible candidates, there was a long silence. Then Napoleon declared in favor of Maximilian.[133] Napoleon himself claimed, "I put forward the name of Archduke Maximilian."[134] It may be concluded that Eugenie mentioned Maximilian's name first, but it was Napoleon who made the final decision. In one of his silences, for which he was famous,[135] he let his mind follow its own course of ideas.[136] He himself had mentioned Maximilian to Wyke earlier that year.[137] Napoleon now decided that Maximilian was the most suitable of the candidates mentioned. He had excellent personal qualities,[138] and his governorship of Lombardy–Venetia had given him experience in government.[139] He came "from a Great Power that is not a Maritime Power" and would "not offend the susceptibilities of the great Maritime Powers" about to intervene in Mexico. He was married to the daughter of the King of the Belgians, whose friendship with Queen Victoria would make him "a natural bond between France and England." It was "in good taste" to propose a candidate from Austria, with which France had been at war so recently.[140] That war ended without the inclusion of Venetia in recently united Italy. Napoleon had promised Venetia to Cavour. Now Napoleon believed he might persuade Austria to cede to Italy the province demanded by it in return for French assistance in establishing Maximilian on a Mexican throne.[141] The means whereby Maximilian would be established in Mexico would be a tripartite intervention, which would permit "a considerable party in Mexico" to "seize power, to call a national assembly, and to proclaim a monarchy."[142]

The idea of a "national assembly" was one of the British mediation proposals of 1860 that Thouvenel proposed in his instruction to Flahault on 9 September. Since it is unlikely that Thouvenel made such an important proposal without the approval of the Emperor, the questions are raised how and when Napoleon III made his approval known to Thouvenel. No conclusive answers can be given to these questions. One difficulty is setting the exact date of the Biarritz decision.[143] Another difficulty is that the only documentary clue is merely dated "September 1861," and therefore Thouvenel could have been instructed to make the proposal of a national assembly before or after Maximilian was selected as a candidate.[144]

The first overture to Austria was not through Estrada, as first intended by Hidalgo,[145] but through Walewski, in whom Eugenie confided.[146] On September 16 Walewski wrote Metternich from Biarritz:

> The Empress is again keenly interested in the Mexican proposal which she discussed with you at Etiolles. She now thinks that it may be possible to arrive at an understanding as to the candidate. Here at Biarritz they would be quite prepared to support the candidature of the Archduke Maximilian should Vienna consent. In that event I believe they would even be willing when the proper moment arrives, to take the initiative in the necessary negotiations with England and Spain. Send me a line so that I may be able to inform the Empress how Vienna views the matter, as her interest in the proposal shows no sign of diminishing.[147]

Metternich took Walewski's letter to Vienna[148] and referred the project to the Austrian Government.[149] Then he went on a leave of absence to his estate, skeptical that the project would be approved by his Government[150] and yet uneasy that Eugenie took such a great interest in the matter.[151]

During his leave of absence, Metternich left Count Muelinen in charge of the Austrian Embassy in Paris. On 27 September Estrada called on Muelinen. Estrada claimed he represented Napoleon III and conveyed a confidential message. Napoleon would be willing to take the initiative in negotiations necessary for an Austrian Archduke to become King of Mexico. Estrada wanted an assurance that Austria would consider such a possibility so that appropriate measures could be taken at the same time that preparations were being made for a tripartite claims-collecting expedition to Mexico. Muelinen at once sent a telegram to inform Rechberg.[152]

On 24 September Cowley communicated the British reply to Thouvenel's proposal made two weeks previously.[153] The British rejection of a "national assembly" must have been a severe disappointment to Thouvenel. A few days before he had written Flahault a private letter that the "calling of a congress, preceded by an amnesty, as I have proposed to Lord Russell," would be the means whereby the "honest and sensible people in Mexico" could express their desire for a monarchy. The collection of debts was merely a pretext:

> Of course the only legitimate pretext for an armed demonstration comes from our grievances, but I believe that it would be in the general interest to make of it the means whereby the Mexican Nation itself could profit of the circumstances . . . .[154]

Instead of making these views known to Cowley, Thouvenel expressed concurrence with British views, but remarked:

> . . . that as Your Lordship (i.e., Russell) seemed to be of opinion that the measures suggested some time ago for the

pacification of Mexico were inapplicable to the present state of affairs, he should be glad to receive from you the plan of action which you now propose to follow.[155]

Accompanying his instruction sent to Cowley on 23 September, Lord Russell sent a copy of a despatch[156] received that very day from Lord Lyons,[157] the British Minister to Washington. On 10 September, Lord Lyons reported, Seward told him that the American Minister to Mexico had been authorized[158] to conclude a convention with Mexico, whereby the United States would pay 3 per cent interest on the foreign debt of Mexico during the Mexican moratorium proclaimed on 17 July.[159] As a mortgage for the repayment of this loan, and 6 per cent interest on it, Mexico would pledge the public lands and minerals of certain Mexican provinces.[160] The convention Corwin was to negotiate, Seward told Lyons, would only be put into effect if the European Powers promised not to take any measures against Mexico until the loan convention could be submitted to the Senate, which would resume sessions in December 1861. In short, Seward hoped to prevent a European intervention in Mexico by means of a loan to Mexico, so urgently proposed by Corwin ever since June 1861.[161] Although Seward's proposals were known by the British Foreign Office on 23 September, they apparently were not taken into consideration by Russell and Palmerston in their reply to Thouvenel's overtures sent the same day. Lyon's despatch was sent to Lord Palmerston that day,[162] but he only made his views known to Russell the next day.[163]

After informing Thouvenel of Russell's instructions of 23 September, Cowley told the French Minister of Foreign Affairs the substance of Lyon's despatch,[164] for Thouvenel had heard nothing of the scheme.[165] He at once perceived how it endangered Napoleon's plan of establishing a monarchy in Mexico, and "expressed himself very strongly" against Seward's proposal. Thouvenel claimed that:

. . . it was tantamount to making over Mexico to the United

States, and that it seemed to him that before any concert should be established between Gt. Britain, France and Spain as to the course to be pursued with the Mexican Government, the proposition of the U.S. must first be disposed of.[166]

While the transaction could not be prevented, Thouvenel urged that Great Britain and France not recognize it in any way. Cowley was asked to obtain Russell's views. Cowley suggested, and Thouvenel agreed, that no reply be given to such an overture from the American Minister to Paris, should he make it, until Cowley ascertained Russell's views.[167]

On 24 September, before knowing Thouvenel's reaction to Seward's proposed loan treaty, Lord Palmerston sent his Foreign Secretary a private letter, commenting on Lyons' despatch. The British Prime Minister saw serious objections to the American plan and suggested it be countered by an invitation to the United States to cooperate with the European Powers about to intervene in Mexico :

The views of England, France and Spain are plain enough; all three have claims unsatisfied and all three are willing to join in enforcing compliance. But the Washington Government inspired by a chivalrous sense of justice, not satisfied with its own enormous expenditure on account of the civil war, proposes to undertake to pay the interest on the foreign debt of Mexico, I forgot how long, taking a mortgage upon all the mineral wealth of Mexico. This scheme . . . makes no provision for the satisfaction of the money claims of the three European Powers, nor for the punishment of the Mexican murderers of the subjects of the Three Powers, and in the next place it lays the ground for foreclosure by this new creditor, and raises a serious political question, and then further it tends to continue the present state of anarchy in Mexico . . . . Perhaps the best answer to the Washington proposal would be a counter proposal to the U.S. Government to join the Three Powers, whether morally or physically—our action ought to begin in November, and the United States Convention even if it were to cover the whole case would not be voted until it had obtained the approval of the Congress which does not meet till the 2 December and often amuses its self for weeks in discussing and voting the choice of a speaker before it enters upon business. The Congress will probably have plenty to do about the war, and this Mexican Convention if concluded, might not be discussed and approved for some time after Congress had met.[168]

Like Thouvenel, Palmerston feared the United States would foreclose the mortgage. He also did not want to wait until December, or longer, for the Spanish Government had already made known that it would not defer its expedition beyond November. Finally, the loan would only pay the interest on claims recognized by international conventions and did not "cover the whole case." There remained the unrecognized claims of redress for British persons and property.[169] The reference to the possibility of preventing a continuance of anarchy in Mexico did not mean that Palmerston wanted a change of Government in Mexico. He believed it "would be very desirable to see a settled government established in Mexico" but "greatly doubted the possibility" that such a change could be effected by the intervening powers.[170] They could, however, "require security for the lives, and respect for the property of British subjects in Mexico."[171]

On 25 September the American Minister to London, Charles Francis Adams, saw Russell. Adams warned that a "direct intervention with a view to organize a new government in Mexico, and especially the active participation of Spain in such an enterprise, would excite strong feelings in the U.S." The United States had always opposed such European interference in the internal affairs of the New World. There was "a sort of understanding that so long as European Powers did not interfere in America the United States might abstain from European alliances." If a "combination" of European Powers organized a government in Mexico, the "United States would feel themselves compelled to choose their allies in Europe, and take their part in the wars & treaties of Europe." All this could be avoided, Adams told Russell, if France and Great Britain agreed to Seward's loan proposal. Russell replied that "our

demands embraced not only the payment of interest on a debt
. . . but also . . . satisfaction for the injuries done to British
subjects." Such claims could hardly be transferred to the
United States "without raising an infinite number of questions
of detail upon which Great Britain and Mexico would have to
appeal to the equity of the United States." Russell feared "that
our friendly relations might be endangered if we increased the
number of points upon which we might come into collision."
He was as anxious as Adams, Russell went on to say, "of an
attempt to build upon the foundation of debts and injuries a
claim to organize a new government in Mexico." Such an
attempt could "be guarded against by defining terms of cooperation with Spain which would exclude interference in the
internal affairs of Mexico." This was Russell's "counter proposition" to the American loan to Mexico. The United States
should join in a combined expedition, founded on two principles:

> I.   The combined Powers, France, Great Britain, Spain and
> the United States, feel themselves compelled by the lawless
> . . . conduct of the authorities of Mexico to seek from those
> authorities protection for the persons and property by the
> Republic of Mexico towards their Governments.
> II.   The said combined Powers hereby declare that they do
> not seek any augmentation of territory or any special advan-
> tage and that they will not endeavour to interfere in the in-
> ternal affairs of Mexico or with the free choice of its form of
> Government by its People.

Such a combined intervention would be a "better course than
leaving Spain to seek her own vindication and afterwards
opposing the results of her operations." Further to calm American fears, Russell read Adams parts of one of Crampton's
despatches[172] "to show . . . that Marshal O'Donnell was by no
means desirous of undertaking the reconquest of the Indies."[173]
   At the same time that Russell tried to calm Adams' fears of
a Spanish attempt to interfere in the internal affairs of Mexico,
the British Foreign Secretary received reports that Spain did

indeed hope that a combined expedition would result in a change of Government in Mexico. The Spanish Ambassador to London invited British cooperation in a claims-collecting expedition and added :

> A combination of this kind would perhaps avert the repetition of such scandals, and contribute to the recognition by the Mexicans of the necessity of constituting a Government which would give security at home and sufficient gurantees abroad.[174]

Russell also received a telegram from Madrid in answer to his inquiry whether Spain would wait pending Anglo–French negotiations.[175] Crampton relayed O'Donnell's reply that Spain would wait until the beginning of November. Thus there was time for concert among the three Powers for "a joint intervention for the immediate vindication of their respective rights." This was all Spain proposed "in the first instance." Afterwards, however, Spain was ready :

> . . . to take into consideration with England and France what measures might be expedient for placing the government of Mexico in a position to fulfill its international obligations for the future.[176]

On 26 September Lord Russell had Cowley's despatch requesting a "plan of action"[177] and Crampton's telegram that Spain would not wait longer than the beginning of November to commence operations against Mexico.[178] The British Foreign Secretary was also under pressure to provide the United States with a "counter proposition." On that day Russell wrote the First Lord of the Admiralty that it would be necessary to prepare a naval expedition to be sent to Mexico.[179] The next day the Duke of Somerset replied that the appropriate orders would be sent.[180]

On 27 September Russell sent Lord Cowley a summary of the talk with Adams, with the instruction to "read this despatch to Monsieur Thouvenel and give him a copy of it."[181] Lord

Russell also sent Crampton observations on the overture made by the Spanish Ambassador to London, commenting specifically on the words, " 'which would give security at home and sufficient guarantees abroad.' " The British Government was "persuaded" that :

> . . . any attempt to effect this desirable purpose by foreign arms would fail in its purpose. If the force were Spanish, one of the contending parties would be fiercely opposed to it; if it were English the opposite party would be as strongly its antagonist; nor is any other foreign force likely to be received with favour. The Mexicans themselves can alone put an end to the anarchy and violence which have torn Mexico to pieces during the last years.

Crampton, however, was to make known to the Spanish Government that Russell was prepared to cooperate with Spain and France to obtain redress from Mexico, but there were two essential conditions :

> The first is that the cooperation of the United States should be invited.
> The second is that the combined Powers should not interfere by force in the internal Government of Mexico.[182]

Then, still on 27 September, the British Foreign Secretary informed Queen Victoria that "it will be necessary to despatch a naval force to the coast of Mexico." Russell stated that he intended to invite the United States to cooperate with the three European Powers and to "declare openly" that Great Britain had "not intention of interfering in the internal government of Mexico." He justified such a declaration by stating it was impossible to act otherwise, that it was a traditional British policy, and that it would be unwise to offend the Monroe Doctrine :

> To do so (i.e., interfere in Mexican internal affairs) would be to meddle in a bitter struggle between two violent factions,

equally cruel, unjust and unprincipled. To depart from this principle of non intervention—which is our usual rule of conduct—(is) to offend not only the government but the whole people of the U.S., who are opposed to any intervention in the internal affairs of America.

Queen Victoria approved this course, "subject to any further observations which Lord Palmerston may submit," and she directed Russell to instruct the Admiralty accordingly.[183] Russell decided to delay sending instructions to the Admiralty until France and Spain agreed to his conditions.[184] September ended with Russell sending telegrams to Paris[185] and Madrid[186] that a despatch "will be sent in four or five days" concerning Mexico.

After asking Cowley to request concrete proposals from Russell on 24 September, Thouvenel could do nothing but wait for a reply. He still didn't have one on 27 September, when the American Minister to Paris referred Seward's loan proposal to him.[187] Thouvenel replied that he had to confer with the British Government, but could say that he wanted the principal, as well as the interest. When Dayton protested that the United States would not permit Mexico to be subjugated, Thouvenel ironically countered that the United States was the only nation that had taken such action in the past. The French Government only wanted to collect debts[188] and to call "Mexico . . . to account in case of ill treatment of any French subjects."[189]

At the end of September Thouvenel thought it was premature to discuss the possibility of monarchy in Mexico through Anglo–French diplomatic channels, although he wrote Flahault privately that Austria had enough archdukes to be able to spare one for Mexico.[190] Before receiving any further news of Russell's views, Thouvenel went to the country after talking with Dayton. When Cowley received a summary of Russell's conversation with Adams and instructions to give Thouvenel a copy, the French Minister was still absent from Paris. Cowley then sent a copy of the Russell–Adams conversation to Thouvenel in the country, but received no answer in September.[191]

## 3.  THE NEGOTIATION OF THE TRIPARTITE CONVENTION OF LONDON, PART II, OCTOBER 1861

In the years before 1861 the reluctance of Great Britain to intervene with force in Mexico was the chief reason that no combined European expedition was sent to Mexico. The Mexican moratorium of payments on foreign claims recognized by conventions caused the British Foreign Office to contemplate coercion in September 1861. For Lord Russell the moratorium was a "shameless breach of faith, which cannot be in the slightest degree excused by the Pretenses put forward" by the Mexican Government.[1] Wyke's reports of outrages against British subjects and their property, Russell believed, could not "be extenuated by any condition of anarchy or civil war which may exist in Mexico."[2] To put pressure on the Mexican Government to grant redress, Lord Russell and Lord Palmerston were favorably impressed by the proposals of Sir Charles Wyke and Captain Aldham to seize the Vera Cruz Custom House. The British Admiralty, however, foresaw that a considerable force would be required at the very time that Great Britain could not easily supply such a force. Combined operations with France and Spain would lighten the military burden for Great Britain. But a tripartite custom house intervention, proposed both by France and Spain in September, gave rise to serious difficulties. Lord Russell and Lord Palmerston objected to the proposals of the French and Spanish Governments that a tripartite expedition should be the means of permitting the Mexicans to establish a "stable" government. Confidentially Thouvenel, the French Minister of Foreign Affairs, let Lord Russell know that the French Government favored the creation of a Mexican monarchy. The project of offering the throne to

Maximilian, however, was kept secret. To forestall any French or Spanish territorial aggrandisement or interference in Mexican internal affairs and to counter Seward's loan proposal, Lord Russell and Lord Palmerston formulated several principles in September 1861 :

1. The United States would be invited to join the European expedition.
2. The combined military and naval forces would seize the Vera Cruz Custom House to put pressure on the Mexican Government to grant redress of grievances.
3. The sole aim of the combined operations was to obtain Mexican recognition and payment of claims recognized by conventions, and personal and property claims, all recognized by International Law.
4. The allies would disclaim any intentions of obtaining Mexican territory.
5. The allies would disclaim any desire of obtaining special advantage in Mexico.
6. The allies would disclaim any intention of interference in Mexican internal affairs.
7. The Mexican people would be promised their right to choose the form of government they wanted.

By the end of September 1861, Lord Russell had formally proposed points one and six to the Spanish Government as the basis of negotiations and explained the British attitude on point seven. All seven points were covered by the Russell–Palmerston despatch of 23 September or by the observations of Russell to Adams. The former was directly communicated to Thouvenel by Cowley, the latter mailed to the French Minister of Foreign Affairs, who was in the country at the end of September.

In September Lord Russell and Lord Palmerston summarily dismissed Thouvenel's proposal that the British mediation plan of 1860 be renewed. In reply to Thouvenel's request that Lord

Russell make his own "plan of action" known, the British Foreign Secretary observed that the British "suggestions" of 1860 were "friendly counsels proffered to two contending parties which such party was at liberty to accept or reject." Thouvenel's proposal, as Russell understood it, was "to impose, or to influence by an armed force an arbitration in the internal affairs of Mexico." Great Britain was opposed to "such a forcible intervention in the internal affairs of an independent nation." Mexico might be considered an exception to this general principle, because "few cases of internal anarchy, bloodshed & murder can exceed the atrocities perpetrated in Mexico." Even admitting this, Russell added that "there is no case in which a remedy by foreign interference appears so hopeless." The Liberals would dislike Spanish interference "from a fear that the power of a dominant church might be restored with the abuses & religious intolerance which accompany it." British interference, for "opposite reasons . . . would be just as odious to the Church party." The factions in Mexico were "spread over a vast extent of country." They were "split into fragments, each of which robs pillages & murders on its own account." A foreign military force would not be "likely to establish any permanent or passaday authority over these scattered bodies." Finally, the United States and the Confederacy would be greatly alarmed if European Powers interferred in the "domestic quarrels of an American independent Republic." Without yielding to the "extravagant pretensions implied by what is called the Monroe doctrine," it would be "unwise to provoke the ill feeling of North America, unless some paramount object were in prospect and tolerably sure of attainment." Russell concluded that he would rejoice if the contemplated debt-collecting expedition should lead to the creation of good government in Mexico, provided the Mexicans were not coerced :

The Spanish Govt, are of opinion that the successful actions of Gt. Britain, France and Spain to enforce their just demands would induce the Mexicans to institute a government more capable than any which has lately existed to resume the relations of peace and friendship with foreign powers.

Should such be the indirect effect of naval and military operations H(er) M(ajesty's) Government would cordially rejoice. But they think this effect is more likely to follow a conduct studiously observant of the respect due to an independent nation than to be the result of an attempt to impose by foreign force the domestic institutions of Mexico.[3]

In September Thouvenel had proposed that France and Great Britain send identical instructions to their Ministers in Mexico as the basis of Anglo–French cooperation in Mexican affairs. Lord Russell, however, feared that such a procedure, based on an exchange of notes, was not enough security to prevent French and Spanish designs to interfere in the internal affairs of Mexico. A convention would be more binding, and, limiting the scope of operations, it could be defended before Parliament. On 2 October Russell drew up a memorandum to this effect for Lord Palmerston :

The advantage of a Convention is that all parties are equally bound by it.

If we send a note to Paris or Madrid I fear the answer would reserve in some oblique way the power of changing the government of Mexico. I fear it is hopeless to think, as Sir Charles Wyke and many in this country do, of a moderate third party. In any change the rancerous (?) Church Party would take the place of the rancerous (?) Constitutional Party. We should be powerless in such a case, or we should be involved in a contest with France and Spain.

It is true a Convention is not a perfect security, but it is at all events a producible security, and would justify us in the eyes of Parliament.

However in either case France and Spain if bent on interference might find quarrels to do so in the lamentable state of Mexico.

If therefore Lord Palmerston prefers an exchange of notes I am ready to take that course.[4]

Provoked as he was by the actions of the Juarez Government,

Lord Russell saw in it the lesser of two evils. The Conservatives were no better, and, Russell believed, would restore the religious intolerance he so much detested. A convention, with appropriate disclaimers, would serve as reasonable security that France and Spain would not return the Conservatives to power. The reference to the persons in Great Britain who placed their hopes in a Mexican moderate party was to over one hundred "British Merchants Trading with Mexico and Owners of Mexican Bonds." In a petition to the Foreign Office, they urged that Great Britain and France assume a joint protectorate over Mexico to restore order to permit moderate Mexicans to organize a government.[5] Russell replied that he had no evidence of a "large and numerous" moderate reforming party in Mexico, "prepared to avail itself of foreign aid." The British Government, therefore, "must confine their action to the clear and legitimate purpose of demanding from the de facto government of Mexico, however constituted, respect for the persons and property of British subjects, and the fulfilment of recorded obligations."[6]

Lord Palmerston made a notation on Russell's memorandum on 4 October that the reasons "in favor of a Convention sound good."[7] The next day the British Foreign Office had a draft convention ready.[8] By this time Lord Russell had answers from Paris and Madrid to his "principles," and he reformulated them as the bases of a tripartite convention.

Cowley had an opportunity on 2 October to see Thouvenel, returned from the country. Cowley read the French Minister of Foreign Affairs Russell's despatch, enumerating the objections to a forcible intervention in Mexican internal affairs. Thouvenel replied that he had made no proposal "to impose or to influence by armed force an arbitration in the internal affairs of Mexico." He only thought it likely that the employment of force for the "legitimate purposes" the British and French Governments had in view might "encourage" the "well disposed" Mexicans to form a better government. Should this happen, and prove to be "decidedly popular," Thouvenel believed this movement should be supported by the Powers seeking redress of grievances. While agreeing with Russell "in principle" about the "inexpediency of forcing interference in the internal affairs of an independent nation," Thouvenel drew a distinction between forcible interference and "indirect encouragement." This "encouragement" given the Mexicans to emerge from "odious tyranny" would arise out of the "presence of forces called to those shores for other purposes." To this distinction between direct and indirect influence, Cowley replied that this was possible if there were only one intervening Power. If more Powers were involved, there would be jealousy. One Power might consider a Mexican movement to be a popular one, while "another might deny it." One Power might favor a monarchical form of government, while another might prefer a republic. Thouvenel was not "disposed" to admit any such difficulties. He said that he would rejoice to see the Mexicans adopt a monarchy, but he would not interfere if they decided on a republic. Cowley, however, was not convinced. He reported to Lord Russell that Thouvenel's "predilection" might lead him, perhaps without his knowing it, to "look upon the cause which he advocates, when in reality the contrary might be the case." This possibility assumed greater probability for Cowley with respect to Thouvenel's comments on Russell's remarks to Adams. While Thouvenel had nothing to say against the principles evoked by Russell, the French Minister of Foreign Affairs "could not but regret that so positive a declaration with regard to non-interference in the internal affairs of Mexico should be contemplated." Such a declaration, Thouvenel feared, would "damp the spirits of the well meaning, if there are any such in Mexico, and will encourage the United States in their designs upon that country." It was the last chance, Thouvenel asserted, of preventing the United States or the Confederacy from annexing Mexico. An attempt to prevent this might fail, "but it was worth trying."[9] Confidentially Thouvenel told Cowley that an Austrian Prince might be placed on a Mexican throne, and this "might facilitate an arrangement respecting Venetia!" Thouvenel claimed it was his personal opinion and that he "had not said a word to the Emperor upon the subject." Cowley reported this confidence to Russell in a private letter and commented that "French influence will be exerted to the utmost to endeavour to establish a monarchical form of Government in Mexico." Cowley also believed that "Spain will be quite ready to assist."[10]

On 4 October Russell received a telegram from Madrid giving the Spanish comments on his two conditions that the cooperation of the United States be sought and that there be no interference in Mexican internal affairs. O'Donnell told Crampton, the British Ambassador to Madrid, that the question of cooperating with the United States was still being considered by the Cabinet. While disclaiming any design of an "armed intervention in the internal government of Mexico," the Chief Spanish Minister gave his opinion that a change of government was necessary in Mexico:

> . . . the Powers which propose to seek redress for wrongs would do so to no purpose if they desisted before they saw some prospect of the establishment of a government in Mexico able to fulfil its engagements and affording some prospect of future respect for their rights and the safety of their Subjects.[11]

Similar remarks were made at the beginning of October to Barrot, the French Ambassador to Madrid. O'Donnell stated his "personal opinion" that the Powers intervening in Mexico "must not only obtain satisfaction for the past but also complete security for the future." The form of government "to be established and maintained in Mexico will consequently be one of the principal questions to examine in advance or to resolve later according to events." Replacing the Juarez Government with another giving better prospects of future behavior suited French plans of establishing Maximilian in Mexico. Someone, therefore, pencilled brackets around this section of Barrot's report of his conversation with O'Donnell.[12]

On 5 October Lord Russell sent identical telegrams to Paris

and Madrid. He proposed the signing of a convention and gave
its general outline :

> The Queen is prepared to enter into a convention with
> France and Spain for the purpose of obtaining reparation from
> Mexico for the injuries received by their respective subjects
> and of securing the fgulfilment of the obligations entered into
> by Mexico towards their respective governments.
>
> It must be provided in the Convention that the forces of
> the contracting parties will not be employed for any ulterior
> object and especially that they will not interfere with the
> internal Govt. of Mexico.
>
> The Government of the United States should be invited to
> adhere to this Convention.   But no delay in commencing
> active operations should be permitted on this account.[13]

As predicted by Russell, both Thouvenel and O'Donnell had
reserved a change of government in Mexico in "some oblique
way." On 4 October Palmerston approved a convention in
preference to an exchange of notes. The next day, with a draft
convention ready, Russell proposed signing a convention. He
directed Cowley[14] and Crampton[15] to make known to the
the French and Spanish Governments that the overture had
been made to both governments, and that, if they were willing
to sign such a convention as outlined, a draft of it would be
forwarded. On 5 October Russell received a despatch from
Cowley stating that Thouvenel proposed sending three heavy
frigates and a detachment of about 1000 troops to Mexico.
Cowley also forwarded Thouvenel's request to know what forces
Great Britain intended to send to Mexico.[16] Russell sent Cowley's despatch to the British Admiralty and instructed it to
inform the British Admiral on the Atlantic Station to be ready
to go to Vera Cruz in the middle of November.[17] On 5 October,
therefore, the preliminary aims had been exchanged, and the
negotiation of the Convention of London began.

In the evening of 5 October Cowley received Russell's telegram proposing a convention, but the late hour prevented the
British Ambassador from seeing Thouvenel before his depar-

ture for Compiègne, where Napoleon III was being paid a visit by the King of Prussia.[18] Cowley waited two days, then wrote Thouvenel, who replied that he could not discuss the proposals with Napoleon until 9 October.[19] On 10 October Cowley saw Thouvenel upon his return to Paris.[20] By now Russell had what he considered a satisfactory answer from the Spanish Government and had sent additional instructions to Cowley to hasten negotiations.

Russell received a telegram from Madrid on 8 October that the Spanish Government was willing to sign a convention with Great Britain and France. Crampton reported that there was no difficulty about an agreement that "no active or armed intervention in the internal Government of Mexico should be attempted." The Spanish Government also agreed to invite the cooperation of the United States but could "not . . . delay operations on that account." The only "shadow of difference" was that the Spanish Government reserved "moral influence" to put an end to anarchy in Mexico :

> . . . the Spanish Government think the three Powers ought to endeavour to exercise a moral influence for putting an end to the civil strife prevailing in Mexico without however seeking to recommend any particular form of government or support any particular party or prolonging the occupation of the Mexican ports.[21]

Just what was meant by "moral influence" was detailed by Crampton in a despatch that only reached the British Foreign Office two weeks later. Collantes told Crampton that the arrival of the allied expedition in Mexico could not fail to exercise a "great influence" on the Mexicans. The allies ought to "profit" by this impression upon the Mexican people :

> . . . to exercise a moral influence upon the contending Parties with a view of inducing them to lay down their arms, and come to an understanding for the formation of a government which would offer some guarantee to the allies for the fulfilment of the engagements of Mexico towards their respective

governments, for a better observance of her international duties in future, and one which would afford some prospect at least of a cessation of the miseries to which that unfortunate country had so long been exposed.

Crampton replied that the British Government would not hesitate to endorse this view "if by moral influence was meant the offer of advice to the Mexican Government to refrain from civil strife." If more were meant, Crampton could not see how any real change could be effected in Mexico "without the application of actual force, or without exerting the influence of the intervening Powers in favour of one or the other of the contending factions." Collantes "confessed that he agreed . . . as to the little hope we could entertain of effecting internal reforms in Mexico either by force or persuasion." He insisted, however, that the Allies "make at least a demonstration of their desire to effect some amelioration" in Mexico. If anarchy continued in Mexico, Collantes told Crampton, "the country would relapse into something of the same condition in which it was found by Hernan Cortes." The "germs of civilization" planted by Spain would disappear. The European Powers ought to make at least an effort to prevent it.[22] This display of a desire to end anarchy in Mexico would also conciliate the Spanish Opposition, which claimed that "Spanish civilisation" and the "Spanish race" in Mexico would vanish before the "force of the Anglo–Saxon race."[23]

In September the Spanish Government had already made known to Russell that an allied expedition to Mexico might lead to the creation of a respectable and stable government in Mexico.[24] Lord Russell had no objection then if the change were effected by the Mexicans themselves without foreign coercion.[25] Since the Spanish Government renounced force and only reserved "moral influence" or advice, Russell was "quite satisfied" with the Spanish answer to his convention proposal.[26] He sent Crampton a telegram requesting that Isturiz, the Spanish Ambassador to London, be sent full powers to sign a convention in London.[27] Since the "Spaniards . . . are quite agreeable to our proposals," Hammond, the British Under-Secretary of State, wrote Cowley, "we are only waiting for M. Thouvenel's answer."[28]

Russell expected a favorable French reply to his proposal of a convention. On 7 October he sent Cowley a copy of a draft convention and stated that instructions to communicate it to Thouvenel would follow in the course of the week.[29] Two days later, when Cowley still hadn't seen Thouvenel, Russell had an answer from the British Admiralty to Thouvenel's request to know what forces Great Britain intended to send to Mexico. Russell elaborated on the Admiralty information and sent Cowley an outline of allied operations. The Admiralty letter to the Foreign Office stated that the forces required could not be determined until the Lords Commissioners of the Admiralty knew the scope of operations contemplated. Should an attack on the forts of Vera Cruz be proposed, the Admiralty advised sending two ships of the line, four frigates, and ". . . a proportion of small vessels which operate in shallow waters."[30] Russell instructed Cowley to inform Thouvenel that this was the force the British Government intended to send to Mexico. Cowley was also directed to tell Thouvenel that it was intended that the Mexican Government surrender the forts of Vera Cruz and Tampico to the allies. Their forces would hold them "until reparations for . . . wrongs is obtained." Reparations would be obtained by Commissioners named by the intervening Powers and who would assume control of the Custom Houses of Vera Cruz and Tampico. If the Mexican Government refused these terms, "the combined forces must attack the forts of Vera Cruz and Tampico and obtain possession of them." The forts would then be held as "securities for the indemnities and reparations required." Russell did not propose to institute blockades of the Mexican coast," as the valuable commerce of Mexico, and the exportation of its mineral wealth would thereby be suspended." The Naval Commanders, however, would be given a discretion to have recourse to blockade if they believed it "expedient in the failure of other measures."[31]

While waiting for a reply from Thouvenel to his proposals, Russell received information that even a coastal operation against Mexico could be very dangerous. The British Admiralty reported that "vomito" and yellow fever[32] might cause high mortality.[33] Amidst the deluge of private letters received by the British Government,[34] there was one that Lord Palmerston particularly recommended to the attention of Lord Russell. A Mr. Farlane observed that Vera Cruz "is one of the four most unhealthy Ports on the whole coast washed by the Atlantic Ocean." Yellow fever and the "Black Vomit" caused death to twenty per cent of all Europeans treated by the most modern methods. About sixty miles north of Vera Cruz, however, the cooler highlands of Jalappa afforded a pleasant climate, "which approximates to that of an English summer."[35] In addition to the poor health conditions on the Mexican coast, the British Admiralty foresaw tactical difficulties in seizing Tampico.[36]

During the morning of 10 October Cowley was able to see Thouvenel, returned from Compiègne.[37] By now, however, the secret French overture to the Austrian Government that Archduke Maximilian become ruler of Mexico had resulted in Maximilian's provisional acceptance, with the approval of Emperor Franz Joseph and the Austrian Government.

Count Rechberg, the Austrian Foreign Minister, visited Maximilian at his residence of Miramar on 4 October to inform him that he was Napoleon III's candidate for a Mexican throne.[38] Rechberg added that Franz Joseph was granting his brother complete freedom to accept or refuse.[39] The Austrian Minister stressed that, if Maximilian were invited by the "great majority of the nation . . ." to become ruler of Mexico, "he must not think of propping up his throne by foreign troops." Although it might be necessary at first to have a foreign army, which could be raised in Germany or Switzerland, it must be "bona fide a Mexican army acting under the flag of that country." Rechberg advised Maximilian to avoid contracting a loan "under the guarantee and protection of foreign Powers," in order to render the "new government independent of foreign interference." Rechberg urged, if Napoleon's overture assumed a more "serious form," Maximilian should "on no account embark in this hazardous business unless he felt certain that he possessed the entire confidence and sympathy of the nation."[40] Maximilian discussed the matter with his wife, Charlotte, and they agreed not to reject the French overture, qualified by Rechberg's observations. At the same time Maximilian considered the "matter as yet quite undecided and my hands . . . still quite free."[41]

In view of the later fiasco of Maximilian's Empire in Mexico, the questions arise why Franz Joseph and the Austrian Government even referred Napoleon's proposal to Maximilian, and why he did not at once reject it. Lord Bloomfield, the British Ambassador to Vienna, believed the Austrian Government " would not be sorry if the arrangement came to pass," because Maximilian was a "continual embarrassment."[42] Metternich, the Austrian Ambassador to Paris, confided to Lord Cowley that "neither the Emperor of Austria nor his ministers regret Max's decision, as they were not satisfied with his management of the fleet, the expenses of which have been very great."[43] As Lord High Admiral, Maximilian himself complained that those "whom I praised were usually passed over, and those whom I removed received conspicuous marks of favour."[44] Maximilian's governorship of Lombardy–Venetia, beginning in 1857, had not been satisfactory to Franz Joseph, who had his brother relieved in 1859.[45] Thereafter Maximilian was in constant financial difficulties.[46] Finally, his reputation as a liberal[47] and a possible stimulus for liberal reforms within a conservative monarchy could hardly please his imperial brother. Maximilian, however, could not be permitted to embark on a "rash and ill-conceived adventure to the hazards of which no Prince of the Imperial Family could entrust his person and the honour of his House."[48] On the other hand, the project had been laid before the Austrian Government "in terms so delicate and friendly on the part of the Emperor (i.e., Napoleon III), and His Majesty evinced such anxiety for its success" that the Austrian Government thought it "polite not to give offense by rejecting it." By answering Napoleon directly, however, there was a danger that he would seek a favor in return for French assistance in the monarchy scheme. Specifically, Napoleon might demand that Venetia be ceded to Italy. Somehow the Austrian Government had to be sure that Maximilian's candidacy "was not connected with any scheme for a territorial change in Europe."[49] Rechberg saw a way out of the dilemma by treating the offer to Maximilian as an unofficial one made by the Mexican exiles, provisionally accepting the overture, and reserving the right to "fix the final conditions." On 7 October Rechberg directed Count Muelinen, the Austrian Chargé d'Affaires left in charge of the Austrian Embassy in Paris during Meternich's absence, to answer Estrada's overture. While Estrada's proposals of the previous July had lacked any "practical value," his new overture gave "a much clearer picture of the attitude which France has adopted towards his plan to place an Archduke on the throne of Mexico." It appeared France and Great Britain planned an expedition to Mexico. Such an expedition would "in all probability, facilitate the plans of the monarchist party in whose name M. Gutierrez speaks." An Austrian refusal would "compromise a real chance of success, and we should certainly regret thus to remove every possibility of seeing an Archduke called beyond the seas, there to add fresh lustre to the glory of his noble House." Franz Joseph, therefore, would not repulse a serious proposal," and Maximilian would . . . "likewise not refuse eventually to yield to the desire of the Mexican nation." Two guarantees had to be obtained in advance :

1.  That the Mexican throne shall be guaranteed the support—not only the moral, but also the material and effective support—of the two great maritime Powers of Great Britain and France.

2. That there shall be a clearly expressed invitation to the Archduke from the people of Mexico themselves.

Without these guarantees, the success of such an "ambitious" enterprize was "more than doubtful." Muelinen was to "impress upon M. Gutierrez the absolute necessity of fulfilling these preliminary conditions." In addition, there were other conditions the Austrian Government reserved the "right to enumerate in the event of the plan assuming a more definite form." Until a "formal offer," based on the two preliminary guarantees, should be made to the Austrian Government, it would remain "completely passive." It did not regard it "compatible with the dignity of Austria to take the initiative in any negotiations with either . . . of the two maritime Powers." In the meantime it was up to Estrada and the party he represented "to take what steps they may think wise." If a formal proposal were made to the Austrian Government, it "would make a thorough examination of the plan and fix the final conditions on which would depend the definitive acceptance of the Emperor and of His Imperial Highness the Archduke."[50] Thus Napoleon's overture was not rejected, and he could not be offended. Rechberg's reply went through an unofficial channel, and only provisionally agreed to the French offer. Thus Metternich could boast to Lord Cowley, "We have taken care that he (i.e., Napoleon III) shall have no hold upon us."[51] The two preliminary conditions, Rechberg believed, would protect Maximilian and the Austrian Government from embarking on a fiasco that would compromise their dignity. Finally, the possibility remained that Maximilian might one day cease being an embarrassment by departing from Austria to become ruler of Mexico, there to add "lustre" to the House of Hapsburg and achieve a "signal victory in the New World" for the "monarchical principle, now so gravely endangered in Europe."[52]

Maximilian claimed that from the first he saw difficulties in connection with the monarchy plan, specifically the "danger of an unlimited extension of French power, both before and after the actual execution of the monarchy scheme."[53] King Leopold of Belgium later insisted that his daughter Charlotte, Maximilian's wife, "had very clearly seen the perils of the position."[54] Yet a Mexican throne was an attraction for Maximilian and Charlotte. The only outlets for Maximilian's "adventurous disposition"[55] after being relieved of his Governorship of Lombardy–Venetia in 1859[56] were writing about his travels and occupying himself with the Austrian navy.[57] As Leopold put it, Maximilian, "being second in rank in the Empire, had the inconveniences of this position, without even having the pecuniary resources that could have rendered this position better."[58] Even his retreat of Miramar, overlooking the Adriatic, was only built by his going into debt.[59] The weeks before Rechberg came to call at Miramar were spent in a usual fashion. In August Maximilian was in Southampton.[60] In September he and Charlotte visited Franz Joseph. At the end of the month Maximilian and Charlotte returned to Miramar, and Maximilian occupied himself with shipbuilding in Trieste.[61] Such a life thwarted Charlotte's desire to be active and useful. She herself admitted that she regarded the French overture as a means to end the boredom of Miramar :

> Put yourself in my place and ask yourself if the life at Miramar is preferable to that of Mexico. No, a hundred times no! and I prefer for my part a position that offers activity and duties, even difficult ones, if you will, instead of contemplating the sea from the rocks until the age of seventy.[62]

Maximilian also wanted "very actively" to go to Mexico.[63] He and Charlotte, while attracted by the monarchy proposal, did not, however, immediately and unsuspectingly accept without any further question. On 8 October Maximilian wrote his father-in-law that the matter was "quite undecided" and asked Leopold I "his enlightening counsel at this difficult moment."[64] Later in the mouth Maximilian sent his private secretary to

Paris to make an estimate of the ideas of Estrada and the other Mexican exiles.[65]

On 9 October 1861 Count Muelinen communicated the contents of Rechberg's answer to Estrada's proposals to the Mexican exile.[66] Estrada was beside himself with joy.[67] and said he had never dared to hope for "so glorious a prospect." He would communicate the Austrian conditions to Napoleon III, who would know how to fulfill them.[68] "To put the matter in a nutshell," Estrada told Muelinen, "Austria's attitude resembles that of an eligible young lady, and her rôle is modestly to wait until her hand is sought." Muelinen replied that the metaphor was apt, but "there must be no demand for *a dowry*." Estrada made appropriate disclaimers,[69] and then sought out Hidalgo, who left Paris that evening to go to Compiègne to convey the news to Napoleon III and Eugenie.[70] At the same time Estrada wrote Thouvenel to tell him of the new development.[71]

Upon learning Rechberg's views and conditions, Napoleon III at once made a personal attempt to win British support of Maximilian's candidacy by sending a private letter to the French Ambassador to London. Napoleon claimed he was expressing his ideas "frankly" and wanted Count Flauhault to communicate them to Lord Palmerston so that an "understanding" would result. Both Great Britain and France had an interest to see Mexico "pacified and endowed with a stable government." There were economic, political, and humanitarian reasons:

> Not only has this country, endowed with all the advantages of nature, attracted much of our capital and our nationals whose existence is menaced without intermission, but, by its regeneration, it would form an insurmountable barrier to the encroachments of North America; it would afford an important market for English, Spanish, and French commerce by exploiting its own resources; finally it would render great service to our industries by extending its cultivation of cotton. These various advantages, as well as the spectacle of one of

the finest countries of the world delivered over to anarchy and threatened by approaching ruin, are the reasons that have always so deeply interested me in Mexico.

A few years before "important" Mexicans proposed to Napoleon that only the establishment of a monarchy could save Mexico. Napoleon had then answered that he had no "pretext" to intervene in Mexico, did not want to "risk a falling out with the United States," and could not act without British cooperation. Now "unforeseen events" had changed the situation:

> The war in America has made it impossible for the United States to interfere in the matter, and above all the outrages committed by the Mexican Government are legitimate grounds for England, Spain, and France to intervene in Mexico.

A convention among France, Great Britain, and Spain would "only establish the redress of our legitimate grievances as the ostensible purpose of our intervention." But it was necessary to "foresee what could happen and not benevolently to tie one's hands in a manner to prevent a solution that would be in the interest of all." Napoleon had information that as soon as the allied fleet appeared before Vera Cruz, "a considerable party in Mexico is ready to seize power, to call a national assembly and to proclaim a monarchy." If this happened, the "important" Mexicans had asked Napoleon who was his candidate for such a throne. Napoleon had then replied that Archduke Maximilian was "animated with the spirit of the times, endowed with enough intelligence and steadfastness." His candidacy had other advantages:

> . . . his connection, through his wife, with the King of the Belgians, a natural bond between France and England, the fact that he comes from a great Power that is not a Maritime Power—all these things appeared to me to meet all the desirable conditions. On my side I thought it was in good taste for me to propose an eventual candidate a prince belonging to a dynasty with which I was recently at war.

The "Mexicans" were "impatient to see events precipitated" and had sounded the Austrian Government. As though he had not sanctioned this overture, Napoleon stated that, according to what he had been told, the Austrian Government "accepted" the proposal of the "Mexicans." There were two conditions, that Great Britain and France "support" the candidacy and that "the will of the Mexican people be frankly and loyally expressed." Napoleon did not mention Rechberg's reservation of making additional conditions. Such was the background of the idea of the establishment of Maximilian in Mexico. Flahault could "very well see" that Napoleon had only "one objective in this whole question : that of seeing French interests protected and safeguarded for the future through an organization which would save Mexico." Napoleon was "far from having any selfish preferences." He was "only seeking to do good, convinced that to try to render a people prosperous is effectively to work for the prosperity of all." These unselfish objectives could be accomplished by an intervention by France, Great Britain, and Spain for the "ostensible objective" of "redress for our grievances." Napoleon was willing to sign a convention providing for such an intervention, but it was impossible for him to engage himself "not to support, at least morally, a change" that he desired with all his heart.[72] Napoleon drew up this important communication without consulting his Minister of Foreign Affairs, Thouvenel[73] Napoleon also sent a similar private letter to Leopold I of Belgium so that he would use his influence with Queen Victoria on behalf of the candidacy of his son-in-law.[74]

Upon returning to Paris, Thouvenel had a meeting with Lord Cowley on 10 October.[75] The British Ambassador summarized Russell's telegram of 5 October, offering to sign a convention.[76] Thouvenel's reply closely followed the line of reasoning contained in Napoleon III's private letter to Count Flahault. While accepting the offer to sign a convention and the principles laid down to guide the actions of the contracting parties, Thouvenel "questioned the propriety of making a public declaration that there would be no interference in the internal affairs of Mexico." Such a declaration, Thouvenel feared, would discourage those Mexicans who might be encouraged by the allied debt-collecting expedition to inaugurate "a better system of government." The French Government would not interfere with the choice of the Mexican people, but "did not see the necessity of making any mention in a convention of what the Allies did not intend to do."[77] The proposed convention should merely state the aims of the contracting parties, redress of legitimate grievances, and the means to achieve these aims. All other events were uncertain and "on which it would be time to consult when they should come about."[78] Technically speaking, Thouvenel observed, a convention "ought to be made for the objects to be attained, and not for the purpose of disavowing intentions." Cowley could not see any objection to proclaiming a principle upon which it was determined to act. It would be a satisfaction to the Mexicans to state it and "would probably go far to reconcile the government of the United States to the expedition." Thouvenel, however, refused to say any more on the subject before seeing the wording of the British draft convention.[79] When Cowley outlined Russell's proposed measures to obtain control of the Custom Houses of Vera Cruz and Tampico,[80] Thouvenel claimed he could give no official answer until he had a chance to speak with the Minister of Marine and Colonies.[81] Accompanying his despatch summarizing this interview with Thouvenel, Cowley sent Russell a private letter, stating that the French Minister had a "great repugnance to introducing into the Mexican Convention any declaration respecting non-interference."[82]

On 10 October Thouvenel spoke to Mon, the Spanish Ambassador to Paris, in the same sense as to Cowley.[83] Thouvenel already knew that the Spanish Government favored a change of government in Mexico and reserved "moral" influence to this end. The form of government, according to O'Donnell, would be a "principal" question "to examine in advance or to resolve later according to events."[84] In this connection Thouvenel informed Mon that the French Government did not wish to oblige itself in advance, "being ignorant of the future."[85]

The day after speaking with Cowley and Mon, Thouvenel went to see Napoleon to inform him of the status of negotiations.[86] By now Napoleon had his private letter to Flahault ready for communication[87] and gave it to Thouvenel to forward.[88] Thouvenel believed—whether he told Napoleon is unknown—that the Emperor of the French "overestimated the numbers of the party which looked to the establishment of a monarchy."[89]

Thouvenel sent Flahault the private letter from Napoleon on 12 October, together with instructions that it might be communicated to Russell and Palmerston. They might not agree with the opinions of the Emperor, but they could "not fail to respect the sincerity with which the ideas . . . are expressed." Thouvenel added that he was ". . . not putting too much faith in England's agreeing." Yet it "would be something if only not to have to struggle against its opposition."[90] On the same day Mon, just having received instructions, called on Thouvenel. The French Minister then related a conversation he had had with Napoleon the previous day. The Emperor believed that the "joint expedition of the three powers must have as its aim the obtaining of reparation for known offenses." The arrival of hte allied forces in Mexico, however, might encourage the Mexicans "to establish order in the government and in their country." Then the allies "must lend them whatever aid possible." By means of a "Congress" or a "spontaneous vote" the Mexicans might wish to establish a monarchy. Then too the allies would have to aid the Mexicans. The French Government, however, foresaw this "eventuality" with perfect impartiality and disavowed in advance "any candidacy of a prince of the (French) imperial family and does not doubt that the other powers will do likewise." Since Maximilian had already provisionally accepted the throne of Mexico, it was easy for Thouvenel to make this show of "impartiality." He also attempted to make use of it to force the Spanish Government to disclaim the candidacy of a Spanish Bourbon. If the Mexicans didn't want any aid from the allies, Thouvenel observed that then "we must be content to press and to obtain reparation of our griefs." Mon answered that these views were in harmony with the instructions he had just received from Collantes.[91]

A detailed report of a conversation the French Ambassador to Madrid had with Collantes reached the French Ministry of Foreign Affairs on 13 October. Collantes, the Spanish Minister of Foreign Relations, had told Barrot that the conditions attached to Russell's offer to enter a convention only "imperfectly" permitted the end in view. This end was the establishment of a stable Mexican government:

> . . . so constituted to be able to assure foreigners residing in Mexico this security without which all commercial transactions are impossible, which has been lacking until now and which will not be assured them so long as one thinks of palliatives for the past without thinking seriously of the future.

Collantes proposed achieving this end by sending enough troops to Mexico to "force" the Mexican "parties" to lay down their arms and "give the country the right of establishing a provisional government and appeal to the national will for the formation of a definitive government." Once established, this government would have "complete freedom of action." Collantes told Barrot that the "active employment" of the forces sent to Mexico would not be necessary. Their "moral action" would suffice. Barrot's impression was that, if the British Government rejected the Spanish view, the Spanish Government would accept the British conditions.[92]

Thouvenel had told Cowley on 10 October that if the Mexicans should decide on a monarchical form of government, the French Government would "see with pleasure the choice of the Mexicans, and the approval of the Powers, bestowed on a

prince of the house of Austria."[93] Cowley, however, thought
this suggestion of so little importance that he did not mention
it in his reports to Lord Russell.[94] Three days later Thouvenel
had Barrot's report that Collantes favored "thinking seriously
of the future" and supporting a change of government in
Mexico. The same day Thouvenel saw Mon again and specifically mentioned Archduke Maximilian. If the Mexicans wanted
a monarchy, the French Government had no candidate to
propose, but, "if it happened, an archduke of Austria would
have our approval." Such a choice would have the "advantage
of removing from the collective action . . . all cause of clashing
or of national rivalry."[95] The Archduke Maximilian presented
himself "in the first place as the most apt" of Austrian archdukes.[96] In a further attempt to obtain Spanish support of
French plans to circumvent Russell's demand that a convention
disclaim interference in Mexican internal affairs, Thouvenel
sent Barrot summaries of conversations with Cowley on 10
October[97] and with Mon on 13 October.[98] Thouvenel observed
that the Spanish and French Governments were in almost perfect agreement:

> In accordance with what Calderon Collantes has told you
> about what action he thinks the three Powers must take con-
> cerning the internal organization of Mexico, it seems to me
> that we are quite close to complete agreement on this point. I
> would learn with pleasure that the cabinet of Madrid equally
> agrees about how the Government of the Emperor sees what
> concerns the eventuality of the return of Mexico to mon-
> archy.[99]

On 12 October Lord Russell authorized Lord Cowley to
communicate the British draft convention to Thouvenel. Concerning Thouvenel's remarks that it was unnecessary to introduce a disclaimer not to interfere in Mexican internal affairs,
Russell observed that "H(er) M(ajesty's) Govt. consider an
engagement not to interfere by force in the internal affairs of
Mexico to be an essential part of the Convention."[100] The

Spanish Government agreed that force should not be used, but reserved "moral influence," which, Russell commented, "is not excluded by the terms of the convention."[101] A few days later he sent his draft convention to Crampton in Madrid, with no comments except that the British draft be communicated to the Spanish Government.[102]

The Preface of the British draft convention[103] stated that the British, French, and Spanish Governments agreed to take joint action against the "lawless and flagitious conduct" of Mexico. Specifically the European Powers sought protection for the "persons and properties of their subjects, and a fulfilment of the obligations contracted by the Republic of Mexico" towards the three allies. Article I outlined coercive measures. The Allies would make arrangements for:

> . . . dispatching to the coasts of Mexico, on the Atlantic Ocean, a combined Naval and Military Force, the amount of which shall be determined hereafter by communications between Their respective governments, sufficient to capture, to occupy, and to hold, the several fortresses, and military positions on the said coasts, and to enforce a rigorous blockade of the Cities, Ports, and Harbours of the same; such occupation to be enforced in the name and on behalf of the High Contracting Parties conjointly, irrespectively of the national character of the Force by which that occupation shall be carried out.

At the time Russell authorized Cowley and Crampton to communicate the draft convention to the French and Spanish Governments respectively, the British Foreign Secretary had changed his mind twice about a blockade and was himself no longer certain of its desirability. In a memorandum prepared for Lord Palmerston in August, Lord Russell proposed that Vera Cruz and Tampico be seized. Then pressure could be put on the Mexican Government to grant redress by threatening to hold these ports or threatening a blockade.[104] Palmerston's comment was:

This issue(?) that blockade by stopping commerce would for a time stop the source from whence payments to us *ought* to be made but neither from that source nor from any other *are* they made, and a blockade would stop the source from whence the Mexican Government and Mexican Politicians derive a great part of their public income and private profits.[105]

Possibly influenced by this argument, Russell stated in the draft convention that the allies would initiate a blockade. Then, on 9 October, Russell sent Cowley a despatch that it was "not advisable to institute blockades . . . as the valuable commerce of Mexico . . . would thereby be suspended."[106] Article II of the draft convention sketched the method by which coercion would lead to redress of grievances. Once in possession of Vera Cruz and its forts, the allied commanders would offer to negotiate with the "Authorities exercising Power in the Republic of Mexico." These authorities would be invited to grant redress to the subjects of the allies and to fulfill conventions made with their governments. It was to be "intimated" that coercive measures "will be maintained, and in case of need, extended" until satisfaction, "under sufficient guarantees," be granted. Furthermore, the allies reserved "the right of taking such steps as they may deem advisable for watching over and enforcing the execution of such arrangements." Such negotiations would be with the *de facto* government, which was, in Russell's estimate, that of Juarez. The French and Spanish Governments, however, had taken the view that the civil war and its party strife still existed in Mexico and that a change of government was necessary. Articles III and IV contained disclaimers to which the allies bound themselves, doubly renouncing interference in Mexican internal affairs. Article III bound the Allies not to use their military forces "for any other objects than those specified in the Preamble . . . and, specifically . . . not . . . for the purpose of interfering with the Internal government of the Republic." By the terms of Article IV the allies engaged not to seek :

. . . any augmentation of territory nor any special advantage; neither will they endeavour to interfere in the Internal affairs of Mexico, or with the free choice on the part of the people of Mexico of the form of Government to be maintained in Mexico.

Article V provided that, once the European Powers had signed the convention, the United States would be invited to join the expedition and sign an identical convention, with the exception of this article. Article VI, the final Article, was merely a form outline providing for an exchange of ratifications.

The British draft convention made no provision for determining the validity or amount of the claims to be pressed by the Allies. Nor was it foreseen that the allies might have to divide any monetary satisfaction granted by Mexico. In the very instruction directing Cowley to communicate the draft convention, Russell commented that provision for these eventualities had to be inserted in the convention.[107] The most common means of obtaining redress from Mexico in the past had been the mortgaging of a percentage of Mexican custom duties.[108] Article II of the draft convention merely referred to "arrangements," but Lord Russell intended to obtain redress in the form of Mexican custom duties. Just before authorizing Cowley to communicate the draft convention, Russell instructed him to inform Thouvenel that the Mexican Government would be asked to turn over the Custom Houses of Vera Cruz and Tampico to allied "Commissioners."[109] The draft convention was submitted to the British Lord Chancellor. In an incisive commentary, he summarized all these difficulties and proposed an addition to the draft convention.[110] The Chancellor's impression was that it was intended to seize Mexican ports and then collect custom duties with which to liquidate claims. A "rigorous blockade," however, was "at variance with . . . encouraging Commerce with a view to derive Funds therefrom." If a "blockade be by no means intended, this Article (I) should be altered in expression." If it were intended to obtain money from Mexican Custom Houses, then:

Mutual arrangements as to mode of levying and collecting the Dues of Customs, the deposit of the monies received, the payment of the expenses occurred, and distribution of the clear surplus will be requisite. Nothing of all this is indicated by the Convention as it stands.

Even if Mexico agreed to pay the allied claims, it was improbable that they would be paid in full. Then grave difficulties might result if not foreseen by the convention :

> Whatever is recovered from Mexico, if not enough to pay the whole, must be distributed and apportioned among the Contracting Parties. But by whom and in what ratio? What degree or extent of mutual engagement between the Contracting Parties, as to the mode of ascertaining and liquidating their respective claims, is involved in their joining in this common action? The Convention does not seem to contemplate any such consequences, for it makes no provision for them. But they are inevitable, and, unless provided for, may become a fruitful source of disagreement.
>
> I am afraid it will be found to be a necessary consequence of this joint action, that each of the Contracting Parties may be entitled to see that the claims of the other two, *not already admitted by* Mexico, are such as International Law may be maintained, and are also just in point of amount.
>
> If this is not intended to be conceded, it should be guarded against, by expressly excluding any such implication.

During a joint occupation of Mexican ports, many non-military questions "will necessarily arise . . . and will require some mutually constituted authority to determine on the spot." The Lord Chancellor suggested that provision be made in the convention for the creation of a body to regulate such questions :

> . . . It may tend to prevent future embarrassment if some such general provision as this (were) inserted, viz—
>
> 'A Commission shall be appointed to consist of three/or six) Commissioners one (or two) to be named by each of the Contracting Powers, who shall have full authority to determine all questions that may arise as to the application or distribution of any money, that may be received, or recovered, in, or

from, Mexico, having regard to the respective rights of the three Contracting Parties.'

Considering the state of affairs in Mexico and the terms of the draft convention, the Lord Chancellor warned Russell that "the whole proceeding is of an anomalous character, & the Convention consequently seems to require the greatest care & caution."

The Lord Chancellor's remarks were written on 17 October,[111] when Russell had already decided not to insist on a blockade. By then he also realized the necessity of making an addition to the convention along the lines proposed by the Lord Chancellor's note. On it Russell made a marginal notation:

> Some provisions for a Commission must no doubt be introduced. My idea has been that the Commission should either consist of three of whom Sir Charles Wyke should be one, or if six of whom the Admiral and Sir Charles Wyke should be two.
> In any case the demands must be made on the de facto government.[112]

Count Flahault read Lord Palmerston the private letter of Napoleon III on 14 October. Palmerston remarked that he "quite agreed with the Emperor that it would be very desirable to see a settled government established in Mexico, and that a Monarchy is much more stable than a Republic." Maximilian would be a "good and unobjectionable sovereign for Mexico." The British Prime Minister, however, "greatly doubted the possibility of any such arrangement." A spontaneous monarchist uprising was unlikely. Palmerston recalled that Mexican exiles had approached him years ago. When he questioned them about the practicability of their schemes, "it came out that they required a Prince of a reigning European family, many millions sterling, and 20,000 European troops to give any chance of success."[113] Flahault also approached Russell, who said he had nothing against Maximilian but doubted the feasability of the plan.[114] The Foreign Secretary was convinced that no efforts would be made by the Mexicans to form a "party more honest than those which contended for power" in Mexico.[115] It was highly unlikely, therefore, that Great Britain would "actively" support Maximilian's candidacy, one of the two preliminary conditions made by the Austrian Government. The most Russell promised Flahault was that if an orderly government, "be it even a monarchy," should be established by the Mexicans themselves, the British Government "would not probably refuse to give . . . it's moral support."[116] At the same time Flahault's overtures reinforced British determination to include self denials in the convention. Hammond, the Under-Secretary of State, privately wrote Cowley that it was to be hoped that Napoleon III "will not dwell too much on his Mexican Scheme." Provided the convention "contains a self-denying Article," it did not "much signify" if the Emperor wanted to be a "new Pizarro."[117]

Lord Cowley received Russell's authorisation to communicate the draft convention to Thouvenel after the French Minister again left Paris to see Napoleon III at Compiègne. On 15 October Cowley sent Thouvenel a copy of the draft convention to permit him to show it to Napoleon. In this way, Cowley reported to Russell, no time would be lost, for Thouvenel "certainly would not give me an answer without taking the Emperor's orders upon the subject."[118] The next day Cowley was able to see Thouvenel in Paris and remarked that Russell had proposed to the Spanish Government that the convention be signed in London. Thouvenel had no objection and said he would ask Napoleon that evening. Thouvenel wanted to detail his objections to the British draft convention,[119] but Cowley urged him to refer his remarks to Russell through the French Ambassador to London. Since the convention would be signed in London, Cowley observed, a "double negotiation would only produce confusion."[120] The same day, 16 October, Flahault, acting on old instructions, tried "in

vain" to convince Russell that a clause disclaiming interference
in Mexican internal affairs was "useless." In a report of his
conversation with Russell, Flahault stated that the ideas of the
British Foreign Secretary were still the same as those already
communicated by Cowley to Thouvenel. The only new devel-
opment was that Russell wanted a convention concerning
Mexico to be signed in London. A report received from
Madrid,[121] Russell told Flahault, indicated that the Spanish
Government had no objection.[122] The next day Thouvenel
received this despatch,[123] forwarded it to Napoleon at Compiègne,[124] and sent a copy of the British draft convention to
Flahault in London, together with observations on it.[125] Article
I "exclusively assigns the action of the combined forces of the
Powers to the Atlantic coast." It seemed to Thouvenel that
"we must not limit our action in advance" to forbid operations
on the Pacific coast of Mexico "or in the interior of the country,
if the security of our nationals demands it." He wanted to omit
Article II of the draft convention altogether. The details of
what would be done when the allies arrived at Vera Cruz,
Thouvenel suggested, could be put into instructions. Articles
III and IV, containing the promises that the allies had no
purposes other than gaining redress, ought to be edited and
combined into one Article. For his objections to Article III
and IV he referred Flahault to a previous instruction, wherein
Thouvenel had objected to stating in a convention what the
allies would not do.[126] Now he added that the French Government had no desire to interfere in the interal affairs of Mexico.
At the same time the allies should not discourage, by "absolute
declarations," the attempts that Mexicans might make to end
anarchy. Thouvenel had no objection to the invitation to the
United States, forming Article V of the draft convention.
Article VI, concerning an exchange of ratifications, was so
standard that he made no comment on it. Having obtained
Napoleon's permission that a convention agreed upon be signed
in London,[127] Thouvenel instructed Flahault to communicate
this information to Lord Russell.[128] In order to gain Spanish

support for these views, Thouvenel sent the French Ambassador to Madrid a copy of the despatch to Flahault to communicate to the Spanish Minister of Foreign Relations. In view of what Barrot had "already found out of the dispositions" of the Spanish Government, Thouvenel hoped it would send instructions in the same sense to the Spanish Ambassador to London.[129]

Flahault saw Russell on 18 October and informed him of Thouvenel's comments on the British draft convention. The French Ambassador added that, in his opinion, Article III had to be revised. He proposed omitting the reference that the allied forces " 'specifically, shall not be employed for the purpose of interfering with the internal Government of the Republic.' " Russell replied that he would wait for Thouvenel's wording of the Article before deciding, but he agreed that Articles III and IV might be combined into a single Article. He also agreed to suppress the words, "on the Atlantic ocean," from Article I. This alteration, Russell observed, would give the necessary latitude.[130]

Before having a reply to his proposed alterations of the British draft convention, Thouvenel received a despatch from Flauhault in answer to older instructions. This was the despatch which stated that Russell absolutely refused to sign a convention with the French Government unless it agreed to a clause renouncing intervention in Mexican internal affairs.[131] Napoleon's telegraphic comment to Thouvenel was to ask whether "the treaty is to be modified." The Emperor could not "in honour sign it as it is."[132] Thouvenel replied shortly after noon on 18 October that suggested changes had been sent to London and Madrid the day before.[133] That same afternoon Thouvenel saw Cowley[134] and informed him that the "Treaty . . . might contain . . . a clause to meet the desire of Her Majesty's Government with regard to non-intervention in the internal affairs of the country."[135] He hoped to find, Thouvenel told Cowley, a "phrase" to which the Emperor would agree and which would "satisfy" Russell.[136] In addition to this "phrase," Thouvenel was willing to include what he had already accepted, "the renunciation of all interested motives." The convention might also state the "object of the expedition . . . but all other matter alluded to in the (British) draft" Thouvenel wanted "to insert in the instructions to the Commanders-in Chiefs (*sic*)."[137]

Late in the evening of 18 October a telegram arrived in Paris from Flahault, who gave a brief summary of his discussion with Russell that day concerning the draft convention.[138] The next day Thouvenel sent Flahault a telegram that his full powers and a draft convention would be sent when approved by Napoleon III. Thouvenel added, "Your telegraphic despatch of yesterday gives me the hope of a complete understanding."[139] Flahault informed Russell that Thouvenel was preparing a draft convention. The French Ambassador also gave his own opinion that Article IV of the British draft convention ought to be edited. He suggested omitting the words, "in the internal affairs of Mexico or."[140] These words were as "useless" as the ones he had suggested dropped from Article III. Without these words it would still be indicated "sufficiently" that the allies would respect the liberty of the Mexicans to retain or to change their government.[141] Russell crossed out the words of Articles III and IV of the British draft convention to which Flahault objected and noted on the original draft that these two Articles would be combined to form a revised Article III. It would read :

> The High Contracting Parties mutually agree that the forces to be employed by them, in pursuance of the terms of the present convention, shall not be employed for any other objects than those specified in the Preamble thereof; and (omitting here, "specifically, shall not be employed for the purpose of interfering with the internal Government of the Republic") the High Contracting Parties further engage, that, in the employment of the coercive measures provided for in this Convention, they will not seek for themselves any augmentation of territory nor any special advantage, neither will they endeavour to interfere (omitting here, "in the internal affairs of

Mexico or") with the free choice on the part of the people of Mexico of the form of Government to be maintained in Mexico.

To indicate more clearly that force would not be used "to interfere with the free choice on the part of the people of Mexico of the form of Government to be maintained in Mexico," Russell inserted "forcibly" before these words. He also made other changes to the original draft convention. In the Preamble he substituted that the allies would "demand" instead of "seek" or "ask" redress of grievances.[142] He crossed out "on the Atlantic Ocean" in Article I, as suggested by Flahault. The expressions, "rigorous blockade" and "Cities, Ports," were redundant, and so Russell crossed out "rigorous" and "Cities." He also altered two words for stylistic reasons, but these changes in no way changed the meaning of Article I.[143] The next Article, which Thouvenel wanted to omit, stated originally that, once the allies were in possession of Vera Cruz, a communication would be sent to the Mexican "Authorities" to demand redress. Even if "arrangements" were made, the allies reserved the right :

. . . of taking such steps as they may deem advisable for watching over and enforcing the execution of such arrangements.[144]

By these parts of Article II it was intended to make it clear that the allies would attempt negotiations with the *de facto* government of Mexico,[145] and Russell intended to retain these sections.[146] He did, however, cross out the words :

and the said Commanding officers shall intimate to the Authorities of the Republic that the coercive measures which they may have adopted will be maintained and, in case of need, extended, until such times as the arrangements aforesaid shall have been approved by the Governments of (the High Contracting Parties).[147]

This omission of what the allies would do if the Mexican Government refused to grant redress could be inserted in instructions, as suggested by Thouvenel. By dropping a reference to the possibility that operations might be "extended," Russell may have intended to prevent French use of such a clause to permit operations in the interior of Mexico.[148] In place of Article IV of the original British draft convention, combined with Article III, Russell inserted an Article based on the one suggested by the Lord Chancellor.[149] A Commission of three persons, one named by each of the allies, would settle any questions that might "arise" from the distribution of money "recovered in, or from Mexico, having regard to the respective rights of the Three Contracting Parties." These Commissioners, in cooperation with the Commanders-in-Chief of the allied forces, would make the demand for redress or grievances envisioned in Article II. Articles V and VI, concerning an invitation to the United States and the exchange of ratifications, were unaltered by Russell.[150]

The British draft convention, as amended by Russell, was sent to Lord Palmerston for his approval on 19 October.[151] The Prime Minister suggested the reference in Article I that the allies would "enforce a blockade" be qualified with the words, "if it shall be found necessary." A disclaimer not to interfere "with the free choice on the part of the people of Mexico of the form of Government to be maintained in Mexico" was adequate in the new Article III without placing "forcibly" before such a statement. To do so was to "enter . . . upon nice distinctions." It would be "next to impossible" for forces occupying Mexican territory to "abstain from all Interferences of every sort in the internal affairs of the Country." For example, the allies would "naturally and necessarily be communicated with by Powers engaged in forming a government." Palmerston also suggested a few stylistic changes, in most cases involving the substitution of nouns for pronouns whose antecedents might not be clearly indicated.[152] The changes suggested by Palmerston were made,[153] and the resulting (second) British draft convention, dated 21 October 1861, was printed[154] so that copies could be "placed before the negotiators."[155]

At the same time that a second British draft convention was in preparation, Thouvenel prepared a draft convention as a counter proposal to the first British draft convention. Since Napoleon had no objection to stating the "ostensible" purpose of the allied expedition, Thouvenel merely translated the Preface of the first British draft convention into French.[156] No change was intended,[157] but the French words, *"arbitraire et vexatoire,"*[158] were used to translate that the "lawless and flagitous"[159] conduct of the Mexican authorities was the cause of the allied expedition. The French word, *"exiger,"*[160] was used to translate "to seek" in the statement that the allies intended "to seek . . . protection for the persons and properties" of the subjects of the allies and a "fulfilment of the obligations" contracted by Mexico toward the allies.[161] The infinitive, *"exiger,"* was used in the special sense "to exact" or "to require" redress. The British Government considered *"arbitraire et vexatoire"* a change[162] but had no objections, and "arbitrary and vexatious" replaced "lawless and flagitious" in the definitive Convention signed 31 October.[163] When the French draft convention reached Russell,[164] he had already decided to substitute "to demand" for "to seek" or "to ask" in his first draft convention, and so he had no objections to the French Preface. In the definitive Convention, *"exiger"* was simply translated as "to demand."[165]

The Articles of the (first) British draft convention were based on the assumption that the objective stated in the Preamble, redress of legitimate grievances, was the only intention of the allies. Napoleon, however, hoped to utilize the expedition in such a way that Maximilian would be established as ruler of Mexico. The means by which this would be done had to be provided for in some way in the convention agreed upon by the European Powers. Similarly, any provisions of the convention that strictly limited the use of the expedition for the purposes stated in the Preamble had to be eliminated or modified.

As stated in his private letter to Flahault, Napoleon claimed it was "necessary to foresee what could happen and not benevolently to tie one's hands." [166]

Article I of the (first) British draft provided that the allies send a force to Mexico sufficient to seize and hold Mexican coastal positions on the Atlantic Ocean and initiate a blockade of that coast. [167] Thouvenel did not believe that the suppression of the words, "on the Atlantic Ocean," indicated "precisely" enough the "latitude" that had to be left the Commanders-in-Chief of the allied expedition. [168] Therefore, in addition to omitting these words from his Article I, Thouvenel inserted an elastic paragraph in the midst of the Article:

> The Commanders of the allied forces will, in addition, be authorized to undertake other operations which will be judged on the spot the most appropriate to accomplish the ends specified in the preamble of the present convention and especially to assure the security of foreign residents, wherever menaced. [169]

Article I of the (first) British draft convention ended with the statement that the occupation of Mexican coastal positions on the Atlantic Ocean was "to be enforced in the name and on behalf of the High Contracting Parties conjointly, irrespective of the national character of the Force by which that occupation shall be carried out." [170] Article I of the French draft convention ended with a similar statement referring not to the occupation of coastal positions, but to "All measures contemplated in this article." [171] This statement, by following the authorization of "operations" decided "on the spot" — to protect foreigners in Mexico "wherever menaced" — would allow the French Commander sent to Mexico to lead his troops into the interior to "protect" foreigners on behalf of the allies. If the result of such operations were that Maximilian should be named King of Mexico, even this, conceivably, might be acclaimed in the name of the allies.

Just what would be done once the allied expeditionary force

landed in Mexico was stated nowhere in the French draft
convention. Article II of the (first) British draft convention,
concerning a demand for redress to be made to the Mexican
"Authorities," completely disappeared from the French draft
convention.[172] Even the reference to a blockade, in Article I of
the (first) British draft,[173] was omitted in the corresponding
French Article.[174] In explanatory instructions to Flahault, Thouvenel stated that matters concerning redress of grievances
would be covered by instructions to the Commanders-in-Chief
of the expedition.[175] It was unnecessary to state the right of
blockade, as it was an inherent right of the commanders of the
allied forces.[176]

Article II of the French draft convention, stating what the
allies would not do, was intended to satisfy Russell's insistence
that the allies bind themselves not to interfere in Mexican
internal affairs. The disclaimers, however, had to be general
enough so that Napoleon could "in honour" sign the convention. Flahault's report had been received that he believed
Russell was "disposed" to omit the last part of Article III of
the (first) British draft convention, stating that the allied forces
would not be employed to interfere "with the Internal government of the Republic."[177] Napoleon, however, objected to the
first part of the British Article that the forces of the allies "shall
not be employed for any other objects than those specified in
the Preamble thereof."[178] Consequently, Article III of the (first)
British draft was omitted from the French version.[179] For
Napoleon the objectives stated in the Preface were only the
"ostensible" ones, to which he did not want to be bound so
rigorously. There was, however, no objection to the first part of
Article IV of the (first) British draft convention, whereby the
allies engaged themselves not to seek any acquisition of territory or "special advantage."[180] If Maximilian were established
in Mexico, France would not gain any territory, and since he
was not French, France technically would not gain any special
advantage. The French Article II, therefore, made these disclaimers without qualification.[181] The last part of Article IV of

the (first) British draft convention could not be omitted from
the French version without omitting all reference to non-interference in Mexican internal affairs in the entire French draft
convention. The British version stated:

> neither will they (i.e., the High Contracting Parties) endeavour
> to interfere in the Internal affairs of Mexico, or with the
> free choice on the part of the people of Mexico of the form
> of Government to be maintained in Mexico.[182]

Even this the French version "abridged," as Thouvenel put
it.[183] The word, "or," in the British version, made this statement
two disclaimers: not to interfere in Mexican internal affairs
and not to interfere with the free choice of their government
by the Mexicans. The last half of the second French Article
reduced the British version to one disclaimer, that did not
necessarily eliminate *all* interference in Mexican internal
affairs. The allies engaged themselves:

> not to exercise in the internal affairs of Mexico any influence
> of a nature to prejudice the right of the Mexican nation to
> choose and to constitute freely the form of its government.[184]

Article IV of the (first) British draft convention,[185] the invitation to the United States, became Article III of the French
draft convention,[186] with minor changes to shorten it.[187] Article
IV of the French draft provided for an exchange of ratifications.[188]

The French draft convention was written in ink on the left
hand side of pages submitted to Napoleon III. On the right
hand side of these pages was a copy of the (first) British draft
convention. On the top of the left hand side of the first page
Napoleon wrote in pencil: "Accepted" and "I approve the
counter proposal," followed by "N"(apoleon). It is likely, therefore, that the other pencil marks on these pages were also made
by Napoleon. An "x" and a line were marked alongside the
insertion in Article I, of the French version, that authorized

operations decided upon "on the spot" to protect foreigners, "wherever menaced." There were also pencilled diagonal lines and an "x" alongside all of Article III of the British draft, denying the allies to use their forces for any other purposes than those "specified in the preamble" and "specifically" renouncing "interfering with the Internal government of the Republic."[189] If Napoleon did not make these pencil marks, he did, however, consider the omission of the British Article III and the insertion of authorization of "on the spot" decisions of the highest importance. In a private letter written to Flahault on 25 October, Thouvenel stated :

> The Emperor is not going to renounce his right to indicate in the convention his desire to protect our nationals wherever their security may be endangered.  His Majesty will not consent to the phrase by which the high contracting powers *would engage themselves to employ coercive measures only for the ends stipulated in the preamble.*[190]

Thouvenel sent the French draft convention to Flahault on 21 October.[191] The next day a copy was sent to the French Ambassador in Madrid.[192] By now the British and French Governments had each prepared revisions of the (first) British draft convention, but neither government had as yet received despatches from their Ambassadors in Madrid concerning the Spanish reaction to the (first) British draft convention.[193] Russell had sent a copy to Madrid on 14 October,[194] and Thouvenel had done likewise on 17 October, when he also sent a copy of a despatch outlining his objections.[195] It took a week or more to receive answers to instructions sent to Madrid from Paris and London. Long instructions were not sent by telegraph, and so Collantes' comments on the (first) British draft convention, presented to him by Crampton on 19 October, only reached the British Foreign Office on 24 October. Crampton reported that Collantes was "generally disposed to agree in the propriety of the terms in which the draft of the convention is drawn up." He suggested one alteration, the addition of a clause :

> . . . expressing the intention or desire of the High Contracting
> Parties to exercise a moral influence on the affairs of Mexico,
> with the object of effecting a suspension of the civil contests
> raging in that country, and bring about an understanding
> between the contending factions in regard to the constitution
> of a government offering some guarantee for the fulfilment of
> its engagements and the preservation of peace.

Crampton remarked that, although the draft convention did
not contain such a clause, there was nothing in the draft to
prevent the use of moral influence for the ends Collantes had
in mind. While admitting this, Collantes maintained that the
insertion of the clause he outlined was desirable:

> . . . as manifesting to the world the desire of the Three Powers
> to ameliorate a state of things which seemed every day to be-
> come more at variance with the interests of civilization and
> humanity.[196]

After he had received the British draft convention, Collantes
saw the French Ambassador to Madrid, who summarized
Thouvenel's objections to that British draft. Collantes agreed
"completely." He claimed he would "rather abstain than go to
Mexico under the conditions proposed by the English treaty
project." It was "an act of distrust . . . that nothing . . . could
justify." The "limits" it set "paralyzed" measures that might
have to be taken in Mexico and would "discourage" the "men
of order," who were in the majority, from attempting to form
a stable government. Without such a change of government in
Mexico, the allies might merely obtain a promise to grant
redress. Then a revolution might bring in a new government
not accepting these promises. Collantes placed his hopes for
guarantees for the future in a conservative government. Such a
government would never he formed if the allies made "useless"
and "premature" declarations of their subjects there, and it
would be necessary to protect them, as well as to obtain redress
for past wrongs. The Spanish Government, Collantes told
Barrot, would support the French views in all these respects.

If their "common ideas" could not be made "to prevail," the Spanish Government, however, would have to accept the British "clauses."[197] But the Spanish Government did not intend to assist in the establishment of Maximilian in Mexico. If Mexico desired a sovereign, Collantes wrote his Ambassador to Paris on 22 October, "it would be in conformity with historical tradition and with hte bonds which unite the two peoples if a prince of the House of Bourbon, or closely associated with it, should be preferred."[198] The same day Collantes sent identical comments on Article III of the (first) British draft convention to his Ambassadors to Paris and London :

> Article III . . . is in entire conformity with the views which the government of the Queen has always manifested. It has always thought that the Mexicans should be left entire freedom to constitute their government in the manner most conformable to their interests, their habits, and their beliefs . . . .

Yet the Spanish Government believed that the Mexicans ought to be "put . . . in a position to examine without passion or self-deception the situation in which their errors have placed them, in order that they may adopt the most suitable means for improving it."[199] The day after these instructions were sent, the full powers for the Spanish Ambassador to London to sign a convention were forwarded,[200] almost two weeks after Russell had requested by telegram that this be done.[201]

Flahault saw Russell on 22 October and gave him a copy of the French draft convention and received a copy of the (second) British draft convention.[202] Negotiations then came to a standstill until 26 October, when Flahault received[203] Thouvenel's comment[204] on the (second British draft convention. In the interval full powers and instructions[205] to support the French objections to the (first) British draft convention[206] were underway from Madrid to Isturiz, the Spanish Ambassador to London. Flahault showed Isturiz the French draft convention, and he highly approved.[207]

Thouvenel and Napoleon III had no objections to the

Preamble of the (second) British draft convention, since it was almost identical to the French draft.[208] Napoleon, however, would not accept Article I of the British convention without the insertion of the authorization of "on the spot" decisions to protect foreigners, "wherever menaced."[209] He had already authorized Thouvenel to drop from the French draft the references to what would be done upon arrival in Mexico. Since Article II of the (second) British draft still contained some of the statements of Article II of the (first) British draft convention, Thouvenel was still determined that this Article would have to be eliminated.[210] Napoleon would not agree to bind himself to limit operations for the purposes stated in the Preface, a provision of Article III of the (second) British draft convention.[211] Nor would he accept this Article if this reference were omitted. He inserted on substituting Article II of the French draft for it.[212] In an instruction to Barrot, enclosing the (second) British and French draft conventions, Thouvenel stated that the French Article II was "indispensable." The French Government did not want to give up "in an absolute manner" the right "to lend our force, at least moral, to the efforts that Mexico may make to obtain a stable government."[213] Napoleon III had his doubts about the creation of a Commission to distribute money among the allies. provided for by Article IV of the (second) British draft convention. He was "very unwilling" to place the Commander-in-Chief of the French forces under the control of a "civil commander." He saw a way out of the difficulty by assuming that these "diplomatic agents" would merely present demands for redress to the Mexican Government.[214] The French demands would be so "excessive" that the Mexican Government would refuse to accept them.[215] Then the "Commissioners" would report their inability to obtain redress to the allied commanders. The functions of the Commissioners would then cease, and the commanders would decide what measures to take.[216] With these mental reservations, Napoleon authorized Thouvenel to accept Article IV of the British draft convention.[217] The Articles concerning an invitation to the United States and an exchange of ratifications were almost the same in the French and British versions. No difficulties, therefore, resulted from these Articles.[218]

Lord Russell opposed the paragraph in the first Article concerning "on the spot" decisions.[219] A long pencil line was drawn alongside this paragraph of the French draft convention presented by Flahault. The words, "wherever menaced" (*partout ou elle se trouverait menacé*), were crossed out.[220] Russell believed this expression "seems to imply the military occupation of Mexico."[221] Article IV, concerning Commissioners, was cut out of the printed (second) British draft convention and pasted on the French draft convention.[222] The British Commissioner, Russell told Flahault, would be Sir Charles Wyke, the British Minister to Mexico.[223]

On 25 October Thouvenel sent Flahault observations on the (second) British draft convention. The French Government had no objections to the Preamble, the creation of a Commission (Article IV), and an invitation to the United States to adhere to the convention after its signature in Europe (Article V). Article II, concerning what would be done when the allies arrived in Mexico, should be omitted and "find its place" in instructions to hte commanders of the allied forces. Article I of the French draft convention was preferable to the British one in that the French Article gave the necessary "latitude" to the commanders to make "on the spot" decisions to protect the French subjects residing in the "interior" of Mexico. Flahault was referred to previous instructions for the objections to the British Article III, stating what the allies would not do. The Emperor would not permit the substitution of this Article for the French version, which permitted "moral support to efforts of reorganization attempted by the country itself."[224] In a private letter accompanying these instructions, Thouvenel stated he was sure that Isturiz, the Spanish Ambassador to London, would assist in persuading Russell to accept what Napoleon considered two important changes in the (second) British draft convention. These were the omission that the allies

promised not to use their forces for any purposes not stated in
the Preamble (Article III) and the insertion in Article I of
"on the spot" decisions.[225] The next day Thouvenel wrote to
the French Ambassador in Madrid in the same sense.[226]

Acting on instructions, Flahault communicated Thouvenel's
comments on the (second) British draft convention to Russell
on 26 October. The British Foreign Secretary agreed to accept
the French draft convention "with the simple omission of the
words, 'wherever menaced' " in Article I. The only other
change demanded by Russell was the insertion, as Article III,
of the British Article providing for the creation of a Commission. The French Articles III and IV would then be renum-
bered IV and V.[227] Russell had a favorable reply[228] from the
British Admiralty to his proposal that Marines be sent to
Mexico to hold the main fortress of Vera Cruz after seizure.[229]
Therefore Russell told Flahault that, if the French Government
agreed to revise its draft convention, the British Government
intended to send seven hundred Marines, two ships, four
frigates, and some "light" boats.[230] The seven hundred Marines
would be "supernumerary,"[231] an addition to those regularly
carried by British warships and yet part of those ship's companies.[232] Consequently Russell[233] and Palmerston[234] believed it
was self-evident that these Marines would remain in the vicinity
of their ships. They would merely assist in capturing Vera
Cruz, if necessary, and perform garrison duty. "Our Marines,"
Russell observed after the convention was signed, "will not go
beyond Vera Cruz." Russell, therefore, never intended the
British Commander-in-Chief to invoke the authorization to
make "on the spot" decisions to protect foreigners in the
interior of Mexico. Furthermore, Russell believed, the French
would not be in a position to use this authorization to send
their troops into the interior of Mexico. They were "too small
a number for conquest, and . . . are required for the custom
houses and ports."[235]

Upon receiving Flahault's despatch summarizing Russell's
proposed changes to the French draft convention. Thouvenel

went to Napoleon III "to get orders." Napoleon consented to omit "wherever menaced" as a "concession . . . to reach agreement with the English cabinet." Thouvenel sent Flahault an instruction on 28 October to inform him of this decision. This omission, however, was not without reservations:

> It suffices for us that the security of the foreign residents be stipulated; the commanders of our forces can take advantage of this stipulation when necessary according to their means and within the limits of the possible. We will not admit that our nationals could be exposed to the dangers that menace their existence at any place that the protective action of our armed forces could reach, and we are convinced that the Government of Her Britannic Majesty will not permit its nationals to be exposed in any way any more than ours.

A previous instruction, Thouvenel observed, already stated that the French Government agreed to the British Article establishing a Commission.[236] In the evening of the same day that Thouvenel sent these instructions to Flahault, the French Ambassador to Madrid telegraphed that the Spanish Government gave its "complete adherence" to the French draft convention and would inform Isturiz in London that very evening.[237]

Thouvenel's authorization to accept Russell's alterations of the French draft convention reached Flahault on 29 October. Since Russell was not in London that day, Flahault wrote him that the French Government agreed to omit "wherever menaced." The next day Flahault received a reply that " *we will certainly try to protect our nationals in all parts of Mexico but not by a military occupation.'* "[238] In Russell's absence, Flahault saw Hammond, the British Under-Secretary of State, and obtained his approval of a French translation of the British Article concerning the establishment of a Commission. The last sentence was omitted, because it referred to an Article of the (second) British draft convention that was omitted from the French convention.[239] Flahault also saw Isturiz, who had his full powers and was ready to sign the convention. On 30 October Flahault sent a report of these developments to Thouvenel, together with the French translation of the Article approved by Hammond.[240] That evening Flahault received a note from Russell that he intended to sign the convention at 3.00 P.M. the next day. Flahault immediately telegraphed Thouvenel:

> If you approve the version that is proposed by my despatch that will reach you tomorrow morning, telegraph me or indicate the modification to make to it.[241]

That same day, 30 October, the British Foreign Office sent a telegram to the British Ambassador to Madrid. The terms of the convention agreed upon with Flahault were summarized. Crampton was instructed to inform O'Donnell and ask him what forces he intended to send to Mexico.[242] At the same time an instruction was drafted that the Admiralty get seven hundred supernumerary Marines ready.[243]

Just before noon on 31 October Thouvenel sent a telegram to Flahault. He was referred to the instruction authorizing the omission of "wherever menaced" for the "interpretation" attached by the French Government to this omission. Furthermore, no "official" value was to be attached to Russell's note to Flahault that a "military occupation" would not be the means to protect foreigners in Mexico:

> . . . in connection with expressing my sentiments on the necessity of a military occupation of such and such a part of the interior, I would not know how to exclude in advance, and in an absolute manner, recourse to this measure. Consequently we accept Article I, as it is drawn up and without attributing an official value to the restriction that the note of Lord Russell would appear to apply to it.

With these reservations, Thouvenel authorized Flahault to sign the convention.[244] When this telegram arrived in London, the British Foreign Office already had a despatch from Cowley, reporting Napoleon's interpretation of the functions of the Commissioners.[245] Since Cowley did not yet know Napoleon's intention that the French Commissioner would present "excessive" claims,[246] Russell saw no objection to the personal opinion of Cowley that had "satisfied" Thouvenel. Cowley had said that he believed the British Government proposed nothing further :

> . . . than the association of the commissioners with the commanders in chief in any negotiations which might take place with the Mexican Government . . . .[247]

Without a reply[248] to the telegram to Crampton of the day before, Russell signed the convention in the afternoon of 31 October 1861. Flahault then sent a telegram to Thouvenel :

> Lord Russell having given satisfactory explanations in the sense of your telegraphic despatch of this morning, we have signed the convention.[249]

All that remained to be done was an exchange of ratifications, the drawing up of instructions to the commanders of the expedition so that it could get underway, and sending an invitation to the United States to join the expedition.

# IV
# The Beginnings of the
# European Intervention in Mexico

## 1. THE INSTRUCTIONS OF THE ALLIES TO THEIR DIPLOMATIC REPRESENTATIVES AND COMMANDERS-IN-CHIEF

THE CONVENTION OF LONDON WAS A COMPROMISE, AND, AS such, it did not fully satisfy any of the contracting parties. The three allies disagreed about the purposes of an expedition to Mexico. For Napoleon the intervention would be the means of establishing Maximilian in Mexico. The Spanish Government wanted to gain popularity at home by an active Mexican policy designed not only to obtain redress for Spanish claims but also to return the conservatives to power in Mexico. The British Government intended to limit the intervention to a debt-collecting expedition. The Convention was made vague enough to satisfy all, each believing his viewpoint was provided for, or not excluded from, the terms of the Convention. The various interpretations of the objectives of the expedition led directly to a difference of opinion of just how the expedition should be employed. Just what operations should be carried out were completely omitted from the Convention. The British and Spanish Governments accepted Thouvenel's explanation

216

that these matters would be included in the instructions to the representatives of the allies.

The Convention of London specified that the strength of the allied expeditionary forces was to be determined by communication among the allies. At the beginning of October Thouvenel had already stated to Cowley that the French Government intended to send three heavy frigates and about one thousand troops.[1] From the British Admiralty Russell had learned that two ships of the line, four frigates, and some smaller vessels were considered adequate to attack Vera Cruz.[2] The Admiralty warned, however, that British Marines used for garrison duty in Vera Cruz had to be replaced by a colored West India Regiment in April, when the unhealthy season began.[3] The day before signing the Convention, Russell sent a telegram to his Ambassador to Madrid. Crampton was to tell O'Donnell that Great Britain intended to send two ships of the line, four frigates, some smaller vessels, and seven hundred Marines. The British Admiral on the American and West India Station would rendezvous with the Spanish and French expeditions at a place yet to be agreed upon. Crampton was to discover what forces the Spanish Government intended to send to Mexico and whether Spanish troops could remain in Vera Cruz after April.[4] In the evening of 31 October Russell had a telegraphic reply from Crampton. Twelve to fourteen warships of various sizes, two large troop transports, and four to five thousand troops would be sent. The troops were "accustomed to the climate of the West Indies" and therefore "able to remain after April if required."[5] Such was the military situation as known to Lord Russell shortly after signing the Convention of London.

The latest estimate of what British subjects were demanding in compensation for personal and property injuries was six months old.[6] Since these claims were largely uninvestigated[7] and claimants often made exorbitant demands,[8] Russell was in no position to specify which claims Mexico would be asked to recognize or how much reparation was just. With respect to recognized claims, Russell assumed that the allied expedition would force Mexico to recognize the validity of conventions already concluded and to resume assignments of the appropriate percentage of custom house receipts to liquidate allied claims.[9] Mexico had never fully or simultaneously complied with the terms of all these conventions.[10] Were this done, 87 per cent of Mexican import duties would be turned over to the allied claimants.[11] Then there would not be enough revenue left to pay the costs of running the Mexican Government.[12]

On 31 October Russell drew up instructions to the British Admiralty and Sir Charles Wyke, the British Minister to Mexico. The Admiralty was directed to send the ships and Marines Russell had decided upon to Vera Cruz. The Marines would be "landed and employed on shore, if circumstances should require it." The Admiral or Senior Naval Officer in command of these forces was to communicate with the Commanders-in-Chief of the French and Spanish forces and with them demand :

1.   Full satisfaction and reparation for the wrongs suffered by the Three nations; and
2.ndly That the Forts of Vera Cruz should be at once delivered up to the forces of the three Nations, as a guarantee for the performance of such conditions as may be agreed upon.

The allies would name a Commission to act in concert with the Commanders-in-Chief to "frame . . . the Articles an assent to which will be demanded of the Mexican Government or of the persons exercising authority in Mexico." The British Commissioner, Russell informed the Admiralty, would be Sir Charles Wyke. The allied forces would "remain in possession of the forts of Vera Cruz and other forts, if taken, until further order." Admiral Maitland, operating off the western coast of North America, should be instructed by the Admiralty to seize Acapulco harbor or another port on the Pacific coast of Mexico "with a view to secure the objects of the Convention."[13] The Admiralty was also requested to propose an appropriate rendez-

vous for the allied expeditions.[14] Then, still on 31 October,
Russell drafted instructions for Wyke. Copies of the Convention of London and the directive to the Admiralty were
enclosed. The only instructions to Wyke that were not merely
a repetition of what was stated in those to the Admiralty were
contained in one paragraph :

> You will instruct Her Majesty's Consuls at the Ports which
> may be determined on, to collect in concert with the French
> and Spanish Consuls at those Ports the Custom Duties, and to
> pay them over according to such rules as the Commissioners
> may jointly lay down.[15]

The next day Russell drafted another instruction for Wyke :

> You should be most careful to observe with strictness the
> Second Article of the Convention signed yesterday . . . by
> which it is provided that no influence shall be used in the
> internal affairs of Mexico, calculated to prejudice the right of
> the Mexican Nation freely to choose and establish it's *(sic)*
> own form of Government.
> Should any Mexican or party in Mexico ask your advice
> on such subjects, you will say that any regular form of Govern-
> ment which shall protect the lives and properties of natives
> and of foreigners, and shall not permit British Subjects to be
> attacked or annoyed on account of their occupation, their
> rights of property or their religion will secure the moral sup-
> port of the British Government.[16]

On 1 November Russell received the Admiralty's proposal
that the allied fleets rendezvous fifteen miles Northwest of
Cape St. Antonio, off the western coast of Cuba[17] Immediately
upon receipt of this letter, Russell sent copies of it,[18] his instructions to the Admiralty,[19] and the two instructions to Wyke[20] to
the British Ambassadors in Paris and Madrid for communication to the French and Spanish Governments. The British
diplomats were also instructed to inform the French[21] and
Spanish[22] Governments that Wyke would be directed to retire
to Jamaica to await instructions and that the British Minister

to Washington would be informed of the invitation to be made to the United States Government. The mail packet that left Southampton on 2 November[23] only carried one instruction for Wyke that pertained to the Mexican expedition. He was ordered to board a ship of war to be sent to Vera Cruz for him and to proceed to the flagship of Admiral Milne, probably at Bermuda. Milne, in command of the American and West India Station, would then give Wyke further instructions.[24] These were the instructions already drafted and not sent by Russell,[25] who wanted to wait for the comments that the French Government might make.[26] Instructions to the British Minister to Washington to invite the United States to join the European expedition were despatched.[27] Lord Lyons was "not to conclude this matter . . . without coming to a complete and clear understanding with the French and Spanish Ministers."[28]

Lord Russell's instructions to Wyke and the Admiralty were based on the assumption that the only objective of the allied expedition was to obtain redress of grievances. By sending copies of the instructions to Wyke, containing remarks about Article II of the Convention, to the French and Spanish Governments, Russell made it clear to his allies that he would not tolerate any forcible interference with the right of Mexicans to choose their government. The means to obtain redress of grievances was a custom house intervention. The allied fleets would rendezvous and proceed to Vera Cruz. The city, forts, and Custom House would be occupied. British ships in the Pacific Ocean would be used to seize Acapulco or some other Mexican harbor on the west coast of Mexico. The claims of the allies would be detailed in an ultimatum prepared by the Commanders-in-Chief and Commissioners of the allies. This ultimatum would be presented to the *de facto* government of Mexico. It would accept the terms of the allies, and monetary redress would be obtained in the form of Mexican custom duties collected by the Consuls of the allies in the various Mexican ports. The allied Commissioners would decide the details of this arrangement. Vera Cruz would be held "until further order" as a guarantee for the fulfillment of Mexican pledges. That the Mexican Government would refuse to enter into an agreement was an eventuality that Russell had not even considered. When the French Government suggested this possibility,[29] Russell admitted that it was something of which he "had not taken notice."[30] He had considered, however, that the employment of British Marines might entail some difficulties. An occupation of Vera Cruz might be necessary even after April 1862, when the unhealthy season usually began on the Atlantic coast of Mexico. Then the British Marines would have to be withdrawn. On 1 November Russell requested to know from the Colonial Office whether one of the "black West India regiments" would be available in April if needed for garrison duty in Vera Cruz.[31] Both Russell and Palmerston intended that the British Marines garrison St. Juan d'Ulloa, the main fortress defending Vera Cruz from an island just offshore, and that there be no unified command over all the allied forces sent to Mexico. The two British Ministers assumed that the Admiralty would give command of the British expedition to Admiral Milne, the Commander of the American and West India Station. In an instruction to the Admiralty drafted by Russell and Palmerston jointly, it was stated that Admiral Milne should :

> . . . propose to his Colleagues of France and Spain that his share in the occupation of the Mexican Forts and positions should consist in placing a garrison of British Marines in the Fortress of St. John d'Ulloa & he should urge this on the ground that it is manifestly undesirable that the troops of the 3 Allied Powers should be mixed up together . . . & that as the British Marines form properly speaking part of the complement of the Ships of the Squadron it would be a great convenience to the service of the British Force that the Ships & the Marines should be in close and easy communication with each other.[32]

In no eventuality did Russell and Palmerston wish the Marines to be employed in mixed garrisons :

As there will be several Forts and Stations to be occupied it seems reasonable to expect that the proposed arrangement will not be objected to by the French and Spanish Commanders. But at all events & in any case, Admiral Milne should insist upon having a separate position allotted to the Marines of his Squadron.[33]

Before Lord Cowley could communicate the correspondence sent him by Lord Russell to Thouvenel,[34] Napoleon III took steps to divert the expedition to the purpose of establishing Maximilian as ruler of Mexico. The Austrian Government was assured that Palmerston agreed to this plan. On 2 November Count Walewski, the Emperor's cousin and Minister of State, told the Austrian Chargé d'Affaires that the British cabinet approved the Emperor's private letter to Flahault.[35] a copy of which had already been sent to Count Rechberg.[36] Palmerston had put nothing in writing in order not to offend the United States and "certain sections of British opinion, notably the School of Bright."[37] That Palmerston approved the French draft convention, Walewski told Muelinen, was proof enough that the British Minister would support the monarchy scheme :

But as my Sovereign has explained his views to Lord Palmerston, and has informed him of his intentions, and has signed the Convention in the form in which it was proposed by France, we are justified in considering that the British support the plan.[38]

On 2 November Thouvenel received a telegram from Madrid that the Spanish Government intended to send four to five thousand troops to Mexico and proposed Havana as a rendezvous for the allied fleets.[39] The next day a report arrived from Flahault, enclosing a copy of the rendezvous proposal of the British Admiralty[40] supplied by Russell.[41] Napoleon reconciled the Spanish and British proposals by deciding that the French fleet being assembled at Toulon would proceed to Havana, join the Spanish expedition there, and then both would proceed to the rendezvous proposed by the British

Admiralty to join forces with the British squadron.[42] The French Minister of Marine and Colonies made preparations[43] so that the French ships could start leaving Toulon on 11 November. It was estimated that they would reach Havana between 15 and 20 December, take on supplies and then proceed to meet the British ships off Cape St. Antonio between 20 and 25 December.[44]

Even before the signature of the Convention of London, Napoleon III had decided that six to seven thousand troops would be necessary for operations in the interior of Mexico, "sufficiently near the capital to afford moral support" to the "party of order."[45] On the assumption that the Spanish Government would not object to the employment of its troops in such a manner,[46] Napoleon decided to increase the French expeditionary force from one to two thousand troops[47] so that six to seven thousand troops would be available for a march toward Mexico City. Admiral Jurien de La Gravière was named Commander-in-Chief of the French forces. He was well known by British naval officers for his "tact, moderation and conciliatory disposition."[48] Consequently it was intended that he use his influence to prevent the British naval authorities sent to Vera Cruz from objecting to Franco–Spanish military operations beyond Vera Cruz. He was even instructed to try to obtain British cooperation if possible.[49] Jurien saw Napoleon and suggested sending a detachment of Zouaves in addition to two thousand troops "to infuse energy into the whole" French expedition.[50] Hidalgo and Eugenie also urged the Emperor to increase the size of the French expeditionary force.[51] Napoleon then gave permission to Jurien to pick up five hundred Zouaves from Algeria on his way to Havana.[52] "Faced with the suspicions of England," Napoleon wrote in a private letter, he "did not at first dare to send any more troops overseas."[53]

When Cowley gave Thouvenel the copies of Russell's instructions to the Admiralty and Wyke, the French military and naval forces were making final preparations to leave from Toulon, but Thouvenel had not yet drafted instructions for

Jurien. Cowley was informed of the increase of French forces, their intended movements before arriving at the British rendezvous point, and that Jurien had been named Commander-in-Chief. Thouvenel expressed "full concurrence" with the special instructions to Wyke warning him to abide by Article II of the Convention of London and not to interfere in Mexican internal affairs. Concerning the other instructions of Russell, Thouvenel reserved his opinion. He explained that he had yet to draw up instructions for Jurien and Saligny, who would be the French Commissioner. Instructions would also be sent to the French Minister to Washington concerning an offer that the United States join the European expedition.[51] After seeing Cowley, Thouvenel sent a telegram to the French Ambassador to Madrid in the evening of 5 November. Barrot was informed that the French force of 2,500 would arrive at Havana about 20 December. The rest of the telegram was classified confidential. It stated how Napoleon hoped to make use of the paragraph of Article I of the Convention of London concerning "on the spot" decisions to authorize a French march into the interior of Mexico. Barrot was to make sure the Spanish Government took a similar view :

> Reach a confidential understanding with Marshall O'Donnell and M. Collantes so that the instructions of the French and Spanish Commanders-in-Chief authorize them to march on Mexico City, if circumstances appear favorable to them. A previous accord in this respect would be impossible with England owing to the situation before Parliament; but if France and Spain jointly give the broadest interpretation to the second paragraph of Article I of the Convention which foresees the necessity of protecting foreign residents, there is every reason to believe that their Commanders-in-Chief will not encounter opposition on the part of the English Admiral.[55]

Thouvenel received a telegram from Barrot on 6 November that O'Donnell promised "that elastic and discretionary instructions will be given to the Spanish Commander-in-Chief and . . . a private letter in the sense of the desire expressed by the Government of the Emperor."[56] Thouvenel delayed writing instructions for Jurien and Saligny until after Barrot's full report arrived in despatch form. O'Donnell had seen no objection to granting the Spanish Commander discretionary powers to march to Mexico City, if circumstances seemed favorable. Collantes, the Spanish Minister of Foreign Relations, raised difficulties. The British Commander, in spite of a Franco–Spanish agreement, might say such a march to Mexico City was contrary to his instructions. Great Britain might then stop its joint action with Fance and Spain. The United States, even with its internal difficulties, might cause "embarrassment." Barrot then replied that, if foreigners were threatened, the British would go to their protection. This eventuality had not been elaborated upon in the Convention of London owing to :

> . . . the situation of the English Cabinet before Parliament and the impossibility in which the Cabinet found itself of admitting, in advance, a hypothesis as a principle in a public document which would be in opposition to the system of non-intervention that it has so often proclaimed.

As to the United States, Barrot observed, its opposition had always been foreseen, more or less, by the contracting parties. If it had not been able to prevent the accord of the allies, it would not be able to make any opposition to the accomplishment of their mission. At last Collantes said he agreed with O'Donnell, but proposed that the French troops sent to Mexico be placed under the command of the Spanish Commander-in-Chief. "Spain," Collantes told Barrot, "would regard it as the greatest glory."[57] Thouvenel received this report on 10 November. The next day he had his instructions ready for Jurien and Saligny.

Jurien's "official" instructions were communicated to the British[58] and Spanish[59] Governments. His confidential instructions and the instructions to Saligny, however, were kept secret. Napoleon's secret instructions to Jurien were partially made known to the Austrian Government but not to France's allies.

A comparison of all these directives shows what Napoleon wanted the Spanish, British, and Austrian Governments to believe and what he really intended.

The official instructions for Jurien took as their text the Convention of London.[60] After outlining the terms of the Convention, Thouvenel stated that Mexican coastal positions would be occupied, by force if necessary. These positions would be held until "a complete solution of the difficulties to be settled, and the collection of custom duties is made . . . under the surveilance of deputies installed for that purpose." These custom duties would be used to liquidate claims examined and approved by the allied Commission, in which Saligny would represent French interests, and the Commanders-in Chief. So that Jurien might sign all "acts and conventions," he was granted plenipotentiary powers on a par with those of Saligny. Jurien alone was to have military command of the French expeditionary forces. He was also allowed discretion concerning "the movement of troops, the opportunity and the means of occupying such or such points of Mexican territory." Operations beyond the coast might be required if the Mexican Government refused to grant redress or if the security of foreigners were threatened :

> . . . the Mexican Government may refuse to enter into relations with you. The latest news which has arrived from Mexico, that Vera Cruz may be demilitarized, seems to lend credence that such really could be the plan adopted by President Juarez. Renewing a strategy already employed by one of his predecessors in the war with the United States, he would retire into the interior of the country. The allied Powers would not allow themselves to be checked by such an expedient; they would not be able to occupy the coastal positions indefinitely, if this occupation could not furnish them with a means of direct and immediate influence on the Mexican Government. The interests of our dignity and considerations of climatic conditions on the coast combine to force us to obtain a prompt and decisive result. It is principally in view of this eventuality that there has been placed at your disposal a corps of landing troops, which, joined to the other military contingents, would furnish

the allies the means to extend the circle of their operations. The Government of the Emperor foresees that, to strike at the Mexican Government or to render more effective the coercion exercised on it by the seizure of its ports, you may have to make a march into the interior of Mexico, even to Mexico City if necessary. I need hardly add that there is another reason for such operations. It would be to provide safety for our nationals, should they be menaced in any part of Mexico that can be reasonably reached.

The allies did not wish to "intervene in the internal affairs of the country, and especially not to exercise any pressure upon the wishes of the people as to the choice of their government." The arrival of the European expedition, however, might encourage the "sane part of the population" to form a stable government. Then it would not be necessary to "have recourse to periodical and expensive expeditions to remind ephemeral and senseless regimes of the duties of governments." Consequently Jurien was to give his "moral support" if :

> . . . by the position of the men who should take the initiative in this direction and by the sympathy that they might ellicit from the mass of the population, they should have a chance of success to establish an order of things to assure foreign residents the protection and guarantees which have been lacking until the present.[61]

What would be done if the Mexican Government accepted the terms of the allies corresponded to Russell's instructions to the British Admiralty and Wyke, communicated by Cowley to Thouvenel. The observations concerning non-interference in Mexican internal affairs, with a reference to "moral support," corresponded roughly to Russell's special instruction regarding Article II of the Convention of London. Jurien, however, was given the right to initiate his moral support, while Wyke was only authorized to offer comments if questioned by Mexicans. Russell could hardly have any objections to these sections of Jurien's instructions. The eventuality of having to protect foreigners in the interior of Mexico was defined in the narrow sense that Russell had made known to the French Government just before signing the Convention of London. Instead of protecting their nationals "wherever menaced," Thouvenel stated the allies would protect them in those parts of Mexico that "can be reasonably reached." In a private letter to Flahault, Thouvenel admitted that he feared Russell would object to the reference to the possibility of a march to Mexico City. Napoleon III had insisted on making this "allusion" so that his "interpretation" of the Convention of London would be known.[62] The Spanish Government had been asked to give its Commander-in-Chief discretionary powers to cover such an eventuality. Since this "official" instruction to Jurien was communicated to the Spanish Government, it was impossible to omit this "allusion." At the same time it served as a trial balloon to determine the reaction of the British Government and to prepare it for things to come. It also explained the increase of the French expeditionary forces as a measure to provide the allied expedition with enough troops for possible extended operations. By making Jurien a "Plenipotentiary," Thouvenel had an argument against placing the French forces under the command of the Spanish Commander. Thouvenel told the Spanish Ambassador to Paris that, as a "Plenipotentiary," Jurien "could not receive orders from anyone." To soothe Spanish disappointment, Thouvenel added that, since the Spanish forces were larger than the French, he saw no objection if a detachment of French troops might obey the orders of the Spanish Commander-in-Chief.[63]

Thouvenel's confidential instructions to Jurien noted that the Convention of London stated the "legal ground" for the European intervention. Napoleon had an "idea" that went "further." To learn what this was, Jurien was directed to read the enclosed private letter of the Emperor to Flahault. The British Government had given "full justice to the ideas of the Emperor, but . . . didn't believe it necessary to promise its active concurrence to execute them." The Spanish Government was "more inclined in this respect," but it probably was "not a very warm partisan of the eventual candidature of the Archduke Maximilian." Thouvenel did not believe that the British and Spanish Governments would place any "obstacles" in the way of a "considerable" Mexican Monarchical party. He anticipated that it would "appear" upon the arrival of the expeditionary forces in Mexico. Jurien's main task was to determine whether this party had such chances of success that no "adventure" would be risked by France:

> Does this party exist in a state manifesting its intentions with nearly certain chances of success? This is the point, my dear Admiral, which will have to be your first object of your interviews with M. Dubois de Saligny and of your most serious investigations. Just as it would be generous and useful to aid a nation to leave the abyss, just so it would be rash in itself and contrary to our interests to risk an adventure. Therefore it is to inspire the honest and peaceable portion of the Mexican people the courage to make its voice known that our efforts must be held out; if the nation remains inert, if it doesn't realize that we offer it an unexpected staff of safety, if it doesn't give itself a practical sense and morality to our protection, it is evident that there is nothing we can do but remain within the terms of the Convention of 31 October and only occupy ourselves with the specific interests for which it was concluded.

Whatever Jurien decided about the chances of success of the Mexican monarchists, it was desirable to make a march to Mexico City:

> Things would be incomplete, however, unless, once the forts are occupied, an expedition were directed into the interior and really as far as Mexico City.

The British Government "broached this eventuality only with an extreme repugnance." "Parliamentary considerations" could explain this "negative response." Consequently Thouvenel believed it "unwise" to try to force the British Government "to commit itself in advance." The French Government, however, had made known that it reserved its "right to do what is necessary to protect the security of our nationals." The Convention of London, furthermore, could be interpreted to permit operations in the interior of Mexico.

> . . . the terms of Article I of the Convention are sufficient for us in that they permit the Commanders-in-Chief to adopt on the spot the measures the most appropriate to attain the ends of the expedition. These terms are broad enough to justify the interpretation that we want to give them.

The Spanish Government agreed with the French interpretation. Marshall O'Donnell had promised to give "very discretionary instructions" to the Spanish Commander. He would be given a private letter authorizing him to agree with Jurien "on a march to Mexico City, if the circumstances should appear favorable." Jurien should try to "obtain the participation of the Britannic Commander-in-Chief in this movement in as far as he is able." If he refused, Jurien should propose that the British hold the forts of Vera Cruz "as a mark of reciprocal confidence" while the French and Spanish extended operations. "Old memories" might make the Spanish unpopular in Mexico. Two steps should be taken to prevent difficulties in this connection. The French troops should "occupy, in as far as possible, the head of the column of the expeditionary corps," advancing toward Mexico City. Before beginning these operations, a proclamation should be issued "to reassure completely the Mexican nation against any idea of conquest and any attempt against its independence as to the choice and form of its government." While Saligny was recommended for his "exact knowledge of men and things in Mexico," all decisions, military and diplomatic, were reserved, in the last resort, to Jurien.[64]

Thouvenel's instructions to Saligny almost exclusively concerned French claims he was to press as French Commissioner. Saligny was granted a complete discretion:

There isn't anything more to discuss with the Mexican Government. It must accept purely and simply the amount at which we should evaluate the sum of our claims. I don't have the necessary means to determine it. But it isn't the same for the Legation (in Mexico), which has the facts concerning all the claims submitted by our nationals under one heading or another; therefore I am leaving the decision up to you to set the total indemnity which would seem to be enough to satisfy all our legitimate claims. It will constitute, with those of the English and Spanish Commissioners, the ultimatum that the Mexican Government will be sent to accept after occupation of the coastal forts, peacefully or by force. It is always probable that you won't be able to put yourself in accord with your colleagues, without being mutually informed of the justice of your demands. I don't want to decide in advance whether a certain sum ought to be added under the title of war indemnity for the Three Powers, but I leave the question to your examination.

Thouvenel concluded his instruction by stating that he was leaving it to Admiral Jurien de La Gravière to inform Saligny of the "views" of the French Government with respect to the allied intervention.[65]

Before he left for Mexico, Jurien saw Napoleon III,[66] who provided him with secret instructions that took account of the possibility that a considerable monarchist movement in favor of Maximilian might not materialize in Mexico. The instructions show that Napoleon III knew that monarchists were probably not in the majority in Mexico. A general election, therefore, was out of the question. On 15 November Prince Metternich, having resumed his duties as Austrian Ambassador to Paris after a leave of absence, visited Napoleon at Compiègne. In order to prepare the Austrian Government not to expect a plebiscite in Mexico, the Emperor related part of his secret instructions to Jurien. The Emperor's remarks were then reported by Metternich to his Government:

Either the Mexicans will immediately acclaim the Prince who will be named for them at the right time, or they will try to perpetuate the state of anarchy we wish to stop. In the first case, everything is settled, but we must reflect on the second possibility. Above all, what is to be avoided is that the Archduke's name is mentioned before the right time. This precaution must be taken, because a powerful dynasty is not acting *on its own account or alone.* In order to safeguard its dignity, it should only have to *answer yes or no* to a proposal made on behalf of those who have influence *(de ceux qui agissent et du peuple qui décide).*

.         .         .         .         .         .         .         .

The instructions that the Emperor has given to the French Admiral Jurien de la Gravière . . . are to assemble his forces at Havana and then proceed to Vera Cruz. It seems settled that the English will occupy this seaport and that six to seven thousand French and Spanish troops will go to Mexico City. It is anticipated that the monarchical party will rise immediately and co-operate with the commanders of these troops. What is especially noteworthy is that the Emperor does not want to carry out his plans by means of a general vote. He told me that *such an election could never be acceptable to an Austrian Archduke.* The Admiral has secret instructions to induce the monarchical party *to summon a sort of Constituent Assembly,* representing all the Mexican provinces, but not elected by them, and to have it express its wishes to the Allied Powers.[67]

Napoleon gave Metternich assurances similar to those the Austrian Chargé d'Affaires had received from Walewski. The British Government had been "extremely suspicious" at first. The private letter to Flahault, however, changed everything. Palmerston and his cabinet now "unresevedly" supported French plans. Palmerston had not made a written reply, but he "intimated his approval" by "adopting" the Emperor's ideas.[68] The whole affair was being managed secretly to spare British susceptibilities.[69] Napoleon tried to give Metternich assurances to "put the question on a footing agreeable to Austria."[70] All "inopportune connection" of the Austrian Government with French plans would be avoided. All that was expected was that "Austria accept, for one of its Princes, the rule of a great country that must be saved from anarchy."[71]

Napoleon implied, without promising, that he expected no return favor. Metternich reported :

> The Emperor is very anxious to convince us that to France the Mexican affair is first and foremost a question of trade and commerce, and he has the tact to utter no word which might suggest that his efforts are deserving of our gratitude.

He realized, Napoleon told Metternich, what a "sacrifice" Maximilian would make by going to Mexico.[72]

Napoleon's secret directions, perhaps only verbal, to Jurien were intended to cover possibilities not foreseen by Thouvenel's instructions to Saligny and Jurien. By following these instructions, the French representatives might be stymied. If the Juarez Government accepted Saligny's ultimatum, as well as Spanish and British terms, the main "legal" foundation of the expedition would no longer exist. Jurien might not encounter numerous Mexican royalists, even if he went all the way to Mexico City. In such an eventuality, Thouvenel's confidential instructions informed Jurien that he was to stay within the strict limits of the Convention of London and only obtain legitimate redress.

A mixed commission, consisting of Mexicans and representatives of claimants, was the normal device used to investigate the justice of claims against Mexico and to set the amount of compensation.[73] According to Thouvenel's instructions, Saligny would assume all these functions himself and arrive at a total indemnity for all French claims. It would be stated in the ultimatum presented to the Juarez Government at the same time that the British and Spanish demands were forwarded. Although Saligny was instructed to make arbitrary decisions that could hardly be approved by the Mexican Government, it might submit to them when supported by force. Napoleon anticipated this possibility and hoped to forestall it with secret instructions, perhaps only made known to Jurien at the time,[74] that Saligny would make his demands so "excessive" that the Mexican Government would refuse to accept them.[75]

Following the instructions, that Napoleon made known to Metternich, Jurien was relieved of the necessity of deciding whether, as Thouvenel put it, the monarchist party had "nearly certain chances of success." Jurien would merely suggest to the monarchists who *did* approach him that they should assemble "influential" monarchists from all the Mexican provinces. This apparently would be the "right time" to mention Maximilian and have the notables declare in favor of him. There still remained the possibility that monarchists would not spontaneously present themselves to Jurien. They might be afraid to approach a foreign invader, whose intentions were unknown to them. To assure that Jurien *would* be contacted by Mexican royalists, Napoleon III decided to send one of the Mexican exiles to Mexico as a confidential agent to inform the Mexican monarchists there of Maximilian's candidacy.[76] The last ship of the French expedition, however, left Toulon on 29 November[77] before Napoleon could make the final arrangements for sending such a propaganda agent.[78]

The means by which Napoleon III hoped to make Maximilian ruler of Mexico and obtain Spanish, British, and Austrian approval were based on a series of assumptions. Coal was purchased in various ports and provision made to send it to Havana to refuel the French ships after crossing the Atlantic Ocean.[79] No means of transport, however, were provided for the march of the French troops to Mexico City[80] Napoleon assumed the necessary tents, carts, horses, and mules would be supplied by the Spanish expeditionary force. The Spanish Government had agreed to grant its Commander-in-Chief discretionary powers to extend operations in Mexico. Napoleon, therefore, believed that, with its supplies in Cuba "so near" Mexico, the Spanish fleet would leave Havana with transportational facilities necessary for land operations beyond Vera Cruz.[81] After taking on coal at Havana, the French ships would set out for Vera Cruz in company with the Spanish fleet. Underway a rendezvous would be effected with the British Admiral off Cape St. Antonio. Vera Cruz would be occupied.

Saligny would then set an arbitrary and "excessive" total of monetary compensation for French claims. The British and Spanish Commissioners might demand being informed of the justice of Saligny's demands. It was assumed that Saligny would be able to make plausable explanations. The inflated French demands, which Napoleon expected would be rejected by the Mexican Government, would be sent to Juarez' Government as well as the British and Spanish terms. Saligny's ultimatum was also intended as a means to overthrow the Juarez Government. Such a "firm demand," Napoleon believed, would :

> . . . have opened the eyes of the people to the misdoings of their chiefs and then there might have been a hope that the better thinking among them would have resolved on effecting a reform.[82]

The ultimatum despatched, Napoleon expected that Jurien would convince his British and Spanish colleagues that a march toward Mexico City was necessary. The instructions of the Spanish Commander would permit him to take such a step. The instructions of the British Admiral might deny him the authority to order his Marines to accompany the French and Spanish forces. Jurien was then to justify the extension of French and Spanish operations on the pretext that foreigners were threatened in the interior of Mexico. This "interpretation" of the Convention of London would be justified by the paragraph in Article I concerning such "on the spot" decisions. The British Admiral would then hold Vera Cruz to protect the base of supplies for the advancing Spanish and French troops. Such an advance might even be made simultaneously with sending the ultimatums to Juarez.[83] To sooth Mexican "susceptibilities," the French would lead the column, if possible. A proclamation would be issued that the allies intended no conquest or any interference in the selection by the Mexicans of their government. Somewhere beyond the unhealthy coastal lowlands, the Spanish and French forces would halt "to see the effect produced on the Mexican people."[84] It was expected that the Mexican monarchists would approach the French and Spanish Commanders-in-Chief, go to Mexico City with them, assemble notables from the Mexican provinces, and proclaim Maximilian ruler of Mexico. Jurien was given $10,000 to cover "special cases" that might arise during his mission.[85] Should any difficulties arise, they would be solved by the propaganda agent Napoleon intended to send to Mexico.

That six or seven thousand European troops were not enough to make a march to Mexico City was the opinion of Mexican, Spanish, and French military authorities. General Santa Anna, living in exile in St. Thomas in the Virgin Islands, had been the Chief Executive of six Mexican Governments. He had over thirty years of experience fomenting revolutions and fighting both Europeans and Americans.[86] When he learned that eight thousand Europeans had landed in Vera Cruz and that a march to Mexico City was intended, Santa Anna wrote Estrada a confidential letter. According to Santa Anna, twenty-five to thirty thousand troops were needed. After garrisoning Vera Cruz, Jalappa, Puebla and other Mexican cities, the allies, however, would only have three to four thousand troops with which to capture Mexico City.[87] General Serrano, the Captain-General of Cuba, believed that a "smaller force than from 20,000 to 25,000 men ought not . . . to march a single pace into the interior of the Republic." Although Mexico did not "possess an organized army properly so-called, the inhabitants entertain a profound aversion to the Spaniards." Serrano drew the conclusion that Mexican "hatred" and "despair" might "lead to disastrous and terrible results."[88] Although the opinions of Santa Anna and Serrano were not known to Napoleon III in 1861,[89] his aide-de-camp, General Fleury, tried to impress the Emperor with military problems that might arise. Napoleon replied with arguments furnished, Fleury believed, by Hidalgo and Almonte via Eugenie.[90]

In September 1861 Hidalgo had told Napoleon and Eugenie

that Mexicans would " rise as one man" in favor of a European intervention and Maximilian.[91] At the end of October Hidalgo and Almonte, who went to Mexico in 1862 as Napoleon's agent,[92] were as enthusiastic as ever.[93] The news from Mexico was also encouraging. In a report from Saligny that arrived in Paris on 30 October, the French Minister to Mexico claimed he saw "less and less" that could stop a "corps of 4,000–5,000 European soldiers from marching right to Mexico City without encountering any resistance." Someone who read this report thought this opinion so important that he made pencil lines in the margin alongside this comment.[94] At the beginning of November, however, Hidalgo started having doubts. When he learned that the Spanish Commander-in-Chief would be General Juan Prim, the Mexican exile went to Compiègne to see Napoleon and Eugenie. Hidalgo gave his opinion that Prim was a man "bent upon cutting a great figure anywhere, whether at home or abroad." It would be believed in Mexico that a Spanish conquest was contemplated. Consequently Hidalgo urged sending a few more French "red trousers"[95] and preventing Prim's appointment. Napoleon replied that he had no influence to prevent Prim from going to Mexico. At first Napoleon refused to send more than two thousand troops[96] in order not to arouse Brritish "suspicions."[97] When Eugenie supported Hidalgo's suggestions[98] and Jurien asked that some Zouaves be sent to increase morale, Napoleon gave permission to Jurien to pick up five hundred Zouaves at Algiers.[99]

Should a "Constituent Assembly" in Mexico City proclaim Maximilian ruler of Mexico, Napoleon II would then have to obtain a "yes" from the Austrian Government and somehow win the approval of the British and Spanish Governments. Preparations for the final implementation of Napoleon's schemes were haphazard and tentative. The Austrian Government had stated that the preliminary conditions for Maximilian's candidacy were a "clearly expressed invitation" from the "people of Mexico" and the "active" support of Great

Britain and France.[100] To prepare the Austrian Government
not to expect a general election in Mexico, Napoleon told
Metternich that an assembly of notables was more dignified.
A copy of Napoleon's private letter to Flahault was sent to the
Austrian Government so that it would know that its demands
had been made known to the British Government. Metternich
and Muelinen were told that the British Government gave its
"tacit" approval.

The "Parliamentary considerations" argument was used to
persuade the Spanish Government that the British Government
would not object to a march to Mexico City. The Spanish
Government had often stated, during the negotiation of the
Convention of London, that it desired to see a "stable government" replace that of Juarez. The French and Spanish
Governments, therefore, agreed that the Liberal Government
in Mexico should be upset. Spain probably would not be a
"warm partisan" of Maximilian's Kingdom. This difficulty
had been anticipated by Thouvenel even before signing the
Convention of London. He made assurances that no *French*
Prince would be permitted to be a candidate for a throne in
Mexico so that there would be no rivalry among the European
allies. The Spanish Government, however, would not make a
similar disavowal. Whether it would accept the decision of the
Mexican notables was problematical. If Great Britain accepted
the *fait accompli*, the Spanish troops could return to Cuba
after having assisted in Napoleon's monarchy project. The
approval of the Spanish Government, in the last resort, was not
necessary to obtain an Austrian "yes."

To a certain extent there was reason for Napoleon to believe
that Palmerston and Russell secretly approved French plans
outlined in the private letter Flahault had shown them. As he
had already made known to Napoleon early in 1861,[101] Palmerston said he had no objections to Maximilian as ruler of
Mexico, should he be chosen by the Mexican people.[102] Both
Russell and Palmerston told Flahault that they could not give
any material aid to assist in the implementation of a project

they considered impractical and, at any rate, could not be defended in Parliament.[103] Since Russell and Palmerston did not tell Flahault all their objections,[104] his report of what they did tell him could be interpreted as containing all the British objections.[105] Napoleon had made preparations to meet the anticipated difficulties connected with his plan. If the operations of the French and Spanish troops in Mexico resulted in Maximilian's becoming King, the British Government had to grant his regime *de facto* recognition. This was the least that the Austrian Government probably would require to fulfill its condition that Great Britain "actively" support Maximilian. How Napoleon would convince the British Government that the notables represented the Mexican people was left for the future. In the opinion of Baron Beyens, the Belgian Ambassador to Paris who knew many of the secrets of the Second Empire, the Liberals would not have a chance to make their desires known :

> It is true that the convention which is about to be concluded at London will contain a nonintervention clause . . . without which the British cabinet had not wanted to sign. But in giving in to this demand, France only gives in to appearances. . . . In effect, the seizure of the custom houses of Vera Cruz and Tampico will entail, of necessity, the fall of the present government. The Powers, not finding anyone with whom to negotiate any more, will be led by the situation to give supremacy to the party having persons with whom they will consent to negotiate. Thus they will indirectly dominate the movement which will be directed in a monarchical sense.[106]

Napoleon and Thouvenel did not leave everything to chance and the future. In addition to the Emperor's private letter to be shown to Russell and Palmerston, other steps were taken to bring pressure on the British Government and to prepare it for the expected sequence of events. A letter similar to the one written to Flahault was sent by Napoleon to Leopold I of Belgium, Maximilian's father-in-law.[107] Leopold's reply was non-commital about what he would do, but he stated he shared

Napoleon's views about Mexico.[108] As anticipated by Napoleon, however, Leopold did write Queen Victoria:

> I had a rather kind letter from the Emperor Napoleon about the state of Mexico. I fear he will find his wishes to see there a stable Government not much liked in England, though his plans are *not* for any advantage France is to derive from it.[109]

At the end of October Thouvenel had a conversation with a British Under-Secretary of State who happened to be visiting Lord Cowley.[110] Even then Thouvenel spoke of the possible necessity of a march towards Mexico City and granting "moral support" to Mexican conservatives. The reasons with which Thouvenel hoped to win British support of these measures were to gain redress of grievances, protect foreigners, and prevent American aggression against Mexico. In a private letter Layard reported the conversation to Lord Russell:

> In speaking of Mexico, he (i.e., Thouvenel) said that he had received the most earnest representations from French Merchants and Mexicans both in Mexico and here, against a mere occupation of the ports. Such a measure, they urged, would lead to no other result than the ill treatment of foreigners, and perhaps even their massacre, that no opposition would be made by the Mexican Government to the seizing of imports, and that if the allies raised the Custom Duties, they would only be raised a second time in the interior. Thouvenel observed that he agreed very much in these views and felt convinced, that we should only succeed in bringing about some definite settlement by marching six or seven thousand men inland, that there we should give encouragement and moral support to a party strong enough to restore order and to establish a permanent government—which party could do this, under any circumstances, he could not, he said, tell me. The Mexicans at Paris assured him that there was a considerable Monarchical party, but he had not sufficient information to allow him to form a decided opinion upon the subject. He says that the allied troops could establish themselves at Tapic or Tepeine, a position in the highlands about half way between Mexico (City) and Vera Cruz, which affords healthy

quarters for Europeans, and is at the same time, sufficiently near the capital to afford moral support to this party of order to which he alludes.

.       .       .       .       .       .       .       .

He said he felt convinced, and the Emperor shared his conviction, that unless we were prepared to give our moral support in aid of the formulation of a strong government in Mexico— of whatever form that government might be—that country would very shortly be annexed by the United States, if the union were restored, or by the North or the South if they were divided, and that this annexation of so large a territory would neither suit England or France.[111]

Thouvenel's observations to Layard were made in the course of a private conversation. The first important official French trial balloon after the signature of the Convention of London was made on 11 November. Then Thouvenel sent Flahault the "official" instructions to Jurien.[112]

While Lord Russell was waiting for Thouvenel to send him a copy of Jurien's instructions, the Spanish Ambassador to London received a telegram from Collantes proposing that the Spanish Commander-in-Chief be given command of all the allied forces.[113] Since Russell was in the country,[114] Isturitz communicated the Spanish proposal to Hammond, the British Under-Secretary of State.[115] He immediately informed Lord Palmerston, who wrote his Foreign Secretary a private letter that the suggestion "must be absolutely refused." The Spanish Commander "might order our Marines to march to the City of Mexico . . . or send them in some unhealthy place where he would not like his Spaniards to be." The official answer was to be the "general objection" that "we never allow any British force . . . to be placed under the command of any foreign officer."[116] At the same time it was expected that the French Government would also refuse the Spanish proposal. Hammond wrote Cowley to ask whether a similar proposal had been made by the Spanish Ambassador to Paris. Hammond added that he ". . . should like to see the Emperor's face on receiving it."[117] On 12 November, after receiving another telegram that

Prim had been named the Spanish Commander-in-Chief,[118] Isturitz saw Russell. He approved Prim's appointment but said that the question of separate commands had already been decided.[119]

Flahault saw Russell on 13 November and showed him Jurien's "official" instructions. The French Ambassador was surprized to find the Foreign Secretary not as opposed as expected to the reference of a march to Mexico City. Russell was still "preoccupied" with the Spanish proposal and told Flahault that the British Government would not place its forces under the command of a Spaniard. When Russell asked for a copy of Jurien's instructions to study them more carefully, Flahault refused,[120] because Thouvenel had not specifically directed that this was intended.[121] On 15 November, when ratifications of the Tripartite Convention were exchanged in London,[122] Flahault had received telegraphic permission from Thouvenel to give Russell a copy of Jurien's instructions.[123] A reading of these "official" instructions led Russell to draft additional instructions for Sir Charles Wyke on 15 November. Enclosing Jurien's instructions, Russell commented that the "French Government have contemplated a case of which I had not taken notice." It was that a march to Mexico City would be necessary if the Mexican Government refused to "enter into any agreement or negotiation whatever." Russell had "nothing to say against this reasoning or the measures in contemplation." The seven hundred British Marines, however, were not to take part in a march toward Mexico City. They were too small an amount and, technically, not "land forces." Although Wyke should decline to cooperate in extended operations, it was "essential that uniformity should be preserved in the demands to be made upon the 'de facto' authorities of Mexico." Concerning other "hypothetical cases," including the erection of interior custom houses that Thouvenel had mentioned to Layard, the British Government had "reliance" on Admiral Milne and Wyke's judgement:

I do not think it necessary to give you more detailed information. It may or may not be expedient to occupy Tampico. It may or may not be expedient to institute a Blockade of some part of the Mexican Coast. It may be found necessary to prevent by stipulation or even by force the establishment of Mexican Custom Houses between the coast and the upper country of Mexico. It may be advisable to send detachments to particular points where the lives of Europeans are threatened, when it can be done without weakening the main body of the allied forces. Upon these and similar points Her Majesty's Government have entire reliance upon your judgement and discretion. They would be unwilling to fetter that discretion by minute directions upon hypothetical cases. They would prefer in regard to operations of much difficulty, where concert is necessary and the aspect of affairs may vary from day to day, to leave you to the guidance of your Judgement, enlightened as that judgement will be by local information and experience. Her Majesty's Government are confident that Sir A. Milne and yourself will be in the performance of your present arduous duties be guided by that zeal for the public service and by that judgement and discrimination of which you have both given satisfactory proof.[124]

An instruction, almost word for word the same as the one for Wyke, was also sent to the Admiralty on 15 November.[125] On 14 November the First Lord of the Admiralty wrote Russell a private letter suggesting he alter the instructions that Admiral Maitland seize a port on the Pacific coast of Mexico. The Duke of Somerset commented that it was not clear what Maitland was to do then: "Is he to appoint some person to collect customs and to retain the proceeds to be divided between the allied powers?" Furthermore, it might not be necessary for Maitland to seize any port at all if the Mexican Government acceded to the demands of the allies. Somerset suggested instructing Maitland to "hold himself in readiness" to seize Mexican Pacific ports. He could do this when so instructed by Sir Charles Wyke, who "should then acquaint him with the further steps to be taken when he has possession of the ports in the Pacific."[126] Russell took this advice and sent appropriate instructions to the Admiralty on 15 November.[127]

A copy was enclosed in an instruction drawn up for Wyke the same day. He was directed to send orders to Maitland, approved by Wyke's French and Spanish colleagues, if the Mexican Government did not oppose the occupation of Vera Cruz, declined to "enter into any Convention" and directed its "exports to the ports on the Pacific." [128]

It was typical of Lord Palmerston to make foreign policy decisions without informing the cabinet. [129] On 7 October, after an offer had been made to sign a convention with the Spanish and French Governments, Lord Palmerston suggested to his Foreign Secretary that a "cabinet" should be held "before the Convention is signed." [130] Even then the Prime Minister only made this decision, because the First Lord of the Admiralty suggested it. [131] He had learned of the intended expedition from the letters of the Foreign Office to the Admiralty requesting military information. When a cabinet meeting was called shortly before the Convention of London was signed, the Secretary of State for War commented in a private letter that "it might as well not have been called." Sir George Lewis explained :

> Nominally, we were summoned in order to decide upon the Mexican question; but practically the question was already decided, for proposals had been made to the French and Spanish govts., by which we were bound, and which engaged us. . . . [132]

The initial instructions to Wyke and the Admiralty of 31 October and 1 November were approved by Palmerston and Queen Victoria without reference to the cabinet. [133] The fact that all Russell's instructions of 15 November were laid before the British Cabinet [134] gives special emphasis to the concern that Jurien's instructions caused Palmerston and Russell.

The British Foreign Office received a long statistical study from the "London Bondholders" [135] concerning their claims on 26 November. [136] The next day a report from Wyke arrived. It summarized his unofficial negotiations [137] with the Mexican

Government in October for the settlement of British claims.[138]
All this information about British claims, and the complications
involved, suggested to Russell that it was essential that his
French and Spanish allies only demand legitimate redress from
Mexico. He had never asked what claims the French and
Spanish Governments would support. When he drew up
instructions for Wyke on 28 November, Russell admitted he
could not give "detailed instructions" concerning British
claims. Wyke would have a "difficult task to perform." He
should state in writing to his French and Spanish colleagues:

First—The written engagements and Conventions with
Mexico to which the British Government has been a party.
Secondly—The several injuries inflicted on British Subjects
for which redress has not only not been given but has been
deliberately refused, or studiously evaded.
Thirdly—The Robbery by Miramon and his Ministers,
Colleagues, and officers of 660,000 Dollars from the House of
the British Legation at Mexico (City).

"In discussing and condoning the claims of France and Spain,"
Wyke was to act "in a conciliatory spirit." Yet he should be
careful that the joint demands sent the "de facto" government
rested on "firm grounds of justice."[139] Such an investigation
might take a long time. The deadline for the stay of the
British Marines in Vera Cruz was April 1862. The Secretary
of War informed Russell that "with the existing force of black
troops, a black regiment could not be spared" to replace the
Marines in Vera Cruz in April, when the unhealthy season was
expected to begin.[140] Consequently Russell decided to save time
by persuading the French and Spanish Governments to state
their claims in advance. On 28 November he summarized
Wyke's negotiations of October in an instruction to the British
Ambassador to Madrid. Crampton was directed to inform the
Spanish Government that the terms already obtained by Wyke
generally fulfilled the requirements of the British Government.
There was no security that these terms would be carried out

by the Mexican Government, but the clearness with which British claims were formulated would facilitate drawing up the British demands to be supported by the allied expedition. The time of negotiation with the Mexican Government would be shortened if the Spanish Government would formulate its demands in as precise a manner.[141] A similar instruction was sent to Lord Cowley on 2 December.[142] The answer from Paris came first. Thouvenel told Cowley that the information was lacking "to form an opinion." Most of the French claims were "provided for by the convention which the Mexican Government had set aside."[143] As to other claims, Thouvenel had to "leave it to the discretion of the Commissioners to examine into and settle their amount."[144] Crampton's report, which arrived in London on 22 December, was more satisfactory. Collantes had said that nothing could be easier than to state with precision the terms which Spain would require of the Mexican Government. These terms were fulfillment of conventions and reparation for personal injuries, together with "punishment upon the perpetrators." The "readiest way" of coming to an understanding proposed by the British Government, Collantes suggested, was that :

> . . . the Commissioners of Spain and England should be instructed by their respective Governments to communicate to each other the terms which each would think it necessary to insist upon in satisfaction for past wrongs, and as security for the future observance of international duties by Mexico.[145]

A few days after receiving this despatch, Russell enclosed it in an instruction to Wyke. He was ordered to follow Collantes' suggestion and to communicate a "summary" to the French Commissioners.[146]

When he learned that an expedition would be sent to Mexico, General Juan Prim asked the Spanish Government to appoint him as its Commander-in-Chief.[147] Although he was one of the leaders of a political group in the Spanish coalition government,[148] Prim had no important political post.[149] He had an excellent military reputation[150] and was looking for an opportunity to increase it.[151] In order to avoid a conflict of authority between Spanish military and diplomatic representatives,[152] the Spanish Government named Prim Commander-in-Chief[153] and Plenipotentiary to settle Spanish claims against Mexico.[154]

The causes for sending a Spanish expedition to Mexico, Prim's "official" instructions[155] stated, were Mexican failure to comply with "solemn" conventions and "continual violences committed against Spanish subjects." The Spanish Government only issued orders to prepare an expedition after it had offered to cooperate with France and Great Britain when it seemed they would act without Spain.[156] To gloss over this, Collantes observed that the Spanish Government, from "time to time," wanted "to send a fleet from Havana with debarkation troops to guarantee our claims." Since France and Great Britain found themselves in the "same situation" and had the "same claims," it was "thought necessary to combine the action of the three powers." The Convention of London provided for this common action. Prim's attention was called to the disclaimers of the allies contained in an enclosed copy of the convention :

. . . Spain, France, and England renounce any acquisition of territory to prove their disinterestedness and that they obligate themselves not to interfere in the internal affairs of Mexico, in which the Mexicans will retain a complete liberty of choosing the form of government which is best suited for them. The three powers are content to combine their efforts for the only end of guaranteeing to their respective subjects an indispensable protection against the arbitrary acts of the Mexican authorities by obliging them to respect the international engagements contracted by their government.

Prim's first duty would be to cooperate with the British and French Commanders to occupy Mexican coastal positions. There probably would not be any Mexican resistance. The Spanish Government had information that Juarez intended to demilitarize Vera Cruz and its forts. The intention, "without doubt," was to "carry the theatre of the campaign into the interior of the country." Then extended operations would be necessary, but provision for this "slight delay" had been made. The allied forces were "sufficient . . . to bring the expedition to a satisfactory end no matter where the operations must be conducted." The Mexicans might refuse to fight. The Mexican Government might intend :

> . . . only opposing by passive resistance the action of the three powers and . . . leave to the climate and all the inconveniences tied up with distant expeditions the time required to decimate the troops and to put off indefinitely the solution of the question.

Then the allied forces would have to go to Mexico City to force the Mexican Government to recognize the "justice of the demands presented by the three governments." In this connection, as in all eventualities, Prim was to act in "perfect harmony" with the British and French Commanders. Another cause for extended operations might be the "renewal of excesses that has made Mexican soil bloody" and had been directed against foreigners. Article I of the Convention of London provided for the protection of the subjects of the allies if their security were threatened. Then the "allied commanders would have the duty and would find themselves in the necessity to go to their aid and to defend them against the exaltation of popular passions." After enumerating these possible difficulties, Collantes admitted that it "would not be impossible that the Mexican Government . . . should accede to the just claims of the allies." As the Spanish Plenipotentiary, Prim would have to draw up the terms that Collantes considered the "*sina qua non* of the treaty of peace." The first condition contained in the outline of Spanish demands that Collantes made for Prim was a "public and solemn satisfaction" for the expulsion of Pacheco, the last Spanish diplomatic representative to Mexico. This demand was primarily connected with Spanish domestic politics. Collantes believed that Pacheco's misfortunes were the results of his own mistakes.[157] Collantes had dismised Pacheco instead of accepting his resignation, accompanied with a condemnation of the apathy of Spain's Mexican policies.[158] The opposition press took up Pacheco's cause,[159] and it was correctly expected that he would attack the Spanish Government in the Cortes.[160] Three specific personal and property claims were to be included in Prim's ultimatum as a "special condition for the honor and interest of Spain."[161] Other claims were left to Prim to formulate after reading the "justificatory documents" presented by Spanish claimants. In every case he was directed to demand punishment of the Mexican culprits. In addition to recognizing the validity of personal and property claims that Prim might consider just, the Juarez Government was expected to put into operation a convention concluded in 1859 by Spain with Miramon's Government, at that time the rival of Juarez during the Mexican Civil War.[162] This convention recognized not only certain Spanish claims, but also similar previous conventions concluded but in a state of suspension in 1859. Arrears of payments to recognized claimants had accumulated, and Juarez' refusal to consider himself bound by the terms of the 1859 convention had added to the confusion[163] Prim was directed to calculate the arrears of interest payments guaranteed by all these conventions to Spanish claimants and to demand payment in full. Collantes admitted Prim's task would not be easy and estimated that the sum might be as high as $500,000.[164] Should the Mexican Government accept Prim's ultimatum, as well as those of his French and British colleagues, the next problem would be a distribution of Mexican custom duties among the allies. This Collantes left to the Allied Commission, in which Prim would represent Spanish interests. This same Commission would also decide how to distribute funds received directly from the Mexican Government or appropriated from Mexican custom houses with or without Mexican consent. Having instructed Prim about the military and diplomatic aspects of the Spanish expedition, Collantes then outlined Prim's "political" mission. Although the allies did not "want" to interfere in Mexican internal affairs and intended to remain "aloof" from the "party strife" in Mexico, they could not "hide the sincere and ardent desire to see an end to this bloody struggle without truce." Anarchy in Mexico would only cease with the establishment of :

> . . . an enlightened and strong power, animated with the firm desire to reestablish and maintain internal order with sufficient means to organize the Administration, protect foreign subjects and offer guarantees of good faith for the observation of treaties in order not to oblige the governments that sign conventions with Mexico to have recourse to censorious and always disagreeable measures for their accomplishment.

By "sympathies of race, by reason of politics, and by reason of reciprocal congruity" Spain had special reasons to see a "strong durable" government established in Mexico. To assist in bringing about such a change, Prim should only use an "influence purely moral." To put special emphasis on the seriousness and sincerity of this order, Collantes added that the Queen of Spain herself had made such a statement before the Cortes. Just what Prim was to do was vague if considered literally. He should "accord the greatest consideration to the influencial persons of the country and to those who are trying to establish a government in harmony with national interests." He was also "to judge with the greatest impartiality the political phases that could develop during" his "stay in Mexico."[165]

The central idea of Prim's instructions was the desirability of encouraging the conservatives in Mexico to overthrow the Juarez Government. In 1859 it had negotiated treaties with the United States that, O'Donnell and Collantes had feared, would bring the conquests of Cortez under the American sphere of influence and serve as a barrier to trade between Spain and Mexico.[166] Juarez refused to settle Spanish claims.[167] The inconclusive negotiations with the Juarez Government in the summer of 1861[168] were just another proof for Collantes of the bad faith of Juarez.[169] Even if Juarez wanted to act in good faith, Collantes reasoned, the Mexican President did not have the financial resources to pay Spanish claimants.[171] Both Collantes[171] and O'Donnell[172] hoped that the arrival of the allied expeditionary forces in Mexico and the presentation of the claims of the allies would lead to a political crisis which would end after a revolution started by the "party of order." The Juarez Government, Collantes and O'Donnell expected, would be replaced by a government of Mexican conservatives.

The overthrow of the Juarez regime and the expected better chances of a settlement of Spanish claims would have direct connections with Spanish internal affairs. The opposition, of conservatives and reactionaries, to O'Donnell's Liberal Union would be deprived of the Mexican question as a political issue. Charges of "apathy" in the opposition press[173] would cease. The expected storm of protest in the Cortes[174] could be countered. The fall of the Juarez Government would be hailed with enthusiasm in many political circles in Spain. For Spanish reactionaries the Mexican Liberal Party of Juarez was "red" and "anti-Spanish."[175] In a Spain ruled by a monarchy and where only Catholics were permitted the right of public worship,[176] the Indian republican of Mexico, who nationalised church property and permitted religious toleration, was intensely hated by many Spaniards. All injuries suffered by Spanish subjects in Mexico were sometimes unjustly blamed on Juarez. He was "the Assassin of Spaniards, the personification or reckless spoliation and revenge and of all the atrocities which had ever been committed against Spain in the New World."[177] Although the Spanish reactionaries and right-wing conservatives were not in power, they were represented by courtiers who counselled Queen Isabella II.[178] Carl Schurz, the American Minister to Madrid, was convinced that there was an intrigue to make Don Sebastian, the Queen's uncle, ruler of Mexico.[179] Baron Beyens, the Belgian Ambassador to Paris, believed that "the court of Madrid" had "a secret desire to favor the pretensions of a Prince of the House of Bourbon."[180]

Although it has sometimes been claimed that the Spanish Government intended to utilize the tripartite intervention in Mexico to establish a Spanish Bourbon on a Mexican throne, those who have made this charge have not given any conclusive documentary evidence to substantiate their assertions.[181] It is true, however, that Collantes believed, at the beginning of the negotiations leading to the signing of the Convention of London, that more was intended by a tripartite intervention in Mexico than just obtaining promises from Juarez to pay debts owed the European Powers.[182] Such promises, Collantes believed, could have been obtained by the mere sending of an "energetic note" to Juarez.[183] Russell was suspicious when the Spanish Government proposed allowing Mexicans an opportunity to form a "stable government," and the British Secretary of Foreign Affairs made it clear that only "moral support" could be given to such a political change in Mexico.[184] Since the French Government seemed to favor a political change, the Spanish Government proposed to agree in advance on the form of government to be established in Mexico.[185] This proposal was rejected by Thouvenel,[186] because he could not expect the British and Spanish Governments to approve Maximilian's candidacy. The Spanish proposal, rejected in October 1861 by Thouvenel, was intended to form the basis of an agreement for the ousting of the Juarez Government. It is not clear, however, whether the Spanish Government expected a Mexican conservative government to invite a Spanish Bourbon to rule in Mexico. When the French Government dropped hints about Maximilian[187] and suggested that each of the European allies renounce members of their royal families as candidates for a Mexican throne,[188] the Spanish Government feared that it would be used as a "tool" to implement French plans for Maximilian.[189] No renunciation of the candidacy of a Spanish Bourbon was made. Instead, as a counter to the candidacy of Maximilian, the Spanish Government made it known that, if its French and British allies put forward a candidate, Spain reserved the right also to put forward a candidate.[190] To avoid difficulties with the French Government, O'Donnell and Collantes made a pretense of believing that Maximilian's candidacy was not supported by Napoleon III.[191]

O'Donnell was disappointed that the British Government intended to limit operations to the Mexican coast.[192] In that way Mexican conservatives would be afforded inadequate encouragement. O'Donnell considered it a diplomatic victory, therefore, that France and Spain had "led England to insert the clause (i.e., in the Convention of London) that the allied powers would take all measures they had in view."[193] Prim's instructions, consequently, authorised operations in the interior of Mexico,[194] an authorization requested by Thouvenel.[195]

Before Prim left for Mexico, he was given confidential instructions by O'Donnell. It is possible to reconstruct the general outlines of these verbal instructions, if not their exact details. Maximilian's candidacy was discussed. O'Donnell "spoke" to Prim on the subject and gave him the "necessary" instructions.[196] Almost certainly Prim was then, as later,[197] directed not to support the project. Prim probably was also instructed to encourage Mexican conservatives to upset the Juarez Government.[198] Even before he left Spain, Prim decided neither to aid in the establishment of Maximilian in Mexico, nor to assist the Mexican conservatives. As a progressive, Prim professed a faith in constitutional monarchy, but he regarded the Mexican conservatives, upon whose assistance Mexican monarchy schemes had always depended,[199] as "reactionary."[200] The very month Prim was given command of the Spanish expedition to Mexico, Prim's wife's uncle became Juarez' Minister of Finance.[201] Although Prim later insisted that such ideological and family considerations had nothing to do with the policies he supported in Mexico,[202] he intended, from the beginning, to follow a policy opposed to the intentions of the Spanish Government. In November 1861 Prim told Carl Schurz, the American Minister to Madrid, that monarchy in

Mexico was an absurdity. He did not care, Prim said, what the Spanish Government might think. He would not work for the clerical party in Mexico, but for a free election. Juarez probably would win, and that would be that.[203] Prim's remarks to Schurz imply, but do not necessarily prove, that the Spanish Government intended to put forward the candidacy of a Spanish Bourbon. What Prim told Schurz, however, clearly implies that Prim probably was instructed to support the Mexican conservatives in more than a "moral" way. Any such instructions, if given, were worthless, because Prim did not intend to follow such a policy.

## 2. THE ARRIVAL OF THE EUROPEAN EXPEDITIONARY FORCES IN MEXICO: EUROPEAN AND AMERICAN REACTIONS

On 29 November 1861 the last ship of the French expeditionary forces left Toulon for Mexico.[1] The monarchy scheme now depended chiefly on Jurien. Thouvenel was confident that the Admiral had enough "prudence" not to "compromise anything." The French Minister of Foreign Affairs also stated in a private letter that he was "as happy as surprised at the facility with which Lord Russell has approved my instructions to Admiral Jurien." A certain skepticism about the existence of a royalist party, stressed in Jurien's "official" instructions, still remained. "If there really exists in Mexico a party that wishes to leave anarchy," Thouvenel wrote Flahault, "we now have all the means to help bring that about." That the British Marines would not be permitted to go inland[2] was no cause for alarm. The "principle" was that there be no opposition to the movement of French troops, and "today the most simple thing is to keep quiet and wait."[3] When Thouvenel received a copy of Prim's "official" instructions, they were sent to Jurien with the remark that they didn't differ "in their general spirit" from his own.[4] While crossing the Atlantic Ocean, Jurien considered

his instructions from Thouvenel and Napoleon III and decided
how best to carry them out with the small French forces being
sent to Mexico. Jurien personally did not expect a monarchist
uprising until he reached Mexico City:

> I don't put much stock in any sympathies that could be mani-
> fested in our favor until we are under the walls of Mexico
> City. This isn't a demonstration; it is rather a war that we
> are going to wage. I am preparing myself for it with the
> greatest confidence . . . .

He attached an "extreme importance," Jurien wrote Thouvenel, to "the organization of our little artillery." It was by
the "mobility and audacity" of the American artillery in 1847
that "the American army won all its battles." Jurien also had
faith in three other things: "the bravery of our soldiers, the
weakness of the Mexicans, and the correctness of the opinions
of the Government of the Emperor."[5]

The expedition to Mexico made no impression on the French
public at large in 1861 that could be detected by the *Procureurs
Généreaux,* Napoleon's administrative agents charged with
reporting on opinion in their districts.[6] Nor was the independent
press sharply critical. Although complications with the United
States and its Monroe Doctrine were sometimes foreseen,[7] it
was reassuring that the United States was invited to join the
intervention.[8] Generally it was assumed that the expedition
would lead to satisfaction for French claims[9] and the end of
violence against Frenchmen in Mexico.[10] Prévost-Paradol, a
liberal writing for the independent *Journal des Débats,* believed
the intended operations did not go far enough. A simple occupation of the coast would only cripple Mexican commerce and
endanger the safety of French subjects in Mexico. Prévost-
Paradol suggested a temporary occupation of Mexico as a
means to restore order and sane finances, both of which were
necessary for the economic development of Mexico and safe-
guarding French interests there.[11] Although an occasional
reference to Mexican affairs was made in November[12] and

December[13] French press interest in Mexican affairs subsided for lack of any determined opposition to the French Government and its failure to supply any news. The semi-official press, supplied with information by the French Government,[14] made almost no references to Mexican affairs.[15] At the beginning of October *Le Constitutionnel* featured the alleged assassination of Saligny[16] and printed the protest of the diplomatic corps in Mexico to the Government of Juarez.[17] In view of the generally favorable reaction of the independent press, the French Government, no doubt gratified, maintained general press silence in November and December. On 22 November the official *Moniteur* merely quoted an imperial decree promulgating the Convention of London.[18] As Thouvenel put it, it was best "to keep quiet and wait."

Before the signature of the Convention of London, the British Admiralty made preparations for an expedition to Mexico. Admiral Milne, the Commander of the American and West India Station, who had intended to winter his squadron at Halifax,[19] was ordered to send ships to Jamaica for operations in the Gulf of Mexico. A Marine officer who had made a plan of the fortifications of Vera Cruz was sent to Admiral Milne from England.[20] After the signature of the Tripartite Convention, Russell ordered the Admiralty to send a man-of-war to Vera Cruz to pick up Sir Charles Wyke and bring him to Milne's flagship[21] to receive the instructions that Russell had held up pending Thouvenel's comments on them.[22] It was expected that the French ships leaving Toulon would stop at Jamaica on the way to Havana.[23] Therefore Russell instructed the Admiralty to order Milne to assemble his ships at Port Royal, Jamaica. There Milne could arrange with the Commander of the French squadron, enroute to Havana, when the ships of the three allies should rendezvous off Cape St. Antonio to proceed in company to Vera Cruz.[24] All these arrangements were made. In the middle of November Captain Von Donop of the *Jason* left Halifax, proceeded to Nassau and Havana, took a man-of-war under his orders, and arrived off Sacrificios on 5 December.[25] He then sent a letter to Wyke in Mexico City,[26] and the British Minister to Mexico replied that he would be in Vera Cruz approximately 25 December.[27] Meanwhile Admiral Milne proceeded to Bermuda from Halifax.[28] He sent orders to the Senior Naval Officer in Port Royal to prepare the British ships there to rendezvous off Cape St. Antonio on 29 December.[29] After receiving a copy of Jurien's official instructions, Russell released his instructions for Wyke,[30] accompanied with full powers for him to negotiate as a plenipotentiary.[31] The Admiralty was directed to send these instructions to Admiral Milne, with orders that he give them to Sir Charles Wyke.[32] Russell also instructed the Admiralty to inform Milne that he was to allow Wyke's opinions to "prevail" should there be a difference about British claims.[33] At the same time Russell revised Admiral Maitland's instructions so that he should not undertake any operations on the Pacific coast of Mexico without orders from Wyke.[34] The Admiralty replied that a ship would be sent to Jamaica from Portsmouth on 20 November.[35] In a private letter to Russell, the First Lord of the Admiralty commented that he could not "send another vessel without adding to the risk of an excess on the sum voted by Parliament for the service of the Navy." He already had more men on active duty than the number voted by Parliament and "should be sorry to have to go to the House of Commons for a supplementary vote on account of Mexico."[36] With the departure of the *Phaeton* from Portsmouth, therefore, ended the preparations to initiate the British intervention in Mexico. Operations were considered safe enough, however, that Queen Victoria permitted Prince Alfred to go to Mexico to observe them.[37]

Lord Palmerston believed that "there are two Powers in this Country (i.e., England), the governmt and Public Opinion and that both must concur for any great and important steps."[38] The "public opinion" of the voters who elected the members of the House of Commons was particularly important. While only a few British subjects were enfranchised in 1861, they included in their numbers many of the bondholders and merchants who had vested interests in Mexico and who were vociferous in their demands that the British Government support them. In the summer of 1861 Russell had promised to support those claims of the London Bondholders that he con-considered justified by International Law, but he completely ignored their demands that Mexican public and nationalized church lands be given in payment.[39] When Russell received similar proposals at the beginning of September,[40] he replied to the bondholders that "Her Majesty's Government cannot undertake to support all the claims which the Bondholders may consider themselves justified in making."[41] When Liverpool and Manchester merchants trading with Mexico exerted pressure on their Chambers of Commerce, these organizations sent letters to Russell to ask him to protect British subjects and property in Mexico."[42] He replied that the matter was under "serious consideration."[43] Russell made similar replies[44] to letters from individual merchants,[45] bondholders,[46] and claimants.[47] With rumors in the financial circles of the "City" in London that Great Britain intended to seek redress from Mexico in cooperation with Spain and France,[48] these private letters to the British Foreign Office could be expected. The curt replies to them tend to indicate that they exerted little influence. It was a different matter, however, when one J. D. Powles, who had been engaged in Mexican mining operations, started circulating a petition[49] among British mercantile companies, bondholders, and creditors. By the end of September Powles had one hundred and forty-two signatures, for the most part representing British vested interests located in London, Liverpool, and Manchester.[50] Before the petition was presented to the Foreign Office,[51] the *Times* published it on 18 September and commented that twenty-three British subjects had been murdered in the last twelve months in Mexico, which owed Englishmen "upwards" of $60,000,000.[52] Powles' petition stated that "interposition" was the only hope to gain redress from Mexico. Great Britain should collect Mexican custom duties to pay British claims until they were settled in full. To prevent further violence to British interests in Mexico, a small army should be sent there to maintain peace until Mexicans constituted a stable government. While Great Britain had more money invested in Mexico than France, there were more French than British subjects residing in Mexico. Therefore Great Britain should seek French aid "in the attempt to throw the shield of a joint protectorate over that rich country and thereby rescue it from the state of degradation into which it has fallen."[53] Four days after the publication of this petition, the Chairman of the London Bondholders wrote Russell that interference by force of arms alone could save Mexico from destruction and the property of foreigners from absolute ruin. Robertson observed that from $150,000,000 to $200,000,000 "belonging to British subjects are involved in the matter."[54] The widespread excitement in British business circles led the *Times* to make comments on 27 September. It did not support the London Bondholders, for two months before it had already stated that a "man who lends his money to a foreign State does so at his own risk."[55] Now the *Times* stressed the necessity of gaining redress for personal and property claims. That the European Powers were at last considering an intervention for this purpose, it was predicted, "will cause neither surprise nor dissatisfaction." The suspicion that advantage would be taken of the American Civil War to violate the Monroe Doctrine was unfounded. It was said that President Lincoln fully approved the expedition to Mexico. Without specific reference to Powle's petition, the *Times* foresaw difficulties in British cooperation with France and Spain. Those two Powers favored the Conservatives in Mexico, while Great Britain preferred the Liberals. Whatever happened, the "Priest Party" should not be returned to power :

. . . for to the barbarism and superstition of the Mexican Church are owing nearly all the evils which affect the country. Its power has been curtailed by the Government now in office, and this benefit to civilization some what atones for many of its shortcomings.

Perhaps, the *Times* suggested, the mere appearance of the European squadrons in the Gulf of Mexico, or the seizure of some ports, would encourage the Juarez Government to make more strenuous efforts to maintain internal order.[56]

On 30 September Powles' petition was officially presented to the British Foreign Office.[57] A few days later Russell made a reply[58] that was soon made public.[59] Although the British Government would exercise its right, recognized by International Law, to demand the execution of conventions and security for the lives and property of British subjects, there would be no interference in the internal affairs of Mexico. It was a mistake to believe that a small army could maintain order, and a large army would also fail of its purpose:

> This is a task that the Mexicans must accomplish for themselves. There are very few cases in which foreign interference can be beneficial, and in those few cases there must be a large and numerous party in the country prepared to avail itself of foreign aid.
>
> I am concerned to say that I see no proof of the existence of such a party in Mexico.

The day after Russell sent his reply to the petitioners, the *Times* published an article that generally repeated Russell's observations. A European intervention, while it should force the "factions" to make peace, should be based on the principle of no permanent occupation. Juarez was praised for granting religious toleration, and the British Government was urged not to aid France and Spain to restore intolerance. These comments were in the nature of tentative suggestions. Essentially Russell's views were supported:

> But this must be left to the future. All that we have to do now is to save the lives and properties of our countrymen, endangered by the anarchy into which the Republic has fallen. The rest time must settle.[60]

The attitude of the *Times* and the flood of requests that Great

Britain intervene in Mexico were reassuring. In a private letter to Russell, Palmerston wrote on 7 October that he thought "we were quite right about Mexico and that public opinion is with us."[61]

The promise of an intervention in Mexico, fears that the United States would obtain Mexican public lands, and a press attack increased the pretensions of the London Bondholders. When their agent in Mexico reported that the United States was negotiating for the public lands of Mexico,[62] the bondholders demanded that Russell instruct Wyke to obtain $1034 from the United States for each square league of territory it obtained.[63] At the beginning of October a mercantile company that had carried on commercial relations with Mexico for over thirty years sent a protest to Lord Russell against Powles' petition. It was charged that bondholder claims would "postpone the satisfaction of *bona fide* British claims and to prejudice British interests."[64] Not receiving an immediate reply from the Foreign Office,[65] McCalmont, Brothers, and Company published their protest in five London newspapers on 18 October.[66] David Robertson, the Chairman of the London Bondholders, published a pamphlet in rebuttal. He claimed "a first lien on all the property and revenues" of Mexico in virtue of "absolute legislative agreements . . . and conventions, which no . . . authority can set aside." The bonds were held almost entirely by Englishmen. A few bonds only had been sold to "Dutchmen and Germans . . . ever ready to buy . . . at depreciated rates."[67] Richard Garde, a "Barrister-at-Law of the Middle Temple,"[68] wrote a letter to Russell and was able to have it inserted in the *Morning Herald* of 22 October. Garde stated that the bondholders, with the exception of a few Dutchmen, were reputable British subjects:

Many of them are men eminent in the Church, the Navy and the Army, the Law and Medicine—gentlemen who regard the term speculator as synonymous with thief.[69]

A month later Garde published a pamphlet in the form of an open letter to Russell, entitled "on the *Absolute* right of the Mexican Bondholders."[70] The Bondholders also sent Russell a long statistical opus,[71] claimed "priority" for their claims, and demanded Mexican church and public lands in addition to what the Mexican Government had promised them.[72] Lord Russell's replies to the bondholders and to McCalmont,[ ] Brothers, and Company merely stated that the British Government would only support formal conventions and agreements to which it had been a party. Russell refused to "cancel" these arrangements for McCalmont.[73] The bondholders were informed that there was a "big distinction" between their claims based on such agreements, "ratified by the Crown," and their claims based on private transactions with Mexico.[74]

The *Times* remained aloof in the controversy about the London Bondholders. On 8 November it announced that the British Government had caught up with public opinion by signing a convention with France and Spain. Outrages to foreigners were no longer endurable when neither Mexican party could end the "savagery of interminable war." A "single frigate" would have been enough to have claims recognized, and so it was assumed that the European allies, though favoring different Mexican parties, would force the opposing factions in Mexico to reach a compromise to establish a stable government.[75] When the official *Gazette* published the text of the Convention of London,[76] the *Times* was disappointed and became critical. It saw the main difficulty in finding a government in Mexico with which to negotiate and which would remain in power long enough to fulfill promises of redress. The convention bound the allies to respect the desires of the Mexican people, but it was "like undertaking to respect the order of Chaos." It was "wrongly" assumed in the convention that its signatories agreed about the "existence" of a government in Mexico, and the three allies probably would never agree among themselves which government to respect. Another difficulty would be the distribution of money collected. Disillusioned that

Lincoln had not yet approved the expedition, the *Times* predicted Americans would be "distrustful."[77]

On 11 September a Royal Order was prepared for General Francisco Serrano, the Captain-General of Cuba, to prepare an expedition to be sent to Mexico.[78] In October the *Concepcion* and *Sealtad,* the last warships needed by Serrano to make up his squadron in accordance with the order of 11 September, left Cadiz.[79] Although the Spanish Government promised to delay operations pending the conclusion of a tripartite convention to allow the three Powers to join forces, no orders to delay the Spanish expedition were sent in September or October. The November mail packet left for Havana without such orders. That ship merely brought Serrano a copy of a British draft convention.[80] Two fast warships, the *Alva* and *San Quinitin,* left Spain for Havana on 5 and 12 November, but no orders for Serrano were sent by them.[81] On 24 November the *Concepcion* and *Sealtad* arrived at Havana,[82] and Serrano's squadron was complete. By reading the British draft convention, Serrano knew that there were negotiations to send an allied expedition to Mexico, but he also had his orders of 11 September to send the Spanish forces to Vera Cruz. He decided that "it would look very bad" for the Spanish squadron to arrive "in the waters of Vera Cruz after the arrival of the other two Squadrons."[83] Therefore Serrano ordered the Spanish expedition to depart for Vera Cruz, and this was done between 29 November and 2 December.[84] When General Prim arrived in Havana on 23 December,[85] the expeditionary forces he was to command were already in Vera Cruz,[86] and Serrano had just received orders to suspend operations.[87] There is inconclusive evidence for and against the thesis that the Spanish Government purposely delayed sending orders to Serrano so that he would act on those of 11 September and thereby win glory for Spain by taking Vera Cruz without aid from Spain's allies.[88]

The news that Spain would cooperate with Great Britain and France in sending an expedition to Mexico, the Spanish opposition press insisted, came too late to make up for past apathy. It appeared that the Spanish Government had permitted Spanish subjects to suffer in Mexico and was now only taking "advantage of being seconded by two stronger powers . . . in order to avenge our bitter wrongs." It was lamented that no prince of the Spanish dynasty would ever rule in Mexico if a monarchy were established there, because Great Britain and France were stronger than Spain. Instead a member of one of the reigning families of Spain's allies would probably rule the "future Monarchy of Mexico." British or French "customs, usages and influence . . . would predominate, extirpating sooner than is believed the remains which exist there of Spanish civilisation, and even the Spanish race."[89] In a speech opening the sessions of the Cortes on 8 November, Queen Isabella II attempted to answer these charges. Her Government, she commented, "had already in readiness" the means to force redress for broken treaties and violence to Spanish subjects when Great Britain and France also decided to use force. These "two Great Nations, whose forebearance . . . could not be attributed to weakness, became the objects of fresh violence." Since the "injuries" of the three European Powers were "common," their "action ought to be collective." Isabella predicted that the European intervention in Mexico would lead to the establishment of a strong government. It would restore order and then Spanish civilization would not disappear in Mexico:

> The presence of . . . land and sea forces at the most important points on the coast of Mexico cannot but lead the parties which are tearing that unhappy country to pieces to reflect. If peace should spring up again in her under the shadow of a firmly constituted government, we should congratulate ourselves on having contributed to give her formerly the life of civilization, and now that of order together with independence and liberty.[90]

After the opening of the sessions of the Cortes, the Senate prepared an answer to the speech from the throne. In a debate on Mexican affairs, Pacheco claimed that he had been "undeservedly disavowed" by the Spanish Government. Collantes replied that Pacheco had acted in a way "to expose himself to the affront which he had undergone."[91] Although it was proposed on 2 December to censure the ratification of the Convention of London, this motion was dropped after a second reading.[92] On 4 December[93] the grandees, dignitaries, and a large number of recent appointees of the Queen to the Senate[94] endorsed the Queen's speech by a vote of 111 to 21.[95] In the Congress of Deputies the vote was 206 to 80 in favor of the administration.[96]

During 1861 Great Britain, France, and Spain were the only European States that had Ministers in Mexico. Belgium and Prussia each had a Chargé d'Affaires in Mexico. Belgium was neutral, and William I's main interest when he became King of Prussia in 1861 was to introduce army reforms in spite of opposition in the Diet. All the other European Powers also had internal problems that did not allow an active Mexican policy. The liberation of the serfs in 1861 pushed Russian foreign policy into the background. The Russian Minister of Foreign Affairs wrote a friend that "the internal question dominates all the others." Gortchakov confessed that he was only following a *"defensive* policy" to prevent "groupings that could hurt us."[97] He received reports that France was cooperating with Great Britain in Mexican affairs in order to cement Anglo-French relations. Gortchakov was so impressed with these reports that he showed them to Bismarck, then Prussia's diplomatic representative in Russia.[98] It was feared that Napoleon III would create a "disturbance" about Russian suppression of Polish uprisings. A "defensive" maneuver in September 1861 was to inform Lord Palmerston of Russian fears and to ask his assistance to prevent French meddling.[99] In a private letter concerning Mexican affairs, the Austrian Ambassador to Paris observed, "We are too much occupied with our home affairs to allow ourselves to drift into Californian dreams."[100] Hungarians, Czechs, and Poles within

Austria were protesting constitutional reforms made early in 1861. Furthermore, the Austrian Government was extremely suspicious about Napoleon III's proposals to Maximilian. Rechberg refused to carry on "official" negotiations and warned Maximilian to reveal nothing to the press.[101] The Italian Government was busy organizing the new state it represented, but unofficially Great Britain was asked to act on behalf of Italians in Mexico. The reply was that it would be inconvenient to support Italian claims. The British Government suggested that an Italian vessel, with someone aboard to whom Italians could submit their claims, might accompany the tripartite expedition. There was no intention, however, that Italy should become a third European ally of Great Britain and "enter into any Convention."[102] At the end of November 1861 Russell was informed that an Italian warship and a Chargé d'Affaires would be sent to Mexico to obtain redress and to observe operations against Mexico. Accompanying this information was a request for the "good offices" of British diplomatic and military authorities in Mexico. On this request Russell made a notation that good offices would be given "if the claims appear to be just, and so far as is consistent with the engagements of the convention of 31 October with France and Spain."[103] Then Russell sent the necessary instructions to Sir Charles Wyke[104] and the Admiralty[105] Although the Italian Government was informed of these directives,[106] it sent no ship to Mexico.[107]

In 1861 Peru tried to rally the Latin American republics to oppose any European encroachment upon Mexican independence. In November a circular was sent to suggest collective resistance to prevent the realization of any ulterior motives of the European Powers about to intervene in Mexico.[108] Those American republics that answered saw no immediate danger. Argentina and Chile blamed Mexico for its predicament and saw no threat to Mexican independence. Bolivia foresaw that any Spanish designs would be frustrated by Great Britain and France.[109]

Mathias Romero, the Mexican Minister to Washington, frequently saw Secretary of State Seward at the end of 1861 and tried to impress him with the dangers that could result for the whole Western Hemisphere from a European intervention in Mexico.[110] When Romero learned of the Convention of London, he wrote Seward that it was a threat "not only against the Mexican nation, but against republican institutions in America, and the autonomy of this continent."[111] The real intention of the European allies, Romero insisted, was to "subvert the form of government which actually exists in Mexico, and to overthrow the constitution which the people of that republic freely chose for itself."[112] All of Romero's efforts to obtain the active assistance of the United States were unsuccessful. When Dr. Manuel Nicolas Corpancho arrived in the United States under orders to see Seward before going to Mexico as Peru's diplomatic representative, Romero acted as translator. Corpancho proposed an alliance of the United States with all the South American states to oppose a European intervention in Mexico. Seward was informed that Peru was ready to supply five to six thousand troops to assist Mexico, but the American Secretary of State was noncommittal.[113] Several months of diplomatic experience, Lincoln's moderating influence, and the force of circumstances had completely altered Seward's belief at the beginning of 1861 that he could avert all internal difficulties by arousing a feeling of patriotism with a war against one or more European Powers. Just before the Confederates started bombarding Fort Sumpter in Charleston Harbour, Seward wrote "Some Thoughts for the President's Consideration" on All Fools Day. It was suggested to Lincoln that he had to "CHANGE THE QUESTION BEFORE THE PUBLIC FROM ONE UPON SLAVERY, OR ABOUT SLAVERY, for a question upon UNION OR DISUNION." Public excitement in favor of "union" could be aroused by a foreign war:

I would demand explanations from Spain and France, categorically, at once.

I would seek explanations from Great Britain and Russia, and send agents into Canada, Mexico, and Central America to rouse a vigorous continental spirit of independence on this continent against European intervention.

And, if satisfactory explanations are not received from Spain and France,

Would convene Congress and declare war against them.[114]

President Lincoln refused to take these "Thoughts" seriously.[115] Two months later he cancelled Seward's instructions to Charles Francis Adams in London that he suspend diplomatic relations with the British Government until Lord Russell promised not to see Confederate agents, even unofficially.[116] Lincoln's restraining influence had its effect on his Secretary of State. In June 1861 Seward wrote his wife: "There is but one vote in the cabinet and that is cast by the President. . . . The President is the best of us all."[117] In May 1861 Spain annexed Santo Domingo.[118] Seward was forced to beat a retreat after taking a stand far beyond any that he could support.[119] The rout of the Union army at the First Battle of Bull Run on 21 July probably also had a sobering effect on Seward.[120] A month later he wrote his Minister to Mexico that the United States "cherishes the actual independence of Mexico as a cardinal object to the exclusion of all foreign political intervention." The "present moment," however, did not appear "opportune" to make such policy statements to foreign nations:

> Prudence requires that in order to surmount the evils of faction at home we should not unnecessarily provoke debates with foreign countries, but rather repair as speedily as possible the prestige which those evils have impaired.[121]

On 30 November the British, French, and Spanish Ministers to Washington sent Seward a collective note proposing he accede to the enclosed Convention of London.[122] Seward refused and renewed his proposal, already rejected by the European Powers,[123] that the United States make a loan to Mexico so that it could pay the arrears on the interest of its debts. Seward replied to the collective note that the United States was "happy" to believe that Great Britain, France, and Spain saw the desirability of not interfering with the internal affairs of Mexico and not seeking Mexican territory. In accordance with the traditional attitude of the United States,[124] Seward did not question the right of the European Powers to resort to war to obtain redress of grievances. But it was "inexpedient" for the United States to accede to the Convention of London. The reasons given were the ones contained in Washington's Farewell Address and implied by the Monroe Doctrine. The United States, "so far as is practicable, prefer to adhere to a traditional policy recommended to them by the father of their country, and confirmed by happy experience, which forbids their making alliances with foreign nations." By implication the world was divided into two parts, republican and monarchist. The United States was disinclined to make war on a neighboring republic:

> . . . Mexico being a neighbour of the United States on this continent, and possessing a system of government similar to our own in many of its important features. The United States habitually cherish a decided goodwill towards that Republic, and a lively interest in its security, prosperity, and welfare.

"Animated by these sentiments" the United States did not:

> . . . feel inclined to resort to forcible remedies for their claims at the present moment, when the Government of Mexico is deeply disturbed by faction within, and exposed to war with foreign nations; and of course, the same sentiments render them still more disinclined to allied war against Mexico than to war against her by themselves alone.

The American Minister to Mexico was negotiating a loan convention "to satisfy the just claims and demands" of the European allies "and to avert the war" agreed upon by them. Should Corwin's negotiations "offer any sufficient ground on which to justify a proposition to the High Contracting Parties in behalf of Mexico" Seward would "hasten to submit such a proposition" to Great Britain, France, and Spain.[125] The day after writing this answer to the collective note, Seward instructed Corwin to convert the draft convention he had forwarded[126] into a formal convention.[127] In the meantime the draft convention was submitted to the Senate for previous advice.[128] His hands tied by the Civil War, Seward clung to the hope that a loan to Mexico might forestall the impending European intervention. As the British Minister to Washington put it, Seward's policy was to find "expedients" to postpone the question until a "favorable turn in . . . domestic affairs" permitted reverting to the "old tone of defiance towards Europe."[129] Lord Lyons also had to admit, however, that Seward had lost "many of his illusions." He no longer believed:

> . . . in the return of the South to the arms of the North in case of a foreign war; in his power to frighten the nations of Europe by great words; in the ease with which the U.S. could crush rebellion with one hand and chastise Europe with the other; in the notion that the relations with England in particular are safe playthings to be used for the amusement of the American people.[130]

On 19 December the Foreign Relations Committee of the United States Senate held a meeting to discuss the difficulty of raising money to loan Mexico, but did not arrive at any decision.[131] The Senators, as well as Northern newspapers,[132] were more interested in domestic affairs than Mexico's plight.[133] The burning foreign policy issue at the end of 1861 was whether the "Trent Affair" would lead to a war between the United States and Great Britain. The removal of the Confederate agents, Mason and Slidell, from a British ship, the *Trent,* by Captain Wilkes of the *San Jacinto* off Havana did not lead to hostilities,[134] but the incident affected the Mexican policy of Great Britain and France. Even before the "Trent Affair," Lord Palmerston feared a war with the United States. Seward was a "vapouring blustering ignorant Man" who might seize Canada to "make up for ill success against the South."[135] In mid-1861 troops were sent to Canada,[136] and their arrival in the fall aroused mistrust and fear in the United States.[137] The news of the Confederate victory at the First Battle of Bull Run convinced Palmerston of the necessity of sending more reinforcements to Canada.[138] While Palmerston doubted Seward and Lincoln would "draw the Sword against us . . . they have shewn themselves so wild, that any act of intemperance may be expected from them."[139] On 27 November 1861 the news of the seizure of Mason and Slidell reached London.[140] A few days later Russell decided that half of the ships of the line and frigates ordered to Vera Cruz should not proceed there.[141] These three ships were intended to strengthen Admiral Milne's squadron on the American and West India Station. It was "possible," Russell believed, that "we may be at war before long with the United States."[142] To permit the British Admiralty to instruct Admiral Milne to remain at Bermuda and prepare for naval operations against the United States,[143] Russell prepared plenipotentiary powers to be forwarded to the officer Milne would designate to command the British ships to be sent to Vera Cruz.[144]

Napoleon III saw in the Trent Affair a chance to grant the British Government a favor by supporting its protest to the United States. The Emperor of the French expected British reciprocation in the form of acquiescence in French plans for Mexico. When this did not happen in 1862, Napoleon was disillusioned. In a conversation with Slidell in July 1862, Napoleon "spoke freely of the Mexican question." He "said he had reason not to be well satisfied with England" which "had not appreciated as she should have done his support in the Trent affair."[145] Even what on the surface appeared purely French domestic concerns were utilized to improve Franco–British relations. Both the appointment of Achille Fould as Minister of Finance to carry out financial reforms and Napoleon III's renunciation of the right to make "extraordinary" expenditures shortly after the negotiation of the

Convention of London[146] were intended by Napoleon as means to cement relations with Great Britain. Beginning in 1859 Lord Palmerston started believing that increases in the French army and navy necessitated British "preparations for the gale which the political Barometer . . . indicates."[147] Lord Cowley personally informed Napoleon of British suspicions.[148] At a meeting of the Council of Ministers at Compiègne in November 1861, Napoleon stated that he hoped Fould's financial reforms would serve to eliminate "fear and suspicion" of French military preparations:

> I . . . wanted to destroy this notion which they pretend to hold abroad that I hold all the wealth of France in my hands, and that I can dispose of it as I please even for my personal needs . . . . This is one of the main causes of the fear and suspicion which France causes abroad, because it is believed that suddenly, without any previous discussion, and hence without any publicity, I can secretly acquire huge sums, for example to make military preparations. I wanted all the world to know that this was impossible . . . .[149]

Seward's refusal to accede to the Convention of London came as no surprise for Thouvenel in December 1861.[150] At the beginning of November the American Minister to Paris told Thouvenel that it was too late to seek the cooperation of the United States, because it had not been given an opportunity to participate in drawing up the terms of the agreement to intervene in Mexico.[151] Thouvenel had predicted Seward's "probable reserve" six weeks before:

> . . . in my opinion, wouldn't it be a question of our getting everything in order without waiting for the cooperation of the United States? At present it has other fish to fry than Mexicans . . . .[152]

Seward's loan scheme as an alternative to a European intervention in Mexico could not be accepted by the French Government, for then there would be no chance to establish

Maximilian in Mexico. Furthermore, Thouvenel regarded the American plan merely as an attempt "to assure the Texas frontier and to put hands on territories coveted for a long time."[153] In September Thouvenel believed that American hostility might have to be aroused anyway in another connection. The anticipated cotton shortage, resulting from Lincoln's blockade of the Confederacy, soon would necessitate Anglo–French measures opposed to the interests of the North:

> . . . it seems to me almost impossible that the question of cotton will not force England and France in the next three months to consider, above all, a vital interest for the prosperity and the tranquility of their industrial cities.[154]

Three months later, when the British Government still refused to support French "King Cotton Diplomacy,"[155] Thouvenel received Seward's refusal to join the intervention in Mexico. Anticipating an American mediation proposal, Thouvenel instructed Jurien to reject such a plan.[156] When Napoleon III read Seward's refusal, the Emperor commented, "This is only a bit of Yankee shrewdness."[157] Later Napoleon believed that, "as America had recognized the Empire of Brazil, why could she not also recognize the Empire of Mexico?"[158]

Lord Russell and Lord Palmerston did not expect Seward to cooperate in an intervention in Mexico. The British Government sponsored the offer to Seward as a show of honorable intentions toward Mexico and as a counter proposal to what was considered an unrealistic loan proposal veiling American designs on Mexican territory. Lord Russell would have welcomed American cooperation, if only in the form of a "single corvette," as a curb on possible French and Spanish ulterior motives.[159] Any tangible improvement in Anglo–American relations might have decreased Palmerston's fears, that no amount of assurances could calm,[160] of a Northern invasion of Canada.

During the negotiation of the Convention of London the Spanish Government was reluctant to approve the British proposal to invite the United States to intervene in Mexico. O'Donnell clearly saw that the intention of the British Government was to give proof of no desire for "exclusive advantage" and observed that the Spanish Government gave "sufficient proof" by "inviting England and France to join with her."[161] Russell's proposal was only accepted so that Great Britain and France would not act without Spain.[162] Such a turn of events would be difficult to explain in the Cortes.[163] O'Donnell did not believe that he made a great concession. The United States "was probably too much engrossed in its internal affairs to be able to direct its attention elsewhere."[164] In order to expedite allied operations against Mexico so that they would be initiated before the opening session of the Cortes,[165] the Spanish Government made a proviso that the expedition to Mexico should not be delayed through an invitation to the United States.[166] British pressure,[167] the Spanish domestic situation, and an expected negative response from the United States were the chief reasons that the Spanish Government consented to the British proposal. Seward's rejection of this offer, therefore, was expected and probably not unwelcome.

Between 30 November and 2 December 1861 a Spanish squadron of twenty-six ships under the command of Admiral Rubalcava and six thousand troops, commanded by General Gasset, left Havana for Vera Cruz.[168] The expedition arrived off Vera Cruz in two sections, on 8 and 10 December. Captain Von Donop of the *Jason,* waiting for Wyke's arrival in Vera Cruz to bring him to Admiral Milne, and the Captain of a French frigate at Vera Cruz paid the Spanish Admiral a complementary visit.[169] Admiral Rubalcava said his orders were to ask the cooperation of any British and French ships he encountered in order to seize Vera Cruz and the fort of St. Juan d'Ulloa. This offer was refused, and Captain Von Donop suggested that nothing be done until the French and British squadrons arrived. Rubalcava claimed his orders and the health of his men made any delay impossible.[170] On 14 December the surrender of Vera Cruz was demanded within twenty-four hours.[171] The inhabitants started to evacuate Vera Cruz,[172] and there were no signs that the fort of St. Juan d'Ulloa would resist.[173] Brisk breezes prevented the first landing of Spanish troops[174] until 17 December. In order to encourage his troops, General Gasset issued a "General Order" that recalled the feats of Cortez and then announced :

> Our present Mission is also glorious : it is intended to demand satisfaction from the Mexican Government for the insults offered to our flag, to extract the fulfilment of treaties, to prevent the repetition of acts of violence towards our countrymen and to prove . . . that Spain is never insulted with impunity, and that distances disappear when Her Honour is called in question.

Gasset's appeal was not only to patriotism, but also to the bravery of his soldiers :

> On taking command of this Division, I did not hesitate to guarantee the success of the enterprise, because I know that an appeal is never made in vain to your valour and enthusiasm[175] . . . .

At noon on 17 December the Spanish flag was flying over Vera Cruz and St. Juan d'Ulloa,[176] the Mexicans having offered no resistance.[177] General Gasset issued a decree proclaiming a "state of siege," establishing a Military Commission for police purposes, and directing Mexicans to surrender fire arms within twenty-four hours.[178] A proclamation, stating Spanish intentions, was made to calm the local population :

> Inhabitants of Vera Cruz : The Spanish Troops who occupy your city have no mission of conquest, no interested views. They are led solely by the Duty of demanding satisfaction for the non fulfilment of treaties, and for the acts of violence committed upon our fellow countrymen, as well as by the necessity of obtaining guarantees that similar outrages shall not be repeated.
> Until these objects are obtained the Spanish Army, both here and wherever events may lead it, will be enabled by

means of vigorous discipline to preserve public tranquility at whatever cost, to afford protection to the pacific inhabitants, and to punish with severity the disturbers of order . . . ."[179]

Before the arrival of the British and French squadrons in Vera Cruz, both Wyke and Saligny came to Vera Cruz from Mexico City. They were hardly on speaking terms after their quarrels of the last few months.[180] In a private correspondence with Serrano, Saligny denounced Wyke's negotiations with the Mexican Government as the *"diplomacy of negroes,"*[181] illustrating the *"simplicity* of perfidious Albion"[182] and Wyke's "duplicity and stupidity."[183] In his turn, Wyke denounced Saligny in a private letter to Lord Russell as "violent, imprudent, and . . . unscrupulous in his assertions, having told every body here (i.e., in Vera Cruz) . . . that I was disgraced and recalled."[184]

On 23 December 1861 General Prim arrived at Havana.[185] He was soon approached by three Mexican conservatives: Padre Miranda, an exile corresponding with Estrada in Europe.[186] General Miramon, Juarez' rival in the Mexican Civil War,[187] and a representative of Zuloaga and Marquez, two leaders of conservative and robber bands in Mexico.[188] All three Mexicans "dwelt upon the number of their friends and fellow politicians" in Mexico and wished to "treat" with the European allies. A year later Prim recalled his answer in the Senate of the Cortes:

I said to them . . . that the Allies could not treat except with the Government which they found constituted. And upon this text I gave them such a host of arguments that they owned themselves vanquished. Nevertheless I added the following remarks, which are word for word, because, foreseeing then what might happen, I wrote them down: "Since you are so numerous, take advantage of the Government forces being massed at Chiquihuite and Cerro Gordo to show a front to (the) Allies; make an effort and march upon the capital and seize it; for if you are there when our Commissioners arrive, the Allies will treat with you."

Could I have replied otherwise? Could my language have

been more in harmony with the principle of non-intervention which the three Governments had imposed upon themselves? To have acted otherwise would have been to sweep away this principle . . . .

Vice Admiral Jurien fully approved the reply I had given to the Mexican Commissioners. . . .[189]

Jurien reported similar remarks made to him by Prim at Havana. The Spanish General wanted to treat with the *de facto* government of Mexico. He also wanted to avoid hostilities. Spanish, French, and British officers would be sent to Mexico City to present their ultimatums demanding redress. The Mexican Government would be given four or five days to reply. If the allied terms were accepted, Prim intended to "support" the party in power:

No matter which party is in power, the General (Prim) would want to offer it the support of the allied arms if this party accepts the conditions of the ultimatum and if it agrees to consult the people by means of universal suffrage. The General admits that the monarchical form is the only form of government that could guarantee in Mexico the interests of the country and those of foreigners, but he looks in vain for a candidate for this new throne who would appear acceptable to him. He realized with me the necessity of not allowing negotiations to drag out. Moreover, the stay at Vera Cruz being without danger for the troops during the months of January and February, he wouldn't see grave inconveniences in not beginning a march into the interior until the first days of March. The ambition that he proclaims loudly is to arrive at Mexico City, if he can, without combat. "Juarez himself can," he said, "desire our presence there; he can see that by resisting us he will only assure the triumph of the party of Marquez and Zuloaga." If one can't go to Mexico City in accordance with the wishes of the Mexicans, if it is necessary to open a way to this city by force, the General still believes it preferable to maneuver in such a way as to avoid positions that could only be taken at the expense of a loss of much blood. In a word, the General wants to avoid, as far as he can, any chance of a violent campaign, a campaign that would be of a nature to revive the hatred of the Mexicans against the Spanish race.

Jurien believed that the Mexican Government would reject any negotiations with the European allies on any other basis than the "prompt and complete evacuation of the territory (i.e., seized by them)."[190] Prim's whole line of reasoning puzzled Jurien and made him suspicious. There were rumors in Havana that Prim was "following a chimerical policy."[191] In a private letter to Estrada, Miranda elaborated. Prim's liberal ideas and the fact that his uncle was Juarez' Minister of Finance "would cause us many more enemies."[192] Jurien foresaw complications and wrote Thouvenel, "Would it be possible that General Prim should bring a personal ambition to Mexico?"[193]

In view of the possibility of hostilities between Great Britain and the United States, owing to the Trent Affair, Admiral Milne directed Commodore Hugh Dunlop to assume command of the British ships and marines to be sent to Vera Cruz. Should "hostilities with the United States . . . break out," Commodore Dunlop was to leave one ship to "represent the British element in the combined operations in Mexico." The other British ships under Dunlop's command would be held ready to blockade the American coast west of Florida.[194] For Milne the "Mexican question" was "comparatively unimportant."[195]

At the end of December 1861 and the beginning of January 1862, Dunlop, Jurien, and Prim left Havana, arriving at Vera Cruz between 6 and 8 January 1862.[196] While the Mexicans offered no resistance at Vera Cruz, General Uraga, commanding the "Army of the East,"[197] was fortifying the mountain passes at the edge of the Mexican coastal plain.[198] Juarez published a decree that any Mexican aiding the Spaniards would be treated as a traitor.[199] A "Presidential Manifesto to the Nation" stated that Mexico, while ready to give satisfaction for just claims, would "meet force with force." Should either Mexican independence be threatened, or there be an attempt to interfere in Mexican internal affairs, Juarez called on all Mexicans to defend their country.[200] Wyke decided that hostilities against Mexico under such circumstances "would be little short of madness."[201] On 3 January 1861 Wyke wrote General Doblado, heading the Mexican cabinet, to suggest he negotiate instead of commencing hostilities:

> Everything now depends upon the manner in which this Intervention is received. If it is accepted in a friendly spirit, there is every reason to hope that great good to all parties concerned will derive from it. If by you it is looked on as hostile much blood will probably be shed, and Mexico have to succumb to the dictation of so formidable a coalition. In my humble opinion, you ought not to hesitate for a moment in the choice you have to make, as your future fame and the real interests of your country demand an amicable adjustment of your pending difficulties with the allied Powers.

Clinging to the hope he had had in 1861 that an intervention in Mexico would cause the Mexicans to form a stable government,[202] Wyke wrote Doblado that "until a respectable and strong gov't is formed . . . there can be no well-founded hope for the future prosperity and peace of the Republick."[203]

On 8 January Prim and Jurien called on Wyke and discussed the means to achieve the objectives of the allied intervention. Prim agreed with Wyke that conciliation ought to be tried before resorting to force. Both Prim and Jurien agreed with Wyke that their first "duty" was:

> . . . to aid and assist the Mexicans in obtaining such a Government as was likely to afford more efficient protection to the lives and properties of foreigners resident in the Republick, before exacting from such a Government the execution of those engagements towards foreign Powers which their present penury and hopeless state of disorganization does not permit them to fulfil.[204]

After his bickering with Saligny, Wyke was "much pleased" with Prim and Jurien.[205] There appeared to be a harmony of ideas. The next morning, 9 January, the French and British forces began to land in Vera Cruz.[206] Prim issued a General Order declaring himself Commander-in-Chief of the Spanish

forces, "not come to conquer . . . but . . . to demand reparation
for offenses done us." For the same purpose were present the
"valiant sons of enthusiastic France, and the no less brave
soldiers of England."[207] Prim, Jurien, and Dunlop, the military
commanders, inspected the various corps,[208] and then joined
Wyke and Saligny for the first official conference.[209] By a coincidence Admiral Maitland, charged with British operations on
the west coast of Mexico, also met his French counterpart,
Admiral Larrien, on 9 January 1862.[210]

## 3.  THE INTRIGUES OF THE MEXICAN EXILES,
## OCTOBER–DECEMBER 1861

In Mexico, as in most of Latin America in the nineteenth
century, the political struggle was between conservatives and
liberals. The former supported the vested interests of the
Catholic Church and tried to establish a strong executive. The
liberals were anti-clerical and wanted to check the executive
with the legislature. In general, the wealthy property holders,
merchants, and the clergy were conservatives. In Mexico the
"Reaction" largely represented the wealthy families of the
cities,[1] and the clergy.[2] The "Priest Party" denounced Juarez'
"red republicans" and "ultra-liberals" for nationalizing church
property, proclaiming liberty of conscience, and attempting to
establish democratic institutions. Yet party lines were blurred.
The white descendants of Europeans and even the *mestizos*
sneered at Juarez, because he was an Indian. Mr. Mathew,
Wyke's predecessor, commented that "the dregs of Spanish
society and those of mixed blood . . . ludicrously arrogate to
themselves the higher social position in Mexico."[3] In 1861
bands of a few thousand roved Mexico. They included those
hostile to Juarez, adventurers, and sometimes just robbers looking for a pretext to plunder.[4] In November 1861 even Saligny,
who detested the Mexican liberals, had to admit that "the
reaction . . . does not appear . . . to have struck much root in

the Country."[5] The conservatives, as in the past whenever their position was threatened or they were out of power, hoped for European aid or intervention. This was the origin of many monarchy schemes.[6] Hidalgo, Almonte, Estrada and his "Committee" in Paris—Wyke referred to them as the "travelled branch" of the Mexican conservatives[7]—were not the only Mexican exiles working in this sense in 1861. Exiled Mexican bishops established headquarters in Rome. Ex-President Santa Anna lived in St. Thomas in the Virgin Islands. Other exiles "travelled." Madrid, New York, and Havana were the standard asylums where plots were made against Juarez. When Estrada's life-long dream of monarchy for Mexico seemed near realization, he tried to utilize this web of intrigue to obtain a privileged position for himself and to prepare the way for Maximilian.[8]

Just before Maximilian's provisional acceptance of a Mexican crown was known in Paris,[9] Gutierrez de Estrada wrote him a flattering letter appealing to his "noble heart" to make a "generous response."[10] Estrada's next letter to Maximilian was filled with *"Helas!"* and predicted that his acceptance of Napoleon's overture would prevent the complete ruin of Mexico.[11] These were the first two letters Maximilian received from a Mexican.[12] The Archduke was curious to learn more about Estrada and the other Mexican exiles in Paris. On 24 October Sebastian Schertzenlechner, Maximilian's private secretary, set out for Paris. Three days later he met Gutierrez in Paris and asked him to state his opinions confidentially. He related his creed and efforts on its behalf. Schertzenlecher was impressed. Estrada's views seemed "noble, elevated, patriotic and seemingly practicable." Nevertheless, Maximilian's secretary "gently" hinted that Estrada was the only Mexican working for a Mexican monarchy. He stoutly denied it and affirmed he had the confidence of all reputable Mexicans. In the course of the next few days Estrada introduced Almonte and Hidalgo to Schertzenlechner. He concluded that Almonte was an "honest and cultured gentleman." Hidalgo was "of the

noblest character and a man of outstanding ability." Estrada
confided that Hidalgo was "that channel, hitherto undiscovered by the official (Austrian) diplomatists, by which the
Mexicans communicate with the Empress Eugénie." At the
same time Gutierrez tried to win a similar position of influence.
He suggested that Maximilian should have an agent in Paris
to represent him and make his opinions known to Napoleon III
and Eugenie.[13] To show Maximilian how many Mexican
friends he had in Europe, Estrada drew up a eulogistic
"Address" on 30 October. The Mexican people, Estrada wrote,
would "bless" Maximilian "from the bottom of their hearts."
His work of regenerating Mexico might even ". . . be the will
of the Almighty."[14] Before sending this panegyric to Maximilian, Estrada and his son Fernando signed it. Gutierrez could
only find five other Mexicans, including Hidalgo and Almonte,
to sign. They were all conservative diplomats disavowed by
Juarez.[15]

Estrada's letters to Maximilian, the hint to his secretary,
and the "Address" were preliminary moves made by Estrada
before unfolding his plans of how he proposed to establish in
Mexico the Prince for whom he had been searching for twenty
years. Estrada approached Count Muelinen, the Austrian
Chargé d'Affaires in Paris, and proposed Maximilian should
accept the throne of Mexico from the Mexicans residing in
Europe. Everything could be settled quickly "from here" without waiting for an invitation from the Mexicans in Mexico.[16]
Gutierrez could muster a few more Mexicans than his little
"Committee" in Paris. He corresponded with Mgr. de Labastida, the exiled Bishop of Puebla residing in Rome.[17] He had
been waiting for the "intervention or mediation of Europe" in
Mexico, for he believed that the Mexican conservatives were
"without sufficient strength" to overthrow the liberals.[18] Learning of Estrada's "Address," Labastida and the other Mexican
bishops in Rome intended to send Maximilian a similar one.
Cardinal Antonelli, the Papal Secretary of State, suggested to
the bishops that they wait in order to do nothing prematurely.

Yet the Cardinal did arrange a meeting for Labastida with the Austrian Minister to Rome.[19] Baron Bach then reported to Rechberg that the Mexican bishop approved a European intervention in Mexico to assist the conservatives "to put an end to anarchy." The "bulk of the clergy and landowners" would cooperate in an undertaking that could only be successful with outside aid.[20] In private letters to Estrada, Labastida approved Maximilian as the future monarch of Mexico. After reading these letters, Estrada sent them to Maximilian.[21]

At the beginning of November 1861 Gutierrez not only planned to offer Maximilian the throne of Mexico on behalf of the Mexican exiles in Europe, but also to publish a pamphlet suggesting the Powers aid in the establishment of a Mexican monarchy.[22] Estrada intended to share the honors with Santa Anna and Padre Miranda, not with Hidalgo and Almonte. Estrada never forgot that Santa Anna, when President of Mexico, had given him a commission to find a European to reign in Mexico.[23] On 31 October Estrada wrote to Santa Anna in the Virgin Islands that at last a monarch had been found in the person of Maximilian.[24] Estrada placed great faith in the good results of the ex-President's cooperation. He was "the only man capable of executing a great enterprise such as the establishment of monarchy in Mexico."[25] Padre Miranda in New York City was also notified by Estrada,[26] who counted on his aid for "the success of our cause in Mexico." [27]

Estrada's plans for Maximilian did not coincide with those of Napoleon. The Emperor told Metternich that Gutierrez was "too zealous, and too liable to lose his head now that his dream of twenty years seems likely to come true." The Mexican had to be told not to interfere or to publish a pamphlet giving his own views.[28] Metternich agreed that the veteran exile was "too optimistic and zealous,"[29] but believed the French rejection of his plans had another cause. It would "certainly not suit their plans that the proposal to establish a Mexican throne should appear to be advanced by a Mexican residing in Europe."[30] Rechberg was also alarmed. He wrote Maximilian that there was "a world of difference between a candidature supported by a small body of Mexicans living abroad, and one supported by the nation as a whole."[31] In response to a request from Maximilian for advice from his father-in-law,[32] Leopold I of Belgium had already written in October, "Until Mexico herself declares her wishes, *you must remain free*."[33] Maximilian accepted Leopold and Rechberg's advice. In answer to Estrada's "Address," the Archduke stated that he was "disposed to take into consideration" the wishes of the Mexican people, but he had to be sure that they really wanted him as their King:

> . . . it would be necessary, before all, that I should be very certain of the will and co-operation of the country. My co-operation in favor of the work of governmental transformation . . . could not be determined, unless that a national manifestion should prove to me, in an undoubted manner, the desire of the nation to see me ocupy the throne.
> Then, only, would my conscience permit me to unite my destinies with those of your country. . . .[34]

Maximilian responded more favorably to the overture that he appoint a confidential agent. He wrote Rechberg that "Gutierrez de Estrada himself would, in virtue of his wide experience, be pre-eminently fitted for the post."[35] Maximilian asked Rechberg to send the Mexican a "written authorization."[36] His functions would be to "keep in touch with the Mexican leaders and with the French." He would also, "as circumstances demand, and of course whilst preserving the closest understanding with His Majesty's respective (Austrian) Embassies, treat on my behalf with the English and Spanish Governments."[37] Although Maximilian opposed an immediate visit of his agent to Miramar to see him on account of the possible publicity, Rechberg was asked to inform Estrada that an opportunity for a meeting would be sought in the next few weeks.[38] Gutierrez was well on the way to establishing his influence with Maximilian in a similar way that Hidalgo had done so with Napoleon and Eugenie. Maximilian was already beginning to act like a Sovereign and Estrada as his Chief Minister. Schertzenlechner was sent off to Pope Pius IX with a letter asking the "active co-operation of the Holy See . . . and the sacred blessing which is so absolutely essential."[39] The Pope replied that "all Christian souls" in Mexico "eagerly look forward to the time when peace shall again be restored, and such a peace as will enable the Church of Jesus Christ and the Nation of the Mexicans to prosper." Pius IX trusted that the "Lord will favour your undertaking with His blessing, and we earnestly bid you and your illustrious Archduchess to be of good heart."[40] After Schertzenlechner returned from Rome with this letter, he was sent to Vienna to see Estrada,[41] summoned there in early December by Rechberg, who cautiously wanted to give the Mexican verbal instead of written instructions.[42]

Late in November 1861 Miramon arrived in Paris[43] to complicate further the cross purposes of the Mexican exiles. He was a conservative exile, Juarez' rival as President of Mexico during the Mexican Civil War. In this capacity Miramon had appointed Almonte as his diplomatic agent to negotiate with the Powers of Europe.[44] When Juarez entered Mexico City, Miramon fled to Havana in the company of Pacheco, the Spanish Minister expelled by Juarez early in 1861.[45] From Havana Miramon went to Paris. In March 1861 he saw Napoleon III,[46] who was flattered that it was said the Mexican admired him.[47] From Paris Miramon went to Madrid,[48] in the hopes that a Spanish intervention in Mexico would restore him as President.[49] When he learned of negotiations for a joint expedition to Mexico and heard rumors of the establishment of a monarchy in Mexico, he made no secret of his belief that there "is no monarchist party in Mexico."[50] The Spanish Government had no intention of assisting his return to power and warned General Serrano in Havana to be on the lookout for Miramon, who intended to return to Mexico via Cuba.[51] Before setting out for Havana, Miramon stopped at Paris again. As in Madrid, he said there were no monarchists in Mexico.[52] He approached Almonte, his former subordinate, and asked him to arrange an audience with Napoleon. Almonte refused, giving as a pretext that "he was no longer in office." Then Miramon made a written request, but it was refused by Napoleon.[53] Lord Cowley believed Napoleon did not want his name mentioned by Miramon in any transactions he might undertake upon returning to Mexico.[54] It is also likely that Hidalgo and Almonte defamed Miramon for his lack of monarchical enthusiasm.[55] Metternich wrote Rechberg privately, "The Empress hates Miramon and has informed me that her husband did not receive him."[56] Unable to obtain any promises of assistance in Europe for his reestablishment as President, Miramon booked a passage to New York City.[57] In December he continued on to Havana, where other exiles were already gathering.[58]

On 10 December 1861 Gutierrez arrived in Vienna.[59] Schertzenlechner, Rechberg, and Franz Joseph took turns for two weeks in trying to impress the Mexican with the need for caution. At first Estrada was dejected that he was not allowed to publish his pamphlet, which he hoped would have had "a most powerful effect on the European cabinets." Maximilian's secretary explained that "in this affair everything depends on Napoleon." The "opinion of Russia and Prussia is wholly, or almost wholly, a matter of indifference." Estrada was then "calmer." Rechberg advised "watchful discretion" and arranged a meeting between Estrada and Franz Joseph, who reiterated Rechberg's advice. Schertzenlechner reported to Maximilian, "Gutierrez is now completely tame, and for the moment at any rate, his zeal is no longer dangerous."[60] His pamphlet rejected, Estrada made a new proposal. He suggested sending some of the Mexican bishops in Rome to Mexico "— in the wake of the European expeditionary force." The bishops could exert their influence on the Mexican clergy, already favorable to monarchy. In particular Estrada mentioned Mgr. de Labastida as already a keen supporter of Maximilian.[61]

Rechberg approved the plan and instructed Metternich to ask Napoleon's opinion.[62]

After two weeks in Vienna, Estrada still expressed his desire to see Maximilian, who overcame his fear of publicity and permitted him to visit Miramar. Maximilian feared that "a further repulse would have humiliated and insulted this devoted man."[63] On Christmas Eve Estrada arrived and stayed almost a week.[64] Maximilian stressed his dependence on the French army and the support of the Mexican people. Later Estrada recalled :

> . . . I visited the Archduke Maximilian . . . . He did not throw cold water on my plans, but he required, as preliminaries, an unmistakable requisition from the Mexican people, and the support of the European powers. "Austria," he added, "is too poor and too busy to take up your cause. Unless a French army will keep in check the anarchical party, we cannot commit ourselves."[65]

Throughout his stay at Miramar Gutierrez stressed the importance of enlisting the cooperation of Santa Anna,[66] whose letters Estrada brought with him.[67] Shortly before leaving Paris Gutierrez had received a letter that "the remedy must be to substitute a Constitutional Emperor for this buffoonery that is called the Republic."[68] While at Vienna, Estrada received a letter from Santa Anna that he would support Maximilian, who was "without equal."[69] In view of these letters and his faith in the ex-President, Estrada urged that Santa Anna should be the President of a regency, including two other persons, until Maximilian arrived in Mexico.[70] Maximilian favored the idea of a regency, "for as short a time as possible." It would include "in any event Santa Anna and a Bishop, perhaps also Miranda."[71] Maximilian did not commit himself about Mgr. de Labastida, but considered inviting him to Miramar.[72] A private letter received by Estrada a few weeks before from Padre Miranda in New York may have merited Maximilian's consideration of him for a position in the regency. Miranda requested a biography and a picture of the Archduke to be used "to try to make this Prince known to our populations."[73] In an attempt to show what important connections he had, Estrada mentioned a certain Rafael Rafael[74] whom Miranda trusted and whose headquarters were in New York City.[75]

On 27 December,[76] when Estrada was still at Miramar, Maximilian received a letter from Rechberg. Enclosed was a report from Metternich of a conversation he had had with Napoleon III on 21 December.[77] Napoleon believed there were three problems and wanted to know Maximilian's views on them. The easiest problem to solve, Napoleon told Metternich, would be the financial one. A loan would have to be raised to establish the monarchy in Mexico, but the Emperor did not offer any more detailed advice. Secondly, provision would have to be made to bring Maximilian to Mexico. Perhaps he might want to go on a ship of the Austrian Navy. This decision would have to be made by Franz Joseph. The last problem was "the most difficult, the most delicate and the most important." It was the necessity of providing Maximilian with a military force to support his regime once he arrived in Mexico. Napoleon gave his opinion that the Powers that assisted the Archduke in obaining a Mexican crown ought to guarantee it to him. Furthermore, Napoleon promised to provide five hundred troops. They would be an elite corps around which to build up an army of Mexicans loyal to Maximilian.[78] In the course of the conversation Metternich brought up Estrada's proposal of sending Lambastida and other Mexican bishops to Mexico. Napoleon heartily approved utilizing such "religious and conservative elements" and said he would instruct Jurien to "co-operate with them."[79] Immediately after learning of Napoleon's observations, Maximilian asked that "his unqualified" appreciation should be conveyed by Rechberg to Metternich.[80] At the same time Maximilian sent Rechberg a telegram to make Estrada's plans for Santa Anna known to Napoleon and ask him to give Jurien instructions to aid the Mexican living in exile in the Virgin Islands.[81] Two days later Rechberg

sent a telegram in reply that Napoleon had assured Meternich that Jurien would receive "careful instructions" concerning Santa Anna.[82] Then Estrada and Maximilian parted
company. The Mexican started his return trip to Paris, stopping at Trieste long enough to write Rafael Rafael of the
latest developmens.[83] Maximilian went to Venice to see Franz
Joseph to discuss the proposals of Estrada and Napoleon III.

On New Year's Eve Maximilian had a long discussion with
Franz Joseph in Venice. The two brothers took up Napoleon's
three "problems." Maximilian had already drawn up a letter
to the Emperor of the French.[84] Therein Maximilian proposed
obtaining a loan of $25,000,000 and added he would appreci-
ate the influence of the French Government with "the great
banking-houses" to "facilitate" this loan. Maximilian proposed to go to Mexico on a ship of the Austrian Navy. He did
not want to be at the mercy of Mexican "generals" and therefore intended to take with him "a small body of troops . . .
enlisted in Europe . . . thus forming the nucleus of a native
army."[85] It was agreed that this letter should be handed to
Napoleon by the Austrian Ambassador to Paris.[86] Metternich
was also authorized to communicate verbally the substance of
a letter from Maximilian to Rechberg, summarizing some of
the New Year's Eve conversation.[87] The loan might be raised
by Rothschild, but it was hoped British and French financiers
would assist. Franz Joseph promised $100,000 out of the
"Family Fund" so that Maximilian could "employ agents" and
finance "journalistic enterprises." Should the European
Powers recognize the Confederacy, it was desirable that a prior
condition be that it "bind itself to respect the independence
and integrity of the Mexican Monarchy."[88] Estrada's proposal
of a regency, already referred to and seemingly approved by
Napoleon, was discussed. It was agreed that decrees issued by
this body would be subject to ratification by Maximilian.[89]
Other matters discussed by Maximilian and Franz Joseph were
not made known to Napoleon. Franz Joseph promised "guns,
bridging equipment and artillery officers." Volunteer Austrian

reserve and active officers would be permitted to go to Mexico (only Catholics, but not Italians) with the assurance of later reinstatement in the Austrian Army. Leopold I would be asked to permit the recruiting of Belgians. The loan of $100,000 from Franz Joseph would be repaid out of Maximilian's appanage. Miramar and Charlotte's property would be sold. The questions of the succession to the Austrian throne and Maximilian's successor in the Austrian Navy were left for future discussion. Schertzenlecher would go to Mexico with letters for Santa Anna, Miranda, and Rafael Rafael, perhaps first stopping in England to see Lord Palmerston. Santa Anna would be given the same salary he received as President of Mexico and the title of Duke of Vera Cruz or Tampico. He would accompany Maximilian to Mexico City. Austrians were considered for the posts of "Obersthofmeister" and "Obershofmeisterin." The Archbishop of Mexico would be made a Cardinal or a Patriarch. Maximilian would assume the title of "Fernando" and not "Maximiliano." Orders of San Fernando and Maria Carlotta would be established.[90] The ostensible purpose of the conversation of the Hapsburg brothers was to discuss Napoleon's remarks to Metternich. The conversation went much further and concerned minute details as if Maximilian were about to leave for Mexico. It was a reflection of Estrada's contagious optimism. The persons discussed—Labastida, Santa Anna, Miranda, Rafael Rafael—were all Estrada's friends. The Mexicans Eugenie and Napoleon trusted were only briefly mentioned. In a memorandum of the conversation Maximilian noted, "How to make the acquaintance of Almonte and Hidalgo?"[91]

In November 1861 Miranda went from New York City to Havana.[92] He left Rafael Rafael behind to influence newspaper opinion in favor of Maximilian, but a month later Miranda reported to Estrada that Rafael was "unable to move in this direction for the moment as his affairs are grave and complicated."[93] Miranda also encountered difficulties in Havana. He could not obtain the "cooperation" of the newspapers "without some subsidy."[94] Although he expected little Mexican resistance to the European intervention,[95] Miranda failed to see how a mere occupation of Mexico's Gulf ports would lead to any good results.[96] Mexico could export and import across its northern frontier and through its Pacific ports.[97] Miranda feared that the allied forces proceeding to Mexico might not be large enough.[98] Even before Prim arrived in Havana, Miranda predicted the General's reputation as a liberal and his family connections in Mexico would be a hinderance to the realization of Estrada's plans.[99] Miranda saw the Bishop of Havana and learned that the Spanish Government probably would not support Maximilian's candidacy. The Bishop showed Miranda a letter from O'Donnell, the Chief Minister in the Spanish cabinet :

> Napoleon wants to sweeten the lips of Austria with honey, and has worn us out by sending us letter upon letter. But we don't have any esteem for him. Almonte is working in the same sense, but the letters about him that I have seen do not agree.[100]

When Prim arrived in Havana, he did not refuse to see Miranda. Prim reasoned that it was unwise to alienate the Mexican conservatives, to whom he might have to turn if the Juarez Government refused to negotiate.[101] For the same reason Prim prevented General Serrano, the Captain-General of Cuba, from arresting Miramon when he arrived in Havana. Prim even urged Serrano to give Miramon a passport if he should want to go to Mexico.[102] Prim saw Miramon and Miranda but refused to "treat" with them. This he would do, Prim told the exiles, if they were able to form a "de facto" government in Mexico City.[103] Not knowing the attitude of the French Government toward Miramon, Jurien refused to reveal anything to the Mexican.[104] Miranda knew about Napoleon's plans for Maximilian from Estrada and was cordially received by Jurien, who was naturally "perfectly in accord" with Miranda's views.[105] Miranda was unable to do anything further in

Havana and decided to go to Vera Cruz, but he did not have ". . . any hope of being able to do anything worthwhile."[106] There were too many "saviours" for Mexico.[107] Serrano gave Miramon a passport made out to "M. Fernandez."[108] The ex-President gathered some thirty adherents and made preparations to go to Vera Cruz.[109] Miranda warned Estrada that ex-President Santa Anna also merely wanted to restore himself to power in Mexico. Then he would seize the "remnant" of Mexican finances and persecute his old enemies.[110]

Santa Anna wrote Estrada at the end of November 1861 from exile in the Virgin Islands, "Praise be to God that our hopes are being realized." Santa Anna unreservedly gave his support to Maximilian. Estrada was authorized to tell the Austrian Archduke and "our friends, but with every caution, because you know that in politics there are things that one can't announce until the opportune time." Convinced that the "moment to act" had arrived for him, Santa Anna was "inclined to return to the soil of my country as soon as possible, determined to work with all my powers until the realization of this affair."[111] A month later he feared that the small number of European troops would encounter stiff Mexican resistance.[112] He had the same doubts that Miranda had about Prim's liberalism and relatives in Mexico.[113] Santa Anna, therefore, cautiously remained in the Virgin Islands and sent his son "Angel" to Vera Cruz to survey the situation. He wanted to go to Vera Cruz himself, Santa Anna wrote Estrada, but was in bed with "fever."[114]

# V

# The First Disagreements Among the European Powers After the Arrival of the Allied Expeditionary Forces in Mexico

## 1. THE NEGOTIATIONS OF THE EUROPEAN REPRESENTATIVES IN MEXICO, JANUARY–FEBRUARY 1862

AT THE FIRST CONFERENCE OF THE ALLIED COMMISSIONERS in Vera Cruz on 9 January 1862, Wyke introduced Commodore Dunlop to Prim, Jurien, and Saligny.[1] Although plenipotentiary powers for Dunlop had not yet arrived,[2] it was agreed that he should act as a British Commissioner in the place of Admiral Milne. General Prim then suggested that the Commissioners issue a proclamation to the Mexican people to point out the "justice" and the "amicable" spirit of the intervention. Prim produced a draft proclamation.[3] There were no objections to it,[4] and it was published.[5] The purposes of the intervention were to put into effect "broken" treaties and to assure the "personal safety of our countrymen." There were no "hidden plans of conquest, of restorations, or of intervention in your policy of administration." Although the "primary interest" was to obtain satisfaction for legitimate claims, there was also a "higher interest." It was to "stretch a friendly hand" to the Mexican people, suffering under "the violent action of civil war and perpetual convulsions." Without any "menace" or "intervention of foreigners," the Mexican people were urged "to constitute yourselves in a solid and permanent manner." It would be the urgent "work of regeneration" that had to be done "now or never." The Europeans who had just arrived in Mexico were the "anchor of salvation," but they would only be "lookers-on," happy to "preside at the grand spectacles of your regeneration." The justice of this advice would be conceded by all "true patriots," who only needed to "appeal to reason, which is that which should triumph in the 19th century." Prim hoped that the assurances of the honorable intentions of the allies and the "conciliatory and generous tone" of the proclamation would "calm excitement." By the "friendly hand" Prim merely meant that the allies suggested that the "civil war . . . terminate as soon as possible" and would "help . . . to that end" by suggesting it. He did not want the allies to overthrow the Juarez Government:

> The allies had necessarily to treat with the Government of Juarez, because had they not done so, they would have broken every stipulation (i.e., of the Convention of London). And if they had destroyed the existing government to create another, what greater intervention could there be?
>
> .  .  .  .  .  .  .  .  .
>
> To establish another government than that of Juarez was to intervene; it was the same as declaring war, since reparation could not have been demanded from subaltern authorities.[6]

After his proclamation was approved, Prim proposed that a collective note be sent to the Mexican Government. French, Spanish, and British ultimatums would be enclosed. It would be demanded that they be accepted "without discussion." Prim's colleagues promised to draw up such ultimatums.[7]

Wyke agreed with Prim's views. The British Commissioner believed conciliation was the only realistic policy:

Without transport of any sort, it would have been impossible to march so small a force into the interior of the country to dictate terms to its government, and owing to the intense hatred felt . . . against the Spanish element . . ., we should have roused the whole population against us had we attempted to do so.[8]

Wyke believed that General Doblado was already "engaged in forming his Cabinet from the best men he could find, irrespective of their political opinions." All he needed was a little "time" to change some of the personnel of the government.[9] Wyke did not expect the proclamation to incite Mexicans to revolt against the Juarez Government. The triumph of the liberals in the Civil War[10] "clearly proved them to represent the wishes and feelings of the majority of their countrymen."[11] The proclamation, therefore, was "harmless" even if it did mention "regeneration."[12] Wyke was happy, however, that the proclamation showed the "good faith" of the allies in "declaring that we did not intend to interfere in the political affairs" of Mexico.[13] Commodore Dunlop believed that the reference to "regeneration" was "confined to giving our moral support to the formation of a strong gov't, from which we might hope for a redress of grievances."[14] Saligny and Jurien did not want to form a minority and therefore approved Prim's suggestions.[14] Saligny did not believe that negotiations would accomplish anything. Prim would soon be forced to admit the "enormity" of his "hopes and illusions." The Mexican Government would only negotiate to gain time to permit the "murderous climate" to force the allied troops to withdraw.[16] Jurien appreciated the "deep intelligence" of Saligny, but the Admiral inclined "more . . . towards prudence."[17] He did not want to compromise his mission "with too much impatience."[18]

After Prim's proclamation and proposal to send ultimatums to Mexico City were approved at the first meeting of the Allied Commissioners, it was decided to rotate the garrison of the fortress of St. Juan d'Ulloa every two weeks but to let the French, British, and Spanish flags wave above it regardless of the nationality of the garrison force.[19] Although Russell had recommended that the fortress be occupied exclusively by the British Marines, Commodore Dunlop's inspection of St. Juan d'Ulloa convinced him that its dampness was unhealthy. The British Commissioners, therefore, agreed to share the "obnoxious duty" of garrison duty in the fort.[20] Sanitary conditions in Vera Cruz were little better. Every street had an open sewer.[21] The city was overcrowded with European troops.[22] Two hundred Spanish troops were already hospitalized, some with yellow fever, when the French and British arrived.[23] As the number of Spaniards on the sick list increased,[24] Prim's "hair stood on end," for he foresaw that "thus an army melts away as if it were made of butter."[25] Mexicans in the environs of Vera Cruz were afraid to supply it with food, and there was a danger that provisions would be cut off altogether.[26] The Mexican soldiers on lookout duty outside Vera Cruz tried to prevent the peasants from bringing food to Vera Cruz.[27] Prim and Jurien, therefore, proposed making a reconnaissance to two nearby towns to determine whether some of the Spanish and French troops could camp there for reasons of health[28] and to prevent any interruption in the provisioning of Vera Cruz.[29] Wyke and Dunlop stated that their instructions did not permit them to order the British Marines beyond Vera Cruz. Jurien and Prim replied that, if British Marines did not take part in the reconnaissance, the Mexicans "would be sure to attribute their absence to some disunion among the allies." Both Wyke[30] and Dunlop[31] saw some justice in this reasoning. Since Tejeria and Medellin, the objectives of the reconnaissance were only some twenty miles from Vera Cruz, Dunlop agreed to allow one company of his Marines to accompany the French and Spanish forces.[32] He foresaw that, if he had to move the British Marines inland in the future to escape the unhealthy coastal climate, it would not be "consistent with our character to do so after the ground had been cleared for us."[33] Dunlop stipulated, however, that his Marines would return to Vera Cruz and stay there unless the Mexicans attacked the French and Spanish outposts.[34] The Commissioners agreed to postpone the discussion of the collection of custom duties and the occupation of the Pacific ports of Mexico, and the first conference ended.[35]

At the second conference of the Allied Commissioners, held on 10 January, it was agreed that a Spanish officer, Colonel Menduinas,[36] should act as Governor of Vera Cruz. For important matters he was to be assisted by a Council, composed of the three consuls of the allies in Vera Cruz. The Governor and his Council would have no jurisdiction over crimes committed by French or British military personnel, who would be subject to their own military authorities. It was also agreed that the collective note and ultimatums, not yet ready, should be brought to Mexico City by French, Spanish, and British officers who would wait no longer than eight days for a reply.[37] Then Prim, Jurien, and Dunlop led a reconnaissance beyond Vera Cruz. A small Mexican cavalry detachment was encountered, but it retreated without offering resistance.[38] Some 4,200 French and Spanish troops were left at Tejeria and Medellin, and two thousand Spaniards pitched tents just outside the gates of Vera Cruz.[39] That left approximately two thousand French and Spanish troops in Vera Cruz, of whom five hundred were hospitalized Spaniards.[40] The seven hundred British Marines were all lodged in Vera Cruz in a building the Mexicans had used as a hospital.[41] The next day seventeen were put on the sick list. Within two weeks the number rose to seventy-seven.[42]

After the Commanders-in-Chief returned to Vera Cruz, they held a third conference, on 13 January, with Sir Charles Wyke —Saligny was ill and absent from the meeting—to discuss the collective note to be sent to the Mexican Government.[43] It was agreed to address this note to President Juarez and that enclosures, the three ultimatums of the demands of the allies, be sent to the Mexican Minister of Foreign Relations.[44] Prim then suggesed that the ultimatums be read aloud.[45] Prim had with him his ultimatum, drawn up in accordance with his instructions, and Jurien had an ultimatum drafted by Saligny, who also had his instruction.[46] Wyke had drafted an ultimatum without reference to any recent instructions. He only had Russell's instructions relative to the allied expedition through 15 November 1861,[47] none of which gave any detailed directions about British claims.[48] The instructions of what classes of British claims Wyke was given discretionary powers to press[49] and that it was intended that the Commissioners communicate their ultimatums to each other[50] had been sent to Jamaica. There instructions were sent without such forwarding directions that had accompanied Russell's previous instructions.[51] It was assumed that Wyke would stop at Jamaica on his way to meet Admiral Milne and leave directions at the places he stopped for the forwarding of mail. Wyke never went to Port Royal, and the British Senior Naval Officer there merely retained Russell's instructions.[52]

Prim's ultimatum[53] demanded the immediate execution of conventions guaranteeing payment to Spanish claimants,[54] the payment of arrears of interest, and a promise to "recognize" the right of Spain to demand :

> . . . compensation for the injuries suffered by subjects of Her Majesty (i.e., the Queen of Spain) in consequence of the oppressive acts and outrages which have been committed, or may be committed, against them; the exemplary punishment of the perpetrators of those crimes, and of the authorities who, though able to do so, did not attempt to prevent them, and the solemn promise that for the future the repetition of such atrocious excesses will be avoided.

Prim did not desire to press specific claims "without ascertaining whether the facts are real." He believed the common practice was for claimants to demand three or four times the legitimate amount of redress.[55] In accordance with his instructions,[56] his ultimatum, however, did list a few claims for specific recognition,[57] because the facts were well known and negotiations concerning them in the past had been fruitless.[58] The only specific amount of redress mentioned in the Spanish ultimatum was $40,000 for the *Concepcion,* a Spanish ship seized by the Juarez Government.[59] The ship was burned in Vera

Cruz harbor at the first appearance of the Spanish squadron in December 1861.[60] The only other condition contained in Prim's ulimatum was that a Mexican agent be sent to Spain to give satisfaction for the expulsion of Pacheco, the last Spanish Minister to Mexico. Jurien had no objections to Prim's ultimatum.[61] Wyke considered it "fair and just."[62] Dunlop agreed that Prim's views were "most moderate."[63]

Wyke's ultimatum[64] demanded the "due and punctual fulfilment of all the stipulations contained in the various Treaties, Conventions, and Agreements at present existing between England and Mexico." Wyke believed the Convention of London was "clear and easily understood." on this point.[65] The word, "Agreements," was intended to cover the claims of the "London Bondholders," technically not recognized by "Treaties" or "Conventions."[66] Thus Mexico would have to recognize a debt of $63,000,000 to the London Bondholders[67] and $4,000,000 to the British "Convention Bondholders,"[68] compared with $9,000,000 owed Spanish bondholders.[69] While these debts would be retired gradually from custom duties, Wyke demanded the immediate repayment of the $660,000 stolen from the British Legation and the $279,000 still owed the "Laguna Seca" claimants.[70] Wyke also wanted the Mexican Government to turn over to the Convention and London Bondholders those custom duties withheld from them in virtue of the law of 17 July 1861, which suspended these payments. The Mexican Government was also asked to permit the appointment of British "Interventors" in Mexican ports to assure that the Convention and London Bondholders obtained their percentage of custom duties guaranteed them. These Interventors would have the power to reduce import duties up to 50 per cent if considered necessary. All these demands were almost in perfect accordance with instructions Russell had written in August 1861.[71] Wyke went beyond these most recent instructions in his possession[72] that outlined British claims in detail, because he thought that each ultimatum should contain "all the demands" of the respective Powers. In addition to the claims mentioned by Russell five months before,[73] there were many personal and property claims. Some of these were recognized as valid by the Mexican Government. Other claims were unrecognized or even uninvestigated. The second category presented a problem:

> Amongst the . . . foreign residents . . . 19 out of every 20 have a claim of some sort or other against the Government: many of them are really founded in justice, whilst others have been trumpted up and fabricated as good speculations to obtain money as compensation for some imaginary injury . . .[74]

Wyke solved the difficulty by demanding, in his ultimatum, that British claims "already acknowledged by the Mexican Government shall at once be liquidated." Other claims would be "fully examined" and, "if founded in justice and right, be also acknowledged as valid when such has been proved . . . and paid with as little delay as possible." Prim saw "no difficulty whatever in allowing" Wyke's ultimatum to claim such an "enormous sum." It was "the result of conventions and of legal settlements which had already been in the course of liquidation." Nor did Jurien object.[75]

Saligny's ultimatum[76] was read by Jurien after Prim and Wyke had read theirs. Saligny demanded the execution of a French convention[77] and the immediate payment of $11,000, the reparation still due the family of the French consul murdered in 1859.[78] Mexico would be "held to the full, loyal, and immediate execution of the contract contracted . . . between the Mexican Government and the House of Jecker."[79] For all other French personal and property claims, up to 31 July 1861, Saligny demanded $12,000,000. He made no stipulation for an investigation of these claims. This total was submitted for the "pure and simple acceptance of Mexico." Furthermore, he reserved the right to fix another total of reparations for losses sustained since 31 July 1861. Saligny announced that he himself would claim reparation for the (alleged) attempt against his life in August 1861 and for "outrages" inflicted on him by the Chief of Police of Mexico City in the following November. "Exemplary punishment" of the perpetrators was demanded, as well as the prosecution of all the culprits involved in crimes against Frenchmen. Saligny demanded the right for himself "to assist, in every kind of case . . . for this purpose, in all examinations opened by the criminal justice of the country."[80] France would have the right to occupy Vera Cruz, Tampico, and other Mexican ports. "Commissioners" would be appointed there. They would supervise the collection of Mexican custom duties to pay claims and have the power to reduce import duties up to 50 per cent. "Additional" duties, paid on imported merchandise after leaving the custom houses and amounting approximately to 80 per cent of the import duties,[81] under no "pretext" hereafter would exceed 15 per cent of import duties. The division of custom duties among claimants and additional conditions to "guarantee" the fulfillment of the French ultimatum would be decided by the Allied Commissioners. Wyke believed that the terms of the French ultimatum were "perfectly outrageous, and . . . so insulting as to render . . . acceptance by the Mexican Government impossible."[82] He would not sanction the demand for $12,000,000, because he did not know how Saligny had arrived at this total.[83] The other objection Wyke made to the ultimatum was that it supported Jecker's usurous claim. Prim recalled that, when Jurien read this part of the ultimatum, Wyke and Dunlop said:

. . . with one voice : "That claim is inadmissable; the Mexican Government will never accept it, before tolerating it they would go to war, and the arms of England will never support such great injustice."[84]

Prim was unacquainted with the details of the claim and asked Wyke to explain them. Wyke replied :

. . . the house of Jecker, which was of Swiss origin, but which had recently taken out French letters of naturalization, had given Miramon, when he was President, and during the last period of his office, 750,000 dollars in money, clothes, provisions and other effects, receiving in payment 15 millions of dollars in Treasury bonds, and that this sum was claimed by the French ultimatum.[85]

Jurien tried to give explanations, but the British Commissioners considered them unsatisfactory,[86] and it was decided to adjourn the discussion until Saligny's health permitted him to take part in it.[87]

The third conference of the Allied Commissioners was reopened on 14 January, when Saligny was able to attend. He said that he had fixed $12,000,000 as the total reparation for unsettled claims without examining them. Such an examination would take at least a year. His instructions directed him to name a total sum for the liquidation of French claims, and he considered the figure he had chosen an "approximation to their value by a million or two more or less." Wyke believed that "this is a very loose way of handling such a question as this, and the more so as . . . this and other claims shall be paid . . . by the Mexican Government, which is . . . debarred from having the justice of the claims examined into either by themselves or by some third party."[88] Prim had similar doubts.[89] Both Wyke and Prim objected to the Jecker claim and proposed that, pending the receipt of answers to requests for instructions from Europe, the ultimatums should only demand the execution of treaties and conventions. It was "clear" from a reading of the Convention of London that this demand should be made. Saligny replied that such a proceeding was not permitted by his instructions.[90] Prim feared that he would compromise the Spanish Government by permitting the French ultimatum to be sent to the Mexican Government,[91] because he understood that the Convention of London bound each of the allies to support the claims submitted by the other two. Wyke was not sure whether this was the intention in signing the Convention of London, and Russell's instructions did not "bear on this point." Saligny refused to modify his ultimatum in any way, and the only agreement that could be reached was that the ultimatums should be retained until the receipt of instructions about them from the British, French, and Spanish Governments. It was also agreed to recommend to these governments that they appoint a "Sub-Commission" of three lawyers and an accountant. Their function would be to "report . . . the fair amount to be claimed by each Government, which, when thus ascertained, should then be insisted on in the name of all three."[92] Throughout this discussion of claims, Dunlop supported Wyke's "view of the case" and expected that the French Government would modify Saligny's ultimatum so that it would "assume an entirely different character."[93] Jurien agreed to put the issue of claims aside for the moment in order "not to break today an alliance so laboriously formed." The Commissioners had to "be content to agree on the general ends of the combined intervention in Mexico."[94] Saligny had two sets of instructions about claims, those of Thouvenel giving him a complete discretion and those of Napoleon III that French claims be made "excessive."[95] It is probable that Thouvenel was unaware of Napoleon's instructions. This would explain why Saligny wrote Thouvenel that a lack of personnel prevented an immediate examination of all French claims. Saligny added that he hoped $12,000,000 were sufficient.[96] A French Ministry of Foreign Affairs memorandum on Saligny's ultimatum noted that $12,000,000 "seems very high." The "Department" had "estimated . . . what is known of the total of debts" and "only arrived at 10 million francs ($2,000,000) *maximum*."[97] In view of this memorandum and a confidence of Saligny, it is probable that Napoleon himself set the figure of $12,000,000. Prim was told by Saligny that he believed French claims amounted to $10,000,000, but he was directed to ask for $12,000,000 and had no choice in the matter.[98]

When it was decided not to send the ultimatums to the Mexican Government, an escort and safe conduct for the officers, already selected,[99] to carry these ultimatums had been requested of General Uraga, the Commander of the Mexican Army of the East. The escort was waiting at Tejeria for the European officers. Jurien, therefore, suggested that it was "indispensable to find a mission for these officers and to draft instructions that we want to send."[100] Prim produced the collective note he had drafted[101] and which had been approved the day before as a suitable one to which to append the ultimatums.[102] This note stated that the purposes of the intervention were to enforce treaties, insure the safety of "fellow countrymen," and to make "just claims." A "friendly hand" was offered, for it was time to end "anarchy" and respect the rights of Mexicans and foreigners. There was no reason to fear that there would be an interference with the form of government or the independence of Mexico. The allies were ready to show the "road" to "prosperity," but it was up to Mexico "alone" and "without foreign intervention" to "take that road." Then it would be easy to fulfill "international obligations" and to maintain "order and liberty."[103] Wyke approved the "extremely conciliatory tone" of the note and agreed with Prim that "persuasion" should be attempted before using force.[104] Wyke, Prim, and Dunlop all agreed that it was undesirable to start immediate hostilities. They believed that it was necessary to gain time until instructions about claims arrived from Europe.[105] The Mexicans hated the Spanish invaders and would offer stiff resistance.[106] None of the expeditionary forces had means of transportation to go into the interior.[107] Great losses could be expected at the first engagement at the beginning of the plateau at the end of the coastal plain, for the Mexicans were fortifying the mountain passes there.[108] The day after having approved Prim's note and when it had been decided not to enclose the ultimatums, Jurien gave his opinion that negotiations would lead to no satisfactory result, and the health of the allied forces would be jeopardized at Vera Cruz. Such a Mexican strategy would be assisted "through our differences of opinion." Jurien suggested that possession of the healthier Jalapa Plateau be demanded of the Mexican Government. If refused, Jurien proposed taking the cooler highlands by force.[109] In the interests of "unity of action,"[110] Dunlop stated that, in spite of his instructions not to permit his Marines to go beyond

Vera Cruz, he would assume full responsibility, in the interests of his men, for leading them to a healthy location if the French and Spanish troops were moved there[111] His decision pleased Jurien,[112] but Prim remarked that the situation was grave. He did not believe that such a march, on the way to Mexico City, would be permitted by the Mexican Government. Then the allied forces would have to be prepared to advance to save face. There would be guerrela attacks, and the hatred of all Mexicans for Spaniards would be directed against all the allied troops. While Jurien had stated that the Americans reached Mexico City with 10,000 troops during the Mexican War (1846–1848), he had failed to say that the Americans had had 30,000 troops in Mexico at the time. The humiliation of defeat also had to be taken into consideration. Jurien replied that he had more confidence in success. The alternative was that the European troops would have to leave Mexico to avoid the deadly climate. If this were the result of the conference, Jurien said he would immediately send a frigate to France with a request for more troops.[113] Wyke and Prim believed that an attempt to force a passage through the fortified mountain passes leading to the healthy plateau beyond probably would result in a loss of a third of the allied forces. Even then a retreat might be necessary.[114] Then Jurien proposed a compromise. Prim's proposed collective note should be modified by removing from it the sections "too favorable to the present government of Mexico, to entrust this note to our delegates, adding to it the verbal order to demand the occupation of Jalapa for our troops." Such measures would "reserve our complete liberty of action and would permit us to wait for reinforcements or new orders."[115] The insertion in Prim's draft note of the following was suggested:

We come here to be the witnesses and in case of need the protectors of the regeneration of Mexico. We come to help in Mexico's definitive organization without wanting to intervene in any way in the form of her Government or in her internal administration.[116]

Saligny agreed to sign this altered version. He considered the original draft too "benevolent, of an excessive confidence," and would only have agreed to it if his ultimatum had been enclosed[117] Prim believed that the altered version of his draft note was a departure from the strict interpretation of the Convention of London by not making the primary purpose of the intervention "the claims," but he agreed in view of "the difficulty in which we . . . found ourselves placed."[118] Wyke accepted the "harmless" insertion of "regeneration" in order to gain time. He did not believe that he bound himself to assist in this "regeneration" by signing the note.[119] He believed the note to be conciliatory in spite of the French alteration of the original.[120] Dunlop was willing to make sacrifices of "forebearance" to the "extent of even yielding occasionally minor points for the sake of preserving harmony of action," and he assumed that he "could not be held responsible for every sentiment and high sounding word that found its way into the collective notes addressed . . . to the Mexican Authorities."[121] In the course of the altering of Prim's original draft of the collective note, Jurien made clear what was meant by the "regeneration of Mexico." He said that he would advise any Mexican, who should ask what kind of government was most suitable for Mexico, that "monarchical government" was "the only form of government that could put an end to the dissensions of which Mexico has for so long given us a sad spectacle." Prim doubted the practicality of such advice :

> The Mexicans wouldn't ever want monarchical government. As a subject myself of a monarchy . . . I could only give your advice, but I would give such advice without the least hope of seeing it listened to.

Jurien replied that "we have every interest to permit ourselves time to enlighten ourselves on the true sentiments of the country."[122] This talk of monarchy worried Wyke. He reported to Russell that the French Commissioners reluctantly agreed to send the collective note to Juarez. The reason was Saligny's "extreme hostility . . . to the Juarez Government, which Admiral de la Graviere seems also anxious to get rid of, with the hope of establishing a monarchy in its place." Wyke believed the allies should not interfere to bring about such a change :

> Whether such a change would be beneficial or not remains to be proved; but if it does take place, it should proceed from the will of the nation itself, as any suggestion coming from us on such a subject could only be looked on by the Mexicans as an unwarrantable interference on our part.

On 14 January, when the third conference ended, a delegation of officers left Vera Cruz for Mexico City with the collective note and instructions verbally to ask for healthy encampments for the allied troops, suggesting the cities of Jalapa and Orizaba.[123]

While the Allied Commissioners waited for a reply to their collective note, Saligny wrote Thouvenel that there was no reason to fear that "peaceful" or "satisfactory arrangements" would be made. The Mexican Government would answer that the first basis of negotiations would be the evacuation of all the European troops from Mexico. Prim was responsible for holding up hostilities and had obtained the support of Wyke. Saligny was under no such "illusions," for "three thousand French troops could have been able to go all the way to Mexico City by a rapid march without hardly a shot fired."[124] While waiting in Vera Cruz, Saligny carried on his "correspondence with the interior."[125] He attempted to persuade two Mexican officers, General Uraga and General Robles, to form a triumvirte with General Doblado to overthrow Juarez and to proclaim a monarchy.[126] Saligny had met General Uraga, the Commander of the Army of the East, at Mexico City in November 1861. Saligny believed him to be "false to the last degree, and as deceitful as a Mexican."[127] Saligny also believed that General Doblado, Juarez' Chief Minister, was dishonest[128] and intended to start a revolution against Juarez.[129] Saligny received regular letters from General Robles, who predicted a rupture between Juarez and Doblado.[130] When Saligny went to Vera Cruz from Mexico City, General Robles continued writing him letters in this sense.[131] Just before Prim, Dunlop, and Jurien arrived in Vera Cruz, Saligny saw Uraga outside Vera Cruz and urged him to join Robles in asking Doblado to overthrow Juarez and proclaim a monarchy.[132] Under the mistaken impression that Uraga would cooperate,[133] Saligny was overjoyed that he was "getting along with the General-in-Chief of the Army of the East!"[134] Saligny also believed he could count on General Robles, "the only General and perhaps the only man of honour in the Country."[135] Saligny convinced Jurien of the trustworthiness of Robles,[136] and "very compromising" letters were sent to him.[137] General Uraga later made public that Saligny offered him a Marshal's baton and the title of duke in return for disavowing Juarez. Uraga did not publish his correspondence with Saligny, but challenged him to do so.[138] Saligny ignored the challenge.[139] Although he initiated these intrigues on his own authority,[140] they were later approved by Thouvenel.[141]

Just the reverse was happening of what Jurien's instructions[142] anticipated. Prim was reluctant to march inland although permitted to do so by his instructions, and Dunlop was willing to lead his men beyond Vera Cruz in spite of his instructions. Jurien complained to Thouvenel that "war would have been declared," had it not been for Prim.[143] On 17 January Jurien saw Prim and tried to explain what the Admiral termed the two objectives of the intervention. Spain was to be given a chance to regain the prestige lost in Europe. The second purpose in coming to Mexico was that "our presence could encourage the men in Mexico who want to substitute a stable government for a government of anarchy in Mexico."[144] Prim liked Jurien and was sorry that he was not the only French Plenipotentiary, for Prim believed that the French Admiral was more "in harmony with me . . . than he was with his Colleague M. Saligny."[145] Nevertheless, Jurien obtained no promises from Prim to march inland to upset the Juarez Government. A few days later Jurien wrote Thouvenel, "The only thing to do is wait, always insist to lead our troops to Jalapa, then to Puebla, and finally to Mexico City."[146]

The holding back of the ultimatums put Prim in a precarious position. There was no longer any basis upon which to negotiate with Juarez except to ask permission for an advance to healthier quarters. Even if such a request were approved, there would still be difficulties. None of the expeditionary forces brought any means of transportation for a move beyond Vera Cruz. The British and French didn't even have tents. The French troops at Tejeria slept under ship sails.[147] In view of the urgent necessity of leaving the unhealthy coast, Prim sent a request to the Captain-General of Cuba to send means of transportation and provisions for two months.[148]

Immediately after the third conference of the Allied Commissioners, Commodore Dunlop wrote to the Secretary of the Admiralty to request discretionary powers to advance the British Marines inland for their health and suggested a "black regiment" replace them for garrison duty in Vera Cruz. Then Dunlop set his men to work sewing tents[149] from duck cloth carried aboard British ships.[150]

On the same day that the third conference ended, Wyke wrote Hammond, the British Under-Secretary of State, a private letter to complain of a lack of recent or detailed instructions. Wyke also complained that Saligny's "violent and unreasoning hostility against the Mexicans individually and collectively" made him "a very difficult person for one to act cordially with in circumstances requiring great tact and conciliation."[151] A few days later Wyke wrote Russell that the allied forces in Mexico were not large enough to commence hostilities. Since Great Britain, of the intervening Powers, had the most at stake, it was impossible to stand by idle and let Spain and France fight for British interests, should it be necessary to resort to force. To provide for such an eventuality, Wyke suggested that a few "black regiments" be sent to gar-

rison Vera Cruz. "Europeans" just could not stay in Vera
Cruz, beyond the coastal plain "the climate is delightful and all
danger from sickness . . . disappears."[152]

A fourth meeting of the Allied Commissioners was held on
18 January. It was agreed that the previous meeting of 13–14
January be considered unofficial. Copies of the proposed
ultimatums were exchanged to be sent to the respective European Governments "to judge their fitness, and whether they
should be sustained or not." Prim and Wyke again urged
Saligny, in the meantime, to limit all three ultimatums to
demand the "fulfilment of all Treaties and engagements," but
he refused. It was agreed to suggest the appointment of a
"Sub-Commission" by the French, Spanish, and British Governments to investigate and to settle "the amount of the special
claims not included in the general terms of the Treaty (i.e., of
London)." It was then decided that if, as rumored, General
Doblado came to Orizaba to treat with the Allied Commissioners, he would be informed that they did not:

> . . . intend to press . . . claims at present, but to use . . . best
> efforts to secure the existence of a firm and respectable
> Government; and that in the meantime a more healthy and
> convenient position should be granted to the allied forces than
> Vera Cruz. . . .

Dunlop stated that he intended to accompany the French and
Spanish forces with his Marines to remove them from the
danger of yellow fever at Vera Cruz if such an arrangement
"could be peaceably obtained." Transportational difficulties
were discussed, and it was decided to send a ship down the
coast to Alvarado to purchase mules, carts, and harnesses. Prim
suggested that instructions be sent to the British and French
Admirals off the Pacific coast of Mexico. It was agreed they
should be instructed not to seize any Mexican ports until
they "had learnt, by reliable information, that hostilities had
actually begun here between the allied forces and those of
Mexico."[153]

After the fourth conference, Saligny wrote Thouvenel that Wyke had used "violent" language in condemning French claims. Instead of recommending a "Sub-Commission," Saligny proposed that a French committee investigate French claims so that he would not be "responsible" for them. The committee would be composed of the French consul at Vera Cruz, a Secretary of the French Legation in Mexico, and a merchant.[154] Saligny also used various excuses to make Jurien responsible for reporting the key conferences of the Allied Commissioners.[155]

When the Spanish originally landed in Vera Cruz in December 1861, they found the custom house abandoned, and Spaniards were placed in charge. Since transactions were in Spanish, the British and French Commissions left the Spaniards in sole charge of the Vera Cruz Custom House. General Prim financed administrative expenses from funds he brought with him for military operations.[156] At the opening of the fifth conference on 25 January, Prim gave an account of difficulties encountered in custom house operations. The merchants importing goods were claiming that they could not pay duties in cash. They offered "bills" and threatened that, if these were not accepted, the merchandise would be placed in bond and the allies held responsible for losses and damages. Prim admitted that there was a scarcity of money in Vera Cruz, but he believed the merchants exaggerated. He claimed their "bills" were "worthless." He needed ready money to administer the custom house. Prim commented that this was a difficulty the French, British, and Spanish Governments had overlooked. They had "imagined" that:

> . . . the collection of the revenue would be the simplest thing in the world—a supposition which, theoretically, looked well enough, but practically, and in the actual state of the country, could not be acted upon.[157]

The protests of the merchants were legitimate to a great extent. Philip Baker, an ex-agent of the British bondholders, had warned Lord Russell of this difficulty in a private letter four weeks before the Convention of London was signed. Import duties were payable in Mexico City, because there were high charges for escorting money to the coast to protect it from robbers.[158] In view of the receipt of so many private letters at the time, Russell merely acknowledged Baker's letter,[159] and it was filed with the others[160] After Prim reported the difficulties involved in custom house operations, the Allied Commissioners decided that their consuls in Vera Cruz were best qualified to find a solution. Therefore the problem was referred to the Council of consuls associated with the Governor of Vera Cruz.[161]

Before the fifth conference Wyke and Dunlop had heard a rumor that General Miramon could be expected in Vera Cruz soon and that he would place himself at the head of the Conservative Party,[162] to "raise the standard of revolt."[163] The British Commissioners decided that Miramon's connection with the robbery of the British Legation in 1860 denied him the right of taking sanctuary in Vera Cruz so long as the British were there. To permit him to organize a following against Juarez seemed a "bitter and unworthy sarcasm" on the Proclamation to the Mexican people and the collective note sent to Juarez.[164] The matter was brought up in the fifth conference of 25 January. Dunlop stated that he would arrest Miramon on arrival for having permitted the robbery of the British Legation.[165] Jurien expressed surprise,[166] and Saligny said he would protest in the name of his Emperor against any interference with Miramon after he set foot in Vera Cruz, over which the French flag was flying.[167] Prim asked Wyke and Dunlop not to arrest Miramon,[168] because it was unwise to alienate the Conservative Party. The Commissioners might have to turn to it if the Juarez Government refused to negotiate.[169] Wyke replied that, if Miramon were permitted to land and to invade Mexico with an expedition of his own, negotiations with the Juarez Government would be compromised :

. . . we should as certainly utterly disgust the present Government, to whom we are now making overtures of peace and conciliation, for they would never believe we were friendly in our intentions towards them, if we thus allow a fresh element of strife and discord to be introduced into the country when we might so easily have prevented it.

Wyke's argument "had its weight with General Prim . . . was only half admitted by Admiral de la Graviere, and still opposed by M. de Saligny." [170] Wyke and Dunlop then proposed a compromise. They would only arrest Miramon if he arrived on the British mail packet. [171] It was not proposed to arrest Miramon's adherents, rumored to arrive with him, [172] because the British Commissioners believed that they could never persuade their colleagues to agree. [173] If Miramon arrived on a ship other than the British packet, Prim would suggest to him, [174] in the name of the Allied Commissioners, [175] not to enter a city over which flew "the flag that he personally had offended." [176] Jurien agreed to make this "last concession," he wrote Thouvenel, "in the interests of maintaining good harmony among us." [177] Isolated, Saligny agreed to the compromise. He considered that he thereby reached "the last limits of possible concessions." [178]

Miramon and thirty of his followers arrived at Vera Cruz on 27 January [179] aboard the British mail packet *Avon*. A British Admiralty agent, Lt. Charles Slaughter, was also aboard. He gave orders not to permit Miramon to disembark. Then Lt. Slaughter went to see Commodore Dunlop and informed him that Miramon was aboard the mail packet with a passport carrying the alias "M. Fernandez." [180] In the meantime the captain of one of Dunlop's ships boarded the *Avon* [181] with someone who had been located in Vera Cruz and who was willing to identify Miramon. [182] The ex-President was arrested, taken aboard a British warship, and held prisoner. [183] Wyke wanted Miramon to leave with the mail packet, but Dunlop feared that Miramon's accomplices were numerous enough to seize the ship and to force its captain to land them somewhere on the Mexican coast. Wyke didn't approve holding Miramon beyond the departure of the *Avon*, and so Dunlop assumed responsibility for the orders he gave concerning his prisoner.[184] He would be sent to Havana on board a British warship. The captain of this ship would give the Captain-General of Cuba a letter from General Prim that Miramon was to be prevented from boarding another ship leaving for Mexico.[185] Then Dunlop wrote Admiral Milne to justify Miramon's arrest. Had Miramon been permitted to land in Vera Cruz, Dunlop reasoned, the "Liberal Party" probably would have broken off negotiations, and hostilities would have resulted. Then Mexicans would have believed that the allies wanted to support the "Church Party," a "fanatical and bigoted minority." Dunlop did not desire to make such an impression, for it would make Mexicans believe that the allies wanted to impose a particular government on them:

> We have come here to assist the Mexicans to inaugurate a new era, as well as to demand our just rights, and these objects can only be gained by keeping ourselves free from all party grounds for suspicion that we wish to dictate to Mexico by whom she is to be governed.[186]

Wyke wrote Russell that the news of Miramon's "being frustrated in his designs cannot but be productive of the very best results." The reason was that "the great majority of the nation is Liberal" and "violently opposed" to the principles Miramon "pretends to support." In reality Miramon was "only thinking of his own personal ambition."[187] Miramon's partisans landed in Vera Cruz and tried to purchase arms and military supplies, but Prim put a stop to it. He also sent a message to the Mexican General Uraga to be on the lookout for this revolutionary group that might attempt to "penetrate inland." Wyke heartily approved[188] and believed that there was no harm done so long as Miramon's followers remained in Vera Cruz.[189]

The British, Spanish, and French officers, who had been sent to Mexico City with the collective note, arrived in Vera Cruz on 28 January with a Mexican reply.[190] The officers had seen President Juarez, who received them courteously and who was given the collective note. Captain Thomasset, the French officer, saw Juarez' Minister of Foreign Relations and told him that the allies would march into the interior no matter what kind of a reply they received to their request to do so.[191] While the allied delegation waited for a reply to carry back to Vera Cruz,[192] rumors were circulated that Brigadier Milans del Bosch, Prim's representative, had pronounced against monarchy. A dinner was held at the Prussian Legation. There Brigadier Milans remarked that the allies came to Mexico with "good faith and . . . disinterestedness." Then he drank a toast to the health of the Mexican ladies present.[193] Spaniards resident in Mexico City[194] spread a rumor that Milans "disclaimed against Monarchy and drunk to the Universal Republic." This rumor reached Madrid[195] and Paris. The form in which Napoleon III heard the rumor was that Milans "replied to those who displayed a desire for the return of the monarchy *that there would soon be no monarchies left in Europe* !"[196]

Juarez directed General Doblado, his Chief Minister and Minister of Foreign Relations, to make a reply to the allies. At great length Doblado enlarged on the theme that he did not need the "support" of the European troops. They were not required to "consolidate" his regime. It was obeyed by all the states of Mexico and was supported by the "general will." The truth of these assertions was in no way "lessened by the existence of some bands of rebels." They were unable to hold a single village and "remain in the mountains." Doblado declined any military assistance, because it would "excite ambitions which now are smothered by . . . public opinion." Then the "peace . . . now being enjoyed" would be disturbed. The European troops were also unnecessary for the purpose of "obtaining justice" for pending claims. The Mexican Government had "the will and the means to satisfy completely . . . just claims." Doblado promised to send Commissioners to Orizaba to treat with the representatives of the allies, who could bring two thousand troops as a "guard of honour." The remaining troops should be reembarked. Otherwise Mexicans would reject any agreements made "as wrung from them by means of armed force, and as agreed to without free-will on the part of the Mexican Government." Since he did not want to do the allies the "injustice" of assuming that they had any other "view" than what was stated in the collective note, Doblado foresaw no reason for the rejection of his "proposition."[197] With the intention of preventing "ambitions" from being "excited" against him, Juarez had a Presidential Decree published before the allied officers were able to return to Vera Cruz. This decree was later utilized against Maximilian at his trial before Mexican authorities who condemned him to death in 1867.[198] All persons, Mexicans and foreigners in Mexico, were placed outside the law and in advance sentenced to death, should they in any way assist foreign invaders or in any other way jeopardize Mexican independence.[199]

When Doblado's "proposition" arrived in Vera Cruz on 28 January, Prim had already sent six hundred sick Spaniards back to Havana.[200] Prim realized that worse could be expected in a few weeks when the "terrible climate" would get worse and the "period . . . of death" began. He decided that his troops had to be moved inland, but he still wanted to avoid declaring war on the "constituted" government and "entering the land with fire and sword." Prim believed Doblado's note was a "frank reply" that his Government "acknowledged that they had committed faults which they were ready to repair." The Spanish Commander-in-Chief decided, therefore, that negotiations should be continued to avoid bloodshed.[201] Wyke agreed. He could not consent to reembark any of the allied forces, but he believed that permission to march two thousand European troops beyond the fortified mountain passes "proves that they would rather treat with than fight us." Private letters from Mexico City led Wyke to believe that :

> . . . all the high-sounding phrases the note contains are meant less for us than as a means of preventing the Opposition from

accusing the present Administration of giving the country up, bound hand and foot, to an armed intervention.

Wyke concluded :

> I believe that General Doblado . . . is anxious to arrange matters amicably with us if he can only succeed in appeasing . . . the violent animosity that is felt throughout the country against the Spaniards.[202]

On 28 January there were seventy-one British Marines on the sick list.[203] Dunlop decided that he would be unfit for his post if he did not take the responsibility upon himself to find sanitary quarters for his men. They could not be reembarked, for this would defeat the purpose of the intervention. Dunlop conferred with Wyke, and they agreed that British Marines would march inland with French and Spanish troops, either to accompany the Commissioners to Orizaba for negotiations or to seek sanitary quarters when decided that this had to be done.[204] Some of the British Marines were still sewing tents, while others were building a "four gun battery" for "field service."[205] Jurien thought Doblado's note was "ambiguous," but the French Admiral was not ready to commence hostilities at once in order to avoid bloodshed.[206] It would be the first step toward reaching Mexico City if he could reach Jalapa "peacably."[207] With "calmness and patience" Jurien hoped to arrive at Mexico City, where he would "watch developments."[208] At this time Wyke reported to Russell that Jurien was a "charming person, but . . . at present, still under the influence of . . . Saligny, to whom . . . he goes for information." Prim could not be praised enough for his "prudence and tact . . . without which we should already have been at open war with the Mexicans."[209] General Prim, therefore, assured a "majority of one" in favor of Wyke and Dunlop, as opposed by Saligny and Jurien. Yet, as Wyke observed a month later, the British–Spanish solidarity was :

> . . . gradually strengthened and made practically useful by the thoroughly amiable and prudent bearing of the Admiral, who

could not avoid feeling that a peaceful line of policy should
be adopted before rushing into hostilities with a government
at the head of eight millions of people, who might be persuaded to grant by persuasion that which they would refuse by
threats.[210]

Saligny complained to Thouvenel that he also had to "submit"
to the "majority" regarding Juarez' decree. Wyke said it wasn't
important, and Prim claimed it could be ignored, because it
was not officially communicated to the allies.[211]

An "unofficial" conference of the Allied Commissioners was
held on 28 January to discuss Doblado's answer to the collective note. Jurien reported that the meeting was "cold and
constrained (*gênée*)." It was merely agreed that the allied
troops should be gotten ready to march, that each of the allies
would supply fifty men in rotation to garrison St. Juan
d'Ulloa,[212] and that one hundred men from each of the three
expeditionary forces would remain in Vera Cruz.[213] The same
day Jurien and Saligny met Zamacona, an ex-Minister of
Foreign Relations sent to Vera Cruz by Doblado. Jurien told
Zamacona that the allies were determined "to go to Jalapa
peaceably or by force." The Mexican replied that the French
and British could go there, but the Spanish would impinge on
"national susceptibilities." Then Jurien asserted that the allies
were determined to make good their claims. Perhaps a general
election or calling a congress of notables would result in a
suggestion for "the solution of the difficulties against which
Mexico has been fighting for fifty years." The "notables,"
Zamacona observed, represented the past that the liberals
would not permit to return.[214] Saligny's only comment on the
conference was that he found Zamacona "under the sway of
the same ideas and the same illusions."[215] Two days later Zamacona dined with Jurien, who outlined his "program." Although
he did not want to spill blood, he insisted, "Whatever happens,
we will go to Jalapa, and we will lead all our forces there."
The next day, 31 January, Jurien told Zamacona in front of
Wyke that the allied troops could not stay in Vera Cruz and

had to go to Jalapa. Both Wyke and Zamacona should understand the "necessity to be finished with . . . ambiguous replies."
Zamacona replied that he was certain the Mexican Government would change its decision. Then Jurien reported the
conversation to Thouvenel and commented that "patience"
would bring results.[216]

At the end of January 1862 the European intervention
in Mexico had reached a seeming stalemate. The Mexican
Government refused to allow all of the European troops to
advance from Vera Cruz to the healthier highlands. The "hot"
season was approaching, when, according to the Municipal
Register of Vera Cruz, at least 12 per cent of the inhabitants
died. The Surgeon attached to the British Marine Brigade
predicted that "we must be prepared for a much greater mortality than people who are acclimated."[217] The allied forces could
not be reembarked, as suggested by Doblado, because that
would be a fiasco. Lack of transportation prevented a march
forward. As a pamphlet published the next year aptly put it,
"A strange situation of not being able to advance, nor to withdraw, nor to stay!"[218] The Allied Commanders-in-Chief —
Prim, Dunlop, Jurien — agreed to continue negotiations with
the Juarez Government in order to obtain healthy encampments for their men before resorting to war. Negotiations would
be with General Doblado, Juarez' Minister of Foreign Relations and his Chief Minister in the cabinet. The crux of all the
difficulties of the Allied Commissioners was how they regarded
Juarez' Government. Prim considered Juarez to have constituted a government "*de facto* and *de jure.*" Prim believed that
this government "was recognized by the allies the very moment
they entered into official relations with it."[219] Dunlop agreed
that negotiations had to be with the Juarez Government,
because it represented "the majority of the Mexican people."[220]
Wyke believed that he perceived a change in the composition
of the Juarez Government. The Mexican Civil War had ended
in a manner that proved Juarez' Liberal Party represented the
majority of Mexicans. In 1861, however, the "scum was

thrown to the surface," and the leadership of the Liberal Party was assumed by a "set of noisy and violent demagogues who . . . thought only of utterly destroying the influence of the Priests." [221] Armed with emergency powers granted him in December 1861, [222] Doblado was attempting to "turn a deaf ear to the clamours of the mob." [223] Wyke foresaw that his hopes of 1861, that an intervention in Mexico would lead to the creation of a government of "Moderates," [224] might be realized by Doblado's reforms. He was appointing dictators in the various states and "giving a death blow to the federal system, that prevented the establishment of a strong and respectable govt." Wyke expected Doblado to continue reforms along these lines :

> Doubtless ere long he will have filled . . . important posts with persons devoted to his policy. The Intervention is thus indirectly bearing its fruits, and I trust that we may soon have in this country a strong and intelligent government willing to treat with us. . . . [225]

In a private letter accompanying this despatch to Lord Russell, Wyke suggested that it might be necessary to give *direct* aid to Doblado. Such a move might be necessary, because Russell had not accepted Wyke's advice to intervene in Mexico without allies :

> If we mean to sustain the demands of France and Spain as well as our own, it becomes quite evident that until the country is regenerated, its resources will never be sufficient to satisfy them and the sooner therefore we set about helping them to effect this regeneration the better. Had we looked only to our own interests the plan I proposed was the best, viz., to act *alone,* when by seizing the ports on both coasts simultaneously we should have held the Government in a vice, and forced them not only to fulfil their Treaty obligations to us but also to have settled the claims of such British subjects as were really and truly entitled to compensation for injuries inflicted on them.

> .      .      .      .      .      .

> The whole question is a very serious one calling for the mature consideration of Her Majesty's Government, for things

have now taken such a turn as may require an intervention or armed protectorate to enable the respectable people in this country to triumph over mob rule and to establish such a government as will offer us a secure guarantee for the future that the lives and property of our Subjects shall be respected and our treaty stipulations duly fulfilled.[226]

Saligny had no sympathy for a policy of moderation. He wanted to start hostilities to overthrow the Juarez Government. From the "very first day," Prim asserted, Saligny's "aim . . . to settle the question by fire and sword was well known."[227] Wyke also complained that Saligny made "the solution . . . in the sense of moderation and peace one of particular difficulty." He had "personal feelings of dislike to the Ministers of the present administration,"[228] without "the downfall of which he can see no hope for the future."[229] When Saligny's views were not shared by his colleagues, he "adopted the system," in Prim's ironic words, "of grumbling at his own house and of throwing discredit . . . upon what he had done at the Conferences, and had sanctioned by his presence and his signature."[230] Saligny also talked "most imprudently," Wyke wrote Russell, "about the establishment of a Monarchy here."[231] Wyke and Dunlop were "annoyed" and went to Prim to suggest demanding an "official explanation." Prim, while "irritated," tried to "calm" his British colleagues, and the conferences of the Allied Commissioners continued into February "in at least official harmony."[232]

Saligny's correspondence "with the interior" and Jurien's instructions from Thouvenel and Napoleon III[233] were all based on the assumption that Mexicans would initiate a monarchist uprising in favor of the European intervention. Jurien found no indications that such a conspiracy was underway.[234] All that he could do was to try to reach Mexico City in accordance with Napoleon's instructions in hopes of encountering monarchists along the way.[235] According to Captain Thomasset, the French officer who had been a member of the delegation that brought the collective note to Juarez, the monarchists existed, but they feared to make themselves known so long as the European troops remained at the coast:

> In such a state of anarchy it is easy to understand the almost universal fervent desires in favor of the intervention. All honorable foreigners, all Mexicans not compromised, all men of property are calling for the arrival into the Capital of the foreign troops, but they fear to let these aspirations be known; corrupt, but energetic, men can only lose by the establishment of a regular order and dominate by terror the masses who only demand support to express their sentiments. I saw men of very different political shades and of all nations, and all said the same thing: "There isn't a man in Mexico who has enough strength to dominate; there isn't any party that can rally the other parties to itself. Moderate and honest men of all shades are ready to rally around a strong power, around a monarchy supported for some time, some years perhaps, by the troops of the allied forces." This is the opinion of all the foreign political agents, and furthermore it is not difficult to see that no matter what the pretensions of certain men of Mexico are to proclaim themselves Republicans, the aristocratic principle remains everywhere in this country.

> .     .     .     .     .     .     .     .

> I will add that it would be illusory to count on the parties that I said were ready to aid us. Until our bayonnets give courage to these masses that are trembling, no one will pronounce himself for us; no one will come to assist us in our march into the interior.

Thomasset estimated that 15,000 infantry and 1,000 cavalry would "suffice" for operations to capture Mexico City. He proposed that 2,000 troops should be stationed in Puebla and at least 1,500 each in Orozaba and Jalapa to maintain communications with Vera Cruz. Thomasset believed 8,000 troops should be used to attack Mexico City itself. Jurien had Thomasset put his opinions in writing and forwarded the report to Thouvenel.[236] The one thing, therefore, that all the Allied Commissioners were agreed upon at the end of January 1862 was that, either to support or to overthrow the Juarez Government, it was necessary to advance beyond Vera Cruz.

Admiral Maitland, the Commander of the British squadron

operating off the Pacific coast of Mexico, arrived at Callao in Peru on 9 January 1862. There he found his French counterpart, Admiral Larrien. Maitland summarized his instructions, including the modified ones to await instructions from Wyke. Larrien had instructions to cooperate with Maitland, but had not yet received the "modified" orders. The French Admiral promised to wait for these orders at Callao and then join Maitland at Panama.[237] The British Admiral proceeded to Toboga Island, Panama, arriving there on 30 January.[238] There he learned that the Acting Governor of Sinaloa had published a proclamation that, when an enemy force arrived, Mexicans should offer no resistance, destroy anything that might be of use to the invaders, and retire to the interior.[239] In anticipation of such a tactic, Maitland considered it necessary to send to the Mexican coast all the provisions and coals needed by ships commencing hostilities there. In accordance with his instructions and in order to know the extent of operations before sending provisions and ships, Maitland waited at Toboga Island for directions from Wyke. Admiral Larrien also waited there, because his instructions were to cooperate with his British colleague. Both sent orders to the single French and three British ships off the Pacific coast of Mexico not to commence hostilities except in self defence. After waiting over three weeks in daily expectation of a communication from Wyke, Maitland wrote him that it would take almost a month to reach the western coast of Mexico from Toboga Island. Within eight weeks after that time, "the wet and unhealthy season commences, and except Acapulco (which is very unhealthy in the wet season), there is no secure port for large ships." Although Maitland assured Wyke that the Mexican ports could be seized, "they cannot be held without a Military Force if the Mexicans are determined to resist."[240] A day later[241] Maitland had Wyke's instructions, written on 31 January[242] in the sense agreed upon by all the Allied Commissioners.[243] Maitland was instructed not to take possession of any of the ports on the Pacific coast of Mexico until the breakdown of negotiations between the Mexi-

can Government and the allies. In the meantime Maitland was
to proceed to a Mexican port best suited for communication
with the British consul in Mexico City. Correspondence
between Maitland and Wyke would then go via Mexico City.
Maitland proceeded to Acapulco, arrived there on 17 March,
and then sent a courrier to Mexico City to announce his
arrival.[244]

The mail packet that brought Miramon and his followers
to Vera Cruz did not bring any instructions from Russell to
Wyke. In desperation Wyke persuaded Dunlop to send one
of his ships to Jamaica to discover whether Russell's instructions were being held up there, as in reality had happened.[245]
Wyke decided not to wait for the return of Dunlop's ship
before again asking Doblado to permit the allied forces to
advance to Jalapa and Orizaba. Such a move from Vera Cruz,
Wyke believed, had to be made before the end of February.[246]
A sixth conference of the Allied Commissioners was called on
2 February to approve such a demand to be made of Doblado.
The Commissioners tentatively approved the suggestion of
their consuls to reserve 20 per cent of custom house receipts for
administrative expenses incurred by running the Vera Cruz
Custom House to relieve Prim from defraying these costs.[247]
Then Prim submitted a draft note to be sent to Doblado.
Saligny opposed it as having "a spirit of excessive conciliation."
Jurien produced a draft note, supported by Saligny as being
"more firm and . . . avoiding any useless discussion."[248] The
purpose of the intervention was "to accomplish a mission of
civilization." The allies hoped to accomplish it "without spill-
ing a drop of Mexican blood." A "healthy camp site" was
required by the European troops, and the "necessity" was
brought to Doblado's attention "of beginning a march of the
allied armies, towards the middle of February, towards Orizaba
and Jalapa, where the undersigned Representatives hope that
they will receive a genuinely friendly reception."[249] As a concession to the French Commissioners, their colleagues approved
Jurien's draft, and it was sent off on 4 February.[250]

Doblado's answer to Jurien's note, approved by all the Commissioners, arrived in Vera Cruz on 9 February.[251] Permission for the advance of the allied troops was refused on the ground that the Mexican Government did not know the intentions of the allies. They had "only announced friendly but indefinite promises, whose real object nobody unravels." Doblado proposed, therefore, that the allies send a Commissioner to Cordova to meet a Mexican representative and to explain the intentions of the intervening Powers with "clearness and precision." Such a meeting could take place before the middle of February. After arriving at a preliminary understanding about negotiations to be initiated later, Juarez was willing to allow the allied forces to advance. Otherwise, the Mexican Government could not, "without compromising the national independence, grant a permission which now would be considered treason."[252] Accompanying this note was a private letter to Prim from Juarez' Minister of Finance. Gonzales Echeverria, the uncle of Prim's wife, explained that the Mexican Government feared being accused of treason, because the public believed that there was going to be an attempt to establish monarchy in Mexico.[253]

A conference—the seventh—of the Allied Commissioners was called on 9 February. Although discouraged themselves,[254] Wyke and Dunlop proposed to make a last effort to prevent hostilities by suggesting Prim see Doblado personally to give the explanations demanded by the Mexican Government.[255] The French Commissioners proposed to stop all further correspondence with the Mexican Government and to march on Jalapa and Orizaba.[256] Prim supported the British proposal, and Jurien finally agreed, because he believed war would soon be declared anyway.[257] Saligny once again isolated in the conference, a note was drafted suggesting Doblado meet Prim on 18 February at the Rancho de la Purga, midway between Tejeria and La Soledad. Prim would make "explanations," but the allies would not modify their determination to begin "to march in the middle of February."[258] In an attempt to influence

the Mexican Government to be careful not to force the allies
to decide on hostilities, Prim wrote Gonzales Echeverria a
private letter :

> Can you possibly have supposed that our respectful, digni-
> fied and friendly language is the effect of weakness? Is it be-
> cause we do not dare to attack the fortified positions of
> Chiquihuite and Cerro Gordo? I blush at the idea that such a
> thought can have been entertained. And I banish it from my
> mind, because reason tells me that you cannot have mortified
> me to such an extent.
> You know me well, my Uncle and friend, and you know
> that I am not boastful nor a bragster. Well then : listen to the
> words of a man of war who flatters himself he knows his pro-
> fession, who because he is a good Christian, fears God, but
> who fears no one and nothing else . . . The Mexican Govern-
> ment cannot prevent the allied troops from going to Orizaba
> and Jalapa, the Mexican soldiers will defend valiantly the
> positions which the government may entrust to them, but the
> allies will lose 1000 men and Jalapa and Orizaba will remain
> in our hands. What will happen afterwards God knows, and
> you and we may conjecture, but assuredly it will be nothing
> good for the country, nor for its present Government.

Prim believed that the "tone" of his letter was "determined"
and was :

> . . . equivalent to saying : "we are going forward : if you agree
> to it good; we shall be very glad because then there will be
> no bloodshed; but if you do not wish it we will go at oll
> events, because we must get out of this pestilential region, and
> it is better that we should lose in a day of battle the men
> whom we should have to lose in one or two months by sick-
> ness.[259]

Jurien had no such hopes of a peaceable solution. On the same
day that it was agreed to invite Doblado to meet Prim, Jurien
wrote Thouvenel that war would be declared and that an
attempt would be made to enlist the support of the groups
opposed to Juarez :

> Until now we have denied ourselves any appeal to the efforts
> of the conservative party, but when the war is declared, we

will resolutely take part in the civil war, and not fear proclaiming the fall of the Government of Mexico City. There are in the arsenals of the Custom House of Vera Cruz 4,000 guns that could be distributed to our auxiliaries.

.     .     .     .     .     .     .     .

Until now nothing has indicated to us the power, let alone the existence of the conservative party. What would be even more desirable would be to rally, besides this party, under the flag of the intervention all the wise people that could be detached from the liberal party.[260]

While waiting for a reply to the proposal that Prim have a meeting with Doblado, Dunlop sent a British officer to Havana to purchase mules, wagons, and stores needed by the British Marines to reach the tablelands beyond the coast.[261] To minimize expenses Dunlop put his men to work making harnesses, pack saddles, and carts.[262] The ships that Prim sent to Havana with sick Spanish troops—1,000 by the end of February—returned with mules, carts, and provisions provided by the Captain-General of Cuba.[263] The French also purchased means of transportation in Havana.[264]

On 10 February the eighth conference of the Allied Commissioners was held to discuss a letter received from a Mexican officer commanding troops near Vera Cruz.[265] General Zaragoza warned that, should the allied troops advance beyond their present positions, he would not "remain a passive spectator of these new insults." Zaragoza's letter was considered insolent. A reply was sent that nothing justified his "uncourteous" and "aggressive" language and that he would be held responsible for all his actions. At the same time this correspondence was sent to Doblado, of whom the Allied Commissioners demanded assurances of the "subordination" of Zaragoza to the Mexican Government. Otherwise Prim would not be able to meet Doblado.[266] Wyke feared "affairs" would "take a hostile turn."[267] Jurien believed hostilities would start soon. He read over his confidential instructions and copied a portion of them to serve as a proclamation to the Mexicans to inform them of the support the intervention would give to a political change:

If the Mexican nation remains inert, if it doesn't realize that we offer it an unexpected staff of safety, if it doesn't give a practical sense and morality to our protection, it is evident that there is nothing we can do but remain within the terms of the Convention of 31 October and only occupy ourselves with the specific interests for which it was concluded.[268]

On 14 February, when it was still unknown in Vera Cruz whether Doblado agreed to meet Prim, a conference (number nine) of the Allied Commissioners was held. Jurien read his Proclamation and proposed that it be published if Doblado refused to permit the allies to move their troops from the coast. Although a decision was postponed,[269] Jurien believed that the "principle" was accepted.[270]

Two letters received from Doblado on 15 February were read in the tenth conference assembled that day by the Allied Commissioners for that purpose. In one letter Doblado stated that he had Juarez' sanction to meet Prim, asked to delay the interview one day to give Doblado time for his journey from Mexico City. Doblado's other letter gave assurances that there was no reason to expect "insubordination" from General Zaragoza, who would not interfere.[271] There was nothing more to do, except to wait for Prim to try to convince Doblado to postpone negotiations for the redress of claims and to permit the European troops to advance in the meantime. Instructions about the ultimatums held back had not yet arrived from Europe.[272] The ship Dunlop had sent to Jamaica returned to Vera Cruz with some instructions written by Russell since mid-November 1861,[273] but these instructions afforded Wyke no solution of his difficulties. He was directed to suggest to the French and Spanish Commissioners that the allied representatives show each other their ultimatums.[274] Wyke summarized these instructions at the last conference (number eleven) held before Prim's departure to see Doblado,[275] but the ultimatums had to be retained. Russell's advice had already been followed and had led to the differences about claims.

Prim met Doblado on 19 February, and they then proceeded

to La Soledad for their conference. Prim believed Doblado was sincere, because he did not hide his difficulties. The Governors refused to obey his orders. A "considerable party" existed that was just looking for a pretext to start a revolution against the Mexican Government, should it "depart in the least from legality." There were "false rumours" that France wanted to establish a monarchy and that Spain intended a reconquest of Mexico. The arrival of the allied expedition had caused "excitement" that would be difficult to calm. Swayed by "passions," the majority would not listen to the minority of sensible persons who realized that the European troops were more than sufficient to impose terms. Doblado was ready to make "pacific arrangements" and to allow the European troops to advance into the interior. Certain precautions were necessary. The "national dignity" could not be sacrificed, and the "malcontents" should not be allowed an opportunity to accuse the Mexican Government of treason. The allies should "contradict" rumors and permit the Mexican Government "not to accept the help . . . offered by the foreign forces to re-establish peace and order." Doblado claimed that his Government had "at its disposal sufficient means to obtain these results," as well as to give satisfaction for legitimate claims, the "principal object of the allied expedition." Prim replied that there was no intention "of imposing on Mexico a form of government contrary to the wishes of the country." Although all the Allied Commissioners represented constitutional monarchies and would recommend such a form of government, there would be no "attempt to force on the country our ideas and opinions." It was "absurd" to suppose that the Spanish Government "had the most remote pretension to rule this country." The "independence" and "integrity" of Mexico, Prim assured Doblado, would be respected. As proof that the Allied Commissioners were loyal to the Convention of London and did not wish to interfere in Mexican internal affairs, Prim remarked that he and his colleagues were "treating with the established Government." The two generals then drew up a "preliminary" convention stipulating the future settlement of claims and the conditions under which the allied forces would be permitted to advance beyond the first line of Mexican defenses without causing alarm. Doblado asked that the allies recognize his Government. Saligny and Jurien could hardly be expected to approve. Therefore Prim tactfully suggested that "such an express recognition was not possible, of which . . . the present Government had no need, since it declares that it possesses sufficient strength to constitute itself in a solid and permanent manner." Doblado consented, provided it be made known that the allies agreed to negotiate with his Government and to stop offering "help." Article I resulted:

> As the Constitutional Government which at present rules in the Mexican Republic has made known to the Commissioners of the Allied Powers that it is not in want of the help that they have so benevolently offered to the Mexican people, since it possesses in itself the elements of strength and of public opinion sufficient to preserve itself against any intestine revolt whatever, the allies from this time enter into negotiations(*entran en el terreno de los tratados*) in order to adjust (*formalizar*) all the claims that they have to make in the name of their respective nations.

Without setting a date for the beginning of negotiations to settle claims—instructions from Europe had to arrive first— it was agreed that the Allied Commissioners would treat with Mexican representatives at Orizaba. The same Article (II) stated that the allies "protest . . . that they will attempt nothing against the independence, sovereignty, and integrity of the territory of the Republic." Prim had no fear that Saligny and Jurien would refuse to sanction these promises, which they had already approved by signing the "first communication to the Mexican Government." Doblado agreed to permit the European troops to be quartered in Cordova, Orizaba, and Tehuacan during negotiations (Article III). Should these negotiations fail and hostilities begin, the allies would have obtained a military advantage by peaceably having passed the fortified mountain passes between Vera Cruz and the three Mexican cities in the interior. In order not to render these defenses "useless" and that it might not "in the most remote degree be believed that the allies have signed these preliminaries in order to obtain the passage of the fortified positions," Prim agreed to Doblado's proposed Article IV. In the "unfortunate" event of a breakdown of negotiations, the troops of the allies would return to a position in front of the first Mexican defenses before commencing hostilities. In such an eventuality, Prim foresaw that he would jeopardize the lives of any of the sick by moving them. Therefore he persuaded Doblado to agree (Article V) that, in the event of hostilities, the hospitals established in Cordova, Orizaba, and Tehuacan would remain in these places "under the protection of the Mexican nation." Prim had a special reason to use the word "nation" instead of "Government." It was to prevent the enemies of the Juarez Government "from committing, in order to do it injury, outrages, and misdeeds, the responsibility of which falls upon it." To soothe Mexican susceptibilities, Doblado proposed that a final Article (VI) provide that the Mexican flag be hoisted alongside those of the allies at Vera Cruz and the fort of St. Juan d'Ulloa as soon as the European troops started to march toward Cordova, Orizaba, and Tehuacan. Prim explained that the Mexican garrisons took their flags with them when they left Vera Cruz and its forts. Since the Mexican flag would wave over the three cities in the interior where the allied troops would be quartered, Prim saw no objection to acceding to Doblado's request. Doblado also suggested returning the Custom House of Vera Cruz to Mexican authorities, but Prim refused. Although the allies obtained "nothing" from trying to collect custom duties themselves, Prim considered Doblado's proposal "too serious" to be decided before prior approval by the British and French Commissioners.[276]

After his meeting with Doblado, Prim returned to Vera Cruz the same day and called a conference (number twelve) of the Allied Commissioners at 11:00 P.M. After summarizing his conversation with Doblado, Prim read the Preliminaries he had negotiated. Before even allowing a discussion of the convention, Saligny suggested that the Allied Commissioners demand the abrogation of Juarez' Decree of 25 January. Saligny gave several reasons, but he did not mention that fear of the death penalty might make Mexicans hesitate to assist the French troops to upset the Juarez Government. Even Jurien hesitated to support Saligny. It was "tardy" to demand the abrogation of the decree "after having exchanged with the (Mexican) Government several communications, in which not the slightest mention was made of it." Although Jurien did reverse himself and agreed to Saligny's proposal, the French Commissioners had to "submit" to the "majority" and drop the matter. The Preliminaries of La Soledad were then approved with hardly any discussion. Wyke asked the meaning of a few words in one of the articles that the Allied Commissioners could appoint representatives to carry on negotiations at Orizaba. Prim explained that the Allied Commissioners could refer "details of little importance" to the "examination of delegates . . . named for that purpose." Jurien proposed not to salute the Mexican flag when hoisted in Vera Cruz and St. Juan d'Ulloa, because he did not want it believed that the allies were making a "reparation." Prim stated it was not necessary, because it was not stipulated. Another reason for not making a salute was "that the Spanish forces on entering Vera Cruz did not find any flag." Prim was not opposed to Doblado's suggestion concerning the Vera Cruz Custom House, because the "inefficiency" of the Spanish officials, who had replaced the Mexican ones, had only led to "negative results." Prim had already disbursed $8,000 to pay administrative costs. Wyke saw no objections to the return of the Mexican officials, provided three allied "interventors" supervised custom house operations. Saligny objected to making a "step backwards" that would "have a very bad effect in Europe." Should the Allied Commissioners not follow his advice, Saligny proposed that the Mexican Government "engage not to establish interior

Custom-Houses." A few remarks about the necessity that
articles imported by the allies should be duty free ended the
discussion without any agreement about the Vera Cruz Custom
House. The Commissioners signed the Preliminaries, and an
officer was immediately sent with the document to bring it
to Doblado.[277] Juarez' signature would complete the ratification
of the convention and permit the allied troops to march to
Cordova, Orizaba, and Tehuacan.[278]

Immediately after signing the Preliminaries of La Soledad
Jurien wrote Thouvenel:

> The arrangement concluded with General Doblado is the best
> result that one could hope for from a situation dominated by
> the complete entente that had been established between the
> Representatives of Spain and those of England. It reserves, in
> the most absolute manner, the question of the respective
> claims and has the advantage of separating the three armies.[279]

Even if the Mexican Government agreed to satisfy French
claims, Jurien still saw a reason to remain in Mexico:

> What, in effect, can come of the conferences to be held at
> Orizaba? Even admitting the Mexican Government accepts
> our claims without discussion, the question of guarantees al-
> ways remains, for armed occupation alone can offer us suf-
> ficient guarantees. I don't see, therefore, how the Convention
> of Soledad could have restricted our action. The Convention
> . . . does not impose any obligation on us that we have to
> regret.[280]

The advantage of the Preliminaries was that fighting was
avoided. If the Spanish troops took part in hostilities against
the Mexicans, Jurien predicted, "we would have found ourselves engaged in a way, the end of which would be impossible
to see."[281] Saligny considered that his signing the Preliminaries
was "one of the saddest sacrifices . . ." he ever was forced to
make.[282] "Outrages" against foreigners in Mexico, Saligny
reasoned, might be used as an excuse to make the Preliminaries
"a dead letter."[283]

Prim considered the Preliminaries a "giant's step" toward a "pacific solution." The allies were bound to "nothing," because all questions were left "intact" and "to be settled at the Conference of Orizaba, where peace or war was the issue." By then instructions would have arrived from Europe. In spite of the confidence in victory in the event of hostilities that he expressed in his letter to Echeverria, Prim feared to expose "the arms of Castile to a catastrophe." The small European forces, large numbers of which were already sick, had inadequate means of transportation. In this connection Prim would "always say: 'God bless the Preliminaries of Soledad, which spared us so many victims, Spanish, French, and English.' "[284]

On the day that Prim negotiated the Preliminaries of La Soledad more British Marines, making a total of one hundred and seventeen, were sent aboard a British ship being used as a hospital. The disorders were fever, "bowel disease," and "ulcer." Fifty-seven British Marines were on the sick list ashore on 19 February, and two Marines had already died.[285] Both Wyke[286] and Dunlop[287] justified the Preliminaries of La Soledad and the decision, against instructions, to move the British Marines inland on the grounds of the poor health conditions at Vera Cruz. Dunlop was relieved that hostilities were avoided, because he did not believe that "honor" could have allowed him to keep his Marines in Vera Cruz if the French and Spanish troops left to fight the Mexicans.[288] The "favorable turn" brought about by the Preliminaries,[289] Wyke wrote Russell, would permit Doblado to take steps to restore order and to satisfy claims:

If Doblado relies on the moral support he might derive by accepting our intervention in a friendly spirit, then he may succeed in reestablishing order and respect for life and property, and that once done, the resources of the country are so great that it would soon right itself, and its government be enabled eventually to fulfil all their engagements, thus relieving us from a task which under other circumstances we should find both hazardous and difficult to perform without the presence of an armed force very much more considerable than the one we now have at our command.[290]

. While waiting for the ratification of the Preliminaries of La Soledad, the Allied Commissioners held conferences about the operation of the Vera Cruz Custom House. At an official conference (number thirteen), held on 24 February, definitive approval was given to the suggestion, already tentatively accepted on 2 February, that 20 per cent of import duties collected would be reserved for administrative expenses incurred.[291] At an unofficial conference the next day the Commissioners agreed to return the Custom House of Vera Cruz to the Mexicans, provided that three allied "Interventors" supervise operations to assure the payment of the proper percentage of custom duties mortgaged by conventions to claimants.[292]

In the morning of 26 February a courrier arrived in Vera Cruz with the ratifications of the Preliminaries of La Soledad.[293] A conference (number fourteen) was immediately called. After communicating the ratifications to his colleagues, Prim read a letter from Doblado requesting that the Vera Cruz Custom House be returned to the Mexicans. One "Interventor" would be permitted to assure that 50 per cent of import duties would be reserved to pay foreign claimants. Doblado also asked to know when the conferences to settle claims could begin at Orizaba. British creditors alone had a lien against 59 per cent of the import duties collected in Vera Cruz. It was decided, therefore, to demand that three "Interventors," one representing each of the allies, assure that the proper amount of import duties guaranteed by conventions, including amounts in excess of 50 per cent, be reserved by the Mexican authorities for the various creditors. The Allied Commissioners also agreed to demand, before returning the Custom House of Vera Cruz to the Mexicans, that articles imported by the allies be duty free.[294] Prim, Wyke, and Dunlop suggested that the conferences at Orizaba open on 25 March, but Saligny insisted that he could agree to no date earlier than 15 April. This date was agreed upon when he explained that he wanted to allow time for instructions to arrive from Europe.[295] After the conference ended, Prim wrote Doblado to inform him of the decisions made.[296] Wyke wrote Russell that the custom house arrangement would only be "a temporary arrangement until further negotiations."[297] The same day, 26 February, Jurien left Vera Cruz with his troops for Tehuacan.[298] As the first French soldiers started marching, the Mexican flag was hoisted alongside those of the allies,[299] and the first phase of the European intervention in Mexico ended.

## 2.  MAXIMILIAN AND NEGOTIATIONS AMONG THE EUROPEAN POWERS, DECEMBER 1861– FEBRUARY 1862

At the end of December 1861 the Spanish Government made known to its British and French allies that instructions to hold up the Spanish expeditionary forces in Havana arrived too late. Although the Spanish squadron had arrived in Vera Cruz alone, the British and French Governments were assured that all measures taken before the arrival of their forces in Vera Cruz would be in the name of the allies.[1] Lord Russell immediately requested,[2] and obtained,[3] assurances that the Spanish expeditionary force would not attempt to march to Mexico City. In a private letter the British Foreign Secretary revealed that he still[4] feared there would be a Spanish attempt to persecute Protestants in Mexico. Russell hoped "the Spaniards are not going to throw the fat in the fire, or the heretics in the fire in Mexico." If the allied fleets had appeared simultaneously at Vera Cruz, the Mexicans would have offered no resistance. Arriving alone, the Spaniards probably would find that the "Mexicans will not put themselves again under the yoke of Spain." Then the "fat" might be in the "fire," and the success of the allied intervention would be jeopardized at the beginning. The British Marines would not go beyond Vera Cruz. The French troops were "too small a number for conquest, and those . . . are required for the custom houses and ports."[5] When the Spanish Ambassador to London sent Russell assurances that the Spaniards in Vera Cruz would not extend operations before the arrival of the British and French,[6] Russell replied that he could not understand why the Spanish expedition was the first to reach Vera Cruz.[7] Isturiz explained that Serrano had not known where the rendezvous of the allied fleets was, and instructions arrived too late.[8] Russell then ended discussion of the matter with Isturiz by stating that, "although . . . not entirely satisfied with the explanation," the British Government "consents . . . to accept the declaration" that the Spanish Government would act "strictly" in accordance with the Convention of London.[9]

Thouvenel wrote his Ambassador to Madrid that, without wishing to examine motives, the isolated action of Spain was to be regretted.[10] Barrot saw the Spanish Minister of Foreign Relations, who claimed he also regretted the initiative taken by the Captain-General of Cuba. There was no premeditation on the part of the Spanish Government. Serrano had acted independently of its desire and control.[11] Barrot believed these assurances.[12] He also believed that Serrano was jealous that Prim had been appointed Commander-in-Chief and had acted before his arrival in order to obtain a share of the military glory.[13] In spite of assurances given Barrot by O'Donnell, the Spanish Chief Minister, that Serrano could not have known of Prim's appointment when the decision was made to send the Spanish forces to Vera Cruz,[14] Thouvenel agreed with Barrot's theory. The Spanish Government, Thouvenel told the British Ambassador to Paris, was in an embarrassing situation, which would be made worse by Prim, "who will find the laurels which he expected to gain already gathered by Marshal Serrano."[15] Cowley admitted that it was an "awkward" situation. He could "hardly see how . . . we can consent to play second fiddle and garrison the forts taken by them (i.e., the Spaniards)."[16]

Napoleon and Eugenie wanted Spain included in an intervention in Mexico so that Spain could regain its "place" in Europe,[17] but the French imperial pair did not want France to be reduced to the position of an auxiliary. At the New Year's reception of the diplomatic corps Napoleon made the Spanish Ambassador sense French displeasure. Eugenie was in a dreadful "rage" (*fuchsteufelswild*). Metternich, the Austrian Ambassador, reported that she "says that, if the worst comes to the worst, France will undertake the whole business by herself."[18] Like Russell, Napoleon III feared that the Mexicans, supposing they only "had to deal with the Spaniards," would make a "greater resistance."[19] There were other reasons for sending French reinforcements to Mexico. As Thouvenel put it, the Spanish "seemed to us to want only to have their own way and to exalt themselves a little too much with memories of Ferdinand Cortez." It was necessary "to reestablish the equilibrium" and not "to expose ourselves to a check."[20] That the Spanish wanted "their own way" probably referred to Collantes' answer at the beginning of December 1861 to a proposal Thouvenel made during the negotiation of the Convention of London. In answer to Thouvenel's suggestion that the allies renounce members of their dynasties as candidates for a Mexican throne, Collantes replied two months later that the Spanish Government intended to permit the Mexicans the choice of their government. Should it be a monarchy, the Spanish Government could not "disguise" that:

> . . . in this case an account of the historical traditions and the links which will join the two Nations (i.e., Mexico and Spain), they (i.e., the Spanish Government) would prefer that a Prince of the Bourbon dynasty, or one intimately allied with it should be preferred. . . .[21]

It was unlikely, therefore, that the Spanish Government would support Maximilian's candidacy. It was also to be feared that Wyke and Saligny would not agree. On 2 and 6 January 1862 reports from Saligny arrived in Paris. Saligny revealed his bitterness and personal animosity toward Wyke, who was condemned for negotiating with the Mexican Government in October and November 1861 to settle British claims.[22] Among Saligny's reports was one that Juarez probably could muster four to five thousand troops.[23] If the French troops in Mexico might have to "undertake the whole business," they would be outnumbered two to one. Even the Spanish troops, Hidalgo told Napoleon, were not entirely an asset. Prim's reputation of seeking glory, Hidalgo believed, would cause the Mexicans to resist what would be believed was intended to be a Spanish reconquest.[24] Napoleon's plans for Maximilian could not be implemented if the French troops remained on the coast. Letters from Estrada's friends in Cuba and Mexico forwarded to Thouvenel already expressed disappointment, because it was believed the allies would only seize Mexican ports.[25] Napoleon decided to send a Mexican propaganda agent to Mexico,[26] and he would need military protection from Juarez' partisans. Another reason for sending more French troops to Mexico was Maximilian's letter to Napoleon, summarizing parts of the New Year's Eve conversation with Franz Joseph. Maximilian stated his determination not at first to rely on Mexican auxiliaries.[27] Without previous consultation with Thouvenel,[28] Napoleon III sent orders to his Minister of War on 9 January to send 4,168 troops and 332 horses to Mexico. Napoleon himself picked out which units would be sent.[29] With a strange penance or feeling of compensation, Napoleon purposely chose those regiments that had seen the most action against the Austrians in the Austro-Sardinian War of 1859. Lord Cowley commented:

> One singular fact . . . is that the Emperor has taken it into his head that the Archduke Maximilian shall owe his throne to the troops who most distinguished themselves in depriving His Imperial Majesty of Lombardy.[30]

Napoleon's decision to send more French troops to Mexico was not immediately made known to the British and Spanish

Governments. In the meantime clandestine negotiations with Maximilian continued. On 8 January Napoleon saw Metternich and discussed the conclusions Maximilian and Franz Joseph had reached during their New Year's Eve conversation in Venice. Napoleon expressed complete concurrence. He even believed making recognition of the Confederacy conditional upon its guaranteeing the integrity of Mexico an excellent idea. Then Napoleon proposed that the Mexican exile, General Almonte, go to Mexico as Maximilian's paid agent to work in his interests. Napoleon suggested that the Mexican go to Miramar to see Maximilian before leaving for Mexico.[31] Maximilian agreed to see Almonte,[32] whom the Archduke was already curious to meet.[33] On 15 January Almonte left Paris[34] with a letter of introduction from Napoleon III. Almonte was a "very excellent fellow" and a "very capable man." Maximilian was urged to give him "full powers" as "principal agent," because Almonte was "about to start for Mexico" where his "presence . . . will . . . be very useful."[35] By a coincidence Mgr. de Labastida, the exiled Bishop of Puebla, also set out for Miramar on 15 January from Rome at Maximilian's invitation to talk over Estrada's plan to send the Mexican bishops in Rome back to Mexico to preach monarchy for the Austrian Archduke.[36] Before Almonte reached Miramar, Estrada wrote Maximilian that Almonte was "incapable" of acting as Maximilian's agent. Santa Anna would never submit to "one who has always been his subordinate." At most Almonte could be an adviser *"under"* Santa Anna.[37] Even then Estrada feared that Almonte would attempt to "erect a centre of intrigue even in the Regency itself."[38] Before leaving for Miramar, Almonte even told Estrada that "replacing Santa Anna" might be necessary.[39] Estrada was furious. He wrote to Maximilian's secretary that there was "no question" that Santa Anna was more important than Almonte. The latter only had a "lifelong desire to wield the supreme power," but "very few people in Mexico know of General Almonte as a politician, and his monarchical sympathies are known to no one."[40] In the interests of "unity of procedure," Estrada urged Maximilian to decide who "of us must be regarded by the rest" as being Maximilian's "instrument."[41] Even greater humiliations were in store for Estrada. On 16 January he saw Napoleon and Eugenie, made the mistake of informing them that he did not think much of Almonte,[42] and emphasized how important it was to use religion as an "influence . . . in Mexico . . . of regenerating society."[43] After the interview Eugenie told Hidalgo that Estrada's views were "very reactionary." Should he return to Mexico, Mexicans would think that Philip II and the inquisition were arriving. Lord Palmerston would never agree with such views, and Hidalgo was asked to tell Estrada that he was not again welcome until he changed his viewpoint. Estrada refused to recant and wrote Maximilian, "there is a conspiracy against me, and . . . Hidalgo . . . is the instigator of it." He was "unbelievably false and hypocritical." Hidalgo, Estrada bemoaned, "points out to me, with the merest pretense at disguise, that at the Palace my advice and my assistance are scorned."[44]

On 17 January Thouvenel told Cowley that an additional three to four thousand French troops would be sent to Mexico under the command of General de Lorencez, an officer of equal rank with General Prim. Napoleon III believed that the solitary arrival of the Spanish expedition in Vera Cruz would cause greater Mexican resistance than would have resulted from the simultaneous arrival of the three allies. The Emperor of the French "could not risk the chance of a disaster to the french troops, which would certainly now have to march into the interior." Another reason for sending more troops was that "the french nation" could not "brook any superiority of numbers on the part of the Spaniards."[45] These were the "official" reasons. Thouvenel also told Cowley, and asked him to report it only by private letter, that Napoleon had "other reasons." Certain "negotiations" had been "continued" with Maximilian. The Austrian Government was "anxious" that he become "Sovereign of Mexico." Napoleon "would be very glad if this was the result of the expedition, and hopes that Her

Majesty's (i.e., the British Queen's) Government will not interfere to prevent it." Cowley objected to any attempt to coerce the Mexicans, but Thouvenel denied such intentions. In a private letter to Russell, Cowley commented that "there is evidently an intention *to advise*, and french advice sometimes Flahault to inform Russell that three thousand French troops resembles coercion."[46] On 17 January Thouvenel instructed would be sent to Mexico, because French "dignity" was wounded by the early departure of the Spanish forces from Havana.[47] In a private letter accompanying these instructions, Thouvenel gave additional reasons. It was necessary for the British Government to understand "a real political interest to prevent this great country from falling under the yoke of the Americans, *united* or *separated*." All the French Government asked was that there be no British interference :

> So if the contrivance in favor of Archduke Maximilian about which the Emperor is thinking is successful, would not they have something to congratulate themselves about in London? I don't think they suspect our intentions there and that if parliamentary considerations do not permit the English ministers to accept the idea openly, they will apply to us the doctrine of *"laissez faire, laissez passer."* That is all we ask.[48]

Thouvenel telegraphed, still on 17 January, his Ambassador to Madrid that three thousand more French troops would be sent to Mexico.[49] As an afterthought Thouvenel wrote Barrot that the ease with which the Spanish forces took possession of Vera Cruz showed that "it is to Mexico City itself" that the allies had to go to dictate terms. Consequently an augmentation of the French forces was needed for operations in the interior.[50] Thouvenel told the Spanish Ambassador to Paris that more troops were needed in view of Saligny's reports of Mexican hatred against foreigners residing in Mexico.[51] At the bottom of all French explanations, therefore, was the pretext that the premature arrival of the Spanish expedition at Vera Cruz necessitated sending more French troops to Mexico. Napoleon

III himself tried to reconcile General Prim to the arrival of the French reinforcements. Prim's attitude was especially important, because Napoleon received some confirmation of Hidalgo's fears about Prim. Estrada forwarded a letter from Miranda in Havana to Thouvenel that stated that Prim's reputation as a liberal and the fact that his wife's uncle was a member of Juarez' cabinet would result in difficulties for Maximilian's cause.[52] In a personal letter to Prim, Napoleon recalled their meeting at Vichy in 1861,[53] claimed that he learned of Prim's appointment "with pleasure," and recommended him to General de Lorencez, arriving with more French troops. "Your dream of Vichy," Napoleon added with a personal touch, "is being realized: here are Spanish and French troops fighting side by side for the same cause."[54]

Upon receipt of Cowley's report and private letter[55] about the increase of the size of the French expedition in Mexico, Russell telegraphed Cowley that the British Government was greatly concerned, for it appeared that a prolonged occupation of Mexico was contemplated. It was strange that the French Government now demanded parity with the Spanish expedition, the size of which was known from the beginning.[56] In a private letter to Cowley, Russell revealed his "concern" more clearly:

> This attempt to set up a Monarchy in Mexico will never do. Let the Franch have an equal number of men with the Spaniards, but let them keep to the Convention.
> If they act otherwise we shall not be able to defend our Convention in Parliament.[57]

Palmerston's attitude toward a Mexican monarchy at this time is less precise. He wrote Russell a private letter on 19 January:

> As to the monarchy scheme if it could be carried out it would be a great blessing for Mexico and a godsend to all countries having anything to do with Mexico. . . . It would also stop the North Americans whether of the Federal or Confederate States in their projected absorption of Mexico. If the North

and South are definitely disunited and if at the same time
Mexico could be turned into a prosperous monarchy I do not
know any arrangement that would be more advantageous for
us. We cannot with our seven hundred marines take part in
such an enterprize, but if France and Spain can manage it
and the Arch Duke Max. could become king, I do not see that
we need complain.[58]

One biographer of Palmerston quotes this letter to show that
"England's prime minister was hardly more true to the spirit
of the agreement (i.e., the Convention of London) than was the
French emperor."[59] Such an interpretation is not justified by
Palmerston's letter and fails to take into consideration Palmerston's opinions before and after 19 January. Palmerston did not
state how France and Spain would "manage" the "monarchy
scheme." Either the French and Spanish troops would maintain order to permit a free election, or else Maximilian would
be imposed on the Mexicans. During the negotiation of the
Convention of London, it was Palmerston who suggested that
an article disclaiming interference in Mexican internal affairs
be inserted to prevent any of the allies from imposing a
particular government on the Mexicans.[60] A week after writing
the private letter to Russell, and when information had been
received that Napoleon intended to impose Maximilian on the
Mexicans by force,[61] Palmerston approved Russell's instructions
to Wyke,[62] a copy of which was sent to the French Government.[63] This document hardly justifies the assertion of Bell that
Palmerston was "pleased that France, by violating" pledges of
non-intervention in Mexican internal affairs, "should draw
certain British chestnuts from the fire."[64] The crux of Wyke's
instructions was:

> If the Mexican people by a spontaneous movement place the
> Austrian Archduke on the Throne of Mexico, there is nothing
> in the Convention to prevent it. On the other hand, we could
> be no parties to a forcible intervention for this purpose. The
> Mexicans must consult their own interests.[65]

Both Russell[66] and Palmerston[67] personally believed monarchy to be the best means of ending anarchy in Mexico, but they did not desire to violate the traditional British policy of non-intervention in the internal affairs of a sovereign state by permitting their Spanish or French allies to violate the Convention of London.

Collantes, the Spanish Minister of Foreign Relations, had no objections to the reasons given for the increase of the French forces in Mexico,[68] and the French Ambassador to Madrid was able to report that the news was received "with apparent satisfaction."[69] Rumors in Madrid had it that Maximilian would establish a monarchy in Mexico with French aid. The news of the augmentation of French troops caused even more "agitation,"[70] and the opposition press bemoaned that Spain would be reduced to an inferior position in the intervention in Mexico.[71] Collantes suspected that the French Government would soon announce that the rumors were true. The Spanish Minister had to protect himself against the fury of the Spanish nation, which "would never brook the notion that it had been used as a tool to . . . forward other political designs."[72] On 22 January Collantes wrote instructions for Prim. He was not to permit a monarchy to be forced upon the Mexican people :

> . . . it is right that Y(our) E(xcellency) should know the project of establishing a Monarchy in Mexico takes larger proportions every day. Some of the natives of that Country resident or established in Europe are working in that sense : but neither has the Government of the Emperor (i.e., Napoleon) made any formal proposal to that of H(er) M(ajesty the Queen of Spain) on this point, nor is it possible to set aside the fundamental principle of Spanish policy in America, viz : to give full liberty to its inhabitants to establish the Government best suited to their necessities and belief.[73]

To calm public excitement in Spain Collantes announced in the Chamber of Deputies of the Cortes on 25 January that the British and French Governments had been informed that Serrano had received orders too late to hold up the Spanish expedition in Havana. Spain's allies, Collantes insisted, were

satisfied that everything was done in accordance with the
Convention of London. Collantes also mentioned that three
thousand additional French troops were being sent to Mexico
and gave assurances that each of the allied Commanders-in-
Chief retained command of his own troops.[74]

On 19 January the French Ambassador to London informed
Russell that more French troops would be sent to Mexico. The
premature arrival of the Spaniards in Vera Cruz implied the
intention to assume a leading role and would incite the Mexicans to resist it. It was now "inevitable" that the "Allied forces
must advance into the interior of Mexico." The "force at
present agreed upon . . ." was insufficient for this purpose.
Furthermore, Napoleon "could not allow the French force to
be in a position of inferiority to that of Spain, or to run the
risk of being compromised." Russell replied that he "very
much regretted this step, for it seemed to portend operations
in Mexico on a greater scale than was originally contemplated." Nevertheless, Russell had no "objection" to the
"argument" that France had to have parity with Spain.[75] He
assumed, Russell told Flahault, that it was understood that no
new instructions would be sent to the French Commander-in-
Chief.[76] Russell added that the British Government was unable
to send any more forces to Mexico.[77]

Cowley wrote Russell on 21 January that Thouvenel had
been informed of British "apprehension" about the additional
French forces being sent to Mexico. Such concern was dictated
by anticipated "consequences of a prolonged occupation of
Mexico, which the French Government appeared to contemplate." Thouvenel repeated the now familiar arguments and
glibly added that he "expressed regret, that the question of
the respective forces . . . had not been more narrowly examined before the signature of the convention."[78] Therewith
probably would have ended Russell's requests for explanations,
had there not been a leak of information about Napoleon's
intentions on the very day that Cowley wrote his report to
Russell. In the morning of 21 January Colonel Claremont, a

military attaché of the British embassy in Paris, talked with
Colonel Valazé, who was going to accompany General de
Lorencez, the commander of the French reinforcements being
sent to Mexico. Valazé "distinctly" told Claremont that :

> . . . the Emperor had informed him they were going for the
> purpose of proclaiming the Archduke Maximilian of Austria
> King of Mexico, and he is under the impression that this
> has been agreed upon with Her Majesty's Government who
> are to furnish a proportionate contingent of troops. He also
> tells me they have positive orders not to remain twenty four
> hours at Vera Cruz but to push on at once to Puebla.[79]

Cowley brought up the matter with Thouvenel, who said he
was not present when General de Lorencez was received by
Napoleon. Thouvenel remarked, however, that the Emperor
had always said that he would "rejoice if the Mexicans would
place themselves under the sovereignty of the Archduke Maximilian but that it must be their own act." Cowley asked
whether there were any negotiations between France and
Austria for this purpose. Thouvenel "replied in the negative."
Only Mexicans had made overtures, which "had been taken
up with an appearance of readiness by the archduke."[80]

On 22 January Cowley sent Russell a telegram summarzing
Valazé's comments to Claremont,[81] and on 25 January Russell
had Claremont's full account and Thouvenel's remarks on it.[82]
By then Russell also had received a clipping from the official
French *Moniteur,* also sent by Cowley. Without mentioning
Maximilian, the *Moniteur* predicted that the "honest and calm
part" of the Mexican nation desired a "modification of the
political regime" as "the only means of stopping . . . an anarchy
become intolerable."[83] All this information alarmed Russell.
He asked the British Admiralty to send specific instructions
that the British Marines not go beyond Vera Cruz.[84] The
British Ambassador to Vienna was instructed to report what
he could find out about Maximilian as a candidate for a
Mexican throne.[85] The British Ambassador to Madrid was

instructed to read O'Donnell and Collantes the preamble of the Convention of London and the article defining the intentions of the intervention and what would not be done. Crampton was to "point out" that the allied force would not be used to deprive the Mexicans of their right to choose their government. Any coercion in this respect would force each of the allies to choose between withdrawal from the joint intervention and extending operations beyond the scope and intention of the Convention of London. To mitigate the bluntness of these observations, Crampton was directed to make clear that the good faith of the Spanish Government was not being called into question. Rather the representatives of the allies in Mexico were "acting at a distance" and had "to be very closely watched lest they should commit their principals to unwarranted proceedings." As an example of such "rashness" Russell gave the premature departure of the Spanish expedition from Havana.[86] Before the monthly mail packet left, Russell instructed Wyke not to assist in any plan to coerce the Mexicans to accept Maximilian as their monarch. In connection with the arrival of French reinforcements in Mexico, Russell commented that it was "supposed that these troops will march at once with the French and a part of the Spanish troops already there, to the City of Mexico." In view of the instructions the British Admiralty would send, Russell directed Wyke not to object to orders from British naval authorities for "the withdrawal of the Marines from Vera Cruz when the unhealthy season shall arrive."[87] A copy of these instructions was sent to the British Admiralty with directions to send appropriate orders to Commodore Dunlop.[88] An information copy was also sent to Thouvenel so that he would know that the British Government would not be a party to any scheme to force Maximilian on the Mexicans.[89]

While Russell was taking steps at the end of January 1862 to prevent the allied troops in Mexico from supporting Maximilian's candidacy, Napoleon carried on negotiations with Maximilian through General Almonte. The Mexican exile arrived at Miramar and spent five days[90] conferring with Maximilian and Mgr. de Labastida,[91] invited to discuss the project of sending the exiled bishops to Mexico.[92] On 22 January Maximilian gave Almonte a copy of a "Protokoll"[93] of the conversations to bring to Napoleon.[94] Before Almonte left for Paris, he signed the Protokoll at Maximilian's request,[95] Almonte, Labastida, and Santa Anna were tentatively named the members of the "Regency."[96] A special article of the Protokoll stated the necessity of cooperating with the regents and that they maintain harmony among themselves:

> XII. Perfect harmony between all who have an interest in the Mexican enterprise, and their willing co-operation with General Santa Anna, General Almonte and Mgr. de Labastida, are indispensable to success.[97]

The purpose of this article was to prevent any antagonism, as predicted by Estrada, between Almonte and Santa Anna. In a letter to the Austrian Ambassador to Paris, Maximilian commented:

> This article puts forward as an indispensable condition of success, not only the complete harmony among themselves of the Conservative leaders in Mexico, but also their co-operation with Santa Anna. Since Almonte recognizes the importance of all I have said on this point, and since he has himself signed the document, everything possible has been done towards the attainment of our end.[98]

Maximilian accompanied the Protokoll with an explanatory letter to Napoleon. Maximilian's justification of his decision to subordinate Almonte to Santa Anna and of the need for Article XII of the Protokoll clearly reflects the influence of Estrada. All Estrada's efforts on behalf of Santa Anna — showing Maximilian letters from the ex-President, the constant praise lavished on him, the predictions that the whole monarchy scheme would be jeopardized by Almonte's insubordination — were not in vain.[99] Maximilian wrote Napoleon:

I have felt it my duty to incorporate in this document an article laying down the necessity of a perfect understanding between Mexican Conservatives and their co-operation with General Satnta Anna. So far as I am able to judge, it is most important to secure up to the end the co-operation of that person, who enjoys such a great reputation in his country. He has repeatedly promised his assistance, in the most explicit terms; he has, moreover, everything to gain by the establishment of a monarchical regime, and would have everything to lose if he dreamt of opposing the will of Europe. It therefore seems to me, and M. Almonte appeared to be of my opinion, that we should risk nothing by placing Santa Anna at the head of the Regency which would have to conduct the administration of the State until the arrival of the sovereign.[100]

In addition to approving Estrada's suggestion of making use of Santa Anna, Maximilian agreed to Estrada's plan to send some of the exiled Mexican bishops to Mexico. Mgr. de Labastida volunteered to leave at once,[101] and it was decided that "at least three of the Bishops (exiled in Rome) should at once set out for Mexico"[102] It was also agreed to suggest to the Pope that he appoint a nuncio to go to Mexico.[103] Maximilian renewed his proposal that the signatories of the Convention of London refuse to recognize the Confederacy unless it agreed to "guarantee the integrity of the Mexican territory."[104] The "different points" that Napoleon "indicated" to Almonte were also discussed. There were military and financial problems. Almonte related that the "doubtful attitude of the Spaniards" caused Napoleon to send reinforcements to Mexico. Napoleon, Almonte told Maximilian, believed Mexican Church property might be used to raise money.[105] At Miramar it was estimated that Maximilian would require at least 10,000 troops to "maintain order." Until Maximilian procured such an army, of which five to eight thousand eventually might be Mexicans, the "French army must remain in the country."[106] Mgr. de Labastida suggested that no definitive decisions be made about the property of the Mexican Church before informing the Pope. Maximilian agreed and decided to send Labastida to

Rome to "treat directly with His Holiness on this point, as well as the other religious questions touched upon in our conversations."[107] In the meantime it was tentatively agreed that church property not yet nationalized be offered as security to pay 5 per cent interest on a loan to be obained from a financial house. It would also be desirable that "the three Powers which signed the Convention of London . . . guarantee . . . purely and simply . . . to compel the government (i.e., of Maximilian), if need be, to carry out its engagements." At least $200,000 of such a loan would be necessary "to secure the services of the leaders of the Conservative party, and possibly also the services of the leaders of other parties." Maximilian also authorized bribery in the form of thirty titles of nobility that Almonte might distribute "with discretion" and with the proviso that they were subject to Maximilian's subsequent approval. Finally, Maximilian would establish a Senate, a Chamber of Deputies, and a Council of State, all having similar powers to "those which the corresponding bodies possess in France." No concessions would be promised and only "granted . . . from time to time, as occasion demands."[108]

Within a month after Almonte and Labastida left Miramar most of the decisions reached there were discarded or became meaningless. Although Pope Pius IX approved Labastida's departure for Mexico,[109] the Bishop of Puebla did not leave Europe. When he arrived in Paris, Hidalgo refused to obtain letters of introduction to Jurien and Saligny. Hidalgo explained that it had "been decided that the clergy shall be prevented from exercising too great an influence in Mexico." Without the protection of the French in Mexico, Labastida feared for his "dignity" and his "person," neither of which he wanted to be at the "mercy of . . . General Almonte."[110] Therefore one of Maximilian's regents remained an exile. At the end of January 1862 Estrada received a letter from Santa Anna that illness prevented him from going to Vera Cruz. His son had been there and "found the greatest opposition on the part of the Spanish General (i.e., Prim)."[111] Estrada was in "great distress" and wrote Maximilian that he was sending Senor Andrade, one of Estrada's "Committee," to see Santa Anna to "inspire him with confidence."[112] In the meantime Regent Santa Anna stayed in the Virgin Islands. General Almonte, as Napoleon had all along intended, left for Mexico as "principal agent." Soon afterwards Hidalgo told Estrada that *what is desired here* is not a Regency but a provisional Government . . . of one person only." Estrada believed that "before General Almonte left Paris it had been decided that he should be that person." In this lament to Maximilian, Estrada observed that in this way "they will succeed in pushing aside both Mgr. de Labastida and General Santa Anna."[113] Estrada had not expected that his plans would be rejected in spite of his refusal to recant what Napoleon and Eugenie considered clerical and reactionary ideas. Pope Pius IX declined to name a nuncio "until the whole affair has reached a successful conclusion."[114] Although the Pope agreed to consider using Mexican Church property as security for a loan if an "annuity" be paid the Church of Mexico,[115] he demanded that all previous nationalization of its property be declared null and void.[116] After seeing Queen Victoria, Leopold I reported to Maximilian that there was no hope for financial aid or guarantees for the proposed loan from the British Government.[117] Without a loan, Maximilian could not supply $200,000 for bribes. On his way to Paris, Almonte stopped at Vienna and asked Franz Joseph for this sum, but the Emperor refused on the grounds that the whole affair was still uncertain.[118] Napoleon tried to force Maximilian to pay the "bill."[119] but he declined by saying that Almonte "is not being sent by me but by the Emperor Napoleon."[120] Rechberg wholeheartedly agreed with Maximilian's decision as being in accordance with the "principle" that "we cannot take any initiative . . . nor to undertake any considerable expense." Rechberg informed Metternich of Maximilian's decision, adding instructions that Metternich "elude" any further overtures that Napoleon might make.[121]

Even before receiving instructions to report on Maximilian's candidacy,[122] Lord Bloomfield, the British Ambassador to Vienna, reported rumors and a conversation with Count Rechberg. Bloomfield first mentioned Maximilian's possible connection with Mexico in a private letter written to Russell on 16 January 1862. Bloomfield reported that he was unable to learn the "truth" of rumors that Maximilian would make a trip to Mexico or to Egypt.[123] Two weeks later—still before the receipt of Russell's instructions—Bloomfield was concerned with rumors that Estrada and Almonte had proposed to Maximilian that he become ruler of Mexico. Bloomfield asked Rechberg to supply information, and the Austrian Minister of Foreign Affairs replied that a "confidential communication" had been received from the French Government, as well as a proposal from Santa Anna. Rechberg added that no definitive reply could be given in view of the "confused" state of Mexico. Franz Joseph, therefore, reserved his opinion. Asked what Maximilian thought of the offer, Rechberg said the Archduke would demand guarantees from Great Britain and France.[124] After the receipt of Russell's instructions, Bloomfield referred the British Foreign Secretary to the comments of Rechberg just reported. Bloomfield then saw Rechberg again and tried to find out through what channel the French offer had come, but all that Bloomfield was able to report was that the overture came "*indirectly* and not officially." The British Ambassador gave his opinion, in his report to Russell, that the Mexican exiles in Paris were the originators of the plan and that "not . . . much value is attached here to their opinions." The Austrian Government, Bloomfield believed, would "object" to the election of Maximilian unless he "had been really called to Mexico by the unanimous feeling of the population."[125] A few days later Bloomfield talked with the French Ambassador to Vienna, who gave assurances that "all had passed quite unofficially and in fact that the Emigrants at Paris were the prime movers of the whole affair." The Duc de Gramont identified himself as the "*indirect* organ" referred to by Rechberg and denied rumors that "Mexico was to be considered as a set off against Venetia, and a compensation to the Austrians for the cession of their Italian possessions."[126]

In Paris Cowley was able to obtain much more accurate information at the beginning of February 1862 than Bloomfield in Vienna. Cowley asked Thouvenel whether it was true that Maximilian and Napoleon were corresponding about Maximilian's acceptance of a Mexican throne. In spite of Thouvenel's denial of any such knowledge, Cowley was convinced that he "never saw more visible embarrassement in any one's manner than this question created in M. Thouvenel's." The French Minister could only say that "Almonte and some other Mexicans" had made proposals to Maximilian. It was "very probable" that Napoleon "signified" to Maximilian through Metternich, in the same manner as the Emperor informed the British Government through Flahault, that it was to be hoped that the "presence" of the allied forces in Mexico would lead to a monarchy under Maximilian. To calm Thouvenel, who spoke with "some warmth," Cowley explained it was his duty to learn if there was reason that the agreement about non-interference in Mexican internal affairs "was possibly about to be overstepped." In spite of Thouvenel's denial that this was true, Cowley reported to Russell that "I happen to know" that Thouvenel "is cognisant of the letter addressed by the Archduke Maximilian to the Emperor."[127] Further confirmation that the monarchy plan was not put forward by the Mexican exiles alone came from a conversation Cowley had with Metternich and reported to Russell. Metternich told Cowley in strict confidence the "transactions" concerning Maximilian. Cowley concluded that there was "no doubt that this project originates entirely with the Emperor (Napoleon) and that it was with His Majesty's sanction, that the first communication upon the subject was made to the Archduke." Metternich also told Cowley that Maximilian had accepted "with the consent of the Emperor of Austria and his government."[128]

At the end of January 1862 the British Ambassador to

Madrid saw both O'Donnell and his Minister of Foreign Relations, Collantes. Crampton read aloud Russell's instructions[129] stressing the importance of checking the "rashness" of the allied representatives in Mexico to prevent any possible interference with the free choice by the Mexicans of their government. Russell's threat was that the alternative was to choose between withdrawing from Mexico or violate the Convention of London. As instructed, Crampton tried to read pertinent parts of the Convention of London to O'Donnell. The Spanish Minister stopped him and said it was unnecessary. The Spanish Government had no desire to impose a particular government on the Mexicans, as evidenced by General Gasset's proclamations upon arrival in Vera Cruz. The only plan to coerce the Mexicans that O'Donnell knew about was "agitated by some persons" in favor of Maximilian, but the French Government had made no official communication to the Spanish Government on the subject. Crampton was assured by O'Donnell that "were such a plan to be proposed to him, it would be met with his decided disapproval." The whole scheme was "so extravagant as to be scarcely worthy of consideration." As Captain-General of Cuba, O'Donnell had observed the "political habits" of Mexico and could say with conviction :

A Monarchy under an European Prince if not guaranteed by Europe would not last a year—if guaranteed and supported by Europe it would be a fruitful cause of struggles between European Powers and those of America who had adopted Republican Institutions and repelled European Interference in the New World.

Collantes protested to Crampton that there "had been no 'arrière pensée' on their part from the beginning, nor was there now." A "candid" presentation of the "facts" would be sent to the Spanish Ambassador to London.[130] Crampton sent a telegram to Russell summarizing Spanish assurances,[131] and Russell immediately sent a telegram in reply that "entire reliance" was placed on the Spanish "declarations."[132] Upon receipt of this telegram, Crampton made its contents known to Collantes, who showed "evident satisfaction."[133] Then Collantes himself demanded explanations. He claimed that Russell had an indirect allusion to some plan of interference in the affairs of Mexico not consistent with the Convention of London. The Spanish Government had no plan to establish a Spanish Prince as monarch of Mexico and hoped the French reinforcements being sent to Mexico would not soon be followed by the announcement of an ulterior motive. Spain would not consent to be the "tool" to establish a candidate for a Mexican throne whom the French Government might select. Collantes asked whether Leopold I of Belgium had made an overture to the British Government that a member of the Belgian royal family, the Duc de Flandres, be established as the future monarch of Mexico. Crampton made denials and promised to obtain assurances from Russell.[134] After talking with Crampton, Collantes wrote the Spanish Ambassador to London that there was no intention to "deviate" from the Convention of London "directly or indirectly." Collantes was worried about Russell's threat to withdraw from the intervention in Mexico. It would be difficult to explain before the Cortes and would leave Spain without an ally to oppose Maximilian's candidacy. Isturiz was informed, therefore, that the allies should all limit themselves to stating their wish for a "firm and durable" government in Mexico. Then there would be no "fear" that any of the allies would be placed in the "necessity of withdrawing from the expedition or of extending their intervention beyond the limits agreed upon."[135]

At the beginning of February Crampton brought Collantes a telegram from Russell[136] that Leopold I had made no such overture as suggested and that the British Government would "abide strictly by the terms of the Convention (i.e., of London)." Collantes said he could not reconcile Russell's telegram with one just received from the Spanish Ambassador to London. Isturiz reported that the French Government had asked the British Government to approve Maximilian as ruler of Mexico. According to Isturiz, Russell had had no objection to the arrangement. Collantes commented that, under these circumstances, he would have to decide what was best for Spanish interests. Asked whether he believed himself at liberty to put forward his own candidate, Collantes replied :

> Most certainly . . . but that is not the question, for if each Power was to propose a Candidate of its own, the result would be a confusion of conflicting claims; what I mean is that if the idea of a monarchy is favored by any one of the Powers it could not be acted upon to any good purpose, unless it was agreed to, and put forward in the name of all the Three.[137]

Russell refuted Isturiz' accusations and restored official harmony between the British and Spanish Governments. Russell telegraphed Crampton :

> I do not understand that the French Government have proposed the Archduke Maximilian as a candidate for the throne of Mexico. They have not made any such proposal to the British Government. They have asked whether in case the Mexican People should choose the Archduke for their King Great Britain would oppose such a settlement. Her Majesty's Government said they would not oppose the wish of the Mexican People but they should not take any part in promoting such an arrangement. You can not too plainly say that Great Britain adheres to the Convention, and will not consent to any modification or addition to it.[138]

Russell's explanation included a refusal to consider the Spanish hint that the allies might agree on a candidate, a suggestion branded as a "modification" of the Convention of London. O'Donnell and Collantes approved Russell's views. O'Donnell promised that, should a French overture be made, he would make a reply identical to the one Russell had made. The Spanish Government would never approve a government established by a "faction" representing a minority of the Mexican people. Crampton commented that a Mexican government established by "pronunciamento" was not to be confused with the "bona fide" desires of the Mexican people. O'Donnell said that was his meaning "exactly." The British and Spanish Governments, he observed, had "identical" views.[139]

O'Donnell and Collantes were true to their promises not to further the scheme in favor of Maximilian. At the beginning of February O'Donnell told the Austrian Ambassador to Madrid that it was incomprehensible that Maximilian could wish to "embark in that *aventureuse galère*."[140] A few days later O'Donnell wrote Prim:

> Our conduct must be most loyal as regards the engagements contracted with France and England; but opposed to imposing a Monarchical form of Government and Prince Maximilian as a candidate, on the Mexican Nation.
> If the Mexicans of their own free will, and without being coerced by anyone, should choose that form of Government, we ought to respect their sovereign will, but not contribute to a form of sham sovereign congress, which would usurp the will of the people.[141]

At the same time Collantes instructed Prim "to carry out the convention and leave the Mexicans full liberty to dispose of their fate." This intention was to be made "evident on every occasion."[142] After seeing Maximilian at Miramar and before leaving Europe for Mexico, Almonte saw O'Donnell.[143] O'Donnell told Almonte:

> I think you have made a mistake and that you arrive late . . . you conceived a project in Paris and went to Vienna to get it accepted. You now wish us to sanction what was agreed upon in Paris and Vienna, and that is not possible. The Count of Reus (i.e., General Prim) has ample powers: he will study the country and give us information. I can do nothing more until I receive it.[144]

The Spanish Government was forced to make its attitude toward Maximilian known not only to the British Government

and Almonte, but also to the Spanish Cortes. On 5 February
Castro, a member of the opposition in the lower house, summarized an article that appeared in the British *Morning Post*[145]
of the previous day. Mexicans were "praying to be delivered"
from the yoke of the Juarez Government. It was "little better
than an organised association of rival brigands, who are the
worst tyrants by which almost any people have ever been
afflicted." This tyranny did not permit a "free manifestation
of . . . opinions." A "republican policy" was "quite unsuited
to the interests of all classes. . . ." The "dominant nationality"
in Mexico was "of Spanish blood which has nearly always
supported the principle of monarchical government." The
European allies intervening in Mexico had "determined" to
send their armies to Mexico City. The Juarez Government
would "fall" and the Mexican people would be consulted.
"And when we say people," the *Morning Post* commented,
"we can hardly go further than the European or semi-Euro-
pean races." They would accept "cheerfully" a "constitutional
Sovereign presented to them by the common voice of their
deliverers." This Sovereign would be Maximilian.[146] After summarizing the article in the *Morning Post,* Castro asked Collantes whether the Convention of London denied the Mexican
people the right to select a member of the Spanish royal family
as their king. Collantes replied that the allies intervening in
Mexico did not intend to impose any particular form of government on the Mexicans, who had to decide their own fate. The
allies had "entered into no engagements for the future." The
Mexicans, therefore, were free to select a king from any
dynasty. If a march into the interior of Mexico should be
considered necessary to protect foreigners or to achieve the
objectives of the Convention of London, such operations would
be decided upon by all the Commanders-in-Chief, whose
actions would be common. The rumors printed by the *Morning
Post* and French newspapers might "be spread, but it is probable that they will be inexact like the present one."[147]

At the beginning of February Leopold I of Belgium, Maximilian's father-in-law, saw Queen Victoria in England.[148] At the suggestion of Napoleon and Eugenie, Metternich had sent requests to Leopold to use his influence with the British Government on behalf of Maximilian.[149] When the French imperial couple read the article in the *Morning Post,* both jumped to the conclusion that it should be attributed to the influence exerted by Leopold.[150] Convinced of Leopold's great powers in England, Eugenie wrote Metternich on 7 February to suggest that a "simple letter" to the King of the Belgians could prevent a discussion on Mexico in the British Parliament. Eugenie asked the Austrian Ambassador to "put the matter before the King" through Baron Beyens, the Belgian Ambassador to Paris.[151] Metternich at once saw Beyens, and a telegram was sent to Leopold.[152] In a private letter written in England on 7 February to Maximilian, Leopold expressed very little confidence. Public opinion was "not bad," but in England "people are amazingly impressed with the difficulty of the affair." Queen Victoria cherished the memory of the recently deceased Prince Albert, who had never been in favor of the monarchy scheme. Napoleon's interest in Maximilian was regarded with suspicion, and no British financial aid could be expected.[153]

After reaching an understanding about Maximilian with the Spanish Government, Russell received reports about the Archduke's candidacy from Vienna and Paris. From Bloomfield's reports received at the beginning of February Russell learned that Rechberg and the French Ambassador to Vienna admitted "indirect" French overtures about Maximilian. Cowley's reports from Paris made it clear that Napoleon was corresponding with Maximilian, that the Archduke was favorable to the plan of sending him to Mexico, and that the Austrian Government approved his decision. Other reasons for alarm were the insinuations of the official French *Moniteur* and the conjectures of the French press. Although Napoleon's speech opening the sessions of the legislature on 27 January only made a passing reference to the expedition to Mexico,[154] the *Moniteur* of a few days later expressed hope that the intervention in Mexico would create a "healthy crisis" leading to a "reorganization."[155] The semi-official *Patrie* predicted an exchange of a Mexican crown for Austrian cession of Venetia.[156] Acting under instructions, Metternich saw Thouvenel and protested such "false insinuations." Metternich asked that Thouvenel make it known "through . . . the French Press" that Maximilian had not definitely accepted the crown of Mexico. The Austrian Government had merely permitted a "confidential exchange of ideas" between Napoleon III and Maximilian. The final decision depended on "the attitude of the Mexican population and on the course of future events."[157] The *Moniteur* of 1 February made a statement designed to satisfy Metternich and at the same time prepare the French public for things to come :

> What the sane part of the population wants is the unification of the country under an independent and constitutional monarchy. A foreign prince would rally all sympathies without doubt; but the allied powers must guard themselves from putting forward for themselves any demands that, implying the idea of conquest, would not fail to wound national pride *(amour-propre)*.

The *Moniteur* went on to imply that war would be declared on the Juarez Government. The Mexican "troops would not be able to repel the . . . Europeans." The "first bayonnet charge" would be "strange and formidable" for the Mexicans.[158] The prospect of such an easy campaign probably was also intended to calm fears of an extended and expensive campaign. The independent press had already expressed alarm.[159] Cowley believed the "Parisian public" was dissatisfied that reinforcements were being sent to Mexico. This move was "criticised as at variance with the economy promised."[160] Cowley's military attaché reported opinion in the French Army was that the expedition to Mexico was "unnecessary." It was a "piece of Quixotic interference to attempt to establish a Kingdom there."[161] Cowley was constantly on the lookout for more information about Maximilian to report to Russell. The

British Ambassador to Paris forwarded a copy of the *Moniteur* of 1 February[162] and somehow learned of Metternich's conversation with Thouvenel about Venetia. Cowley reported to Russell that the Austrian Government "have now taken care to have it well understood that their consent to . . . Maximilian becoming a candidate . . . is not to imply . . . the intention on their part to consent to any modification of their own territorial position in Europe."[163] In a private letter to Russell, Cowley gave his opinion that the Austrian Government "counts without her host if she thinks, that should the intrigue prove successful, the Emperor (i.e., Napoleon) will not by and bye to put it in the scale against Venetia."[164]

The reports of Cowley and Bloomfield prompted Russell to make it clear to the Austrian Government that it should not expect British approval or support of Napoleon's plans for Maximilian. Bloomfield was instructed to inform Rechberg that the British Government intended to abide "strictly" to the terms of the Convention of London.[165] In answer to Bloomfield's observation that the Mexicans in Paris were the originators of the scheme in favor of Maximilian, Russell observed that this "class of People are notorious for unfounded calculation of the strength of their Partisans in their native country." Making use of Spanish support of his views, Russell noted that O'Donnell believed that "the notion of establishing by foreign intervention a Constitutional Monarchy in Mexico is very chimerical." The British Government would never "lend . . . support to such a project." Should Maximilian "assume the crown," he "would have to rely wholly on the support of the French Troops." Even assuming it could be done, it would take a "long time" to render Maximilian independent of foreign assistance. If such assistance were withdrawn in the "meantime," the "Sovereign might possibly be driven out by the Republicans of Mexico and the United States." Then Maximilian's "position would not be dignified or safe."[166] Russell saw Apponyi, the Austrian Ambassador to London, and complained that he had kept it a secret that negotiations concerning

Maximilian's candidacy were being carried on between the Austrian and French Governments. The private letter from Napoleon to Flahault, that the French Ambassador had shown Russell and Palmerston in October 1861,[167] was mentioned. Russell informed Apponyi that that letter was not taken seriously. Both British Ministers had declined to give the support demanded by Napoleon. In reply Flahault had said that the whole scheme could be considered as abandoned. He had even asked Russell and Palmerston not to make the contents of Napoleon's letter known to the other British cabinet members. With the "greatest surprise," Russell told Apponyi, it was now known that the French and Austrian Governments were taking the matter seriously.[168]

Rechberg received Apponyi's report about Napoleon's private letter to Flahault shortly after Bloomfield made it known that Russell would adhere to the Convention of London.[169] The Austrian Minister of Foreign Affairs could not bring himself to accept the conclusion that there was a "deliberate" French design to mislead him. Perhaps the British Government "was never made acquainted with the steps taken by the Emperor Napoleon to execute his plans." Rechberg resolved to be on his "guard . . . and especially see to it that we do not trust ourselves unreservedly to the well-meaning, but too precipitate zeal of the promoters of the Mexican enterprise."[170] A week later, on 26 February, Bloomfield read to Rechberg the observations of Russell concerning the dangers to Maximilian's dignity and safety should he go to Mexico. Rechberg replied that he had warned Maximilian to be sure he "possessed the entire confidence and sympathy" of the Mexican nation. The throne should not be supported by "foreign troops." At first an army raised in Germany and Switzerland might be necessary, but "it must be bona fide a Mexican army acting under the flag of that country." Asked whether he really believed there was a strong monarchical party in Mexico, Rechberg said that he believed that "the result of an appeal to the people of Mexico would be favourable to the ADk." Mexicans were "weary of confusion" and "would willingly try a new system of government." Bloomfield reported to Russell the belief that Rechberg "is merely repeating the impressions which have been transmitted from Paris."[171]

Rechberg was not so naïve as Bloomfield believed. The Austrian Minister of Foreign Affairs followed a cautious policy of "watch and wait." As he told Bloomfield, "official" negotiations were not being carried on between Vienna and Paris. Maximilian's preliminary conditions were made known to Estrada, not directly to Napoleon III.[172] Maximilian's *private* secretary contacted the exiles in Paris. Rechberg refused to consider Estrada's plan that his friends in Paris offer the throne of Mexico to Maximilian. Rechberg insisted on giving Estrada, as Maximilian's "agent," verbal instead of written instructions and invited him to Vienna to "restrain" him. Although Maximilian was permitted to start a correspondence with Napoleon in January 1862 — to make known the results of the conversation with Franz Joseph at Venice[173] — Rechberg insisted at that time that the Austrian Government had to "restrict itself to working only by indirect methods."[174] Rechberg rejected Maximilian's request for permission that Estrada "treat on my behalf with the English and Spanish Governments."[175] The only negotiations Rechberg would allow were with the French Government and Napoleon.[176] Metternich was instructed to make it clear to Thouvenel that the Austrian Government did not consider the scheme "connected with any scheme for a territorial change in Europe."[177] When the French official and semi-official press started a campaign in January 1862 in favor of a Mexican monarchy and even mentioned that Austria might give Venetia in compensation, Metternich protested to Thouvenel that Maximilian's candidacy was conditional on the attitude of the Mexican people and "future events." Any "attempt to link the question of Venice with the Mexican question" was "false."[178] In February 1862 Rechberg wrote Maximilian to suggest he cease using Estrada as an agent. He lacked circumspection, and the Austrian Government was not ready to initiate official negotiations.[179]

Apponyi's report and Rechberg's interviews with Bloomfield caused the Austrian Minister of Foreign Affairs to depart from his policy of not communicating with the British Government about Maximilian. Rechberg sent his Ambassador to London an information copy, for Russell, of the conditions of Maximilian's candidacy communicated to Estrada in October 1861.[180] Gradually Russell learned more about the monarchy plan. In addition, his inquiries and explanations created an Anglo–Spanish front against a French violation of the Convention of London in favor of Maximilian. Not only Rechberg, but even Maximilian, decided to be more cautious in dealings with Napoleon. Apponyi's report was sent to Maximilian, who saw in it proof that "England was very far from giving her tacit consent to the Mexican plan — as had continually been asserted in Paris." Maximilian felt "compelled to exercise redoubled caution."[181]


## 3. THE REACTIONS OF THE EUROPEAN POWERS TO THE INITIAL NEGOTIATIONS OF THEIR REPRESENTATIVES IN MEXICO

The Spanish Government, of the three allies intervening in Mexico, was the first to receive news of what the Allied Commissioners were doing in Vera Cruz. In the middle of February 1862 a report, written by Prim on 15 January and relating the steps taken by the Allied Commissioners until then, arrived at Madrid.[1] Prim's despatch was published in the official *Gazette* on 17 February, and the British Ambassador to Madrid sent a copy to Russell.[2] The contents of Prim's report were also made known to Thouvenel, together with the observation of the Spanish Government that claims should have been pressed.[3]

On 20 February Thouvenel received a single report, dated

15 January, from Saligny. Saligny enclosed his proposed ultimatum and the collective note sent to Juarez. Saligny referred
Thouvenel to Jurien's reports for the details of "difficulties
greater than could be foreseen in Paris." None of Jurien's
reports accompanied Saligny's despatch, which stated that
Prim was "resolved to use a great benevolence and an extreme
regard "toward the Juarez Government. Prim's objective was
"to arrive through the means of negotiations at peaceful and
satisfactory arrangements of the present difficulties." Saligny
gave his opinion that Prim, who was supported by Wyke,
would soon be disillusioned. The Mexican Government would
merely negotiate to gain time to let the unhealthy climate
decimate the allied forces.[4]

On the same day that Saligny's report arrived in Paris,
Thouvenel made the French position known to the British and
Spanish Governments. A telegram was sent to the French
Ambassador to Madrid that the French Government regretted
that the representatives of the allies in Mexico did not demand
redress instead of making "illusory" negotiations with the
Mexican Government. Barrot was directed to make known
that the French Commander-in-Chief would be instructed to
act with "promptitude and energy" and that it was desirable
that Prim be similarly instructed.[5] The proclamation to the
Mexican people and the collective note to Juarez, Thouvenel
observed in instructions in letter form sent to Barrot, failed to
state that the primary aim of the allies was to obtain redress.
Claims should have been pressed instead of expressing "confidence" in the Juarez Government and stated a willingness
to negotiate. There should be no difficulty about claims, Thouvenel observed, because it was "understood" that the "entente"
merely concerned distribution of sums recovered. Each of the
allies was not responsible to the other two for the list of claims
presented to the Mexican Government.[6] Thouvenel saw Cowley
on 20 February and said that the proclamation and collective
note deviated from the Convention of London. Since its preface
stated that the "arbitrary" conduct of the Mexican authorities

was the cause of the intervention, Thouvenel could not understand why:

> ... the Commissioners had taken upon themselves to say that
> they had no cause of complaint against the Mexican Govern-
> ment, and why it was made to appear that the intervention of
> the three Powers was rather for the purpose of obtaining a
> stable government in Mexico, than for the redressment of past
> wrongs to their respective subjects.

Thouvenel could not "conceive" why the allied troops had not
yet begun a march into the interior. He hoped that it was not
"the intention of the Commissioners to await the formation of
a settled Government, before they sent in their Ultimatums."
Napoleon III was equally vexed, Thouvenel told Cowley, and
had given the order that Saligny and Jurien should be informed
of the disapproval of their actions. Cowley shrewdly saw
through this attempt to veil the real cause of Napoleon's displeasure. In his report of the conversation with Thouvenel,
Cowley commented that the Emperor of the French was
angered:

> ... by the very solemn declaration made that there is no
> intention on the part of the Allied Governments to interfere in
> the internal government of Mexico, whereby he fears that the
> interests of the Archduke Maximilian may be jeopardized.[7]

In a private letter, Cowley stated his suspicion that Napoleon
was irked the Mexicans had been invited to choose a government "before the troops (i.e., of the allies) are at Mexico (City)
to *help* them in their choice."[8]

A telegram sent on 21 February to the French Consul at
Cadiz verifies Cowley's suspicions. These instructions for Jurien
and Saligny, to be sent from Cadiz to expedite arrival in
Mexico, also reveal that Napoleon III did not desire satisfaction for French claims in order to have a pretext for the
French troops to march to Mexico City. In the last extremity,
if the Spanish and British representatives in Mexico decided to

settle differences amicably, Jurien and Saligny were given discretionary powers to act independently of their colleagues:

> The last post only brought me one despatch of M. De Saligny, dated 15 January. The announced (illegible word) is lacking.
>
> The Emperor regrets that instead of immediately seeking the redress of grievances of the three Powers, the Plenipotentiarie: addressed a note to the Mexican Government that furnished it the means, by gaining time, of organizing resistence and of putting on the wrong scent, with the aid of the appearance of consultation, as concerns the real wishes of the nation. It is only after the occupation of Mexico City, or at least the approaches of this city, that the political question of the reorganization of the country can be usefully posed and resolved. His Majesty hopes that one will not let himself be stopped by an evasive and fallacious reply of the Government of Juarez and that one would have marched on the Capital with as much promptitude as the means at one's disposal permits.
>
> Your concessions for the good entente with our allies does not have to go so far as to accept satisfaction that would be in your eyes really less than our legitimate claims and our sacrifices to obtain them. If however the Plenipotentiaries of England and Spain should accept for themselves conditions of this nature, Admiral Jurien and M. De Saligny, always being careful to take into an exact account the necessities of our military situation and of the general state of things in Mexico, would be authorized to let their colleagues treat separately and to seek alone the reparations due France. The gravity also of this resolution indicates that it should only be taken in the last extremity, and after making a calculation of the chances of our isolated action.[9]

In view of Napoleon's instructions to Saligny that he make "excessive" demands likely to be rejected by the Mexican Government,[10] the reference to "legitimate claims" indicates either that Thouvenel was as yet uninformed of Napoleon's intentions or that it was feared to put in writing what Napoleon probably only told Jurien verbally before he left for Mexico.[11]

Lord Russell received Cowley's report of Thouvenel's objections to the first proceedings of the Allied Commissioners on 22 February.[12] On the same day Thouvenel sent instructions to the French Ambassador to London that he make Napoleon III's opinions known. The Emperor believed that the representatives of the allies should not have entered into a discussion with the Juarez Government on the political reorganization of the country. Instead, redress of grievances should have been demanded. Negotiating with the Mexican Government merely gave it "the means of gaining time and to organize resistance." [13] Flahault informed Russell, who said he would send instructions to Mexico so that redress would be demanded instead of continuing an attempt to reorganize Mexico politically. Russell had little choice, Flahault commented in his report to Thouvenel, because the French objections were made in such a way that they appeared to be in harmony with the spirit of the Convention of London.[14] Russell did not receive Wyke's reports until 2 March.[15] What knowledge the British Foreign Secretary had about events in Mexico was derived from Flahault's remarks and Cowley's report. Russell also had a copy of Prim's despatch of 15 January, published by the Spanish Government and forwarded by the British Ambassador to Madrid.[16] Russell was concerned and wrote instructions for Wyke on 24 February:

> Not having received your Despatches I am unable to form a decided opinion as to the course taken by the Commissioners of the allies at Vera Cruz. But so far as I can judge, the Commissioners appear . . . to have insisted too little on the reparation of the wrongs which the allied nations have sustained, and too much on the reorganization of the Mexican Government.
>
> I have to repeat to you, therefore, that the objects for which the Allies have sent their naval and military forces to Mexico are stated fully and explicitly in the preamble to the Convention of the 31st of October.
>
> Her Majesty's Government are at all times ready to give their moral support to a Government which can maintain relations of amity and punish assassins who murder Foreign Residents. But the construction of the form of government

capable of fulfilling these conditions is a matter for the consideration of the Mexicans themselves.

The Convention takes no notice of the form of Government in Mexico except to disavow any intention to interfere with the right of the Mexican people to choose their own Government.[17]

A day later Russell wrote to Wyke in connection with the proclamation to the Mexican people, published in newspapers, which also related the first negotiations leading to the Preliminaries of La Soledad :

> H(er) M(ajesty's) G(overnment) cannot approve, indeed they strongly disapprove this Proclamation.
>
> The Newspapers of this Country as well as those of France state that the Allies asked permission of the Mexicans to occupy a healthy position for their encampment.
>
> It appears . . . that your course was clearly before you. Vera Cruz having been evacuated by the Mexican Forces, the Allies should have sent, by proper messengers, to Mexico (City), the terms they demanded for the wrongs enumerated in the preamble of the Convention.
>
> Subsequent proceedings should have depended on the answers received. But if an encampment out of Vera Cruz, or an advance to Jalapa, should, for sanitary or military reasons, have become necessary, it should have been asked for in terms which should have inspired respect, and not in a way to encourage resistance. But on this point I wait for your explanations before forming a final opinion.[18]

Palmerston approved both sets of instructions to Wyke,[19] copies of which were sent to Cowley to communicate to Thouvenel.[20] To provide sanitary quarters for the British Marines, Russell instructed the British Admiralty to send orders that they be reembarked or sent to Jalapa.[21] A month before, when concerned about Colonel Valazé's remarks that the French reinforcements would march into the interior of Mexico to establish Maximilian as king, Russell had already instructed the Admiralty to send orders that Dunlop remove the British Marines from Vera Cruz at the approach of the unhealthy season.[22]

On that occasion the Admiralty had sent instructions that the British Marines be reembarked at Dunlop's earliest convenience.[23] So, at the end of February, the Admiralty informed Russell of having made this decision[24] and sent more instructions to make sure the Marines would be reembarked instead of moved inland.[25]

On 21 February Barrot saw O'Donnell, the Chief Spanish Minister, and informed him of the contents of Thouvenel's telegram of the previous day,[26] that it was desirable to instruct Prim to act with "promptitude and energy." O'Donnell promised to send Prim instructions identical to those that would be sent to Jurien in this respect. O'Donnell observed that Prim already had instructions to adapt his policy to local circumstances in Mexico. When Barrot countered that negotiations with the Juarez Government would only cause a loss of time, O'Donnell replied that such a decision was not made by Prim alone, but in a conference of all the Allied Commissioners. The collective note had been sent to the Mexican Government without enclosing ultimatums, because there were differences among the Commissioners about the claims Saligny wanted to press. A further cause of delays was the difficulty of obtaining transportational facilities.[27] A few days later Barrot received Thouvenel's instructions objecting to the proclamation to the Mexican people and the collective note sent to the Juarez Government.[28] Barrot obtained an interview with Collantes, the Spanish Minister of Foreign Relations. Collantes agreed that negotiating with the Juarez Government was an "error." The result would be a loss of "precious time" and affording the Mexicans an opportunity "to organize means of defense." Collantes also agreed with Thouvenel that it had been "decided" that each of the allies "would formulate the claims that it had to present against the Mexican Government and that the two others would abstain from any appreciation of the total and the nature of these claims." The "contrary," Collantes told Barrot, had happened. Wyke objected to Saligny's claims, and all the Commissioners decided not to send ultimatums with the collective note to the Mexican Government. Sending the collective note was senseless, because it only informed the Juarez Government what it already knew, that the allies had claims against it. The reply would be to ask what claims would be pressed. Prim's participation in the affair was "mitigated," because he "acted in concert with his colleagues, with whom he had been recommended always to act in accord." Collantes also condemned the request the Allied Commissioners made to obtain a healthy place to stay during negotiations. Three great Powers did not send a joint expedition to Mexico "to open illusory negotiations with a Government that has already given so many proofs of its bad faith." The allied troops were sent "to force the Mexican Government . . . to give immediate and complete satisfaction for claims." In addition, the representatives of the allies were to take "measures" to prevent the recurrence of outrages to foreigners in Mexico. It was not intended that the Allied Commissioners would go to Mexico "to ask a Government, which must be treated . . . as an enemy, for very useless permission to establish themselves on such or such a point of its territory." Collantes then went on to explain what the Spanish Government had expected would result from the allied expedition to Mexico. Negotiations should never have been initiated with Juarez. He would only make promises, "already so often made and so often violated." Even if he wanted to act in good faith, he could not. He wanted to obtain a loan of $6,000,000 from the United States, giving Mexican territory as security, but such an American loan would be insufficient to pay the claims of the allies. They should not end their intervention, satisfied with having obtained what "probably would not have been refused them," after the presentation of an "energetic note" from any one of them. The collective action of the allies was something unique, which "would not happen again." It was necessary, Collantes urged, "to act in such a way to obtain all the results one had in view." A "grave mistake" had been made, but with redoubled "activity and energy" it was still possible to "regain the time already lost."

What Collantes meant was that it was necessary to replace the Government of Juarez with one "which can give to Mexico this prosperity for which nature has provided all the elements for this privileged land, and to assure there the property and existence of foreigners." After having begun negotiations with Juarez, the allies would be inconsistent it they asked him to relinquish power. He would say his government was "stable" and could give "guarantees." Even if he should resign his position and agree to permit the Mexican people to express its wishes, this "renunciation" would give him a "moral force" greater than he ever had. It was not desirable to "peel power from him momentarily only to see it fall into his hands again under conditions infinitely more favorable." It was wrong to suppose that, once Juarez ceased being President, the "party of order" would "begin a movement to choose another form of government or another man." That was now impossible, because negotiations with Juarez had begun. Juarez would only have been driven from power if :

> . . . when arriving on the coasts of Mexico, the Powers had clearly stated that they did not want to treat with Juarez and that they were making an appeal to the Mexican nation that it should choose immediately a government with which the dignity of the allied Powers permitted them to negotiate; but, from the moment that we openly recognized the Government of Juarez by negotiating with it, by that alone we discouraged the sane part of the population; we repelled its aspirations towards a better order of things, and it is to be feared that it will be very difficult now to revive the hopes that are only based on the certainty of the moral, and if need be, material cooperation of the three Powers.

Collantes told Barrot that, in spite of this situation, there was still hope to obtain "results." The three European allies "cannot, come what may, abandon an enterprise for which they have united their forces." The Spanish Government was "determined" to "do in Mexico" what the allies "have proposed to do there."[29]

At the end of February Cowley gave Thouvenel copies of Russell's instructions, of 24 and 25 February, to Wyke.[30] Thouvenel did not comment on Russell's injunctions to permit the Mexican people complete freedom in the choice of a government. The French Minister of Foreign Affairs said he agreed with Russell's objections to the proclamation issued by the Allied Commissioners. Thouvenel promised to write to Saligny in the same sense. Disapproval would not be expressed so "strongly" as by Russell, because the French Commissioners had already objected to the proclamation and only signed it to maintain harmony with their colleagues.[31] Confidentially Thouvenel told Cowley that Wyke and Prim were responsible for the proclamation. Its purpose was "to maintain the present President and Government in their places." Prim, in particular, seemed determined to keep on good terms with the Juarez Government. Perhaps, Thouvenel suggested, the Spanish General had "ambitious views" of his own.[32] Thouvenel also complained that Wyke had objected to Saligny's ultimatum and that that was contrary to the Convention of London:

> His (i.e., Thouvenel's) conception of the engagements existing between the three governments was that they were generally to support each other's demands. Of course if any one of them put forward claims which in the opinion of the other two were extravagant or ill founded and the settlement of the claims of the two were thereby to be delayed, it could not be expected that they would join in what they might consider to be an act of injustice, to the detriment of their own claimants. It would be open to them to express their opinions, and, if not listened to, to proceed with their own affairs. But this could not invalidate the claims of the third Power who might prosecute them alone, it being however clearly understood that the said Power was still bound by the article of the convention of October 31st abjuring all particular and special advantages.[33]

Referring the whole question of claims to Europe, Thouvenel asserted, was undesirable, because then there would be no end to the delays that would result.[34]

The opinions that Thouvenel stated about the motives of

Wyke and Prim were the same as contained in reports from Saligny already received when Thouvenel had his conversation with Cowley. In January 1862 copies of the letters exchanged between Wyke and Saligny in November 1861 arrived in Paris.[35] These letters were written in connection with Wyke's negotiations with the Juarez Government for a settlement of claims even after Wyke had received instructions to present an ultimatum. Saligny predicted that the "bad faith" of the Juarez Government would cause these negotiations to come to nothing. Wyke's letters showed that he was willing to negotiate with the Mexican Government until all means of reaching a pacific settlement were exhausted.[36] Saligny's report of 15 January, received 20 February, stated that Prim was extremely anxious to negotiate a settlement with Juarez without resorting to hostilities, "illusions" with which Saligny could not associate himself.[37] Jurien's report of a conversation with Prim at Havana, before going to Vera Cruz, stated that Prim would "support" Juarez if he would be willing to negotiate a settlement of claims.[38] Hidalgo had been opposed to Prim's appointment from the very beginning, because he was "bent upon cutting a great figure anywhere."[39] A letter from Miranda, forwarded to the French Ministry of Foreign Affairs by Estrada in January 1862, also expressed anticipated difficulties, because Prim was famous as a liberal and related to Juarez' Minister of Finance.[40] Napoleon III read everything about Mexican affairs that reached the Ministry of Foreign Affairs,[41] and Thouvenel's comments to Cowley about Prim reflected the ideas of the Emperor himself.[42]

On 1 March Russell wrote Cowley to answer Thouvenel's complaints, related in reports received that day.[43] Russell passed over the question of whether the allies should pass judgement on each other's claims. The Foreign Secretary stated that, while it was possible that Wyke might have objected to some French claims, reports from Mexico had not yet arrived in London. In answer to Thouvenel's objection that Prim and Wyke were acting in a friendly way toward the Juarez Government, Russell protested that "it was never understood that the government de facto of Mexico was not to be treated with." If the Mexican people showed a "preference to the existing government," Russell warned, "it would be a violation of the Convention (i.e., of London) to interfere with the Right of the Mexican People in that Respect."[44]

All the reports that Wyke wrote in January 1862 arrived at the British Foreign Office on 2 March.[45] The next day Russell sent Cowley a copy of Wyke's report, giving an account of the conferences about Saligny's proposed ultimatum. Cowley was directed to call Thouvenel's attention to the contents of Wyke's despatch and point out that Russell agreed with Wyke's two objections:

> The demand of twelve millions of dollars . . . formed without any account on a rough guess, and the demand of the full and immediate execution of a contract for the payment of bonds to the amount of fifteen millions of dollars in return for seven hundred and fifty thousand dollars advanced to a nominal government just in the act of falling appear to Her Majesty's Government to be items of the ultimatum of which the Government of the Emperor cannot approve.
>
> But Her Majesty's Government would be glad to learn the views of the French Government before they reply to Sir Charles Wyke.[46]

Cowley saw Thouvenel on 4 March and made known Russell's opinion of Saligny's proposed ultimatum, but Thouvenel asked that a discussion on the matter be delayed a day, because he only had had a chance to glance at the voluminous reports from Mexico.[47] Cowley sent a report of this conversation to Russell the same day,[48] together with a private letter. While expressing a hope that Thouvenel would not support Saligny's ultimatum, Cowley gave his opinion that the French Minister of Foreign Affairs was "a mere cypher in this question." It was Eugenie who "governs the Emperor's decision upon it."[49]

On the very day that Cowley tried to obtain explanations

from Thouvenel on Saligny's ultimatum, only two reports from Saligny arrived in Paris.[50] The voluminous reports referred to by Thouvenel were from Jurien,[51] to whom Saligny left the task of reporting conferences of the Allied Commissioners. The whole bundle of reports was forwarded to Napoleon III.[52] He was impressed by a private letter from Baron Wagner, the Prussian Chargé d'Affaires in Mexico City, to Saligny.[53] Wagner was considered "impartial,"[54] and Napoleon took his comments seriously that "the monarchist party is making remarkable progress."[55] Great value was also placed on the report of Thomasset, the French officer who was a member of the delegation that carried the collective note of the Allied Commissioners to Mexico City. Pencil lines were made in the margin next to Thomasset's remarks that only Juarez' terroristic measures prevented the "masses" from expressing their "sentiments." Pencil lines were also made alongside Thomasset's statement that only the protection of French "bayonnets" would give "courage" to "these masses that are trembling" and would not "pronounce" in favor of a monarchy unless protected from Juarez.[56] Pencil marks were also drawn along the margin of a letter from Santa Anna, forwarded to Thouvenel on 5 March by Estrada, that "men of property will remain silent and indifferent if they do not see a positive objective in the intervention, because these people can not triumph by themselves."[57] Napoleon and Eugenie took pride in obtaining information outside official diplomatic channels. A report of anarchy in Mexico from the captain of a French warship anchored in Vera Cruz at the time of the first arrival of the Spanish expedition at Vera Cruz[58] especially impressed Eugenie. She found his report "remarkable," because he was "unaware" of Jurien's instructions and "yet found . . . the germ of the idea which it only remains for us to develop and lead to a happy issue, by God's help."[59] Both Jurien and Saligny blamed Prim that the allied expeditionary forces were still at Vera Cruz, instead of in the interior, and that negotiations were being carried on with Juarez.[60] While a report written by Jurien on 9 February stated that a march into the interior would begin after a meeting between Prim and Doblado, regardless of the result of the meeting, Jurien also stated that "nothing has indicated to us the power, let alone the existence of the conservative party."[61] Napoleon was not discouraged that Jurien found no monarchists in Mexico. One of Saligny's reports mentioned the receipt of a letter from General Robles that predicted a rupture between Juarez and Doblado.[62] Saligny's attempt to rally Doblado, Uraga, and Robles to the monarchist cause[63] seemed likely soon to be successful.[64] Since Saligny was furthering the monarchist cause in Mexico, Napoleon concluded that Jurien was being tricked to support Prim, who was judged chiefly responsible for negotiations with Juarez. There were persons in Mexico who would rally to a monarchy, Napoleon believed, but they were afraid to act so long as the allied expedition remained at Vera Cruz and could afford them no protection. Baron Beyens, the Belgian Ambassador to Paris, discovered that Napoleon "flatters himself, in accordance with secret information, that not only will Spain formally condemn the conduct of its General, but that it will go so far as to recall him."[65] The "secret information" could have been Barrot's report, received 2 March, of Collantes' condemnation of the proclamation issued by the Allied Commissioners, the theory that the allies judge each other's claims, the language of the collective note, and the requesting of permission to move inland. All these steps, Collantes had said, only supported Juarez' regime.[66] General Fleury, Napoleon's aide-de-camp, gives further confirmation in his memoirs that Collantes' remarks probably led Napoleon to believe that Prim would be recalled. The proclamation drawn up by Prim, Fleury wrote, made "an appeal for good understanding to an unworthy government." It was, "the Spaniards themselves said, 'the height of madness.' " Such an appeal was "to support what was to be pulled down . . . to rally to the liberals . . . it was treason."[67] On 7 March Napoleon wrote

Maximilian the interpretation given to all the information studied :

> I . . . was waiting to receive news from Mexico. . . . That which has arrived is not very good, for General Prim seems to be animated by motives of personal ambition, and has caused Admiral Jurien to take a number of rash steps; fortunately the arrival of my reinforcements will alter the situation. But we cannot hear from him for a month. Instead of marching onward and adopting an authoritative tone, General Prim has, so to speak, abased himself before Juarez' Government. The aide-de-camp whom he sent to Mexico (City) replied to those who displayed a desire for the return of the monarchy *that there would soon be no monarchies left in Europe!*—In spite of this the Prussian Minister writes to M. de Saligny that the monarchist party is making remarkable progress; a more recent communication from Admiral Jurien, dated February 9, announces that the expedition is at last about to advance. The elements in the country seem to be all ready, all that is necessary is to know how to take advantage of them, and I am distressed to see that my Admiral is allowing himself to be tricked by General Prim. It is very unfortunate that Spain has entrusted this weighty mission to such a man; I am going to send another general to examine the situation and see whether Admiral Jurien ought not to retire. Finally, I have great hopes of the moral effect which will be produced by the arrival of General Lorencez, for, according to all the accounts I receive, the French are as much loved as the Spaniards are detested.
>
> I have made a point of giving Your Imperial Highness these details so that you may know that I am making every effort for the success of the plan which we have conceived.[68]

Eugenie agreed with Napoleon's interpretation of the course of events in Mexico. Metternich reported, "She spits fire and flame at her Spanish fellow countrymen (*Elle jette feu et flamme contre ses compatriotes.*)."[69] Eugenie's "Private Reader," who seems to reflect the Empress' ideas, wrote memoirs, in which Prim was criticized as "looking after his personal influences." The premature arrival of the Spanish fleet at Vera Cruz was the beginning of all the difficulties.

Mexicans were "alarmed," and the result was a reception "different" from the one expected.[70]

In spite of Thouvenel's fears of "complaints" from the Spanish Government,[71] Napoleon had a condemnation of Prim published in the official *Moniteur* of 7 March, in the hope that Prim's actions would be disapproved by the Spanish Government, which might also be encouraged by the article to recall him. Jurien, the *Moniteur* asserted, had expected Prim to take the lead in marching into the interior, because the largest part of the expeditionary forces was Spanish. Such a march was "indispensible to assure our political influence, to negotiate with advantage, finally to remove our troops from the littoral, which is an uninhabitable torrid zone after the month of April." Prim had compromised the dignity of the European allies by negotiating "on enemy territory" and using his "influence" to obtain the agreement of the French and British representatives in Mexico:

> . . . General Prim, to our great surprise, is no longer this general whose spirit of adventure one feared, but a prudent, almost fearful, negotiator. By his influence he has led the English and French commanders into a proceeding that certainly will be approved neither in Paris nor in Madrid, because one must very well believe there that the prestige of the three powers is compromised when fifteen thousand men, arriving on enemy territory, instead of demanding the government to do justice, within twenty-four hours, to their grievances, not only commences to parlay, but goes so far as to ask permission of this same government to go to Jalapa or to Orizaba to find a healthy encampment.

All the Spanish officers and soldiers wanted to march forward, and, the *Moniteur* added, "you can understand that our zouaves agree." Prim's inactivity was also discouraging the "friends of the intervention" in Mexico. They were "in the majority," but they "will not declare themselves until they see the allies acting with vigor against this handful of persons who pillage and levy contributions in this unfortunate country." To "remedy" the false starts, it was necessary that :

. . . the three powers take without delay energetic measures to send precise and identical instructions to their representatives; it would be especially necessary that the Emperor send reinforcements, for it is chiefly on us that they are counting in Mexico to get this unfortunate country out of the state of complete disorganization in which it finds itself.[71]

While Russell supported Wyke's views about Saligny's ultimatum, the Foreign Secretary disapproved the references to "regeneration" that found their way into the proclamation to the Mexican people.[72] Russell explained, in instructions to Wyke, that the British Government did not desire to give "even the appearance of interference in the internal affairs of Mexico." The political fate of the Mexicans was for them to choose themselves :

> If the Mexicans can establish a strong central Government, capable of maintaining order at home, and of protecting merchants, the moral support of the British Government will be willingly given to Mexico, whatver the particular form of the Mexican Government may be.[73]

Russell also disapproved Wyke's reports, suggesting Mexico would be "regenerated" by a government of moderates, "encouraged" by the intervention and organized by Doblado.[74] "I cannot," Russell wrote Cowley in a private letter, "go along with Wyke about Mexican Regeneration."[75] Wyke was instructed that Doblado had to depend only on his own "energy" in forming a Mexican government :

> If Senor Doblado has the energy for which credit is given him, he will form a government whose strength will maintain order and punish adequately miscreants who have robbed and murdered with impunity the subjects of the Sovereigns of Great Britain, France and Spain.[76]

With reference to Wyke's complaint that he had no instructions dated later than mid-November 1861, Russell replied that he did not understand it. At any rate, the "instructions which you did receive were precise and, read with the Convention, they clearly set forth the policy of Her Majesty's Government and the course by which you were to carry that policy into effect." Instead of acting on these instructions, Wyke and Dunlop "attributed to Her Majesty's Government views and intentions diametrically opposed" to these instructions. Since the British Commissioners were "following out" their "fancies," they were "naturally without any instruction to guide" them "in a course which Her Majesty's Government had no intention" to "pursue."[77] The sense of Russell's objection was expressed in a letter he sent to the British Admiralty, a copy of which was forwarded to Wyke.[78] From the reports of Wyke and Dunlop, Russell wrote the Admiralty, the British Government learned with regret that the British representatives "are impressed with the belief that the 'regeneration' of Mexico is the primary object to which the efforts of the Allied Forces are to be directed." This was a belief "wholly unwarranted by the terms of the Triple Convention and by the instructions to H(er) M(ajesty's) servants for carrying them out." Redress of grievances of British subjects "was the sole inducement of H(er) M(ajesty's) G(overnment) to enter into the convention."[79] Hammond, the British Under-Secretary of State for Foreign Affairs, wrote Wyke a private letter reiterating Russell's comments. Hammond also expressed his "sincere hope that the affair will end better than it has begun."[80] The way this would be done, Russell instructed Wyke, was to negotiate a settlement. With the exception of the "absurd proposal of the re-embarkation of the Allied Forces," Doblado's answer to the collective note was "tolerably satisfactory." A continuation of these negotiations, Russell hoped, would lead to an amicable settlement:

> The meeting of the Commissioners at Orizaba, and the assembly of the whole Force of the Allies at Jalapa and Orizaba, will, Her Majesty's Government hope, afford means of arriving at an amicable conclusion of these difficult affairs.[81]

Cowley saw Thouvenel on 5 March and informed him of

Russell's objections to Saligny's proposed ultimatum. Thouvenel said that the only claims the allies were bound to support mutually were those already recognized. Unrecognized claims, for which no amount of redress had been set, were not covered by the Convention of London. Each of the allies pressing such claims was the "sole judge" of them. If France's allies "could not conscientiously countenance" some of the French claims, Thouvenel expected no "support" for these claims, but the French Government "must take its own means for enforcing them." A "division of action" was to be regretted, but Thouvenel "saw no help for it, and in such case each Government must be left to conclude its own treaty with the Mexican Government." Such treaties ought to be in harmony with the "general principle of obtaining no special advantages." Thouvenel told Cowley that the Spanish Government also objected to submitting its claims to the French and British Governments for approval. Thouvenel read Cowley Barrot's report of the conversation with Collantes, about how the allies should press claims, and Cowley admitted that Collantes seemed to disapprove Prim's failure to endorse Saligny's ultimatum. Cowley observed, however, that Thouvenel could hardly approve a demand for $12,000,000, "formed . . . on a rough guess, and another demand for the payment of fifteen millions of dollars in return for an advance of seven hundred and fifty thousand dollars." Thouvenel explained that it was impossible for him to check the fairness of the demand for $12,000,000. The documents concerning French claims were in Mexico. All he could do, Thouvenel said, was to instruct Saligny to examine every claim carefully. A mixed commission to study claims, as suggested at one of the conferences of the Allied Commissioners, was out of the question. Thouvenel made a counterproposal, suggested by Saligny, that a French Commission decide the merits of French claims. If it were found that $12,000,000 was too high an estimate of French claims, this figure could be decreased. When Cowley asked whether Thouvenel would be satisfied if the Mexican Government agreed to accept the decisions of the French Commission without a specific sum named in advance, Thouvenel even objected to "this slight modification." As to the Jecker bonds, Thouvenel claimed, the question was not that much more was being demanded than was loaned originally to the Mexican Government. A "number of French subjects" had "advanced money to Jecker on bonds issued by him on the strength of this contract." The Mexican Government, therefore, was being asked for the "repayment of bonds for which value had been given." Cowley replied that "no Government which had any respect for itself could countenance such a monstrous abuse, as this transaction in all probability covered." All the difficulties would have been avoided if Saligny, like Wyke, had only demanded that the Mexican Government agree to pay all just claims. In his report to Russell of this conversation, Cowley admitted that "M. Thouvenel's answer admits with difficulty of a reply." The French Minister claimed that no reliance could be placed on Mexican promises after all the "experience" the allies had had with Mexican bad faith. Cowley countered that Mexico could not pay all the claims in full at once and the allied expeditionary forces could not remain in Mexico until its government paid "every farthing." The French Government, Cowley charged, had no desire to settle differences with Mexico and only used them as an excuse to keep French troops in Mexico until the accomplishment of other objects, such as placing Maximilian on a throne there. Thouvenel admitted that that was probably the intention of Napoleon III :

> M. Thouvenel defended himself but feebly, if indeed at all. He said that no doubt such was the Emperor's wish, but the other commissioners, he thought, had also plans of their own. He was not sure that General Prim did not entertain the ambitious design of becoming President of the Republic, while Sir Charles Wyke was desirous of maintaining the Juarez administration.

To cut off the discussion, Thouvenel remarked that "while the Governments were discussing at home, events were marching in Mexico." It was very difficult, therefore, "to send instructions relating to matters which had occurred two months before the comments on them could be read."[82]

On 8 March Cowley learned from Napoleon himself that Saligny's claims were intended as an excuse to keep the expeditionary forces in Mexico. Napoleon started the conversation by stating his objections to the first proceedings of the Allied Commissioners in Mexico :

> His idea had been, that the expeditionary forces should have possessed themselves of Vera Cruz, and that the Commissioners should then have sent in their demands for redress, taking up with the troops such a forward position, as circumstances might have ordered necessary. This done, they should have waited to see the effect produced on the Mexican people by their presence, which he (the Emperor) had hoped would have shown itself in a desire to reform the Mexican institutions. But, said His Majesty, the Spaniards have spoilt everything, and General Prim has evidently designs of his own. The Commissioners ought never to have signed the proclamation which he drew up, and which had strengthened the Government of Juarez, and alarmed the Mexican people, by giving the one cause to assert, and the other to believe, that the main intention of the Allies was to interfere in the internal concerns. A firm demand for redress would have opened the eyes of the people to the misdoings of their chiefs and then there might have been a hope that the better thinking among them would have resolved on effecting a reform.

Cowley observed that Saligny had put forward "preposterous" claims, and they were the cause of difficulties among the Allied Commissioners. Cowley asked Napoleon not to support Saligny's claims, and Napoleon replied that "excessive" claims were being pressed at his command :

> I intimated a hope that His Majesty would not encourage these claims, but His Majesty avowed, that it was he who had desired they should be made excessive *(aussi vives que possible (sic))*. It was necessary to begin with high terms, said His Majesty *(il fallait commencer par le gros bout (sic))* or otherwise the Government of Juarez would at once have accepted

the conditions proposed, and the Allies having no further excuse to remain, must have taken their departure, to be treated in all probability with the same disdain as before as soon as their backs should be turned. The Emperor declared, that in acting as he had done he had no selfish policy in view, he wished to see the riches and resources of Mexico thrown open to the commerce of Europe—he was convinced that this could only be effected by the establishment of a monarchical form of government in that country, and therefore he had not concealed his opinions.

Cowley warned the Emperor that, unless the Mexican people really wanted a monarchy, "Mexico might become a second Rome," because French troops would have to support the monarchy created. Napoleon replied by hedging:

> . . . he felt that the whole question must be left to the Mexican people, only he considered, that the presence of the Allied troops, by maintaining tranquillity, would give the country an opportunity of considering their present position and their future destiny.[83]

In spite of these assurances to Cowley, Napoleon had sent Almonte to Mexico a month before with orders to collect "notables" to proclaim Maximilian ruler of Mexico.[84]

Russell received Cowley's report of Thouvenel's proposals concerning and justification of Saligny's ultimatum on 7 March.[85] Russell agreed that French demands were a "pretext for a continued occupation of Mexico, and the assumption of the Government of the Country by a Foreign Power."[86] A cabinet meeting was called on 8 March,[87] and it was decided to instruct the Admiralty to send orders to Dunlop to reembark the British Marines at the "first opportunity," even if they had been marched inland already.[88] Russell sent appropriate instructions to the Admiralty.[89] Russell also sent another letter to the Admiralty, commenting on Dunlop's report justifying the seizure of Miramon. In this despatch Dunlop justified the seizure by stating:

We have come here to assist the Mexicans to inaugurate a new era, as well as to demand our just rights, and these objects can only be gained by keeping ourselves free from all party grounds for suspicion that we wish to dictate to Mexico by whom she is to be governed.

Russell approved the arrest of Miramon, but complained that Dunlop did not arrest Miramon's adherents. Calling attention to Dunlop's words, Russell commented that the Commodore was not to "suppose that H(er) M(ajesty's) G(overnment) have undertaken to inaugurate a new era or to attempt the regeneration of Mexico."[90] With respect to Dunlop's suggestion that a "black regiment" replace the Marines during the unhealthy season,[91] Russell informed the Admiralty that the Secretary of State for War had stated that no such troops could be spared for service in Mexico.[92] The Admiralty immediately sent orders to Admiral Milne, the Commander of the North American and West India Station, to relieve Dunlop of his duties in Mexico. Milne was given a discretion to go to Mexico to relieve Dunlop, or to send Admiral Dacres, the Senior Naval Officer at Port Royal, as Dunlop's replacement. A copy of Russell's instructions that Dunlop be informed not to interfere with Mexican internal affairs was enclosed, and attention was called to previous instructions from the Admiralty, dated 1 and 28 February, that the British Marines be reembarked. Milne or Dacres would carry out these orders, sending the British Marines to Bermuda to await further instructions. A British naval force would be kept in the Gulf of Mexico for the purpose, if need be, to protect British lives and property in Mexico.[93] Russell approved the decision to relieve Dunlop,[94] and, if the orders of the Admiralty were carried out, the British intervention in Mexico would be reduced to the position of being represented in Mexico by Wyke and either Admiral Milne or Dacres, supported by a few British warships in the Gulf of Mexico.

Thouvenel sent Flahault a summary of the explanations of Saligny's ultimatum given Cowley on 5 March.[95] Thouvenel also forwarded to Flahault instructions for Saligny, written for the purpose that they be sent to Flahault and that it would appear that the French Government only desired to press just claims. Saligny's instructions, written on 28 February, stated that the Allied Commissioners had no power to judge each other's ultimatums. They could act jointly only concerning *"the employment and the distribution of sums of money that will be recovered from Mexico."* Since Prim and Wyke objected to the $12,000,000 demanded by Saligny, he might be "less rigorous on this point" in the interests of maintaing harmony among the Allied Commissioners. Concerning the Jecker bonds, Saligny was directed to make a "distinction" between what "touches directly on our interests and what is foreign to them." Saligny was to "separate what . . . can really compromise the interests that we have to protect and what has a completely different character."[96] Instructions written for Jurien on 28 February were not sent to Flahault. These instructions referred Jurien to the orders sent on 21 February to Mexico via Cadiz. The French Commissioners were not to permit the British and Spanish Commissioners to delay operations by discussion of French claims, which were not subject to approval by the allies of France. If difficulties in this connection continued, Jurien was to examine the possibility of operations independent of France's allies. "It is to Mexico City," Thouvenel urged, "that you must go . . . to demand straightforward the satisfactions that are due us."[97] Thouvenel's instructions to Flahault stated that he was to call to Russell's attention the concessions made in the instructions to Saligny of 28 February concerning the $12,000,000 and the Jecker claim. As another concession, Thouvenel wrote Flahault, a French Commission would examine French claims. It was important, however, that the Mexican Government be given no opportunity to "discuss the obligations that will have to be imposed." If this were done, only general principles of a liquidation would be agreed upon, and Mexico would contest the details after the departure of the allied expedition. Such a predicament would be avoided "if our claims are formulated very precisely right away."[98] In addition to the necessity that the Mexican Government accept, without discussion, the French claims, drawn up in detail, it was also important a stable government be formed in Mexico. Such a government was "the only guarantee for the future." Without a political change in Mexico, no claims of the allies would be settled, and Mexico would revert to barbarism and eventually be annexed by the United States.[99] Thouvenel sent Flahault a private letter at the same time that the official instructions about claims were forwarded. Thouvenel made it clear that the whole elaborate explanation of claims and how they should be pressed was only designed to afford a means of upsetting the Juarez Government, a change to be effected by French troops and, it was hoped, with British passive approval:

> ... I am convinced that at the point at which things are, the only thing to do is to push them energetically, and all I ask of England is to let us use our forces in a way she certainly wouldn't have to regret, if Mexico is saved at the same time from anarchy and the covetousness of the United States.

Although Wyke and Saligny "have not been getting along for some time," it was possible that this "difficult" situation could be improved. Dunlop and Jurien "understood each other wonderfully."[100] Wyke might also be won over to further French plans. Thouvenel's proposal was based on two assumptions. The first was that Wyke was in favor of the establishment of a Mexican monarchy and would work for its implementation. The basis of this assumption was that Wyke had seen Napoleon III and Thouvenel in 1861 before going to Mexico and had said that Latin America was "ripe" for monarchical institutions.[101] Thouvenel's second assumption was that Doblado, as reported by Saligny and his friend Robles, was about to have a falling out with Juarez.[102] Thouvenel's proposal to Flahault was:

Wyke, whom I saw last year, told me that with his experience with the people of South America he believed that only monarchy would bring a solution to the abyss. If he were authorized to express confidentially the same opinion to General Doblado, he would without doubt demand nothing better than to play the profitable role of Monk and everything would soon be finished.[103]

Flahault saw Russell on 10 March. The accounts of the meeting by Russell[104] and by Flahault[105] make no mention that Thouvenel's suggestion concerning Wyke and Doblado was discussed. Flahault summarized the official instructions from Thouvenel and read parts of them.[106] Russell concurred that "the allies could not examine each other's claims without a great loss of time, and . . . would not be able to judge of the validity of each particular demand." But when a demand was "exorbitant on the face of it" and appeared to be only a "pretext for war," the British Government could not support such a demand. The Jecker bonds and the demand for $12,000,000 seemed to be demands of this nature.[107] Russell agreed to accept Thouvenel's compromise that a French Commission adjust the demand for $12,000,000 by making a thorough investigation of French claims.[108] Concerning the Jecker bonds, Flahault stated that Thouvenel's instructions to Saligny permitted him to modify his stand on this claim.[109] Russell promised to send instructions to Wyke not to object to French claims, provided a French Commission were established and the Jecker claim "abandoned."[110] Russell ended the conversation by stating that the British Marines would be reembarked when the unhealthy season began in Vera Cruz. He explained that this was not a change of policy, because it had been understood all along that the Marines were not land forces and would not be able to march beyond Vera Cruz.[111]

On 12 March Thouvenel received Flahault's report of the agreement made with Russell on 10 March. Flahault's summary of his conversation with Russell failed to state Russell's condition about the Jecker claim.[112] Because Flahault told Russell that Saligny would receive orders to modify his position with regard to the Jecker claim, the British Foreign Secretary assumed that the Jecker claim would not be supported by Saligny any more. Russell drew up instructions for Wyke to cease his opposition to the French claims provided Saligny carried out the agreement reached with Flahault that a French Commission be established and that the Jecker bonds no longer receive French support, as promised by Flahault. The French Commission, no doubt, would be "fair" in its investigation of French claims. It was never "contemplated" that the "Commissioners of the Allies should constitute themselves into a Mixed Commission for determining on the merits of their respective claims before they were pressed on the Mexican Government." Such a procedure would have caused "interminable delay" and probably resulted in "serious disagreement between the Commissioners." The Commissioners, therefore, "should generally support the demands of each other, when these demands appear fair and reasonable." Since it appeared that Saligny had acted on instructions when drafting his ultimatum, Russell wrote Wyke, there was no "ground for attributing personal motives to your French Colleague or for your ceasing to act with the utmost frankness and cordiality with him." Russell did not care to discuss questions of a "personal character" concerning Saligny that Wyke mentioned in his correspondence. Wyke was directed to prevent such "personal feelings" on his part from impairing the "Joint action of the Allied Commissioners."[113]

Having received Russell's version of the agreement reached with Flahault,[114] as well as a copy of Wyke's instructions[115] based on that understanding, Cowley saw Thouvenel on 13 March and summarized these documents. Thouvenel objected that the Jecker claim was not being waived. The reasons Thouvenel gave were that:

... he was not sufficiently cognisant of the terms of the Jecker contract, which he had never seen, to form any opinion about it, that he did not know how far French interests were engaged in it, and therefore he must leave the whole matter to the appreciation of M. Dubois de Saligny. . . .

When pressed further by Cowley, Thouvenel stated that he could give Saligny "no orders upon the subject." Thouvenel merely promised to inform Saligny of the terms of Wyke's instructions and to suggest that Saligny not permit personal disagreements to interfere with his public duty to maintain cordial relations with Wyke.[116] Thouvenel admitted the truth of Russell's reasons why the British Marines would be reembarked, but expressed the hope that the Marines be permitted to stay at Jalapa should they already be there.[117]

Russell was sorry that Thouvenel supported "Jecker and his fraudulent loan and the culpable French who robbed the Mexicans so shamelessly."[118] Wyke's instructions were altered to inform him that the French Government did not waive the Jecker claim and that the French arrangement was to be supported, barring the Jecker claim.[119] The difficulties resulting from claims brought Russell to the realization that it was recognized as legitimate by the Mexican Government or ones desirable that he himself know what British claims Wyke would press. Wyke's proposed ultimatum only enumerated a few important claims. The other claims were characterized as ones that would be found to be legitimate.[120] Therefore Wyke was instructed on 15 March to draw up a list of all British claims, to state which were "absolute" and which were not yet investigated, and to give the amount of monetary compensation for each claim.[121]

On 14 March, the day after Cowley told Thouvenel that Wyke would be instructed not to support the Jecker claim, the French Minister of Foreign Affairs wrote instructions for Saligny. He was not directed to establish a French Commission. He was merely asked to "study this contrivance again." It was left to Saligny's discretion, in this connection, whether "too great a rigor on our part would not be, in the last analysis, more inconvenient than some concessions that would contribute to maintaining an intimate concert among the representatives of the three courts." Concerning the "Jecker affair," Thouvenel suggested making a "distinction" between what "should legitimately claim our protection and the foreign interests that we have . . . no mission to safeguard." This remark about the Jecker claim probably was inserted, because these instructions were intended for publication.[122] Saligny did not have to take the suggestion about making such a "distinction" seriously, because in the same instructions Thouvenel stated that he was convinced of the "perfectly thought out and justified character of our ultimatum." Presenting it to the Mexican Government should cause no difficulties, because Russell "completely agreed with us that the demands formulated by one of the representatives of the Allied Powers were not subjected to the obligation of first being approved by the the two others." Russell's only qualification was that the Allied Commissioners were permitted to express "advice on the ultimatum of their colleague."[123] Thouvenel also wrote instructions for Jurien on 14 March. Although Thouvenel could not "foretell" what would happen when the French troops advanced toward Mexico City, there might be less "manifestation" against the Juarez Government than originally expected. In making preparations for "the establishment of monarchy in Mexico," Jurien was to take into consideration whether the "appeal" to him by Mexicans for a monarchy represented enough "energy" to proceed with the scheme. If there were "apathy," Jurien was instructed to apply "only moral force."[124]

At the end of January and the beginning of February 1862 the British and Spanish Governments reached an entente to oppose any French attempts to force the Mexican people to submit to being ruled by Maximilian.[125] At the beginning of March, when Russell made known that he objected to the proclamation issued by the Allied Commissioners and the Jecker claim,[126] the Spanish viewpoint reported to Russell was so similar to his own that he did not request further explanations. Collantes told the British Ambassador to Madrid that

the language of the proclamation, and the collective note to
Juarez, was to be regretted. Instructions had already been sent
to Prim to adhere strictly to the Convention of London. Collantes agreed that the Jecker claim was "exorbitant," but
Prim had been directed to refrain from examining any claims
put forward by the British and French Commissioners. Reciprocal examination of claims would only cause confusion and
delay.[127] The only real misunderstanding between the British
and Spanish Governments in March was quickly adjusted.
Under the impression that Dunlop had arrested Miramon
without the consent of all the Allied Commissioners, the Spanish Government directed its Ambassador to complain to
Russell. Russell promised to instruct Wyke to act in concert
with the other Commissioners, then paged through Wyke's
correspondence, and found that the conditions under which
Miramon had been arrested had been approved in advance by
all the Commissioners. Then Russell instructed the British
Ambassador to Madrid to inform the Spanish Government
of the details.[128]

At the end of February Collantes revealed to the French
Government that it was desirable that a conservative government replace that of Juarez, but that the first acts of the Allied
Commissioners in Mexico made such a change improbable,
because negotiations had started with the Juarez Government
and given it a sort of recognition. Collantes also made clear
that he agreed with the French view that an ultimatum
presented by one of the Allied Commissioners could not be
judged by the other Commissioners.[129] On 8 March, when
Barrot's report of Collantes' observations had arrived in Paris
and when Thouvenel and Russell were already exchanging
views about Saligny's ultimatum, Thouvenel wrote his Ambassador to Madrid to express satisfaction that the French and
Spanish Governments agreed.[130] Thouvenel also enclosed some
reports from Mexico that complained that Prim had entered
into a coalition with the British Commissioners against Jurien
and Saligny.[131] Barrot's answer did not arrive until 21 March.[132]

Napoleon believed that it was a good sign that no reports were received from Madrid for over two weeks. He was pleased that the Spanish Government did not protest the defamation of Prim in the *Moniteur*. It was a good indication that Prim would be recalled.[133] The hostility to Juarez that Collantes had expressed to Barrot at the end of February was also a cause for satisfaction. Baron Beyens, the Belgian Ambassador to Paris, reported that Napoleon was "counting on the absence of opposition to his projects on the part of Spain."[134]

On 19 March the French Consul at Cadiz sent a summary of the contents of the Preliminaries of La Soledad to Paris.[135] Napoleon was furious[136] that this "capitulation"[137] had been made and blamed Prim.[138] Without waiting for the arrival of the official text of the Preliminaries or the explanations of Jurien and Saligny, Napoleon ordered Jurien's recall. Three telegrams were sent on 20 March to the French Consul at Cadiz for transmittal to Mexico. The French Minister of Marine and Colonies relieved Jurien of command of the French forces and gave him the choice of retaining command of the French ships in Vera Cruz or returning to France.[139] The Minister of War gave General de Lorencez, who had been sent with reenforcements, the command of which Jurien was relieved.[140] Thouvenel's telegram informed Saligny that all previous instructions were still valid. In consequence of the Preliminaries, "one does not know how to judge here the situation that resulted." Lorencez was in sole military command, and the "whole political direction" was entrusted only to Saligny. Thouvenel added that "the Emperor counts on your prudence as well as your zeal." Saligny was given a complete discretion of how to implement French policy:

> What we demand from the Mexicans is, above all, the redress of our grievances and a government which gives us guarantees for the future. As to the form or the personnel of this government, we do not lay claim to impose them. What must or can happen depends absolutely on local circumstances and on the estimation of the wise men and friends of their country, as, for example, General Almonte.[141]

The disclaimer that it was not intended to "impose" a government on Mexico was meaningless in view of the fact that a general election was never intended. The "wise men" were the notables Almonte had been directed to assemble and gather to proclaim Maximilian ruler of Mexico,[142] and, as Thouvenel's telegram stated, all previous instructions were still valid. The disclaimer made by Thouvenel, therefore, merely left Saligny free not to press Napoleon's plans if "local circumstances" did not permit the implementation of the scheme in favor of Maximilian.

Thouvenel informed the British[143] and Spanish[144] Governments of Jurien's recall and French disapproval of the Preliminaries of La Soledad. The Spanish Government waited for the arrival of Prim's reports[145] before writing instructions to Prim.[146] Although Prim's conduct was approved, objection was made to certain articles of the Preliminaries.[147] On 23 March the French Ambassador to Madrid was permitted to see Prim's instructions[148] and given a summary of them.[149] Upon receipt of Barrot's report, enclosing the Spanish summary,[150] Thouvenel sent an outline of Spanish objections to Flahault in London.[151] On 30 March Thouvenel had a reply from Flahault that Russell agreed with the Spanish view of the Preliminaries.[152] The next day Thouvenel wrote instructions for Saligny that all three allies disapproved the Preliminaries. Saligny was ordered to inform Prim that the purpose of the Preliminaries was to break off negotiations with Juarez, by placing the allies in the situation foreseen by Article IV.[153] This article provided that, in the event of a failure of negotiations for redress, the allied forces would withdraw to a position on the coastal side of the first Mexican defenses before commencing hostilities.[154] By "demanding redress of grievances," Thouvenel instructed Saligny, this eventuality would become a certainty. If Prim refused to cooperate, Saligny and Lorencez were directed to consider whether they had the means to commence hostilities by themselves.[155] On 2 April, still under the impression that the British and Spanish Governments disapproved the Preliminaries, the French Government published a statement in the *Moniteur* that the Preliminaries were disapproved as contrary to the "dignity" of France.[156]

The British Government did not disapprove the Preliminaries, as at first believed by Thouvenel. On 31 March Wyke's reports arrived in London, and Russell approved Wyke's proceedings and the Preliminaries. Russell was pleased that the Preliminaries disclaimed interference in Mexican internal affairs. There was no more talk of "regeneration," and affairs were being conducted in accordance with the Convention of London by merely seeking redress. The advance permitted into the interior was approved as necessary for the health of the allied troops. If negotiations failed, it was only just that a retrograde movement be made. It was hoped, however, that a pacific solution would be reached, for then no coercion would be required. Although it was to be regretted that the Mexican flag would wave over Vera Cruz, this provision was approved, because the allies remained in sole possession of that city. These British views were stated in instructions to Wyke[157] and to the British Ambassadors in Paris[158] and Madrid.[159]

The Spanish Government approved Prim's conduct in general, but objected to some of the provisions of the Preliminaries. Objections were to Articles I, V, and VI. Article I gave the Juarez Government a "moral force that it did not have, seeing that in adding faith to its declaration that it possessed all the elements of force and backing of opinion to maintain itself, one enters immediately upon the ground of treaties and negotiations." That could have been done "without including it as a declaration." It was to be regretted that, by Article V, hospitals would "remain in the power of the enemies" in the eventuality of hostilities, "even though they have taken a solemn engagement to respect" these hospitals. Least justified was that the Mexican flag be hoisted in Vera Cruz (Article VI), because this city was under the authority of the allies and not of the Mexicans. The retrograde movement in case of a rupture was only approved in view of Prim's explanation that "one cannot maintain by force what one has obtained by negotiation."[160] This part of the instructions for Prim was read to Barrot,[161] who sent an outline to Thouvenel,[162] together with a Spanish "summary" supplied.[163] This "summary" outlined that part of Prim's instructions shown Barrot, with the exception of the remarks on hospitals. The "summary" ended with the order and comment that :

> . . . the Queen's Government . . . order him decisively to act with the greatest promptitude and energy, setting aside every system of temporisation, if the result of the conferences should not be completely satisfactory.
> The next mail will inform us of that result and until then every decision would be premature and hazardous.

The last part of the instructions actually sent to Prim directed him to commence hostilities, should the conference of Orizaba lead to no satisfactory result. Then Mexicans probably also would realize that the Juarez Government was not deserving of support. The "presence" of the allied troops and the "cooperation of all honorable men" would lead to the establishment of a stable government willing to grant redress of grievances to the allies. Such a government would protect the "independence" of the Mexican people and afford them internal order.[164] The meaning attached to the directions not included in the "summary" were made known to the French Ambassador to Madrid. O'Donnell told Barrot :

> We had counted, . . . upon arriving in Mexico, on the support of the conservative party. Now this party did not give signs of life. One looked for signs of it in vain. . . .

Collantes told Barrot that one cause of difficulties in Mexico was Maximilian's candidacy, attributed to be put forward by the French Government. Rumors of such a plot had alarmed the Mexican people and made it difficult to convince them that :

. . . the Allied Powers only came to obtain from . . . an oppressive government redress of grievances . . . and to offer the party of order and sensible men of this country an occasion to manifest their wishes with all the plenitude of their independence and to establish a government strong enough to assure foreign residents in Mexico sufficient guarantees of security and provide the Mexican people with a wise and liberal administration . . . and the peace needed so badly after so many years of discord.[165]

When Thouvenel received Barrot's report,[166] the French Minister of Foreign Affairs believed that the Spanish Government disapproved the Preliminaries. Thouvenel sent Barrot instructions that the French and Spanish Governments were in agreement[167] Thouvenel also forwarded to Barrot a copy of Flahault's report that stated that Russell also disapproved the Preliminaries.[168]

On 3 April Cowley informed Thouvenel that the British Government approved the Preliminaries.[169] Thouvenel, Napoleon, and Eugenie were surprised and angry. Cowley reported that Eugenie was even more excited than Napoleon.[170] Thouvenel told Cowley that "the British force having withdrawn, each government must do the best it could for itself."[171] Russell's answer was:

The Emperor is at liberty to try a march in Mexico for the objects of the Convention. He is not free to skip away from the original Convention altogether as Thouvenel observed. . . .[172]

Although a report had arrived from Madrid that the Spanish Government protested the defamatory remarks directed against Prim in March in the *Moniteur*,[173] Thouvenel still believed the Spanish Government disapproved the Preliminaries.[174]

Russell sent Crampton a telegram on 2 April stating that the Preliminaries were approved by the British Government, "as it is desirable to try negotiation, and the health of the troops is secured."[175] The next day Crampton saw O'Donnell, who said that the *Moniteur* of 2 April showed that the French Government did not agree with the views taken by its allies.

In order to clear up any misunderstanding, including the interpretation of the Convention of London, O'Donnell proposed consultation by representatives of the allies. A conference could take place in Paris, London, or Madrid.[176] O'Donnell told Barrot that the allies did not agree about the Preliminaries. Barrot was asked to suggest to Thouvenel the desirability of calling such a conference as proposed to Crampton in order to settle in advance questions that might arise from the negotiations of the Allied Commissioners at Orizaba.[177] Russell saw in the Spanish proposal a desire "to stick to the Convention (i.e., of London)" and was willing to define it "more clearly."[178] Thouvenel rejected O'Donnell's proposal on 5 April. The meetings at Orizaba would result in a rupture or in a treaty settling claims. Discussions were useless in Europe until the text of such a treaty arrived.[179] The reference O'Donnell had made to the differences of opinion of the Preliminaries was interpreted by Thouvenel to apply to British approval of the Preliminaries.[180]

Barrot saw Crampton on 8 April and showed him a copy of Flahault's report that claimed Russell disapproved the Preliminaries. Barrot also stated that he had seen the instructions to Prim and that the Spanish Government also disapproved the Preliminaries.[181] The next day Crampton saw O'Donnell and informed him of Barrot's remarks. O'Donnell said Prim's conduct was approved in general. Although the Spanish Government disapproved of parts of the Preliminaries, it was not intended to disapprove the entire agreement. O'Donnell promised to send a copy of Prim's instructions to the Spanish representative in London to communicate to Russell so that he could judge for himself.[182] Crampton at once telegraphed this information to Russell.[183]

Forced by the opposition in the Cortes to take a stand on the Preliminaries,[184] Collantes stated on 9 April:

> Well then, Gentlemen, I say here that Her Majesty's Government have approved the conduct of General Prim and the Preliminaries of Soledad. The terms . . . and all . . . the

documents . . . the Government will in due time present to the Cortes. . . .[185]

Barrot read this speech in the official *Gazette*[186] and went to Collantes and O'Donnell to protest that they had reversed themselves. To calm Barrot, Collantes and O'Donnell claimed that Prim's actions, but not the Preliminaries, had been approved. Barrot was told that Collantes had said in the Cortes that the Spanish Government:

> . . . has approved the conduct of General Prim, and the Preliminaries of Soledad, the terms . . . and all . . . the documents . . . the Government will in due time present to the Cortes. . . .[187]

When Barrot produced the Gazette, which did not place a comma after "General Prim," Collantes and O'Donnell said the speech had to be taken as a whole.[188] Barrot tried to convince O'Donnell that only a monarchy could give stability to Mexico. Maximilian's candidacy was not a "fixed project," because the Convention of London forbade interference in the internal affairs of Mexico. The whole scheme was only a "project to examine." O'Donnell's laconic answer was that the Spanish Government would be faithful to the Convention of London.[189] After seeing Barrot, Collantes sent Crampton the "summary" of Prim's instructions that had already been given Barrot, and the British Ambassador to Madrid forwarded this document to Russell, who received it on 18 April.[190]

Russell sent Crampton a telegram on 10 April to rectify Barrot's assertion that the British Government disapproved the Preliminaries. The Spanish representative in London, Russell stated, had read him a copy of Prim's instructions, and the British Government:

> . . . agree in substance with the Government of Her Catholic Majesty. They think a false step was taken at first in saying so much of the regeneration of Mexico, and they approve the Convention of Soledad as retrieving that false step.[191]

When Thouvenel learned about Collantes' speech in the Cortes, the French Minister of Foreign Affairs wrote Barrot of "our surprise." The explanations of Collantes and O'Donnell were "equivocal." The Spanish Government had approved the Preliminaries "without qualification." It was to be regretted, and all that could be hoped for was that Prim would obey his instructions to act with "vigor" and contribute to the unity of action "demanded by the community of interest which has brought us to Mexico."[192]

On 16 April Russell received an extract of the *Gazette*, containing Collantes' speech in the Cortes on 9 April and stating that the Spanish Government approved "the conduct of General Prim and the Preliminaries."[193] Two days later the "summary" of Prim's instructions, given Crampton by Collantes, arrived at the British Foreign Office.[194] The "instructions" to Prim that were read to Russell by the Spanish representative in London were probably identical to the "summary" Crampton sent Russell. On 21 April Russell sent a copy of the "summary" to Cowley and remarked that the last part implied that the Spanish Government seemed to imply that no further negotiations would be carried on with the Juarez Government if it refused to agree to reasonable demands put forward at Orizaba. Russell directed Cowley to ascertain whether the French Government considered the Preliminaries disavowed or binding.[195] Thouvenel's reply was that the French Government disapproved the Preliminaries but considered them binding.[196] Although Eugenie pleaded with Napoleon to disavow the Preliminaries,[197] the Emperor and Thouvenel decided to leave it to Saligny to break off negotiations with the Juarez Government, to make the retrograde movement provided for by the Preliminaries, and then to commence hostilities with Prim's aid. If Prim refused, Saligny was permitted by his instructions to take independent action. Thouvenel did not tell Cowley these plans, but a few hints were dropped. Thouvenel promised that the provisions of the Preliminaries would be respected if negotiations were broken off between the Allied

Commissioners in Mexico and the Juarez Government. Thouvenel also "intimated" that :

> . . . the Commissioners would have to decide the moment when the negotiations should be broken off, if at all, whereupon the Convention signed in London on the 31st October last, would naturally be the guide for their future proceedings.[198]

The positive and negative reactions of the British, French, and Spanish Governments to the first proceedings of their representatives in Mexico were directly related to what each of the allies hoped to accomplish in Mexico. The British Government approved all steps leading to a pacific solution of the issue of claims if those steps did not involve interference with Mexican internal affairs. The French Government considered all such proceedings as obstacles to the establishment of Maximilian in Mexico. The Spanish Government took a position overlapping and yet opposed to the British and French views. The Spanish Government had never hoped to carry on negotiations with Juarez, but was determined not to assist in the scheme in favor of Maximilian.

# VI

# The Breakdown of the Convention of London

## 1 THE BREAKDOWN OF THE CONVENTION OF LONDON IN MEXICO

THE MAIL PACKET THAT ARRIVED AT VERA CRUZ ON 27 February 1862 brought General Almonte, Napoleon's propaganda agent.[1] With him came Miranda[2] and a few other Mexican exiles.[3] Almonte then contacted and organized into a following the adherents of Miramon,[4] who had not been arrested. In contrast to Miramon, Almonte was acting under instructions from Napoleon III.[5] After he landed in Vera Cruz, Almonte sought out Prim and told him that the French Government intended to overthrow the Juarez Government and establish a monarchy under Maximilian. According to Almonte, it would all be settled within two months. The Mexicans would "rise as one man when they see the Monarchical flag raised." Prim asked how the Mexican people would be consulted, and Almonte replied:

> By an assembly of notables as all the rest are not worth reckoning upon; but we will begin by upsetting the Juarez Government.

404

Almonte added that he counted on the support of the Allied Commissioners. The British Government, Almonte told Prim, had already approved the plans of the French Government. Almonte added that he had seen Collantes and O'Donnell before leaving for Mexico. The Spanish Ministers had not made any promises, but they had stated that they were waiting for Prim's report on the "state" of Mexico.[6] The same mail packet that brought Almonte to Vera Cruz also brought instructions for Prim that, in view of the growing proportions of the project of a monarchy for Mexico, he allow Mexicans full liberty to choose the government they wanted.[7] Prim knew, therefore, that he could count on the support of the Spanish Government by replying, as he did, that Almonte's proposal was contrary to the Convention of London and "even absurd from its impracticability." The allies were not in Mexico to topple governments, and Mexicans did not desire a monarchy. Nor could Almonte count on British support. Almonte replied that he could "reckon" with the support of French arms.[8] Prim then warned Almonte not to go beyond Vera Cruz with French troops, because it would compromise the negotiations of the Allied Commissioners with Juarez.[9]

After seeing Prim, Almonte talked with Dunlop,[10] who had just received instructions from the British Admiralty. Dunlop was informed that the French reinforcements under General Lorencez were going to Mexico and had orders to march into the interior of Mexico within twenty-four hours after landing. Dunlop was directed not to permit the British Marines to go beyond Vera Cruz and to reembark them as soon as the unhealthy season commenced in Vera Cruz.[11] On the same day Dunlop received his instructions, Wyke received instructions from Russell that no objection be made to Dunlop's reembarking the Marines. Russell also informed Wyke that French reinforcements would arrive and probably would march to Mexico City. It was "said" that Mexicans would invite Maximilian to "place himself on the Throne of Mexico." In this connection, Wyke was not to be a party to a "forcible" intervention. The Mexicans had to "consult their own interest."[12]

Prim wrote Napoleon III a private letter that very few Mexicans would support a monarchy. It was logical, because the Mexicans knew monarchy only in the persons of viceroys who ruled on behalf of Spain. The neighboring United States had influenced Mexico to adopt republican habits and customs, even republican "expression of thought." If logic were not enough, Prim added, his assertions were proved by the fact that, during the two months that the allied expeditionary forces were in Mexico, "neither the conservatives nor the partisans of monarchy have made the slightest demonstration which might lead the allies to believe that such partisans exist."[13] Dunlop wrote Admiral Milne that a monarchy was only favored by the "Church Party," which "merely sees no other prospect whatever of retaining influence of the Mexican people." This "bigoted and fanatical" party in Mexico was "detested by the great majority of the people who are in favour of a liberal policy."[14] Wyke's remark to Russell, about the possibility that the Mexican people would accept Maximilian, was that there "never was a greater fallacy than this!" Some of the wealthy families of the Mexican cities were "reactionary" and desired to see Juarez replaced by a nominee of the "Priest Party," but the party of Juarez represented the Mexican people. Although the "scum" of this party assumed the leadership of the party in 1861, General Doblado's cabinet now united the elements of the country that were "supported by what remains here of public opinion." Wyke suggested that the allies respect the wishes of the Mexican people by supporting Doblado and giving his time to reestablish peace and order. Otherwise redress could never be expected for claims. Wyke proposed more than just moral support. Mexico wanted:

> . . . a helping hand and judicious aid in the shape of a Protectorate for two or three years to come, to enable it to right itself and eventually become of immense commercial importance to us.

For this purpose Wyke proposed that the British Government send a military force "worthy of the position of England in the triple alliance." When achieving a position of equality with Spain and France, England could assist in accomplishing "a great end by regenerating a country which . . . would soon learn how worthily to occupy its place in the great family of nations."[15]

After the negotiation of the Preliminaries of La Soledad, the Allied Commissioners intended to quarter the French troops at Tehuacan, the Spanish at Cordova, and the British Marines at Orizaba.[16] On 26 February Jurien left Vera Cruz for Tehuacan, and two days later the first Spanish forces left Vera Cruz.[17] After Wyke and Dunlop received orders not to permit the British Marines to leave Vera Cruz, a conference of the four Allied Commissioners still in Vera Cruz was called. Dunlop made known his intention to reembark all but one hundred and fifty Marines, who would perform garrison duty in Vera Cruz and San Juan d'Ulloa.[18] Having no need for the mules and carts purchased, Dunlop made arrangements to sell them to the French at the price he paid for them.[19] Wyke remarked that it was undesirable that Almonte proceed into the interior of Mexico, because "his presence would suffice to revolutionize the country."[20] After the conference Saligny wrote to Paris that he had no intention to make this "concession."[21] The departure of the British Marines, Saligny believed, was a good sign that all the British and Spanish forces would be withdrawn after Wyke and Prim negotiated a settlement of claims. That would "leave the field free for us." It would render the situation "more simple and more plain."[22] Wyke reported that Prim regretted the departure of the British Marines, "as he fully appreciated the advantage of having English troops associated with his own." Wyke believed that his "status" would decline without any British military support. If the French Commissioners should support Almonte's scheme, Wyke recommended that "we . . . retire from our Alliance." But if the French Commissioners caused no "mischief" and a settlement were negotiated with the Juarez Government, Wyke hoped Russell would send a "Brigade" to maintain order in the Mexican cities. Then the Mexican garrisons there could "be employed in . . . clearing the country of . . . swarms of highway robbers." With the restoration of peace, Wyke hoped to "get paid back the sums owing to us."[23]

It was agreed that Wyke and Prim would follow Jurien inland and that Dunlop and Saligny stay in Vera Cruz to await instructions from Europe before going to Orizaba for the conferences, to begin 15 April, with Mexican representatives of Juarez to settle claims.[24] Before Wyke and Prim left Vera Cruz, news arrived in Vera Cruz that the Mexican Government had levied a tax on all capital savings. A conference was called, and Wyke said he could not agree to giving the Mexican authorities control of the Custom House of Vera Cruz, as requested by Doblado,[25] until Juarez desisted collecting such a tax. Wyke considered it could not be justified, because the allies had shown their friendly intentions by negotiating the Preliminaries of La Soledad. Saligny and Prim agreed, and a note was sent to Doblado.[26] At the same time Wyke sent private letters to Doblado[27] and Corwin,[28] the American Minister to Mexico City, in order to facilitate a settlement of differences. At the same time Wyke[29] and Prim[30] left Vera Cruz for Orizaba, with the intention of going on to Puebla to meet Doblado to give him "good advice."[31]

While Dunlop, Wyke, and Prim all received specific instructions, Jurien received discretionary instructions. General de Lorencez arrived at Vera Cruz on 5 March[32] with a letter from Napoleon III for Jurien. Jurien was informed that it was "necessary to remain firm in our resolutions without wanting, however, in any way to force the public opinion if it was not what one said it was."[33] Jurien also received another letter from Napoleon, stating that "since one could not foresee events from such a distance," the implementation of the monarchy scheme was up to Jurien.[34] Thouvenel's instructions of 30 January 1862 stated that, "in what concerns the political direction of the expedition, absolutely nothing has changed."[35] Jurien concluded that Napoleon "will continue to place confidence in me."[36] Jurien believed that the best policy was to be patient[37] and avoid hostilities. If the Spanish troops had fired a shot, "we would have found ourselves engaged in a way, the end of which would be impossible to see."[38] Although "initiated into the intimate thoughts of the Emperor," Jurien failed to discover, even when at Orizaba on his way to Tehuacan, any genuine Mexican support for Maximilian:

> I am neither able to contest nor to affirm the strength of the conservative party, because no serious effort has yet revealled the existence of it to me. I do not put into the ranks of this party the people of property who are evidently tired of anarchy, and who have not ceased, for so many years, to put their faith in a foreign intervention. The conservative party, of which one can compose an army against the present government, is composed today, as far as I can judge, of the band of Marquez and Zuloaga. That this band, encouraged by our presence, could make itself master of Mexico by force is not materially impossible, perhaps, for Mexico is the country of unforeseeable eventualities. Without doubt, it is not necessary to count this possibility among coming eventualities, but it is not necessary to confound in advance our cause with that of a party that appears to me to have against it the majority of the country.[39]

When Jurien learned of Almonte's arrival, Jurien supplied him with $20,000, but wrote Thouvenel that "I am counting more on our efforts than those of the General."[40]

Saligny's views differed from those of Jurien. Saligny talked with Almonte and then reported to Thouvenel, "I am happy to say that our views on the situation and on the steps to follow are in complete agreement." Almonte was very important, because he could have "a great influence on the course of events."[41] The most recent instructions from Thouvenel informed Saligny that his efforts to form a triumvirate of Doblado, Robles, and Uragua in favor of monarchy were approved. Thouvenel approved Saligny's attempts to obtain:

. . . the personal services of the different military or political leaders who are now playing an active role in the affairs of Mexico. . . .[42]

On 5 March General de Lorencez arrived at Vera Cruz[43] with 4,573 troops.[44] He had orders from Napoleon to proceed toward Mexico City by way of Jalapa[45] and to afford protection to Almonte and the other exiles.[46] Saligny was certain that "the more our troops advance into the interior, the more the population will receive them with cordiality."[47] Saligny told Lorencez that his military forces were sufficient to advance in accordance with Napoleon's orders. The sity of Puebla had been taken and retaken twenty times during the Mexican Civil War (1857–1860) by Mexican forces never comprising more than two to three thousand men.[48] From Saligny's and Almonte's comments, Lorencez concluded that the people of Puebla called for his soldiers "with anxiety, and . . . would rush out to embrace" them.[49] The difficulty as Lorencez saw it was that the allies had negotiated the Preliminaries of La Soledad, but Saligny suggested that the "outrages" perpetrated by the Mexican Government might be a pretext to make that agreement a "dead letter."[50]

Shortly after their arrival at Orizaba, Wyke and Prim received a communication from Doblado that the Mexican Government had ordered the arrest of all "traitors" who might attempt to go to Cordova, Orizaba, and Tehuacan with the hope of obtaining the protection of the intervening European Powers.[51] Prim sent a copy of Doblado's letter to Jurien at Tehuacan on 12 March and suggested a conference of all five Commissioners be assembled to reply to what both Wyke and Prim considered Doblado's "reasonable and just" letter.[52] At the same time Wyke wrote to Dunlop in Vera Cruz.[53] If necessary, Jurien observed, he would declare negotiations with Juarez severed before begun and make the retrograde movement provided for by the Preliminaries of La Soledad in order to gain freedom of action. On 13 March Jurien sent a letter to Saligny in Vera Cruz to inform him of Doblado's letter forwarded by Prim. Jurien proposed that Saligny leave Vera Cruz to take part in a conference of the Allied Commissioners, and, at the same time, Jurien informed Saligny that it was undesirable for Almonte and his friends to leave Vera Cruz before the proclamation of a general amnesty.[54] The same day Jurien wrote Prim that Saligny had been informed of Doblado's letter, that a conference of the Commissioners should assemble, and that a general amnesty should be demanded.[55] If the Mexican Government could be persuaded to grant an amnesty, Jurien reasoned, hostilities would be avoided, and Almonte and his friends could visit the allied camps and try to persuade the local population of the desirability of a monarchy. If Almonte were successful, then negotiations could be broken off with Juarez, a retrograde movement be made in accordance with the Preliminaries, and hostilities could begin.

Saligny decided not to attend the conference proposed by Prim and Jurien. Prim was informed that the persons proscribed by the Mexican Government were under French protection.[56] His poor health, Saligny let Jurien know, prevented a departure from Vera Cruz.[57] Almonte was angry that Jurien wanted to carry on further correspondence with the Juarez Government. In a private letter to Napoleon, Almonte complained of Jurien's "incomprehensible attitude" and urged his recall. Jurien should have consulted Saligny. He was "the only person who knows my native land." If Napoleon wanted his plans carried out, he should "leave the whole direction of the policy . . . in Mexico" to Saligny. Almonte lamented that so much time had been lost, for it would have been so simple to have reached Mexico City.[58] As Prim had told Almonte, he would be executed if he advanced beyond Vera Cruz without military protection. Miranda was aware that the Presidential Decree of 25 January 1862, condemning all traitors to death, was not to be taken lightly. He blamed Prim for not protesting the decree. It proved, Miranda wrote Estrada, that Prim had plans for his "personal elevation."[59] If he could go into the interior, Miranda believed, a "conservative revolution" would be encouraged.[60] Saligny thought that, if Lorencez marched forward and took Almonte with him, the Juarez Government would be overthrown by the "conservative or monarchical party" before the opening of the conferences at Orizaba on 15 April.[61] As substantiation for this belief, Saligny had a private letter from the Prussian representative in Mexico City. Baron Wagner wrote Saligny there was a desire "more and more universal for the establishment of a monarchy." All Mexicans wanted the allied troops to "come as soon as possible to Mexico City itself."[62]

Obeying orders from Napoleon,[63] Lorencez gave Almonte and the other exiles the protection of a French detachment of soldiers, commanded by Commandant Mangin.[64] Without Dunlop's knowledge,[65] Mangin, his troops, Almonte, and the other exiles left Vera Cruz on 19 March.[66] The next day Lorencez himself left Vera Cruz.[67] Although Saligny agreed with the wisdom of Lorencez' decision, Saligny wrote Thouvenel that it was a serious matter, but Lorencez had not hesitated to assume the responsibility.[68] Just as Saligny had let Jurien assume the responsibility for reporting most of the conferences of the Allied Commissioners in January and February, Saligny now diverted responsibilities to Lorencez. When Dunlop discovered that Almonte had left Vera Cruz, the Commodore protested to Saligny, who replied that "General de Lorencez was acting in this matter, as far as General Almonte is concerned, under direct orders from the Emperor."[69] Then Dunlop wrote to inform Wyke and Prim at Orizaba.[70]

On 16 March Jurien saw Colonel Cautelenne, the senior Mexican officer at Tehuacan. Jurien said he had instructions that foresaw that the "sane" part of the population might be encouraged by the presence of the allied forces to constitute a stable government. Thouvenel's instructions directed Jurien not to discourage such a change, but rather to assist those attempting it, if they had a chance of success, with "moral force." These instructions explained the arrival of Almonte. Unless the Mexican Government granted a general amnesty,

Jurien would make the retrograde movement, provided for by the Preliminaries, and then commence hostilities:

> . . . I cannot subscribe to your laws of proscription whereby you are going to deny such a considerable man, who has the special esteem of the Emperor, the entry into the territory of the Republic. General Almonte will come to join me with the troops of General de Lorencez. If the Mexican Government finds fault with this, I am ready to execute the Convention of La Soledad loyally and to retrograde with my troops beyond the passes of Chinquihuite in order to start, twenty-four hours later, a campaign the results of which cannot be in doubt. General Doblado only has one means of preventing this, and that is to proclaim a general amnesty at once. . . .

Asked what Almonte would do if the ban against him were lifted, Jurien replied that Almonte would go to Mexico City after Jurien had taken measures for his safety. That same day Cautelenne sent an officer to Mexico City to inform Doblado. In his report of his doings to Thouvenel, Jurien explained that he hoped his threat would not lead to hostilities. "I would be profoundly sorry," Jurien wrote Thouvenel, "to be obliged to come to an open rupture with the Mexican Government."[71]

Jurien wrote Prim on 17 March in an attempt to win his support for the monarchy project. Jurien asked assistance "to do things here by amicable means." He was sure that he still had the Emperor's confidence, Jurien wrote, but "we want some more noble object here, than that entertained by exacting creditors."[72] When Prim received Jurien's letter, the Spanish General wanted to continue amicable negotiations with the Juarez Government, but Prim was also angry that he was being "mocked"[73] by measures taken by the Mexican Government. If need be, Prim was ready to fight if Juarez refused to reverse two steps already taken and a third threatened. The tax on capital savings continued to be collected, from Mexicans and from foreigners. The Juarez Government also demanded forced loans from six commercial houses, stock of one of which belonged to Prim's wife.[74] Doblado's threat was that, if the Vera

Cruz Custom House were not returned to Mexican authorities, goods passing through it would not be permitted to pass beyond a barrier made in the interior by the Mexican Government.[75] Prim wrote to Doblado to demand explanations. Since Prim expected Doblado would answer in a "high tone," Prim decided to answer Jurien's letter of 17 March to ask him to take part in a conference to discuss Doblado's reply. Prim wanted no part of Jurien's "noble object" and decided that "if hostilities had to be undertaken, they had better be so in the interest of our fellow citizens, instead of for unjust causes."[76] Prim believed that, as in the past, all decisions should be made in a conference of all five Allied Commissioners. Wyke agreed, and a summons was sent to Dunlop in Vera Cruz, and Prim wrote to Saligny.[77] Prim answered Jurien's letter of 17 March three days later. Prim reproached the Mexican Government for the levy on capital, the forced loans, and the threat to erect a barrier in the interior. Prim claimed that he could not tolerate such defiance, urged Jurien to take part in a conference, and stated that the Mexican measures were serious enough to "burn our papers and march as soldiers!"[78]

Jurien completely misunderstood the meaning of Prim's letter of 20 March. The Admiral believed Prim wanted a pretext to start hostilities. Jurien replied that he understood that Prim was "very differently disposed than I had a right to expect." Consequently Jurien confided his plans. It was necessary to avoid "embracing a party which constitutes the minority in too apparent a manner." Nevertheless only a monarchy could restore order to Mexico. To arrive at this "result," Jurien had signed the Preliminaries of La Soledad "in the belief that a truce would give us time to work on men's opinions without appearing to wish to force them." For his part in bringing about the situation, Prim was praised for avoiding a war "in which the national sentiment would have arisen against us." Prim had prevented "disastrous consequence" to an "expedition conceived with too great confidence." Before starting negotiations at Orizaba, Jurien proposed to demand the "adoption of the principle of the military occupation of Mexico by the allied forces." This principle, Jurien wrote Prim, was inherent in the Preliminaries. If the Mexican Government refused to recognize this "principle," Jurien intended to make the retrograde movement provided for in the Preliminaries and then to commence hostilities. If Wyke and Prim wanted a better pretext, Jurien was willing to use one of the "injuries" suffered by foreigners in Mexico. Jurien announced that, while willing to cooperate with Prim, the French reinforcements that had arrived changed the situation. The intervention no longer had an "exclusively Spanish colouring." Although he claimed he had not been so instructed, Jurien believed the reinforcements showed that Napoleon wanted to "free the action of France, and reserve full liberty." Jurien wanted it understood that "our expedition is a French expedition, and under orders of no one." "I am resolved," Jurien wrote in summary, "to continue, whatever happens, until I arrive at the end I propose to attain." The "true sympathy" for France would assist him to carry out his plans. Jurien was willing to see Prim, but there was no French officer of sufficient rank to entrust with the command of the French forces at Tehuacan. Jurien promised to arrange a meeting after Lorencez arrived at Tehuacan.[79] Jurien sent a private letter with this "semi-official" one which Prim was authorized to send to the Spanish Government. In the "private" letter Jurien stated that he had already made it known "here" in Tehuacan that he would not allow any interference with persons "protected by the Emperor." Jurien had also made it known that, if the Mexican Government refused to make an "agreement," Jurien would be forced to "seek for allies amongst . . . enemies" of the republic. He added that he was ready to "break" the Preliminaries, but he wanted to confer with Prim first. The main topic of that conference would be the establishment of a "Monarchy in Mexico," for Jurien could not regard his mission at an end until he carried out his "old chimera."[80]

Jurien's "semi-official" and "private" letters of 20 March

reveal the Admiral's predicament. He did not believe the Mexicans wanted a monarchy, but he knew Napoleon wanted to establish Maximilian in Mexico. Jurien approved of Prim's moderation, but the premature arrival of the Spanish expedition in December 1861 had led to Lorencez' arrival in March 1862 with reinforcements to prevent a "Spanish colouring." Almonte was under orders from Napoleon to "consult" the Mexican people, but Jurien wanted to avoid hostilities by obtaining an amnesty to permit Almonte to advance beyond Vera Cruz. Time was passing, and Jurien did not want to wait until 15 April to use "excessive" claims as a pretext to break off negotiations with Juarez. If Jurien could obtain his ends without war, he would do so, with or without Prim's aid. If war were declared, Jurien hoped Prim would assist him.

When Prim received Jurien's two letters of 20 March, the Spanish General was angry that Jurien showed a determination, in the last resort, to act without his British and Spanish colleagues and to establish a monarchy.[81] Prim replied that he was not seeking any pretexts to break the Preliminaries of La Soledad. He only meant that, although not wanting to resort to force, he would not permit Juarez to mock the allies by making exactions of foreigners in Mexico and threatening to blockade the transfer of imported goods into the interior. If Jurien believed that the allied expedition had really been a Spanish one in the past, it was to be supposed that the Admiral now intended to make the intervention in Mexico a French one. It was impossible, Prim concluded, to demand amnesty for persons who wanted to enter the country to overthrow its government. Prim answered Jurien's proposals concerning a monarchy by stating that Jurien was wrong in believing the Mexicans liked the French. Mexicans preferred the Spaniards, who did not want to impose what the Mexican people did not desire. In contrast to Jurien, Prim did not want to make the Mexicans "happy" by means of "cannon shots."[82]

Prim soon abandoned any ideas of "burning his papers" and fighting. Juarez sent Gonzales Echeverria, the Mexican Minister of Finance and Prim's wife's uncle, and Don Jesus Teran, the Minister of Justice, to Orizaba to confer with Wyke and Prim. Teran and Echeverria agreed to stop the levy on capital and the forced loans, and Prim and Wyke accepted these "solemn promises" to be able to negotiate a settlement of all differences between the allies and the Juarez Governmnt at the conferences scheduled to begin at Orizaba on 15 April. The question of turning over the Custom House of Vera Cruz was put on the agenda of topics for discussion at those conferences.[83]

In answer to Prim's letter that he was seeking no pretexts to commence hostilities, Jurien replied on 22 March that Almonte could not be "abandoned," because he had the "confidence" of Napoleon. Although Jurien had wanted to cooperate with Wyke and Prim, the Admiral confessed that the "French Government . . . have foreseen the case in which I am not to respect the agreements of the conference."[84] At 11.00 P.M. that evening Jurien sent Prim a second letter. That very day, 22 March, Jurien had told Colonel Cautelenne, the senior officer at Tehuacan, that Almonte would be "here" on 31 March. Jurien also informed Cautelenne, and asked him to forward the information to the Juarez Government, that the French forces would make the retrograde movement, provided for by the Preliminaries, on 1 April. Jurien's letter ended, "Goodby my dear General."[85] Jurien considered his conversation with Cautelenne a "threat" to force Juarez to grant an amnesty. On 23 March Jurien wrote Lorencez, "I have good reason to believe that they will be little disposed to permit me to execute my threat."[86]

On 23 March Prim answered Jurien's first letter of the day before by stating that it showed a "fixed determination" to violate the Convention of London and adopt a policy independent of France's allies and their Commissioners in Mexico:

The act of conducting the political exiles into the interior of the country—so that they can organize a conspiracy intended to destroy both the existing government and political system, at the same time that you advance as a friend and are waiting for the coming conference—is something without precedent and incomprehensible to me.

If Jurien were acting under orders, Prim could not recognize their "wisdom" and "justice." That Jurien acted independently would make "the friendly relations of England and Spain for France less cordial." When Prim had written this far, he received Jurien's second letter of 22 March, marked 11.00 P.M. After reading it, Prim finished writing his reply to Jurien's first letter, first stating that he had just received Jurien's second letter. Prim continued that both he and Wyke agreed that they could not "be disregarded except by an official act." An official letter from Wyke and Prim was enclosed, proposing a conference of all the Allied Commissioners for the purpose of verifying the rupture officially in the last meeting. Prim concluded, "As of today, I am making preparations for reembarking my troops as soon as we have held our last conference."[87] The official enclosure of Prim's letter reiterated his statements in polite but firm diplomatic language and proposed a conference at Orizaba.[88]

While Prim and Jurien were carrying on a correspondence between Orizaba and Tehuacan, Almonte advanced from Vera Cruz to Cordova.[89] While Almonte was still at Cordova, Lorencez arrived at Orizaba, and both Wyke and Prim complained that Almonte's presence at Cordova under French protection was a violation of the Convention of London. Lorencez expressed a willingness to send Almonte and his party back to Vera Cruz. Lorencez also agreed to send orders to Mangin, who was escorting Almonte, not to permit the Mexican exiles to leave Cordova until the views of Jurien were obtained.[90] After seeing Wyke and Prim, Lorencez, believing the British and Spanish Commissioners also spoke on behalf of Jurien, sent an order to Mangin on 24 March. This order stated that all the Commissioners agreed that Almonte should return to Vera Cruz and that Jurien would send an escort for Almonte.[91] While Almonte was at Cordova, Robles left the small town near Real del Monte where he had promised the Juarez Government—suspecting his connections with Saligny—to stay, and he was arrested near Tehuacan on his way to join Almonte at Cordova. When Wyke and Prim learned of Robles' arrest, they urged, as an act of humanity, that Teran and Gonzales, then still at Orizaba, send orders to General Zaragoza not to execute his prisoner. The road was very bad, the night rainy, and the orders that would have saved Robles arrived two hours after his execution.[92]

On 24 March Captain Thomasset, one of Jurien's officers, informed the Admiral of Robles' execution.[93] Thomasset also gave Jurien a report of a conversation with Almonte. The propaganda agent of Napoleon had said that "military action" was not yet necessary. Almonte would tell Jurien "when the time is right." The "political task" was more important at the moment. Almonte had money so that it was unnecessary for "those who would serve us to live off the land." The "masses" had appreciated Jurien's "conciliatory" and "friendly" measures, and therefore friendly feelings evoked by Jurien should be taken "into the greatest account." In the written report of his conversation with Almonte, Thomasset stated that he feared Robles had been arrested "with very compromising papers."[94]

Apparently before learning of the execution of Robles on 24 March, Jurien sent a reply, dated 24 March, to the official note of Wyke and Prim that proposed a conference at Orizaba. The conference would have to be delayed, because Saligny's health did not permit him to leave Vera Cruz until instructions arrived from Europe. Lorencez had direct orders from Napoleon to give protection to Almonte and the other returned exiles. Jurien could only "ratify," therefore, what had been done without his "participation." Almonte was no conspirator. He only wanted to make known "to his fellow countrymen the totally peaceful end of our intervention." Should hostilities break out, Jurien would favor no party. He would accept the aid of all Mexicans favorable to the European intervention. Jurien intended to adhere with a "scrupulous fidelity" to the provisions of the Preliminaries. Before the conference of the Allied Commissioners, Jurien intended to withdraw his troops to the coastal side of the first Mexican fortifications, as provided by the Preliminaries. An alternative to his retrograde movement would be Mexican approval of certain conditions. After declaring an amnesty, the Juarez Government should permit the Allied Commissioners to examine and decide the "best means to follow to consult the sincere and true voice of the country." Then Jurien was prepared to go to Mexico City with the French troops in Mexico "to protect public peace there in the name of the three Signatory Powers of the Convention of 31 October." Since the French troops would obtain a better reception in Mexico City than the Spanish troops, Jurien hoped that it would be agreed that Prim's men not go to the Capital. If his proposals were not accepted by the Mexican Government by 1 April, Jurien wrote Wyke and Prim, the French forces would start their retrograde movements. The other Allied Commissioners, Jurien observed, would see the advantages of his proposals, which would "tend to preserve Mexico from the calamities of war and to bind together the bonds of an alliance which must certainly open a better road for this country."[95] In a letter to Prim, also written on 24 March, Jurien asked whether it was still possible, in view of Robles' execution, to propose to the Mexican Government that French forces go to Mexico City to maintain public peace. Jurien added that he hoped that, by observing the Preliminaries, he would be in agreement with Prim again.[96] What Jurien meant was that the execution of Robles was an excellent reason not to negotiate with the Juarez Government. At 11.00 P.M. on 24 March Jurien wrote to Lorencez that first the French had to obtain "freedom of action" by making the retrograde movement. Then Jurien intended to announce that the killing of Robles made it impossible to negotiate with Juarez. Within a month, Jurien wrote Lorencez, "we will be in Mexico City."[97]

Jurien believed that by being "faithful" to the Preliminaries of La Soledad, he would win Prim's cooperation. The retrograde movement, after which Jurien would have a freedom of action to start war, was intended, by the terms of the Preliminaries, only to take place *after* the failure of negotiations between the allies and the Juarez Government.[98] By making such a move before the conferences opened at Orizaba, Jurien would violate the spirit of these Preliminaries and jeopardize negotiations with Juarez by making it appear that the French intended war instead of settling claims amicably. On 25 March Jurien even sent a confidential letter to Prim, enclosing a letter the Admiral intended to send to Doblado.[99] The proposed letter to Doblado was advance dated to 26 March and stated that, in view of the unfavorable prospects of a negotiated settlement at the conference to begin on 15 April, the French forces would retire to the coastal side of the Mexican defenses on 1 April.[100] Although Jurien never sent the note to Doblado,[101] he did send another one to Doblado announcing the intention to make the retrograde movement on 1 April. Upon the receipt of a letter from General Zaragoza, stating that he had orders from the Mexican Government to arrest Almonte and the other "traitors,"[102] Jurien replied on 27 March that he was not responsible for Almonte's having left Vera Cruz with French protection, but "this protection once granted imposes duties on us that no French soldier has ever misunderstood." Jurien also informed Zaragoza of the intention to withdraw French troops to regain their "liberty of action."[103] Then Jurien wrote a letter to Doblado, enclosing Zaragoza's letter and the reply to it, to state that the French would commence their retrograde movement on 1 April.[104] On 27 March Jurien also sent a letter to Prim, enclosing Zaragoza's letter, to observe that the "direct communication" received from a "fanatical and violent" Mexican General proved "better than anything that the Mexican Government is not the veritable master in this country."[105]

On 27 March Prim visited Jurien at Tehuacan in an attempt to convince the Admiral to send Almonte and his friends back to Vera Cruz and to persuade Jurien not to make the retro-

grade movement.[106] Prim spent hours without convincing
Jurien that he should withdraw the French protection given
Almonte. Because Jurien had a "mania . . . to go to the
Capital, because he believed that he would find multitudes of
royalists there," Prim said, "half joking and half serious," that
he would permit Jurien his "intrigue" on behalf of Maximilian.
The allies could demand that their forces be permitted to go
to Mexico City and hold it as a guarantee for the carrying out
of treaties to be made with the Mexican Government. Jurien
was overjoyed and embraced Prim, who then added, seriously,
that Almonte could not be permitted to make the journey to
Mexico City to "sow conspiracy, revolt, and destruction," on
the way there.[107] Prim believed that the possession of Mexico
City should be demanded as a guarantee for the fulfillment of
treaties. He also believed that it would be necessary to establish
Commissioners in the custom houses of Mexico to insure that
mortgaged custom duties be handed over to the allies. He
did not believe, however, that the Mexicans had a desire for a
"Monarchical system." Jurien was unconvinced, and Prim
reported :

> . . . the three Allied Governments were agreed with respect to
> the candidature of the Archduke Maximilian, and both Sir
> Charles Wyke and myself would soon receive positive orders
> to associate ourselves with the plans of France : I assured him
> in vain that I had positive proof that such were not the views
> of the Spanish Government, whose firm resolve it was not to
> deviate a jot from the Convention of London : I failed to
> uproot his error.[108]

Prim and Jurien did reach a provisional compromise. Almonte
would remain in Cordova, and the French forces at Tehuacan
would retire to Cordova, instead of proceeding all the way to
below the mountain passes fortified by the Mexicans.[109] The
argument Jurien used for not sending Almonte back was that,
since Almonte was at Cordova, "there he must stay."[110]

Before the last conference of the Allied Commissioners on
9 April at Orizaba, instructions arrived from Europe. Contrary

to Jurien's expectations, Prim and Wyke received instructions not to impose Maximilian on the Mexican people. Both Prim and Wyke were instructed to observe the provisions of the Convention of London by not interfering in Mexican internal affairs.[111] Wyke and Prim believed the protection afforded Almonte was an interference in Mexican internal affairs.[112] Instead of overthrowing the Mexican Government, the British and Spanish Commissioners wanted to negotiate with it.[113]

Dunlop was able to attend the conference of 9 April with full powers, as one of the British Commissioners. When Admiral Milne received instructions to relieve Dunlop, the British Admiral assumed responsibility not to recall the Commodore. Since Dunlop had decided to remove the Marines from Mexico, Milne reasoned, Dunlop could not compromise the British Government. Dunlop's latest reports stated that negotiations would start with Juarez on 15 April. The "regeneration" of Mexico, Milne concluded, had been abandoned. Even if Dunlop were relieved, his replacement would arrive after the beginning of negotiations between the Allied Commissioners, and confusion would result.[114]

Before the last conference of the Allied Commissioners Jurien and Saligny received instructions, so anxiously awaited, to continue on behalf of Maximilian, independently of the Spanish and British allies if necessary and feasible. Both Saligny and Jurien were directed not to permit a reciprocal approval of the ultimatums to be presented to the Mexican Government. It was of the utmost importance to press Saligny's "just" ultimatum and to advance immediately to Mexico City or its vicinity in order to effect the political reorganization of Mexico.[115] Jurien only learned that he had been recalled after he took part in the final conference of the Allied Commissioners.[116] Wyke received Russell's instructions not to support the Jecker claim four days after the British Commissioners had made their definitive decision to withdraw from the intervention in Mexico.[117] Wyke did not learn that the

British Government approved the Preliminaries of La Soledad until 29 April.[118]

The instructions that arrived from Europe convinced Saligny that his policy was approved. He alone, Saligny wrote Thouvenel, always wanted to demand immediate redress and then march to Mexico City. He could not understand, Saligny claimed, why Jurien was negotiating with the Mexican Government to obtain an amnesty. Saligny complained that Jurien was acting independently. Such could be expected from the British and Spanish Commissioners, but Jurien's attitude was incomprehensible. If the Spanish and the British Commissioners did not receive instructions to maintain the "entente" established among the allies, Saligny predicted a rupture of the alliance. Saligny placed his hope in the reinforcements Lorencez brought.[119]

Jurien was surprized that the French Government intended that he act more vigorously than he had expected. Thouvenel's instructions, Jurien wrote the French Minister of Foreign Affairs, did not permit :

> . . . any doubt about the firm intention of the Government of the Emperor to break as soon as possible the negotiations from which he expected no result and to furnish to the Mexican people, by a vigorous demonstration, the occasion of manifesting their true sentiments.[120]

In a personal letter to Napoleon III, Jurien remarked that he had thought that he had the confidence of the Emperor. Thouvenel's instructions made it clear, however, that Jurien was not bold enough :

> . . . I have not been able to hide from myself that it entered into the views of His Majesty to adopt in Mexico a policy more bold and more decided than that of which I have been until now the only interpreter. Consequently I have just taken the great determination for which I have been preparing for a month.

Still Jurien was skeptical :

. . . if the attitude of the Mexican people does not respond to our efforts, the success of our enterprise will perhaps be less prompt than Your Majesty had hoped.[121]

The questions that the five Allied Commissioners had to settle on 9 April at what turned out to be their last conference were whether the French were to continue to offer their protection to Almonte and whether to continue negotiations with the Juarez Government. The British and Spanish Commissioners insisted that the Juarez Government was *de facto* and that negotiations with it continue. French protection given Almonte was a violation of the Convention of London, because it was not intended to interfere with Mexican internal affairs. The intention of making a retrograde movement of the French forces before the conferences, scheduled to begin with Juarez' representatives on 15 April, was a violation of the Preliminaries of La Soledad. These were the views of the British and Spanish Commissioners. They would withdraw from the intervention in Mexico if Saligny and Jurien did not approve. Furthermore Jurien was asked to explain why he had taken it upon himself to act without obtaining the approval of the other Commissioners.

Jurien claimed that he had not violated the Convention of London or the Preliminaries. Since the stay of the French troops at Tehuacan was "incompatible" with the protection afforded Almonte, Jurien had decided to withdraw his troops to "neutral" ground. There protection could be given to a person who had the confidence of Napoleon. Wyke and Prim protested that forcing a particular government on the Mexican people and introducing enemies of the Mexican Government were violations of the Convention of London. Jurien replied that he assumed responsibility for his interpretation of the Convention of London. A "mild" policy was not regarded with favor in Europe, and Jurien had reason to believe Napoleon approved the proposals Saligny had made. Almonte was an exile, and the French flag always would protect such persons. It was without precedent that protection, once granted, should be withdrawn. Prim commented that the protection referred to by Jurien was reserved for persons "vanquished and who are in danger, not for people who came from the outside with hostile intentions against the established Government, with which the allies have started negotiations." Jurien's answer was that there was a civil war in Mexico and that Almonte had come to preach "harmony." Almonte also wanted to explain the "generous views of Europe." There was reason to expect the Mexicans to establish a monarchy. Wyke interrupted to say that Almonte had no authority to act on behalf of the allies. When Jurien claimed that Almonte had no such "pretensions," Prim and Dunlop recalled Almonte's proposals to them about Maximilian. Almonte's remarks could not "pass for a simple conversation."

After failing to reach an agreement about Almonte, the Commissioners discussed negotiations with the Juarez Government. Saligny claimed that the arbitrary extortions made by Juarez and the violence he permitted against foreigners were reasons to break off negotiations and proceed to Mexico City to protect foreign residents there. Prim observed that the Commissioners only had to wait six days to "test" the sincerity of Juarez' promises to grant redress. Saligny refused to wait for the opening of the conferences with Juarez' representatives, because violence to French subjects in Mexico was so serious that "numerous" additional French claims had arrived. Wyke asked to be informed of the nature of these claims and why they had not been made known to him. Saligny refused to give details and added that "naturally French subjects do not address themselves to the British Legation to make good their claims." Jurien agreed with Saligny that it was impossible to have any sympathy for the Juarez Government, which permitted "bloody executions" and published "edicts of proscription."

Prim asked Saligny to explain remarks he had made to the Spanish consul at Vera Cruz, and its Governor. Prim protested assertions that he intended to be "crowned Emperor of

Mexico" and that that was why he was opposed to Maximilian. Saligny claimed he had "proof." He had seen a letter of one of Prim's partisans. Prim himself had said that "the candidature of an Austrian Prince for Mexico was absurd, but perhaps there were chances of success for a successful soldier." Finally, there were articles in Prim's personal newspaper, *El Eco de Europa*. Prim replied that he had made "allusion to a successful Mexican soldier." Although *El Eco de Europa* printed nothing without his permission, that paper had never proposed Prim as ruler of Mexico.[122] What Prim said about *El Eco de Europa* was true. Although Saligny did not mention to which copies of *El Eco de Europa* he was referring,[123] he probably had in mind the ones of 6 March and 19 March. Saligny had already sent these to Thouvenel, and they attacked the belief that a monarchy could be established in Mexico. Maximilian's candidacy was especially ridiculed.[124]

After Prim answered Saligny's charges, a note received from the Mexican Government was read.[125] Doblado demanded that Almonte, Miranda and the other exiles leave Mexico.[126] Then Jurien read the reply he intended to send.[127] Almonte would stay in Mexico, because he was authorized to go to Mexico City with "words of conciliation" for his fellow countrymen. His mission was to make known the "benevolent aim that the European intervention had proposed." Since the Mexican Government had issued edicts of proscription, Almonte was given protection to save his life, and such protection could never be withdrawn once given. Since the signing of the Preliminaries of La Soledad, French subjects in Mexico had suffered "new vexations." Violent measures were only adopted "with a view of stiffling the expression of the wishes and the true public opinion of the country."[128] For the next part of the note Jurien and Saligny proposed to send to Doblado, the French Commissioners took as their text Thouvenel's instructions of 21 February 1862 and even copied a phrase from Thouvenel's orders. Thouvenel's instructions read:

The Emperor regrets that instead of immediately seeking the redress of grievances of the three Powers, the Plenipotentiaries addressed a note to the Mexican Government that furnished it the means, by gaining time, of organizing resistance and of putting on the wrong scent, with the aid of the appearance of consultation, as concerns the real wishes of the nation. It is only after the occupation of Mexico City, or at least of the approaches of this city, that the political reorganization of the country can be usefully posed and resolved. His Majesty hopes that one will not let himself be stopped by an evasive and fallacious reply of the Government of Juaıez and that one would have marched on the Capital with as much promptitude as the means at one's disposal permits.[129]

The note Saligny and Jurien wanted to send Doblado stated :

One thus (i.e., by "stiffling . . . the wishes and the true public opinion") hoped to succeed in putting Europe on the wrong scent and to make it accept the triumph of an oppressive minority, as the only element of order and reorganization that could still be found in Mexico.

The French forces, therefore, would retreat to Paso Ancho to "regain all their freedom of action."[130]

Wyke, Dunlop, and Prim refused to sanction the reply to Doblado, and Jurien remarked that Juarez was the leader of a "regime of terror weighing on the population and keeping it under a yoke of iron." Saligny agreed, but Wyke countered that the majority of Mexicans supported Juarez and that there were few monarchists in Mexico. The real majority, Jurien claimed, was composed of the "sane and moderate party" whose freedom of expression was being suppressed by Juarez. Wyke denied this and stated that the Juarez Government was composed of "moderates." All discussion was useless. Jurien and Saligny would not change their minds, and the British and Spanish Commissioners presented their *sine qua non* for a continuation of an allied intervention in Mexico :

. . . if their French colleagues persist to refuse to remove the Mexican exiles, refuse to take part in the Conferences that must take place at Orizaba on the 15th of April, the English and Spanish Commissioners will retire with their troops from Mexican territory, considering this stand of the French Commissioners a violation of the Convention of London and the Preliminaries of La Soledad.

Jurien and Saligny refused these conditions,[131] and the last official document signed by all five Commissioners was drafted and sent to the Mexican Government:

The Plenipotentiaries of Her Majesty the Queen of Great Britain, of Her Majesty the Queen of Spain and of His Majesty the Emperor of the French have the honor to inform His Excellency the Minister of Foreign Relations of the Mexican Republic, that, not having been able to agree on the interpretation to give under actual circumstances to the Convention of 31 October 1861, they have resolved to adopt henceforth an action completely separate and independent.

Consequently the Commander of the Spanish Forces is going to take immediately the measures necessary to re-embark his troops.

The French army will concentrate itself at Paso Ancho as soon as the Spanish Troops will have passed this position, that is to say, probably about the 20th April, and will commence operations on the spot.[132]

Minutes were made of the meeting of 9 April and read to the Commissioners.[133] They approved what now became an official document,[134] copies of which were sent to the British,[135] French,[136] and Spanish[137] Governments. Saligny sent a personal representative to Napoleon to offer explanations.[138] Wyke sent one of the members of his legation to answer any questions Russell might have.[139] Prim ordered two of his aides-de-camp to proceed to Spain, to obtain an audience with Queen Isabella, and to justify Prim's decision to withdraw his troops from Mexico.[140] The allied intervention in Mexico was now at an end if the British, Spanish, and French Governments approved the decisions of their representatives.

## 2.   THE BREAKDOWN OF THE CONVENTION OF LONDON IN EUROPE

Russell approved all the decisions made by Wyke and Dunlop at the conference of 9 April that ended the collective intervention in Mexico.[1] Since Dunlop supported Wyke's views, Russell decided that Admiral Milne made a wise decision not to recall Dunlop.[2] The British Foreign Secretary wrote to the British Admiralty that Dunlop deserved the "highest credit"[3] and was restored to favor.[4] A bill for $48,133.21 was sent to the French Government for the means of transportation Dunlop had sold the French in Mexico.[5] In Parliament an Under Secretary of State for Foreign Affairs stated that Wyke had only made two decisions contrary to his instructions:

> The first mistake consisted in his issuing a proclamation, stating the object of the intervention was the regeneration of the country; and the second was the attempt to place the Marines on the same footing with the French and Spanish force, and send them into the interior to co-operate with them.[6]

In answer to Wyke's complaint that the Allied Commissioners should have been instructed, from the beginning, how to regard each other's claims, Russell stated that there were two reasons why the British Government did not give precise orders. If the Allied Commissioners had been directed to support each other's claims, any unreasonable claims pressed would have been supported by all three allies. If claims had been pressed separately, the Mexican Government would have been able to find a means to cause a division among the allies. In such a situation, Russell believed the course adopted was the best, that the Commissioners decide "on the spot."[7] Russell did notify Wyke, however, that he deserved "credit" for the policy he had carried out under "great difficulties."[8]

Cowley[9] and Crampton[10] were instructed to inform, respectively, the French and Spanish Governments that the Convention of London would not be at an "end," but merely "suspended," if Saligny and Jurien refused to reverse their policies. After having made this policy statement on 29 April 1862, Russell received the minutes of the 9 April meeting of the Commissioners.[11] He believed those minutes to be a "very extraordinary document"[12] and sent a letter to the British Admiralty that the Convention of London was "suspended."[13] Queen Victoria's reaction was :

> The conduct of the French is everywhere disgraceful. Let us only have *nothing* to do with them in future in any proceedings in other countries.[14]

At the end of May 1862 Flahault brought Russell a private letter from Napoleon III. A summary of the contents of this letter has been preserved. Russell wrote Cowley a private letter that Napoleon proposed "that we should make the redress of our wrongs in Mexico merely an ostensible object and that our real object should be the setting up of a Monarchy in Mexico." After reading the Emperor's letter, Russell told Flahault "that we could never concur in such a course." At Flahault's request, Russell "did not even mention the letter to the Cabinet." He had much cause, Russell wrote Cowley, "to complain of the conduct of the Emperor in regard to Mexico." Russell explained what his own Mexican policy was :

> The whole foundation of my policy consists in non-intervention and I would never concur in a flagrant project of intervention.
>     I had hoped in spite of the mission of General Almonte to create a civil war in Mexico that we might keep a force at Vera Cruz.
>     But the declarations of Saligny and Jurien de la Graviere that they must march on Mexico (City) on the pretext of outrages the nature of which they would not present to their colleagues of England and Spain have de facto suspended the Convention of the 31st October last. We can now only wait in silence till the French or we are (unreadable letters)ated by events.

Cowley was instructed that "all conference on the subject should be avoided, as it would merely renew agitation."[15] A month later Russell wrote Cowley another private letter that Saligny had "entirely set aside" the Convention of London. Therefore the British Foreign Secretary was "not likely" to involve himself "in any new engagement with regard to Mexico."[16]

Throughout 1862 Russell rejected Spanish overtures to renew the tripartite alliance. In May O'Donnell told the British Ambassador to Madrid that a conference "as to the future conduct of the affairs of Mexico would at present be useless." But O'Donnell added that "some communication between the governments of the Three Powers in regard to what has taken place is necessary to remove the appearance of a misunderstanding between them on account of the disagreement of their agents in Mexico."[17] Russell replied, "When the French troops shall have left Mexico we may consider what is next to be done."[18] During negotiations between the Spanish and French Governments for the reestablishment of a common policy toward Mexico,[19] Queen Isabella made a speech to open the sessions of the Cortes on 1 December 1862. She stated:

> I hope that the difficulties which the disagreement of the Plenipotentiaries in Mexico has opposed to the execution of the Treaty of London will terminate in a satisfactory manner. The unforeseen obstacles which have prevented this have not altered my desire to fulfill it, and to realize the idea which formed its basis.[20]

The meaning of these remarks, O'Donnell told Crampton, was that the Spanish Government was willing to renew a tripartite policy toward Mexico if the French Government took the initiative in inviting British and Spanish cooperation.[21] Russell replied that he agreed, but he had to make another condition. It was that "France should distinctly refrain from any interference in the internal concerns of Mexico."[22]

The only precedent for Napoleon's policy in Mexico, Russell informed Cowley with irony, was the Emperor's Italian policy:

The intention of entering Mexico (City) by force of arms, in order to enable the Mexican people to say what Government they would like to have has its only precedent in the expedition to Rome. According to this precedent the Roman People have had for 12 years the choice of their own Government.[23]

In order to make it clear to the members of Parliament and the British people that his policy was opposed to such forcible interference in the internal affairs of another sovereign nation, Russell had a large part of the British diplomatic correspondence concerning Mexico published and submitted to Parliament.[24] As Russell told Hammond, " 'Our case must be brought out however much the French may be irritated'."[25]

Before Collantes and O'Donnell received Prim's reports of the decisions made at the last conference of the Allied Commissioners in Mexico, the Spanish Ministers could not believe that Prim had ordered his troops to leave Mexico. The British Ambassador was told that Prim had no authority to take such a step without specific authorization from the Spanish Government.[26] Prim had taken precautions, however, to prevent his being disavowed. His two aides-de-camp saw Queen Isabella and convinced her that it was not in the interests of Spain to participate in a war to implement French designs to make Maximilian ruler of Mexico.[27] On 19 May Collantes announced in the Cortes that Prim's decisions had been approved by the Spanish Government, and the French Ambassador telegraphed the information to Thouvenel the same day."[28] The next day Barrot sent another telegram to Paris that O'Donnell considered the Convention of London "suspended but not broken."[29]

The Spanish Government was in a dilemma. It had never intended to assist French projects in favor of Maximilian. At the same time Collantes and O'Donnell had not intended that the intervention be confined to the purpose of settling claims. It was hoped that an expedition proceeding beyond Vera Cruz would encourage the Mexican conservatives to overthrow Juarez. On 12 May O'Donnell told the French Ambassador

to Madrid that, during the negotiation of the Convention of
London, the Spanish Government had proposed agreeing upon
the objectives of the intervention.[30] Although O'Donnell did
not mention that the French Government at the time had
rejected this proposal,[31] he recalled that the British Government
had tried to limit joint action to the occupation of Mexican
coastal positions. It had been a victory for France and Spain
to "have led England to insert the clause that the allied powers
would take all measures they had in view."[32] Since the Mexican
policy of Spain was opposed both to the aims of Russell and
Napoleon, the Spanish Government could not side with one
against the other. At the same time the opposition in the
Cortes could be expected to launch a campaign against the
Spanish Government's Mexican policy. Collantes' announcement in the Cortes that Prim's decisions were approved was in
reply to a proposal of a vote of censure.[33] Although Prim had
intended to negotiate with the Juarez Government and had left
a Chargé d'Affaires in Mexico after departing with the Spanish
troops, the Spanish Government had no desire to recognize
Juarez' regime or negotiate a settlement of claims with it.
Lopez de Ceballos, whom Prim had left in Mexico, was
instructed by Collantes not to enter into any "official" relations
with the Juarez Government, and in particular Ceballos was
neither to recognize the Liberal Government nor to negotiate
a treaty with it.[34] In this way Prim's intentions to support
Juarez were frustrated. In order to calm criticism in the Cortes
that the whole expedition was a miscarriage, Collantes took
the stand that Spain had never deviated from a strict observance of the Convention of London.[35] Collantes also stressed
that the British Government was in complete agreement with
the views he expressed.[36]

Rather than do nothing, and thereby permit Napoleon to
continue his project in favor of Maximilian and perhaps
arouse violent criticism in the Cortes, the Spanish Government
attempted the thankless task of renewing an understanding
among the three Powers that had signed the now suspended

Convention of London. Efforts in this direction were rejected by Russell. On 21 May Collantes directed his diplomatic representative in Paris to propose "consultation" to settle differences.[37] At the same time it was made known to Thouvenel that Prim was not responsible for the difficulties that had arisen. They had been caused by the "independent" proceedings of the French Commissioners.[38] Thouvenel replied by stating that his representatives in Mexico were not acting independently. They were implementing loyally the proclamation issued by all the Allied Commissioners upon arrival in Mexico. The French Government could not be accused of attempting to impose a government on the Mexican people, because the proclamation forbade that. Indirectly Thouvenel refused the offer to "consult." Since the Spanish Government intended to follow a policy of "conciliation and caution," with which the French Government could not associate itself, it was to be regretted that the French forces in Mexico would have to "accomplish alone a task we would have been happy and proud to share with the glorious Spanish army."[39]

Even the refusal of Russell and Thouvenel to "consult" did not put an end to Spanish attempts to reach an understanding with the French and British Governments. In July 1862 copies of instructions for Ceballos were sent to London and Paris. Ceballos was directed not to "negotiate any private treaty and thus to separate themselves (i.e., the Spanish Government) from the friendly nations which have taken part in one and the same cause."[40] On 27 July 1862 Queen Isabella signed a decree declaring Prim's mission to Mexico at an end and expressing satisfaction with the "real loyalty and intelligence, with which he has fulfilled" his diplomatic duties.[41] On the same day the official *Gazette* published a royal decree naming General Concha Spanish Ambassador to Paris.[42] Two days later Collantes wrote instructions for Concha. Since the Convention was only "suspended," the Spanish Government hoped to "establish it in full force and vigour by an understanding amongst the three powers which signed it." For this purpose, Collantes

proposed "conferences." But first the French Government had
to accept three preliminary conditions. British cooperation had
to be invited. The Mexican people should be guaranteed the
"integrity of their territory and . . . the independence . . . to
enable them to constitute the form of Government best suited
to their wishes, habits and necessities." Lastly, the three Powers
"should sustain the demands which each may present to the
Government of Mexico." If the French Government accepted
these conditions, the exact details of a renewed tripartite intervention should be agreed on in advance in order to avoid
difficulties in the future.[43] At the same time the objectives of
Concha's mission were made known to the British Government.[44] Since Russell would never agree to support the Jecker
claims pressed by the French Government, there was no hope
that the British Government would send a representative to
the "conferences." Napoleon was not willing to guarantee to
the Mexican people their right to select a government in
accordance with their "wishes, habits and necessities." It
sounded too much like a Bourbon restoration in Mexico. The
French reply was that conferences would have to be delayed
until after the final victory of the French army in Mexico.[44]

On 2 May Cowley told Thouvenel that Russell approved
Wyke's views of the differences among the Allied Commissioners in Mexico. Thouvenel replied that it was not intended
to impose a government on the Mexicans. Although Napoleon
had ordered that the French army afford protection to
Almonte, the protection given the other exiles was disapproved.[45] Both Napoleon,[46] and Eugenie[47] at this time blamed
Prim as chiefly responsible for the difficulties in Mexico. Before
the arrival of a telegram from Madrid on 19 May[48] that the
Spanish Government approved Prim's policy in Mexico,
Napoleon believed that Prim's policy would be at least disavowed, if he were not recalled in disgrace. Devious means
had already been employed to win Spanish approval of French
designs. On 18 April Hidalgo had written a letter to a Mexican
exile residing in Spain, and what was made to appear a private

letter appeared in the *Epoca* of 25 April 1862. As a sop to Spanish susceptibilities that an Austrian would become ruler of Mexico, Hidalgo stated that the other countries of Latin America would follow the example of Mexico and proclaim enough monarchies to provide several thrones for members of the Spanish Bourbon family.[49] There was some reason for Napoleon to believe that Prim would be recalled. On 10 May the French Ambassador to Madrid sent a telegram to Thouvenel :

> I have good reason to believe, if the Government of the Emperor expressed the intention of confiding the Command-in-Chief of the allied forces to Marshal Serrano, the Spanish Government would little hesitate to recall General Prim.[50]

The Spanish Chargé d'Affaires in Paris believed that the Spanish Government would be very "disappointed" that Prim was withdrawing his troops from Mexico.[51] On 19 May Napoleon saw Cowley and expressed "great irritation" that Prim's decisions had been approved.[52] Cowley also talked with Thouvenel on 19 May, and the French Minister of Foreign Affairs expressed surprise that the Spanish Government continued to have confidence in Prim. Thouvenel "certainly had expected a contrary result."[53]

After Napoleon learned that Prim would not be recalled, the Emperor believed the British Government might support his Mexican policy. At the end of May Napoleon proposed to Russell by means of a private letter that the British Government make redress of grievances a pretext to establish a monarchy in Mexico.[54] At the same time Napoleon told Cowley that the British Government should "take some step" to show that it would not make "common cause with Spain."[55] Even after Russell refused to act under a "pretext," Napoleon believed that the British Government would not oppose the establishment of Maximilian in Mexico. On 7 June Napoleon wrote to Maximilian, "The English will, I think, be much pleased if it succeeds, but they do not want to help us pick the

*chestnuts out of the fire."* Since Maximilian could not expect
"active" British support, Napoleon stressed that the other condition of Maximilian's candidacy would be fulfilled :

> Being at war with the Mexican Government, I have not been
> willing to treat with it. I have told my representatives there
> that there was no question whatever of impsing any kind
> of government upon the Mexicans, but only of supporting a
> monarchy if it found partisans in the country and a prospect
> of stability. This course of action was quite simple and straight-
> forward, and yet attempts have been made to distort my inten-
> tions and misinterpret the character of the intervention.[56]

On the same day that Napoleon wrote to Maximilian, Eugenie
wrote to Charlotte with greater enthusiasm :

> *. . . here we are, thanks to God, without allies!* It is a very
> significant fact that so long as three of us were acting together,
> not a single Mexican was in favour of us, not even Juarez, for
> whom the treaty, or rather the preliminaries, were *(sic)* a
> triumph; but since our action has been freed from all con-
> straint, the country feels safe enough to express its wishes, and
> all men are grouping themselves round Almonte, who, but
> yesterday an exile, is today the dictator of the provinces
> through which we have just advanced. The next mail will
> probably bring the news of the arrival in Mexico City.[57]

In mid-June 1862 Thouvenel was so eager for information
that he persuaded Bismarck, then Prussian Ambassador to
Paris, to provide some of the reports of Baron Wagner, the
Prussian Chargé d'Affaires in Mexico. A map of Puebla,
enclosed in one of Wagner's reports, was copied.[58] Since Wagner believed that the monarchist cause was making progress in
Mexico,[59] he probably stated this opinion in his reports that
Bismarck gave Thouvenel. Some confirmation for this likeli-
hood is that Thouvenel asked permission to send some "interesting passages" of Wagner's reports to the British Government.
Bismarck sent a report to the Prussian Government on 15 June
and observed that neither Prussia nor Wagner would receive
any "thanks" if Thouvenel's request were granted.[60] Wagner's

reports, since a map of Puebla was enclosed in one report, probably related that Lorencez had attempted to capture Puebla on 5 May and had been forced to retreat. On 15 June Napoleon wrote Lorencez:

> I have approved with pleasure the . . . attack on Puebla. It . . must not be a discouragement. . . . The honor of the country (i.e., France) has been engaged and you will obtain all the reinforcements you need. Express to the troops under your command my entire satisfaction with their courage. . . . I have approved your conduct, although it does not seem to be understood by everybody. You did right to protect General Almonte; being at war with the existing government of Mexico, all who will wish to take refuge under our flag will have the same right to our protection. But that must not influence our policy in the future. It is against my interests, my origin, and my principles to impose any government whatsoever on the Mexican people. Let them choose in all freedom the form of government best suited to them; I have only asked sincerity of the Mexican people in their foreign relations, and I only desire one thing, the well being and independence of this fine country under a stable and regular government.[61]

If Napoleon was now sincere about letting the Mexicans choose their own government, as he stated in the letter to Lorencez, the Emperor rationalized that the means he intended to follow were compatible with the "freedom" that would be permitted the Mexican nation. On 29 June a report arrived from Saligny relating the failure of Lorencez to capture Puebla on 5 May. Saligny enclosed an order Lorencez issued to his troops on 21 May:

> You were told a hundred times that the city of Puebla called you with anxiety, and that the inhabitants would rush to embrace you, and crown you with flowers.
>
> .    .    .    .    .    .    .    .
>
> You have been deceived, as well as His Majesty the Emperor.[62]

Commenting on Lorencez' order, Saligny said that he had said that Puebla had been taken and retaken twenty times during the Mexican Civil War (1857–1860) by forces of Mexican volunteers, never comprising more than two to three thousand men. But, although Lorencez blamed his defeat on "false information supplied," he could not have expected a good reception until after entering the city, the most reactionary of all Mexico.[63] On the same day that Saligny's report arrived, Napoleon wrote to Randon, his Minister of War. Randon was instructed to write to Lorencez in the following sense:

> He (i.e., Napoleon III) blames your attitude toward M. de Saligny; whatever may be his faults, he is the representative of the Emperor and has the right to have your respect *(droit à vos égards)*. Likewise you must have the same respect and kindness not only toward General Almonte, but even toward all Mexicans who come to us. You will not gain adherents by talking harshly: the Spanish character is very sensitive; it is by good gentlemanly manners that one wins them over. It is necessary to pay and arm the Mexican auxiliaries and show them confidence. General Forey will soon come to take the general command.[64]

The armed and paid "Mexican auxiliaries," it would seem, were inconsistent with the desire Napoleon had expressed earlier that month in letters, both to Maximilian and Lorencez, that the Mexicans would be "free" to choose the government they wanted. Randon's reply to Napoleon's directions of what orders to send Lorencez did not change the Emperor's opinion of Saligny. Randon wrote:

> In reading the despatches of M. de Saligny . . . on the ease and appropriateness of a march to Mexico City wit the weak column that Admiral Jurien commanded . . . one is certainly permitted to smile and not to take very seriously the reasons he (i.e., Saligny) employs to criticize the operations of the troops that Your Majesty has entrusted to General de Lorencez.[65]

In November 1862, when Mexico City still had not been captured, Napoleon still trusted Saligny. Drouyn de Lhuys, Thouvenel's successor, told Cowley that Napoleon "protected" Saligny in a way that "astonished" Drouyn.[66]

At the end of June 1862 Napoleon's Mexican policy entered a new phase. He became extremely interested in and disturbed by the military situation in Mexico. His Mexican policy now no longer had the direct connection, as before, with the Mexican policies of Spain and Great Britain. As Napoleon had written Lorencez, the defeat at Puebla engaged French honor and required vengeance in the form of French military victories. When Metternich saw Napoleon at the end of June and brought up the question of the conditions Maximilian had made for his candidacy, Napoleon answered that the military question was more important than the political one. With a map of Mexico lying in front of him, Napoleon assured Metternich that Maximilian could still count on the Emperor of the French.[67] The victories were also necessary to calm French public opinion. In a conversation at the end of August 1862, Napoleon made it clear that he needed "one or two battles, to restore . . . lustre to the French arms, and to cause public opinion more readily to accept the necessity of so considerable an expenditure of force."[68]

One thing that Napoleon judged correctly in 1861 and 1862 was that the United States at that time was unable to oppose the French intervention in Mexico. Although Seward made protests from time to time, he wrote in his diary:

> Attention has been directed to the extraordinary proceedings which are taking place in Mexico. We shall be just to ourselves, and at the same time shall practice the prudence that will avert any new complication in our affairs.[69]

Seward's refusal to take active measures against Napoleon's Mexican policy was also an important reason for the failure of the Latin American states, under the leadership of Peru, to assist Mexico to resist what was regarded aggression against republican ideas in the Western Hemisphere.[70]

No account of the tripartite intervention would be complete

without an account of Jurien's fate upon returning to France. Cowley saw the Admiral at the end of June 1862 and questioned him. Cowley reported in a private letter:

> He got at last so entangled in his explanations that he could only get out of the dilemma by fairly stating that he had not been his own master, the Emperor having given positive orders that the Government of Juarez was to be upset at all hazards.[71]

Upon returning from Mexico, Jurien was given a warm welcome by Napoleon, much to the surprise of the Imperial Court.[72]

# VII
# Conclusions

DURING THE FORTY YEARS BETWEEN 1821, WHEN MEXICO became independent of Spain, and 1861, when Napoleon proposed to Maximilian that he become ruler of Mexico, many attempts were made by or on behalf of Mexican conservatives to win European support for the establishment of a member of the European nobility as ruler of a Mexican monarchy. All these plans were frustrated by the refusal of the British Government to intervene in the internal affairs of Mexico, fears that the United States would defend the Monroe Doctrine, and events in Europe that diverted attention from the New World. Napoleon interested himself in Mexico in the 1840's while a political prisoner in the fortress of Ham. When he became Emperor of the French, his interest in Mexico continued, but he hesitated to implement the proposals made by Hidalgo and other Mexican *émigrés* and exiles. Napoleon would not act independently of Great Britain, feared complications with the United States, had no "pretext" to intervene in Mexico, and could not find a suitable and willing candidate for a Mexican throne.

The chaos in Mexican internal affairs before 1861 led to the accumulation of personal and property claims of foreigners residing in Mexico. A series of treaties negotiated with various Mexican governments recognized some of these claims and provided that the claimants be given compensation in the form of bonds. The interest and retirement of these bonds were guaranteed by a percentage of Mexican custom duties. Such arrangements were made on behalf of British, French, and Spanish subjects by their respective governments. A group of British subjects lent money to the Mexican Government in the 1820's, and they made similar arrangements for repayment. These "London Bondholders" negotiated directly with the succeeding Mexican governments. These governments, both conservative and liberals, constantly failed to comply with the terms they and their predecessors had made. Diplomatic protests, the suspension or severing of diplomatic relations, the sending of naval forces to demonstrate before Mexican ports, and the signing of new agreements were the usual consequences of Mexican inability or unwillingness to stop defaulting in payments to claimants.

There was an accumulation of European claims against Mexico during the Mexican Civil War (1857–1860). All plans to intervene in Mexico came to nothing, because the British Government, in spite of the pleas of its diplomatic representative in Mexico, refused to accept such projects seriously. The Buchanan administration, in an attempt to prevent European intervention in Mexico, negotiated the McLane–Ocampo treaties with Mexico in 1859, but they were never ratified by the United States Senate, occupied with internal affairs. These treaties indirectly encouraged a European intervention in Mexico, because the British, French, and Spanish Governments saw in the McLane–Ocampo treaties an American attempt to gain exclusive influence in Mexico and to exclude the European Powers politically and commercially from the New World. In 1860 a European mediation proposal was rejected by both contending parties in Mexico, and the relations of the European Powers with Mexico returned to their normal and unsatisfactory status.

In 1861 Juarez established his government in Mexico City, and his rival entered the ranks of the Mexican exiles. Although the civil war was over, bands of conservatives and robbers roamed the country. More claims were filed in the dossiers of the foreign legations, and both the French and British Ministers to Mexico appealed to their governments to use force to obtain redress of grievances from Mexico. The expulsion of the Spanish diplomatic representative from Mexico by Juarez ended official Mexican–Spanish diplomatic relations. The situation was similar to what had happened in years before, but the suspension of claims conventions by the Juarez Government in July 1861 brought even the patience of the British Government to an end. Palmerston and Russell decided to make a custom house intervention, as proposed by their Minister to Mexico, to obtain funds to pay British claimants. The proposals of the "London Bondholders" to extend the scope of the intervention were rejected. Contrary to Wyke's suggestions, the British Government decided to accept French cooperation. Napoleon would not be acting independently of Great Britain. The Jecker bonds and the Mexican law of July 1861 were good "pretexts," and the American Civil War could be counted on to prevent any interference by the United States. Only a candidate for a Mexican throne failed. Throughout 1861 Napoleon and Eugenie considered various candidates, including Maximilian. In July 1861 Estrada made an overture to the Austrian Government, which refused to consider the matter seriously for the time being. Two preliminary conditions were unofficially made : Anglo–French support and the clearly expressed desires of the Mexican people. Only during the negotiation of the Convention of London did Eugenie and Napoleon make the final decision on behalf of Maximilian at Biarritz. Napoleon hoped that the Austrian Archduke would establish a stable government in Mexico so that commercial intercourse between Europe and Mexico would flourish. The imperialism of the United States would be blocked. Cotton that failed to reach Europe, owing to the Northern blockade of the Confederacy, would be planted in Mexico. Napoleon also expected that Austria could be persuaded to cede Venetia to

Italy in return for the crown received by Maximilian. Napoleon hoped that he would be assisted to gain British support of French plans through the influence with Queen Victoria of of Leopold of Belgium, Maximilian's father-in-law. Eugenie saw in the creation of a Mexican monarchy the chance for the restoration to their former positions of the Catholic Church and the Spanish civilization of her ancestors. Her compassion for suffering also was an important factor in Eugenie's desire to see an end to strife in Mexico. By including Spain as an ally of France and Great Britain in an intervention in Mexico, Eugenie hoped, the influence of Spain as one of the powers of Europe would be increased.

Russell and Palmerston insisted that a convention should be the basis of a tripartite intervention in Mexico. Although such a convention was not considered a perfect means to prevent Spanish and French interference in Mexican internal affairs, the two British Ministers could find no better barrier to suspected ulterior intentions than to include disclaimers not to interfere in Mexican internal affairs in such a convention. Spanish proposals to encourage the establishment of a "stable" government in Mexico, Thouvenel's suggestion to renew the mediation proposals of 1860, and Napoleon's private letter to Flahault — shown to Russell and Palmerston and proposing Maximilian as a candidate for a Mexican throne — only strengthened the determination of Russell and Palmerston to insert disclaimers in the convention. The British Ministers permitted the French Government, however, to define these disclaimers less rigorously than in the first British draft convention and to insert loopholes in the convention to permit operations beyond the coast of Mexico. The Spanish Government was happy that such operations would be permitted so that the conservatives in Mexico might be encouraged to overthrow the Juarez regime. It would be a diplomatic victory for O'Donnell and his Liberal Union, which would not have to fear any more attacks on the Mexican policy of Spain by the opposition press or opposition representatives in the Cortes.

The changes made to a series of draft conventions gave Napoleon the leeway he desired. That the British Government permitted these changes encouraged the Emperor in the belief that the British Government would not oppose his plans, if not assist in their implementation. Russell did not believe the changes made between the first draft convention and the final convention were important, because he did not think the size of the allied expeditionary force being sent to Mexico was large enough for operations beyond Vera Cruz.

The Convention of London was important for what it did not contain. The redress of grievances the allies would demand of Mexico were not defined with precision. It was not stated whether the allies would support each other's claims. The instructions to the allied military and diplomatic representatives were very little more precise. The confusion of claims was such that the British and Spanish Governments did not know exactly what claims were justified. The British and Spanish instructions, therefore, granted large discretionary powers. Napoleon did not want French claims to be recognized by the Juarez Government so that there would be a pretext for the European troops to remain in Mexico. Instructions were given Saligny, therefore, to make "excessive" demands of the Mexican Government.

In one respect the Convention of London broke down partially before the arrival of the first European troops in Mexico. As a counterproposal to the American offer of a loan to Mexico to prevent a European intervention, an article of the Convention of London provided for an invitation to the United States to join the European allies after the signature of the convention. The United States was not invited to take part in the negotiations leading to the signing of the convention, because no delays could be permitted so that the European troops could be sent to Mexico during the "healthy" season on the Mexican coast. Since the Spanish Government had given October or November 1861 as the deadline for the departure of the Spanish forces from Havana for Mexico, Russell and

Palmerston wanted to sign a convention quickly. They foresaw that it might take months before a convention, even if agreed upon by Seward, would be put to a vote in the Senate of the United States. The rejection of the European invitation by Seward was expected, although Russell would have been happy to obtain American cooperation to foil any possible ulterior aims of France and Spain.

After the signature of the Convention of London, the intentions of the British and Spanish Governments were relatively simple. Russell and Palmerston expected that Vera Cruz would be seized. The representatives of the allies would decide "on the spot" what demands to make of the Juarez Government. If these demands were refused, the allies would collect custom duties themselves and decide, again on the spot, how to divide the money collected. The Spanish Government did not expect Juarez to be able to afford redress and hoped a crisis in Mexican internal affairs would lead to the establishment of a government of conservatives. To "encourage" such a development, General Prim, the Spanish representative sent to Mexico, was given discretionary powers, at the request of the French Government, to proceed beyond the coast with his troops.

Napoleon intended to implement his plans to establish Maximilian in Mexico by typically conspiratorial means. Napoleon devised these means chiefly by himself and acted to a large extent outside official diplomatic channels, including his own Ministry of Foreign Affairs. The allied forces would seize Vera Cruz. Ultimatums would be sent to the Juarez Government. From Saligny's reports of the bad faith of that government, it could be expected that no satisfaction would be obtained. To make sure that this would happen, the French demands would be excessive. Even if these demands were accepted, there still remained the excuse to protect foreigners threatened in Mexico, the loophole Napoleon had had inserted in the Convention of London. Since Prim had discretionary powers to advance beyond Vera Cruz, Admiral Jurien de La

Gravière, the Commander-in-Chief of the French forces, would convince Prim to act on this discretion. If the British Commander refused to march his small force of seven hundred Marines beyond Vera Cruz, they could stay there on garrison duty. Napoleon had no illusions that the Mexicans would rise "as one man" in favor of Maximilian, as predicted by Hidalgo. A general election was out of the question. Jurien and Saligny would gather some "notables" willing to make the appropriate invitation to Maximilian. Although Thouvenel warned Jurien to avoid an "adventure" by making sure that there was widespread support for Maximilian, Napoleon had less qualms, but he gave Jurien discretionary powers to decide when the right "moment" arrived to mention Maximilian. Napoleon believed that the British Government would accept the *fait accompli*. Russell and Palmerston had not refused to change their original draft convention. They had no objections to Maximilian. The provision that he be the genuine choice of the Mexican people was an obstacle, but Napoleon hoped that by personal letters to the British Ministers he would change their minds. King Leopold was also expected to exert an influence. Napoleon had seen Wyke, the British Minister to Mexico, early in 1861. Since Wyke believed that Latin America was "ripe" for monarchical institutions, it was hoped he would cause no difficulties. Jurien had a reputation for moderation among British naval officers, and it was expected that he could exert influence on Commodore Dunlop, the British Commander-in-Chief sent to Mexico. To lure Maximilian from the reserve imposed on him by the Austrian Government, Almonte was sent to Miramar to try to involve Maximilian more directly. Then Almonte was sent to Mexico to contact conservatives and to prepare the way for Maximilian. Before leaving Europe, Almonte saw O'Donnell and Collantes, the Spanish Ministers, in an attempt to influence them to favor Maximilian's candidacy. Napoleon confided many of his intrigues to Metternich, the Austrian Ambassador to Paris. When Cowley informed Metternich of the "fantastic" claims being pressed

by France, the Austrian replied by giving an excellent general
outline of Napoleon's schemes. Cowley reported Metternich's
remarks in a private letter to Russell:

> He (i.e., Metternich) remarked that these demands were made
> purposely, and he then went on to tell me that nothing in his
> Diplomatic life had amused him so much as to follow the
> Emperor's proceedings with regard to Mexico. It had given
> him, he said, a greater insight into His Majesty's character
> than years of common intercourse would have afforded. It was
> impossible to conceive all the dodges which His Majesty had
> imagined, or how perseveringly he carried them out. It seemed
> a regular amusement to him. He had sent enormous sums of
> money to Mexico, and he had planned all the measures to be
> taken to insure the election of the Archduke. Whenever a
> difficulty arose, it was immediately met by some fresh man-
> oeuvre or devise. In short, said Metternich, he is "un pres-
> digitateur de premier ordre."

The premature arrival of the Spanish expedition at Vera
Cruz before the French and British expeditionary forces
afforded Napoleon a pretext to send reinforcements to Mexico.
A leak of information about orders given the officers in charge
of these reinforcements caused Russell to renew his efforts to
prevent Maximilian from being imposed on the Mexican
people. An Anglo–Spanish agreement was reached in January
and February 1862 to oppose any such plans. At the same time
the Austrian Government was disillusioned to learn that the
British Government had not agreed to Napoleon's plans, as
previously had been made known by Napoleon to the Austrian
Government. Meanwhile, in Mexico, the allied expeditionary
forces had no means of transportation needed to proceed
beyond the coast. The "healthy" season was found to be
extremely unhealthy for Europeans, and the British and Spanish Commissioners would not approve the "excessive" French
demands. Cautious by nature and not finding any evidence of
the existence of a monarchical party in Mexico, Jurien refused
to support the proposals of his French colleague, Saligny, to
commence hostilities. The result was a deadlock, and, while

instructions from Europe were awaited, the Preliminaries of La Soledad were negotiated. The allied forces were permitted to advance to healthy cities in the interior of Mexico on the promise that, if negotiations for a settlement of claims broke down, the European troops would withdraw to the coastal side of the first Mexican fortifications before commencing hostilities.

Before instructions arrived in Mexico concerning the Preliminaries of La Soledad, Almonte arrived at Vera Cruz and proceeded inland under the protection afforded him by the French troops by order of Napoleon III. When Jurien realized that Napoleon intended that a vigorous implementation of his plans was intended, the Admiral sought pretexts to break off negotiations with Juarez and refused to permit Almonte to be shipped out of Mexico. The British and Spanish Commissioners demanded that negotiations with Juarez be continued and regarded the protection afforded Almonte contrary to the provisions of the Convention of London disclaiming to interfere in Mexican internal affairs. When Jurien and Saligny refused to accept these views, the Convention of London was suspended in Mexico.

The issues of negotiating with Juarez and the protection of Almonte caused the suspension of the Convention of London in Europe, as in Mexico. The British Government regarded the Juarez Government as the *de facto* government of Mexico and the introduction of Almonte into Mexico to spread propaganda in favor of Maximilian as a violation of the Convention of London. Napoleon and Eugenie should have seen the hopelessness of the situation, but they blamed Prim for the miscarriage of their plans. The Spanish General had merely frightened the Mexican monarchists, and they remained silent. The reports of Saligny, the assurances of Hidalgo, the letters of Mexican exiles, the private letters of the Prussian Chargé in Mexico, and a blind belief that the British Government would still reverse itself gave Napoleon and Eugenie hope that their plans might still be carried out. Contrary evidence and advice were ignored. Thouvenel's caution was regarded as unrealistic. Cowley's remarks were not considered seriously. The comments on the seriousness of the military situation by Fleury and Randon were rejected. Napoleon and Eugenie became obsessed by their illusions which they could not dismiss. They might still have had the chance to abandon the affair if the French troops had not been defeated before Puebla on 5 May 1862. That defeat by the Mexican republicans obliged France to continue in the name of *"l'honneur."* Disillusioned that Prim was not recalled as expected, Napoleon rejected all Spanish overtures in 1862 to renew joint tripartite intervention in Mexico. The attempt to obtain Spanish and British support for Maximilian's throne in 1861–1862 turned out to be a fiasco.

# Appendix A

*The British Convention Bondholders, 1842–1861*

On 15 October 1842, the British Minister to Mexico, Pakenham, signed a convention with Mexico for the payment of fifteen British claims. They amounted to $287,412.09, formed into a consolidated fund, to be retired, capital and 12 per cent interest thereupon, by 2 per cent of the custom duties of Vera Cruz and 1 per cent of those of Tampico.[1]

By 1851 Mexico had paid the "Convention Bondholders" $291,654.95, but since interest since 1842 amounted to $160,804.45, Mexico still owed $156,561.59. This balance still due the original fifteen claimants was included in the Doyle Convention of 4 December 1851, that also provided for the payment of other British claims recognized since 1842, so that a consolidated fund of $4,984,914.84 was established. A sinking fund of 5 per cent (to be raised to 6 per cent in 1857) was provided for the retirement of the bonds issued the claimants. Mexico promised to pay 3 per cent interest (to be raised to 4 per cent in 1857). To meet payments, Mexico mortgaged 12 per cent of all its custom receipts.[2]

Two days after Mexico signed the Doyle Convention, the "Padre Moran" Convention was concluded with Spain. $983,000 in Spanish claims were recognized. The other terms of the Spanish Convention were identical with those obtained by Doyle.[3] The following February a single Mexican custom

453

order set 12 per cent of custom receipts aside for both conventions.[4] Since each convention provided that such an order be considered as part of the convention itself, two custom orders should have been issued. Messrs. Martinez del Rio were the agents for both the British and Spanish Conventions. The Mexican custom order provided that 12 per cent of custom duties be made over to them, not 24 per cent, as was required for the two conventions. Martinez del Rio handed one-sixth of each assignment to the Padre Moran claimants and five-sixths to the British Convention Bondholders. As greater percentages of Mexican custom duties were mortgaged to the British bondholders in the following years, Martinez del Rio handed one-sixth of these assignments over to the Padre Moran claimants. As Wyke complained, when he discovered the tangle in 1861, the agents of the two conventions merged them into one, and ". . . Her Majesty's Government, this legation, and British ships of war, have been labouring on behalf not only of British, but of Spanish interests. . . ." It was not until 1861 that Martinez del Rio ". . . breathed a word . . ." about what they had done.[5] At that time they asked to know whether the latest increase of custom house assignments to the British Convention Bondholders also applied to the Padre Moran Convention.[6] For Wyke it was proof that Martinez del Rio always must have had doubts about their amalgamating the Spanish and British Conventions. Consequently, Wyke could not ". . . acquit Messrs. Martnez del Rio of great and culpable negligence." Wyke blamed the origin of the whole entanglement on the Mexican Government:

. . . the Order on the Custom-Houses was simply a piece of trickery on the part of the Mexican Government, nobody took the trouble to counteract it, and we alone have been the dupes, to our own prejudice, but to the profit of others.[7]

In less than a year after the signature of the Doyle Convention, Mexico was $124,622.87 in arrears. To pay this deficit, Doyle signed a "Sub-Convention" with Mexico on 27 November 1852. A further custom house assignment of 3 per cent was set aside solely to make up this deficit.[8] But thereafter, for practical purposes, the 12 per cent of the Doyle Convention became 15 per cent, for arrears continued to accumulate. While interest payments of $1,494,147.34 were properly, though not promptly, paid from 1852 until 1861, Mexico fell behind on capital (sinking fund) payments. Whereas $1,246,228.70 should have been paid between 1852 and 1857, Mexico only paid $810,634.84. After 1856 the semi-annual payments of $149,547.45 ceased completely. On 1 January 1861, Mexico was $1,482,426.01 in arrears on capital payments. But the $2,304,782.18 (interest and capital payments) paid the British Convention Bondholders from 1852 until 1861 only represented five-sixths of the sums received by Messrs. Martinez del Rio, who turned over $452,706.39 to the Padre Moran claimants during this period.[9]

In 1857, by the terms of the Doyle Convention, the interest on the "Convention Bonds" was raised from 3 per cent to 4 per cent, the sinking fund from 5 per cent to 6 per cent. The increase of 3 per cent of custom duties to make up arrears, provided for by Doyle's Sub-Convention, continued, and the British mortgage of Mexican custom duties stood at 15 per cent. But when Otway, Doyle's successor, signed a convention with Mexico on 10 August 1858, raising the interest rate from 4 per cent to 6 per cent, everyone was so confused that Article II of his convention provided that the British mortgage on Mexican customs would "remain" at 16 per cent.[10]

On 7 February 1859 Captain Dunlop, the British Senior Naval Officer in the Gulf of Mexico, reached an agreement with the Juarez Government whereby an additional 8 per cent of Mexican custom duties would be reserved to pay the arrears on the sinking fund.[11] The British mortgage on Mexican custom duties now stood at 24 per cent, but Dunlop's 8 per cent did not apply to custom duties collected from French vessels.[12]

In 1860 Juarez "occupied" over $300,000 in mortgaged custom duties.[13] In December 1860 Captain Dunlop's successor,

Captain Aldham, reached an agreement with Juarez for the repayment of these withheld funds. An additional 5 per cent of the custom duties of Vera Cruz and Tampico were reserved for these arrears, but customs on French cargoes were not exempted.[14]

According to the Doyle, Otway, Dunlop, and Aldham agreements and conventions, the mortgage on Mexican custom duties would revert to the original 12 per cent once arrears were paid. When he studied the history of these negotiations, Wyke observed that the arrangements after Doyle's original convention were for nothing. Wyke estimated that the annual Mexican import duties amounted to $7,000,000 to $8,000,000 a year. Even taking the low figure of $5,000,000, in no one year, Wyke insisted, was the original assignment of 12 per cent met.[15]

In August 1861 Wyke, having convinced himself that Messrs. Martinez del Rio were guilty of negligence, wrote Russell to suggest that Consul Glennie, the auditor of the British Convention fund, become its agent.[16] Shortly afterwards Messrs. Martinez del Rio resigned, whether through Wyke's influence is not clear from the British Minister's despatches. At a general meeting of the Convention Bondholders, to elect a new agent, it was agreed that Wyke be consulted. He hinted that Consul Glennie might be a suitable agent.[17] Mr. Edward Perry, a former partner of Martinez del Rio, however, canvassed for votes,[18] and on 14 October 1861 he was elected.[19] Thereupon Wyke wrote the Secretary of the Bondholders to protest Perry's election. The Bondholders should never have asked his advice, Wyke complained, if they were going to disregard his views. Mr. Perry, however, had no intention of waiving his election in favor of Mr. Glennie[20] and accepted the position of agent.[21] Finding that Wyke was opposed to his election, Perry offered to share the post of agent with Glennie. Wyke replied that this arrangement was impossible, owing to Perry's past connection with Martinez del Rio.[22] On 1 November 1861 Perry resigned, giving as a reason the desire not to disturb the harmony between the Bondholders and Her Majesty's Legation,[23] and then Glennie was elected.[24]

Russell did not entirely approve Wyke's proposals concerning the change of agents for the Convention Bondholders, but the instructions from London came too late to prevent Wyke's interference. In answer to Wyke's original proposal in August that Glennie replace Martinez del Rio, Russell observed that ". . . it seems to me that the moment is hardly favorable for making such a change."[25] A summary of Wyke's despatch relating his objections to Perry's election was made by someone in the British Foreign Office. On it Hammond, Under-Secretary of State, noted, "I should be inclined to let the parties interested appoint their own agent. . . ." Russell also made a note after Hammond's notation: "The communications with Mr. Perry must be very guarded, but we cannot assume the proper functions of the Bondholders."[26] These notes formed the basis of an instruction to Wyke, but it only reached him in February 1862, when the problem of an agent for the Convention Bondholders no longer was an issue in Mexico.[27]

# Appendix B

*The London Bondholders, 1823–1861*

In 1823 Mexico contracted a loan of $16,000,000 from the financial house of B. A. Goldschmidt & Co. of London at 5 per cent interest.[1] The following year another loan of $16,000,000 was obtained from Barclay, Richardson & Co., also of London, at 6 per cent interest.[2] For both loans Mexico pledged the whole of the revenues of the nation, in particular two special taxes[3] and one-third of maritime custom duties.[4]

Through these two loans, Mexico became liable for $32,000,000, but it only received $13,749,315,[5] of which $1,654,160 was delivered in the form of high-priced mititary goods.[6] The remaining $18,250,685, for which Mexico became liable but did not receive, were losses sustained in that the bonds issued by the financial houses were sold below par[7] and losses through commission charges in connection with floating the loans.[8] To the $18,000,000 that Mexico lost in the very act of negotiating the loans of 1823 and 1824 must be added the $315,000 Mexico lent Columbia in 1823, never repaid except for a small token payment,[9] and the $1,500,000 Mexico lost when Barclay, Richardson & Co. went into bankruptcy.[10] Thus Mexico, by the loans of 1823–1824, became indebted for $32,000,000, while only receiving a little more than $11,000,000.[11]

By 1837, through arrears of interest, Mexico's indebtedness

458

had risen from the original $32,000,000 to $43,679,620.46.[12] In that year the Mexican Government drew up a plan for the liquidation of the two debts of 1823 and 1824, half to be redeemed by lands in Texas, Chihuahua, New Mexico, and California.[13] The advantage was that Mexico would reduce by one half its indebtedness through land grants instead of cash. There was also a political motive. A Committee of Public Credit of the Mexican Chamber of Deputies, in a report on the history of the debts contracted in London, stated that it was hoped that ". . . in a short time the waste lands of New Mexico, California, and Sonora, would be peopled by an industrious and laborious race." This colonization would prevent the encroachments of the United States:

> This measure thus involved nothing less than the great political idea of the colonization of the frontiers, in order to prevent that separation of the territories of New Mexico, Texas, and Upper California, which was consummated in 1848.[14]

F. de Lizardi & Co. of London was commissioned to treat with the London Bondholders to make the conversion.[15] On 4 September 1837 a convention was concluded, approved by the Mexican Congress on 1 June 1839. The 5 per cent and 6 per cent loans were converted into one stock. The 5 per cent loan and its dividend (interest) coupons were accepted at par, the 6 per cent loan and its dividend coupons at $112\frac{1}{2}$ per cent, thus giving the latter bondholders a compensation ($12\frac{1}{2}$ per cent) of $2,560,100 for accepting a reduction of interest from 6 per cent to 5 per cent for the twelve years, 1837–1849, a loss of interest amounting to $2,457,540. The total debt of Mexico after the conversion of 1837 was to be capitalized at $46,239,720.46 ($43,679,620.46 plus $2,560,100 "compensation"). Half of this ($23,119,860.23) was to be converted into active bonds, paying 5 per cent interest (until 1849). The other half was to be converted into deferred bonds, which were not to bear interest until 1 October 1847, when 5 per cent interest would be paid. This suspension of interest saved Mexico

$10,114,930. These deferred bonds, during the ten years that they were to bear no interest, could be exchanged for uncultivated lands. Four acres would be granted for each pound sterling ($5.00) in deferred bonds. To make such transactions attractive, 5 per cent interest from 1837 until the time of the exchange of bonds for land was to be paid by Mexico on each deferred bond so exchanged.[16]

The conversion of 1837, had it been carried out as intended, would have given Mexico several advantages:

1. The conversion of the two stocks into one simplified accounts and payments.
2. The lowering of the rate of interest on the active bonds to 5 per cent and the suspension of interest on the deferred bonds saved Mexico $10,012,370.[17]
3. Mexico decreased its interest payments for the future, and consequently there were better prospects that there would be no defaults.
4. If the deferred bonds were exchanged for Mexican public lands, Mexico would be freed of one half of its obligations without paying them in cash. If settlers formed colonies on the Mexican frontiers, this, it was hoped, would prevent annexation by the United States.

The conversion of 1837 was not approved by the Mexican Congress until 1839, and in the interval the $\frac{1}{6}$ of the custom duties of Vera Cruz and Tampico, as provided for by the 1837 conversion agreement, was not set aside. No interest was paid in cash, but some certificates were given on the Mexican custom houses of Vera Cruz and Tampico.[18] To settle these defaults, Lizardi & Co. signed a convention with the Committee of Bondholders on 11 February 1842.[19] The Bondholders surrendered half of their coupons for four years, taking a loss of $2,311,980. The remaining interest was covered by custom house certificates already issued by the Mexican Government, non-interest bearing documents ("debentures") to be issued, and the promise of ready cash by increasing the amount of custom duties to be set aside in the custom houses of Vera

Cruz and Tampico from one-sixth to one-fifth. Adding the
$10,012,370 saved by Mexico in 1837 to the $2,311,980 in
dividend coupons surrendered by the Bondholders in 1842,
Mexico saved, and the Bondholders lost, $12,324,350.

The conversion agreement negotiated with the Bondholders
in 1837 provided for issues of active and deferred bonds in
equal amounts, totalling $46,239,720.46.[20] In view of the fact
that Lizardi & Co. issued bonds in excess of this figure, it is
important to determine just how much should have been
issued. On 10 April 1844 $46,027,284.81 $\frac{1}{2}$ of the old 5 per
cent and 6 per cent bonds were cancelled, and it was estimated
that $214,235.24 16/100 of bonds had not then been pre-
sented for conversion, making a total of $46,241,520.05 $\frac{2}{3}$.[21]
Other estimates of how much in bonds should have been issued
by Lizardi & Co. have varied from $46,235,000 to $46,240,000
as the correct amount of bonds that ought to have been issued,
to be divided equally into deferred and active bonds.[23]

Instead of $23,120,000 each in active and deferred bonds,
Lizardi & Co. received $27,500,000 of each category from and
signed by D. Augustin Iturbide, the Mexican Chargé d'Affaires
in London,[24] an excess of $8,756,000. The original decree of
4 April 1837 did not state the amount of Lizardi's commission,[25] and his financial house simply assumed "excess" bonds
would cover the commission. On 5 November 1842 Lizardi &
Co. made a clandestine issue of bonds in excess of those necessary for the conversion.[26] Rumors to this effect spread on the
London Stock Exchange the same month, and the Secretary
of the Stock Exchange asked Lizardi & Co. to furnish a statement in writing of the number of bonds ssued and their serial
numbers. Lizardi refused to furnish this information. Being
further pressed by Mr. Robinson, the Chairman of the Committee of Spanish–American Bondholders, Lizardi & Co. stated
that it had received $27,500,000 in active bonds and the same
amount in deferred bonds from Iturbide. Mr. Robinson protested this excess, but D. Manuel José Lizardi said he had acted
in accordance with instructions from the Mexican Govern-

ment and that the "excess" bonds represented his commission.[27]
The "instructions" Lizardi referred to actually arrived after
the issue of excess bonds. The monthly mail packet left Vera
Cruz early in November 1842 and carried two orders, both
dated 10 October 1842, from the Secretary of Finance to
Lizardi. He was granted a commission of $2\frac{1}{2}$ per cent on the
1837 conversion ($1,156,000) and 5 per cent on the arrange-
ment of 1842 ($231,195) concerning defaulted interest pay-
ments.[28] When Lizardi's claim for $133,520 for charges in
addition to commissions is admitted, Lizardi could expect
$1,520,715 from Mexico. This was a handsome profit when it
is recalled that Chili, Venezuela, and New Granada paid their
agents one half of 1 per cent for the conversion of their debts.[29]
The two orders of 10 October 1842 granted permission to
issue bonds to cover Lizardi's commissions, but no limit was
placed on how many bonds Lizardi was to issue. Since the
lowest price the Lizardi bonds brought on the London market
in 1842 and 1843 was a fraction above 31 per cent,[30] the sale
of no more than $4,905,532 of these bonds would have
sufficed to pay the $1,520,715 Mexico owed Lizardi & Co.
When the $458,250 of excess deferred bonds used by Lizardi
to meet an interest payment due the Bondholders in April
1843[31] is subtracted from the $8,756,000 of excess bonds issued,
$8,297,750 of excess bonds remain that Lizardi sold and for
which he refused to furnish the vouchers, showing the price at
which he sold the bonds.[32] In December 1842 Lizardi had the
audacity to inform the Mexican Government that it still owed
him $206,804 for his commissions and expenses.[33] Probably
in an attempt to pay this $206,804,[34] a Presidential Decree
dated 22 February 1843 stated that 5 per cent of the custom
duties of Vera Cruz, Tampico, San Blas, Mazatlan, and Guay-
mas should be assigned to Lizardi & Co. for the payment of
what was still due it for commissions and for advances that it
had or would make to the Mexican legations.[35] Up to 1844
Mexico also sent Lizardi $56,995 in cash payment of com-
missions.[36] A decree dated 28 July 1843 supplemented the one

of 22 February 1843 and declared that the 5 per cent referred
to in the earlier decree was to be applied to the payment of
dividends and the redemption of bonds which had or were
still to be issued by Lizardi & Co. The limit of these bonds was
placed at $1,000,000.[37] In pursuance of this decree, the Mexi-
can Ministry of Finance sent an order, dated 26 January 1844,
to Mr. Murphy, the Mexican diplomatic representative
in London, to direct him to sign bonds to the amount
of $1,000,000 to be issued by Lizardi & Co. Murphy
refused to sign the bonds, because he considered that Lizardi's
commissions were included in the issue of active bonds to the
amount of $27,500,000.[38] Murphy was then replaced by
Dr. José Luis Mora, who signed the $1,000,000 in bonds,
which Lizardi & Co. issued as active bonds in addition to the
$27,500,000 already issued.[39] These issues of bonds by Lizardi
& Co. in connection with its "commissions" largely nullified
the $10,012,370 gained by Mexico through the 1837 con-
version. To pay Lizardi's commission, Mexico increased its
indebtedness by $5,230,000 : $4,230,000 of excess active bonds
plus $1,000,000 in active bonds issued by virtue of the decree
of 28 July 1843. Mexico also paid over $50,000 in cash in
payment of these commissions. The $3,921,750 of unauthorized
excess deferred bonds simply was not recognized by Mexico
in the next conversion of 1846. The holders of these bonds
kept this worthless paper that Lizardi & Co. had sold them.[40]
As a Committee of Public Credit of the Mexican Chamber of
Deputies observed, in spite of the sacrifices on the part of the
London Bondholders, Mexico found its debt increased by each
conversion :

. . . between the Mexican Government and the Bondholders
there have always been interposed third parties, who have
reaped all the advantages, and who have profited by the
sacrifices of the creditors.[41]

But it was also admitted that part of the fault was in Mexican indifference and failure to demand strict accounting of the financial transactions:

> The business of the foreign debt . . . has been looked upon with so much apathy and indifference, that up to the present date (i.e., 1850) not a single account of the agents had been audited, nor have . . . books of account been opened for these transactions; all the data bearing on the subject being confusedly dispersed among the general accounts of various offices.[42]

The occasion of the April 1843 dividend of interest to the holders of active bonds resulted in the issue of more bonds by Lizardi & Co. Foreseeing that there might not be enough cash to pay this dividend, the Mexican Government, by an order of 22 February 1843, instructed Lizardi & Co. that, if it had insufficient funds, it was to pay half of this dividend in cash, the other half by converting "deferred" into "active" bonds. Instead Lizardi paid $\frac{1}{3}$ of the dividend in cash, the remaining $458,250 by converting "excess" deferred bonds to that amount into active bonds. In July 1843 the Mexican Government approved this transaction, expressed surprise that Lizardi & Co. had disobeyed the order of 22 February 1843, and ordered that in the future all dividend payments should be made in cash.[43]

On 15 December 1843 the Mexican Government issued a law stating what it recognized as its debt to the London Bondholders.[44] Except for "excess" deferred bonds, all the bond issues of Lizardi & Co. were legalized:

| | | |
|---|---|---|
| Active bonds | $27,500,000 | ($23,120,000 for the 1837 conversion, plus $4,380,000 for Lizardi't commissions and expenses) |
| Deferred bonds rendered active | 458,250 | (to pay $\frac{2}{3}$ of April 1843 dividend) |
| Debentures | 2,495,480 | (non-interest paper issued to meet various dividend payments) |

Deferred bonds    23,120,000    (thus $3,921,750 of "excess"
                                deferred bonds were not recog-
                                nized)

Active bonds in                 (issued for Lizardi's commis-
virtue of law of                sions and advances made or to
28 July 1843       1,000,000    be made by Lizardi to Mexican
                                legations)

In December 1844 there was a change of government in
Mexico, and on 5 April 1845 Lizardi & Co. was relieved as
financial agent of Mexico and replaced by Schneider & Co.
Lizardi & Co., however, would not hand over papers and funds
it held, giving as a reason that Mexico owed the company
money. Thereupon the Committee of Bondholders started
legal proceedings. Then Lizardi settled out of court, with the
agreement that Schneider & Co. was to accept bills to the
amount of $328,255, being the proceeds of the customs of
Vera Cruz and Tampico which had come into the possession
of Lizardi & Co.[45] When Schneider & Co. demanded the
$3,921,750 of "unauthorized" "excess" deferred bonds, Lizardi
refused to produce them, even when Schneider & Co.'s demand
was supported by an order of the Mexican Minister of Finance,
dated 27 June 1846.[46] Nothing more came of it. The 1846
conversion did not recognize these bonds. At least $1,263,000
of these bonds had been sold by then by Lizardi & Co., for
holders of deferred bonds to that amount were then refused
the conversion of their bonds, because the amount accepted by
Mexico as valid ($23,120,000) had already been converted.
Just how many excess deferred bonds were sold by Lizardi is
not known.[47]

The conversion of 1837 was followed by Mexican defaults
in dividend payments, and this difficulty was aggrivated by
disputes, difficulties, and obstacles raised by Lizardi & Co. On
1 October 1847 the deferred bonds were to start bearing 5
per cent interest (none, apparently, were exchanged for Mexican public lands), and it was necessary that a new arrangement

be reached between Mexico and the London Bondholders so that the accumulation of dividend arrears would not accelerate with the added interest burden. The new arrangement was a conversion agreed upon in 1846. Mexican indebtedness was recognized at $51,208,250.[48] Both the Mexican and Bondholder versions of this conversion agree that in 1846, before the conversion, the London Bondholders held, and Mexico was in debt for, the following sums of bonds issued by Lizardi & Co.:

| | |
|---|---|
| Active bonds | $27,958,250[49] |
| Deferred bonds | $23,120,000[50] |

According to Mexican statistics there were $2,495,000 in debentures issued in lieu of interest,[51] $2,495,480 according to the statistics of the London Bondholders.[52] The $2,495,480 is probably the correct figure, as the Bondholders admitted receiving new bonds of the 1846 conversion for debentures to this amount. By the conversion the active bonds were exchanged at 90 per cent of par, the deferred bonds and debentures at 60 per cent of par.[53] Consequently the Bondholders received new bonds, totalling $40,531,713 and sustained losses of $13,042,017 through this conversion.[54] The Bondholders claimed they also lost $5,500,000 of dividend arrears on the active bonds.[55] The Mexicans, however claimed the interest owed was only $2,466,345 and that the net gain by Mexico through the conversion was $4,811,826.[56] Subtracting the $40,531,713 of new stock issued the London Bondholders from the new capitalization of the Mexican foreign debt of $51,208,250 still leaves over $10,000,000 in bonds unaccounted for. Something over this amount was issued by Mexico in bonds to Manning & Mackintosh & Co. for transactions relative to the conversion. Although this company gave Mexico various bonds and paper in return, the middle man again made a huge profit of almost $5,000,000.[57] The $3,921,750 of Lizardi's excess deferred bonds was not recognized, and holders of deferred bonds who presented their bonds for conversion after the recognized total of $23,120,000 had been converted — and there was no way to differentiate genuine from "excess" bonds — found that they held bonds that could not be converted or sold. Years later they were still protesting to the British Foreign Office.[58]

The new bonds authorized by the 1846 conversion were to bear 5 per cent interest, to be paid semi-annually. In addition $500,000 was to be paid annually by Mexico to retire the bonds. The funds to make these payments were to come from the Mexican tobacco revenue, the duty on the exportation of silver from Mexico, and 20 per cent of the custom duties of Vera Cruz and Tampico.[59]

From 1846 to 1848 Mexico was at war withe United States and made no dividend payments to the London Bondholders.[60] At the end of the war Mexico received an indemnity from the United States for the cession of territory, and the Chairman of the Committee of Bondholders requested that part of the indemnity be used to pay dividend arrears. The Bondholders took the view that the land ceded by Mexico to the United States (for which the indemnity was granted) really belonged to the Bondholders in virtue of the 1837 conversion agreement. Consequently the Bondholders had a right to part of the indemnity Mexico received from the United States.[61] The Mexico reply was that no part of the American indemnity would be used to pay the Bondholders. Whatever claims the Bondholders had had to Mexican territory in virtue of the 1837 conversion, the Mexicans insisted, were renounced through the conversion of 1846.[62] Continued negotiations, however, led to a Mexican law of 14 October 1850, accepted by the Bondholders on 23 December 1850, providing for a new conversion of bonds.[63]

The 1850 arrangement provided that the Mexican debt should remain capitalized, as by the 1846 conversion, at $51,208,250. The Mexicans apparently learned their lesson from the excess bond issues of Lizardi, for specific provision was made that no bonds in excess of this figure should be issued.[64] Furthermore, Mexico agreed to the new conversion only when it was agreed that it would pay nothing for commissions or brokerage charges connected with the conversion. Mexico set $15,000 as the annual limit of its expenses for the distribution of dividends to the Bondholders in the future. The interest rate was reduced from 5 per cent to 3 per cent. The Bondholders calculated that this was equivalent to a reduction of principal to the amount of $20,483,300.[65] They accepted this interest reduction in the hope that the semi-annual interest payments of $768,123.75 would be ". . . made with *unfailing punctuality.* . . ." the first of each January and July.[66] There was some foundation for this hope in that Mexico promised to set aside considerable custom duties for the payment of the 3 per cent interest : 25 per cent of the import duties of its maritime and frontier custom houses, 75 per cent of export duties of its Pacific ports, and 5 per cent of its export duties in its Gulf ports. To facilitate the payment of these duties to the Bondholders, they were permitted to appoint agents to Mexican ports to receive these funds. If these duties were insufficient to meet interest payments, Mexico promised to make up any deficiency from other national revenues. Should the custom duties, on the contrary, provide a surplus, it was to be applied to form a sinking fund to retire the bonds. This arrangement concerning a sinking fund would cease in 1857, when Mexico was to start providing $250,000 annually for the retirement of the bonds.[67] The agreement of 1850 further provided that all arrears of interest — Mexico had made no interest payments since the 1846 conversion — were considered paid up to date. Mexico promised to pay $2,500,000 of the American indemnity to the Bondholders if they accepted the new arrangement. The sundry assets given by Mexico, however, when realized, left the Bondholders with a loss of interest amounting to $6,452,240.[68]

The Bondholders calculated that they lost $26,935,540 by the 1850 conversion.[69] In 1852 Payno, the Mexican Minister of Finance, in a *comte rendu,* calculated the advantages to Mexico at $25,581,570. The difference between this figure and the one of the Bondholders resulted from Payno's estimating some of the assets Mexico gave the Bondholders at a higher value than was realized.[70] In return for these sacrifices the Bondholders hoped the custom duties pledged them would enable Mexico to meet its interest payments promptly. The Bondholders also considered the reduction of interest from 5 per cent to 3 per cent as merely temporary. Furthermore, they somewhat naïvely hoped that means would be found to compensate this concession through ". . . gratuitous grants of the public lands of the Republic."[71] They still believed they had a claim to Mexican public lands by the 1837 conversion agreement, even though Mexico claimed the 1846 conversion nullified such claims.

The first six semi-annual dividend payments of $768,123.75 each (1 July 1851 through 1 January 1854) were paid by Mexico with an ever-increasing tardiness, so that the last of these dividends was paid in full by a payment made by Mexico on 10 October 1861.[72] The 1 January 1854 dividend was the last dividend paid by Mexico by the time of the tripartite intervention in 1861. Nor were the $250,000 annual sinking fund payments, that were to start in 1857, ever made. The capitalization of Mexico's debt to the London Bondholders, therefore, remained at $51,208,250. The arrears of dividends and sinking fund payments just before and after the signing of the Tripartite Convention of London of 31 October 1861 were as follows:

| | | |
|---|---|---|
| Dividend arrears | $11,829,105.75[73] | $12,289,980.00[75] |
| Sinking fund arrears | 1,000,000.00[74] | 1,250,000.00[76] |
| Total | $12,829,105.75 | $13,539,980.00 |

While Mexico was falling into arrears, the London Bondholders withdrew from the Committee of Spanish–American Bondholders and formed their own Committee of Mexican Bondholders, under the chairmanship of William P. Robertson.[77] This Committee held general meetings at the London Tavern and drew up reports of how much Mexico was in arrears. At the same time they estimated how much Mexico was receiving in custom duties. In 1854 the Bondholders estimated that their share of Mexican custom duties could produce $2\frac{3}{8}$ per cent interest ". . . IF IT WAS ONLY COLLECTED, ACCOUNTED FOR, AND REMITTED (*sic*)."[78] Two years later they estimated that their share of Mexican custom duties was more than enough to pay the 3 per cent dividend.[79] These reports, stating how much Mexico was in arrears, and an occasional memorandum of statistics,[80] were sent to the British Foreign Office. The policy of the British Government, however, was to consider the claims of the London Bondholders as private transactions that could not be supported officially. In 1854 Lord Malmesbury drew up a memorandum that summarized past views of the British Government and which substantially remained those of the British Government in the following years:

> The only interference of Her Majesty's Government on behalf of the Bondholders has ben semi-official : that is to say, Her Majesty's Government have never supported their claims on the ground of Right, because the contracts having been considered private transactions between Individuals and the Mexican and other Governments. Her Majesty's Government have held that they ought not to press them under international law. Short of this, however every assistance has been given to the Bondholders, but upon one occasion (in 1848) Lord Palmerston wrote a despatch to the effect that if the Spanish American Governments did not soon make arrangements with their Bondholders, the Public voice in this country would force Her Majesty's Government to take more active steps than before to get the matter settled.[81]

When Lord Palmerston became Prime Minister in 1859, it might be added, the British Foreign Office did not revert to his 1848 position. In July 1862 the Under-Secretary of State for Foreign Affairs stated in the House of Commons that, when persons chose to lend their money to foreign countries, ". . . they did so at their own risk."[82]

The London Bondholders had two chief proposals in the

1850's to obtain their dividends from Mexico with the "semi-official" aid of the British Foreign Office. One proposal was to obtain title to Mexican public lands. The other was to empower the "agents" permitted by the 1850 agreement as "interventors" to collect custom duties due the Bondholders.

The idea of receiving Mexican public lands in payment of what was owed the Bondholders seems to have originated with the 1837 conversion plan of exchanging deferred bonds for such lands. In 1848 the Bondholders insisted they had a right to compensation for territory ceded by Mexico to the United States, but Mexico denied the existence of such a right. In 1857 a plan to pay the Bondholders with Mexican waste lands was made known to the British Foreign Office, which offered no objection to the project.[83] Nothing came of the scheme. The next year Mr. Otway, the British Minister to Mexico, reported that there was no hope for the payment of the overdue interest owed the Bondholders, unless Mexican monastic property were nationalized :

> Certainly if that property is to be confiscated, I do not see how they could apply part of it to a better purpose than paying off their Foreign Creditors and thus clearing off all incumbrances of their revenue.

On the back of this despatch Lord Malmesbury, the British Foreign Secretary, wrote that the British Government ". . . cannot act officially in this matter but Mr. Otway can give his advice and employ his personal influence."[84]

Provision was made by the 1850 conversion agreement for agents of the Bondholders to receive the appropriate percentage of Mexican custom duties for the Bondholders. By an order of 1852 of the Mexican Minister of Finance to the Collectors of Custom Duties, they were directed to render monthly accounts of the produce of the revenues assigned the Bondholders.[85] No accounts, however, were furnished the Bondholders.[86] Further orders from the Mexican Government make it clear that the Custom Collectors misappropriated the funds due the Bond-

holders. An order of 1854 to all Mexican Custom Houses stated
that no funds belonging to the London Bondholders ". . . be
again touched. . . ." no matter what the emergency.[87] An order
two years later made all Mexican public officers, civil and
military, personally responsible for laying hands on the funds
of the Bondholders.[88] The agents of the Bondholders had so
little authority that their very existence was called into question, and a decree of 23 January 1857 was necessary to
reaffirm the right of the Bondholders to appoint such agents
to receive custom revenues for the Bondholders.[89] In 1858 Mr.
Robertson, the Chairman of the Bondholders, proposed to the
British Foreign Office that the collection of custom duties due
the Bondholders be transferred to them by agents appointed
under the supervision of the British Consuls in Mexico.[90] The
Foreign Office approved the plan,[91] and Lord Malmesbury
instructed Mr. Otway to support the appointment of "Interventors." They would receive bills, which the Collectors of
Customs drew on the importers, for the payment of that
portion of duties allowed the Bondholders. These bills would
be converted into cash and handed over to the Consuls,
". . . so as not to pass through the hands of the Mexican
Authorities at all." Lord Malmesbury suggested that the Interventors might also act for the "Convention Bondholders."[92]
But by the end Mr. Otway reported that there was no hope
of any arrangement in favor of the Bondholders.[93]

So long as the claims of the London Bondholders were based
on agreements with the Mexican Government, its decrees and
orders, and even the laws passed by Mexican legislatures, the
British Government did not consider the claims of the Bondholders as founded upon International Law. If these claims,
however, were recognized by a convention between Mexico
and Great Britain, duly ratified by both contracting parties,
those claims would be grounded in an international instrument
recognized by International Law. The London Bondholders
almost accomplished such a transformation of the nature of
their claims. In February 1859, when a Civil War was in

process between Conservatves and Liberals in Mexico, Captain Dunlop, the British Senior Naval Officer in the Gulf of Mexico, arrived at an agreement with the Liberals concerning the claims of the Convention and London Bondholders. The right of the London Bondholders to 25 per cent of Mexican import duties was recognized. Article 12 of the agreement stated that if the Liberals should be recognized diplomatically by foreign Powers (as did happen in 1861), then the articles of the Dunlop agreement should form the basis of a Diplomatic Convention.[94] Another agreement, made in December 1860 by Captain Aldham, Dunlop's successor, with the yet unrecognized Liberals promised to abide by the Dunlop agreement. Furthermore, the Liberals agreed to set aside 5 per cent of the import duties of Vera Cruz and Tampico to pay arrears of interest due the London Bondholders.[95] The only loophole of the Dunlop and Aldham agreements was that they were not conventions, but merely contained a promise to convert the terms of the Dunlop agreement into a convention. The Bondholders did not fail to perceive the implications. At a general meeting on 4 July 1861 they passed a resolution that an international convention contemplated by Article 10 of the Dunlop agreement be made in such a manner as ". . . to make it in future impossible for the Mexican government to escape from their engagements."[96] Lord Russell, the Foreign Secretary in 1861, in his initial instructions to Sir Charles Wyke, the British Minister to Mexico, had not foreseen that Mexco would cause any difficulties with regard to this technicality. Lord Russell instructed Wyke that, through the Dunlop and Aldham agreements, the claims of the London Bondholders had ". . . acquired the character of international obligations. . . ." Consequently, Wyke was to insist on punctual fulfilment of the obligations thus contracted.[97] Russell, therefore, counted on the good faith of the Mexican Government. But on 29 July 1861 the British Foreign Office received Wyke's report that Mexico had suspended payments to the London Bondholders altogether and refused to recognize the Dunlop and Aldham agreements as international obligations.[98] Only three days before the Foreign Office had received a copy of the resolution of the Bondholders concerning Article 10 of the Dunlop agreement.[99]

In addition to interest and sinking fund arrears, the London Bondholders had a claim against Mexico for $660,000 that they had stored in the British Legation in Mexico City and which was seized on 17 November 1860 by the Conservatives in the last days of the Civil War.[100] The Bondholders protested this seizure of their $660,000 as robbery of ". . . *British property*."[101] Lord Russell accepted this view and instructed his Minister to Mexico to recover the money for the London Bondholders.[102]

# Appendix C

*Morny, Saligny, and the Jecker Bonds*

DURING THE FRANCO–PRUSSIAN WAR VARIOUS PRIVATE PAPERS
and documents of Napoleon III were found in the Tuileries.
Among these was a letter from J. B. Jecker to Conti, the "Chef
du Cabinet de l'Empereur," dated 8 December 1869.[1] The
overwhelming majority of historians who have studied this
letter[2] have given credence to the following paragraphs of
Jecker's letter:

> Without doubt you do not know that I had as an associate
> in this affair the Duke de Morny, who had engaged himself
> for 30 per cent of the profits of this affair to make it respected
> and paid by the Mexican Government, as it had been made
> in the beginning. About this there is a voluminous correspon-
> dence exchanged with his agent, M. de Marpon.
>
> In January 1861, I was sought out in Mexico City on behalf
> of these gentlemen to treat of this affair.
>
> This arrangement was made when my house already found
> itself in liquidation, so that all who considered it concerned
> themselves exclusively with it.
>
> As soon as this arrangement was concluded, I was perfectly
> supported by the French Government and its Legation in
> Mexico. The latter had even assured my creditors, in the
> name of France, that they would be completely paid, and
> sent some very sharp notes to the Mexican Government on
> the execution of my contract with it, to the extent that the
> ultimatum of 1862 demanded the execution, pure and simple,
> of the decrees.

Although Jecker threatened, in this letter, to reveal all he knew ". . . in order not to see . . ." himself ". . . thrown in prison for debts . . ." if he received no aid from the French Government, he never did so. According to a letter Conti wrote the *Journal de Bruxelles* on 6 October 1870, Jecker presented his letter personally and never pressed the French Government after being refused on that occasion :

> I only have a word to say about the letter of M. Jecker. This gentleman brought it to me himself, and, after having looked at it in his presence and seeing that it contained a demand for money, under threat, if refused, to release slanderous documents, I threatened him in turn to hand him over to justice as guilty of the offense *of extortion,* and invited him to leave my office. I never saw him since.

That he never published does not necessarily prove that Jecker's assertions were false. He may have regarded such a step as a last resort, and before he could take it, he was shot during the Commune uprising in Paris on 26 May 1871.[4]

Independent evidence confirms Jecker's assertions, except that he entered into the deal with Morny. Marpon was an agent of Morny.[5] Saligny supported the Jecker bonds throughout 1861[6] and prepared the ultimatum in 1862 to which Jecker referred.[7] In 1861 and 1862 Morny interested himself in real estate transactions in Mexico.[8] One biographer of Morny, however, questions the truth of Jecker's claim about the "deal" with Morny and points out that Jecker was an interested witness who tried to justify himself in a *private* letter at a time when Morny was already dead.[9] One historian was told by Morny's son, as might be expected when the Mexican Empire had fallen to pieces, that his father was strongly opposed to the Mexican Expedition, which he considered ill-advized.[10] In 1903, when she was in her late seventies, Eugenie recalled that the Jecker bonds were not the main reason for the Mexican Expedition, but she did not specifically deny that Morny and Jecker entered into the arrangement Jecker outlned in his letter of 1869 :

As for the allegation that the Mexican expedition was undertaken at his (i.e., Morny's) prompting and for base motives, that is a calumny of which he should be entirely cleared. The improper influence of the Jecker bonds counted for nothing in our intervention in Mexico; it merely hooked itself on, exactly as you will always find villanies creeping into the noblest enterprises. Do you suppose that there was nothing but piety in the crusades?[11]

Maximilian has also added to the confusion. In December 1865 he wrote Napoleon III :

If other measures have burdened the budget and have not always merited approval, where does the insistence come from that has morally compelled me to make a difficult arrangement with Jecker, an arrangement to which I only meekly agreed, because I thought to render a service to my best friend, the Emperor Napoleon?[12]

Professor Case believes that this letter implicates Napoleon III himself in the Jecker affair.[13] Just how is not clear from Maximilian's letter.

Ten letters of August and September 1862 to Jecker from his relatives and friends in Europe were intercepted and published by the Mexican Government.[14] Some historians have believed that these letters "speak for themselves."[15] Although circumstantial evidence[16] points to Morny as "our friend," "the new duke," "the influence that sustains our business," and "so great a protection," he is not conclusively identified by these phrases.

It has been asserted that Saligny was a protegé of Morny and was appointed to the Mexican post through the Duke's influence.[17] Schefer, who consulted the archives of the French Ministry of Foreign Affairs, concludes that merely administrative reasons could explain Saligny's appointment,[18] but that ". . . this does not exclude the hypothesis of powerful recommendations."[19] A mystery, then, still surrounds Saligny. He interested himself in the Jecker bonds before leaving France for Mexico and even told Jecker's brother-in-law, Xavier Elsesser, that the bonds would probably be respected.[20] Saligny also called on one Hottinguer, one of Jecker's chief creditors, who said Jecker was ". . . the most honest man that I have met in business affairs."[21]

Before receiving Thouvenel's instructions of 6 March 1861 to support the Jecker bonds, Saligny demanded that the Mexican Government respect them.[22] Saligny's motives are not clear. It has been asserted, without proof, that he himself may have been a holder of Jecker bonds.[23] He may have been acting under orders from Morny, but this presupposes the Jecker–Morny deal of January, which is problematical. Saligny may even have thought the Jecker bonds, usurous as they were, were a means indirectly to lower the high Mexican tariff. By the decrees providing for the issue of the bonds, they were to be respected as part paymnt of tariff duties, and Saligny told Elsesser that this was one of the advantages of the bonds.[24] Another interpretation is that Saligny used the bonds as a means to bring about a French intervention in Mexico. This view is reinforced by an alleged statement Saligny made to Ernest Louet, the Paymaster of the French Expedition. Supposedly Saligny said, "My only merit is in having divined the intention of the Emperor to intervene in Mexico and having rendered the intervention necessary."[25] Sara Yorke Stevenson also records that Saligny said to a friend of hers that his great merit ". . . was to have understood the wishes of the Emperor, and to have precipitated events so as to make the intervention a necessity."[26] Schefer points out that this boast should not be interpreted to imply that Saligny penetrated the ideas of the Emperor and systematically provoked complications sufficient to justify an intervention. As proof Schefer cites Saligny's initial instructions of 30 May 1860 and comments, "Not a word about the establishment of a monarchy."[27] Nor was there a word about the Jecker bonds. It was not until June 1861 that the French Government decided to send naval forces to Mexico.[28] And it was not until 29 July 1861 that Thouvenel wrote Saligny a despatch that French naval forces had been instructed to contact him.[29] Saligny probably received this despatch at the beginning of September, when Wyke received a despatch from Russell dated 31 July.[30] There was nothing to indicate that these naval forces were to be employed for anything other than a show of force to back up Saligny's demands of redress, as he himself requested. The next instructions from Thouvenel were dated 5 September, and Saligny received them in the evening of 30 October.[31] At this time Saligny also learned of an impending Anglo–French intervention in Mexico.[32] There was, therefore, little "divining" necessary to know that Napoleon wanted to intervene in Mexico. Merely following Thouvenel's instructions of 5 September, Saligny presented an ultimatum, which Mexico rejected.[33] Later, when he thought the monarchy scheme was sure of fulfilment, he exaggerated his role in initiating the intervention and boasted he had "precipitated" events.

The fact remains, however, that as early as 6 March 1861 Thouvenel instructed Saligny to support the Jecker bonds.[34] By sheer guesswork that historical romance, *Phantom Crown: The Story of Maximilian and Carlota of Mexico*, may have hit upon the truth. Mrs. Harding, its author, claims that by means of the Jecker bonds ". . . France held suddenly a weapon in her fist which could one day be waved grimly over the struggling Aztec Republic."[35] In July 1861, before the news of the Mexican financial law of 17 July had reached Europe, Thouvenel told an agent of the Mexican Government that France had decided upon a severe coercion to have the bonds respected.[36] The news of the financial law suspending payments on Mexico's funded debts reached France and England at the end of August.[37] The French Governmetn soon learned that this law was viewed as sufficient reason by Great Britain to intervene in Mexico.[38] In September and October, Great Britain, France, and Spain carried on negotiations for a joint intervention, culminating in the Tripartite Convention of London of 31 October 1861.[39] Now the conditions that Napoleon always thought necessary for the establishment of a monarchy

in Mexico were fulfilled. Great Britain was acting with
France. The United States, with its Civil War, could create
few obstacles, and the financial law of 17 July was the "pretext."[40] Napoleon, however, feared that the Mexican Government would accept the demands of the intervening powers.
Consequently, once the allied expeditionary forces were in
Mexico, Saligny demanded that Mexico respect the Jecker
bonds in the hope that Mexico would refuse and that France
would have a pretext to remain in Mexico.[41] The proof of this
"pretext" thesis comes directly from Napoleon, as reported by
the British Ambassador to Paris n a confidential despatch
apparently hitherto overlooked.[42] On 8 March 1862 Lord
Cowley complained to Napoleon of the Jecker bonds and what
the British Government considered a very high figure for other
French claims. Cowley ". . . intimated a hope that His Majesty
would not encourage these claims, but His Majesty avowed,
that it was he who had desired they should be made excessive
(*aussi vives que possible* (*sic*))." Napoleon continued that it
was ". . . necessary to begin with high terms . . . (*il fallait commencer par le gros bout* (*sic*)) or otherwise the Government of
Juarez would at once have accepted the conditions proposed,
and the Allies having no further excuse to remain, must have
taken their departure. . . ."[43]

In addition to the intercepted correspondence of 1862,
Jecker's letter of 1869, and Saligny's "boast," there is a literature of anecdotes and court gossip about Jecker that is interesting, but picturesque rather than authentic. In postumous
memoirs Maxine Du Camp asserts:

> Empress Eugenie, very hare-brained, wasteful, spending money
> foolishly for her dresses, in debt to her tradesmen, was, in
> spite of the liberality of the Emperor, always without money,
> something Morny did not ignore. He brought six millions in
> Jecker bonds to the Empress that the Crédit Mobilier,
> governed by Emile and Isaac Pereire, discounted for four
> million, five hundred thousand francs that were passed into
> "Profits and Losses." The debts of the Empress were paid and
> Morny had, near the ear of the Emperor, an ally who backed

the expedition so well that it was decided on and ended as everyone knows.[44]

Albert Vandam, the famous "Englishman in Paris," claims that Morny's attitude toward the Mexican Expedition changed when he and Walewski both wanted the same opera box, and Morny got it. The affair supposedly came up before Napoleon III, with the result that Morny and Walewski became exasperated with each other:

> In spite of his undoubted interest in the Jecker scheme, or probably because it had yielded all it was likely to yield, De Morny had of late been on the side of Walewski, who strongly counselled the withdrawal of the French troops. But the moment the incident of the opera-box cropped up, there was a change of front on his part. He became an ardent partisan for continuing the campaign, systematically siding against Walewski in everything, and tacitly avoiding any attempt of the latter to draw him into conversation.[45]

Vandam, however, merely reported hearsay and apparently did not have any first-hand information. The same seems to be true of the account of the Confederate agent, John Slidell:

> The creditor (i.e., Jecker) came to Paris and laid his affair before the Duc de Morny, who perceived great political and commercial possibilities in the business. Jecker became a French subject and the Emperor, who had long had his eye on Mexico, needed little inducement to espouse his interests. That country was already giving umbrage to England and Spain by shooting their subjects and not paying their debts and this led to the tripartite convention of 1861, and the despatch of an allied force to teach the Mexicans to mend their ways.[46]

Jecker's change of citizenship as proof of an intrigue was popularized by Comte Emile de Keraltry. J. B. Jecker was born in Porrentray in the Swiss Canton of Berne in 1816, a year too late to possess French citizenship, for until the Treaties of 1815 the area belonged to France. Thus an older brother,

Louis Jecker, born in 1804, was a French citizen, whereas Jean Baptiste was Swiss.[47] Keraltry discovered that the Swiss Consul General informed the Mexican Minister of Foreign Relations on 8 February 1862 that ordinarily, in case of need, Swiss citizens in Mexico had the diplomatic protection of the United States. What amazed Keraltry was that shortly afterward, on 26 March 1862, J. B. Jecer was naturalized as a French citizen.[48] Jecker's naturalization came a little less than three weeks after Napoleon told Cowley that the Jecker bonds were an "excuse." The naturalization, therefore, probably was only to legitimize Jecker as a French excuse.

Although most historians have accepted Jecker's assertion of a deal with Morny and given the Jecker bonds as an important cause of the French intervention in Mexico,[49] a few historians have deprecated the bonds as a motive for the intervention. Albert Guerard believes that the "deal" actually was made, but that it was not the origin of the Mexican affair, and only acted in a negative way by preventing Morny ". . . from using his restraining hand."[50] Daniel Dawson's opinion is :

> . . . it would . . . be wrong to infer that this sordid financial intrigue was the true propulsive force which set in motion the Mexican enterprise. The more we learn of the history of the Second Empire and of the character of the Emperor Napoleon the more does it seem that the bewitching, the irresistable lure was that grandiose vision of a "regenerated" Central America which Louis Napoleon first saw in the prison cell at Ham. That the Jecker bonds played their part there can, we think, be but little doubt; but they probably weighed in the scales only as an added inducement.[51]

Dawson, however, believes that Morny had a connection with Jecker :

> Though there is much which remains obscure concerning their proceedings, and even some question as to their identity, yet enough is known to make it beyond reasonable doubt that somewhere deep down, somewhere very nearly at the bottom of the Mexican affair there were the bonds of the Jecker loan

and the scheming agile brains of M. de Morny and his gambling Parisian friends.[52]

Whether Morny urged Napoleon and Eugenie to undertake the Mexican expedition, Dawson admits, is an open question :

> . . . how far M. de Saligny's arguments as to the desirability of intervention were reinforced and elaborated at the French Court by M. de Morny himself, it is not possible to say : though there can be no doubt but that from this time on it became an object of French policy to obtain for the Jecker bank the fifteen millions.[53]

Guerard and Dawson, while not questioning Morny's connection with Jecker, only depreciate the Jecker bonds as an important motive in Napoleon's Mexican policy. Morny's biographers, not able to find conclusive evidence either to rehabilitate or to defame him, have formulated theories to his discredit. Marcel Boulenger poses the question that Morny may have promised to support Jecker, all the while knowing that there was little hope. Morny may have taken a gambler's chance : he had nothing to lose if the scheme failed.[54] Robert Christophe believes that Morny urged an expedition be sent to Mexico to make a profit for himself and beat a retreat when he saw the folly of it.[55] Maristan Chapman claims that Morny became acquainted with Jecker when he had difficulties about his naturalization and was referred to the Duke. Morny then formed a syndicate to buy the Jecker bonds and ". . . proceeded to try to make them worth something." Morny, Chapman asserts, was against the expedition, but Eugenie appealed to him to support it. Morny, ". . . seeing Napoleon was determined to go on with the scheme, consented."[56]

Stripped of conjecture, guesswork, unfounded accusations, and court gossip, very little documentary evidence remains about a connection between J. B. Jecker and Morny. That they entered a deal in January 1861 is based on the testimony of a single, interested witness, Jecker himself, in his letter to Conti of 1869. No independent corroboration of this connection has ever been discovered, and it remains an open question. The ten intercepted letters of 1862 contain circumstantial evidence of a connection between the Jecker bonds and Morny, but the weakness of such evidence is basic in external criticism.

Whether Saligny was a protegé of Morny, obtained the Mexican post through the Duke's influence, and precipitated the intervention are also open questions. They are, in part, corrolaries to the Jecker–Morny thesis of a deal. A study of chronology, however, appears to indicate that Saligny's "boast," if he did make it, merely applies to his presentation of an ultimatum in November 1861 in accordance with Thouvenel's instructions of September 1861. It is difficult to imagine how Saligny "divined" Napoleon's intention to intervene in Mexico before Napoleon himself made that decision. Saligny's interest in the bonds before he left France and his support of them in Mexico before receiving instructions to do so from Thouvenel remain a mystery, but a plausible reason France supported the bonds is that they served as a pretext to intervene in Mexico. Once the expeditionary forces arrived there, Napoleon III admitted that the bonds were an "excuse" to keep his troops there.

# Appendix D

*Spanish Claims Against Mexico, 1847–1861*

IN 1821 MEXICO GAINED ITS INDEPENDENCE FROM SPAIN. Three years later Mexico passed a statute promising to pay all the debts contracted by the Spanish viceregal governments in Mexico until 17 September 1810.[1] The Spanish citizens, however, who held the titles of this pre-independence internal debt of Mexico could not expect Spanish diplomatic support until 1836, when Spain reluctantly recognized Mexican independence,[2] after an unsuccessful attempt in 1829 to recover the conquests of Cortez.[3] The Treaty of Madrid, establishing diplomatic relations between Mexico and Spain, provided that Mexico assume all the viceregal debts of the revolutionary period in Spanish hands.[4] But it was not until 17 July 1847 that Mexico concluded a treaty with Spain, whereby the amount of public indebtedness of the Spanish Viceroys until 17 September 1810 was fixed at $6,633,000.[5] This treaty was very unpopular in Mexico because it converted an internal debt into a foreign and privileged one, to the prejudice of other creditors. Mexicans also objected to the provision granting the Spanish Minister to Mexico the right to name the personnel to administer a fund established to cover future Spanish claims against Mexico. Some Mexicans doubted the legality of the treaty, because it was negotiated without the consent of Congress. In response to all these objections to the treaty, Mexico didn't put it into operation.[6]

In November 1851 Fernando Ramirez, the Mexican Minister of Foreign Relations, concluded a new treaty with Spain. This treaty protected all the credits previously covered, but Ramirez negotiated under congressional authorization and obtained a new arrangement of liquidating past and future claims. Within a year nineteen Spanish claims were liquidated, and 546,250 pesos in bonds were issued to the Spanish claimants. Then, in October 1852, the Mexican Chamber of Deputies impeached Ramirez when there were rumors that credits of non-Spanish origin were being respected. Ramirez was absolved when the Spanish Minister to Mexico agreed to make Spanish claims of the revolutionary period a matter of future negotiations. Spain, however, refused to discuss these claims again. Then the Mexican Chamber of Deputies stopped the issue of any more bonds to liquidate any more Spanish claims and demanded reconsideration of the treaty with Spain. Interest on bonds already issued, however, continued to be paid.[7]

In May 1853 Louis Aláman, a new Mexican Minister of Foreign Relations, told the Spanish Minister to Mexico that pre-independence credits should not be included in any treaty between the two countries. Spaniards, Aláman insisted, had no right to be treated any better than others who held titles of the internal debt of Mexico. The Marqués de la Ribera, the Spanish Minister, would not negotiate on the basis of this reservation and threatened to depart from his legation if his terms were not accepted by Mexico. Mexico refused the terms, and the Spanish Minister left in October 1853.[8]

On 12 November 1853 Spain and Mexico concluded a treaty which declared the treaty of 1851 subsistant. Debts already liquidated were exempted from revision, but other debts were to be adjusted by a commission. This commission would consider debts of Spanish origin still in Spanish hands. The creditors were to be paid by 8 per cent of Mexican custom revenues to be reserved for them.[9] Mexico interpreted the treaty to mean continuous Spanish ownership was necessary to validate a claim. But Spain insisted that a period of possession by a non-Spaniard between the time of origin and the time of presentation of a claim did not disqualify it.[10] In 1855 Mexico stopped payments and demanded the treaty be suspended, giving as a reason the necessity of ". . . revising certain debts abortively . . ." introduced.[11]

In 1856 Spain sent warships and a new Minister to Mexico,[12] but negotiations came to nothing.[13] At the end of the same year some Spanish citizens were murdered at San Vicente. Spain saw in the murders a political motive and demanded exemplary punishment of the guilty and a large indemnity.[14] Not obtaining the satisfaction he deemed necessary, the Spanish Minister to Mexico severed diplomatic relations in June 1857.[15] Mexico sent a representative to Spain to negotiate, and Spain demanded Mexican recognition of its responsibility to Spain for the titles of the Mexican internal debt in Spanish hands, the issue over which the Treaty of 1853 was suspended by Mexico. Another *sine qua non* demanded by Spain for resumption of diplomatic relations was Mexican acceptance of responsibility for the San Vicente murders. Negotiations broke down on this issue, and diplomatic relations continued to be suspended.[16]

In 1858 General Zuloaga, Juarez' rival during the Mexican Civil War, sent General Almonte to Europe as a special agent to settle differences with Spain. The result was the Mon–Almonte Treaty of 26 September 1859, whereby full force was given the treaty of 12 November 1853. Mexico accepted responsibility to Spain for the San Vicente murders and the bonds of the internal debt of Mexico in Spanish hands.[17]

After the signature of the Mon–Almonte Treaty, Spain sent Pacheco as Minister to Mexico to renew diplomatic relations. He arrived at Vera Cruz in May 1860. The Civil War was still in process. The Liberals held Vera Cruz, but Pacheco obtained permission from Juarez to proceed to Mexico City.[18]

There Pacheco presented his credentials to the Conservative Government of Miramon, Juarez' rival.[19] The Spanish Minister expected and even hoped that the British mediation proposal of 1860 would fail and lead to an intervention by Europe.[20] It was ". . . necessary that Europe not give advice to Mexico but impose on it liberty, discipline, order."[21] Pacheco, in short, favored the Conservatives to the Liberals. Defending his views before the Spanish Senate a year later, Pacheco testified that Juarez' party was ". . . the one that detests us, that sells its country to the Anglo–Americans. . . ." But the party called ". . . reactionary and clerical in Europe is tolerant and liberal . . . even tolerates freedom of religion."[22]

In January 1861 Juarez entered Mexico City, and Miramon, whom Pacheco had recognized, became an exile. One of the first acts of Juarez was to expel Pacheco as an "enemy" of the Republic.[23] Mexico took the view that the expulsion was merely personal and was not to reflect on Spain.[24] Juarez also protested the validity of the Mon–Almonte Treaty on the ground that it was unjust[25] and had been negotiated by a person having no authority to bind Mexico.[26]

Spain regarded the acceptance by Mexico of the Mon–Almonte Treaty as the *sine qua non* of Spanish recognition of the Juarez Government.[27] Collantes, the Spanish Minister of Foreign Relations, drew up a list of Spanish claims in November 1861 for General Prim, the Commander-in-Chief of the Spanish portion of the Tripartite Expedition of 1861–1862.[28] Collantes noted that the Convention of 12 November 1853 was recognized by the Mon–Almonte Treaty. Therefore Prim was not only to demand the execution of the Mon–Almonte Treaty, but also to demand the payment of arrears of interest due the claims recognized by the 1853 treaty. Collantes admitted that this interest ". . . isn't easy to calculate . . ." but might be as high as 10,000,000 *réaux,* or $506,356.31.[29] Collantes apparently overlooked the Padre Moran Convention of 6 December 1851.[30] Perhaps he did not consider it important, because at the time of writing his instructions the Mexicans had

met the last interest payment (due 4 June 1861 and paid
1 May 1861) and had thereby paid the proper interest of
$320,197.99 due Spaniards since the signing of the convention.
On 4 June 1861, however, Mexico was $324,390 in arrears on
capital payments to retire the original debt.[31] On 4 June 1861,
therefore, the Padre Moran Convention was capitalized at
$825,720. The financial confusion of the Spanish–Mexican
Conventions of 1847, 1851 (November, not the Padre Moran
one of December 1851), 1853, and 1859 makes an exact calculation of the Mexican debt to Spain almost impossible. Each
of these conventions (except the initial convention of 1847)
declared the previous one subsistent. The convention of 1847
alone stated a total of claims, given as $6,633,000. According
to Mexican Treasury Department statistics, the total as of 12
July 1862 was exactly $9,460,986.29.[32] On that date the Padre
Moran Convention stood at $875,263.20.[33] Subtracting this
from the sum total of all conventions of $9,460,986.29 gives
$8,575,723.09, the convention (minus the Padre Moran) debt
of Mexico as of 12 July 1862. Subtracting the $6,633,000,
given in the 1847 convention, leaves $1,942,723.09, which
should equal the arrears of interest (to July 1862) and debts
contracted by Mexico by the conventions of November 1851,
1853, and 1859. No such exact figures, however, appear to
have been available to Collantes. The only figure he mentioned
in his instructions to Prim was 10,000,000 *réaux*. In the ultimatum to be presented to Mexico that Prim prepared, based
on these instructions, Prim demanded the ". . . immediate
fulfilment of the Mon–Almonte Treaty, and the payment of
the interest due from the date of the said Treaty."[34] The only
figure Prim cited was $40,000 as an indemnity for the "Con-
cepcion," a Spanish vessel captured and sold by the Juarez
Government.[35]

In addition to approximately $9,000,000, based on con-
ventions Mexico had either suspended or not recognized, Spain
claimed redress for the San Vicente murders and other property
and personal injuries sustained by Spaniards in Mexico. Col-

lantes gave no figures in his instructions to Prim. He was to
". . . read the justificatory documents presented by interested
parties . . ." and then demand appropriate indemnities.[36]
Prim's ultimatum specified $40,000 reparation for the "Con-
cepcion" but further only demanded Mexican recognition of
". . . the right which belongs to Spain to demand compensation
for the injuries suffered by subjects of Her Majesty in consequence of the oppressive acts and outrages which have been
committed, or, may be committed, against them. . . ."[37] Prim
did not state a specific figure, because he had not had time to
examine the necessary "justificatory documents." Even had he
done so, he believed the common practice was to invoke
". . . Spanish nationality . . ." to ". . . demand three or four
times . . ." the appropriate indemnity. Prim, therefore, foresaw
that naming a specific figure might be to act with undue
rashness:

> What I . . . take to be certain is that we . . . accept with a
> precipitation which is perhaps, nay assuredly rash, what the
> Spaniards living in America write to us, for it is enough that
> any of them says that he is persecuted and ill-treated, for a
> hundred voices to be immediately raised, which without seek-
> ing out the truth, and without ascertaining whether the facts
> are real, cry out to the government (of Spain) to lose no time
> in demanding satisfaction for so gross an outrage; and the
> Governments are impressed, and at one time they send a fleet,
> at another time they write notes and then the misunderstand-
> ing is established. The settlement may be a good or a bad one,
> but it is never definitive; and it only serves as a means of get-
> ting out of the scrape until next time.[38]

It is with these qualifications that Ulick Ralph Burke's estimate
of $8,000,000 of Spanish property and personal claims[39] must
be regarded, especially as no agreement was reached between
Spain and Mexico on these claims in 1861–1862.[40]

# Appendix E

## SALIGNY–ZARCO CONVENTION, 26 MARCH 1861
## (NEVER RATIFIED)

THE UNDERSIGNED, MINISTER OF FOREIGN RELATIONS OF THE
Mexican Republic, and the Envoy Extraordinary and Minister
Plenipotentiary of His Majesty the Emperor of the French,
charged with the temporary direction of the Imperial Legation
in Mexico, united in diplomatic conference for the end of
regulating the payment of sums due the subjects of the French
Empire, desiring to proceed according to the sentiments of
loyalty and equity and justice that are the basis of the frank
conduct of the representatives of two nations between which
fortunately exists the best harmony, and to remove all causes
which in the future could alter the friendship which exists
between the two Governments, all the while conciliating
reciprocal interests in so far as particular circumstances permit,
have arrived at the following articles:

### Article 1

A fund for the special retirement of the French debt is
formed.

### Article 2

The French debt includes:
1. The sums remaining due the Convention of 1853.

2. The value of pending orders, that is, orders accepted by custom and other administrations with specification of a special mode of payment.

3. The value of obligations, no matter what kind, under-written by Mexican authorities in favor of French citizens.

4. The sums due, no matter what kind, other than for damages done by Mexican authorities to Frenchmen, for which the latter do not have written documents.

5. The sums due Frenchmen as indemnity and in redress of damages to them caused by illegal or arbitrary acts of Mexican authorities or their agents.

### Article 3

Only claims of French origin will be admitted in the French debt.

### Article 4

The claims for the repayment of which a special mode of payment has been stipulated will be repaid in accordance with the conditions of the relative conventions. Those sums still due as a result of the seizure of the conducta-money of San Luis Postosi and of Laguna-Seca, the order in favor of MM. Gar-ruste-Labadie and Co. and other debts of the same nature, if any exist, will be excluded from the present Convention.

### Article 5

The debts comprised in the first three paragraphs of Article 2 above will be settled in the following manner : those of the first paragraph upon the presentation of account current, those of paragraphs 2 and 3 upon the presentation of titles.

The debts comprised in paragraphs 4 and 5 of said Article 2 above will be arbitrated in accordance with equity and without any rule of procedure by a commission of six members, three named by the Government of the Republic and three named by the French Legation in Mexico.

This commission will be governed by majority rule. In case of a division, the commission will add a seventh member, who will be designated for each special case, be it by common accord, be it by lot.

The interested parties will have the right to present before this commission, in person or by private attorney, explanations. The commission, in addition, will have the right to utilize all means of information judged applicable.

The sentences rendered by the commission will be final. There will not be an appeal, nor recourse against the commission's decisions.

The Mexican Government and the Minister of France will always have the right, during the operations of liquidation, to change, if they think it convenient, the members of the Commission respectively chosen by them.

## Article 6

The funds destined for the retirement of the French debt will be obtained from all the maritime tariffs of the Republic :

1. 25% of the tariff on merchandise imported by French ships, and

2. 8% of the tariff on merchandise imported by ships other than French.

## Article 7

In accordance with their receipt, and every two months, the sums will be sent to the Legation of France, which will be responsible for them and will distribute them among the interested parties as it sees fit.

## Article 8

The Mexican Government engages itself to submit the present Convention for the approval of Congress no later than a month after the next meeting of Congress.

## Article 9

For the execution of the present Convention, as for its interpretation or in the case of omission, the contracting parties engage themselves to act in good faith and in accordance with equity.

Done in duplicate in Mexico City, the twenty-sixth of March, one thousand eight hundred and sixty one.

/s/ Zarco

/s/ Saligny

# Appendix F

NAPOLEON III TO COUNT FLAHAULT, PALAIS DE COMPIEGNE, (9) OCTOBER 1861

My dear Count Flahault,

As I learn from M. Thouvenel that our convention with regard to Mexico is bogged down, I want to express my ideas frankly for you to communicate to Lord Palmerston. When the Prime Minister knows my intentions in this affair, I hope that he will as clearly state to you his inner thoughts and then an understanding and a joint action will result.

It is not necessary for me to dwell at length on the joint interest that we have in Europe to see Mexico pacified and endowed with a stable government. Not only has this country, endowed with all the advantages of nature, attracted much of our capital and our nationals whose existence is menaced without intermission, but, by its regeneration, it would form an insurmountable barrier to the encroachments of North America; it would afford an important market for English, Spanish, and French commerce by exploiting its own resources; finally it would render great service to our industries by extending its cultivation of cotton. These various advantages, as well as the spectacle of one of the finest countries of the world delivered over to anarchy and threatened by approaching ruin, are the reasons that have always so deeply interested me in Mexico.

Several years ago some important persons of this country came to me, described their unfortunate state, and asked my support, saying that only a monarchy could reestablish order in a country torn apart by factions. I think they also appealed to England, but, as that time I could only indulge in barren hopes. In spite of my sympathy, I answered them that I did not have any pretext to intervene in Mexico, that especially in American affairs my policy was closely bound to that of England, that I believed it would be difficult to reach an agreement with the Cabinet of St. James for the objective they proposed, that we would risk a falling out with the United States, and therefore it was necessary to wait for better days.

Today unforeseen events have changed things. The war in America has made it impossible for the United States to interfere in the matter, and above all the outrages committed by the Mexican Government are legitimate grounds for England, Spain, and France to intervene in Mexico. How shall this intervention be carried out? That is the question.

I understand very well the convention among the three Powers, which will send forces to America, will only establish the redress of our legitimate grievances as the ostensible purpose of our intervention, but it is necessary to foresee what could happen and not benevolently to tie one's hands in a manner to prevent a solution that would be in the interest of all. According to the information I have, as soon as the squadrons appear before Vera Cruz, a considerable party in Mexico is ready to seize power, to call a national assembly and to proclaim a monarchy. I was confidentially asked who would be my candidate in this eventuality. I said that I didn't have any but that if one had to be decided upon, he should be a prince animated with the spirit of the times, endowed with enough intelligence and steadfastness to establish a stable order of things in a country stirred by so many revolutions. Finally it was necessary that he must not offend the suscepti-bilities of the great Maritime Powers, and I put forward the name of Archduke Maximilian.

This idea has been happily accepted by the little committee residing in France. The qualities of the Prince, his connection through his wife, with the King of the Belgians, a natural bond between France and England, the fact that he comes from a great Power that is not a Maritime Power — all these things appeared to me to meet all the desirable conditions. On my side I thought it was in good taste for me to propose as an eventual candidate a prince belonging to a dynasty with which I was recently at war.

The Mexicans, who naturally take things with more spirit than I do and who are impatient to see events precipitated, had the Cabinet of Vienna sounded. According to what I have been told, it accepted the overture under two conditions: firstly, that the Prince would have the support of France and England, and, secondly, that the will of the Mexican people be frankly and loyally expressed.

That is how things are now. You can very well see, my dear Monsieur de Flahault, that I only have one objective in this whole question: that of seeing French interests protected and safeguarded for the future through an organization which would save Mexico from a devastation by the Indians or an American invasion. Finally, I am glad to point out that, far from having any selfish preferences or any unjust dislikes, I am only seeking to do good, convinced that to try to render a people prosperous is effectively to work for the prosperity of all.

Summing up, I would ask for nothing better than to sign a convention with England and Spain. The ostensible objective of our intervention will be the redress of our grievances, but it would be impossible for me, without violating good faith and knowing the state of things as I do, to engage myself not to support, at least morally, a change that I wish with all my heart, because it is in the interest of civilization in general.

Croyez, etc.

/s/ Napoleon

# Appendix G

(FIRST) BRITISH DRAFT CONVENTION, UNDATED,
COMMUNICATED TO THOUVENEL BY COWLEY,
15 OCTOBER 1861

HER MAJESTY THE QUEEN OF THE UNITED KINGDOM OF
Great Britain and Ireland, His Majesty the Emperor of the
French, and Her Majesty the Queen of Spain, feeling themselves compelled by the lawless and flagitious conduct of the
authorities of the Republic of Mexico, to seek from those
authorities protection for the persons and properties of their
subjects, and a fulfilment of the obligations contracted by the
Republic of Mexico towards Their Said Majesties, Their
Majesties have agreed to enter into a Convention for regulating
their joint action in the premises, and for that purpose have
named as the Plenipotentiaries, that is to say;

Her Majesty the Queen of Great Britain and Ireland, etc.

His Majesty the Emperor of the French, etc.

Her Majesty the Queen of Spain, etc.

Who, having exchanged their full Powers, etc., have agreed
upon and concluded the following articles:

## Article I

Her Majesty the Queen of Great Britain and Ireland, His
Majesty the Emperor of the French, and Her Majesty the

Queen of Spain, agree that, immediately after the signature of the present Convention, arrangements should be made for dispatching to the coasts of Mexico, on the Atlantic Ocean, a combined Naval and Military Force, the amount of which shall be determined hereafter by communications between Their respective governments, sufficient to capture, to occupy, and to hold, the several fortresses, and military positions on the said coasts, and to enforce a rigorous blockade of the Cities, Ports, and Harbours of the same; such occupation to be enforced in the name and on behalf of the High Contracting Parties conjointly, irrespectively of the national character of the Force by which that occupation shall be carried out.

## Article II

The officers in command of the Allied Forces shall, as soon as possible after the occupation of the City of Vera Cruz and the adjacent forts, address to the Authorities exercising Power in the Republic of Mexico a joint communication declaring the objects for which the Allied Powers have had recourse to measures of coercion, and inviting those Authorities forthwith to enter into arrangements under sufficient guarantees for the execution thereof, for the redress of injuries done to the subjects of the High Contracting Parties, and for the fulfilment of the obligations contracted towards them by the said Republic : and the said commanding officers shall intimate to the Authorities of the Republic that the coercive measures which they may have adopted will be maintained, and in case of need, extended, until such times as the arrangements aforesaid shall have been entered into by the said Authorities and shall have been approved by the governments of the High Contracting Parties, who, moreover, will reserve to themselves the right of taking such steps as they may deem advisable for watching over and enforcing the execution of such arrangements.

## Article III

The High Contracting Parties mutually agree that the Forces

to be employed by them, in pursuance of the terms of the present Convention, shall not be employed for any other objects than those specified in the Preamble thereof; and, specifically, shall not be employed for the purpose of interfering with the Internal government of the Republic.

### Article IV

The High Contracting Parties further engage, that, in the employment of the coercive measures provided for in this Convention, they will not seek for themselves any augmentation of territory nor any special advantage; neither will they endeavour to interfere in the Internal affairs of Mexico, or with the free choice on the part of the people of Mexico of the form of government to be maintained in Mexico.

### Article V

The High Contracting Parties being, moreover, desirous that the measures which it is their intention to adopt should bear no exclusive character, and being aware that the government of the United States have equally with themselves claims upon the Mexican Republic, They agree that, immediately on the signature of the present Convention, a copy thereof shall be communicated to the government of the United States, and it's (sic) accession to the Provisions thereof shall be invited; and in the event of the accession of the United States, the High Contracting Parties will immediately empower Their Ministers at Washington to conclude and sign with a Plenipotentiary to be named by the President of the United States, either jointly or separately, a convention to the same effect and in the same terms, excepting only the present article, as the convention now signed on their behalf by their several Plenipotentiaries. But as by reason of any delay in carrying into effect the Provisions of the 1st, 2nd, 3rd and 4th articles of this Convention, the objects which the High Contracting Parties have in view might be defeated, they agree that they will not, with a view to obtain the accession of the government of the United States, defer beyond the term when the forces of the present High Contracting Parties can be assembled in the neighbourhood of Vera Cruz, the commencement of the operations contemplated by this Convention.

## Article VI

The present Convention shall be ratified, and the Ratifications thereof exchanged at

# Appendix H

## NOTE BY THE LORD CHANCELLOR ON THE (FIRST) BRITISH DRAFT CONVENTION, 17 OCTOBER, 1861, MARKED "FOR THE CABINET" AND MARGINAL NOTE BY LORD RUSSELL

THE CHANCELLOR'S IMPRESSION FROM EARL RUSSELL'S statement was, that the Contracting powers proposed to take possession of all the Mexican Ports on the Atlantic, to encourage . . . commerce there, & to levy duties & take custom dues, with a view thereby to liquidate or ensure the liquidation of, the pecuniary claims of the Three Powers respectively against Mexico.

As it is not probable that there will be soon any settled government in Mexico, able to conclude treaties or to raise or secure an indemnity, the occupation of the three powers will last a considerable time. Mutual arrangements as to the mode of levying & collecting Dues of Customs, the deposit of the monies received, the payment of the expenses occurred, & distribution of the clear surplus will be requisite. Nothing of all this is indicated by the Convention as it stands. Neither the contrary. For the first Article thus defines the objects of the joint enterprise "to capture, occupy & hold the several fortresses & military positions on the said Coast & to enforce a rigorous blockade of the Cities Ports & Harbours of the same." These last words are quite at variance with the Policy of seizing the

Cities Ports & Harbours as a material Security, & encouraging Commerce with a view to derive Funds therefrom.

If ordering military & naval measures be not all that is intended, & if blockade be by no means intended, this Article should be altered in expression.

The claims of the three Contracting Powers against Mexico are distinct & separate. There is no joint demand. But the Expedition is a joint action to enforce the discharge of three separate demands by three several Claimants. It is not probable that Mexico can or will pay each in full. Therefore each Nation has an interest in reducing & limiting the amounts of the demands of the other two.

Whatever is recovered from Mexico, if not enough to pay the whole, must be distributed and apportioned among the Contracting Parties. But by whom & in what ratio? What degree or extent of mutual engagement between the Contracting Parties, as to the mode of ascertaining & liquidating their respective claims, is involved in their joining in this common action? The Convention does not seem to contemplate any such consequences, for it makes no provision for them. But they are inevitable, &, unless provided for, may become a fruitful source of disagreement.

I am afraid it will be found to be a necessary consequence of this joint action, that each of the Contracting Parties may be entitled to see that the claims of the other two, *not already admitted by Mexico,* are such as International Law may be maintained, & are also just in point of amount.

If this is not intended to be conceded, it should be guarded against, by expressly excluding any such implication.

Again, many questions, not of a military nature, will necessarily arise during any joint occupation, and will require some mutually constituted authority to determine on the spot. These difficulties cannot be completely provided for, but it may tend to prevent future embarrassment if some such general provision as this (were) inserted, viz. —

"A Commission shall be appointed to consist of three / or

six / Commissioners one (or two) to be named by each of the Contracting Powers, who shall have full authority to determine all questions that may arise as to the application or distribution of any money, that may be received, or recovered, in, or from, Mexico, having regard to the respective rights of the three Contracting Parties."

If there were a settled Government in Mexico, or if it was the object of the Expedition to establish a govt. there, many of the difficulties I apprehend could be prevented by the Treaty with such govt. that could probably result from the Expedition.

Having regard to the present state of Mexico & to the stipulations in the Convention, the whole proceeding is of an anomalous character, & the Convention consequently seems to require the greatest care & caution.

Russell Note

Some provisions for a Commission must no doubt be introduced. My idea has been that the Commission should either consist of three of whom Sir Charles Wyke should be one, or if six of whom the Admiral & Sir Charles Wyke be two.

In any case the demands must be made on the de facto govt.

/s/ Russell

# Appendix I

FIRST VERSION OF (SECOND) BRITISH DRAFT
CONVENTION, UNDATED, WITH MARGINAL
ALTERATIONS INDICATED, AND NOTES
BY PALMERSTON, HAMMOND, AND
RUSSELL INDICATING THE ORIGINATORS
OF THESE ALTERATIONS

(Crossed out words are italicized, and marginal notations
of changes are enclosed in brackets in the text where
intended to be inserted.)

HER MAJESTY THE QUEEN OF THE UNITED KINGDOM OF
Great Britain and Ireland, His Majesty the Emperor of the
French, and Her Majesty the Queen of Spain, feeling themselves compelled by the lawless and flagitious conduct of the
Authorities of the Republic of Mexico, to *ask* (demand) from
those Authorities protection for the persons and properties of
their subjects, and a fulfilment of the obligations contracted by
the Republic of Mexico towards Their said Majesties have
agreed to enter into a Convention for regulating their joint
action in the premises, and for that purpose have named as
their Plenipotentiaries, that is to say :
Her Majesty the Queen of Great Britain and Ireland ,etc.
His Majesty the Emperor of the French, etc.
Her Majesty the Queen of Spain, etc.

Who, after having exchanged their full Powers etc have agreed upon and concluded the following Articles :

### Article I

Her Majesty the Queen of Great Britain and Ireland, His Majesty the Emperor of the French, and Her Majesty the Queen of Spain, agree that, immediately after the signature of the present Convention, arrangements shall be made for dispatching to the Coasts of Mexico, *on the Atlantic Ocean,* a combined Naval and military force, the amount of which shall be determined hereafter by communications between Their respective Governments, sufficient to capture, to occupy, and to hold the several fortresses and military positions on the said Coast, and to enforce (if it shall be found necessary) a *rigorous* blockade of the *Cities,* Ports, and Harbours of the same; such occupation to be *enforced* (taken) in the name and on behalf of the High Contracting Parties conjointly, irrespectively of the national character of the force by which that occupation shall be carried *out* (into effect).

### Article II

The officers in command of the Allied Forces shall, as soon as possible after the occupation of the City of Vera Cruz and the adjacent forts, address a joint communication declaring the objects for which the Allied Powers have had recourse to measures of coercion, and inviting those Authorities forthwith to enter into arrangements under sufficient guarantees for the execution thereof, for the redress of injuries done to the Subjects of the High Contracting Parties, and for the fulfilment of the obligations contracted towards *them* (the said High Contracting Parties) by the said Republic; *and the said Commanding Officers shall intimate to the Authorities of the Republic that the coercive measures which they may have adopted will be maintained and, in case of need, extended, entered into by the said Authorities and shall have been approved by the Governments of* (and the) High Contracting Parties, *who* moreover, will reserve to themselves the right of taking such steps as they may deem advisable for watching over and enforcing the execution of such arrangements, and entering (retaining) a material guarantee for the same.

## Article III

The High Contracting Parties mutually agree that the forces to be employed by them, in pursuance of the terms of the present Convention, shall not be employed for any other objects than those specified in the Preamble thereof, and, *specifically, shall not be employed for the purpose of inter-fering with the internal Government of the Republic.*

Go on to next article which is to be embodied in this

## Article IV

The High Contracting Parties further engage, that, in the employment of the coercive measures provided for in this Convention, they will not seek for themselves any augmentation of territory nor any special advantage, neither will they endeavour to interfere *in the internal affairs of Mexico or* (forcibly) with the free choice on the part of the people of Mexico of the form of Government to be maintained in Mexico.

## Article IV
### (in Russell's handwriting)

A Commission shall be appointed to consist of three Commissioners one to be named by each of the Contracting Powers, who shall have full authority to determine all questions that may arise as to the application or distribution of any sums (of money) that may be recovered in, or from Mexico, having regard to the respective rights of the Three Contracting Parties. The said Commissioners in concert with the officers in command of the Allied Forces shall draw up the joint communication to the Authorities exercising power in the Republic of Mexico mentioned in Article II of the present Convention.

## Article V

The High Contracting Parties being moreover, desirous that the measures which it is their intention to adopt should bear no exclusive character, and being aware that the Government of the United States have equally with themselves claims upon the Mexican Republic, — They agree that, immediately on the signature of the present Convention, a Copy thereof shall be communicated to the Government of the United States, and its (the) accession (of that government) to the provisions thereof shall be invited; and in the event of the accession of the United States (thereto), the High Contracting Parties will immediately empower their Ministers at Washington to conclude and sign with a Plenipotentiary to be named by the President of the United States, either jointly or separately, a Convention to the same effect and in the same terms, excepting only the present Article, as the Convention now signed on Their behalf by Their several Plenipotentiaries. But as by reason of any delay in carrying into effect the provisions of the 1st., 2nd., 3rd., and 4th Articles of this Convention, the objects which the High Contracting Parties have in view might be defeated, they agree that they will not, with a view to obtain the accession of the Government of the United States, defer beyond the term when the forces of the present High Contracting Parties can be assembled in the neighbourhood of Vera Cruz, the commencement of the operations contemplated by this Convention.

## Article VI

The present Convention shall be ratified, and the Ratifications thereof exchanged at
        In faith whereof, etc.
Palmerston Note of suggested alterations, 19 October 1861, written on First Version of (Second) British Draft Convention

Article 1. insert after "to enforce" "if found necessary"
( „   2) instead of "contracted towards *them*" say "towards
the said High contracting Parties"

Article 4. "forcibly" to interfere "It would be next to impossible that forces so occupying a portion of Mexican Territory
should abstain from all Interferences of every sort in the
internal affairs of the Country. They will naturally and necessarily be communicated with by Powers engaged in forming
a government, and it is not good to enter into an engagement
the fulfilment . . . of which may depend upon nice distinctions.

Article 5. Instead of "its accession" say "the accession of that
government." It might refer to "present convention"
after "United States" insert "thereto"

Hammond Note, 19 October 1861
Lord Russell desires me to send Your Lordship the draft of
Convention with Mexico, with some alterations in pencil, in
his handwriting, suggested verbally by the French Ambassador
/s/ H(ammond) 19 Oct (1861)

Palmerston Notation on Hammond's Note of 19 October 1861
The word *demand* is certainly better than ask
/s/ P(almerston) 19/10/61

Russell Note, 20 October 1861, unsigned but in his handwriting
If Lord Palmerston approves of M. de Flahault's alterations,
an amended draft may be placed before the negotiators. . . .
At all events let the amended draft be submitted to Ld Palmerston, & the Lord Chancellor.

# Appendix J

FINAL VERSION OF (SECOND) BRITISH DRAFT
CONVENTION, 21 OCTOBER 1861, COMMUNI-
CATED TO FLAHAULT BY RUSSELL,
22 OCTOBER 1861

HER MAJESTY THE QUEEN OF THE UNITED KINGDOM OF
Great Britain and Ireland, His Majesty the Emperor of the
French, and Her Majesty the Queen of Spain, feeling themselves compelled by the lawless and flagitious conduct of the
authorities of the Republic of Mexico, to demand from those
authorities protection for the persons and properties of their
subjects, and a fulfilment of the obligations contracted by the
Republic of Mexico towards their said Majesties, have agreed
to enter into a Convention for regulating their joint action in
the premises, and for that purpose have named as their Plenipotentiaries, that is to say: —

Her Majesty the Queen of Great Britain and Ireland, etc.

His Majesty the Emperor of the French, etc.

Her Majesty the Queen of Spain, etc.

Who, after having exchanged their full powers, etc., have
agreed upon and concluded the following Articles: —

### Article I

Her Majesty the Queen of Great Britain and Ireland, His
Majesty the Emperor of the French, and Her Majesty the

Queen of Spain, agree that, immediately after the signature of the present Convention, arrangements shall be made for despatching to the coasts of Mexico a combined naval and military force, the amount of which shall be determined here-after by communications between their respective Govern-ments, sufficient to capture, to occupy, and to hold the several fortresses and military positions on the said coasts, and, if it shall be found necessary, to enforce a blockade of the ports and harbours of the same; such occupation to be taken in the name and on behalf of the High Contracting Parties conjointly, irrespectively of the national character of the force by which that occupation shall be carried into effect.

## Article II

The officers in command of the allied forces shall, as soon as possible after the occupation of the city of Vera Cruz and the adjacent forts, address to the authorities exercising power in the Republic of Mexico a joint communication declaring the objects for which the allied Powers have had recourse to measures of coercion, and inviting those authorities forthwith to enter into arrangements, under sufficient guarantees for the execution thereof, for the redress of injuries done to the subjects of the High Contracting Parties, and for the fulfilment of the obligations contracted towards the said High Contracting Parties by the said Republic; and the High Contracting Parties, moreover, will reserve to themselves the right of taking such steps as they may deem advisable for watching over and enforcing the execution of such arrangements, and retaining a material guarantee for the same.

## Article III

The High Contracting Parties mutually agree that the forces to be employed by them, in pursuance of the terms of the present Convention, shall not be employed for any other objects than those specified in the preamble thereof; and the

High Contracing Parties further engage that, in the employment of the coercive measures provided for in this Convention, they will not seek for themselves any augmentation of territory, nor any special advantage, neither will they endeavour forcibly to interfere with the free choice, on the part of the people of Mexico, of the form of government to be maintained in Mexico.

## Article IV

A Commission shall be appointed, to consist of three Commissioners, one to be named by each of the Contracting Powers, who shall have full authority to determine all questions that may arise as to the application or distribution of any sums of money that may be recovered in or from Mexico, having regard to the respective rights of the three Contracting Parties. The said Commissioners, in concert with the Officers in command of the Allied Forces, shall draw up the joint communication to the Authorities exercising power in the Republic of Mexico, mentioned in Article II of the present Convention.

## Article V

The High Contracting Parties being, moreover, desirous that the measures which it is their intention to adopt should bear no exclusive character, and being aware that the Government of the United States have, equally with themselves, claims upon the Mexican Republic, they agree that, immediately on the signature of the present Convention, a copy thereof shall be communicated to the Government of the United States, and the accession of that Government to the provisions thereof shall be invited; and in the event of the accession of the United States thereto, the High Contracting Parties will immediately empower their Ministers at Washington to conclude and sign with a Plenipotentiary to be named by the President of the United States, either jointly or separately, a Convention to the same effect and in the same terms, excepting only the present

Article, as the Convention now signed on their behalf by their several Plenipotentiaries. But as by reason of any delay in carrying into effect the provisions of Article I, II, III, and IV of this Convention, the objects which the High Contracting Powers have in view might be defeated, they agree that they will not, with a view to obtain the accession of the Government of the United States, defer beyond the term when the forces of the present High Contracting Parties can be assembled in the neighbourhood of Vera Cruz, the commencement of the operations contemplated by this Convention.

## Article VI

The present Convention shall be ratified, and the ratifications thereof exchanged at

In faith whereof, etc.

# Appendix K

## FRENCH COUNTER PROPOSAL ( TO FIRST BRITISH DRAFT CONVENTION), UNDATED, COMMUNICATED TO RUSSELL BY FLAHAULT, 22 OCTOBER 1861

HIS MAJESTY THE EMPEROR OF THE FRENCH, HER MAJESTY the Queen of the United Kingdom of Great Britain and Ireland, and Her Majesty the Queen of Spain, feeling themselves compelled by the arbitrary and vexatious (*arbitraire et vexatoire*) conduct of the authorities of the Republic of Mexico to demand (*exiger*) from those authorities a more efficacious protection for the persons and property of their subjects as well as the fulfillment of obligations contracted toward their Majesties by the Republic of Mexico, have agreed to conclude a convention with a view to combine their common action, and, for this purpose, have named the following as their Plenipotentiaries:

His Majesty the Emperor of the French . . .

Her Majesty the Queen of Great Britain and Ireland . . .

Her Majesty the Queen of Spain . . .

who, after having exchanged their credentials, have agreed to the following articles:

### Article I

His Majesty the Emperor of the French, the Queen of Great

Britain and Ireland, and Her Majesty the Queen of Spain engage to make, immediately after the signature of the present convention, the necessary arrangements for dispatching to the coasts of Mexico, combined naval and military forces, the strength of which shall be determined by a further interchange of communications between their Governments, but of which the total shall be sufficient to seize and occupy the several fortresses and military positions on the Mexican coast.

The Commanders of the allied forces shall be, moreover, authorized to execute the other operations which may be considered, on the spot, most suitable to effect the object specified in the preamble of the present Convention, and specifically to ensure the security of foreign residents, wherever menaced (*partout ou elle se trouverait menacée*).

All the measures contemplated in this Article shall be taken in the name and on the account of the High Contracting Parties, without reference to the particular nationality of the forces employed to execute them.

## Article II

The High Contracting Parties engage themselves not to seek for themselves, in the employment of the coercive measures foreseen by the present convention, any acquisition of territory nor any special advantage and not to exercise in the internal affairs of Mexico any influence of a nature to prejudice the right of the Mexican nation to choose and to constitute freely the form of its government.

## Article III

The High Contracting Parties desiring, moreover, that the measures that they have the intention to adopt not have an exclusive nature, and knowing that the Government of the United States likewise has claims to make against the Mexican Republic, agree that as soon as possible after the signature of the present convention, a copy will be sent to the Government of the United States, that this Government will be invited to accept the stipulations it contains, that, in case the United States accepts, their respective Ministers to Washington will immediately be given full powers to conclude and sign, singly or collectively, with the Plenipotentiary designated by the President of the United States an identical convention, with the exception of the present article, signed today. But, as the High Contracting Parties are opposed to any delay in the execution of articles 1 and 2 of the present convention, thereby failing to achieve the ends that they desire to attain, they have agreed not to delay, with a view to obtaining the acceptance of the United States, the beginning of the operations above mentioned beyond the meeting of their combined forces outside Vera Cruz.

### *Article IV*

The Convention once ratified, and the ratifications exchanged at . . . after the delay of ....................................

In faith of which ...................................................

# Appendix L

CONVENTION BETWEEN HER MAJESTY (THE QUEEN OF THE KINGDOM OF GREAT BRITAIN AND IRELAND), THE QUEEN OF SPAIN AND THE EMPEROR OF THE FRENCH RELATIVE TO COMBINED OPERATIONS AGAINST MEXICO, SIGNED AT LONDON, 31 OCTOBER 1861 (RATIFICATIONS EXCHANGED AT LONDON, 15 NOVEMBER 1861)

HER MAJESTY THE QUEEN OF THE UNITED KINGDOM OF Great Britain and Ireland, Her Majesty the Queen of Spain, and His Majesty the Emperor of the French, feeling themselves compelled by the arbitrary and vexatious conduct of the authorities of the Republic of Mexico to demand from those authorities more efficacious protection for the persons and properties of their subjects, as well as a fulfillment of the obligations contracted towards their Majesties by the Republic of Mexico, have agreed to conclude a Convention with a view to combine their common action, and, for this purpose, have named as their Plenipotentiaries, that is to say : —

Her Majesty the Queen of the United Kingdom of Great Britain and Ireland, the Right Honourable John Earl Russell, Vi-count Amberley of Amberley and Ardsalla, a Peer of the United Kingdom, a Member of Her Britannic Majesty's Privy Council, Her Majesty's Principal Secretary for Foreign Affairs;

Her Majesty the Queen of Spain, Don Xavier de Isturiz y

Montero, Knight of the Illustrious Order of the Golden Fleece, Grand Cross of the Royal and Distinguished Order of Charles III, of the Imperial Order of the Legion of Honour of France, of the Orders of the Conception of Villaviciosa and Christ of Portugal, Senator of the Kingdom, late President of the Council of Ministers, and First Secretary of State of Her Catholic Majesty, and Her Envoy Extraordinary and Minister Plenipotentiary to Her Britannic Majesty;

And His Majesty the Emperor of the French, his Excellency the Count de Flahault de la Billarderie, Senator, General of Division, Grand Cross of the Legion of Honour, His Imperial Majesty's Ambassador Extraordinary to Her Britannic Majesty;

Who after having reciprocally communicated their respective full powers, found in good and due form, have agreed upon the following Articles: —

## Article I

Her Majesty the Queen of the United Kingdom of Great Britain and Ireland, Her Majesty the Queen of Spain, and His Majesty the Emperor of the French, engage to make, immediately after the signature of the present Convention, the necessary arrangements for dispatching to the coasts of Mexico, combined naval and military forces, the strength of which shall be determined by a further interchange of communications between their Governments, but of which the total shall be sufficient to seize and occupy the several fortresses and military positions on the Mexican coast.

The Commanders of the allied forces shall be, moreover, authorized to execute the other operations which may be considered, on the spot, most suitable to effect the object specified in the preamble of the present Convention, and specifically to ensure the security of foreign residents.

All the measures contemplated in this Article shall be taken in the name and on the account of the High Contracting

Parties, without reference to the particular nationality of the forces employed to execute them.

## Article II

The High Contracting Parties engage not to seek for themselves, in the employment of the coercive measures contemplated by the present Convention, any acquisition of territory nor any special advantage, and, not to exercise in the internal affairs of Mexico any influence of a nature to prejudice the right of the Mexican nation to choose and to constitute freely the form of its Government.

## Article III

A Commission composed of three Commissioners, one to be named by each of the Contracting Powers, shall be established with full authority to determine all questions that may arise as to the application or distribution of the sums of money which may be recovered from Mexico, having regard to the respective rights of the three Contracting Parties.

## Article IV

The High Contracting Parties desiring, moreover, that the measures which they intend to adopt should not bear an exclusive character, and being aware that the Government of the United States on its part has, like them, claims to enforce upon the Mexican Republic, agree that immediately after the signature of the present Convention a copy thereof shall be communicated the Government of the United States; that that Government shall be invited to accede to it; and that in anticipation of that accession their respective Ministers at Washington shall be at once furnished with full powers for the purpose of concluding and signing, collectively or separately, with the Plenipotentiary designated by the President of the United States, a Convention, identical, save the suppression of the present Article, with that which they sign this day. But as by delaying to put into execution Articles I and II of the present Convention, the High Contracting Parties would incur a risk of failing in the object which they desire to attain, they have agreed not to defer, with the view of obtaining the accession of the Government of the United States, the commencement of the above-mentioned operations beyond the time at which their combined forces can be assembled in the neighbourhood of Vera Cruz.

### Article V

The present Convention shall be ratified, and the ratifications thereof shall be exchanged at London within fifteen days.

In witness thereof the respective Plenipotentiaries have signed it, and have fixed thereto the seal of their arms.

Done at London, in triplicate, the thirty-first day of the month of October, in the year of our Lord one thousand eight hundred and sixty-one.

> (L.S.) RUSSELL
> (L.S.) XAVIER DE ISTURIZ
> (L.S.) FLAHAULT.

# Appendix M

## THOUVENEL'S CONFIDENTIAL INSTRUCTIONS TO ADMIRAL JURIEN DE LA GRAVIERE, PARIS, 11 NOVEMBER 1861

My Dear Admiral,

The official instructions that I have the honor to address to you under today's date determine, as far as it is possible to do so at a distance, the action that you would have to exercise in concert with the Commanders-in-Chief and the Commissioners of the Allied Powers to realize the aims of the Convention of 31 October. To obtain jointly the redress of similar grievances and to obtain guarantees capable of sheltering foreign residents from new outrages, such is, if I can put it thusly, the legal ground of the accord that has been established among France, England, and Spain. The idea of the Emperor, moreover, moved by an interest of humanity and civilization, has gone further, and it is necessary that you be informed of it.

In this regard I wouldn't know anything better than to communicate to you under the heading of strictly confidential a letter that His Majesty has written to His Ambassador to London, and a despatch that I myself addressed to M. le Comte de Flahault to invite him to call the attention of the Britannic Cabinet to the eventualities that could spring from a demonstration against Mexico and the choice that the interests of this unfortunate country and those of Europe would advize us to take. You will see by the reply, also enclosed, that the English Government has given full justice to the ideas of the Emperor, but that it didn't believe it necessary to promise its active concurrence to execute them. The Cabinet of Madrid, just the reverse, is more inclined in this respect; it is permitted to suppose, however, that it is not a very warm partisan of the eventual candidature of the Archduke Maximilian. Be this as it may, it doesn't appear to me doubtful that if a considerable party appears, under the influence of the appearance of the combined forces, and works for the reestablishment of monarchy, neither England nor Spain will put obstacles in the way of its progress. Does this party exist in a state of manifesting its intentions with nearly certain chances of success? This is the point, my dear Admiral, which will have to be your first object of your interviews with M. Dubois de Saligny and of your most serious investigations. Just as it would be generous and useful to aid a nation to leave the abyss, just so it would be rash in itself and contrary to our interests to risk an adventure. Therefore it is to inspire the honest and peaceable portion of the Mexican people the courage to make its voice known that our efforts must be held out; if the nation remains inert, if it doesn't realize that we offer it an unexpected staff of safety, if it doesn't give a practical sense and morality to our protection, it is evident that there is nothing we can do but remain within the terms of the Convention of 31 October and only occupy ourselves with the specific interests for which it was concluded. Things would be incomplete, however, unless, once the forts are occupied, an expedition were directed into the interior and really as far as Mexico City.

The English Government has broached this eventuality only with an extreme repugnance and it seemed to me that it would be unwise to seek it to commit itself in advance, all the while reserving, in our relations with the English Government, our right to do what is necessary to protect the security of our nationals. Parliamentary considerations, without doubt, would have determined, theoretically, this negative response, and the terms of Article 1 of the Convention are sufficient for us in that they permit the Commanders-in-Chief to adopt on the spot the measures the most appropriate in order to attain the ends of the expedition. These terms are broad enough to justify the interpretation that we want to give them.

It was more essential to know whether the Spanish Government, which is supplying the largest contingent of land troops, would accept this interpretation, and our Ambassador to Madrid, from whom I have demanded a categorical answer, has left no doubt on this subject. Marechal Duc de Tetuan said in satisfactory terms to M. Barrot that very discretionary instructions would be addressed to the Spanish Commander-in-Chief and that he would furthermore send a private letter authorizing him to agree with you on a march to Mexico City, if the circumstances should appear favorable to you both. Naturally you see what will depend on you to obtain the participation of the Britannic Commander-in-Chief in this movement in as far as he is able. If he believes himself unable to join himself to this march, you will propose that he, as a mark of reciprocal confidence, guard the forts of Vera Cruz alone.

In accordance with the information that I have, the popularity of Spain in Mexico would be far from being as great as ours. This would be explained by old memories; but account of it must be taken, and, without wounding any susceptibilities, it would be necessary, I think, that our troops occupy, in as far as possible, the head of the column of the expeditionary corps and that a proclamation of a nature to reassure completely the Mexican nation against any idea of conquest and any attempt against its independence as to the choice and the form of its government, should be diffused through the country before the beginning of operations to the interior. M. Dubois de Saligny, as I say in my official instructions, will not be able, in anything that touches the duties confided in you, neithe to substitute his responsibility for yours, nor to initiate any conflict. This superior agent of my Department has always given enough proof of capacity and good judgement that I do not believe I have to recommend to you to give him the greatest confidence and to profit from advice that an exact knowledge of men and things in Mexico could suggest itself to him.

Accept, my dear Admiral . . . etc.

This letter, and our official instructions, have been read and completely approved by the Emperor (in pencil).

# Appendix N

## COLLANTES' INSTRUCTIONS TO GENERAL JUAN PRIM, 17 NOVEMBER 1861

EXCELLENCY,

The Queen, Our Sovereign, in deigning to entrust to Your Excellency the command of the troops sent to Mexico to obtain the redress of grievances for which the government of this Republic has made itself responsible toward us, also was pleased to name you her Representative in the negotiations for the conclusion of a treaty, in which situation your powers must be justly recognized. In the presence of this situation I must make you acquainted with the circumstances that have obliged Spain to have recourse to the use of force and the conditions to which the Government of Her Majesty will consent in order to renew with Mexico relations now interrupted.

The Government of the Queen could endure no longer the nonexecution of the most solemn stipulations and the continual violences committed against Spanish subjects. It has resolved to send into this country land and sea forces capable of bringing about by force a satisfaction that had been refused to conciliatory measures. From time to time Spain was going to send a fleet from Havana with debarkation troops to guarantee our claims. However, as France and England found themselves in the same situation as Spain, it was thought necessary to combine the action of the three powers. These powers, having the same claims, have the right to the same reparations. For this purpose a treaty signed at London on the 31st of the month of October, and of which I have the honour to send you an enclosed copy, was made among the three governments.

In looking over this document, Your Excellency will see that Spain, France, and England renounce any acquisition of territory to prove their disinterestedness and that they obligate themselves not to interfere with the internal affairs of Mexico, in which the Mexicans will retain a complete liberty of choosing the form of government that is best suited for them. The three powers are content to combine their efforts for the only end of guaranteeing to their respective subjects an indispensable protection against the arbitrary acts of the Mexican authorities by obliging them to respect the international engagements contracted by their government.

In accordance with Article 1 of the treaty, the allied forces will occupy immediately the ports and forts of the littoral of the Republic. In these operations, as in all others, the Commanders named by the three governments will proceed by common agreement in everything concerning military operations. The Minister of War will give to Your Excellency the necessary military instructions and will make you acquainted with the means that he is putting at your disposal in order to obtain a prompt success.

From the news recently received from Mexico, Juarez has given the order to dismantle the chateau of San Juan de Ulloa and Vera Cruz. It appears to indicate that he doesn't intend to oppose the debarkation of the expeditionary troops, without doubt to carry the theatre of the campaign into the interior of the country. In this case, the result of the campaign, despite a slight delay, would be the same, for the allied fleets are carrying sufficient forces to bring the expedition to a satisfactory end no matter where the operations must be conducted.

Your Excellency will see that Article 1 foresees all the eventualities that could occur after the occupation of the

Mexican ports by the allied forces. If the security of the nationals of the three powers should be menaced, if new outrages and new violence are committed against them, it would be impossible to do nothing. The allied commanders would have the duty and would find themselves in the necessity to go to their aid and to defend them against the exaltation of popular passions. Your Excellency will understand that it would be impossible to tolerate the renewal of excesses that has made Mexican soil bloody, when the allied troops would have occupied the places, which they are occupying only to make respected the principles of international law too long violated by the government of this country.

Perhaps the Mexican Government would have the idea of only opposing by passive resistance the action of the three powers and to withdraw its forces into the interior of the country to leave to the climate and to all the inconveniences tied up with distant expeditions the time decimate the troops and to put off indefinitely the solution of the question. In this case, it would be necessary to go to seek out the government even to the place of its residence to impose on it conditions more vigorous than those that it would have obtained by recognizing the justice of the demands presented by the three governments and by ceding to these sentiments of honor, wisdom, and equity.

Your Excellency will understand that the agreement and perfect harmony among the Commanders of the allied forces are always the indispensable conditions to avoid conflict and to attain promptly the aims of the powers .

It would not be impossible that the Mexican Government, deprived by the occupation of its ports of the customs that constitute its chief and almost its only resource, should accede to the just claims of the allies.

In this eventuality Your Excellency would have to formulate the claims of the Government of Her Majesty in accordance to the communication that I sent last 11 September to M le Marechal Serrano, Captain-General of Cuba, a copy of which you will find enclosed. In this document the just claims to which we have a right and that will have to be accorded to use before the conclusion of peace are :

1.   A public and solemn satisfaction for the violent expulsion of the Ambassador of the Queen that was ordered by the Mexican Government, which has already admitted its fault in this question and which has already promised a reparation in accordance with the nature of the offense. This condition must be done in the terms contained in the said communication.

2.   The complete execution of the treaty signed at Paris on 26 September 1859 by Messieurs Mon and Almonte and wherein is included the convention of 12 November 1853 concerning the payment of Spanish debts indefinitely suspended by the Mexican Government.

You will note that the instructions communicated to the Captain-General of Cuba expressly stipulate in favor of the Spanish debts contained in the Convention of 1853 the payment of the interest accrued since the suspension that froze them. It isn't easy to calculate at first the sum of this liquidation, but one can estimate that it could be as high as 10 million *réaux*, a sum that will have to be reimbursed before the signature of any convention. After the establishment of the allied intervention in the administration of customs and the distribution of its proceeds among the creditors of the three countries, Your Excellency will have to seek to destine a fixed amount towards the sum owed Spain to pay the debts in arrears until the formulation of the balance to be established among all the interested parties.

The indemnity owed Spaniards for damages that they have suffered as a result of crimes commited at the estate of San Vicente Chiconcuaque and at the mines of San Dimas must be claimed as a special condition for the honor and interest of Spain.

Lately the subjects of Her Majesty have been exposed to new outrages and vexations, and Your Excellency will have to read the justificatory documents presented by interested parties to demand an indemnity due and the exemplary punishment of those to blame and of the authorities who did not try to prevent this violence.

3. Reimbursement for the "Concepcion," a boat captured by a ship of the Juarez Government, held for some time at Vera Cruz, and finally sold in spite of all our protests.

Such are the conditions that Your Excellency must present and whose acceptance will be a condition *sina oua non* of the treaty of peace.

The Allied Powers have decided to act in perfect accord toward Mexico. They have decided to act in perfect accord toward Mexico. They have decided that all the war operations be made in the name of the three governments without reference to nationality. For this purpose it has been decided to name a commission of three members armed with full powers to resolve questions that could come up with regard to the use and distribution of sums that could be obtained in Mexico, be they obtained from customs that will be appropriated by the Three Powers under the inspection of their deligates designated for this purpose, be they sums received directly from the Mexican Government.

Your Excellency will represent the Queen, Our Sovereign, in this commission, in which His Majesty the Emperor of the French will be represented by his Minister to Mexico, M. le comte Dubois de Saligny, and for Her Britannic Majesty, Sir Charles Wyke, who represents it in the same capacity in this country. The French Government has also conferred the powers of Plenipotentiary for the signature of conventions upon Contre-Admiral Jurien de La Gravière, Commander of the French expeditionary forces, and probably the English Government will give the same rank to the Admiral commanding its squadron.

If the Government of the United States makes its adhesion to the Treaty of 31 October known, in accordance with the stipulations of Article IV, the Minister of Her Majesty to

Washington will inform you of the nomination of the American diplomatic agent who would be designated to take part in the work of the commission and in the ultimate negotiations.

I have already informed Your Excellency that the Allied Powers want to refrain from any intervention in the internal affairs of Mexico and to leave the inhabitants of this country the entire liberty of choosing the form of government that will seem to them to be the most suitable. However, in spite of the intention to remain aloof from the party strife and the interests that oppose each other in the country, the allied governments cannot hide the sincere and ardent desire to see an end to this bloody struggle without truce that disrupts the population of this unfortunate State, and the establishment of an enlightened and strong power, animated with the firm desire to reestablish and maintain internal order with sufficient means to organize the Administration, protect foreign subjects and offer guarantees of good faith for the observation of treaties in order not to oblige the governments that sign conventions with Mexico to have recourse to censorious and always disagreeable measures for their accomplishment. Spain especially by sympathies of race, by reasons of politics, and by reason of reciprocal congruity would see with the greatest satisfaction the establishment in Mexico of a strong and durable government.

We will only seek an influence purely moral in everything concerning the internal government of the Mexican people. This is even in the speech given by Her Majesty before the Representatives of our country. We have given existence and civilization to the great American continent, and, in the middle of prolonged dissensions that are tearing Mexico apart, this would be a new glory for Spain to give these people new pledges of security, independence, order, and liberty.

Your Excellency will have to judge with the greatest impartiality the political phases that could develop during your stay in Mexico.

The mission that is confided to you is both military and

political. As a military mission, it will only cause this country temporary but inevitable injuries that the armed occupation of a part of its territory entails. As a political mission, it must accord the greatest consideration to the influential persons of the country and to those who are trying to establish a government in harmony with national interests. The misfortunes of Mexico can only inspire the Great Powers with the same sollicitude that Spain continues to profess to them. Our flag would appear as a sign of conciliation forty years after the separation of the two countries without bringing neither resentment nor regret for domination, the loss of which has been more baneful for Mexico than for Spain.

Pervaded with these principles and these sentiments, Your Excellency will adhere to the line of conduct I have just traced for you. The best relations and the most cordial accord must be maintained among the Commanders of the allied forces.

Everything depends on the good harmony that must reign among the Powers, which harmony alone can produce good results in an European expedition and which can contain the principle and the basis for procuring for all the peoples of the American continent the tranquillity internally and externally the respect of the civilized world that sees with sadness the deplorable situation to which the intestine dissensions have condemned them.

Palais, 17 (November) (1861), etc., etc.

# Appendix O

## CONVENTION BETWEEN HER BRITANNIC MAJESTY AND THE REPUBLIC OF MEXICO FOR THE SETTLEMENT OF VARIOUS QUESTIONS NOW PENDING BETWEEN THE TWO GOVERNMENTS, SIGNED AT MEXICO CITY, 21 NOVEMBER 1861
### (Never Ratified)

DESIROUS OF PUTTING AN END TO THE PRESENT SUSPENSION of diplomatic relations between the British Legation and the Government of Mexico by an arrangement removing the cause of such suspension, and at the same time settling certain other questions in which the Government of Her Majesty and that of the Republic are mutually interested, they have resolved to conclude a Treaty for that purpose, and have named as their Plenipotentiaries, that is to say :

Her Majesty the Queen of the United Kingdom of Great Britain and Ireland, Sir Charles Lennox Wyke, Knight Commander of the Most Honourable Order of Bath, Her Majesty's Envoy Extraordinary and Minister Plenipotentiary to the Republic of Mexico;

And his Excellency the President of the Republic of Mexico, Senor Don Manuel Maria de Zamacona, Minister for Foreign Affairs, etc.;

Who, having communicated to each other their respective

full powers, found in good and due form, have agreed and concluded the following Articles:

## Article I

The sum still remaining due to British subjects of the moneys abstracted from the conducta at the Laguna Seca, as well as the 660,000 dollars forcibly taken from the British Legation in the month of November last, shall be repaid to the lawful owners thereof by an assignment made for that purpose by the Mexican Government corresponding to 10 per cent. of the import duties, to be taken from that portion of the additional duties commonly known under the denomination of "mejoras materiales."

## Article II

The rate of interest due from the time when the money was taken to be paid on both these sums from the same fund shall be as follows: namely, 6 per cent. per annum on the 660,000 dollars, and 12 per cent. per annum on the remainder of the money due to British subjects from the moneys abstracted from the conducta at the Laguna Seca.

## Article III

All Treaties, Conventions, and agreements heretofore concluded between the two High Contracting Parties shall remain binding in their totality on both parties in all affecting British and Mexican interests; and the Supreme Decrees of the 14th of October, 1850, and the 23rd of January, 1857, do likewise remain in full force and vigour in all that concerns the London bondholders.

## Article IV

Such sums of money owing to the London bondholders and Convention bondholders as were in the hands of the Custom-

House authorities at the time all payments were suspended by the law of the 17th of July last, shall be paid to the owners thereof, together with 6 per cent interest thereon, out of the same fund that is set apart for the Legation and Laguna Seca claims, when those shall have been liquidated.

## Article V

Nothing contained in this Convention shall in any way interfere with the stipulations of other agreements or Conventions by which the goods imported in French vessels are exempt from contributing to British assignments until the French Convention shall have been wholly paid off, as well as the arrears due on other claims as arranged with Admiral Penaud, have been liquidated, whom the quota belonging to the British Convention bondholders shall be augmented, as agreed on, by two per cent. additional.

## Article VI

The British Consular Agents and agents of bondholders at the different ports of the Republic shall be entitled to exact the production of all Custom-House books and papers as may have reference to their clients' interests, and to call for ships' manifests, bills of lading, and all other documents which for the above-named purpose they may consider it necessary to examine.

Every month a statement of the duties incurred, and of the liquidation of the assignments due to the London bondholders and the Convention bondholders at each of the Custom-Houses shall be delivered to the British Consul resident at the port, and in those places where there is no British Consul, such statement shall be given to the agents of the respective funds, provided there be any such on the spot.

## Article VII

In order to ensure with every certainty the fulfillment of the conditions contained in the preceding Articles, the assignments made over to the British crediters shall henceforth be represented by certificates to be issued by the Ministry of Finance, according to the regulations which shall be framed by the said Ministry, and no importer will be permitted in future to pay the duties on his cargo without at the same time paying said assignments, which shall not be paid in cash or in any other form except in the said certificates, under the penalty of a second payment of double the amount, one half in certificates, and the other in cash, which latter half shall be given to the informer of the fraud.

The Minister of Finance shall deliver a sufficient quantity of said certificates to the representatives of both classes of bond-holders in Mexico, who shall be required to keep enough of them on hand, both in this city and the ports, to enable the importers to obtain them with the facility required.

For greater security these certificates must be signed by the representatives of the aforesaid bondholders, as well as by the aforesaid agents, and after liquidation they shall be remitted by the collectors of the maritime and frontier Custom-Houses directly to the Minister of Finance, for the purpose of enabling the Government to take due not thereof in forming the account current of the respective debts.

## Article VIII

The assignment of 10 per cent. of the duties alluded to in Article I for the purposes above specified shall commence from the date of the signature of this Convention; and the assignments belonging to the London bondholders and to the Convention bondholders, secured to them by Article III, shall begin from the first day of January, 1862.

## Article IX

It is understood that the Mexican Government shall be free from the responsibility of a debtor to a creditor in so far as concerns any such sums as shall have been paid by them at the end of each month to the agents of the respective bond-holders, when a liquidation of the sums so paid and received is duly made out and signed by the authorities of the Custom-Houses and the agents at the ports.

## Article X

In settling with the other foreign creditors of the Republic the difficulties to which the law of the 17th of July last has given rise, no advantage shall be accorded to them, with regard to the time at which the payment of the assignments shall be renewed, nor as regards the control that they may have in the Custom-Houses, which shall not by the same act be conceded to the British creditors.

## Article XI

The present Convention shall be ratified by Her Britannic Majesty and by the Congress of the Mexican Republic, and the ratifications shall be exchanged at London as soon as possible within the space of six months.

In witness whereof the respective Plenipotentiaries have signed the same, and have affixed thereto their respective seals.

Done at Mexico this twenty first day of November, in the year of our Lord, eighteen hundred and sixty-one.

           (L.S.)    G. Lennox Wyke.

           (L.S.)    Manuel MA. De Zamacona.

# Appendix P

## PROCLAMATION OF THE ALLIED COMMISSIONERS TO THE MEXICAN PEOPLE, VERA CRUZ, 10 JANUARY 1862

MEXICANS:

The representatives of England, France, and Spain fulfil a sacred duty in letting you know their intentions as soon as they set foot upon the territory of the Republic.

The faith of Treaties, broken by the various Governments which have succeeded one another in your country, the personal safety of our country continually menaced, have made this expedition necessary and indispensable.

Those deceive you who would have you believe that, behind demands as just as they are legitimate, are hidden plans of conquest, of restorations, or of intervention in your policy of administration.

Three nations, who with loyalty accepted and recognized your independence, have a right to expect that you should believe them animated by no illegitimate thoughts, but rather by more noble, elevated, and generous ones. The 3 nations which we come here to represent, and whose primary interest may seem to be satisfaction for the outrages inflicted upon them, have a higher interest, and one that has more general and beneficent consequences. They come to stretch a friendly hand

537

to the people on whom Providence has showered all its gifts, and whom they see, with grief, wasting their strength and destroying their vitality, under the violent action of civil war and perpetual convulsions.

This is the truth, and we, who are charged to lay it before you, do not do so as a war-cry or menace, but in order that you may build up the edifice of your prosperity, which interests us all.

It is for you, exclusively for you, without the intervention of foreigners, to constitute yourselves in a solid and permanent manner; your work will be the work of regeneration, and all will have contributed to it, some with their opinions, with their intelligence, others, with their conscience all! The evil is serious, the remedy urgent; now or never you may make your happiness.

Mexicans! Listen to the voice of the Allies, the anchor of salvation in the dreadful tempest before which you are being driven; intrust yourselves with the greatest confidence to their good faith and upright intentions. Fear nothing on account of the unquiet and restless spirits, who, should they present themselves, your determined and decided uprightness would know how to confound, while we, lookers-on, preside at the grand spectacles of your regeneration, guaranteed by order and liberty.

Thus will it be understood, we are sure, by the Supreme Government to whom we address ourselves; thus will it be understood by the intelligence of the country to whom we speak, and who, as true patriots, will not do otherwise than agree that they should all of them rest on their arms, and that they should appeal to reason, which is that which should triumph in the 19th century.

C. LENNOX WYKE      E. JURIEN DE LA GRAVIERE

HUGH DUNLOP      DUBOIS DE SALIGNY

EL CONDE DE REUS

# Appendix Q

## DUBOIS DE SALIGNY'S PROPOSED ULTIMATUM, VERA CRUZ, 12 JANUARY 1862

THE UNDERSIGNED, REPRESENTATIVES OF FRANCE, HAVE THE honor, as stated in the collective note of this day addressed to the Mexican Government by the Plenipotentiaries of France, England, and Spain, to formulate as an ultimatum, authorized by the Government of His Majesty the Emperor, for the pure and simple acceptance of Mexico:

### Article I

Mexico engages to pay France a sum of 12,000,000 piastres (i.e., dollars), to cover all French claims, for the deeds done until last 31 July, excepting stipulations in Articles II and IV below.

Relative to the deeds accomplished since 31 July last, and for which a reservation is made here expressly, the total amount of claims against Mexico will ultimately be fixed by the Plenipotentiaries of France.

### Article II

The sums still due under the Convention of 1853, which are not part of Article I above, will have to be paid in accordance with the terms of the Convention of 1853.

## Article III

Mexico will be held to the full, loyal, and immediate execution of the contracted concluded February, 1859 between the Mexican Government and the House of Jecker.

## Article IV

Mexico obliges itself to pay immediately the $11,000 (*11,000 piastres*) forming the remaining indemnity which has been stipulated in favor of the widow and children of M. Riche, Vice-Consul of France at Tépic, assassinated in October, 1859.

The Mexican Government fire from its employ and punish in an exemplary manner Colonel Rojas, one of the assassins of M. Ricke, with the express condition that Rojas will never again be invested with any employ, command, or public function whatsoever.

## Article V

The Mexican Government engages itself to seek out and punish the authors of numerous assassinations against the French, especially the murderers of Sieur Davesne.

## Article VI

The authors of the attempts such as the one of last 14 August against the Minister of the Emperor, and of outrages against the Representatives of France in the first days of November, 1861, will be given an exemplary punishment; and the Mexican Government will give France and its Representative reparations and satisfactions due by reason of these deplorable excesses.

## Article VII

To assure the execution of Articles V and VI above, and the punishment of all attempts made or which will be made against the persons of French residing in the Republic, the Minister of France will always have the right to assist, in every kind of case, and by such deligate whom he will designate for this purpose, in all examinations opened by the criminal justice of the country.

He will be invested with the same right relative to all criminal cases intended against his nationals.

## Article VIII

The indemnities stipulated in this ultimatum will carry, until final payment, 6 per cent interest from 17 July last.

## Article IX

To guarantee the carrying out of the financial and other conditions presented in this ultimatum, France will have the right to occupy the ports of Vera Cruz, Tampico, and such other ports of the Republic what France will think appropriate, and to establish there Commissioners appointed by the Impeial Government and having for their mission to assure the return into the hands of the Powers who would have a right to the funds there that must be levied for them, in execution of the foreign Conventions, on the maritime tariff of Mexico and the return into the hands of French Agents of the sums due to France.

The Commissioners will be invested with the power to diminish, be it half or be it in a less proportion according to what they will judge convenient, the duties actually observed in the ports of the Republic.

It is expressly understood that the merchandise having already paid import duties will not be, in any case or under any pretext, submitted by the Supreme Government or by the authorities of the States to any additional custom duties, internal or other, exceeding the proportion of 15% of the import duties.

## Article X

All the measures which will be judged necessary to regulate the division between interested parties of sums levied on the yield of customs, as to the mode and the time of indemnity payments stipulated above, as for the guarantee of the execution of the conditions of this ultimatum, will be resolved on in concert with the Plenipotentiaries of France, England, and Spain.

# Appendix R

## PRELIMINARIES OF LA SOLEDAD, 19 FEBRUARY 1862

### Article I

AS THE CONSTITUTIONAL GOVERNMENT WHICH AT PRESENT rules in the Mexican Republic has made known to the Commissioners of the Allied Powers that it is not in want of the help that they have so benevolently offered to the Mexican people, since it possesses in itself the elements of strength and of public opinion sufficient to preserve itself against any intestine revolt whatever, the allies from this time entere into negotiations (*entran en el terreno de los tratados*) in order to adjust (*formalizar*) all the claims that they have to make in the name of their respective nations.

### Article II

Accordingly, and protesting as do protest the Representatives of the allied Powers, that they will attempt nothing against the independence, sovereignty, and integrity of the territory of the Republic, the negotiations will be opened in Orizaba, to which city will repair the Commissioners and two of the Ministers of the Government of the Republic, except in the case by common consent it be arranged to name representatives delegated by both parties.

### Article III

During the negotiations, the forces of the allied Powers will occupy the towns of Cordova, Orizaba, and Tehuacan, with their natural limits.

### Article IV

In order that it may not in the most remote degree be believed that the allies have signed these preliminaries in order to obtain the passage of the fortified positions garrisoned by the Mexican army, it is stipulated that in the unfortunate event of the negotiations being broken off, the forces of the allies will retire from the said towns, and will place themselves in the line that is beyond the said fortifications, on the Vera Cruze side; Paso Ancho on the Cordova road, and Paso de Ovejas on that of Jalapa, being the principal extreme points.

### Article V

Should the unfortunate event of the breaking off of negotiations take place, and the Allied troops retire to the line indicated in the preceding Article, the hospitals that the Allies may have will remain under the protection of the Mexican nation.

### Article VI

The day on which the Allied troops commence their march to occupy the place marked out in the third Article, the Mexican flag shall be hoisted in the city of Vera Cruz, and on the castle of San Juan de Ulloa.

C. LENNOX WYKE.      EL CONDE DE REUS.

HUGH DUNLOP.      MANUEL DOBLADO.

The above preliminaries approved,

E. JURIEN.

D. DE SALIGNY.

# Appendix S

PROTOCOL OF THE TWELFTH CONFERENCE OF
THE ALLIED COMMISSIOINERS, VERA CRUZ,
19 FEBRUARY 1862

IN THE CITY OF VERA CRUZ, AT 11 O'CLOCK ON THE NIGHT OF
the 19th day of February of 1862, being assembled their
Excellencies the Plenipotentiaries and Commanders of the
Forces of the allied nations, and after the Protocol of the
preceding Conference has been approved, the sitting is opened.

The Count de Reus addresses the meeting, in order to give
an account to his colleagues of what has taken place in the
Conference that he had had that very day, the 19th, with the
Minister of Foreign Affairs of Mexico, and he does so in the
following terms :

"As agreed on, I started from Vera Cruz at dawn, on my
way to Soledad; at a league from the said place Generals
Doblado and Zaragoza were waiting for me with a carriage,
and I continued my journey with those gentlemen, escorted
by a squadron of Mexican carabineers.

"As soon as we arrived at the Soledad, General Doblado and
I went to a separate dwelling, and began our conference.

"I found in the General a superior and intelligent person,
and of very good manners. He seemed to me to be a man well
acquainted with the affairs of his country, and I believe that
in what he said there was sincerity and frankness; for he did

not, as other persons were wont to do, cry up to me the excellencies of his country, nor the superiority of the political party to which he belongs; on the contrary, he made me an exact description, and one not at all inspired by passion, of the Republic.

"He told me, in short, that the Government was surrounded by difficulties from the sort of independence that exists among the States, whose Governors refuse to obey the orders of the Government of the capital; from the excited state of public feeling, and more especially in the present case, which at time prevents the Government, limited as it is in its authority, from dictating the measures which the situation demands, and prudence counsels.

"He observed to me that in this country, for a long time disturbed by intestine revolts, there is a considerable party, composed of persons who have no other employment but war, and who, accustomed to disorder and vandalism, will with difficulty submit themselves to a policy whose object would be to augment the authority of the Government, to re-establish peace, and strengthen order. They desire war, because by it they live, and with it they thrive; and every arrangement that should depart in the least from legality, will be a sufficient pretext for them to rise against the established Government.

"General Doblado admitted that the allied Powers have much more force than is necessary in order to impose any conditions on this country, which is so weakened and divided; and he owned to me that in his opinion, and in that of all sensible people, the military elements that are now in Vera Cruz suffice, and more than suffice, crumple up the forces that the Mexican Government would be able to oppose to them; but the sensible men are in a minority, and the masses which constitute the immense majority do not allow themselves to be guided by reasons, but by their passions. They have seen arrive on the Mexican shores, without previous declaration of war, the troops of the allied nations, which have taken possession of a portion of the Mexican territory, and this has produced in the country an excitement which it will be very difficult to calm down.

"The Government desires to enter into pacific arrangements, and believes that it will be able to do so easily, if the foreign Governments take into consideration what is due to that of the Republic, and do not force it to sacrifice its feeling of national dignity. If, on the contrary, it is forced to adopt precipitately, measures which would authorize the malcontents to accuse it of treason to the country, the nation would again fall into disorder and anarchy, and there will be no means for any party to form a strong and stable Government.

"It is necessary to give time to the majority of the nation to persuade itself that the allied forces do not come with a view to attempt anything against the independence and sovereignty of Mexico; it is necessary to destroy the bad effect produced in the country by the false rumours that have been published, and which the people, in its ignorance, has received as true. It is believed by some that France has the fixed intention of establishing a Monarchy, and others give out as certain that Spain desires to re-establish her ancient dominion in the republic. If the belief in these rumours is not done away with, the ultras of all parties will resist obstinately any arrangement with the Commanders of the Forces which occupy Vera Cruz.

If the allies consent to make a solemn declaration contradicting these rumours; if they give the Government time to go on preparing the minds and modifying the opinion of the country, the Government is, on its part, decided to do everything in order to obtain the prompt and satisfactory arrangement of the pending differences. As the principal object of the allied expedition is to demand reparation for injuries and the fulfilment of Treaties, as the Government offers to do whatever may be just, and to fulfil all its obligations with the allied Powers, seeing that the intentions of England, France, and Spain, are noble, generous, and disinterested; and taking into account that the Mexican nation does not accept the help so benevolently offered by the foreign forces in order to re-establish peace and order, inasmuch as the present Government has at its disposal sufficient means to obtain these results, there is no reason to oppose the commencement of friendly negotiations. But before entering into the whole question, it would be proper to settle some preliminary basis which would render acceptable to the country the entry of foreign troops into the interior of the country.

"To these reasons of General Doblado, I answered that indeed our Governments did not entertain the design of imposing on Mexico a form of government contrary to the wishes of the country. That all the allied Commissioners represent nations governed by constitutional monarchies, and that under the shadow of this system England, France, and Spain prosper and grow great; therefore, if counsel were asked of us, we should recommend constitutional monarchy as the best government, but in no way attempt to force on the country our ideas and opinions.

"I repelled most energetically the absurd supposition that the Spanish Government had the most remote pretension to rule this country. I gave the most formal assurances that the independence and integrity of the Republic would be respected; and I stated to General Doblado that the present Administration possessed unequivocal proofs of our having regulated our conduct in accordance with what was agreed on in the Convention of London, namely, in not interfering in the internal policy of the country, and in treating with the established Government, which has not any ground of complaint against us, since in our relations with it we have taken into consideration all that was due it. After this frank explanation on both sides, we could not fail to agree on the principal points; we had only to settle upon the form best suited to make the preliminary stipulations acceptable to the country.

"As first basis, General Doblado required the recognition of the present Government. I gave him to understand, that such an express recognition was not possible, of which, however, the present Government had no need, since it declares that it possesses sufficient strength to constitute itself in a solid and permanent manner; with which reasons I succeeded in getting General Doblado to desist from this requirement.

"Without opposing the slightest difficulty, I consented to declare that nothing should be attempted against the sovereignty, independence, and integrity of the Mexican nation — a declaration which we made spontaneous in our first communication to the Mexican Government.

"Afterwards the General observed to me, if, when the foreign troops had penetrated peaceably into the heart of the country, an agreement should not be arrived at, we should have succeeded in rendering useless the principal means of defense of the Mexican Government, having passed as friends the fortified points that there are between Vera Cruz and the towns we are to occupy. I assured Senor Doblado that the fortified positions, in which the Mexicans place such confidence, were obstacles of little importance to our troops; that therefore, and so that we might never, nor by anybody, be accused of having entered into the country in a perfidious manner, should the negotiations happen to be broken off, we would return and take up our positions beyond the fortified line.

"The Minister of Foreign Affairs desired to settle a truce or term within which we should not be able to make use of our arms, after we had returned and occupied our former positions; but far from acceding to such a demand, I declared to the General that on the day following that on which we arrived in our retrograde movement at the limit marked out for us, we should take possession of his so much vaunted fortifications.

"Although it had been intended that a portion of the Allied Forces should take up their positions in the city of Jalapa, General Doblado stated that as Tehuacan was on the same road as Cordova and Orizaba, and nearer to this last place than Jalapa, it would, perhaps, be preferable for us to occupy the cities of Cordova, Orizaba, and Tehuacan.

"Foreseeing that we shall have to form, in the points we

occupy, hospitals which will be abandoned the day that, in consequence of a rupture, we evacuate the said towns, I desired to have it stated, among the preliminary stipulations, that the hospitals would remain under the protection of the Mexican nation; it seemed to me right to say the nation, and not Government in order to prevent its enemies from committing, in order to do it injury, outrages, and misdeeds, the responsibility of which falls upon it.

"In conclusion, General Doblado observed to me, that the country in general had taken it very ill that the mexican flag should have disappeared from the town of Vera Cruz, and from the castle of San Juan de Ulloa; that notwithstanding that it might appear a puerile demand, the majority of the mexicans desired ardently that the national flag should again float by the side of those of the Allied nations.

"I stated to General Doblado that, strictly speaking, it was not our fault that the Mexican flag had disappeared, since the garrisons of Vera Cruz and Ulloa, when they abandoned those points on the 15th December, 1861, not only took with them the flags, but also the halyards. As already among ourselves we had touched upon this point, it having reached our ears that for the Mexicans it was of the greatest importance, whilst in our eyes it had not any signification; taking likewise into account that we are about to occupy peaceably Mexican towns, where the Mexican flag will float without our having any right to prevent it, it appeared to me that there was not any inconvenience in acceding to this demand, certain as I was that my colleagues were of the same opinion as myself.

"After having agreed upon these points, Senor Doblado touched upon the advantages of returning the Custom-House of Vera Cruz to the Mexican authorities; but as this demand had not been foreseen, and although in our hands the Custom-House produces nothing, it appeared to me that the question was too serious a one for me to settle, without submitting beforehand this incident to the consideration of my colleagues.

"I now proceed to read the preliminary stipulations agreed

on with General Doblado, so that the Commissioners may make the observations and propose the modifications that they may deem proper.

After the preliminaries have been read the French Minister addresses the meeting, and states the propriety of demanding from the Mexican Government the abrogation of the Decree of the 25th of January, by which all persons composing the allied expedition are placed beyond the pale of the law.

The British Minister reads the said Decree, and expresses the opinion that no importance should be given to the said document, of which the Conference has no official knowledge.

The French Minister does not believe that a Decree in which the penalty of death is imposed on all the individuals who form part of the forces which now occupy Vera Cruz, and its neighbourhood, is of so little importance, and that although this Decree has not been officially communicated to the Allied Commissioners, nobody is ignorant of its existence, since it is to be seen, signed by the President, in the Mexican newspapers.

Admiral Jurien de la Gravière is of opinion that if the abrogation of the said Decree is demanded only for the part touching the Allies, they would be sanctioning, up to a certain point, the barbarous enactments which have reference to the native and foreign persons residing in the country.

The French Minister declares that, for his part, he does not entertain any doubt that the Mexican Government would abrogate without difficulty the enactments of the Decree in question in what touches the Allied forces and their commanders, reserving to themselves the power of re-establishing them should the negotiations be broken off. He desires that it should be stated that he has expressed this opinion, but that if none of his colleagues share the same, he would submit to the decision of the majority.

The admiral points out that the abrogation might have been fittingly demanded at the time that the Decree became known; but after having exchanged with the Government several communications, in which not the slightest mention was made of it, the demand appears tardy and inopportune. He states, nevertheless, that he is not opposed to the total abrogation of the Decree being asked for; since what ought to be avoided is that individuals residing in the interior of the country, and whom the effects of the Decree of January 25 may easily reach, should see themselves exposed to arbitrary acts of barbarity in presence of the flags of three nations who come to this country as representatives of civilization.

Count Saligny observes that in a preceding Conference, and as soon as he knew of the Decree, he called the attention of his colleagues to this document; and also pointed out that it was proper to request its abrogation. He believes that without including this demand in the preliminary bases, the complete abrogation of the Decree can be asked for, the Government retaining the power of dictating another, from which may be excluded every barbarous measure, and those contrary to humanity.

Commodore Dunlop is of the opinion that the part of the above-mentioned Decree which refers to the Allies becomes null and void from the moment that the Government enters into peaceable negotiations with the Commanders of the foreign forces.

The English Minister asks Count de Reus to explain to him the concluding part of Article II of the Preliminaries, in which it is said "except in the case, that by common consent it should be arranged to name Representatives delegated by both parties."

In reply, Count Reus states that, perhaps there will be questions to be decided relating to details of little importance, in which case the Commissioners of the Allied Powers will be able to entrust those questions of less importance to the examination of delegates that shall be named for that purpose.

Admiral Jurien asks if the Mexican flag will have to be saluted, when it is hoisted. For his part, he thinks that such a salute ought not to be made, as it would appear like a reparation.

Count de Reus is of the same opinion, and besides remarks, that in the agreements in which reparations are stipulated, it is generally stated that on the flag being hoisted the salute due it shall be made; but as the preliminary bases agreed on with General Doblado no mention whatever is made of the salute, there is no obligation to make it, and with so much more reason that the Spanish forces on entering Vera Cruz did not find any flag.

With respect to the question of the Custom-House, the French Minister, before deciding, wishes again to consult his instructions.

The Count de Reus states that the instructions of the Spanish Government direct, in a decisive manner, that the Custom-Houses are to be occupied; but, seeing the inefficiency of this occupation, which has caused the military chest of the Spanish army to disburse, up to the present date, 8,000 dollars, he considers himself authorized to adopt any measure which does not give negative results.

Count de Saligny thinks that the giving over of the Custom-House to the Mexican authorities would be a step backwards, and would have a very bad effect in Europe.

The British Minister is of opinion, that if delegates or interventors of the three nations are established, with the faculties to supervise all the operations of the Custom-House, the Allied Governments cannot but approve of this measure, which will be in entire accordance with the stipulations of the Convention of London.

The French Minister thinks that in this case it will be not only prudent, but necessary, that the Mexican Government should engage not to establish interior Custom-Houses.

Count de Reus and Admiral Jurien de la Gravière observe upon the necessity of securing, in case of the giving up of the Custom-House, the importation, free of all duty, of the provisions and articles destined for the expedition.

Count de Reus remarks, that perhaps there would be frauds and abuses; to which M. de Saligny replies, that the intervention of the foreign delegates ought to be a sufficient guarantee that no illegal act will be committed with impunity.

All the Commissioners approve, without any modification, of the six Articles contained in the draft of the preliminary bases presented by Count de Reus, of which four copies are made, which after having been signed by the Count de Reus, and ratified by his four colleagues, are sent immediately by an officer commissioned for the purpose to General Doblado, in order that he may sign them, and return three of them, one for each mission.

The settlement of the other points remains pending for another Conference.

The sitting is raised without fixing a day for the next one.

# Appendix T

## PROTOCOL OF THE FINAL CONFERENCE OF THE ALLIED COMMISSIONERS, ORIZABA, 9 APRIL 1862

Orizaba, April 11, 1862.

THEIR EXCELLENCIES THE PLENIPOTENTIARIES AND COM-manders-in-Chief of the Forces of the Allied Powers finding themselves united in the residence of his Excellency the Count of Reus, the session was opened at 1.00 P.M.

In view of the gravity of the affairs to be considered, their Excellencies decided that the Secretaries of the Missions of England and France would assist the Secretary of the Spanish Mission at this Conference to take full minutes.

His Excellency the Count of Reus speaks to invite his Excellency the Admiral Jurien to explain the object of the Conference, and the latter replies that the chief reason for the reunion is to agree on a reply to a communication from the Mexican Government demanding the reembarkation of General Almonte and the persons accompanying him.

His Excellency Sir Charles Wyke says that is necessary to have new and plain explanations, and his colleagues agree with him.

The Count of Reus adds that it is urgent to know whether it is possible to continue to act together, as done until now.

But he and his colleagues from England think the attitude recently taken by the Plenipotentiaries of His Majesty the Emperor is contrary to the stipulations of the Convention of London, the aim of which, according to them, was, in the first place, to obtain the reparation of grievances that each of the High Powers had against the Mexican Government and to demand the respect of Treaties, then to obtain, by the moral force of the three nations, the establishment of a strong and stable Government in Mexico, offering sufficient guarantees to its own nationals as to those of foreign Powers.

His Excellency recalls to mind that if this principle, concerning the question of grievances, has not appeared on the first line of the Proclamation to the Mexicans and the note sent to President Juarez, it is that the Commissioners had not thought themselves authorized to decide whether there was to be solidarity among them as to their respective ultimatums, and, in consequence, they had thought it necessary to demand new instructions in this respect.

His Excellency desires that it be well established that the line of conduct which has been considered by certain people as a loss of precious time has been but an absolute necessity owing to the total lack of transportation. But, although the three Allied Powers had foreseen that in certain circumstances it would be necessary to advance into the interior of the country, their troops arrived at Vera Cruz without carts, without horses, without mules, without any of the indispensable resources for the transportation of the living, the sick, the artillery. Thus it was in these conditions that a resolution was adopted to limit the occupation to the port of Vera Cruz. However, hardly having landed, the Allies felt the necessity of penetrating the interior of the country, owing to the change in the health of the troops, owing to the complete lack of goods, which the guerillas were not permitting to reach Vera Cruz.

Consequently, the Chiefs of the Allied Forces immediately made an effort to assemble as many means of transportation as possible. These were obtained with difficulty and at the price of gold, and the allies extended, little by little, the circle of their operations in the territory surrounding Vera Cruz.

Admiral Jurien approves what his Spanish colleague has just said and desires that it be established that his artillery and the objects of encampment of two of his battalions were not able to land until the 5th of February.

The Count of Reus believes that it was impossible to act otherwise, that in entering parleys and friendly negotiations with the Mexican Government, the Allies only gained the time that was absolutely necessary for them to prepare themselves to march forward, without permitting themselves to be deceived by the Mexican Government, as might be thought. One did not fear war, but one wanted to avoid in Mexico the misfortunes which result of it and to achieve the aims of the alliance without the shedding of blood. Thus the Commissioners notified the Mexican Government of their intention to march ahead without demanding authorization. While desiring to stay in peace, the Allies decided not to modify this resolution.

It is in this spirit that the Count of Reus, authorized by his colleagues, went, on the 19th of February, to La Soledad to have a meeting there with Doblado, Mexican Minister of Foreign Affairs. The Count of Reus signed at La Soledad the Preliminaries destined to determine the respective situations and to serve as the basis of the line of conduct to follow.

On the 28th of February the Spanish army began to march into the interior. The Admiral, at the head of the French troops, had already started his march on the 26th of February. He encountered no serious obstacles or hostilities. But the two armies left on the road sad traces of their passage — sick, baggage, horses or mules which, not being able to follow the march on terrible roads under a sun of fire, stayed behind and attested to all the difficulties of the affair.

His Excellency adds that, if one had found war around him, a disaster would have been possible, and the European Governments would have demanded a rigorous account of the conduct of their Generals.

But finally the Spanish and French arrived peacefully at their cantonments at Cordova, Orizaba, and Tehuacan, where they were supposed to wait until the 15th April, the day fixed for the opening of Conferences between the Allied Plenipotentiaries and the Mexican Commissioners.

The Count of Reus recalls to mind all the arguments, perhaps not too well grounded, that he had to employ to get the Mexican Government to accept this late date.

Saligny says that it is he who demanded with insistance this delay of the new Conferences to have time to receive awaited instructions from his Government.

The Count of Reus says, in summary, that the time spent at Vera Cruz and that necessary to wait until the 15th April was not really time lost, a fact sufficiently proved by what has just been said.

Finally, everything was going well, and it had been hoped that one would obtain by peaceful means all the satisfaction foreseen in the Convention of London, when the packet of the month of February came, bringing General Almonte, Don Antonio Haro y Zamariz and some other exiles, to throw the apple of discord into the Conference.

In a visit made to his Excellency by General Almonte, the latter declared to him, without evasion, that he was counting on the force of the three Powers to change the Government established in Mexico into a Monarchy and to place the crown on the head of the Archduke Maximilian of Austria. General Almonte declared that he thought the project would be well-received in Mexico, realized perhaps within two months.

Commodore Dunlop says that a few days later Almonte said the same thing to him.

His Excellency the Count of Reus had replied to General Almonte that he was of a diametrically opposed opinion and that Almonte was not to count on the force of Spain. The Count of Reus had declared to Almonte that Mexico, constituted into a Republic for forty years, must necessarily be Anti-Monarchical and would never accept new institutions that it could not know and which were contrary to those which it had adopted and under which it had been living for such a long time.

On the observation of General Almonte that he felt assured of the force of French arms, his Excellency replied that he was sorry that the French Government was engaging itself in Mexico in a policy which was in contradiction to the always great, just, and generous policy of the Emperor. The Count of Reus had added that in the case, very improbable but yet possible, of a check suffered by the French forces following such an enterprise, his Excellency would regard the enterprise as if the misfortune had struck his country or himself. Finally he urged General Almonte not to march forward, for, if he went alone, exiled by a just or unjust decree, he was running to his ruin, and if he were escorted by the troops of one of the Allied Powers, this protection would produce an alarm which would compromise the results of the good policy followed until then by the Commissioners.

Soon, however, one learned at Orizaba and at Tehuacan of the arrival of new French troops; but at the same time one learned that, by order of General de Lorencez, a battalion of light infantry was escorting General Almonte and his companions on the road from Vera Cruz to Tehuacan. Admiral Jurien thought it necessary, in consequence, to give notice to the Mexican Government of his resolution to begin, on the 1st of April, the retrograde movement foreseen in the Preliminaries of La Soledad if the Conferences did not end in a satisfactory result.

Admiral Jurien speaks to explain that he kept within bounds by having given first an indirect notice of his resolution to the Mexican Government, that he did not address an official note on this subject until after having received himself a letter from General Zaragoza which did not permit him any hope of obtaining from the Conference of Orizaba a result conforming to the interests and dignity of France.

The Count of Reus explains that at this time he and his

English colleague were alone at Orizaba, that in receiving the communication of the Admiral they asked themselves if the French Commissioners had the right to escort the enemies of the Government established in Mexico, if the Admiral could act without a decision of the Conference, but they considered this line of conduct as equivalent to a declaration of war and contrary to the Convention of London and the Preliminaries of La Soledad. The English and Spanish Commissioners had been in accord in thinking that the French Commissioners did not have the right to adopt this line of conduct without the assent of their colleagues. Consequently the Spanish and English Commissioners had immediately invited a Conference to meet to decide if they were continuing to act in accordance with the Convention of London, or if instruction of their Government had come to put a stop to the French Commissioners' acting as before with their colleagues, so that in this latter case each had to proceed in the manner that he would think would best reflect the views of his Government.

"For my part," adds his Excellency, "I beg my colleagues to be so good as to make these points clear, for this is the aim of this Conference."

His Excellency the Admiral Jurien replies that he thinks that he has not violated any of the stipulations of the Convention of London any more than those of the Preliminaries of La Soledad.

He has considered as incompatible with the stay of the French troops at Tehuacan the protection accorded to General Almonte by General de Lorencez.

"The boat which brought the Commander of the expeditionary corps and his Major General, adds Saligny, has, on orders from the Emperor, been waiting for General Almonte for four days."

Admiral Jurien explains that his withdrawal from Tehuacan was on his part but a scruple of loyalty to the subject of which he had not to consult his colleagues. Once at Paso Ancho with his troops, he would find himself on neutral ground where he was free to give General Almonte all the protection to which a person had the right who was honored with the good-will (*bienveillance*) of His Majesty the Emperor.

The Counte of Reus and Sir Charles Wyke desire that the root of the question be examined. They assert that the French Commissioners did not have the right to lend their protection to the enemies of the Mexican Government on its very territory. One did not come to Mexico to force on it the particular policy of any of the three nations but only that indicated in the Convention of London. No Commissioner has the right to act in such serious cases without the consent of his colleagues.

The Admiral repeats that the interpretation of the Convention of London is reserved to him and accepts thereby all the responsibility, just as this right belongs to each of the Commissioners, without engaging the Governments which have concluded this Convention. The French Commissioners are thus acting on the interpretation which appears to them the best, and assure in advance all the responsibility for their acts.

Sir Charles Wyke asks that the Admiral be given a reading of Article II of the Convention of London, and the Admiral Jurien persists in believing, after having heard it, that if there was any infraction of the Convention, it was not in the protection given General Almonte, but in the excessive mildness and the great cautions taken toward the Mexican Government, that, moreover, this policy does not seem to have been regarded favorably in Europe. The steps urged by Saligny had been, he believes, more in conformity with the intentions of the Government of the Emperor.

Sir Charles Wyke says that from the beginning negotiation was with the *de facto* Government, that this change of attitude could be considered an inconsistency, that the protection given to the exiles constitutes a real interference in the internal affairs of the country.

Admiral Jurien replies that the protection given General Almonte is only that of the French flag, which never and in no way has been lacking to the exiles of all countries, that it does not in any way constitute an interference in the internal affairs of the Republic, that once accorded, there was never an example of this protection having been withdrawn.

The Count of Reus says that this protection is for persons vanquished and who are in danger, not for people who came from the outside with hostile intentions against the established Government, with which the allies have started negotiations.

The Admiral replies that General Almonte, who is of the same opinion of that general in Europe, that there is a war in Mexico, came to Mexico, not with hostile intention, but, to the contrary, in a spirit entirely peaceful and conciliatory. Almonte came to Mexico to preach harmony to the different parties, and his previous conduct recommended him to explain to his fellow countrymen the generous views of Europe and to help avoid misunderstanding. The posts he had so honorably, his relations with and the esteem of the Emperor were recommendations for Almonte to head this mission. The reasons that the Count of Reus had given, in support of his opinion of the impossibility of establishing Monarchy in Mexico, appeared to Jurien, on the contrary, favorable for this radical change of institutions, since those adopted by Mexico had only made it prey to endless revolutions and to lead it to the deplorable state in which it finds itself today.

Sir Charles Wyke replies to Jurien that it is strange to find General Almonte speaking in the name of the three Allied Powers, for he has not been invested with any power to represent England and Spain and is not the interpreter of the Convention of London.

Admiral Jurien believes that General Almonte has never manifested such pretentions. The Count of Reus again brings to mind the conversation he had at Vera Cruz with General Almonte, adding that General Almonte claimed then to have offered the throne of Mexico, in the name of his fellow countrymen, to the Archduke Maximilian, who had shown himself inclined to accept it.

This declaration made the Count of Reus, just as to Commodore Dunlop, could not pass for a simple conversation, and as nothing was more in contradiction to the spirit of his instructions, the Count of Reus could not cooperate for the success of such projects.

The English Commissioners took exactly the same opinion as their Spanish colleague.

Saligny insists, on this point, that it is not possible to deny that the real and principal object of the Convention was to obtain satisfaction of the outrages lavished on foreigners by the Mexican Government and to force it to observe Treaties, that the system of delay and caution followed up to now was condemned by what was happening every day, for the regime of extortions, of the arbitrary, and of violence had increased and rendered the situation of foreigners entirely intolerable, that there was in them at every moment new proof in the claims without number which were sent to him every day, that the attitude of the allied forces seemed to have increased the audacity of the Government, that he was for stopping negotiation with this Government, that his opinion, firmly resolved upon, was that it was necessary to march on Mexico (City).

The Count of Reus finds what Saligny has just said unjust, and Sir Charles Wyke agrees. If the Mexican Government has hesitated sometimes to give in to the desires of the allies, it was only that it was not able to consider at first as friends the three Powers who occupied the only port from which Mexico drew all its resources, but, after more or less of hesitation, the resolutions of the Mexican Government had always been satisfactory.

There was, however, a time when the Plenipotentiaries of England and Spain thought that it was necessary to change their attitude toward the Mexican Government. They had written in this sense to Saligny and Admiral Jurien and based themselves upon the assurance given Sir Charles Wyke, in a letter from Mexico City, that the tax of 2% was to continue to be exacted of foreigners, and on threat, expressed by Doblado in a letter to the Count of Reus, to interrupt the communications between Vera Cruz and the interior if the custom house duties were not handed over to the Mexican authorities.

A few days later the Mexican Ministers, Gonzales Echeverria and Don Jesus Teran, arrived at Orizaba with full powers, listened to the complaints of the English and Spanish Commissioners, renounced, after many difficulties, the collection of the 2% on foreigners, promised an end of the Decree interrupting communications between Vera Cruz and the interior, made known the intention of the Government to make good its claim to satisfy all the just claims of the Allied Powers. If these promises were not kept, then it would be time to declare war, but it was not necessary to declare war in trusting to futile theories, which would not be justified before the great court of the civilized world.

Why, adds the Count of Reus, do the French Plenipotentiaries refuse to believe these solemn promises? Why will they not consent to put the proof of the sincerity of the Mexican Government to a test, when they only have to wait six days?

The Count of Saligny continues in his opinion and assumes all responsibility for it; it is founded on grievances, each day more numerous, of which his nationals complain all the time, and he has received from Spaniards — he does not know why — a great number of claims, which ought to have been addressed to the Count of Reus, which will be sent by his colleague as soon as he can open the bundles they are in.

Sir Charles Wyke is surprised that the news of these grievances was not made known to him and asks of what nature they are and against whom they have been committed. Saligny replies that naturally French subjects do not address themselves to the British Legation to make good their claims.

Sir Charles Wyke wants to know if it is true that Saligny has said that he considers the preliminaries as not worth the paper on which they were written, and Saligny replies that he has never had any confidence in what came from the Mexican Government, no less the Preliminaries than the other engagements.

Commodore Dunlop asks Saligny why he signed, and how it is that he does not think himself bound.

The French Commissioner replies that he has no explanations to give the Conference on the motives which made him sign the Preliminaries, but he found himself solemnly bound by his signature, if the Mexican Government had not taken care itself to tear up the Preliminaries of La Soledad in a thousand ways.

The Count of Reus asks Saligny about a personal thing. Saligny has said to Colonel Menduina, Governor of Vera Cruz, and to Cortez, Consul of Spain in Vera Cruz, that the Count of Reus was against the project of Mexican Monarchy in favor of the Archduke only because he himself wished to be crowned Emperor of Mexico. Saligny had said that he had proof of it. The Count of Reus came out strongly against such an assertion and asks his colleague to explain himself on this subject. The Count of Reus added that such an absurd statement in the mouth of the common people was not worth much, but coming from Saligny, it was very serious, that if there was any proof of it, he was insisting that it be produced.

The French Commissioner recalls having spoken in this sense, but he was but repeating what was being said highly and publically. The proof to which he had made allusion was firstly, a letter, also seen by the Admiral, which was written by a person who was a partisan of his candidature to the throne of Mexico. Secondly, the idle talk which could support the supposition was that the Emperor was favorable to this project. Finally, there were the articles in the paper, *El Eco de Europa*, to which Saligny would not have attached the slightest importance if his Excellency the Count of Reus had not declared before the Conference at Vera Cruz that this paper was not permitted to print a single word without having received the previous approval of his Excellency.

Saligny recalls something the Count of Reus has said that has stuck with him vividly. The Count of Reus had said that the candidature of an Austrian Prince for Mexico was absurd, but perhaps there were chances of success for a successful soldier.

The Count of Reus says that he made the allusion to a successful Mexican soldier, that he had never authorized anyone to attribute to him a project so insane or to support it, that it was absolutely true that *El Eco de Europa* did not print anything without his approval, but it never printed anything about his candidature to the Throne of Mexico. He is badly wounded by these suppositions. One could offer him Mexico with all its riches, and he would not want any part of it. He preferred infinitely the position he has in Spain. The rewards that he appreciates above all others, and which are enough for his ambition, are the goodwill of his Sovereign and the esteem of his fellow countrymen.

On the observation of the French Commissioners that there was in all this nothing to hurt the Count of Reus, the Count of Reus replies that it was injuring his well-known loyalty as well as to suppose that he cherished such projects in secret.

The Count of Reus desires that one return to the chief object of the Conference, namely, that it be decided if all the Commissioners will continue to act in accord, following the terms of the Convention of London, or whether his French colleagues would adopt another line of action.

The French Commissioners reply that they will continue to stick rigidly to the Convention of London, but they will act in virtue of the interpretation that they find the best, as this is their right and their duty.

The Secretary of the Spanish Mission reads a note of Doblado which demands the reembarkation of General Almonte and his companions.

The Admiral Jurien reads the reply of the French Commissioners, who cannot yield to these demands of the Mexican Government.

The Commissioners of England and Spain do not approve of this action submitted by the Admiral to their approval.

Admiral Jurien declares never having seen in any country

of the world a regime of terror weighing on the population and keeping it under a yoke of iron as he has seen in Mexico. It is the oppression in everything that is odious, the tearing away, under poor pretexts, of a father from his children, of a son from his family, stripping arbitrarily those who own, obstructing even the most timid manifestations of public opinion.

He refers to, among others, the poverty of General Uraya and the rest of General Cenobio, who was shot for trivial relations with the Allies, when they were already negotiating.

Saligny agrees with what his colleague has just said.

Sir Charles Wyke disagrees. He thinks that the majority of the Mexican people favor the Government in power, that it would be difficult to find partisans for Monarchy.

Admiral Jurien signifies absence of mind on the projects relative to Archduke Maximilian; it is not just a question of Monarchy for the time being—that is but an eventuality, which is not a question in the presence of the urgent necessity for the country to have a moral and respectable Government, which will not suffocate, under a systematic oppression, the free expression of the voice of the sane and moderate party of the nation.

This majority exists, but it is not making its opinions known, for it has had reason to believe that the Allied Commissioners would be hostile to it.

The Count of Reus replies that there is no motive to attribute this hostility to the Allied Commissioners. At Havana he declared to General Miramon, Doctor Miranda, and an agent accredited to Marquez and Zuloaga his intention to treat with the Government established at Mexico City and not with guerillas. He clearly told them that these same guerillas had but to enter Mexico City and to constitute a Government, and then they would be treated with, that that would have been easy for them, as all the forces of President Juarez were then at Vera Cruz.

Admiral Jurien thinks that the people really worthy of interest are those, who, without belonging to the ancient classification of the extreme parties, without being under arms, are found especially in the capital, in the towns, in the country, groaning under the oppression, not daring to breathe, but calling for order and peace; this party desires our protection (*appui*), and one would find it especially on the day when there would be the liberty to manifest its real sentiments. The Government of the Emperor, well informed in this respect, wishes, in consequence, to march to Mexico City, and such is the resolution of the French Commissioners.

Saligny says that his nationals are also groaning under this oppression, that he has received several petitions demanding the prompt march of French troops to Mexico City, action considered by the petitioners as the only way to safety, the sole remedy for the evils they suffer and the end of their ruin.

Commodore thinks that the French in Mexico City would see the march of the French army on the capital with great displeasure.

Sir Charles Wyke thinks that among the persons who direct the affairs of the Government of the Republic of Mexico, there are found distinguished members of the real moderate party, that the line of conduct followed up to now by the Allied Commissioners was the best for the consolidation of a Government accepted by all.

The English and Spanish Commissioners think that it is impossible to act in accord if their colleagues will not conform strictly to the Convention of London and the Preliminaries of La Soledad.

Saligny replies that if there is an infraction of the Preliminaries, it is not on account of the Commissioners, but rather from the Mexican Government itself.

Sir Charles Wyke comes back to the Convention of London, and the Count of Reus reads the reply of Billault to the interpellations addressed to him by de Boissy in the Senate on the affairs of Mexico. The substance of this reply is that the Convention of London sets the line of conduct for the Allied Powers.

The Count of Reus brings to mind the right of the Mexicans to oppose any change of their institutions. The Admiral declares he can give no sympathy to a Government to which one came to preach peace and conciliation and which only regards the regard that one has had toward it by permitting bloody executions and by publishing edicts of proscription.

The English and Spanish Commissioners declare themselves unable to act in accord with their French colleagues if the Admiral persists in his retrograde movement, and if the French Commissioners attack this resolution strongly, it will be considered as contrary to reciprocal engagements.

The Admiral replies that armistices can always be denounced in advance by one of the parties. "I have engaged myself to retire in case of rupture, but nothing more. Today I find the rupture completely justified, and I am retiring : my resolution does not bind my colleagues, but it is in conformity with my interpretation of the Convention, and I assume all responsibility, to my colleagues, to my Government, and to the whole world."

The Count of Reus says that one can't have an armistice if there is no war. Saligny replies that there was war from the moment Vera Cruz was occupied.

He repeats that he considers the march of troops to Mexico City as absolutely necessary for the security of his nationals, victims every day of terrible abuse, and he declares again his immovable resolution not to treat with the Government of President Juarez.

The English and Spanish Commissioners reply that they know of no motive to justify this resolution, that they cannot accept the reply addressed by the French Commissioners to Doblado, and they cannot sign the latter.

They declare that, if their French colleagues persist to refuse to remove the Mexican exiles, refuse to take part in the Conferences that must take place at Orizaba on the 15th of April, the English and Spanish Commissioners will retire with their troops from Mexican territory, considering this stand of the

French Commissioners a violation of the Convention of London and the Preliminaries of La Soledad.

Admiral Jurien says that those of the three Powers staying in Mexico would be able to act in the interests of the Allies, and the English and Spanish Commissioners reply that it belongs only to their Governments to decide this question, and as for them, they were not authorized to accept this offer.

The time and means of evacuation of territory by Spanish and English forces is discussed.

Admiral Jurien offers the ships at his command to aid the transport of Spanish troops.

The Count of Reus thinks it necessary not to accept this offer, for all the means will be sent to him from Havana, and, if it is necessary, he will make use of the English ships commanded by Commodore Dunlop.

The sitting in continuing, approval is given of the resolutions taken to the Government of Mexico City and to General Zaragoza.

These minutes have been read in the presence of their Excellencies Sir Charles Lennox Wyke, the Count of Reus, Admiral Jurien, and Commodore Dunlop (The Count of Saligny finding himself absent owing to indisposition), and they have been found true to the original conversation and have been approved by them.

> JUAN A. L. DE CEBALLOS, Secretary of the Mission of Her Catholic Majesty.
>
> COMTE A. DE LA LONDE, Secretary of the Legation of France.
>
> JOHN WALSHAM, Acting Secretary of Her Majesty's Legation.

# Appendix U

Mr. F(rancisco) de A(rrangiz)

My dear Friend: Four days ago I had the pleasure to
receive your letter of the 10th. In it you state that you have
reasons to believe, that Spain will never support the candidature of the Archduke Maximilian to the throne of Mexico,
and that you know without doubt that what would suite the
views of the opposition, would be the proposal of a Spanish
Prince, or that things might be so brought about that a Prince
would be thought of, who would combine the desires of
Mexico, with the recollections of the Spanish dynasty.

One of the best known adherents to the O'Donnell Ministry,
spontaneously made the same declaration to me through a
friend.

As the Mexican question, now fortunately become an
European one, occupies a great deal of attention and gives rise
to a great many opinions, associating with it at every step, the
humble names of those, who like myself, have always taken an
interest in it, I will avail myself of the opportunity offered to
me, to examine this important affair at some length.

But before entering upon the subject of the present state of
the Question, I must be allowed to write a few lines on what

has been done in this matter, from the time I became an adherent of the Monarchical Party and began to work in favour of an European intervention in Mexico.

General Santana (*sic*) being in the plenitude of his power in 1854, as he had just been empowered by the Nation, to give it the best form of Government in his opinion, asked Europe to establish a Monarchy in Mexico under a Prince of Royal extraction. He conferred this delicate mission to Don Jose Maria Gutierrez de Estrada who had so bravely initiated this idea of preservation in 1840; and this gentleman who was already acquainted with my political ideas, honoured me by asking the Government to allow me to remain secretly under his orders for which reason I was named Secretary in Madrid.

I must state here, that it was then desired to have a Spanish Prince, and the Crown was offered to the Enfant Don Juan, whose political principles were not then perverted. My journey to Madrid coincided with the revolution of 1854. Then came the Crimean War, and General Santana (*sic*) went out of power the following year, which put an end to this negotiation.

The rupture of relations between Spain and Mexico in 1857 made us all believe in a War. Mr. Gutierrez and myself set to work ardently in order to prevent its being a War of vengeance. We desired to make it profitable, asking France also to interfere, in order that both Nations being agreed, the nationality of Mexico might be saved; but things took another turn and War was not carried into those Regions. Until then I had merely carried out, with much pleasure, the views transmitted to me from Rome by Mr. Gutierrez; but having gone to France in 1857, I had the honour and good fortune to take the initiative more than once, at the conjunction of affairs which, for the time, put a stop to this negotiation.

I was enabled to appreciate in Paris, how great and sincere was the desire of the Emperor Napoleon to do something in favour of Mexico, but his Policy did not allow him to depart from his intention of acting in union with England in American questions. This Nation, which has never done anything disagreeable to the United States, refused to contribute to put an end to the bloody anarchy in which the Mexican Republic was plunged. The Emperor heard the expression of the feelings of the Mexicans with the greatest kindness. They hoped much from his power and wisdom, but the loyalty of His Policy did not allow us to entertain much chance of success.

There were moments in which we lost all hopes of preserving the nationality of Mexico, notwithstanding that two successive Governments had the patriotism to ask Europe, but in vain, to lend them a helping hand. We who were acting in this sense now ceased our efforts, retaining only a grateful recollection and an imperishable gratitude for the benevolence with which the Emperor Napoleon and the Spanish Govenment had listened to our Prayers and our hopes.

Let us come to the present Question. The horrible events which occurred in Mexico last year, and the Scandalous behavior of the demagogic Government wore out the patience of Europe and She decided to send Her Fleets and Armies. We who had so earnestly and with such good Faith demanded this intervention, as the *only* means of Salvation, saw our hopes renewed and forgetting all the pain and ruinous vengeance which these hopes had occasioned us, set to work with the ardour natural to our convictions and good intentions. We understood, as every one understood, that order and material tranquillity being established by the European Armies, all men of weight, all peacefully disposed persons, seeing themselves free from the attacks of the demagogic Bands, would express their opinion as to the best form of Government for Mexico. The true opinion of the Country was well known to us, by the identical wishes of the three Governments who had demanded European intervention and by the incessant reclamations of all right minded people, who for the last eight years looked upon that as the only means of saving Mexican Society.

It was a question of glory and interest for Europe, more especially for Spain and France. Of Glory, because they saved Mexican Nationality, because they stopped the impious fratricidal shedding of blood and because they saved the Latin Race and Catholicism in those Regions.

Of interest, because Europe cannot for a moment allow the United States to take possession of one of the finest and richest Countries in the World; to be master of both Seas, and to lord it over those Countries to the extent of closing all European industry and commerce. England alone has thought of the future by taking possession of Bermudas in front of the Eastern Coast of the American Union—the Bahamas at the entrance of the Gulf of Mexico, Jamaica and Her West Indian Island.

We were all going to gain them in the Tripartite European Expedition. But We, who during so many years, had considered ourselves as the legitimate representatives of men of order in Mexico, would not and could not lose time.

We acknowledge that we acted loyally to induce these Governments to busy themselves with the question of a candidate. When the three Maritime Powers intervened, we at once understood that it was neither judicious or possible to think of a Prince of one of these Nations, and on laying this question reverently before the Emperor, we had the honour to tell him so. It is necessary to say it, because it is the truth and it has been much disfigured where it ought to have been most respected; the Emperor replied to our respectful remarks, by stating that he had no Candidate and would accept anyone Mexico might choose. It never entered into His Majesty's ideas to propose a Candidate of His own Family, nor into ours to propose an Englishman; and if from our origin and feelings we would have aspired to have a Prince of the Royal House of Spain, or connected with it, we were detained by the Political consideration that the intervening Powers had to remain strangers to all combinations which might give them more influence than others in Mexico, and also it is painful to confess, for people who think and feel as we do, because there are still many people in Mexico who would look on such a candidature as a disguised reconquest by Spain.

It became necessary then to look for a Prince, unconnected with the three Maritime Powers, gifted with high qualities of the heart and feeling, with proved virtue and wisdom, with a varied and profound instruction in the Government of a State, animated with liberal conservative principles, a good Catholic without fanaticism and popular in Europe, including England, (and none was better) than the Archduke Maximilian.

When His Highnesses name was mentioned before the Emperor, His Majesty had just condescended to reply he had no candidate. The candidature was then proposed to the Emperor, and it is well that those who see in it a plan of Napoleon the 3d to exchange Venice for Mexico, should know that such was not the case, as it would have been unworthy of both Emperors.

The truth is that the Emperor Napoleon, knowing the high qualities of the Archduke, found this candidature much to his taste, and nobly forgetting, that two years ago he was at War with Austria, he extended one loyal hand to an enlightened Prince and another to the Country which asked for it, and gave it new life as he did to Spain.

This Candidate, before whose qualifications even England has had to bow, has been asked for by the Conservative Party of Mexico : that party is expecting him anxiously, is counting the days which intervene before his arrival, and no other combination is now possible.

It must not be forgotten that this so called Conservative Party, is all of Spanish origin, that its members have been persecuted, humiliated and insulted for their fidelity to it, when the party which is now in power triumphed, as that Party always joins the cry of down with Spain to that of liberty. If the Conservative Party was not fully persuaded of the ancient sympathy of the Archduke for Spain, they would not have given him their vote, because to be an enemy of Spain is to be an enemy of their race, and the descendants of Spaniards in Mexico would prefer to bow their heads to the

*Yankee* yoke, to naming a Prince an enemy to their race and traditions.

You will perceive from this, my dear friend, that the choice of the Archduke is wise and in conformity with the legitimate interests of Spain, and in the present state of things, we could not if we wished annul what has been done and begin afresh. If we were to attempt it, which we will not do, we would find ourselves alone and deceived. Do not you believe, that knowing this affair as we do, the best of Spaniards would have acted in the same manner.

I cannot close this letter without adding some other considerations which preoccupy me much. If the Allies go, as I hope they will, to the Capitol, there is no doubt but that public opinion will pronounce itself in favor of the Monarchical System. The prompt establishment of a Monarchy in Mexico, will bring about similar movements in the other Spanish American Republics, and then it will be impossible not to take into consideration the merits of the worthy and accomplished Princes you mention. The Monarchy will reestablish the unfortunate Society of Mexico; will put an end to impiety and butchery; will protect Religion, and its shepherds will no longer be persecuted and stoned; Commerce will obtain a brilliant extension; its magnificent and innumerable silver mines will be benefitted, and their immense products would meet the disproportion of precious metals with which Europe is menaced; agriculture with its rich and fabulous fruits, would at given moments, succour astonished Europe; the varied and rich products of that country, such as cotton which is cultivated there without slaves, and is much superior to that of the United States, would be a staple for European industry, and could emancipate Europe from the tutelage of the American Union; immigration would exchange hunger and misery for abundance and happiness, and the latin race, Catholicism and the language of Cervantes would rule over all this.

But if the Allies leave Mexico without having established the Monarchy desired by the Nation, the United States, following up their policy, will at once take possession of the whole country, in order to prevent Europe again invading it, and the gates will be thrown open for them by the demagogues, who will be their first victims. All the produce of that favoured land will serve exclusively for the benefit of the United States in exchange for their industry : the Spanish race, vexed and persecuted, will disappear by degrees, as in California and New Mexico; protestantism will appear triumphant, performing its rites in the very Churches erected by our Fathers to Catholicism; the United States master of all the Northern part of America and of the two seas, closing all Commerce to Europe, will arise gigantic to contemplate Haughtily the catastrophe which the (authors) of its industry will bring about; political equilibrium will be menaced by the triumph of the Monroe doctrine; Spain, with the Key of the Gulf of Mexico in Her hands, will not be able to move from the entrance; Her influence and Her Commerce would soon be at an end. ... France warned by the fact that the most propitious moment to save such high interests in Mexico, has not been duped, will not again expose herself to a fresh deception, and will not renew her expedition, from which she will acquire much glory it is true, but no other profit, because she has declared and given proofs that she does not look for any other profit, because she has declared and given proofs that she does not look for any other on this occasion. England, the enemy of Catholicism and the Spanish race, will calmly see both them and the power of Spain disappear in America.

This is what I picture to myself, I am sometimes sanguine and at others depressed, as the changes in this question alternate in my mind. You who are so well acquainted with American affairs, will tell me whether I am right.

As for me my dear friend, you know that I have long since worked in this question with all my soul, conscience and strength. Under the Spanish point of view or under the Mexican point of view, nothing and no person has proved to me that I am mistaken. The bitterness of the demagogues makes no impression on me. The march of events may afflict me greatly. The erroneous ideas which are taken of the part which has fallen to my lot in this affair may each day cause me more pain; but whether it ends in giving me the happiness to see a throne erected in Mexico, or I have there to look upon the banner of the stars, God, who knows my intentions, will never send me the terrible punishment of remorse.

Do what you like, my good friend, with this letter and receive, etc.

/s/ J(uan) H(idalgo)

# Appendix V

## THE INTERCEPTED JECKER CORRESPONDENCE

Louis Elsesser to J. B. Jecker, Paris, 31 August 1862

MY DEAR UNCLE : I have to acknowledge the receipt of your letters dated in Mexico, the 16th July. . . .

. . . . . . . . . . . . . . . . . . . . . . . . .

Complete *statu quo* — paralyzation of affairs — *inertiae* of Lorencez! Fortunately, Forey is on the way to take the direction of the war, and will be there by the beginning of the last half of September . . . He aspires to a marshalship, and will not sleep on the road.

As this packet brought scarcely any news, I have availed myself of your letter, and that of Javier, to write immediately a short article . . . and I have taken care to make specially apparent the sagacity of the conduct and the correctness of the ideas of Mr. de Saligny with reference to the liability of Juarez and his government. *While Saligny is so useful to us, it is well to employ all possible means to strengthen his credit.* The journals will enlarge upon this theme from patriotism, and will contrast the triumph of his policy with the inefficiency of Prim. In conclusion, I touch lightly upon the affair of the bonds, showing the impossibility of believing in the protests of Juarez against private contracts, celebrated with the solemn guarantee of the legations, when he gives such proofs of his lack of honor. This article, I believe, will produce a salutary effect and will attract attention, being the first to expose the Jesuitism of Juarez, now that the packet brings us no news whatever from Mexico.

As you do not make in your last letter any inquiries to which I have to respond, I will embrace this opportunity to communicate to you some items of information which, I think, will be interesting to the house, and which I have collected with much care. I have had some difficulty in my relations with father's friends on account of my young appearance, and they were inclined to treat me in a formal manner; but, thank Heaven, after some persistence on my part, and some careful conversations to show them how fully I was informed with reference to the business, they have given me their full confidence, and I am now in a position to be useful to the house to the utmost extent of my ability. To proceed : Your letter of the 16th July . . . has been presented entire before the eyes of his Majesty, as has been done with the previous ones *when their tenor has permitted,* and I believe the same has taken place with that received by this packet. His Majesty likes your clear and concise style, and your general observations have attracted his attention. Our friend has particularly recommended to me to charge you to send your letters in two separate sheets, one of which can treat of general matters of observations on the course of events and of their direction, *leaving it to your sagacity to give them such a turn as may be advantageous,* and of producing a close connexion between the interests of the house and the general interests, although without insisting too much upon this point. The other sheet can treat of confidential matters.

The person whom you believed in Orizaba when you wrote your last letter has returned to France since the 16th August. He remained a month at Vera Cruz without being able to go to Orizaba, because being on friendly terms with Mr. de Saligny, and also having very intimate relations with Lorencez, he would not have known what to have done between these two gentlemen. He also remained some time in Martinique. I had a very long conversation with him on the 23d August, the day of his arrival in Paris, to which place I again returned on the 27th, as he was to leave the 2d September, in order to arrive in Mexico in October, as I wrote to my father. The 27th he suddenly changed his mind, and his voyage was deferred without my being able to penetrate the motives of this sudden decision, when all had already left for the campaign, and he only gave as a reason the useless cost of his residence there, when it was perfectly well understood what we had to do by the tenor of his instructions.

However, in the course of the conversation, in speaking of how false his position there would be, the remark was dropped that he had insisted strongly that the influence which we have should be employed to produre for him from the Emperor some official post there, in order that his position might be established, and that in the next visit he would give the reasons for the new decision, although professing that he should continue acting without reserve.

I suppose he has some other motive, but as from want of time I have not been able to take the necessary steps to inform myself with reference to it, my opinion does not rest upon certain data.

There was in Mexico one Mr. Lapierre, an adjutant of Almonte, an insinuating man, accustomed to intrigue, but in bad standing with the French army, from which he had separated under somewhat unfavorable circumstances. Desiring, at any cost, to use his talents, and seeing that Almonte was slipping out of his hands, he commenced, in Mexico, intriguing to gain the confidence of Mr. de C., and even wrote to Paris, desiring, like a prudent man, to have two strings to his bow. He has since returned here, charged to bring to his Majesty the communications and explanations of Mr. Saligny, and has carried his mission to a successful issue.

He renewed his approaches in Paris, whence he left on his return on the 2d July. It is believed that the party solicited, embarrassed by the petition of Mr. de C., has arranged with this individual, who, up to a certain point, had been forced upon him, and who has manifested himself very accomodating, because, being less scrupulous than the other, he counts more upon what the future has in store for him, and has not asked money in advance, which is a good deal, as he fills at the same time another mission. Probably he may be employed *ad interim,* as I believe it is always the intention to send C. to Mexico, when the situation becomes more clearly defined. In fact, "if the policy of Forey is diametrically opposed to that of Saligny on account of different impressions," said C. to me this morning, "and if it becomes necessary for Saligny to return to France, it would be a stupidity on my part to go there now, because, on account of the relations which connect me with him, I should be obliged to associate myself with his fortune, and to return to his company, without the ability to be of any further use to the house. It is better to wait the impression which the first letters of Forey make upon the Emperor, and then I can go in any event; because if Saligny is relieved I can, free from all influence, follow another line of conduct, and still be useful, because I do not believe, counting the time necessary to install a new government, that the business of the bonds will come up before November."

C. has had a very long conversation with his Majesty, in which, according to the established ceremonial, he was limited in replying to the questions put to him. There was no allusion, direct or indirect, to the affairs of the house. The impressions drawn from the interview are the following, which I communicate to you, because they are the views of a man of ability, who, in his visit to Mexico, has formed very correct ideas of men and things, and because they indicate with clearness his ideas of the policy of the Emperor: "His Majesty has not yet been able," he says to me, "to come to a definite resolution, with reference to the affairs in Mexico, in the midst of the contradictory information which he receives. He examines everything that reaches him, and will only form an opinion after consulting all possible sources of information. Notwithstanding, in the midst of all this, the mission of Mr. Lapierre and the efforts of Mr. de Saligny have been attended with complete success, and the unfavorable impressions caused by the communications of Lorencez have been completely removed. This Lapierre has tact, and has labored with energy, and his efforts have gained their object. The letters of Saligny have much pleased his Majesty, and even kept up some respect for Almonte. I insinuated something to him with reference to the probable candidature of Santa Anna, but I was not able to discover in his impassible face any indication of assent. The idea of the Emperor appears to me to be this : Fearing to mark out at such a distance, and with so slight a knowledge of what is passing, a line of policy which might embarrass the triumph of the expedition, provoking dissensions, he has confided almost entirely to Forey to care of establishing such order of things as may be necessary. He has no intention to relieve Mr. de Saligny, but the *role* of the latter is too limited to struggle with the new general. With regard to Lorencez, he will return to obscurity, as he well deserves.

"His Majesty greatly desires one or two battles, to restore their lustre to the French arms, and to cause public opinion more readily to accept the necessity of so considerable an expenditure of force."

Permit me, my dear uncle, notwithstanding this letter is already very long, to state also the opinions of C—— with reference to what should be done by the house. These are valuable, not only from the information he has acquired in his visit, but from the intimate knowledge he has of the men placed at the head of the expedition. I let him continue. "My attention was attracted on arriving by hearing all the world talking of the bond business, on the steamer, at Vera Cruz, and in the camp. No one but knows of it, and the efforts employed to discredit them among the officers of the expedition have been completely successful.

"All the French residents of Vera Cruz are liberals. They

are in constant relations with the soldiers, and for all the evils they suffer they throw the blame always upon the affair of the bonds, because they consider it the cause of the continuation of the war.

"The reactionaries fear their entire and full recognition, because it would burden the treasury. The liberals execrate them, and the French believe the calumnies employed to depreciate them, so that I can truly say *that I have not encountered any one in Mexico but M. de Saligny who sustains them.*

"Forey will arrive meanwhile; Forey, of violent character, caustic, malevolent, and who refers everything to the military standard, which, for him, is superior to all else. By the decree which relieved La Graviere, the military element, which he represented, was made subject to the diplomatic, as Saligny remained invested with full powers during war, which is an occurrence without precedent. It is, therefore, self-evident that Forey will adopt the opinion of the officers who surround him, and that he will look upon the business with an unfavorable eye, to which must be added that all the chiefs also dislike it — Jurien, Roze, Russell, Lacroix, Doazan, etc., etc.

"Saligny cannot struggle against all this, and he will be obliged to return. The business has been strongly recommended to Forey; but it is necessary to bear in mind that the influence that sustains our business, as French, *is very great in high places,* but less among the military chiefs, and Forey, who bears almost unlimited powers, will be a species of viceroy, doing whatever he pleases. The opinion of our friends is that he will be against the business, and that it would have been desirable that there should have gone in his place Trechu, a man as reliable as he is able, and of fine manners."

"I acknowledge," adds C., "that Forey can do nothing more than regard the recognition of the bonds, because the sole judge of their validity is the proper tribunal of Paris, and that it will be impossible to dispute their justice, presenting them thus, that is, not reclamations, nor a payment, nor seventy-five millions, but simply the execution of a law of the treasury of Mexico. We have to insist, also, upon the slight value of Mexican paper, which can never be sold for over fifty per cent.

"I would consent, notwithstanding, were I in the place of the house, to some composition by which the changes and the tediousness that would attend a decision by the tribunal might be avoided.

"Appearances could be saved by stating that no arrangement could be consented to that did not have some other guarantee than the faith of the Mexican government, but that an arrangement under the auspices of France would be accepted with pleasure."

.   .   .   .   .   .   .   .   .   .   .   .   .   .   .   .   .   .   .

I enclose a number of the *Bulletin of Laws,* which contains the decree of your naturalization. It would not have been printed tll the end of October, as there are many others which should have been published first; but as I was aware of its importance, I took such steps with those in charge of its insertion — availing myself also of my friends — that I carried my point. I will send two other copies on the 15th of September.

Adieu, my dear uncle. Desiring that your health may continue good, and taking the most lively interest in the favorable issue of your affairs, I am your affectionate nephew.

LOUIS ELSESSER.

P.S. — I shall not omit any efforts to hasten the departure of Mr. De C., as in your last letter you indicate that you desire it. By way of San Nazarido I will write you anything interesting that I may learn.

Elsesser Jecker to J. B. Jecker, Porentrui, 24 August, 1862.

MY DEAR BROTHER :

.   .   .   .   .   .   .   .   .   .   .   .   .   .   .   .   .   .   .

When you receive the letters by this mail you will already have made the acquaintance of the Zouaves. How consoling is this thought. I congratulate you with all my heart. How interesting will be your letters of the coming month; give me many details.

They say here that General Lorencez is crazy, and that Valaze manages everything for him.

. . . . . . . . . . . . . . . . . . . . . . . . .

. . . the press has received orders not to insert anything with reference to Mexico, and they are completely silent upon this head.

. . . . . . . . . . . . . . . . . . . . . . . . .

Your loving sister,

ELSESSER JECKER

Porentrui, August 27

Feeling itself almost anticipated and closely watched by Wyke, the French government lets nothing transpire with reference to its projects of protectorate, colonization, etc. Not less than eighteen generals go out with the expeditionary corps, for which reason it must be very considerable.

*This affair costs a great deal.* How will the government be indemnified so as to satisfy public opinion, if the revenues of the state (twenty millions per annum) are mortgaged in advance?

X. Elsesser to J. B. Jecker, Porentrui, 24 August 1862.

MY DEAR JECKER:

I believe that affairs are taking a better aspect for us, for a decision has been come to to colonize; forty-five thousand men will be sent out, and, in fine, a complete transportation is treated of.

I believe that as it has afforded the pretext under which to realize all of this, the unfortunate affair of the 5th May is not now so much regretted.

Your letter of the 12th July has reached my hands. That of the 11th, directed to Mr.———, has been shown to his Majesty, as has been done with various of the extracts from former favors of yours.

I trust we shall rise from the abyss, for the news received by our friends is good, and their hopes revive.

Mr. de Chr—— is again back in Paris; he returns to Mexico the 1st September. He has given an account to his Majesty of the state of affairs, and I believe there is reason to congratulate ourselves upon his mission. Our friends think that the bonds will be admitted in Mexico. It is better so, and not that the affair be decided in Europe at the cost of a great sacrifice. Such is my desire. . . . in order that my data may be complete, please send me a statement of your reclamation separate from those of the bonds, resting assured I will make no use of it without consulting you, and that I will divulge nothing, although I see everything has been published since the disgusting correspondence of Wyke has been submitted to Parliament. That diplomat, the instrument of favor, has been your true adversary, and even your deadly enemy. I have promised nothing to your creditors; but have reassured Mr. Hottinger, who affirms that your liquidation has not yet the regular character which it will have after the entry of the French into Mexico. Louis is very exact in his vigilance with reference to whatever may be of interest to you. I shall see the persons who are interested with us. . . .

Your naturalization has been inserted in the Boletin of Laws, and I enclose a copy.

Yours, affectionate,

X. ELSESSER.

P.S. — I have reason to believe that the plans of colonization will be arranged according to the ideas contained on page 481 of Fossey. His Majesty, in his works, had selected the transit of Nicaragua. I have already spoken to you of all this in my previous letters. The time approaches in which this idea may be realized. You will not have forgotten that I delivered the map of the railroad route across the isthmus of Tehuantepec to the new duke. He had raised the objection of the project of the Emperor; but I responded with the works of Rais and Fossey. I cannot enumerate to you the reasons which led me to desire a speedy settlement in Mexico; they are too numerous. The presence of the new agent will contribute to this end, as also that of the Minister Saligny. Do not fear as regards Forey, to whom you are already recommended. It is more than a month since I knew of it; but I had forgotten to speak of it. It will be well to take advantage of the liberty of the press to defend yourself. Do not omit my separate paragraph with reference to naturalization.

The expedition will have relation, also, to the affairs of the United States.

Luis to Javier, Paris, 31 August 1862.

MY DEAR JAVIER:

I hastily wrote you these few lines, as I have written uncle so many, many pages, giving all the information possible, and have delayed so much in writing them, to learn positively whether C. would go or not, that the last moment has arrived for letters to be received for the mail for Mexico.

According to your advice, and with the aid of your letter and that of uncle, I have written an article directed to the *Patrie,* drawing a comparison between the conduct of Prim and that of Saligny. As no letters have arrived from Mexico, and all are ignorant of the course of Juarez, I hope that the article will be favorably received, and will produce the effect we desire of touching the national pride of some of the papers, which is considered as resulting from the course he pursued. Prim is very unpopular in France since the affair of Puebla, which is considered as resulting from the courage he pursued.

I send the package directly to you, according to the advice of Mr. De G., in order to attract less attention, and do not seal uncle's letter, so that you can read it. Read that addressed to him before those of father and mother. It is very interesting for the news it contains, which is too much to repeat to you here.

Seal it — it already has the envelope — and direct it immediately.

Your affectionate brother,

LUIS

Father to Javier, Porentrui, 24 August 1862.

MY VERY DEAR JAVIER:

I have done all I could to tranquillize our creditors, but have succeeded in nothing more. It is true I was mistaken with regard to the amount of the forces confided to Douay, the famous general of the war in Italy, cited by Bazancount; *but I have not deceived you in repeating to you for now more than a year, that there would be colonization, a throne, protectorate,* etc., etc.

. . . . . . . . . . . . . . . . . . . . . . .

You are aware that I have sent to your uncle a memoir which treats of each one of the negotiations projected by him or our friends: First, Tehuantepec; second, Sonora; third, mines; fourth, improvement of forges by the Chenot process; fifth, etc, etc. He has acknowledged receipt without remark. Perhaps that is what has provoked the laugh of his nephew, because there is nothing that now appears to me available except the exchange of the drafts of the army, monopolized in our favor, without the prejudice of dividing the gains without our friends.

Of this Jecker speaks again in a letter to Mr. De N., of which he has sent me a copy.

Mr. De Chevardier will have carried the decree of naturalization; any way it will appear in the *Boletin,* and I will send it to you.

                                        YOUR FATHER

X. Elsesser to Javier, Porentrui, 24 August 1862.

MY DEAR JAVIER:

It is possible that I may have been mistaken as to the forces sent up to the present time; but now it is certain that the misfortune of the 5th of May, prepared by the artifices of Wyke, has only served as a plausible pretext to his Majesty to display his eagles and establish a protectorate, or colonize Mexico, the same as Algeria, which has been much treated of in secret, and I suspected it when I presented to Mr. De——

the memoir upon Tehuantepec, formed from the notes of Raiss, Fossey, etc., etc., and accompanied by a map of the railroad route across the isthmus.

With a man so positive as Jecker, I want myself to be equally positive. For this I have considered as chimerical some of his projects, that is to say, as not available at present, and that they cannot furnish us funds except in certain contingencies; such as Sonora; the isthmus; the lands near Matamoras, contiguous to the Rio Grande del Norte, etc., etc. Of all of them I have made a critical review in order of number. There is no doubt that the future will enable us to realize largely from these values, if for the intermediate time we can count upon the aid of some capitalist not very usurious. Jecker does well in insisting in his letter of the 11th of July upon the theme of the monopoly of the drafts of the army, for this being composed of upward of 45,000 men, the business would be excellent, above all to raise our credit, because under the point of view of gain, as there will be a division, it will not be so brilliant, having only one-half per cent exchange.

Has the house shoulders sufficiently strong? I have not tried them. Our friends have faith in the capacity of Jecker.

The papers are silent with reference to the projects concerning Mexico, for these are very grave and capable of inspiring serious alarm in England, for by reason of his smartness, Wyke has acted like a fool, making a golden bridge and leaving it a free field.

For the present nothing is required but patience, for now only has the horizon been opened to our view.

It is believed here that immediately on the arrival of the French in Mexico your situation will greatly change, and if uncle can be able to pay his interest at the end of the year the result will be superb, above all, for us, because we will receive over 200,000 francs; but he does not speak of it, perhaps remembering that at first he promised too much. Aid him in the articles of J. in Mexico, destined to rehabilitate his bonds. In Paris, for the present, it is better not to wake the cat that sleeps. Wyke has been our real enemy; Juarez should burn a long candle for him.

I do not know if you will publish your defence in Mexico; in any case it will be well to write frequent articles, for the emissaries of Juarez have persuaded the French army that they have only gone to Mexico on our account.

The documents I have received here fully informed me. I have nothing more to say of the business of Corona, and understand perfectly that I have no option, for he has said in Paris that to get his money it would be necessary to put the dagger to Jecker's breast.

Forey is in favor of the colonization of the isthmus. See his note with reference to this point at the end of the book. His Majesty does not insist any longer upon Nicaragua. With 45,000 men submission will follow, and even a pressure will be brought to bear upon the United States, the position of which is not without its influence on what passes.

The character of the Emperor is that of patience; the affair of Mexico has given him much trouble; but nothing has been precipitated thereby.

According to what they say, he has this trace of simularity with Jecker.

The first care of his Majesty concerns the organization of *gens d'armerie* under the charge of Generals Woll and Mirandoi.

When two thousands are had it is calculated that robberies will cease. In fine, we shall even see a visit paid to the viceroy of the south, Alvarez, who will have to keep down the Apache.

Mr. de P. has touched at the Rio del Norte; some of the detachments of the army will also go there. With reference to the organization of the government, Maximilian was nothing more than a pilot balloon without any importance. Almonte can well be laid aside. Who will be placed to govern under the tutilage of France, I cannot say. If I was in Paris I might penetrate certain things, but —

The terrible mystery has at last been discovered; the instructions are first known by the *Presse,* organ of Juarez. They are not very decided, but rather elastic and conditional. For this reason I can understand that they have caused no excitement, although the cabinet of Mexico learned them immediately through Salonde — I mean Selong — who received a copy from Saberbielle, who received them from Noel, sub-editor of foreign relations for America. Abraham begat Jacob, Jacob, etc., etc.

Even if the business of the bonds had been arranged at the time of the recognition of Juarez, I doubt if the house would have come out any better; for it would have been exhausted by forced loans, etc., much aid would it have required.

But now that the affair of the bonds has been discussed by the press of both worlds, Jecker has an universal name, and is from this time inseparable from the war in Mexico.

Juarez knows the power of the press, and no one has made a better use of it in Europe and America, and but for the firmness of Mr. de Saligny, he would have carried his point. This has been affirmed by his consul in Paris, with an assurance that would in the end have imposed upon me.

They say that Mexico will be speedily regulated, and that, after having formed a sufficient nucleus of indigenous force, the French will return by degrees, leaving only the number that may be strictly necessary.

Your loving father, who thinks of you constantly.

X ELSESSER

Luis Elsesser to Uncle, Paris, 14 September 1862.

DEAR UNCLE :

The arrival of the steamer which brings the correspondence from Mexico to San Nazario is not yet signalized, and I cannot, therefore, this time, answer your letters by return of mail.

This letter will be only the complement of the news I gave you in my letter of the 1st instant. Since that time I have not been able to have any private conversation with M. Le Receveur, and consequently am yet uncertain as to the *role* he designs for M. De Che, who has now been detained more than twenty days at Puy by the mutiny of the general council.

On the other hand, he has probably not been able to occupy himself usefully with your affairs, as he must have received your letter at the very moment he was receiving at his house the friend who had gone on the occasion of his new position. Mr. De Che considers what you wrote to father, although I read him only extracts from it, as sufficiently important to communicate to the duke, in order to contrast the conduct of Prim with that of Saligny; and he judges that great advantage may be taken of it to restore the credit of Saligny, for which purpose it is necessary to do everything to influence his Majesty. I have not yet learned the result of the audience, because all these gentlemen are occupied in their preparations for travel, some for the baths of Biarritz, where the Emperor goes, and some to the country.

I believe, however, according to the conversation which I have had with Mr. Che., that the intention of these gentlemen, as I have before stated, is to wait for the first communications of Forey to his Majesty, in order to penetrate the direction he will give to his policy, see his opinion of the conduct of Saligny with reference to the special interests he has sustained, and, if they are favorable to that minister, what effect this may produce upon the mind of his Majesty. On this hypothesis, and if matters should reach a point which would oblige Saligny to resign his post, we shall see Mr. Che, who, then free in his actions and dependent upon any one, as would have been the case with Saligny, from their relations of friendship, can protect the house in its affairs, using there his powerful influence.

. . . . . . . . . . . . . . . . . . . . . . . .

The individual of whom I spoke in my last letter—the attache of Almonte—will probably answer, although he knows but little, and we have not advanced much with him; but there is no necessity for delay on this account; as he is only a person of intrigue. At the beginning of the expedition Jurien de la Gravierra paid him 500 francs monthly for account of the ministry of foreign affairs, under what title we cannot learn.

I have caused Mr. Che, in the last interview I had with him, to understand that it is indispensable to accelerate the decision with reference to the affair of the bonds, giving him in my way the general impression which had been produced upon my mind by the reading of your correspondence. I said to him that all the statements which had been given to these gentlemen were exact, and that there were, in fact, immense resources, but that before all it was necessary to restore to the house its liberty of action, in order to get rid of its creditors, although it might be by the credit these had given it, and that then, like a wagon temporarily stuck, it would again resume its progress without delay. He appeared convinced, and as he was going at once to the duke's, he promised to use with him all his influence in order to convince him that this indefinite doubt and paralysis will be the ruin of the house. This gentleman is on the most intimate terms with the duke, as also with Mr. Receveur or Mr. G. He was in college with him, and has the *entree* of his house at all hours. He possesses some little capital, and has, unfortunately, private affairs which occupy him. Before Mr. Receveur took the sudden resolution of delaying his departure, he had not renewed any relations, and was for all the world still in Mexico, but since he has begun to occupy himself again, and I cannot derive as much advantage as before. He has a fixed salary, and $2\frac{1}{2}$ per cent. of the final result, according to what he has told me. These gentlemen have various projects, some of them rather too ingenious. Here is one they have communicated to me with great secrecy, and from which you will be able to extract some benefit in the future: "When the French army occupies Mexico, there will be a great movement of convoys between Vera Cruz and Mexico (City). The wagons will come up and full and return empty. Persons sustained by powerful influence, and of great estimation with the military chiefs, could, under some gratuitous or slightly onerous concession, obtain the right to a certain amount of freight by the return wagons, say 300 kilogrammes each wagon. *You can easily imagine the rest.* The freight will be in dollars, and thus there could be managed the remission to Europe of all the sums which now go out by conductas, as of course the English and San Nazario lines of steamers would be glad to take the money on its arrival at Vera Cruz, as all would be gratuitious — the mules, the wagons, and the escort — so all would be clear profit."

. . . . . . . . . . . . . . . . . . . . . .

There exists in London, as I have been informed by Mr. de Ch—, a company which has been organized to open the transit route by way of the lakes Nicaraugua and Leon; you will, without doubt, know of it; he has not been able to give me many details, as he only knows of it through the fact that some two months ago propositions were made to his friend, Prince Lucien Murat, offering him the presidency. This latter consulted the Emperor, and I believe has refused it. Mr. de Receveur, who is somewhat hasty, has confounded it with Tehuantepec, and has led Mr. de Ch— into an error, which I will correct when I have a chance to speak with him, and I will get all the further news I can with reference to the affair and communicate it to you. Unfortunately my studies occupy me very much, and, notwithstanding the care I take, I am prohibited going out on foot. I dislike to risk the public vehicles in my feeble state. Father combats the project of Nicaragua in a memoir which he has sent to the duke with reference to Tehuantepec, using the arguments of Raiss, Reichtoffen, Humboldt, Fossey, and derived from his own knowledge of the subject; but I believe the Emperor is set in his opinion.

When he was in the fortress of Ham, in 1842, he occupied himself with the project by way of Nicaragua, and he has himself written a book upon the subject which has been printed, and is still in circulation.

At the time M. Castillon, sent by the states of Panama and Honduras to demand the protection of Louis Philippe, because connected with Louis Napoleon, and after returning to his country maintained a correspondence with him, which has also been printed, in which it is seen that the prince agreed with him with regard to the point of departure for the execution of this work, for which the consent of the authorities was obtained.

.   .   .   .   .   .   .   .   .   .   .   .   .   .   .   .   .   .   .

Adieu, My dear uncle. I hope that my letter will follow and not precede the French in Mexico. Dispose of me for everything.

Your affectionate nephew,

LUIS ELSESSER


Porentrui, September 3, 1862.

MY DEAR XR:

.   .   .   .   .   .   .   .   .   .   .   .   .   .   .   .   .   .   .

Your letters of the 28th of July, and those of your uncle, have been received. Louis, who is in Paris, is the only one who has been able to reply by the same mail, and he has given very grave news to M. J. I believe that I have said to you that, of all the projects with which he has been occupied, there is only one that is possible of realization for the present, and that is to give drafts upon Paris for the army in exchange for the sums paid out to them there; upon this an exchange can be made, and we can divide the profits.

I have told Louis to mention this, and I will myself take charge of the affair, the more readily as I am informed very large sums will not be necessary. I believe that if, upon the entry of the French, the house recovers its credit, that this arrangement can be carried out.

With reference to all the other projects with which, for the the lack of something better we have occupied ourselves so long, I do not see any necessity to dwell upon them for the present, and I have already stated my reasons, because in the state of suffering in which our creditors are, nothing can be done but to procure means to satisfy their clamor. Mr. Jecker has spoken to me of his mines, of the future reserved to Catorce, Tasco, and, I believe, Santa Anna.

. . . . . . . . . . . . . . . . . . .

I can say to you that, in my judgement, if the house had got the real estate of Mr. de——— for half a million francs and 50,000 francs of rent, its situation near Chapultepec would have enabled us to dispose of it without great loss. Luis labors hard for the house, and with good success, I think. I do not believe there has been any indiscretion. Since its beginning, according to the memoir of Oceguera, the causes of so great a protection to a Swiss should have been investigated, and as in Mexico everything is done with money, a thousand conjectures have been formed. When the army, which the people of Juarez have convinced that our house is the cause of the war, shall see the tricolor flag floating over the towers of Mexico, they will no longer hate us, for the country is rich and beautiful, and the army must have suffered much confined in Orizaba.

If Saligny knows how to manage with Forey, who is a bear, all will go well; but I fear some pique, and this is why it is necessary that the affair should terminate speedily, even if some concession has to be made. This is the opinion of Mr. de Ch——r, who has not yet returned here, but who could very easily return by way of St. Nazaire. Luis, who has frequent intercourse with him, looks upon it seriously.

. . . . . . . . . . . . . . . . . . .

A thousand affectionate expressions from all your family and from your brother.

# Notes

## CHAPTER I

### 1. Monarchist Intrigue, 1821–1857

1. But it was not until 1836, after an unsuccessful attempt to reconquer Mexico (1828–1829), that Spain begrudgingly recognized Mexican independence. See Hubert Howe Bancroft: *History of Mexico* (6 v., San Francisco, 1883–1889), V, 71–75. (Hereafter referred to as BANCROFT).

2. H. Montgomery Hyde: Mexican Empire: *The History of Maximilian and Carlota of Mexico* (London, 1946), pp. 108, 112. (Hereafter referred to as HYDE).

3. William Spence Robertson: "Metternich's Attitude Towards Revolutions in Latin America," *Hispanic American Historical Review,* (Hereafter referred to as HAHR). XXI (1941), 538–558.

4. Estrada-Senior Conversation, 27 Apr 1863, Nassau Senior: *Conversations with Distinguished Persons During the Second Empire from 1860 to 1863 by the Late Nassau Senior,* ed. M. C. M. Simpson (2 v., London, 1880), II, 275. (Hereafter referred to as SENIOR).

5. *Ibid.*

6. *Ibid.,* pp. 275–276.

7. *Ibid.,* p. 276.

8. Montluc to Billault, Paris, 19 Jun 1862, Armand de Montluc: *Correspondence de Juarez et de Montluc, Ancien Consul General de Mexique, Accomoagnée de Nombreuses Lettres de Personnages Politiques Relative a L'Expédition Du Mexique,* ed. Leon de Montluc (Paris, 1885), p. 91. (Hereafter referred to as MONTLUC). Montluc sympathized with the Mexican liberals and was writing Billault to protest that liberal ideas had advanced since Estrada's exile from Mexico in 1840, but that Estrada failed to realize this.

9. Estrada to Metternich *(fils),* Paris, 5 Jul 1861, 1861, Vienna, *Haus-Hof-und-Staats Archiv,* Archiv Kaiser Max, (Hereafter referred

to as AKM). Daniel Dawson: *The Mexican Adventure* (London, 1935), pp. 83, 122n. (Hereafter referred to as DAWSON). Dawson refers to the *Haus-Hof-und-Staats Archiv* as the *Wiener Staats Archiv*. For purposes of consistency this source will be referred to in the present investigation as the *Haus-Hof-und-Staats Archiv*. (Hereafter referred to as *HHSA*).

10. Estrada to Metternich *(père)*, Rome, 28 Mar 1846, *HHSA, AKM, ibid.,* pp. 83–84.

11. Estrada to Metternich *(père)*, 28 Mar 1846, Egon Caesar Corti: *Maximilian and Charlotte of Mexico,* trans. Catherine Alison Phillips (2 v., New York, 1928), I, 30–31. (Hereafter referred to as CORTI).

12. Estrada to Metternich *(père)*, Rome, 14 Apr 1846, *HHSA,* DAWSON, p. 84.

13. *Ibid.*

14. Estrada-Senior Conversation, 27 Apr 1863, SENIOR, II, 276.

15. *Ibid*

16. In a private letter, or in a private conversation, Estrada had every inducement to make his role in the past appear greater than it had been.

17. Estrada-Senior Conversation, 27 Apr 1863, SENIOR, II, 276.

18. *Ibid,* Estrada to Metternich *(fils)*, Paris, 5 Jul 1861, *HHSA, AKM,* DAWSON, p. 85.

19. Ray Allen Billington: *The Far Western Frontier, 1830–1860* (London, 1956), pp. 151–152. See also Thomas A. Bailey: *A Diplomatic History of the American People* (4th ed., New York, 1950), p. 259. (Hereafter referred to as BAILEY).

20. BAILEY, p. 239.

21. Polk's revival message was given on 2 December 1845. For highlights of the "withdrawal" of the Monroe Doctrine between 1823 and 1845, see Dexter Perkins: *Hands Off* (Boston, 1941), pp. 69–74.

22. Palmerston Minute, 15 Oct 1861, London, Public Record Office (Hereafter referred to as PRO.), P.R.O. 30/22–21.

23. DAWSON, p. 122.

24. *Ibid.,* p. 84.

25. Estrada-Senior Conversation, 27 Apr 1863, SENIOR, II, 276.

26. DAWSON, p. 85.

27. *Ibid.,* pp. 85–86.

28. CORTI, I, 35–39.

29. Ulick Ralph Burke: *A Life of Benito Juarez, Constitutional President of Mexico* (London and Sydney, 1894), p. 41. (Hereafter referred to as BURKE).

30. Richard A. Johnson: "Spanish-Mexican Diplomatic Relations, 1853–1855," *HAHR,* XXI, (1941), 559.

31. Doyle to Br. Foreign Office (Hereafter referred to as F.O.), No. 117, 3 Dec 1853, PRO, F.O., Mexico, 261, sum. by Dexter Perkins: *The Monroe Doctrine, 1826–1867* (Baltimore, 1933), p. 325. (Hereafter referred to as PERKINS).

32. Levasseur to Fr. F.O., 30 Apr 1853, Paris Ministere des Affaires

Etrangères: *Correspondance Politique* (Hereafter referred to as MDAE: *CP.), Mex.,* vol. 41, ibid., p. 321.

33. *Ibid.,* p. 325.

34. *Ibid.,* p. 321. Perkins concludes that Napoleon III was too busy in Europe to undertake an ambitious program in Mexico.

35. PERKINS, pp. 323–324.

36. Richard A. Johnson: "Spanish-Mexican Diplomatic Relations, 1853–1855," *HAHR,* XXI (1941), 559–576.

37. Estrada produced a French copy of this commission, dated 1 July 1854, for Senior, who copied it. Corti and Duvernois likewise date these full powers 1 July 1854, whereas Perkins dates it 1 July 1853. Schefer dates it 1853. The commission may have been advance-dated, for an entry in Hübner's journal under 8 March 1854 relates a visit of Estrada, who is reported as having the full powers already. See SENIOR, II, 277–278; CORTI, I, 32–33; Clement Duvernois, ed.: *L'Intervention Française au Mexique, Accompagnée de Documents Inèdits et d'un long Memoire addresse par L'Impératrice Charlotte: Précedée d'une Preface de Clement Duvernois* (2 v., Paris, 1868), I, 50–51 (Hereafter referred to as DUVERNOIS); PERKINGS, p. 324; Christian Schefer: *La Grande Pensée de Napoléon III. Les origines de l'expedition de Mexique, 1858–1862* (Paris, 1939), pp. 23–24 (Hereafter referred to as SCHEFER); Alexander von Hübner: *Neuf Ans de Souvenirs D'Un Ambassadeur D'Autriche A Paris Sous Le Second Empire, 1851–1859, Publiés Par Son Fils, Le Comte Alexander de Hübner* (2v., Paris, 1904), I, 220. (Hereafter referred to as HUBNER).

38. CORTI, I, 33.

39. See Appendix U of present investigation.

40. Estrada to Metternich *(Fils),* Paris, 5 Jul 1861, *HHSA,* AKM, DAWSON, p. 85. Hidalgo blamed the failure of the negotiations on the revolution of 1854, the Crimean War, and Santa Anna's fall from power. See Appendix U of present investigation.

41. SCHEFER, pp. 23–24; DAWSON, pp. 86–87.

42. DAWSON, pp. 86–87.

43. PERKINS, p. 333.

44. Murphy Memorial, 17 Feb 1856, MDAE: *CP, Mex.,* vol. 45, *ibid.,* p. 347.

45. SCHEFER, p. 25; Albert Guerard: *Napoleon III* (Cambridge, Mass., 1943), p. 232. (Hereafter referred to as GUERARD).

46. The Marquis de Radepont had been sent to Central America during the reign of Louis Philippe, was recalled during the Second Empire, but stayed in Mexico. See SCHEFER, pp. 25–26.

47. De Gabriac to Fr. F.O., 1 Sep 1856, MDAE: *CP, Mex.,* PERKINS, p. 347.

48. Lettsom to Clarendon, 19 Sep (r. 15 Nov) 1856, DAWSON, pp. 50–51.

49. SCHEFER, pp. 25–26.

50. See footnote 48 above.

51. Clarendon to Lettsom, 18 Nov 1856, DAWSON, p. 51

52. Cowley to Clarendon, 26 Nov 1856, *ibid.*, p. 52.
53. Clarendon to Cowley, 2 Dec 1856, *ibid.*
54. Cowley to Clarendon, 7 Dec 1856, *ibid.*, pp. 52–53.
55. Cowley to Clarendon, 5 Feb 1857, *ibid.*, p. 53.
56. CORTI, I, 79. Corti concludes that Napoleon III seemed really to desire that the project should be carried into effect but that it was not yet clear to him how this was to be done.
57. See Appendix U of present investigation.
58. Cowley to Clarendon, 16 Apr 1857, DAWSON, p. 54.
59. *Ibid.*
60. MDAE: *CP, Mex.,* vol. 45, PERKINS, p. 350.
61. See Appendix F of present investigation.
62. Estrada to Metternich (fils), Paris, 5 Jul 1861, *HHSA,* AKM, DAWSON, p. 85.
63. *Ibid.*

## 2. THE UNITED STATES AND THE AMERICAN CIVIL WAR, 1857–1860

1. Included in the religious reforms was an attempt to free from mortmain the large holdings of the Church.
2. Frank A. Knapp, Jr.: "Parliamentary Government and the Mexican Constitution of 1857: A Forgotten Phase of Mexican Political History," *HAHR,* XXXIII (1953), 66.
3. Forsyth to Cass, Mexico City, 4 Apr (r. 15 May) 1857, William R. Manning, ed.: *Diplomatic Correspondence of the United States: Inter-American Affairs, 1831–1860* (12 v., Washington, 1932-1939), IX, 907–908, (Hereafter referred to as MANNING).
4. At the same time Forsyth completed a postal convention, a treaty of commerce, and a reciprocity treaty.
5. Forsyth to Cass, Mexico City, 4 Apr (r. 15 May) 1857, MANNING, IX, 907–908.
6. Nor were the other three treaties (see footnote 4 above) submitted to the Senate. See J. M. Callahan: "The Mexican Policy of Southern Leaders Under Buchanan's Administration," *American Historical Association Annual Report,* 1910, p. 137.
7. PERKINS, pp. 333–334.
8. Forsyth to Cass, Mexico City, 4 Apr (r. 15 May) 1857, MANNING, IX, 907–908.
9. In his message of 2 December 1845 to Congress.
10. Julius W. Pratt: "The Origin of 'Manifest Destiny'," *American Historical Review,* XXXI (1927), sum. by Ray Allen Billington: *The Far Western Frontier, 1830–1860* (London, 1956), p. 149.
11. Albert K. Weinberg: *Manifest Destiny* (Baltimore, 1935); John D. P. Fuller: *The Movement for the Acquisition of All Mexico, 1846–1848* (The Johns Hopkins University Studies in Historical and Political Science, Ser. LIV, No. 1, Baltimore, 1936).

12. For him the Monroe Doctrine was ". . . no abstraction." See Gadsden to Marcy, Mexico City, No. 60, 3 (r. 16) Apr 1855, MANNING, IX, 751. The United States owed it to her "enlightened institutions," "humanity," and "Civilization" (Gadsden to Marcy, Mexico City, 18 (r. 31) May 1855, MANNING, IX, 771–776) to rescue a Mexico threatened by a plot to erect a throne for a Spanish Bourbon. It was a case of ". . . *Mexico* and the *Castilian blood* to resist the progress of *Anglo Saxon* muscle." See Gaddsden to Marcy, Mexico City, No. 38 *(bis)*, 2 (r. 18) Sep 1854, MANNING, IX, 729.

13. Cass to Forsyth, 17 Jul 1857, Washington, Dept of State: *Instructions, Mexico,* PERKINS, p. 336; DAWSON, p. 31.

14. Congress was installed 8 October 1857, Commonfort as President, 1 December 1857. For details of the Mexican Civil War, the "War of Reform," see BANCROFT, V, 697–795.

15. Zuloaga, a brigade commander, conspired with some governors and issued the "Plan of Tacubaya" on 17 December 1857. It proclaimed that a new congress was to be called by Commonfort to draw up a new constitution and that all authorities refusing to second the plan were to be replaced by those inclined to support it. On the same day Congress made a protest against the Plan and decreed Commonfort's authority at an end. The next day Zuloaga's brigade entered Mexico City. In January 1858 Commonfort fled Mexico City, and Zuloaga had some representatives elect himself President.

16. Juarez, as President of the Supreme Court, claimed himself the legal President of Mexico for the "unexpired" term of office of Commonfort, that ran until 1 December 1861. In May 1858 Juarez established the capital of the liberals at Vera Cruz.

17. Otway to Malmesbury, 30 Apr 1858, DAWSON, p. 32.

18. Such proposals were an embarrassment to the Zuloaga Government, fearing a loss of prestige during its contest with Juarez. In addition, Forsyth's predecessor, James Gadsden, had already discredited any such proposals. He had been in the habit of producing maps with as many as nine or ten boundaries for which proportionate sums were offered. When it was discovered that he had received no instructions to make these proposals, Mexico protested and urged his recall, which was effected in October 1856. See DAWSON, pp. 25–26.

19. For American claims against Mexico, see J. Fred Rippy: *The United States and Mexico* (New York, 1926), pp. 42–125, 168–196. See also Frederick Sherwood Dunn: *The Diplomatic Protection of Americans in Mexico* (New York, 1933), pp. 30–31, 49–52.

20. Forsyth to Cass, Pri., 15 Apr 1858, Washington, Dept of State: *Despatches, Mexico,* J. Fred Rippy: *The United States and Mexico* (New York, 1926), p. 216.

21. When a decree in May 1858 imposed a tax on all capital, Forsyth advized Americans resident in Mexico not to pay unless confronted by force. Solomon Nigel, an American subject, refused to pay the tax and was banished from Mexico. On his own initiative Forsyth suspended diplomatic relations with the Zuloaga Government. See DAWSON, p.

32, and PERKINS, p. 337.

22. Otway to Malmesbury, 4 Nov 1858, DAWSON, p. 32.

23. Otway to Malmesbury, 3 Oct 1858, *ibid.*, p. 38.

24. Cass to Dodge, Confidential, 21 Oct 1858, John Bassett Moore, ed.: *A Digest of Internationl Law, as embodied in Diplomatic Discussions, Treaties, and Other International Agreements, International Awards, The Decisions of Municipal Courts, and the Writings of Jurists, and especially in Documents, Published and Unpublished, Issued by Presidents and Secretaries of State of the United States, the Opinions of the Attorneys-General, and the Decisions of Courts, Federal and State* (8 v., Washington, 1906), VI, 477. (Hereafter referred to as MOORE).

25. DAWSON, p. 36; H. Leonardon: *Prim* (Paris, 1901), p. 43. (Hereafter referred to as *PRIM*). Appendix D of present investigation.

26. PRIM, pp. 43–44. See also Appendix D of present investigation.

27. Mason to Cass, Paris, 30 Jul (r. 21 Aug) 1858, MANNING, VI, 690.

28. Cass to Dodge, Confidential, 21 Oct 1858, MOORE, VI, 477–478.

29. Collantes to Cass, 15 Nov 1858, Washington, Dept of State: *Despatches, Spain,* vol. 41, PERKINS, p. 344.

30. PERKINS, p. 339.

31. J. D. Richardson, ed.: *The Messages and Papers of the Presidents* (10 v., Washington, 1896–1899), V, 512–514.

32. On 2 June 1858 Senator Houston's resolutions that the United States extend a protectorate over Mexico were defeated in the Senate by a vote of 32–16. See PERKINS, pp. 336–337.

33. Cass to McLane, 7 Mar 1859, MANNING, IX, 257.

34. J. M. Callahan: "The Mexican Policy of Southern Leaders under Buchanan's Administration," *American Historical Association Annual Report,* 1910, p. 138.

35. McLane to Cass, Vera Cruz, 28 May (r. 11 Jun) 1860, MANNING, IX, 1190.

36. J. D. Richardson, ed.: *The Messages and Papers of the Presidents* (10 v., Washington, 1896–1899), V, 567–568.

37. Treaty of Transits and Commerce between the United States and Mexico, signed by Robert M. McLane, United States Minister to Mexico, and Melchor Ocampo, Minister of Foreign Affairs of Mexico, at Vera Cruz, 14 Dec 1859, MANNING, IX, 1137–1141. General accounts of the treaty include: W. Stull Holt: *Treaties Defeated by the Senate: A Study of the Struggle between President and Senate over the Conduct of Foreign Affairs* (Baltimore, 1933), pp. 92–93; BANCROFT, V, 773–774; J. Fred Rippy: *The United States and Mexico* (New York, 1926), pp. 212–227; Howard L. Wilson: "President Buchanan's Proposed Intervention in Mexico," *AHR,* V (1899–1900), 687–701; J. M. Callahan: *American Foreign Policy in Mexican Relations* (New York, 1932), pp. 244–277. An account based on the records of the American State Department is J. M. Callahan: "The Mexican

Policy of Southern Leaders Under Buchanan's Administration," *American Historical Association Annual Report,* 1910, pp. 135–151. The published correspondence between McLane and Cass is found in MANNING, IX.

38. Convention between the United States and Mexico to enforce Treaty Stipulations and to Maintain Order and Security in the Territories of each of the two Republics, signed by Robert M. McLane, United States Minister to Mexico, and Melchor Ocampo, Minister of Foreign Affairs of Mexico, at Vera Cruz, 14 Dec 1859, MANNING, IX, 1141.

39. Juarez raised some money by selling war bonds. See Mathew to Russell, Mexico City, No. 37, Confidential, 12 May (r. 27 Jun) 1861, PRO, F.O. 50/352.

40. By Article X. See MANNING, IX, 1140.

41. McLane to Cass, 14 Dec 1859, Washington: Dept. of State: *Despatches, Mexico,* vol. 24, Frederick Sherwood Dunn: *The Diplomatic Protection of Americans in Mexico* (New York, 1933), p. 89.

42. PERKINS, pp. 340–341.

43. It was feared that the United States would have to intervene constantly, contrary to American policy. Attempts were made to show that the commercial advantages were in favor of Mexico. Northerners saw in the treaties a Southern plot to secure more territory from which to erect slave states. See *New York Tribune,* 27, 28, 29 Feb, 5 Mar, 1 Jun 1860; *National Intelligencer,* 4, 11 Jun 1860, sum. by W. Stull Holt: *Treaties Defeated by the Senate: A Study of the Struggle between President and Senate over the Conduct of Foreign Affairs* (Baltimore, 1933), p. 95.

44. Howard L. Wilson: "President Buchanan's Proposed Intervention in Mexico," AHR, V (1899–1900), 696.

45. All in favor (18) were Democrats, and almost all opposed (21 of 27) were Republicans. Actually it was the Treaty of Transits that was defeated. The Convention to enforce Treaty Stipulations was not even put to a vote. See W. Stull Holt: *Treaties Defeated by the Senate: A Study of the Struggle between President and Senate over the Conduct of Foreign Affairs* (Baltimore, 1933), pp. 95–96.

46. McLane to Cass, Vera Cruz, 30 Mar (r. 16 Apr) 1860; Memorandum of a conversation between McLane and Cass, 18 Sep 1860, MANNING, IX, 1172, 1205–1206.

47. Cass to McLane, Washington, 20 Sep 1860, *ibid.,* IX, 290.

48. While the right to demand redress for injuries was acknowledged, it was stated that the ". . . . United States had determined to resist any forcible attempt to impose a particular adjustment of the existing conflict against the will and sanction of the people of Mexico, and also, any forcible intervention by any power which looks to control of the political destiny thereof. . . ." See "La Reintrie Circular," 37th Cong., 2nd Sess., *House Exec. Doc. No. 100,* pp. 17–18, cited by PERKINS, p. 345. La Reintrie was an agent sent to Mexico City by

McLane and who transmitted the circular to the members of the diplomatic corps there.

49. Following a rout of the Conservatives in the Silao Hills in August 1860, the tide turned in favor of the Liberals.

## 3.   EUROPE AND THE MEXICAN CIVIL WAR, 1857–1860

1. See footnote 26 of Section 2 of Chapter I and Appendix D of the present investigation.

2. See footnote 24 of Section 2 of Chapter I of the present investigation. In mid-1857 there were rumors of a Spanish attempt to place a son of the Count Montemolin on a throne in Mexico (Cowley to Clarendon, 8 Jul 1857, cited by DAWSON, p. 54).

3. See William O. Scroggs: *Filibusters and Financiers: The Story of William Walker and His Associates* (New York, 1916). American filibustering activities continued up to the American Civil War. See Ollinger Crenshaw: "The Knights of the Golden Circle. The Career of George Bickley," *AHR,* XLVII (1941), 23–50.

4. The phrase is Thomas A. Bailey's. See BAILEY, p. 294.

5. Lumley forwarded an article published in the New Orleans *Delta,* the personal organ of Mr. Dabis, Secretary of War in Pierce's cabinet, and called attention to the following sentence: "The regeneration of Central America by Walker, in alliance with the United States, would lead to the gradual emancipation of the West Indies from the infamous 'free-negroism' established there by the enemies of American Republicanism." Lumley commented: "You will perceive that a great danger threatens the West India Islands if the Americans are permitted to annex, as they certainly expect to do at some period, not only Nicaragua but the whole of Central America" (Lumley to Clarendon, 20 Nov 1856, cited by DAWSON, p. 27).

6. Napier to Clarendon, 21 Jun 1857, cited by *ibid.,* p. 38.

7. Lettsom to Clarendon, 21 Mar, 30 Apr 1857, cited by *ibid.,* pp. 30, 30–31.

8. Clarendon to Lettsom, 1 Jul 1856, cited by *ibid.,* p. 37.

9. Cowley to Clarendon, Paris, 6 Jun 1856, *Foreign Office Archives,* Repts. from France, cited by *ibid.*

10. Cowley to Clarendon, 10 Apr 1857, cited by *ibid.,* p. 38.

11. Cowley to Clarendon, Paris, 6 Jun 1856, *Foreign Office Archives,* Repts. from France, cited by *ibid.,* p. 37.

12. See Appendix D of the present investigation.

13. Lyons to Malmesbury, Washington, 30 May 1859, cited by Baron Thomas W. Legh Newton: *Lord Lyons: A record of British Diplomacy* (2v., London, 1913), I, 15.

14. Buchanan to Russell, 14 Mar 1860, sum. and cited by DAWSON, p. 39.

15. See text below footnoted by footnotes 102 and 106.

16. See text below between footnotes 107 and 110.

17. See text below footnoted by footnote 107.

18. See Appendix F. of the present investigation.

19. De Gabriac to Walewski, Pri., ? (r. 7 Sep) 1857, sum. by SCHEFER, pp. 37–39; *Ibid.*, pp. 39–40.

20. De Gabriac to French Ministry of Foreign Affairs, 31 May, 8 Aug 1858, MDAE: *CP, Mex.*, XLV, sum. by PERKINS, p. 348.

21. Malmesbury to Cowley, 28 Sep. 1858, cited by James Howard Harris, 3rd Earl of Malmesbury: *Memoirs of an Ex-Minister: An Autobiography* (2v., London, 1884), II, 136.

22. James S. C. Abbott: *The History of Napoleon III, Emperor of the French, Including a brief narrative of all the most important events which have occurred in Europe Since the fall of Napoleon I Until the present time* (Boston, 1869), p. 628. (Hereafter referred to as ABBOTT). Hidalgo made the statement to a friend of Abbott before leaving for Europe.

23. Malmesbury to Otway, 7 Jan 1859, cited by DAWSON, p. 11.

24. Mon to Collantes, Paris, 24 Nov 1858, cited by *Archives Diplomatiques: Recueil de Diplomatie et D'Histoire*, Ser. I, VII, 205. (Hereafter referred to as *AD*): Herbert Ingram Priestley: *The Mexican Nation, a History* (London, 1923), pp. 345–346; Mon to Collantes, 24 Nov, 9 Dec 1858, *Documents communiques aux Cortes sur les affaires du Mexique, 1861–1862*, sum. by Pierre de La Gorce: *Histoire de Second Empire* (7v., Paris, 1894–1905), IV, 17.

25. Mon to Collantes, Paris, 24 Nov 1858, *AD*, Ser. I, VII, 205.

26. *Ibid.*, p. 206.

27. Collantes to Mon, 3 and 10 Jan 1859, *Documents communiques aux Cortes sur les affaires du Mexique, 1861–1862*, sum. by Pierre de La Gorce:*Histoire de Second Empire* (7 v., Paris, 1894–1905), IV, 17.

28. See Appendix D. of the present investigation.

29. Speech of General Prim before Senate of the Cortes, Dec 1858, cited by *PRIM*, p. 44.

30. Donaldson Jordan and Edwin J. Pratt: *Europe and the American Civil War* (Boston and New York, 1931), pp. 245–246; Arnold Robert Verduin:*Modern Spanish Constitutions (1808–1931): A dissertation submitted in partial fulfillment of the requirements for the degree of Doctor of Philosophy in the University of Michigan.* (Typescript, University of Michigan, 1934), p. 129. (Hereafter referred to as VERDUIN).

31. Buchanan to Russell, San Ildefonso, 20 Jul 1859, *Foreign Office Archives,* repts. from Spain, sum. by DAWSON, p. 39.

32. Buchanan to Russell, 24 Aug 1859, sum. and cited by *ibid.*

33. SCHEFER, p. 39; Robert Sencourt: *The Life of the Empress Eugenie* (London, 1931), p. 162.

34. DAWSON, p. 87.

35. See Appendix U of the present investigation.

36. *Ibid.*

37. Eugenie to Duc D'Albe, 12 Dec 1854, cited by Duc D'Albe, ed.: *Lettres Familières de L'Impératrice Eugénie Conservées dans Les*

*Archives du Palais de Liria* (2 v., Paris, 1935), I, 114–116. (Hereafter referred to as ALBE).

38. Hübner to Buol, 20 Nov 1853, *HHSA,* cited by Robert Sencourt: *Napoleon III: The Modern Emperor* (London, 1933), p. 270.

39. Just before her marriage, Eugenie confided to her sister: "Two things, I hope will protect me: the faith I have in God and the great desire that I have to help the unfortunate classes. . . . If the finger of Providence has marked out such an elevated place for me, it is to serve as the mediator between those who are suffering and the one who can remedy it" (Eugenie to Duchesse D'Albe, Jan 1853, cited by Robert Sencourt (?): "Les Financailles de L'Impératrice: Lettres à La Duchesse D'Albe," *Revue des Deux Mondes,* 15 Jul 1932, p. 299). When it appeared that Orsini would be executed, Baron Hübner noted in his journal under 28 February 1858 that Eugenie" . . . spends her time crying and appealing to her husband for mercy to save the life of this miserable one" (HUBNER, II, 119).

40. "Pious without being bigoted, well informed without being pedantic, she talks on all subjects without constraint" (Ms. of Napoleon III of 1868, found in the Tuileries, cited by *Dr. Thomas W. Evans: The Memoirs of Dr. Thomas W. Evans: Recollections of the Second Empire,* ed. Edward A. Crane (2 v., London, 1905), I, 124).

41. These arguments were part of Estrada's creed. See Section I of Chapter I of the present investigation. Hidalgo reiterated them in 1862. See Appendix U.

42. Emile Ollivier: *L'Empire Libéral: Etudes, Récits, Souvenirs* (18 v., Paris, 1895–1912), V, 233. (Hereafter referred to as OLLIVIER).

43. The literature and sources of information about the exiles is reviewed in Chapter III of the present investigation.

44. Emmanuel Domenech: *Histoire du Mexique, Juarez et Maximilien: Correspondances Inédites des Présidents, Ministres et Généraux Almonte, Santa-Anna, Gutierrez, Miramon, Marquez, Mejia, Woll, etc., de Juarez, de l'Empereur Maximilien et de l'Imperatrice Charlotte, par Emmanuel Domenech, Ancien Directeur de la Presse de l'Empereur Maximilien, ex-aumonier de l'Armee Francaise du Mexique* (3 v., Paris, 1868), II, 366. (Hereafter referred to as DOMENECH).

45. This was the so-called "Pastry War" between France and Mexico. The war got its name from the fact that the pastry of a French shop owner had tempted a Mexican mob, a circumstance that the Mexicans seized upon to ridicule all French claims as the pastry claims. See BANCROFT, V, 186–205.

46. "An Old Story Which is Always New," 3 Aug 1843, cited by *The Political and Historical Works of Louis Napoleon Bonaparte, President of the French Republic, Now First Collected, with an Original Memoir of His Life, Brought Down to the Promulgation of the Constitution of 1852, and Occasional Notes* (2 v., London, 1852), II, 213.

47. Eugenie-Paléologue Conversation, 10 Jan 1904, cited by Maurice Paléologue: *The Tragic Empress: Intimate Conversations with the*

*Empress Eugenie, 1901 to 1911,* trans. Hamish Miles (London, n.d.), p. 98. (Hereafter referred to as PALEOLOGUE).

48. "Facsimilie of Prince Napoleon Louis Bonaparte's drawing for the Nicaragua Canal—Drawn at Ham 1845," Jerrold Blanchard: *The Life of Napoleon III, Derived from State Records, From Unpublished Family Correspondence, and From Personal Testimony* (4v., London, 1874–1882), II, facing 328.

49. *Le Canal de Nicaragua, ou projet de jonction des Oceans Atlatintique et Pacificue au moyen d'un canal,* sum. and cited by DAWSON, pp. 48–49.

50. In March 1853 Napoleon received a deputation from an English company formed to join the Atlantic and Pacific Oceans by the Isthmus of Darien. The company's plans and maps were laid before Napoleon, who observed them with particular attention and then said, "I have long appreciated all the advantages of a junction between the two seas . . ." (*Le Moniteur,* 30 Mar 1853; *The Times,* London, 29 Mar 1853, encls. of Rives to Marcey, Paris, No. 198, 31 Mar (r. 18 Apr) 1853, cited by MANNING, V, 650–651).

51. Cowley to Russell, Chantilly, Pri., 9 Dec 1861, PRO, P.R.O. 30/22–56 (original); F.O. 519/229 (letter book). This letter has been published, but without the source given. See Sir Victory Wellesley and Robert Sencourt, eds.: *Conversations with Napoleon III: A Collection of Documents, mostly unpublished and almost entirely Diplomatic, Selected and arranged with introductions* (London, 1934), p. 200.

52. See Appendix U of the present investigation.

53. See Appendix F of the present investigation.

54. CORTI, I, 79.

55. Comte Fleury: *Memoirs of the Empress Eugenie by Comte Fleury: Compiled from Statements, Private Documents and Personal Letters of the Empress Eugenie, From Conversations of the Emperor Napoleon III and From Family Letters and Papers of General Fleury, M. Franceschini Pietri, Prince Victor Napoleon and Other Members of the Court of the Second Empire* (2 v., New York and London, 1920), II, 106–107.

56. Thouvenel-Hidalgo Conversation, Paris, 22 Mar 1860, sum. by Verbal Note, Paris, 22 Mar 1860, encl. of Hidalgo to Thouvenel, 22 Mar 1860, MDAE; *CP,Mex.,* LIII.

57. Hidalgo to Thouvenel, Paris, 12 May 1860, *ibid.*

58. Antonin Debidour: *Histoire Diplomatique de l'Europe depuis L'Ouverture Du Congrès de Vienne Jusqu'a La Cloture Du Congrès de Berlin, 1814–1878* (2 v., Paris, 1891), II, 235n.

59. Almonte to ?, 9 Rue Roqueplan, Paris, 31 Jul 1860, *La Revolucion,* 7 Oct 1860, cited by BANCROFT, V, 788.

60. Forsyth to Cass, 4 Apr 1857. See footnote 8 of Section II of Chapter I of the present investigation.

61. De Gabriac to French Ministry of Foreign Affairs, 22 Apr 1857, MDAE: *CP.Mex.,* XLV, cited by PERKINS, p. 348.

62. De Gabrias to French Ministry of Foreign Affairs, 26 Dec 1858, *ibid.*

63. De Gabriac to French Ministry of Foreign Affairs, 18 Apr 1859, *ibid.,* p. 349.

64. De Gabriac to Thouvenel, Mexico City, No. 442, 11 Apr (r. 1 Jun) 1860, MDAE: *CP,Mex,* LIII.

65. De Gabriac to Thouvenel, Mexico City, No. 444, 24 Apr (r. 31 May) 1860, *ibid.*

66. Montluc to Whitehead, Paris, 31 May 1860, cited by MONTLUC, p. 27.

67. Montluc to Lelong, 31 May 1860, cited by *ibid.,* p. 28.

68. M. F. Maury-Napoleon III Conversation, Biarritz, 1860, sum. and cited by M. F. Maury to Benjamin, 23 Jan 1863, MS., Confederate Archives, cited by John G. Nicolay and John Hay: *Abraham Lincoln: A History* (10 V., New York, 1890), VI, 34–35. Nicolay and Hay make it appear that Schele de Vere had this conversation with Napoleon. Actually it was M. F. Maury. See Beckles Willson: John Slidell and the Confederates in Paris, 1862–1865 (New York, 1932), pp. 40–41, 204.

69. Otway to Malmesbury, 2 Aug 1858, cited by Dawson, pp. 6–7.

70. Otway to Malmesbury, 3 Dec 1858, cited by *ibid.,* p. 8.

71. Otway to Malmesbury, 20 Dec 1858, cited by *ibid.,* pp. 8–9.

72. In round figures, the population of Mexico in 1858 was 8,000,000, comprising 4,500,00 Indians, 2,500,000 of mixed blood, and 1,000,000 whites, mostly of Spanish descent. See Paul Gaulot: *La Vérité sur L'Expédition du Mexique d'après les Documents Inédits de Ernest Louet, Payeur en Chef du Corps Expeditionaire: Rêve d' Empire* (Paris, 1889), p. 24; (Hereafter referred to as GAULOT). Lieutenant-Colonel Charles Martin: *Précis des Evénements de la Campagne du Mexique en 1862, par Ch. Martin, Précéde d'une Notice Géographique et Statistique sur le Mexique par Léon Deluzy* (Paris, 1863). p. 2; Henry M. Flint: *Mexico Under Maximilian* (Philadelphia, 1867), p. 26. Emmanuel Domenech: *Le Mexique Tel Qu'il Est: La Vérité sur son climat, ses habitants et son Gouvernement par Emmanuel Domenech, Ancien Directeur de la presse du Cabinet de S. M. L'Empereur Maximilien, exaumonier de corps expéditionnaire* (Paris, 1867), p. 98.

73. Malmesbury to Cowley, 28 Sep 1858, cited by James Howard Harris, 3rd Earl of Malmesbury: *Memoirs of an Ex-Minister: An Autobiography* (2v., London, 1884), II, 136.

74. Malmesbury to Otway, 16 Sep 1858, cited by DAWSON, p. 8.

75. See text of the present investigation footnoted by footnote 23 above.

76. Malmesbury to Otway, 7 Jan 1859, cited by DAWSON, p. 11.

77. Petition to Queen Victoria, encl. of Otway to Malmesbury, Most Secret and Confidential, 2 Jan 1859, *Foreign Office Archives,* Repts. from Mexico, sum. and cited by *ibid,* pp. 9–10.

78. Otway to Malmesbury, Most Secret and Confidential, 2 Jan 1859, cited by *ibid.,* p. 9.

79. *Ibid.,* p. 14.

80. Otway to Malmesbury, 29 Jan 1859, cited by *ibid.,* pp. 12–13.

81. Malmesbury to Otway, 14 Feb 1859, cited by *ibid.,* pp. 13–14.

82. Malmesbury to Otway, 9 Jun 1859, cited by *ibid.,* pp. 14–15.

83. Russell to Otway, 1 Aug 1859, sum. by *ibid.,* p. 15.

84. Malmesbury to Cowley, 28 Sep 1858, cited by James Howard Harris, 3rd Earl of Malmesbury: *Memoirs of an Ex-Minister: An Autobiography* (2 v., London, 1884), II, 136.

85. See Appendix A of the present investigation.

86. See Appendix B of the present investigation.

87. Mr. Mathew accepted the post ". . . as the avowed stepping stone to a European Mission . . ." (Mathew to Russell, Mexico City, Pri., 12 Jan 1860, PRO, P.R.O. 30/22–74).

88. Mathew to Russell, 12 Oct 1859, sum. and cited by DAWSON, p. 18.

89. Russell to Mathew, 26 Jan 1860, cited by MANNING, IX, 1174.

90. SCHEFER, pp. 52–55.

91. Verbal Note, Paris, 8 Mar 1860, MDAE: *Cp, Mex.,* LIII.

92. "Say we cannot recommend any settlement which shall not include so far as our advice is concerned, religious toleration" (Russell to Murphy, draft, 11 May 1860, PRO, F.O. 96/26). Murphy was Miramon's Minister to London.

93. Throughout this period a difficulty in Spanish-British relations was Spanish persecution of British protestants resident in Spain. In 1861 Hammond related Russell's view that he probably also had in 1860: "Lord Russell says he never could agree to act with Spain in Mexico, as Great Britain never can embark in a crusade against liberty of conscience, and Spain holds that Protestants should be prevented from the exercise of their public worship" (Hammond to Cowley, F.O., Pri., 14 Sep 1861, PRO, F.O. 519/190).

94. See Appendix D of the present investigation.

95. Mathew to Russell, 29 Mar 1860, sum. and cited by DAWSON, p. 20.

96. Munos-Ledo to De Gabriac, Mexico City, 21 Apr 1861, encl. 1 of De Gabriac to Thouvenel, Mexico City, No. 444, 24 Apr (r. 31 May) 1860, MDAE: *CP. Mex.,* LIII.

97. Munos-Ledo to De Gabriac, Mexico City, 12 Apr 1860, encl. 5 of De Gabriac to Thouvenel, Mexico City, No. 443, 16 Apr (r. 1 Jun) 1860, *ibid.*

98. Jose de Emaparan, Acting Minister of Foreign Affairs, to D. W. Cornwallis Aldham, in command of the British Fleet in the Gulf of Mexico, Vera Cruz, 27 Mar 1860, encl. A of McLane to Cass, Vera Cruz, 26 Apr (r. 16 May) 1860, cited by MANNING, IX, 1183.

99. Juarez-McLane Conversation, 30 Mar 1860, sum. by McLane to Cass, Vera Cruz, 30 Mar (r. 16 Apr) 1860, cited by *ibid.,* IX, 1173.

100. Mathew to Russell, 29 Mar 1860, cited by DAWSON, p. 20.

101. Mon-Thouvenel Conversation, reported by Mon and sum. by Collantes to Spanish Ambassadors to Paris and London, Madrid, 18 Apr 1860, *AD,* Ser. I, VII, 211.

102. *Ibid.* VII, 212.

103. Isturitz to Collantes, London, 27 Apr 1860, cited by DUVER-NOIS, I, 5–6.

104. Mon-Thouvenel Conversation, sum. by Mon to Collantes, Paris, 4 May 1860, *AD,* Ser. I, VII, 214.

105. Herbert Ingram Priestley: *The Mexican Nation, a History* (London, 1923), p. 346. The constitution apparently is no longer in existence.

106. Collantes to Spanish Ambassadors in Paris and London, Madrid, 11 May 1860, *AD* Ser I, VII, 215.

107. Russell-Murphy Conversation, related to De Gabriac by Miramon's Foreign Minister, sum. by De Gabriac to Thouvenel, Mexico City, No. 437, 23 Mar (r. 7 May) 1860, MDAE: *CP, Mex.,* LIII.

108. See text footnoted by footnotes 55 and 56 above.

109. "Mexican Affairs, Note for the Minister," Apr 1860, MDAE: *CP, Mex.,* LIII.

110. Thouvenel to Saligny, 30 May 1860, sum. and cited by SCHEFER, p. 65.

111. See footnote 45 of Section II of Chapter I of the present investigation.

112. Russel to Mathew, 28 Jun 1860, sum. by DAWSON, p. 20.

113. MOORE, VI, 479.

114. Trescot, Acting Secretary of State, to Elgee, Secretary in Charge of the American Legation in Mexico, 8 Aug 1860, cited by *ibid.,* VI, 479–480.

115. *Ibid.*

116. Cass to Faulkner, 31 Aug 1860, cited by *ibid.,* VI, 480.

117. Cass to Preston, 7 Sep 1860, cited by *ibid.,* VI, 481.

118. Russell to Mathew, 24 Aug 1860, cited by DAWSON, p. 20.

119. Mathew to Russell, Jalapa, No. 6, 30 Jan (r. 28 Feb) 1861, PRO, F.O. 50/352.

120. Verbal Note, Paris, 4 Sep 1860, MDAE: *CP, Mex.,* LIII.

121. "Note for the Minister," Sep 1860, *ibid.*

122. Cte. A. de la Londe, Interim Chargè, to Thouvenel, Mexico City, 8 May (r. 28 Jun) 1860, *ibid.*

123. Saligny to Thouvenel, Vera Cruz, No. 1, 26 Nov 1860 (r. 4 Jan 1861), *ibid.*

124. From 1831 to 1839 Saligny served in the French diplomatic service in Hanover, Athens, and Washington. Then he became Chargé d'Affaires to Texas, then an independent republic. When Texas was annexed to the United States, Saligny lost his position and obtained no new post until the Second French Republic sent him to The Hague. In 1851 he was recalled and placed in an unassigned status by Napoleon, then Prince-President. The assignment to Mexico was the first post since 1851 for Saligny. See SCHEFER, p. 64.

125. Thouvenel to Saligny, 30 May 1860, sum. and cited by *ibid.,* pp. 64–66.

126. *Ibid.,* pp. 66–67.

127. Thouvenel to Saligny, 5 Jul 1860, sum. by *ibid.*, p. 68.

128. Thouvenel to Saligny, 28 Aug 1860, sum. by *ibid.*, p. 69.

129. A Franco-Mexican Convention of 1853 recognized 28 French claims amounting to about $1,500,000 (Comte Emile de Kéraltry: *La Créance Jecker, Les Indemnités Françaises et Les Emprunts Mexicains* (Paris, 1868), pp. 67–68; BURKE, p. 134). Bonds were issued to be paid from 25 per cent of customs collected from French cargoes. In 1859 a new convention set aside 8 per cent of all import duties for the French bondholders (Saligny to Thouvenel, Mexico City, No. 14, 28 Mar (r. 30 Apr) 1861, MDAE: *CP, Mex.*, LIV). An adjudication in 1860 set $312,431.00 as the sum still owed the French Conventions ("Adjudication of 21 May 1860," encl. 3 of Cte. A. de La Londe, Interim Chargé, to Thouvenel, Mexico City, No. 448, 2 May (r. 28 Jun) 1860, MDAE: *CP, Mex.*, LIII). This was a small sum compared with what was owed the British and Spanish bondholders. (See Appendices A, B, and D of the present investigation. Saligny charged that the French bonds were ". . . adjudicated at about 40% of their nominal value" (Saligny to Thouvenel, Mexico City, No. 14, 28 Mar (r. 30 Apr) 1861, MDAE: *CP, Mex.*, LIV).

130. The decree was signed 27 October and published 29 October. See E. Lefèvre: *Le Mexique et L'Intervention Europeenne, Par Le Citoyen E. Lefèvre* (Mexico City, 1862, p. 108).

131. Jean Baptiste Jecker was born in Porrentruy in the Swiss Canton of Berne in 1816, a year too late to possess French citizenship, for until the Treaties of 1815, the area belonged to France. Thus an elder brother, Louis Jecker, born in 1804, was a French citizen. See Robert Christophe: *Le Duc de Morny: "Empereur" Des Français Sous Napoleon III Paris, 1951)* p. 203.

132. Bonds paying 6% interest were issued to the amount of 75,000,000 francs. In return Miramon was given 3,094,640 francs in cash, 4,344,500 francs in various bonds, custom house orders, military supplies, and 33,000 francs in diverse credits and payments. See Kéraltry: *La Créance Jecker, p. 12.* These figures agree with a "Note on the Jecker Claim" by Montluc. See MONTLUC, p. 49. Montluc gives the sums in dollars, calculated at one dollar to five francs. In 1862 the franc stood at $0.1931 ("Table of Pars of Exchange," Foreign Office Circular, 28 Mar 1862, PRO, F.O. 27/1423).

133. The bonds were to be received in payment of 20% of all duties and taxes to be collected by the Mexican Government, exclusive of payments to the national contingent (Petition of 150 French, Swiss, and Belgian residents in Mexico to Saligny, 31 Dec 1860, encl. of Saligny to Thouvenel, Mexico City, No. 15, 30 Mar (r. 30 Apr) 1861, MDAE: *CP, Mex.*, LIV).

134. BURKE, p. 130; Kéraltry; *La Créance Jecker, p. 13.*

135. On 17 November 1859 the interested Swiss, Spanish and French merchants addressed a petition to De Gabriac to ask whether the Mexican Government would adhere to the agreement. De Gabriac forwarded the petition to the Mexican Government, which replied that

it would observe the arrangement "religiously." The petition and reply from the Mexican Government were then sent by De Gabriac to the French Ministry of Foreign Affairs (Petition of 150 French, Swiss, and Belgian residents in Mexico to Saligny, 31 Dec 1860, encl. of Saligny to Thouvenel, Mexico City, No. 15, (r. 30 Apr) 1861, MDAE: *CP, Mex.*, LIV).

136. Xavier Elsesser to Montluc, Porentruy, 2 Oct 1860, cited by MONTLUC, p. 41.

137. Xavier Elsesser to Montluc, Porentruy, 1 Oct 1860, cited by *ibid.*, pp. 47–49.

138. In October 1861 Saligny approached M. Hottinguer (A. de Morineau to Du Camp, Paris, Aug 1877, cited by Maxime De Camp: Les Convulsions de Paris (4 v., Paris, 1878–1880), I, 512–516). Morineau was a pensioned Consul of France, former manager of the General Consulates of Switzerland and Spain in Mexico. He answered Du Camp's request for information about Jecker in connection with the book being prepared about the Commune, at which time Jecker was shot.

139. See Section 2 of Chapter II and Appendix C of the present investigation.

140. Mathew to Aldham, Jalapa, 2 Dec 1860, PRO, F.O. 50/357; Mathew to Russell, No. 83, 25 Dec 1860, sum. by Russell to Mathew, F.O., No. 13, 7 Feb (r. 29 Mar) 1861, *ibid.*, F.O. 204/153; Aldham to Mathew, 7 Dec 1860, sum. by BURKE, pp. 105–106; DAWSON, p. 21; BANCROFT, V, 787–788.

141. Glennie to Mathew, British Consulate, Mexico City, No. 10, 21 Nov 1860, PRO, F.O. 50/359.

142. Saligny to Thouvenel, Vera Cruz, No. 1, 26 Nov 1860 (r. 4 Jan 1861), MDAE: *CP, Mex.*, LIII.

143. MONTLUC, p. 53.

144. SCHEFER, pp. 74–75.

145. Mathew to Russell, Mexico City, Pri., 29 May 1860 PRO, P.R.O. 30/22–74.

146. Mathew to Russell, Jalapa, Pri., 31 Dec 1860, *ibid.*

147. See Appendix D of the present investigation.

148. See Section 2 of Chapter II of the present investigation.

149. See footnote 70 of Section 1 of Chapter II of the present investigation.

150. See Appendices A and B of the present investigation.

151. Mathew to Russell, Jalapa, Pri., 30 Dec 1860, PRO, P.R.O. 30/22–74.

152. Aldham to Milne, *Valorious* off Vera Cruz, 5 Dec 1860, encl. 3 of Admiralty to Hammond, Admiralty, 2 (r. 3) Jan 1861, *ibid.*, F.O. 50/357.

153. See Section 1 of Chapter II of the present investigation.

## CHAPTER II

### 1.  MATHEW AND WYKE IN MEXICO, 1861

1. The United States on 30 January, Prussia on 3 February. See BURKE, p. 119.

2. Mathew to Russell, Jalapa, No. 6, 30 Jan (r. 28 Feb) 1861, PRO, F.O. 50/352.

3. Mathew to Zarco, 8 Feb 1861, sum. by Zarco to Mathew, National Palace, 12 Feb 1861, encl. 2 of Mathew to Russell, Mexico City, No. 11, 25 Feb (r. 30 Mar) 1861, *ibid*.

4. Mathew to Russell, Mexico City, No. 11, 25 Feb (r. 30 Mar) 1861, *ibid*.

6. Mathew to Russell, Mexico City, No. 11, 25 Feb (r. 30 Mar) 1861, *ibid*.

7. Zarco to Mathew, National Palace, 12 Feb 1861, encl. 2 of *ibid*. Zarco pledged to repay the amounts due British subjects from seizure of the Laguna Seca Conducta, with 12 per cent interest, as requested, in four months from 11 February. He expressed regret for the seizure by way of apology requested by Mathew. As to the due honor to be given the British flag when hoisted at the British Legation in consideration for the insult given it by the taking of the $660,000 from the British Legation, Zarco promised to raise the Mexican flag at the National Palace at the same time the British flag should be raised at the British Legation. The proposed means of restoring the $660,000 was in reply to Mathew's demand that the Mexican Government make a declaration of the most feasible arrangement for prompt repayment.

8. Mathew to Russell, Mexico City, No. 11, 25 Feb (r. 30 Mar) 1861, *ibid*.

9. Mathew to Russell, Mexico City, No. 13, 28 Feb (r. 3 Apr) 1861, *ibid*.

10. Russell to Mathew, F.O., No. 36, draft, 22 Apr 1861, PRO, F.O. 50/351.

11. Mathew to Zarco, Mexico City, 2 May 1861, encl. 1 of Wyke to Russell, Mexico City, No. 2, 27 May (r. 27 Jun) 1861, PRO, F.O. 50/352.

12. Zarco to Mathew, Mexico City, 2 May 1861, encl. 3 of Wyke to Russell, Mexico City, No. 2, 27 May (r. 27 Jun) 1861, *ibid*.

13. Wyke to Russell, Mexico City, No. 2, 27 May (r. 27 Jun) 1861, *ibid*.

14. Russell to Mathew, No. 2, 2 Jan 1861, dated by Mathew to Russell, Mexico City, No. 13, 28 Feb (r. 3 Apr) 1861, *ibid*., and sum. by Mathew to Zarco, Mexico City, 22 Feb 1861, encl. 1 of Mathew to Russell, Mexico City, No. 13, 28 Feb (r. 3 Apr) 1861, PRO, F.O. 50/352 ("To Mr. Mathew and Sir C. Wyke, January-December 1861"). Mathew received these instructions about 22 February, for he says he wrote Zarco upon receipt to inform him of Russell's conditions. See

Mathew to Russell, Mexico City, No. 13, 28 Feb (r. 3 Apr) 1861, PRO, F.O. 50/352.

15. Mathew to Russell, Mexico City, No. 13, 28 Feb (r. 3 Apr) 1861, and encls. 1 and 2 thereof, Mathew to Zarco, Mexico City, 22 Feb 1861, and Zarco to Mathew, National Palace, 23 Feb 1861, PRO, F.O. 50/352.

16. Aldham to Milne, Mexico City, 27 Feb 1861, encl. of Admiralty to Hammond, Admiralty, 15 (r. 16) Apr. 1861, PRO, F.O. 50/357. Russell aproved this recognition (Russell to Mathew, F.O., No. 34, 5 Apr (r. 28 May) 1861, PRO, F.O. 204/153).

17. Mathew to Russell, Mexico City, No. 26, 5 Apr (r. 10 May) 1861, PRO, F.O. 50/352.

18. Mathew to Zarco, Mexico City, 22 Mar 1861, encl. 1 of *ibid.*

19. Mathew to Russell, Mexico City, No. 26, 5 Apr (r. 10 May) 1861, *ibid.*

20. Zarco to Mathew, National Palace, 27 Mar 1861, encl. 2 of *ibid.* At the same time Zarco renounced forced loans and extraordinary contributions, except as ". . . legally established . . ." He also promised liberty of conscience.

21. Russell to Mathew, F.O., No. 15, 7 Feb (r. 29 Mar) 1861, PRO, F.O. 204/153.

22. Mathew to Russell, Mexico City, No. 34, 30 Apr (r. 28 May) 1861, PRO, F.O. 50/352.

23. "List of British Claims against the Mexican Government, which have been sent to Her Majesty's Consulate at Mexico (City) up to the 28th April 1861," encl. of *ibid.* The exact total was $18,583,187.83½. The claims included robbery, illegal taxes, ill treatment, imprisonment, forced loans, breach of contract. There were 84 claims, but more persons were involved. There were 7 question marks for sums that were not given. A note at the end of the report adds that some further claims had yet to be listed. Mathew himself, in the covering despatch, admitted that the list "presents but an approximate total, which cannot possibly be verified at the present moment."

24. Russell to Wyke, F.O., No. 8, draft, 17 Apr 1861, PRO, F.O. 50/351.

25. Mathew to Russell, Jalapa, No. 2, 28 Jan (r. 28 Feb) 1861; Mathew to Russell, Mexico City, No. 21, 27 Mar (r. 29 Apr) 1861, PRO, F.O. 50/352. Bodmer was murdered on 10 January 1861.

26. Mathew to Russell, Mexico City, No. 33, 29 Apr (r. 28 May) 1861, *ibid.* Mathew claimed these conditions were general, except at Vera Cruz.

27. Mathew to Zarco, 23 Mar 1861, sum. by Zarco to Mathew, National Palace, 30 Mar 1861, encl. 1 of *ibid.*

28. Zarco to Mathew, Mevico City, 22 Apr 1861, encl. 4 of Mathew to Russell, Mexico City, No. 33, 29 Apr (r. 28 May) 1861, *ibid.*

29. Mathew to Russell, Mexico City, No. 37, Confidential, 12 May (r. 27 Jun) 1861, *ibid.*

30. See footnote 72 below.

31. Mathew to Russell, Mexico City, No. 37, Confidential, 12 May (r. 27 Jun) 1861, PRO, F.O. 50/352.

32. Mathew to Russell, Mexico City, Pri., 12 Jan 1860, PRO, P.R.O. 30/22–74.

33. Mathew to Rusell, Jalapa, Pri., 30 Dec 1860, *ibid*.

34. See footnote 60 below.

35. Russell to Mathew, 30 Apr 1860, cited by Mathew to Russell, London, Pri., 18 Aug 1861, PRO, P.R.O. 30/22–74.

36. See below in text of this section. See also Section 1 of Chapter III of present investigation.

37. Wyke-Herzfeld Conversation, Carlsbad, Sep 1863, sum. by Herzfeld to Baron de Pont, Carlsbad, 7 Sep 1863 and "Report by H. C. Herzfeld, 13 Sep 1863," *HHSA*, AKM, DAWSON, p. 309. After leaving Mexico, Wyke went to Carlsbad for reasons of health and met his friend, Prince Carl zu Solms, who reported Wyke's views on Mexico to Count Rechberg, who sent the communication to Maximilian. He sent Captain Herzfeld to Carlsbad to see Wyke. With difficulty Herzfeld won Wykes's confidence, and Wyke related his meetings with Napoleon III in 1861. See DAWSON, pp. 307–308. Palmerston's letter book for 1860–1862 in the British Museum Additional MSS. Room (vol. CLXVI) contains no letters to Wyke. There are no letters to or from Wyke in the private collection of Palmerston Papers in the possession of the Mounbatten family (Mrs. Blois, Secretary to Lady Mountbatten (deceased), to author, London, Pri., 4 Dec 1959). There is no mention of Wyke's meetings with Napolecn in Wyke's private letters to Lord Russell (PRO, P.R.O. 30/22–74), in a private letter, Thouvenel, the French Minister of Foreign Affairs, mentioned seeing Wyke in 1861. Thouvenel wrote: Sir Charles Wyke, whom I saw last year, told me that with his experience with the people of South America he believed that only monarchy would bring a solution to the abyss." See Thouvenel to Flahault, Paris, Pri., 7 Mar 1862, L. Thouvenel, ed.: *Le secret de l'Empereur. Correspondance confidentielle et inédite exchangée entre M. Thouvenel, Le Duc de Gramont et le General Comte de Flahault, 1860–1862* (2 v., Paris, 1889), II, 243. (Hereafter referred to as THOUVENEL).

38. Russell to Wyke, F.O., No. 3, draft, 30 Mar 1861, PRO, F.O. 50/351. Marked as seen by Palmerston and Queen Victoria.

39. A delay was undesirable, but "undue eagerness' might encourage the Mexican Government to withhold the concessions Mathew had been instructed to obtain.

40. Encl. of Russell to Wyke, F.O., No. 2, draft, 30 Mar 1861, PRO, F.O., 50/351.

41. The amounts of the recognized claims were to be enumerated, and the manner of payment was to be stated specifically. Wyke was given discretion whether to examine unrecognized claims by a mixed commission.

42. On 27 March 1861 Russell sent a draft of Wyke's instructions to the Colonial Office and asked if the Duke of Newcastle objected to the

references to the boundary between British Honduras and the Mexican frontier. The Colonial Office replied on 9 April that the Duke of Newcastle thought any rumor of negotiations with Mexico for a frontier settlement might stir up the Indians. The Duke did not believe such negotiation should be started before previous consultation with Mr. Seymour, the Superintendent, and Mr. Price, the Acting Superintendent, of the Settlement. On 26 August 1861 the Colonial Office informed the Foreign Office that the Duke of Newcastle foresaw no good object would be gained by opening the question with Mexico, which had no powers over the territory in question, which was in the undisturbed possession of the Indians. See Draft to Colonial Office, F.O., 27 Mar 1861; Rogers to Hammond, 9 (r. 11) Apr 1861; Rogers to Hammond, 26 (r. 27) Aug 1861, and encl., Price to Darling, Belize, 7 Jun 1861, PRO, F.O. 50/357. In reply to Russell's instructions to protest the violation of British territory by Santa Cruz Indians, who carried off some cattle, Wyke stated that application for redress to the Mexican Government would be useless ". . . as they are quite incapable of coercing these Indians who are to all intents and purposes, practically independent. . . ."See Russell to Wyke, F.O., No. 13, 27 May (r. 3 Jul) 1861, PRO, F.O. 204/153. See also Wyke to Russell, Mexico City, No. 17, 11 Jul (r. 29 Aug) 1861, PRO, F.O. 50/353.

43. Mathew had already observed that the ". . . somewhat loose wording of our present treaty has been a cheval de bataille with these knaves. . . ." He had also suggested Wyke be authorized to secure an amended treaty. See Mathew to Russell, Jalapa, Pri., 30 Dec 1860. PRO, P.R.O. 30/22–74.

44. One of the difficulties had been that Miramon levied forced loans in the form of a tax on capital. The additional act was to clarify the disputed Article 10 of the Convention of 1826 and to exempt British subjects from ". . . all extra-ordinary contributions under whatever denominations they may be levied. . . ."

45. A copy is filed in MDAE: *CP, Mex.,* vol. 54.

46. Ocampo to Pacheco, 12 Jan 1861, *L'Estafette des Deux Mondes,* Mexico City, 17 Jan 1861, encl. of Mathew to Russell, Jalapa, No. 2, 28 Jan (r. 28 Feb) 1861, PRO, F.O. 50/352.

47. Wyke to Alston, Vera Cruz, Pri., 2 May 1861, *ibid.*

48. Wyke to Russell, Mexico City, Separate, 26 Jun (r. 29 Jul) 1861, PRO, F.O. 50/353.

49. Mathew to Russell, Mexico City, No. 52, Confidential, 12 May (r. 27 Jun) 1861, PRO, F.O. 50/352.

50. Wyke to Russell, Mexico City, No. 1, 26 May (r. 27 Jun) 1861, *ibid.* It had admitted that it was only a stopgap council and would resign as soon as the deputies met to permit the formation of a "parliamentary" cabinet. Se *El Siglo,* 22 Apr, 2, 11 May, 1861, sum, by Frank A. Knapp, Jr.: "Parliamentary Government and the Mexican Constitution of 1857: A Forgotten Phase of Mexican Political History," *HAHR,* XXXIII (1953), 74.

51. Wyke to Russell, Mexico City, No. 1, 26 May (r. 27 Jun) 1861, PRO, F.O. 50/352.

52. Wyke to Russell, Mexico City, No. 2, 27 May (r. 27 Jun) 1861, *ibid.*

53. Wyke to Russell, Mexico City, No. 1, 26 May (r. 27 Jun) 1861, *ibid.*

54. Wyke to Russell, Mexico City, No. 2, 27 May (r. 27 Jun) 1861, *ibid.*

55. Wyke to Russell, Mexico City, No. 1, 26 May (r. 27 Jun) 1861, *ibid.*

56. Wyke to Russell, Mexico City, No. 3, 27 May (r. 27 Jun) 1861, *ibid.*

57. Wyke to Russell, Pri., 27 May 1861, PRO, P.R.O. 30/22–74.

58. Saligny claimed he was ready to act with Wyke. The French Minister asserted their only means to achieve success was to support each other mutually. See Wyke to Russell, Mexico City, No. 52, Secret and Confidential, 27 Nov 1861 (r. 1 Jan 1862), PRO, F.O. 50/354. Saligny wrote Thouvenel that he hoped to get along completely with Wyke, who had ". . . better spirit . . ." than Mathew. See Saligny to Thouvenel, Mexico City, No. 26, 18 May (r. 30 Jun) 1861, MDAE: *CP, Mex.*, vol. 54.

59. Wyke to Russell, Pri., 27 May 1861, PRO, P.R.O. 30/22–74. This was not true, for it was not until 12 June that Thouvenel sent the Minister of Marine and Colonies Saligny's request for ships to back up his demands. See Thouvenel to Minister of Marine and Colonies, 12 Jun 1861, sum. by Minister of Marine and Colonies to Thouvenel, Paris, 2 (r. 3) July 1861, MDAE: *Cp, Mex.*, vol. 55. Wyke gave Saligny a similar wrong impression. Saligny believed Wyke ". . . is waiting for the arrival of considerable naval forces in the Gulf (of Mexico) that are to arrive shortly." See Saligny to Thouvenel, Mexico City, No. 27, 27 May (r. 30 Jun) 1861, MDAE: *CP, Mex.*, vol. 54. Seemingly the two Ministers, agreeing that force had to be applied, represented to each other that it actually was already authorized.

60. Wyke had spent seven years as Chargé d'Affaires in Guatemala before going to Mexico. Three years had been spent in Honduros and San Salvedor.

61. Wyke claimed that he had arrived at these conclusions before going to Mexico. See Wyke-Herzfeld Conversation, Carlsbad, Sep 1863, sum. by Herzfeld to Baron de Pont, Carlsbad, 7 Sep 1863 and "Report by H. C. Herzfeld, 13 Sep 1863," *HHSA,* DAWSON, p. 309.

62. The decree was dated 29 May and stated that during the suspension Congress would make financial reforms. See Presidential Decree, 29 May 1861, newspaper clipping, encl. 5 of Wyke to Russell, Mexico City, No. 4. 24 Jun (4. 29 Jul) 1861, PRO, F.O. 50/353.

63. Wyke to Guzman, Mexico City, 3 Jun 1861, encl. 1 of *ibid.*

64. Guzman to Wyke, 6, 12, 15 Jun 1861, encls. 3, 8, 11 of Wyke to Russell, Mexico City, No. 4, 24 Jun (r. 29 Jul) 1861, *ibid.*

65. Wyke to Guzman, 7, 14, 18 Jun 1861, encls, 6, 9, 12 of *ibid.*

66. Wyke gave the amount as $285,569.38 with interest. See Wyke to Guzman, Mexico City, 11 Jun 1861, encl. 1 of Wyke to Russell, Mexico City, No. 5, 24 Jun (r. 29 Jul) 1861, *ibid.*

67. Guzman added that if this property did not suffice, each individual claim could be admitted in payment of duties on any future imports or in connection with any other transaction with the Government. He also announced that Don Jose M. Mata and Don Francisco Zarco had been named Commissioners to treat with the interested parties. See Guzman to Wyke, Mexico City, 12 Jun 1861, encl. 3 of *ibid.*

68. Wyke feared the remission of duties might be set aside at any time by decree, founded on the excuse of urgent necessity and that if the Church Party returned to power, it would repudiate grants of church property. Wyke forwarded Guzman's suggestions to the interested parties, but they refused it, on the ground that they needed ready cash to meet engagements. Since the Mexican Government was penniless, Wyke recommended that the claimants listen to further proposals, and they named two representatives, Mr. Whitehead and Mr. Watson. Yet Wyke feared British interests would ". . . again be sacrificed to the reckless folly and bad faith of this government." See Wyke to Russell, Mexico City, No. 5, 24 Jun (r. 29 Jul) 1861, and encl. 4 thereof, Wyke to Guzman, Mexico City, 22 Jun 1861, *ibid.*

69. Wyke to Russell, Mexico City, No. 6, 24 Jun (r. 29 Jul) 1861, PRO, F.O. 97/280. See also enclosures 1 and 2 hereof, Wyke to Guzman, 13, 19 Jun 1861.

70. Technically Guzman was correct, but Article 12 of the Dunlop Agreement stipulated that if the party then in possession of Vera Cruz should be recognized by foreign Powers as the Supreme Government (as did happen), the articles of the Dunlop Agreement should form the basis of a Diplomatic Convention. By the Aldham Agreement Juarez promised to live up to the Dunlop Agreement. See Appendices A and B of present investigation.

71. Wyke to Russell, Mexico City, No. 8, 26 Jun (r. 29 Jul) 1861, and encl. 1 thereof, Wyke to Guzman, Mexico City, 21 Jun 1861, summarizing Guzman to Wyke, 17 Jun 1861, PRO, F.O. 50/353.

72. Mathew to Russell, Mexico City, No. 37, Confidential, 12 May (r. 27 Jun) 1861; Wyke to Russell, Mexico City, No. 3, 27 May (r. 27 Jun) 1861, PRO. F.O. 50/352. Mathew and Wyke Agreed that a large share of the money raised from the sale of church property went to pay Juarez' war debts. Mathew claimed that rumors of a Spanish intervention, attributed to Saligny, caused a loss of confidence so that it was difficult to find anyone willing to buy church property. Wyke believed that some money must have remained after the payment of war debts.

73. Mathew to Russell, Mexico City, No. 33, 29 Apr (r. 28 May) 1861, *ibid;* Corwin to Wyke, Pri., ?, cited by Wyke to Rnssell, Vera Cruz, No. 26, 23 Feb 1861, PRO, F.O., 204/160. Mathew claimed that, with the exception of Vera Cruz, custom house authorities reduced duties capriciously to prevent smuggling. Corwin charged that foreign

merchants in Mexico made "fraudulent arrangement" with the Collectors of Customs so that no more than 20 per cent ad valorum was paid on cargoes from Europe.

74. Wyke to Russell, Mexico City, No. 11, 28 Jun (r. 29 Jul) 1861, PRO, F.O. 50/353; Saligny to Thouvenel, Mexico City, Nos. 31 and 32, (r. 30 Jul) 1861, MDAE: *CP, Mex.,* vol. 55.

75. Wyke to Russell, Mexico City, No. 11, 28 Jun (r. 29 Jul) 1861, PRO, F.O. 50/353; Saligny to Thouvenel, Mexico City, Nos. 31 and 31, 22 and 29 Jun (r. 30 Jul) 1861, MDAE: *CP, Mex.,* vol. 55.

76. *Mexican Extraordinary,* Mexico City, 27 Jun 1861, encl. of Wyke to Russell, Mexico City, No. 10, 27 Jun (r. 29 Jul) 1861, PRO F.O. 50/353. 23 claims of murder, forced loans, arbitrary imprisonment and confiscation or sacking of property were detailed.

77. Wyke to Russell, Mexico City, No. 7, 25 Jun (r. 29 Jul) 1861, *ibid.*

78. Wyke to Alston, Pri., 28 Jun (r. 29 Jul) 1861, *ibid.*

79. Wyke to Russell, Mexico City, Pri., 29 Jun 1861, PRO, P.R.O. 30/22–74.

80. Wyke to Russell, Mexico City, No. 7, 25 Jun (r. 29 Jul) 1861, PRO, F.O. 50/353.

81. Wyke to Russell, Mexico City, Pri., 29 Jun 1861, PRO, P.R.O. 30/22–74.

82. *Ibid.* Wyke stated: ". . . Your Lordship must not suppose that I am favorable to their opponents the Church Party, for they are intolerant and difficult to deal with too, but at all events they have certain fixed principles and endeavour to maintain order after a fashion. . . ."

83. See footnote 86 below.

84. Wyke to Lyons, Mexico City, Pri., 23 Jun 1861, PRO, F.O. 204/162.

85. Wyke to Russell, Mexico City, No. 7, 25 Jun (r. 29 Jul) 1861, PRO, F.O. 50/353.

86. Wyke did not think Corwin would negotiate a treaty with so wretched a Government as that of Juarez, but if the moderates came forward, Corwin might negotiate a treaty with great benefit to them. See Wyke to Russell, Mexico City, No. 9, 26 Jun (r. 29 Jul) 1861, *ibid.*

87. Wyke to Russell, Mexico City, Pri., 29 Jun 1861, PRO, P.R.O. 30/22–74.

88. On 6 July over twenty men attacked H. M. Beale's house in the village of Naples, a few miles from Mexico City. They said it was their mision to kill foreigners. Beale was stabbed and shot so many times that his corpse was a horrible sight. See *Mexican Extraordinary,* Mexico City, 11 Jul 1861, encl. 1 of Wyke to Russell, Mexico City, No. 16, 11 Jul (r. 29 Aug) 1861, PRO, F.O. 50/353.

89. On 28 June Marquez, at the head of nearly 5,000 men, marched on Real de Monte, where there were valuable mines belonging to a mixed English and Mexican company. The Government troops were overcome, and the miners robbed of their savings, $3,898. Marquez

also levied a contribution on the company for $80,000. See Wyke to Russell, Mexico City, No. 25, 28 Jul (r. 29 Aug) 1861, *ibid*. The news reached Mexico City about the same time as the Beale murder (Saligny to Thouvenel, Mexico City, No. 33, 5 Jul (r. 30 Aug) 1861, MDAE: *CP, Mex.*, vol. 55). The mine executives and miners sent a letter to Wyke, asking what guarantee they had for the safety of their lives and property. See Auld, Murray, Skinfill, Griffin, and 120 miners to Wyke, Real del Monte, 16 Jul 1861, encl. 1 of Wyke to Russell, Mexico City, No. 25, 28 Jul (r. 29 Aug) 1861, PRO, F.O. 50/353.

90. Wyke protested the murder and asked what measures would be taken. The reply was that steps would be taken of which Wyke would be informed. Wyke wrote Russell, however, that the murderers would not be brought to justice, ". . . for crime is now triumphant and no judge would dare . . . to vindicate the law, which in matters of criminal jurisdiction has become a dead letter. See Wyke to Russell, Mexico City, No. 16, 11 Jul (r. 29 Aug) 1861, and encls. 2 and 4 thereof, Wyke to Don Lucas de Palacio y Magarola, Official Mayor, Mexico City, 8 Jul 1861, and Palacio to Wyke, Mexico City, 8 Jul 1861, *ibid*.

91. Wyke observed that Marquez evaded ". . . that vain and empty-headed personage General Ortega . . ." with apparent ease. See Wyke to Russell, Mexico City, No. 25, 28 Jul (r. 29 Aug) 1861, *ibid*. In the "Correspondence Respecting the Affairs of Mexico: Presented to both Houses of Parliament by Command of Her Majesty, 1862," this is toned down: ". . . Government troops, under the command of General Ortega, go running about the country, in hope of catching the rebels, who elude their pursuit with the greatest facility." See British Sessional Papers, 1862 (University of Pennsylvania microfilms), LXIV, 157. (Hereafter referred to as BSP).

92. Wyke to Russell, Mexico City, No. 11, 28 Jun (r. 29 Jul) 1861, PRO, F.O. 50/353; Saligny to Thouvenel, Mexico City, No. 31, 22 Jun (r. 20 Jul) 1861, MDAE: *CP, Mex.*, vol. 55.

93. Zamacona was the Sub-Editor of *El Siglo*. Wyke claimed the whole cabinet was unknown to fame, and that no one had faith in its members, whose selection was owing solely to the fact that it was impossible to leave Mexico any longer without a government. See Wyke to Russell, Mexico City, No. 21, 17 Jul (r. 29 Aug) 1861, PRO, F.O. 50/353.

94. These payments had already ceased. The British Consul in Vera Cruz reported that the Director of the Custom House there annulled bills already accepted by Vera Cruz merchants in favor of the London Bondholders and tried to compel the merchants to replace these orders by others payable to his own order. See Gifford to Wyke, No. 6, 25 Jun 1861, encl. of Wyke to Russell, Mexico City, No. 14, 29 Jun 1861, PRO, F.O. 204/154.

95. Law of Congress of the Union, 17 Jul 1861, given in Decree form by President Juarez, National Palace, 17 Jul 1861, *Mexican Extraordinary*, Mexico City, 25 Jul 1861, encl. 2 of Wyke to Russell, Mexico

City, No. 24, 26 Jul (r. 29 Aug) 1861, PRO, F.O. 50/353. Article 1 made the suspension for 2 years. Article 13 doubled the "contraregistro" (duty on the consumption) on foreign goods in the District of Mexico, for the time the Government deemed this necessary for the fulfilment of Article 14, which stated that by means of the "contraregistro" and other taxes, the Government would pay with preference all debts contracted after 29 May 1861 and ". . . all those that it may contract for the reestablishment of public tranquility . . ." British merchants protested to Wyke that Article 13 was unfair, as it applied only to the District of Mexico, not to all districts, and that they would have to pay the increased rate on goods slowly arriving in Mexico City, for which a loss would be sustained, as the goods had been sold in advance. See Messrs. Graham Greaves et al to Wyke, Mexico City, 23 Jul 1861, encl. 16 of Wyke to Russell, Mexico City, No. 24, 26 Jul (r. 29 Aug) 1861, PRO, F.O. 50/353.

96. Zamacona also claimed that the suspension would permit the initiation of administrative reforms to put an end to forced exactions and denied the church property had been squandered. See Zamacona to Wyke, Mexico City, 21, 21, 25, 27 (pri.) Jul 1861, Encls. 5, 7, 12, 20 of Wyke to Russell, Mexico City, No. 24, 26 Jul (r. 29 Aug) 1861, PRO, F.O. 50/353.

97. Wyke also warned that the suspensio would strike at the root of the Mexican Government's credit and commercial prosperity. In reply to quotations of authorities on International Law, Wyke replied that they were quoted out of context. See Wyke to Zamacona, Mexico City, 19, 22, 23, 25, 26 (Pri.) Jul 1861, encls. 3, 8, 9, 10, 15 of Wyke to Russell, Mexico City, No. 24, 26 Jul (r. 29 Aug) 1861, *ibid*. See also Wyke to Zamacona, Mexico City, Pri., 30 Jul 1861, encl. 1 of Wyke to Russell, Mexico City, No. 27, 8 Aug (r. 29 Sep) 1861, PRO, F.O. 50/353.

98. Wyke to Russell, Mexico City, No. 25, 28 Jul (r. 29 Aug) 1861, PRO, F.O. 50/353.

99. Wyke to Russell, Mexico City, Pri., 29 Jul (r. Aug) 1861, PRO, P.R.O. 30/22–74.

100. Wyke to Russell, Mexico City, No. 24, 26 Jul (r. 29 Aug) 1861, PRO, F.O. 50/353.

101. Wyke to Russell, Mexico City, Pri., 29 Jul (r. Aug) 1861, PRO, P.R.O. 30/22–74.

102. Wyke to Russell, Mexico City, No. 24, 26 Jul (r. 29 Aug) 1861, PRO, F.O. 50/353.

103. *Ibid;* Wyke to Russell, Mexico City, Pri., 29 Jul (r. Aug) 1861, PRO, P.R.O. 30/22–74.

104. Wyke to Russell, Mexico City, No. 24, 26 Jul (r. 29 Aug) 1861, PRO, F.O. 50/353.

105. "To anybody thoroughly acquainted with the Mexican question, a direct intervention must appear the best solution of the existing difficulties, but in acknowledging this, I have always felt that in asking too much we might obtain nothing. En attendant *(sic)*, I feel convinced

that an occupation of the principal ports by H.M.'s land and sea forces will bring about a great change for the better, as such a measure will have the effect of not only repaying us in part what is owed, but will also encourage the moderate and really respectable Party in the country to come forward and form a Government that would offer us more guarantees than any other without such support both moral and physical is likely to afford us." See Wyke to Whitehead, Mexico City, Pri., 25 Sep 1861, PRO, F.O. 204/157.

106. Wyke to Russell, Mexico City, No. 24, 26 Jul (r. 29 Aug) 1861, PRO, F.O. 50/353.

107. See Section 1 of the Chapter III of present investigation.

108. See Appendix A of present investigation.

109. Wyke to Russell, Mexico City, No. 33, 27 Aug (r. 29 Sep) 1861, PRO, F.O. 50/354.

110. Wyke to Russell, Mexico City, Nos. 33 and 42, 27 Aug (r. 29 Sep), 29 Sep (r. 30 Oct) 1861, *ibid*.

111. Wyke to Russell, Mexico City, No. 42, 29 Sep (r. 30 Oct) 1861, *ibid*.

112. Wyke to Russell, Mexico City, No. 31, 24 Aug (r. 29 Sep) 1861, *ibid*.

113. Wyke reported that this resulted from the merchants' not removing their goods from the custom houses. See Wyke to Russell, Mexico City, No. 33, 27 Aug (r. 29 Sep) 1861, *ibid*.

114. The decree was published 22 August, applied to all residents of the district, and demanded payments in three installments. The first was due the next day, with a penalty of 50 per cent of the contribution for non-compliance. British merchants in Mexico City protested to Wyke that if the tax were admitted, the Government could call for contributions every few days. Wyke agreed, saw the tax as another form of forced loan, and recommended it only be paid on compulsion and under protest. He observed that the decree was grossly unjust, as many were unaware all of 23 August that the decree had been published and placarded during the night. A meeting of the Diplomatic Corps led to Baron Wagner's caling on Zamacona, who gave the Prussian Chargeé d'Affaires the excuse of dire necessity. See Wyke to Russell, Mexico City, No. 31, 24 Aug (r. 29 Sep) 1861, and encls. 3 and 4 thereof, Graham Greaves et al to Wyke, Mexico City, 23 Aug 1861, and Wyke to Graham Greaves et al, Mexico City, 23 Aug 1861, *ibid*.

115. Judge Jesus Maria de Herrera passed sentence of MM. Isidro Diaz, Francisco Montero, and Teofilo Marin on 3 August. See *Estafette*, 10 Aug 1861, encl. 1 of Wyke to Russell, Mexico City, No. 28, 12 Aug (r. 29 Sep) 1861, *ibid*.

116. Wyke to Russell, Mexico City, No. 28, 12 Aug (r. 29 Sep) 1861, *ibid*.

117. Wyke to Russell, Mexico City, No. 42, 29 Sep (r. 30 Oct) 1861, *ibid*.

118. 51 members of Congress, forming a majority, petitioned Juarez to resign in the beginning of September, and later in the month 52

deputies drew up a counter address asking Juarez to remain as President. Wyke charged that 12 opposition votes were purchased. See Wyke to Russell, Mexico City, Nos. 37 and 40, 8 and 26 Sep (r. 30 Oct) 1861, *ibid*.

119. Wyke to Russell, Mexico City, No. 33, 27 Aug (r. 29 Sep) 1861, *ibid*.

120. Wyke to Russell, Mexico City, No. 40, 26 Sep (r. 30 Oct) 1861, *ibid*.

121. Russell to Wyke, F.O., No. 38, 21 Aug (r. 1 Oct) 1861, PRO, F.O., 204/153.

122. Wyke to Saligny, Mexico City, Pri. 22 Nov 1861, "Correspondence between Sir Charles Lennox Wyke and M. de Saligny the French Minister," encl. of Wyke to Russell, Mexico City, No. 52, Secret and Confidential, 27 Nov 1861 (r. 1 Jan 1862), PRO, F.O. 50/354.

123. Wyke to Russell, Mexico City, No. 56, 28 Nov 1861 (r. 1 Jan 1862), *ibid*.

124. *Ibid*.

125. Wyke to Russell, Mexico City, No. 47, Confidential, 29 Oct (r. 27 Nov) 1861, *ibid*.

126. Wyke to Russell, Mexico City, No. 52, Secret and Confidential, 27 Nov 1861 (r. Jan 1862), *ibid*.

127. *Ibid*. Wyke added that Saligny was ". . . possessed at the same time of great natural shrewdness thought not over scupulous in its employment. . . ." Wyke claimed he had formed this opinion of Saligny shortly after arriving in Mexico.

128. Wyke to Russell, Mexico City, No. 46, 28 Oct (r. 27 Nov) 1861, *ibid*.

129. Wyke to Russell, Mexico City, No. 52, Secret and Confidential, 27 Nov 1861 (r. 1 Jan 1862), *ibid*.

130. Wyke to Russell, Mexico City, Pri., 29 Oct 1861, PRO, P.R.O. 30/22–74.

131. Saligny to Thouvenel, Mexico City, No. 59 *(bis)*, Confidential, 15 Nov 1861 (r. 2 Jan 1862), MDAE: *C.P. Mex.*, vol. 56.

132. Wyke to Russell, Mexico City, No. 52, Secret and Confidential, 27 Nov 1861 (r. 1 Jan 1862), PRO, F.O. 50/354.

133. Saligny to Thouvenel, Mexico City, No. 59 *(bis)*, Confidential, 15 Nov 1861 (r. 2 Jan 1862), MDAE: *CP, Mex.*, vol. 56.

134. Wyke to Russell, Mexico City, No. 52, Secret and Confidential, 27 Nov 1861 (r. 1 Jan 1862), PRO, F.O. 50/354.

135. Wyke to Russell, Mexico City, No. 46, 28 Oct (r. 27 Nov) 1861, *ibid*.

136. Saligny to Wyke, Mexico City, Priv., 23 Nov 1861, "Correspondence between Sir Charles Lennox Wyke and M. de Saligny, the French Minister," encl. of Wyke to Russell, Mexico City, No. 52, Secret and Confidential, 27 Nov 1861 (r. 1 Jan 1862), *ibid*.

137. Wyke to Saligny, Mexico City, Pri., 23 Nov 1861, *ibid*.

138. Wyke to Russell, Mexico City, No. 52, Secret and Confidential, 27 Nov 1861 (r. 1 Jan 1862), *ibid*.

139. Wyke to Russell, Mexico City, No. 46, 28 Oct (r. 27 Nov) 1861, *ibid*. At first Zamacona wanted Wyke to negotiate with Corwin for the settlement of British financial demands, but Wyke woke Zamacona from this "happy daydream" by informing him that his Government must be held responsible for what was owed Great Britain. Then Zamacona reflected that Mexico could obtain money from the United States and hand it over to Great Britain. In the ensuing negotiations, however, Zamacona and Wyke agreed to mortgage Mexican custom duties to Great Britain. But Wyke observed that without the prospect of an American loan, the arrangement would have been impossible.

140. Wyke to Lyons, Mexico City, Pri., 27 Oct 1861, PRO, F.O. 204/162.

141. Zamacona to Wyke, Mexico City, Pri., 20 Oct 1861, encl. 2 of Wyke to Russell, Mexico City, No. 46, 28 Oct (r. 27 Nov) 1861, PRO, F.O. 50/354.

142. Wyke to Russell, Mexico City, No. 46, 28 Oct (r. 27 Nov) 1861, *ibid*.

143. Imports were liable to import duties and "additional duties," amounting to about 81 per cent of the import duties. See "Schedule showing amount of duties that would be paid under the reduced tariff voted on a cargo of merchandise which now pays $100,000 Import Duties," encl. 2 of Wyke to Russell, Mexico City, No. 51, 25 Nov 1861 (r. 1 Jan 1862), *ibid*.

144. Wyke to Russell, Mexico City, No. 46, 28 Oct (r. 27 Nov) 1861, *ibid*.

145. Wyke to Russell, Mexico City, Pri., 29 Oct 1861, PRO, P.R.O. 30/22–74.

146. Wyke to Russell, Mexico City, No. 46, 28 Oct (r. 27 Nov) 1861, PRO, F.O. 50/354.

147. Wyke to Russell, Mexico City, No. 45, 28 Oct (r. 27 Nov) 1861, *ibid*.

148. Wyke to Saligny, Mexico City, Pri., 22 Nov 1861, "Correspondence between Sir Charles Lennox Wyke and M. de Saligny, the French Minister," encl. of Wyke to Russell, Mexico City, No. 52, Secret and Confidential, 27 Nov 1861 (r. 1 Jan 1862), *ibid*.

149. Saligny to Thouvenel, Mexico City, No. 52, 15 Nov 1861 (r. 6 Jan 1862), MDAE: *CP, Mex.*, vol. 56.

150. Saligny to Thouvenel, Mexico City, No. 59 *(bis)*, Confidential, 15 Nov 1861 (r. 2 Jan 1862), *ibid*.

151. Thouvenel to Saligny, No. 12, draft, 5 Sep 1861, *ibid.*, vol. 55.

152. See Section 2 of Chapter III of present investigation, between footnotes 15 and 16.

153. Saligny to Thouvenel, Mexico City, No. 59 *(bis)*, Confidential, 15 Nov 1861 (r. 2 Jan 1862), MDAE: *C.P. Mex.*, vol. 56.

154. Saligny to Wyke, Mexico City, Pri., 23 Nov 1861, "Correspondence between Sir Charles Lennox Wyke and M. de Saligny, the French Minister," encl. of Wyke to Russell, Mexico City, No. 52, Secret and Confidential, 27 Nov 1861 (r. 1 Jan 1862), PRO, F.O. 50/354.

155. Saligny to Thouvenel, Mexico City, No. 59 *(bis)*, Confidential, 15 Nov 1861 (r. 2 Jan 1862), MDAE: *CP, Mex.,* vol. 56.

156. Wyke to Russell, Mexico City, No. 51, 25 Nov 1861 (r. 1 Jan 1862), PRO, F.O. 50/354.

157. Wyke to Russell, Mexico City, No. 55, 28 Nov 1861 (r. 1 Jan 1862), *ibid.*

158. Wyke to Russell, Mexico City, No. 51, 25 Nov 1861 (r. 1 Jan 1862), *ibid.*

159. Wyke to Russell, Mexico City, Pri., 29 Nov 1861, PRO, P.R.O. 30/22–74.

160. Wyke to Russell, Mexico City, No. 51, 25 Nov 1861 (r. 1 Jan 1862), PRO, F.O. 50/354.

161. Saligny to Thouvenel, Mexico City, No. 59 (bis), Confidential, 15 Nov 1861 (r. 2 Jan 1862), MDAE: *CP, Mex.,* vol. 56.

162. Saligny to Thouvenel, Vera Cruz, No. 61, 31 Dec 1861 (r. 30 Jan 1862), *ibid.*

163. Wyke to Russell, Mexico City, No. 51, 25 Nov 1861 (r. 1 Jan 1862), PRO, F.O. 50/354.

164. Address of 29 British Merchant to Wyke, Mexico City, 25 Nov 1861, encl. 1 of Wyke to Russell, Mexico City, No. 53, 28 Nov 1861 (r. 1 Jan 1862), *ibid.*

165. Wyke to Russell, Mexico City, No. 51, 25 Nov 1861 (r. 1 Jan 1862), *ibid.*

165. Wyke to Russell, Mexico City, No. 51, 25 Nov 1861 (r. 1 Jan 1862), *ibid.*

166. Law fixing bases of reduction of tariff, 15 Nov 1861, signed by Juarez 18 Nov 1861, encl. 1 of *ibid.* Horace Johnson, an Attaché of the British Legation, calculated that a cargo paying $100,000 in import duties paid $81,000 in additional duties. Under the new tariff, the same cargo would pay $60,000 in import duties and $46,500 in additional duties, showing a reduction of $74,500, or 41 1/6 per cent. See "Schedule showing amount of duties that would be paid under the reduced tariff voted by Congress on a cargo of merchandise that now pays $100,000 Import Duties," encl. 2 of Wyke to Russell, Mexico City, No. 51, 25 Nov 1861 (r. 1 Jan 1862), *ibid.*

167. Wyke to Russell, Mexico City, No. 51, 25 Nov 1861 (r. 1 Jan 1862), *ibid.* The merchants wanted the tariff changes to go into effect after six months; the Mexican Government desired only a two month waiting period, and so Wyke picked a period between the two.

168. See Appendix 0 of present investigation for the text of this convention.

169. Wyke to Zamacona, Mexico City, 20 Nov 1861; Zamacona to Wyke, Government House, 21 Nov 1861, encls. 4 and 6 of Wyke to Russell, Mexico City, No. 51, 25 Nov 1861 (r. 1 Jan 1862), PRO, F.O. 50/354.

170. Wyke to Russell, Mexico City, No. 51, 25 Nov 1861 (r. 1 Jan 1862), *ibid.*

171. Wyke to Russell, Mexico City, No. 46, 28 Oct (r. 27 Nov) 1861, *ibid.*

172. Frank A. Knapp, Jr.: "Parliamentary Government and the Mexican Constitution of 1857: A Forgotten Phase of Mexican Political History," *HAHR,* XXXIII (1953), 77.

173. Wyke to Russell, Mexico City, No. 51, 25 Nov 1861 (r. 1 Jan 1862), PRO, F.O. 50/354.

174. Frank A. Knapp, Jr.: "Parliamentary Government and the Mexican Constitution of 1857: A Forgotten Phase of Mexican Political History," *HAHR,* XXXIII (1953), 77.

175. Saligny claimed the vote was 75–22, but the *Mexican Extraordinary* gave it as 70–29. See Saligny to Thouvenel, Mexico City, No. 55, 25 Nov 1861 (r. 2 Jan 1862), MDAE: *CP, Mex.,* vol. 56. See also *Mexican Extraordinary,* Mexico City, 28 Nov 1861 (r. 1 Jan 1862), PRO, F.O. 50/354.

176. Lerdo approached Wyke on 28 November and claimed Congress might agree if these articles were revised. See Wyke to Russell, Mexico City, No. 56, 28 Nov 1861 (r. 1 Jan 1862), PRO, F.O. 50/354.

177. The bill was sponsored by Sebastion Lerdo Tejada, Manuel Ruiz, Mariano Riva Palacio, Montes, Dublan, Linarez Pina y Raminez, Blaz, Suarez Novarro, and Chico Sein.

178. Repeal of the Law of 17 Jul 1861, 23 Nov 1861, encl. 1 of Wyke to Russell, Mexico City, No. 56, 28 Nov 1861 (r. 1 Jan 1862), PRO, F.O., 50/354.

179. Saligny to Thouvenel, Mexico City, No. 56, 28 Nov 1861 (r. 2 Jan 1862), MDAE: *CP, Mex.,* vol., 56.

180. Arias to Wyke, Government House, 28 Nov 1861, encl. 4 of Wyke to Russell, Mexico City, No. 56, 28 Nov 1861 (r. 1 Jan 1862), PRO, F.O. 50/354.

181. At this time the Minister of Foreign Relations headed the cabinet.

182. Sebastian Lerdo de Tejada-Wyke meeting, 28 Nov 1861, sum. by Wyke to Russell, Mexico City, No. 56, 28 Nov 1861 (r. 1 Jan 1862), PRO, F.O. 50/354.

183. Wyke to Saligny, Mexico City, Pri., 21 Nov 1861, "Correspondence between Sir Charles Lennox Wyke and M. de Saligny, the French Minister," encl. of Wyke to Russell, Mexico City, No. 52, Secret and Confidential, 27 Nov 1861 (r. 1 Jan 1862), *ibid.*

184. Wyke to Russell, Mexico City, No. 52, Secret and Confidential, 27 Nov 1861 (r. 1 Jan 1862), *ibid.*

185. Wyke to Russell, Mexico City, No. 31, 24 Aug (r. 29 Sep) 1861, *ibid.* The meeting took place on 23 Aug 1861.

186. Wyke to Russell, Mexico City, No. 52, Secret and Confidential, 27 Nov 1861 (r. 1 Jan 1862), *ibid.*

187. Wyke to Saligny, Mexico City, Pri., 21 Nov 1861, "Correspondence between Sir Charles Lennox Wyke and M. de Saligny, the French Minister," encl. of *ibid.*

188. Saligny to Wyke, Mexico City, Pri., 21 Nov 1861, *ibid.*

189. Wyke to Russell, Mexico City, No. 52, Secret and Confidential, 27 Nov 1861 (r. 1 Jan 1862), *ibid.*

190. Wyke to Saligny Mexico City, Pri., 22 Nov 1861, "Correspondence between Sir Charles Lennox Wyke and M. de Saligny, the French Minister," encl. of *ibid.*

191. Saligny to Wyke, Mexico City, Pri., 23 Nov 1861, *ibid.*

192. Wyke to Saligny, Mexico City, Pri., 23 Nov 1861, *ibid.*

193. Wyke to Saligny, Mexico City, Pri., 25 Nov 1861, *ibid.*

194. Wyke to Saligny, Mexico City, Pri., 23 Nov 1861, *ibid.*

195. Wyke to Saligny, Mexico City, Pri., 25 Nov. 1861, *ibid.*

196. Saligny to Wyke, Mexico City, Pri., 24 Nov 1861, *ibid.*

197. Wyke to Saligny, Mexico City, Pri., 25 Nov 1861, *ibid.*

198. Saligny to Wyke, Mexico City, Pri., 25 Nov 1861, *ibid.*

199. Wyke to Russell, Mexico City, No. 52, Secret and Confidential, 27 Nov 1861 (r. 1 Jan 1862), *ibid.*

200. Saligny to Wyke, Mexico City, Pri., 25 Nov 1861, "Correspondence between Sir Charles Lennox Wyke and M. de Saligny, the French Minister," encl. of *ibid.*

201. Saligny to Thouvenel, Mexico City, No. 59 *(bis)*, Confidential, 15 Nov 1861 (r. 2 Jan 1862), MDAE: *CP, Mex.,* vol. 56.

202. Address of 29 British Merchants to Wyke, Mexico City, 25 Nov 1861, encl. 1 of Wyke to Russell, Mexico City, No. 53, 28 Nov 1861 (r. 1 Jan 1862), PRO, F.O. 50/354.

203. "Mr. Glennie's Report of British Claims accompanied by schedule, 5 Apr 1862," encl. 1 of Wyke to Russell, Orizaba, No. 61, 20 Apr (r. 2 Jun) 1862, PRO, F.O. 50/365.

204. *Mexican Extraordinary,* Mexico City, 28 Nov 1861, encl. of Wyke to Russell, Mexico City, No. 54, 28 Nov 1861 (r. 1 Jan 1862), PRO, F.O. 50/354.

205. Wyke to Russell, Mexico City, No. 54, 28 Nov 1861 (r. 1 Jan 1862), *ibid.*

206. Worral claimed compensation for his expulsion from Mexico in 1858 for not paying a tax on capital. Wyke believed the claim was unjustified, because the position of the British Government at the time was that the tax was to be paid, but under protest. See Wyke to Russell, Mexico City, No. 20, draft, 13 Jul 1861, PRO, F.O. 204/154.

207. Wyke to British Merchants, Mexico City, 28 Nov 1861, encl. 2 of Wyke to Russell, Mexico City, No. 53, 28 Nov 1861 (r. 1 Jan 1862), PRO, F.O. 50/354.

208. Wyke to Russell, Mexico City, No. 54, 28 Nov 1861 (r. 1 Jan 1862) *ibid.*

209. Wyke to Russell, Mexico City, No. 51, 25 Nov 1861 (r. 1 Jan 1862), *ibid.*

210. Wyke to Zamacona, Mexico City, 24 Nov 1861, encl. 2 of Wyke to Russell, Mexico City, No. 56, 28 Nov 1861 (r. 1 Jan 1862), *ibid.*

211. Wyke to Russell, Mexico City, No. 56, 28 Nov 1861 (r. 1 Jan 1862), *ibid.* Whereas Russell only demanded Interventors in Tampico

and Vera Cruz, Wyke's convention in substance gained this condition in all Mexican ports. Wyke gained a reduction of the general tariff, instead of in only two ports. His ultimatum demanded the conditions in these instances that he had obtained in his convention and negotiations for tariff reduction.

212. Arias to Wyke, Government House, 28 Nov 1861, encl. 4 of *ibid*.

213. After Zamacona's resignation, Juarez turned to Lerdo, but they could not agree about cabinet membership. Then Juarez sent for Doblado. He insisted that the President's responsibility ended when he appointed someone to form a cabinet. Juarez was reluctant to accept this viewpoint but did so for the time being. See Frank A. Knapp, Jr.: "Parliamentary Government and the Mexican Constitution of 1857: A Forgotten Phase of Mexican Political History," *HAHR*, XXXIII (1953), 78-80.

214. Wyke to Doblado, Mexico City, 13 Dec 1861, encl. 1 of Wyke to Russell, Mexico City, No. 57, 14 Dec 1861 (r. 29 Jan) 1862, PRO, F.O. 50/354.

215. Doblado to Wyke, Government House, 14 Dec 1861, encl. 3 of *ibid*. Congress granted Juarez full powers to make treaties.

216. Wyke to Russell, Vera Cruz, No. 60, 29 Dec 1861 (r. 29 Jan 1862), *ibid*.

217. Wyke to Russell, Vera Cruz, No. 59, 29 Dec 1861 (r. 29 Jan 1862), *ibid*.

218. Wyke to Russell, Vera Cruz, Pri., 31 Dec 1861, PRO, P.R.O. 30/22-74.

## 2. SALIGNY IN MEXICO, 1861

1. Consul General Crawford to Russell, Havana, No. 9, Separate, 5 Mar 1861, encl. of Hammond to Wyke, F.O., No. 5, 10 Apr (r. 29 May) 1861, PRO, F.O. 204/153. Miramon arrived in Cuba with Pacheco on a Spanish Man-of-War.

2. See footnote 46 of the previous section of the present investigation.

3. Saligny to Thouvenel, Mexico City, 26 Jan 1861, encl. 1 of Saligny to Thouvenel, Mexica City, No. 6, 28 Jan (r. 1 Mar) 1861, MDAE: *CP, Mex.,* LIV.

4. Saligny to Thouvenel, Mexico City, No. 7, 4 Feb (r. 5 Mar) 1861, *ibid*.

5. Mathew to Russell, Mexico City, No. 10, 24 Feb (r. 30 Mar) 1861, PRO, F.O. 50/352. Mathew claimed that he heard from a private but sure source of Miramon's proposed escape with the aid of Saligny and Pacheco ". . . *in the mode in which it actually occurred.*"

6. Saligny to Thouvenel, Mexico City, No. 22, 1 May (r. 30 Jun) 1861, MDAE: *CP, Mex.,* LIV.

7. Saligny to Thouvenel, Mexico City, 26 Jan 1861, encl. 1 of Saligny to Thouvenel, Mexico City, No. 6, 28 Jan (r. 1 Mar) 1861, *ibid*.

8. *Ibid*.

9. Saligny to Thouvenel, Mexico City, No. 7, 4 Feb (r. 5 Mar) 1861, *ibid*.

10. Saligny to Thouvenel, Mexico City, No. 15, 30 Mar (r. 30 Apr) 1861, *ibid*.

11. Decree, 5 Feb 1861, *Le Trait d'Union: Journal Francais Universel*, 11 Feb 1861, encl. 2 of Saligny to Thouvenel, Mexico City, No. 12, 8 Mar (r. 30 Apr) 1861, *ibid*.

12. Andres Geguera, First Secretary of the Mexican Legation in Paris, to Count of Persigny, Secretary in the Department of the Interior, Paris, 8 Apr 1861, *ibid*.

13. Saligny to Thouvenel, Mexico City, No. 11, 28 Feb (r. 31 Mar) 1861, *ibid*. In answer to Saligny's original protest, Zarco promised to withdraw the soldiers, but Saligny renewed his protest that afternoon when they were still in the convent. Zarco again promised to withdraw the soldiers, but the next morning two priests informed Saligny the soldiers had not left. Saligny protested again, and an hour later the soldiers departed.

14. Saligny to Zardo, Mexico City, 7 Mar 1861, encl. 3 of Saligny to Thouvenel, Mexico City, No. 12, 8 Mar (r. 30 Apr) 1861, *ibid*.

15. Andres Geguera, First Secretary of the Mexican Legation in Paris, to Count of Persigny, Secretary in the Department of the Interior, Paris, 8 Apr 1861, *ibid*.

16. Saligny to Thouvenel, Mexico City, No. 11, 28 Feb (r. 31 Mar) 1861, *ibid*.

17. Thouvenel to Saligny, No. 4, Confidential, draft, 11 Apr 1861, *ibid*. If the Sisters had been French, Thouvenel observed, their cause would have been taken up. Later that day Thouvenel drew up another instruction approving Saligny's agreement with Zarco to maintain the *status quo* in the affair (Thouvenel to Saligny, No. 5, draft, 11 Apr 1861, *ibid*.).

18. Saligny to Thouvenel, Mexico City, No. 14, 28 Mar (r. 30 Apr) 1861, *ibid*.

19. For the entire convention, see Appendix of the present investigation (Convention of 26 Mar 1861).

20. Saligny to Thouvenel, Mexico City, No. 14, 28 Mar (r. 30 Apr) 1861, MDAE: *CP, Mex.*, LIV.

21. *Ibid*. Saligny wanted the money turned over directly to the French Legation, because he thought the mode of payment in the past had been corrupt. The system of adjudication adopted by the Convention of 1853 ruined, ". . . to the profit of the Mexican Treasury and two or three speculators, some of our nationals, precisely those whose situation was the most worthy of interest." the bonds were adjudicated at about 40 per cent of their nominal value, with a corresponding benefit to the Mexican Treasury of 60 per cent. As a result, ". . . the poorest French, forced to create resources, brought themselves to sell their bonds to any who would buy, and these were speculators."

22. Petition of 150 French, Swiss, and Belgians resident in Mexico

to Saligny, 31 Dec 1860, encl. of Saligny to Thouvenel, Mexico City, No. 15, 30 Mar (r. 30 Apr) 1861, *ibid.*

23. Saligny to Thouvenel, Mexico City, No. 15, 30 Mar (r. 30 Apr) 1861, *ibid.*

25. De La Fuente-Thouvenel Conversation, sum. by De La Fuente to Billault, Senator, Minister in the Department of Foreign Affairs, Paris, 20 Jul 1861, *ibid.*, LV.

26. See Appendix V of the present investigation (Jecker affair).

27. *Ibid.*

28. Napoleon III to Flahault, Compiegne, (9) Oct 1861, *HHSA*, cited by CORTI, I, 362.

29. De La Fuente-Thouvenel Conversation, sum. by De La Fuente to Billault, Senator, Minister in the Department of Foreign Affairs, Paris, 20 Jul 1861, MDAE: *CP, Mex.*, LV.

30. Cowley-Napoleon III Conversation, 8 Mar 1862, sum. by Cowley to Russell, Paris, No. 299, Confidential, 10 (r. 11) Mar 1861, PRO, F.O. 27/1434. Lord Cowley, the British Ambassador to Paris, complained to Napoleon of the Jecker claim and what the British Government considered a very high figure for other French claims. Cowley ". . . intimated a hope that His Majesty would not encourage these claims, but His Majesty avowed, that it was he who had desired they should be made excessive *(aussi vives que possible (sic) )*." Napoleon continued that it was ". . . necessary to begin with high terms . . . *(il fallait commencer par le gros bout (sic) )* or otherwise the Government of Juarez would at once have accepted the conditions proposed, and the Allies having no further excuse to remain, mut have taken their departure. . . ."

31. Saligny to Thouvenel, Mexico City, No. 13, 15 Mar (r. 30 Apr) 1861, MDAE: *CP, Mex.*, LIV.

32. Saligny to Thouvenel, Mexico City, No. 17, Apr (r. 29 May) 1861, *ibid.* Saligny blamed the supposed favoritism on the Minister of Finance, Guillermo Prieto.

33. Saligny to Thouvenel, Mexico City, No. 22, 1 May (r. 30 Jun) 1861, *ibid.*

34. Saligny to Thouvenel, Mexico City, No. 19, 28 Apr (r. 29 May) 1861, *ibid.*

35. Saligny to Thouvenel, Mexico City, No. 23, 7 May (r. 30 Jun) 1861, *ibid.*

36. Saligny-Mata-Zarco Conference, 1 May 1861, sum. by Saligny to Thouvenel, Mexico City, No. 25 *(bis)*, 9 May (r. 30 Jun) 1861, *ibid.*

37. Saligny to Zarco, Mexico City, 2 May 1861, encl. 1 of Saligny to Thouvenel, Mexico City, No. 25, 9 May (r. 30 Jun) 1861, *ibid.*

38. The capital of emission would be reduced to ten million piastres. The bonds, instead of being admitted for twenty per cent of all the duties and customs whatsoever by the Government and the States, would only be admitted for 15 per cent of the payment of Federal Custom Duties, both on imports and exports.

39. Saligny to Zarco, Mexico City, Confidential, 2 May 1861, encl.

2 of Saligny to Thouvenel, Mexico City, No. 25, 9 May (r. 30 Jun) 1861, MDAE: *CP, Mex.,* LIV.

40. Zarco to Saligny, National Palace, Mexico City, 4 May 1861, encl. 3 of *Ibid.*

41. Saligny to Thouvenel, Mexico City, No. 25 (bis), 9 May (r. 30 Jun) 1861, *ibid.*

42. Saligny to Thouvenel, Mexico City, No. 26, 18 May (r. 30 Jun) 1861, *ibid.*

43. Saligny to Thouvenel, Mexico City, No. 27, 27 May (r. 30 Jun) 1861, *ibid.*

44. *Ibid.* See footnote 59 of the previous section of the present investigation.

45. Saligny to Thouvenel, Mexico City, No. 19, 28 Apr (r. 29 May) 1861, MDAE: *CP, Mex.,* LIV.

46. Saligny to Thouvenel, Mexico City, No. 28, 8 Jun (r. 30 Jul) 1861, *ibid.* Saligny gave as an example the proposition of M. Aguirre to accuse Juarez of high treason on 29 May after the Government refused to show the correspondence concerning the McLane Treaty.

47. Saligny to Thouvenel, Mexico City, No. 26, 18 May (r. 30 Jun) 1861, *ibid.*

48. Saligny to Thouvenel, Mexico City, No. 19, 28 Apr r. 29 May) 1861, *ibid.*

49. Saligny to Thouvenel, Mexico City, No. 7, 4 Feb (r. 5 Mar) 1861, *ibid.*

50. On 12 June Guzman told Saligny the convention was submitted to Congress several days before (Saligny to Thouvenel, Mexico City, No. 30, 12 Jun (r. 30 Jul) 1861, *ibid.,* LV).

51. Rieche was thrown in prison and died of treatment given him in October 1859. In November 1860 Captain Levin of the *Serieuse* received at Alcapulco instructions to obtain an indemnity for Rieche's family. In December Levin obtained 10,000 piastres and a promise from the Governor of Sinaloa to search for the male-factors. One of them, Coronado, was dead, and another, Rojas, blamed him for everything. In February 1861 Saligny, apparently not knowing Levin had collected the 10,000, demanded 31,000 piastres from Zarco, who promised to pay 10,000 and explained this was all that could be paid for the time being. In March Saligny reported to Thouvenel that the Mexican Government had paid these 10,000 and, since Levin had collected 10,000, there was only 11,000 to collect (Captain of the Serieuse, P. Levin, to Minister of Marine, Gulf of Fonseca, 12 Feb 1861; Levin to Minister of Marine, Mazotlan, 25 Dec 1860, encls. 2 and 1 of Minister of Marine to Thouvenel, Paris, 21 Mar 1861, *ibid.,* LIV: Levin to Minister of Marine, Mazatlan, 28 Dec 1860, encl. of Minister of Marine to Thouvenel, Paris, 14 (r. 16) Mar 1861, *ibid.;* Saligny to Thouvenel, Mexico City, No. 9, 17 Feb (r. 31 Mar) 1861, *ibid.;* Zarco to Saligny, Mexico City, 16 Feb 1861, encl. 7 of ibid.; Saligny to Thouvenel, Mexico City, No. 14, 28 Mar (r. 30 Apr) 1861, *ibid.*).

52. Saligny to Thouvenel, Mexico City, No. 26, 18 May (r. 30 Jun) 1861, *ibid.*, LIV.

53. Wyke to Russell, Mexico City, No. 11, 28 Jun (r. 29 Jul) 1861, PRO, F.O. 50/353.

54. Saligny to Thouvenel, Mexico City, No. 28, 8 Jun (r. 30 Jul) 1861, MDAE: *CP, Mex.,* LV, and *Ibid.*

55. Saligny to Thouvenel, Mexico City, No. 28, 8 Jun (r. 30 Jul) 1861, MDAE: *CP, Mex.,* LV.

56. See footnote of previous section of the present investigation.

57. Wyke to Russell, Mexico City, No. 2, 27 May (r. 27 Jun) 1861, PRO, F.O. 50/352.

58. Saligny to Thouvenel, Mexico City, No. 30, 12 Jun (r. 30 Jul) 1861, MDAE: *CP, Mex.,* LV.

59. Saligny to Thouvenel, Mexico City, No. 31, 22 Jun (r. 30 Jul) 1861, *ibid.*

60. Saligny to Thouvenel, Mexico City, No. 32, 29 Jun (r. 30 Jul) 1861, *ibid.*

61. Saligny to Thouvenel, Mexico City, No. 33, 5 Jul (r. 30 Aug) 1861, *ibid.*

62. Saligny to Thouvenel, Mexico City, No. 30, 12 Jun (r. 30 Jul) 1861, *ibid.*

63. Saligny to Thouvenel, Mexico City, Nos. 30, 31, 32; 12, 22, 29 Jun (r. 30 Jul) 1861, *ibid.*

64. Saligny to Thouvenel, Mexico City, No. 30, 12 Jun (r. 30 Jul) 1861, *ibid.*

65. Zamacona to Saligny, 13 Jul 1861, sum. and cited by Saligny to Thouvenel, Mexico City, No. 34, 17 Jul (r. 30 Aug) 1861, and dated by Zaligny to Zamacona, Mexico City, 15 Jul 1861, encl. of Saligny to Thouvenel, Mexico City, No. 34, 17 Jul (r. 30 Aug) 1861, *ibid.*

66. Saligny to Zamacona, Mexico City, 15 Jul 1861, encl. of Saligny to Thouvenel, Mexico City, No. 34, 17 Jul (r. 30 Aug) 1861, *ibid.*

67. Saligny to Thouvenel, Mexico City, No. 34, 17 Jul (r. 30 Aug) 1861, *ibid.*

68. Saligny to Zamacona, Mexico City, 23 Jul 1861, encl. 5 of Saligny to Thouvenel, Mexico City, No. 35, 27 Jul (r. 30 Aug) 1861, *ibid.*

69. *Ibid.* Saligny claimed the law was a ". . . new insult, free and premeditated, against France."

70. Zamacona to Saligny, 21, 21, (25) Jul 1861, encls. 3, 4, 8 of Saligny to Thouvenel, Mexico City, No. 35, 27 Jul (r. 30 Aug) 1861, *ibid.* Enclosure 8 is dated "July 1861," but Zamacona dates it 25 July in another letter (Zamacona to Saligny, Mexico City, 25 Jul 1861, encl. 9 of Saligny to Thouvenel, Mexico City, No. 35, 27 Jul (r. 30 Aug) 1861, *ibid.*). Zamacona claimed the law was to permit Mexico to straighten out its finances so that "vexatious exactions" could be abolished forever, that the law did not deny any obligations, and that Mexico was just placing its duties to ". . . Civilization and to Society before duties to the creditors."

71. Saligny to Zamacona, Mexico City, 24 Jul 1861, encl. 6 of Saligny to Thouvenel, Mexico City, No. 35, 27 Jul (r. 30 Aug) 1861, *ibid.* Saligny gave Mexico 24 hours to annull the law. Otherwise France could only defend itself by force, and it was up to Zamacona's Government ". . . to decide whether it will let things come to this extremity."

72. Saligny to Zamacona, 25 Jul 1861, encl. 7 of Saligny to Thouvenel. Mexico City, No. 35, 27 Jul (r. 30 Aug) 1861, *ibid.* After writing this letter, Saligny received Zamacona's reply to the ultimatum that the financial law of 17 July could not be repealed without throwing Mexico into ". . . anarchy and social dissolution . . . (Zamacona to Saligny, Mexico City, (25) Jul 1861; Saligny to Zamacona, Mexico City, Confidential and Private, 26 Jul 1861, encls. 8 and 10 of Saligny to Thouvenel, Mexico City, No. 35, 27 Jul (r. 30 Aug) 1861, *ibid.*).

73. Saligny to Thouvenel, Mexico City, No. 35, 27 Jul (r. 30 Aug) 1861, *ibid.* Parts of this despatch have been quoted by William S. Robertson. See "The Tripartite Treaty of London," *HAHR*, XX (1940), 168. A very edited version appears in the *Livre jaune* for 1861. See Ministère des Affaires Etrangères: *Documents Diplomatiques* (Hereafer referred to as *DD.*), *1861* (Paris, 1862), pp. 113–114.

74. Saligny to Thouvenel, Mexico City, No. 40, 18 Aug (r. 30 Sep) 1861, MDAE: *CP, Mex.,* LV.

75. Wyke to Russell, Mexico City, No. 30, 23 Aug (r. 29 Sep) 1861, PRO, F.O. 50/353.

76. Saligny to Thouvenel, Mexico City, No. 41, 21 Aug (r. 30 Sep) 1861, MDAE: *CP, Mex.,* LV. Since Corwin was in the country for the weekend, the representatives of Belgium and Equador were contacted and a meeting arranged for the next day at Corwin's house.

77. Wyke believed that a shot was fired at Saligny and that the ball struck and flattened against a pillar near where Saligny was passing, and that a fragment of detached stone hit the French Minister on the right arm (Wyke to Russell, Mexico City, No. 30, 23 Aug (r. 29 Sep) 1861, PRO, F.O. 50/353). A collective note of 23 September to Zamacona insisted that Saligny had been fired upon and gave as proof the bullet hole seen by all members of the Diplomatic Corps (encl. 2 of Saligny to Thouvenel, Mexico City, No. 46, 28 Sep (r. 30 Oct) 1861, MDAE: *CP, Mex.,* LV).

78. Thomas Corwin, U.S.A.; Baron Wagner, Prussia; Francisco de N. Pastor, Equador; August Kint de Roodenbeek, Belgium to Zamacona, Mexico City, 16 Aug 1861, encl. 1 of Saligny to Thouvenel, Mexico City, No. 41, 21 Aug (r. 30 Sep) 1861, MDAE: *CP, Mex.,* LV. It was also complained that the Police did nothing about the demonstration before the French Legation.

79. Zamacona to Baron Wagner, Mexico City, 17 Aug 1861, encl. 2 of *Ibid.*

80. Baron Wagner to Zamacona, Mexico City, 21 Aug 1861, and encl., both encl. 3 of *Ibid.* Listed were 6 assassinations, including Bodmer and Beale, 4 attempts with wounds, and 29 attempts against French.

81. Saligny to Thouvenel, Mexico City, No. 41, 21 Aug (r. 30 Sep) 1861, *ibid.*

82. Wyke to Russell, Mexico City, No. 30, 23 Aug (r. 29 Sep) 1861, PRO, F.O. 50/353.

83. Saligny to Thouvenel, Mexico City, No. 42, 28 Aug (r. 30 Sep) 1861, MDAE: *CP, Mex.*, LV. All the diplomats, except Corwin, wanted to protest vigorously, seeing the decree only as a disguised forced loan or a confiscation of property. It was resolved to urge their nationals not to pay, except under protest and pressure. For Wyke's account, see the previous section of the present investigation.

84. Wyke to Russell, Mexico City, No. 31, 24 Aug (r. 29 Sep) 1861, PRO, F.O. 50/354.

85. Saligny to Thouvenel, Mexico City, No. 42, 28 Aug (r. 30 Sep) 1861, MDAE: *CP, Mex.*, LV.

86. Saligny to Thouvenel, Mexico City, No. 40, 18 Aug (r. 30 Sep) 1861, *ibid.*; PERKINS, p. 356.

87. Saligny to Thouvenel, Mexico City, No. 42, 28 Aug (r. 30 Sep) 1861, MDAE: *CP, Mex.*, LV.

88. "Injuries committed against French subjects in 1861," encl. 4 of Saligny to Thouvenel, Mexico City, No. 46, 28 Sep (r. 30 Oct) 1861, *ibid.* Marquez is named as responsible in 2 cases, the Mexican Police for one case of mistreatment, Mexican soldiers for two beatings. All in all, 25 claims were listed: 7 assassinations, 5 wounded, 3 beaten, 3 robbed, 3 tortured, 2 ransomed, 2 jailed.

89. Saligny to Thouvenel, Mexico City, No. 43, 4 Sep (r. 30 Oct) 1861, *ibid.* Saligny related that a week before an inoffensive passer-by was shot in the main street of Mexico by four soldiers, because he did not give the right of way quickly enough. The police did nothing until two hours later, when the body was removed.

90. See footnote 88 above.

91. Saligny to Thouvenel, Mexico City, No. 46, 28 Sep (r. 30 Oct) 1861, MDAE: *CP, Mex.*, LV.

92. "Incident of the French Legation. The Minister of Foreign Relations had had published what follows, Mexico City, 3 Sep 1861. Mariano Arrieta to the Publisher of the *Siglo XIX*," encl. 1 of *Ibid.*

93. Saligny to Thouvenel, Mexico City, No. 46, 28 Sep (r. 30 Oct) 1861, *ibid.*

94. Collective Note of Diplomatic Corps to Zamacona, 25 Sep 1861, encl. 2 of *Ibid.*

95. Saligny to Thouvenel, Mexico City, No. 47, 29 Sep (r. 30 Oct) 1861, *ibid.*

96. See the previous section of the present investigation.

97. See Chapter III of the present investigation.

98. Saligny to Thouvenel, Mexico City, No. 59 *(bis)*, Confidential, 15 Nov 1861 (r. 2 Jan 1862), MDAE: *CP, Mex.*, LVI.

99. See the previous section of the present investigation.

100. Saligny to Thouvenel, Mexico City, No. 49, 16 Oct (r. 28 Nov) 1861, MDAE: *CP, Mex.*, LVI.

101. Saligny to Thouvenel, Mexico City, No. 50, 28 Oct (r. 28 Nov) 1861, *ibid.* On 20 October 1500 Government troops under General Tapia were defeated by Pachuca, 25 leagues from Mexico City, by 3000 men led by Marquez, Zuloago, and Mejia.

102. Saligny to Thouvenel, Mexico City, No. 51, 29 Oct (r. 28 Nov) 1861, *ibid.,* and encl. 3 thereof, *Testimonio de la Averiguacion Practicada por orden del Supremo Govierno Sobre Los Hechos Acaecidos en la Noche Del 14 de Agosto Con el Sr. Ministro Frances de los cuales se Quejo el cuerpo diplomatico* (Mexico City, 1861). The investigation was first published in a newspaper in September. See footnote 92 above.

103. Zarco-Saligny meeting, 28 Oct 1861, sum. by Saligny to Thouvenel, Mexico City, No. 51, 29 Oct (r. 28 Nov) 1861, *ibid.* Zarco said the Government wanted to make a friendly settlement of difference Saligny replied that he had to have the 40,000 piastres taken from the Penaud fund. Asked if he would be disposed to make a settlement if he got the 40,000, Saligny answered there were other things too, such as the two affairs of 14 August. Zarco replied that the money would be returned and that there would have to be a new judicial investigation.

104. Saligny to Thouvenel, Mexico City, No. 59 *(bis),* Confidential, 15 Nov 1861 (r. 2 Jan 1862), *ibid.*

105. Thouvenel to Saligny, No. 12, draft, 5 Sep 1861, *ibid.,* LV.

106. Saligny to Thouvenel, Mexico City, No. 52, 15 Nov 1861 (r. 6 Jan 1862), *ibid.,* LVI. Saligny arranged a meeting with Zamacona for 2 November and gave him three days to accept Thouvenel's demands. Zamacona asked for and obtained a delay of five days.

107. Saligny to Thouvenel, Mexico City, No. 53, 16 Nov 1861 (r. 2 Jan 1862), *ibid.*

108. *Ibid.* Baron Wagner confirms Saligny's account (Wagner to Baron Schleintz, Mexico City, 14 Nov 1861, encl. of Saligny to Thouvenel, Mexico City, No. 53 *(bis),* Confidential, 16 Nov 1861 (r. 2 Jan) 1862, *ibid.* After supper on 3 November Saligny took a walk with Wagner and Pastor, the representatives of Prussia and Equador. Leon and his French mistress approached Saligny, and the French girl asked whether Saligny had said Leon was a robber. Saligny replied yes and kept walking with Pastor, while Wagner placed himself between them and Leon. A few minutes later Saligny was confronted by Leon and a young man who said the Chief of Police wanted an explanation and proposed a meeting.

109. Saligny to Thouvenel, Mexico City, No. 53, 16 Nov 1861 (r. 2 Jan 1862), *ibid.*

110. Saligny to Thouvenel, Mexico City, No. 52, 15 Nov 1861 (r. 6 Jan 1862), *ibid.* See footnote 106 above.

111. Saligny to Zamacona, Mexico City, 9 Nov 1861, encl. 1 of *Ibid.*

112. Zamacona to Saligny, Mexico City, 11 Nov 1861, encl. 2 of *Ibid.*

113. Thouvenel to Saligny, No. 12, draft, 5 Sep 1861, ibid., LV.

114. Saligny to Thouvenel, Mexico City, No. 59 *(bis),* Confidential, 15 Nov 1861 (r. 2 Jan 1862), *ibid.,* LVI. No such documents, however,

are found in MDAE: *CP, Mex.*, LV, where they would have been filed. For the negotiations, see Chapter III of the present investigation.

115. Saligny to Serrano, 22 Nov 1861, DUVERNUIS, I, 61–62. Saligny wrote there would be no negotiation with Juarez and affirmed he spoke in the name of the Emperor. Serrano was the Captain-General of Cuba.

116. Saligny to Zamacona, Mexico City, 12 Nov 1861, encl. 3 of Saligny to Thouvenel, Mexico City, No. 52, 15 Nov 1861 (r. 6 Jan 1862), MDAE: *CP, Mex.*, LVI.

117. Zamacona to Saligny, Mexico City, 13 Nov 1861, encl. 4 of *Ibid.*

118. Saligny to Zamacona, Mexico City, 14 Nov 1861, encl. 5 of *Ibid.*

119. GAULOT, p. 23. Saligny made this statement to Ernest Louet, whose papers Gaulot used. Sara Yorke Stevenson also records that Saligny said to a friend of hers that his great merit ". . . . was to have understood the wishes of the Emperor, and to have precipitated events so as to make the intervention a necessity . . ." *(Maximilian in Mexico: A Woman's Reminiscences of the French Intervention, 1862–1867* (New York, 1891), p. 21). Sara York Stevenson was an American Studying in Paris at the beginning of the French intervention in Mexico. She knew many people at court and went to Mexico in 1862, because a relative was murdered there. Schefer points out that this boast should not be interpreted to imply that Saligny penetrated the ideas of the Emperor and systematically provoked complications sufficient to justify an intervention. As proof Schefer cites Saligny's initial instructions of 30 May 1860 and comments, "Not a word about the establishment of a monarchy." See SCHEFER, pp. 63–66. It was not until June that the French Government decided to send naval forces to Mexico. See Chapter III of the present investigation. It was not until 29 July that Thouvenel wrote Saligny a despatch that French naval forces had been instructed to contact him (Thouvenel to Saligny, Paris, No. 11, draft, 29 Jul 1861, MDAE: *CP, Mex.*, LV). Saligny probably received this despatch at the beginning of September, when Wyke received a despatch from Russell dated 31 July (Russell to Wyke, F.O., No. 35, 31 Jul (r. 4 Sep) 1861, PRO, F.O. 204/153). There was nothing to indicate that these naval forces were to be employed for anything other than a show of force to back up Saligny's demands for redress. The next instructions from Thouvenel were dated 5 September, and Saligny received them in the evening of 30 October. At this time Saligny also learned of an impending Anglo-French intervention in Mexico. There was, therefore, little "divining" necessary to know Napoleon wanted to intervene in Mexico. Merely following his instructions, Saligny presented an ultimatum. Later, when he thought the monarchy scheme was sure of fulfillment, he exaggerated his role in initiating the intervention and boasted he had "precipitated" events.

120. Saligny to Thouvenel, Mexico City, No. 55, 25 Nov 1861 (r. 2 Jan 1862), and encl. 6 therof, "Regular Troops which the Mexican

Government could employ against a foreign army of invasion," MDAE: *CP, Mex.,* LVI.

121. Saligny to Thouvenel, Mexico City, No. 56, 28 Nov 1861 (r. 2 Jan 1862), *ibid.* Saligny received this news on 27 November.

122. Saligny to Thouvenel, Mexico City, No. 58, 29 Nov 1861 (r. 2 Jan 1862), *ibid.*

123. Saligny to Thouvenel, Vera Cruz, No. 59, 22 Dec 1861 (r. 30 Jan 1862), *ibid.*

124. Saligny to General Rollin, Vera Cruz, Pri., 1 Jan 1862, *ibid.,* LVIII. General Rollin was a French General residing in France with whom Saligny maintained a private correspondence. General Robles was in Saligny's opinion ". . . perhaps the only honest man in this country" (Saligny to Thouvenel, Mexico City, No. 55 *(bis),* Confidential, 26 Nov 1861 (r. 6 Jan 1862), ibid., LVI). For Saligny's conspiracy with Robles, see Chapter IV of the present investigation.

125. José L. Uraga to Saligny, Guanajuato, 10 Sep 1862, translation of a Mexican newspaper, encl. 2 of Wyke to Russell, Mexico City, No. 122, 24 Sep (r. 30 Oct) 1862, PRO, F.O. 50/366. Uraga claimed he read in the "Herald" of 29 August 1862 Saligny's correspondence with Serrano, which slurred Uraga. This correspondence was published from papers laid before the Spanish Cortes. Uraga said, as a man of honor, he had said nothing before, but now he challenged Saligny to publish their correspondence. The verdict, Uraga said, he was leaving to men of honor. M. de Chaillé, then commanding the *Foudre,* was present at the meeting on 25 December 1861, Uraga said, and had taken the Mexican General's side when he was "insulted" by Saligny's proposals.

126. Wyke to Russell, Vera Cruz, Pri., 31 Dec 1861, PRO, P.R.O. 30/22–74.

127. Wyke to Russell, Vera Cruz, No. 60, 29 Dec 1861 (r. 29 Jan 1862), *ibid.,* F.O. 50/354

128. Saligny to Thouvenel, Vera Cruz, No. 61, 31 Dec 1861 (r. 30 Jan 1862), MDAE: *CP, Mex.,* LVI.

## 3. *Corwin and Pickett in Mexico, 1861*

1. Jesse Burton Hendrick: *Statesmen of the Lost Cause: Jefferson Davis and His Cabinet* (Boston, 1939), p. 121. (Hereafter referred to as HENDRICK).

2. Addison Peale Russell: *Thomas Corwin: A Sketch* (Cincinnati, 1861), unnumbered page following title page.

3. For his instructions, see J. D. Richardson: *A Compilation of the Messages and Papers of the Confederacy* (2 v., Nashville, 1904–1906), II, 20–26.

4. Jay Monaghan: *Diplomat in Carpet Slippers: Abraham Lincoln Deals with Foreign Affairs* (Indianapolis and New York, 1945), p. 65. (Hereafter referred to as MONAGHAN).

5. *Ibid.*

6. Seward to Corwin, No. 2, 6 Apr 1861, Washington, Dept. of State: *Instructions, Mexico,* XVII, cited by Frank Lawrence Owsley: *King Cotton Diplomacy: Foreign Relations of the Confederate States of America* (Chicago, 1931), pp. 110–111 (Hereafter referred to as OWSLEY); James Morton Callahan: *American Foreign Policy in Mexican Relations* (New York, 1932), pp. 280–281; J. Fred Rippy: *The United States and Mexico* (New York, 1926), p. 254; U.S., *House executive documents* (37th cong., 2nd sess.), VIII, doc. 100, pp. 5–9, cited by John Musser:*The Establishment of Maximilian's Empire in Mexico: A Thesis Presented to the Faculty of the Graduate School of the University of Pennsylvania in Partial Fulfilment of the Degree of Doctor of Philosophy* (Menasha, Wisconsin, 1918), p. 26. (Hereafter referred to as Musser).

7. Saligny to Thouvenel, Mexico City, No. 26, 18 May (r. 30 Jun) 1861, MDAE: *CP, Mex.,* LIV.

8. Wyke to Russell, Mexico City, No. 12, 28 Jun (r. 29 Jul) 1861, PRO, F.O. 50/353.

9. Corwin to Seward, No. 1, 29 May 1861, and encl. G. Washington, Dept. of State: *Despatches, Mexico,* XVIII, cited by OWSLEY, pp. 111–112.

10. Seward to Corwin, No. 8, 3 Jun 1861, Washington, Dept. of State: *Instructions, Mexico,* XVII, cited by OWSLEY, pp. 112–113.

11. Corwin to Seward, No. 2, 29 Jun 1861, and encls., Washington, Dept of State: *Despatches, Mexico,* XXVIII, cited by OWSLEY, pp. 113–114; U.S. *House executive documents* (37th cong., 2nd sess.), VII, doc. 100, pp. 12–14, cited by MUSSER, p. 26.

12. Saligny to Thouvenel, Mexico City, No. 34, 17 Jul (r. 30 Aug) 1861, MDAE: *CP, Mex.,* LV.

13. HENDRICK, p. 123.

14. *Ibid.,* pp. 129–130.

15. *Ibid.,* p. 131.

16. An exception might be Lower California, ". . . .which may become indispensable to the protection of our Pacific possessions."

17. Corwin to Seward, No. 3, 29 Jul 1861, U.S., *House executive documents* (37th cong., 2nd sess.), VIII, doc. 100, pp. 15–16, cited by Rippy: *The United States and Mexico,* p. 256; Washington, Dept. of State: *Despatches, Mexico,* XXVIII, cited by OWSLEY, pp. 113–115.

18. Wyke to Russell, Mexico City, No. 31, 24 Aug (r. 29 Sep) 1861, PRO, F.O. 50/354.

19. Saligny to Thouvenel, Mexico City, No. 42, 28 Aug (r. 30 Sep) 1861, MDAE: *CP, Mex.,* LV.

20. Corwin to Seward, No. 2, 29 Jun 1861, Washington, Dept: of State: *Despatches, Mexico,* XXVIII, cited by OWSLEY, p. 113.

21. Corwin to Seward, No. 4, 29 Aug 1861, *ibid.,* p. 115.

22. Corwin to Seward, 7 Sep 1861, U.S., House executive documents, (37th cong. 2nd sess.), VIII, doc. No. 100, pp. 23–24, cited by MUSSER, p. 27.

23. Seward to Corwin, 2 Oct 1861, U.S., *House executive documents,* (37th cong., 2nd sess), VIII, doc. No. 100, pp. 29–30, cited by MUSSER, p. 27.

24. Seward to Corwin, No. 17, 2 Sep 1861, Washington, Dept. of State: *Instructions, Mexico,* XVII, cited by OWSLEY, p. 116; U.S., *House executive documents* (37th cong., 2nd sess.) VIII, doc. No. 100, p. 22, cited by Rippy: *The United States and Mexico,* pp. 255–256; Callahan: *American Foreign Policy in Mexican Relations,* p. 282. The term of the loan was to be five years. Interest was to be six per cent. If reimbursement should not be made within six years from the time the treaty went into effect, the mortgage would be foreclosed, and the public lands and mineral rights were to ". . . become absolute in the United States . . ." The treaty would only be ratified if England and France promised not to intervene while the treaty was pending ratification and while the interest was being paid upon the Mexican debts after the treaty went into effect. Seward's motives are analyzed in Chapter III of the present investigation.

25. See text between footnotes 138 and 140 of Section I of Chapter II of the present investigation.

26. Colonel John Pickett to Zamacona, Hotel Iturbide, Mexico City, 1 Nov 1861, encl. of Pickett to Wyke, Hotel Iturbide, Mexico City, 4(r.7) Nov 1861, PRO, F.O. 204/158.

27. HENDRICK, pp. 135–137.

28. Corwin to Seward, No. 8, 29 Nov 1861, Washington, Dept. of State: *Despatches, Mexico,* XXVIII, cited by OWSLEY, p. 117.

29. See Chapter III of the present investigation.

30. Lyons-Seward Conversation, 12 Oct 1861, sum. by Lyons to Russell, Washington, No. 553, 14 (r. 28) Oct 1861, PRO, F.O. 5/772.

31. See Chapter III of the present investigation.

32. Lyons to Russell, Washington, No. 787, 21 Dec 1861 (r. 7 Jan 1862), PRO, F.O. 5/777. On 19 December the Foreign Relations Committee of the Senate considered the draft treaty but considered the amount of money to be lent Mexico excessive. The Senators then adjourned. See MONAGHAN, p. 188.


## Chapter III


### 1. The Immediate Background: The Mexican Policies of the European Powers, January-August 1861

1. Time Table for West India Mail Service for the year 1861, encl. of Post Office to Hammond, 30 Jan (r. 2 Feb) 1861, PRO, F.O. 50/357.

2. Russell to Cowley, F.O., No. 95, draft, 21 Jan 1861, PRO, F.O. 27/1372.

3. Cowley to Russell, Paris, No. 121, 22 (r. 23) Jan 1861, PRO, F.O. 27/1384.

4. Saligny to Thouvenel, Mexico City, No. 7, 4 Feb (r. 5 Mar) 1861, MDAE: *CP, Mex.,* vol. 54.

5. Thouvenel to Saligny, draft, 6 Mar 1861, *ibid.*

6. Saligny to Thouvenel, Mexico City, No. 11, 28 Feb (r. 31 Mar) 1861, *ibid.*

7. Thouvenel, to Saligny, Nos. 4 and 5, drafts, 11 Apr. 1861, *ibid.*

8. Saligny to Thouvenel, Mexico City, Nos. 14 and 15, 28 and 30 Mar (r. 30 Apr) 1861, *ibid.*

9. Thouvenel to Saligny, No. 6, draft, 30 Apr 1861, *ibid.*

10. Cowley to Russell, Paris, No. 527, 8 (r. 9) Apr 1861, PRO, F.O. 27/1389; Russell to Cowley, F.O., No. 445, draft, 10 Apr 1861, PRO, F.O. 27/1375.

11. Thouvenel to Saligny, No. 7, draft, 31 May 1861, MDAE: *CP, Mex.,* vol. 54.

12. Saligny to Thouvenel, Mexico City, No. 19, 28 Apr (r. 29 May) 1861, *ibid.*

13. Thouvenel to Minister of Marine and Colonies, 12 Jun 1861, sum. by Ministry of Marine and Colonies to Thouvenel, Paris 2 (r. 3) Jul 1861, *ibid.,* vol. 55.

14. Minister of Marine and Colonies to Thouvenel, Paris, 2 (r. 3) Jul 1861, *ibid.*

15. Thouvenel to Saligny, No. 10, draft, 30 Jun 1861, *ibid.*

16. See Section 1 of Chapter II of present investigation.

17. Wyke to Russell, Mexico City, Nos. 1–3, 26–27 May (r. 27 Jun) 1861, PRO, F.O. 50/352.

18. Russell to Wyke, F.O., No. 28, draft, 1 Jul 1861, PRO, F.O. 50/351.

19. See Appendix D of present investigation.

20. Buchanan to Russell, Madrid, No. 72, 20 (r. 25) Feb 1861, PRO, F.O. 72/1004.

21. Saligny to Thouvenel, Mexico City, No. 27, 27 May (r. 30 Jun) 1861, MDAE: *CP, Mex.,* vol. 54.

22. Edwardes to Russell, Madrid, No. 48, 8 (r. 13) May 1861, PRO, F.O. 72/1005.

23. Encl. of *ibid.*

24. ABBOTT, p. 628.

25. The first order to start preparations was dated 11 September 1861. See Section 2 of Chapter IV of present investigation.

26. See Appendix D of present investigation.

27. Zarco to Almonte, Mexico City, 28 Jan 1861, MONTLUC, pp. 55–56.

28. Zarco to Montluc, Mexico City, 27 Apr 1861, *ibid.,* p. 57.

29. DAWSON, p. 150.

30. *Ibid.,* p. 95.

31. Estrada-Schertzenlechner conversation, sum. by Schertzenlechner to Maximilian, Trieste, 6 Nov 1861, sum. & cited by CORTI, I, 119–120. See also DAWSON, p. 150.

32. Eugenie to Duc D'Albe, Tuileries, 10 Jan 1861, ALBE, I, 210.

33. Eugenie to Duc D'Albe, 14 Apr 1861, ibid., I, 211–212.

34. CORTI, I, 96.

35. *Ibid.,* I, 97.

36. *Ibid.*

37. Wyke-Herzfeld Conversations, Sep 1863, sum. by Herzfeld to Baron de Pont, Carlsbad, 7 Sep 1863 and "Report by H. D. Herzveld, 13 Sep 1863," HHSA, AKM, DAWSON, pp. 308–310.

38. For interesting conjectures, see DAWSON, pp. 99–101.

39. Maximilian to Franz Joseph, Brussels, 2 Jul 1856, CORTI, I, 56–59. See also HUBNER, I, 429, 432.

40. HUBNER, II, 187.

41. *Ibid.,* I, 203–204.

42. Albert to Baron Stockmar, 18 Jun 1857, Theodore Martin: *The Life of His Royal Highness, the Prince Consort* (5v., London, 1875–1880), IV (3rd ed., 1879), 59.

43. Schertzenlechner to Maximilian, Trieste, 6 Nov 1861. This document, from the *HHSA,* is summarized and cited by DAWSON (without reference), pp. 149–150, in greater detail than by CORTI, I, 119–120, but Corti gives the source.

44. See footnote 37 above.

45. Palmerston to Cobden, 94 Piccadilly, Pri., 8 Jan 1862, British Museum Additional MS. Room, Palmerston Papers, 48582.

46. Palmerston to Russell, 13 Aug 1863, Victor Wellesley and Robert Sencourt, eds.: *Conversations with Napoleon III: A Collection of Documents, mostly unpublished and almost entirely Diplomatic, Selected and arranged with Introductions* (London, 1934), p. 223; Palmerston to Russell, Pri., 19 Jan 1862, PRO, Gifts and Deposits, 22–22 (Russell Papers), Herbert C. F. Bell: *Lord Palmerston* (2 v., London, 1936), II, 313.

47. Palmerston to Russell, 19 Jan 1862, PRO, Gifts and Deposits, 22/22 (Russell Papers), Harold Temperley and Lilian M. Penson, eds.: *Foundations of British Foreign Policy, from Pitt (1792) to Salisbury (1902), or, Documents Old and New* (Cambridge, 1938), p. 295.

48. Palmerston Minute, 15 Oct 1861, PRO, P.R.O. 30/22–56.

49. Palmerston to Russell, 94 Piccadilly, Pri., 9 Sep 1861, British Museum Additional MS. Room, Palmerston Papers, 48582.

50. Mathew to Russell, Mexico City, No. 37, Con., 12 May (r. 27 Jun) 1861, PRO, F.O. 50/352.

51. Saligny to Thouvenel, Mexico City, No. 25 (bis), 9 May (r. 30 Jun) 1861, MDAE: *CP, Mex.,* vol. 54.

52. Zarco to Saligny, National Palace, Mexico City, 4 May 1861, encl. 3 of Saligny to Thouvenel, Mexico City, No. 25, 9 May (r. 30 Jun) 1861, *ibid.*

53. "Note on our Griefs end of June 1861," draft, *ibid.,* vol. 55.

54. Minister of Marine and Colonies to Thouvenel, Paris, 2 (r. 3) Jul 1861, *ibid.*

55. Saligny to Zarco, Mexico City, Confidential, 2 May 1861, encl. 2 of Saligny to Thouvenel, Mexico City, No. 25, 9 May (r. 30 Jun)

1861, *ibid.*, vol. 54. See also Section 2 of Chapter II of present investigation.

56. Cowley to Russell, Paris, No. 822, 6 (r. 8) Jul 1961, PRO, F.O. 27/1393.

57. Palmerston note, 19 Jul 1861, attached to *ibid*.

58. Thouvenel, to Saligny, Paris, No. 11, draft, 29 Jul 1861, MDAE: *CP, Mex.*, vol. 55.

59. De La Fuente to Billault, Senator, Minister in the Dept. of Foreign Affairs, 58 Rue du Faubourg St. Honoré, Paris, 20 Jul 1861, *ibid*.

60. See text between footnotes 51 and 54 of Section 3 of Chapter I of present investigation.

61. See footnote 59 of Section 1 of Chapter II of present investigation.

62. Saligny to Thouvenel, Mexico City, No. 27, 27 May (r. 30 Jun) 1861, MDAE: *CP, Mex.*, vol. 54.

63. Thouvenel to Saligny, No. 10, draft, 30 Jun 1861, *ibid*. Thouvenel remarked that Article II should have specified the mode of payment ". . . of such and such a percentage on such and such portion of custom revenue, without which . . . it seems illusory. . . ." Article VII, which provided that Mexico turn reparation money over to the French Legation, would cause difficulties. What, asked Thouvenel, would Saligny do when all the interested parties presented themselves at the same time to collect their money from him?

64. See footnote 60 above.

65. See footnote 60 above.

66. Metternich to Rechberg, 5 Jul 1861, *HHSA,* Berichte aus Paris, DAWSON, pp. 101–102.

67. Estrada to Metternich, 4 Jul 1861, *HHSA,* CORTI, I, 105.

68. Metternich to Rechberg, 5 Jul 1861, *HHSA,* Henry Salomon: *L'Ambassade de Richard De Metternich A Paris* (Paris, 1931), pp. 149–150. (Hereafter referred to as SALOMON).

69. Rechberg to Metternich, Vienna, 28 Jul 1861, *HHSA,* Weisungen nach Frankreich, DAWSON, pp. 102–103. See also CORTI, I, 105.

70. DAWSON, pp. 102–103.

71. Senior-Estrada Conversation, 27 Apr 1863, SENIOR, II, 280.

72. Rechberg to Maximilian, 21 Nov 1861, 4 Jan 1862, *HHSA,* AKM, DAWSON, pp. 153, 193.

73. Metternich-Cowley Conversation, sum. by Cowley to Russell, Paris, Pri., 6 Mar 1862, PRO, P.R.O. 30/22–57.

74. Cowley to Russell, Paris, No. 141, Confidential, 11 (r. 12) Feb 1862, PRO, F.O. 27/1432.

75. DAWSON, p. 103.

76. Metternich to Rechberg, 12 Aug 1861, *HHSA,* SALOMON, p. 150.

77. Cowley-Napoleon III Conversation, 1 Jul 1861, sum. by Cowley to Russell, Paris No. 799, Confidential, 2 (r. 3) Jul 1861, PRO, F.O. 27/1393.

(Saligny to Thouvenel, Mexico City, No. 59 *(bis)*, Confidential, 15 Nov 1861 (r. 2 Jan 1862), MDAE: *CP, Mex.,* vol. 56).

118. SCHEFER, p. 109.

119. De La Fuente to Thouvenel, Paris, 31 Aug 1861, MDAE: *CP, Mex.,* vol. 55. The justification given was that Mexico had to have time to organise its Treasury in order to be able to pay creditors.

120. PRIM, p. 47.

### 2. *The Negotiation of the Tripartite Convention of London, Part I, September 1861*

1. Draft to Admiralty, F.O., Con., 29 Aug 1861, PRO, F.O. 50/357.

2. Hammond to Russell, Pri., 29 Aug 1861, *ibid.,* P.R.O. 30/22–28.

3. Romaine to Hammond, Admiralty, Con., 29 (r. 30) Aug 1961, *ibid.,* F.O. 50/357.

4. Russell Memorandum, 31 Aug 1861, ibid., P.R.O. 30/22–21. See also Section 1 of Chapter III of present investigation.

5. Cowley to Russell, Paris, No. 1083, 3 (r. 4) Sep 1861, *ibid.,* F.O. 27/1396.

6. De La Fuente to Thouvenel, Paris, 4 Sep 1861, MDAE: *CP, Mex.,* LV.

7. Cowley to Russell, Paris, No. 1090, 5 (r. 7) Sep 1861, PRO, F.O. 27/1396.

8. De La Fuente to Thouvenel, Paris, 4 Sep 1861, MDAE: *CP, Mex.,* LV.

9. Thouvenel to Saligny, No. 12, draft, 5 Sep 1861, *ibid.*

10. See previous section of present investigation.

11. See below in text of this section of present investigation.

12. See footnote 5 above.

13. Draft to Admiralty, F.O., 4 Sep 1861, PRO, F.O. 50/358.

14. Cowley to Russell, Paris, No. 1090, 5 (r. 7) Sep 1861, *ibid.,* F.O. 27/1396.

15. Cowley to Russell, Pri., 5 Sep 1861, *ibid.,* P.R.O. 30/22–56.

16. Thouvenel to Saligny, No. 12, draft, 5 Sep 1861, MDAE: *CP, Mex.,* LV.

17. Mon to Collantes, telegraphic despatch, 6 Sep 1861, cited by DOMENECH, II, 379; PRIM, p. 48; Leonardon: "L'Espagne et La Question Du Mexique, 1861–1862," p. 63; PERKINS, p. 376.

18. PRIM, p. 38; Leonardon: L'Espagne et La Question Du Mexique, 1861–1862," p. 63.

19. Collantes to Mon, San Ildefonsok 6 Sep 1861, cited by DOMENECH II, 379–380; Leonardon: "L'Espagne et La Question Du Mexique, 1861–1862," pp. 63–64.

20. DUVERNOIS, I, 32–33.

21. Xavier de Isturiz to Russell, London, 23 (r. 24) Sep 1861, *BSP,* 1862, LXIV, 164.

22. *Diario Espanol,* Madrid, 10 Sep 1861, encl. (with translation) of

Crampton to Russell, San Ildefonso, No. 76, 13 (r. 22) Sep 1861, PRO, F.O. 72/1009.

23. Royal Order, 11 Sep 1861, sum. by Serrano to Collantes, Havana, No. 89, 16 Dec 1861, *Diario de las Sesiones de Cortes* (translated), encl. of Crampton to Russell, Madrid, No. 255, 16 (r. 26) Jun 1862, PRO, F.O. 72/1035.

24. See previous section and Appendix D of present investigation.

25. Barrot to Thouvenel, Madrid, No. 96, 18 (r. 22) Sep 1861, MDAE: *CP, Espagne,* 859.

26. Crampton to Russell, San Ildefonso, No. 93, 24 Sep (r. 11 Oct) 1861, PRO, F.O. 72/1009.

27. Mon to Collantes, 9 Sep 1861, cited by DOMENECH II, 30.

28. Thouvenel to Barrot, No. 33, draft, 10 Sep 1861, MDAE: *CP, Espagne,* 859.

29. In Thouvenel's instruction to Flahault of 9 September, the conversation with Mon is referred to, and this sets the sequence.

30. See footnotes 97 and 98 of Section II of Chapter II of present investigation.

31. See Section III of Chapter I of present investigation.

32. Thouvenel to Flahault, Paris, No. 124, draft, 9 Sep 1861, MDAE: *CP, Angleterre,* 720.

33. Thouvenel to Flahault, Paris, Pri., 19 Sep 1861, cited by THOUVENEL, II, 169.

34. Thouvenel to Barrot, No. 33, draft, 10 Sep 1861, MDAE: *CP, Espagne,* 859.

35. Barrot to Thouvenel, Madrid, No. 96, 18 (r. 22) Sep 1861, ibid.

36. See below in text of this section of this investigation.

37. See below in text of this section of this investigation.

38. See below in text of this section of this investigation.

39. Admiralty to Hammond, Admiralty, 7 (r. 8) Sep 1861, and enclosures (Captain P. W. P. Wallis to Commodore P. Douglas, H.M.S. "Madagascar" at Sacrificios, 28 Dec 1838; extract of Commander Robb to Vice Admiral Sir Chas Paget, H.M.S. "Satellite" at Sacrificios, 28 Nov 1838), PRO, F.O. 50/358.

40. Flahault to Thouvenel, London, Pri., 16 Sep 1861, MDAE: *CP, Angleterre,* 720.

41. Palmerston to Russell, Pri., 17 Sep 1861, PRO, P.R.O. 30/22–21.

42. Flahault to Thouvenel, London, Pri., 16 Sep 1861, MDAE: *CP, Angleterre,* 720.

43. Cowley to Russell, Paris, No. 1113, 10 (r. 11) Sep 1861, PRO, F.O. 27/1396.

44. Cowley to Russell, Paris, No. 1129, 17 (r. 18) Sep 1861, *ibid.*

45. Russell to Crampton, F.O., Telegram, 2:20 p.m., 14 Sep 1861, cited by Russell to Crampton, F.O., No. 51, draft, 14 Sep 1861, *ibid.,* F.O. 72/1002.

46. Crampton to Russell, San Ildefonso, Telegram, 14 (r. 15) Sep 1861, *ibid.,* F.O. 72/1012.

47. Russell to Flahault, Pri.,? (r. 16 Sep 1861), cited by Flahault to Thouvenel, London, Pri., 16 Sep 1861, MDAE: *CP, Angleterre,* 720.

48. Russell to Cowley, Pri., 9 Sep 1861, PRO, F.O. 519/199.

49. See previous section of present investigation.

50. See footnote 56 below.

51. Palmerston to Russell, Pri., 17 Sep 1861, PRO, P.R.O. 30/22–21.

52. Russell to Crampton, F.O., telegram, 18 Sep 1861, cited by Russell to Crampton, F.O., No. 54, draft, 18 Sep 1861, *ibid.,* F.O. 72/1002.

53. In a "Note" for Palmerston, dated 20 September, Russell stated he had "forgotten" the contents of Thouvenel's despatch. See text of present section of present investigation between footnotes 55 and 56. in Russell's draft reply to Thouvenel's overture, the British Foreign Secretary also seemed to have "forgotten" Thouvenel's remarks about the United States. See text below between footnotes 66 and 67.

54. Hammond to Cowley, F.O., Pri., 21 Sep 1861, PRO, F.O. 519/190.

55. Palmerston to Duke of Somerset, 94 Piccadilly, 26 May 1861, Palmerston Papers, 48582, British Museum Additional MS. Room. As recently as 9 September Palmerston expressed the same fear to Russell. See Palmerston to Russell, 94 Piccadilly, Pri., 9 Sep 1861, PRO, P.R.O. 30/22–21.

56. Mathew to Russell, Pri., 17 Sep 1861, with attached note of Russell, 20 Sep 1861, on which Palmerston wrote his comment, dated 22 Sep 1861, PRO, P.R.O. 30/22–74. Mathew had returned to England from Mexico. In his letter to Russell, Mathew warned that "guerrilla warfare" would result from any attempt to "neutralize the existing basis of religious liberty." Mathew also warned that Spanish troops, "under any guise," could not be used to restore peace in Mexico.

57. Cowley to Russell, Paris, No. 1129, 17 (r. 18) Sep 1861, PRO, F.O. 27/1396.

58. Hammond to Cowley, F.O., Pri., 14 Sep 1861, *ibid.,* F.O. 519/190.

59. Cowley to Russell, Paris, No. 1129, 17 (r. 18) Sep 1861, *ibid.,* F.O. 27/1396.

60. Cowley to Russell, Paris, Pri., 17 Sep 1861, *ibid.,* F.O. 519/229.

61. Crampton to Russell, Madrid, Telegram, 3:20 P.M. (r. 9:00 P.M.) 19 Sep 1861, *ibid.,* F.O. 72/1012.

62. Crampton to Russell, Madrid, Telegram, 4:30 P.M., 21 Sep (r. 9:45 A.M., 22 Sep) 1861, marked "Copy to Lord Palmerston," *ibid.*

63. Crampton to Russell, San Ildefonso No. 84, 16 (r. 22) Sep 1861, *ibid.,* F.O. 72/1009.

64. Russell read parts of this despatch to Charles Francis Adams, the American Minister to London, on 25 September 1861. See below in text of this section of present investigation.

65. *Contemporaneo,* 10 Sep 1861, encl. (with translation) of Crampton to Russell, San Ildefonso, No. 76, 13 (r. 22) Sep 1861, PRO, F.O. 72/1009.

66. Crampton to Russell, San Ildefonso, No. 76, 13 (r. 22) Sep 1861, *ibid.*

67. Russell to Cowley, F.O., No. 1005, draft, 23 Sep 1861, with Russell and Palmerston marginal alterations, PRO, F.O. 27/1379. A copy of the despatch in the form sent to Cowley is found in MDAE: *CP, Mex.,* L.V.

68. Russell to Crampton, F.O., telegram, 1.45 P.M., 23 Sep 1861, cited by Russell to Crampton, F.O., No. 57, draft, 23 Sep 1861, PRO, F.O. 72/1002.

69. See Appendix F of present investigation. This letter was written by Napoleon to his Ambassador to London. See Section 3 of Chapter III of present investigation. Napoleon claimed he wanted to reveal his policy "frankly," and Schefer believed the letter was "capital for History," as it shows "imperial arrières pensées." See SCHEFER, p. 135. Henrick N. Boon also quotes this letter, prefacing it with a qualifying remark: "It is impossible to study here to what extent the economic conceptions of Napoleon III influenced the foreign policy of the Empire." See *Rêve et Réalité dans l'oeuvre économique et sociale de Napoleon III* (The Hague, 1936), p. 99. It was a private letter Flahault was to show Russell and Palmerston, and therefore had a propaganda purpose. The importance Napoleon gave to commercial reasons, however, was not new. See Section 3 of Chapter I, especially text between footnotes 44 and 50 and between 67 and 68. Nor was it unusual that Napoleon sometimes said ". . . everything that he thinks . . ." (Note on a conversation between the Emperor Napoleon and me (i.e., Prince Napoleon) on 19 June 1865, at the Tuileries, cited by Ernest d'Hauterive: *Napoléon III et le Prince Napoléon. Correspondance inédite* (Paris, 1925), p. 382.

70. Paléologue-Eugenie Conversation, 10 Jan 1904, cited by PALEOLOGUE, pp. 97–103. Eugenie, while accepting much responsibility, tried to justify the Mexican policy of her husband and herself. Her comments to Paléologue were over forty years after the Biarritz conversation, and she may have forgotten the exact details. Elisabet Esslinger gives Paléologue's account a great prominance in her chapter on Eugenie's part in the Mexican expedition. See *Kaiserin Eugenie Und Die Politik Des zweiten Kaiserreichs* (Stuttgart, 1932), pp. 102–107. (Hereafter referred to as ESSLINGER).

71. Hidalgo's memoirs, "Notes secrètes de M. Hidalgo," were written in 1865, when Maximilian was actually established in Mexico. Hidalgo's purpose in writing these memoirs, unpublished and first discovered and partly published by Count Corti (CORTI, I, 99–102), was for the information of Maximilian to show the part Hidalgo and Estrada played in the establishment of monarchy in Mexico. At the time of writing, Maximilian was established in Mexico, and Hidalgo had a reason to magnify his own role, and to minimize that of Estrada, with whom Hidalgo had now quarrelled. See DAWSON, pp. 87–89. Schefer simply dismisses Hidalgo's memoirs as "picturesque" and "Imaginative." See SCHEFER, pp. 116–117. Corti quotes the memoirs with

apparent satisfaction. A third important scholar, who has tried to reconstruct the Biarritz meeting, simply ignores Hidalgo's Memoirs. See DAWSON, pp. 105–106. A letter of Hidalgo, published in a Spanish newspaper in 1862 (See Appendix U of present investigation), was written with the propaganda purpose of reconciling Spain to the candidacy of Maximilian. Dawson based his account of the Biarritz decision on this letter. See DAWSON, pp. 105–106. Dawson states that it was given to Crampton to Collantes. See DAWSON, p. 104. This is misleading, for the letter was published in the "Epoca," and Crampton's attention was merely called to this already published letter by Collantes. See Crampton to Russell, Madrid, No. 203, Secret and Confidential, 6 (r. 19) May 1862, PRO, F.O. 72/1034.

72. "Notes secrètes de M. Hidalgo," HHSA, cited by CORTI, I, 99–100.

73. See Appendix U of present investigation.

74. Paléologue-Eugenie Conversation, 10 Jan 1904, cited by PALEOLOGUE, p. 101.

75. Paléologue-Eugenie Conversation, 27 Dec 1903, cited by *ibid.*' p. 77.

76. Eugenie to Duchesse D'Albe, Tuileries, 22 Apr 1859, cited by ALBE, I, 163–164.

77. Paléologuc-Eugenie Conversation, 27 Dec 1903, cited by PALEOLOGUE, p. 73.

78. Eugenie to Duc D'Albe, 12 Dec 1854, cited by ALBE, I, 114–115.

79. Eugenie to Duchesse D'Albe, Tuileries, 16 May 1860, cited by *ibid,* I, 171.

80. Hübner to ?, 18 Apr 1862, HHSA, cited by SALOMON, p. 154. See also Comte Fleury: *Memoires of the Empress Eugenie by Comte Fleury: Compiled from Statements, Private Documents, and Personal Letters of the Empress Eugenie, From Conversations of the Emperor Napoleon III and From Family Letters and Papers of General Fleury, M. Franceschini Pietri, Prince Victor Napoleon and Other Members of the Court of the Second Empire* (2 v., New York and London, 1920), II, 105.

81. Eugenie to Charlotte, Paris, 3 Feb 1862, HHSA, cited by CORTI, I, 369.

82. Charlotte to Eugenie, Miramar, 22 Jan 1862, HHSA, cited by ibid., I, 366.

83. Eugenie to Charlotte, Paris, 3 Feb 1862, HHSA, cited by *ibid.,* I, 365.

84. Napoleon III to Maximilian, Paris, 14 Jan 1862, HHSA, cited by *ibid.*

85. Cowley to Russell, Paris, No. 1243, Con., 18 (r. 19) Oct 1861, PRO, F.O. 27/1397. Napoleon had similar ideas about Africa. In 1857 he told Albert, the Prince Consort, that Morocco, Tripoli, Egypt, and Syria were ". . . magnificent countries rendered useless to humanity and civilization by their abominable governments . . ." (Memorandum of Conversation between Prince Albert and Napoleon II (10 Aug 1857),

Osborne, 11 Aug 1857, cited by Theodore Martin: *The Life of his Royal Highness, the Prince Consort* (5 v., London, 1875–1880), IV (3rd ed., 1879), 110.

86. See Appendix F of present investigation.

87. Napoleon III to General Forey, Fontainebleau, 3 Jul 1862, DD, 1862, p. 191. These instructions have been quoted and taken for the purposes of Napoleon from Flint to Rippy. See Henry M. Flint: *Mexico Under Maximilian* (Philadelphia, 1867), pp. 37–40; J. Fred Rippy: *Latin America: A Modern History* (Ann Arbor, Mayflower, London, 1958), pp. 338, 367. While open to the charge that, since these instruction were published in the *DD,* the motives given only served propaganda purposes, these motives agree with those he gave Maury in a private conversation. See Section 3 of Chapter I of present investigation.

88. Napoleon III to Maximilian, Paris, 14 Jan 1862, HHSA, cited by CORTI, I, 365.

89. See Appendix F of present investigation.

90. Arthur Louis Dunham: *The Anglo-French Treaty of Commerce of 1860 and the Progress of the Industrial Revolution in France.* Vol. IX of University of Michigan Publications in History and Political Science. (Ann Arbor, 1930), p. 194.

91. Lincoln's Blockade Proclamation, 19 Apr 1861, cited by James D. Richardson: *The Messages and Papers of the Presidents* (10 v. Washington, 1896–1899), VI, 14.

92. Napoleon III-Cowley Conversation, 1 Jul 1861, cited by F. A. Wellesley, ed.: *Secrets of the Second Empire: Private Letters from the Paris Embassy: Selections from the papers of Henry Richard Charles Wellesley, 1st Earl Cowley, Ambassador at Paris, 1852–1867, Edited by his Son, Colonel the Hon. F. A. Wellesley* (New York and London, 1929), p. 220.

93. Slidell to Mason, 12 Feb 1862, Mason Papers, cited by Louis Martin Sears: "A Confederate Diplomat at the Court of Napoleon III," *AHR,* XXVI (1921), 257.

94. Hubert Howe Bancroft: *Resources and Development of Mexico* (San Francisco, 1893), p. 187.

95. See Appendix F of present investigation.

96. For a popular presentation of this thesis, see Albert Guerard: *Napoleon III* (Cambridge, Mass., 1943), p. 226.

97. See Appendices F and U of present investigation.

98. Thouvenel to Benedetti, 26 Oct 1861, cited by L. Thouvenel, ed.: *Pages de l'Histoire du Second Empire d'Après les Papiers de M. Thouvenel, Ancien Ministre des Affaires Etrangères (1854–1866)* (Paris, 1903), p. 308; Mérimée to Panizzi, 14 Oct 1861, cited by J. M. Thompson: *Louis Napoleon and the Second Empire* (Oxford, 1956), p. 209.

99. HUBNER, I, 205; Lynn M. Case: *French Opinion on War and Diplomacy during the Second Empire* (Philadelphia, 1954), Chs. I and XI. (Hereafter referred to as Case: *French Opinion).*

100. It might also gain popularity with imperialists and nationalists.

For Dawson's speculations that Napoleon may have wanted to please the Pope, see DAWSON, p. 107.

101. Baron Napoléon Beyens: *Le Second Empire vu par un Diplomate Belge* (2 v., Paris, 1925), I, 226–227. (Hereafter referred to as BEYENS).

102. See Case: *French Opinion*, Ch. I.

103. Lynn M. Case: *French Opinion on the United States and Mexico, 1860–1867: Extracts from the Reports of the Procurerus Généraux* (New York and London, 1936), p. 310, summarizing the documents cited (pp. 309–435).

104. *Ibid,* Ch, VI.

105. BEYENS, I, 226–227.

106. HUBNER, II, 51 (23 Sep 1857 entry).

107. Cowley Memorandum, Chantilly, 9 Jan 1862, PRO, P.R.O. 30/22–57.

108. With regard to the expedition to Syria in 1860, Napoleon wrote Persigny that the expedition could not be undertaken alone, ". . . because that would be a big expense . . ." (Napoleon III to Persigny, St. Cloud, 29 Jul 1860, cited by Henry D'Ideville: *Journal d'un Diplomat en Italie: Notes Intimes Pour Servir a l'Histoire du Second Empire: Turin 1859–1862* (Paris, 1872), p. 320).

109. Paléologue asked Eugenie: "At what date did the idea take definitive form in Napoleon's mind? What gave him the final and decisive impetus?" Eugenie replied, "It came in 1861, at Biarritz, from myself" (Paléologue-Eugenie Conversation, 10 Jan 1904, cited by Paleologue, p. 99). Guerard, Dawson, Aubry, Lano, and Esslinger have credited Eugenie with a decisive role, while Stern, Schefer, and Gaulot have given her influence less importance. See GUERARD, pp. 233–234; DAWSON, pp. 88–89; Octtve Aubry: *L'Impératrice Eugénie* (Paris, 1933), pp. 211–212; Pierre de Lano: *The Secret of an Empire: The Empress Eugénie.* Trans. Ethelred Taylor (London, 1895), pp. 129–133; Alfred Stern: *Geschichte Europas von 1848 bis 1871* (10 v., Stuttgart and Berlin, 1894–1924), IX, 18; (Hereafter referred to as STERN). GAULOT p. 21; ESSLINGER, pp. 102–107.

110. Cowley to Russell, Pri., 4 Mar 1862, PRO, P.R.O. 30/22–57.

111. Comte Emile F. Fleury: *Souvenirs de Général Comte Fleury* (2 v., Paris, 1897–1898), II, 266–267.

112. Persigny befriended Napoleon before his seizure of power and held posts as Ambassador to London and Minister of the Interior.

113. "Note for the Emperor, Chamarande," 11 Nov 1867, cited by M. H. de Laire D'Espagny: *Mémoires du Duc de Persigny Publiés Avec Des Documents Inédits, un avant-propos et un épilogue par M. H. De Laire Cte D'Espagne, Ancien Sécretaire Intime Du Duc* (2nd ed., Paris, 1896), p. 393.

114. Clarendon to Cowley, Pri., 21 Jun 1862, PRO, F.O. 519/178.

115. See Section 2 of Chapter II of present investigation. Stern and Wertheimer stress Saligny's reports as a cause of the intervention in Mexico. See STERN, IX, 18; Oskar Von Wertheimer: *Napoleon III.*

*Abenteurer, Frauenheld, Cäsar* (Berlin, 1928), p. 294. In this connection, see Appendix C of present investigation.

116. See Section 2 of Chapter II of present investigation.

117. For Napoleon's secret diplomacy, see OLLIVIER, III, 132–133; DUNHAM, p. 60–61; HUBNER, II, 155. Napoleon also liked to use unofficial agents. During the American Civil War, he obtained news of the battles from his American dentist, who was sent to the United States in 1864 to gather more information. See Dr. Thomas W. Evans: *The Memoirs of Dr. Thomas W. Evans: Recollections of the Second Empire*. Ed. Edward A. Crane (2 v., 2nd ed., London, 1905), I, 49, 156–162. In 1862 used Mr. Lindsay, a British MP, to convey French views on Lincoln's blockade to Russell and Palmerston. At that time Napoleon told Lindsay that ". . . these matters were better managed by private than official hands . . ." (Confidential Minutes of two conversations with Mr. Lindsay, encl. of Cowley to Russell, Paris, Pri., PRO, P.R.O. 30/22–57).

118. See Appendices F and U. Cowley believed Napoleon was " . . . more inclined to wait upon events, instead of erecting them. . ." (Cowley Memorandum, Chantilly, 9 Jan 1862, PRO, P.R.O. 30/22–57).

119. See Section 2 of Chapter I and Appendices F and U of present investigation.

120. See Appendix F of present investigation.

121. "Notes secrètes de M. Hidalgo," HHSA, cited by CORTI, I, 100.

122. *Ibid.*, I, 100–101. See also Appendices F and T of present investigation.

123. See Appendix U of present investigation.

124. See Appendix F of present investigation.

125. Paléologue-Eugenie Conversation, 10 Jan 1904, cited by PALEOLOGUE, p. 101.

126. *Ibid.*, p. 100.

127. See Section 1 of Chapter III of present investigation.

128. "Notes Secrètes de M. Hidalgo," HHSA, cited by CORTI, I, 101; Paléologue-Eugenie Conversation, 10 Jan 1904, sum. by PALEOLOGUE, p. 100.

129. See Section 1 of Chapter III of present investigation.

130. "Notes secrètes de M. Hidalgo," HHSA, cited by CORTI, I, 101–102.

131. Ibid.

132. See Appendix U of present investigation.

133. Paléologue–Eugenie Conversation, 10 Jan 1904, sum. by PALEOLOGUE, p. 100.

134. See Appendix F of present investigation.

135. Comtesse Stéphanie de Tascher de la Pagerie: *Mon Séjour aux Tuileries, 1852–1858* (Paris, 1893), pp. 179–180; HUBNER, I, 141.

136. "He . . . gives loose to his ideas, lets them follow one another without exercising over them his will, till at last something pleases his imagination; he seizes it, and thinks himself inspired" (Madame

Cornu-Senior Conversation, 7 Apr 1862, cited by SENIOR, II, 116).
See also Grimblot-Senior Conversation, 20 May 1855, cited by Nassau
William Senior: *Conversations with M. Thiers, M. Guizot, and Other
Distinguished Persons, During the Second Empire, by the Late Nassau
William Senior* (2 v., London, 1878), II, 21.

137. See Section I of Chapter III of present investigation.

138. See Appendix F of present investigation. Dawson believes that
it is probable that Napoleon made up his mind before, but no proof is
produced. See DAWSON, pp. 106–107.

139. Paléologue-Eugenie Conversation, 10 Jan 1904, sum. by PALE-
OLOGUE, p. 100.

140. See Appendix F of present investigation.

141. "Finally, I shall not hide from you that, in my husband's
thoughts the elevation of an Austrian archduke to the throne of Mexico,
would one day serve him as an argument to obtain from Francis Joseph
the cession of Venice to Italy" (Paléologue-Eugenie Conversation, 10
Jan 1904, cited by PALEOLOGUE, p. 100. On 2 October 1861
Thouvenel told Cowley that ". . . an Austrian Prince might be placed
on the throne, and that might facilitate an arrangement respecting
Venetia!" (Cowley to Russell, Paris, Pri., 2 Oct 1861, PRO, P.R.O.
30/22–56). In 1863 Eugenie told Metternich that she would like to
see Austria cede Venetia to Italy (Metternich to Rechberg, Paris, 22
Feb 1863, cited by Count Caesar Egon Corti: "Les idées de l'Impératrice Eugénie sur le Redressement de la Carte de L'Europe, d'après
des rapports du Prince Richard de Metternich," *Révue des Etudes
Napoléoniennes: Les Origines de l'europe Nouvelle*, IIe Année, 11
(1922), p. 153.

142. See Appendix F of present investigation.

143. Dawson estimates that it took place between 10 and 15 September 1861. See DAWSON, p. 122.

144. A "Note of General Almonte" (MDAE: *CP, Mex.*, LV) was
sent to the French Ministry of Foreign Affairs. The "Note" proposed
a "general amnesty" and the "calling of an extraordinary congress"
after France, Great Britain and Spain seized Tampico and Vera Cruz.
Since Almonte's Note was merely dated "September 1861," it could
have been transmitted to Thouvenel before or after the Biarritz decision. While Hidalgo telegraphed Almonte, who was in Paris, to
notify him of the decision of making Maximilian a candidate (CORTI,
I, 101), there is no evidence that Almonte was directed to give any
instructions to Thouvenel. There are no marginal notations on the
Almonte Note, but some lines are drawn through wordy sections.

145. At the same time that he telegraphed Almonte (see footnote
143 above), Hidalga telegraphed Estrada that he would have to go to
Vienna on Mexican business. See CORTI, I, 102.

146. *Ibid.*

147. Walewski to Metternich, Biarritz, 16 (r. 17) Sep 1861, HHSA,
cited by DAWSON, p. 108.

148. DAWSON, p. 112.

149. Metternich to Pierre de Lano, Chateau de Koenigswart, Pri., 23 Sep 1861, cited by Pierre de Lano: *The Secret of an Empire: The Empress Eugenie*. Trans. Ethelred Taylor (London, 1895), pp. 132–133.

150. *Ibid.*

151. Metternich to Baron Aldenburg, Koenigswart, Pri., 25 Sep 1861, HHSA, cited by CORTI, 1, 106.

152. Muelinen to Rechberg, Telegram in code, Paris, 27 Sep 1861, HHSA, AKM, sum. by DAWSON, pp. 108–109.

153. Cowley to Russell, Paris, No. 1157, 24 (r. 26) Sep 1861, PRO, F.O. 27/1397.

154. Thouvenel to Flahault, Paris, Pri., 19 Sep 1861, cited by THOUVENEL, II, 168.

155. Cowley to Russell, Paris, No. 1157, 24 (r. 26) Sep 1861, PRO, F.O. 27/1397.

156. Cowley acknowledged receipt the next day. See *ibid.*

157. Lyons to Russell, Washington, No. 481, 10 (r. 23) Sep 1861, ibid., F.O. 5/770.

158. Seward had sent Corwin the authorization on 2 September 1861. See Seward to Corwin, No. 17, 2 Sep 1862, Washington, Dept. of State, *Instructions, Mexico,* XVII, cited by OWSLEY, p. 116.

159. In his instructions to Corwin, Seward stated the United States would pay this interest for five years from 17 July 1861. See footnote 158.

160. In his instructions to Corwin, Seward stated Lower California, Chihuahua, Sonora, and Sinaloa would be pledged. See footnote 158.

161. See Section III of Chapter II of present investigation.

162. Hammon to Russell, Pri., 23 Sep 1861, PRO, P.R.O. 30/22–28.

163. Palmerston to Russell, 94 Piccadilly, 24 Sep 1861, *ibid.,* P.R.O. 30.22–21.

164. Cowley to Russell, Paris, No. 1157, 24 (r. 26) Sep 1861, *ibid.,* F.O. 27/1397.

165. The American Minister to London made Seward's proposal known to Russell on 25 September, and the American Minister to Paris on 27 September. See below in text of present investigation. Mercier, the French Minister to Washington, was on tour with Prince Napoleon in the United States and had not reported the scheme to Thouvenel. See Cowley to Russell, Paris, Pri., 24 Sep 1861, PRO, P.R.O. 30/22–56.

166. Cowley to Russell, Paris, Pri., 24 Sep 1861, PRO, P.R.O. 30/22–56.

167. Cowley to Russell, Paris, No. 1157, 24 (r. 26) Sep 1861, PRO, F.O. 27/1397.

168. Palmerston to Russell, 94 Piccadilly, Pri., 24 Sep 1861, PRO, P.R.O. 30/22–21. Part of this letter has been cited by C. F. Bell: *Lord Palmerston* (2 v., London, 1936), II, 312–313.

169. Hammond observed that Seward's scheme " . . will practically prevent us from enforcing our claims for redress for wrongs due to

British subjects . . ." (Hammond to Russell, Pri., 23 Sep 1861, PRO, P.R.O. 30/22-28).

170. Palmerston Note, 15 Oct. 1861, PRO, P.R.O. 30/22-56.

171. Russell to Cowley, F.O., No. 1005, draft, 23 Sep 1861, PRO, F.O. 27/1379. For further verification, see Section 3 of present investigation.

172. See Text above, between footnotes 65 and 66.

173. Russell to Cowley, F.O., No. 1023, draft, 27 Sep 1861, PRO, F.O. 27/1380.

174. Xavier de Isturiz to Russell, London, 23 (r. 24) Sep 1861, *BSP,* 1862, LXIV, 164.

175. See footnote 68 above.

176. Crampton to Russell, Madrid, Telegram, 11.30 P.M., 24 Sep (r. 6:00 P.M., 25 Sep) 1861, PRO, F.O. 72/1012.

177. See footnote 153 above.

178. See footnote 176 above.

179. Sum. by Duke of Somerset to Russell, Admiralty, Pri., 27 Sep 1861, PRO, P.R.O. 30/22-24.

180. Duke of Somerset to Russell, Admiralty, Pri., 27 Sep 1861, ibid., P.R.O. 30/22-24.

181. Russell to Cowley, F.O., No. 1023, draft, 27 Sep 1861, *ibid.,* F.O. 27/1380. A copy is found in MDAE: *CP, Mex.,* LV.

182. Russell to Crampton, F.O., No. 64, draft, 27 Sep 1861, PRO, F.O. 72/1002.

183. Russell to Queen Victoria, copy, 27 Sep 1861, with undated notation by Queen Victoria, *ibid.,* P.R.O. 30/22-14.

184. Russell Memorandum, 28 Sep 1861, ibid., F.O. 50/358.

185. Russell to Cowley, telegram, 28 Sep 1861, cited by Russell to Cowley, F.O., No. 1029, draft, 28 Sep 1861, *ibid.,* F.O. 27/1380.

186. Russell to Crampton, F.O., telegram, 28 Sep 1861, *ibid.,* F.O. 72/1002.

187. Cowley to Russell, Paris, No. 1166, 27 (r. 28) Sep 1861, *ibid.,* F.O. 27/1397.

188. Dayton to Seward, No. 51, 27 Sep 1861, Washington, Dept. of State, *Despatchs, France,* L, cited by OWSLEY, pp. 116–117.

189. Cowley to Russell, Paris, No. 1166, 27 (r. 28) Sep 1861, PRO, F.O. 27/1397.

190. Thouvenel to Flahault, Paris, Pri., 26 Sep 1861, cited by THOUVENEL, II, 175–176.

191. Cowley to Russell, Paris, No. 1181, 2 (r. 3) Oct 1861, PRO, F.O. 27/1397.


### 3. The Negotiation of the Tripartite Convention of London, Part II, October 1861

1. Russell to Wyke, F.O., No. 44, draft, 10 Sep 1861, marked seen by Palmerston and the Queen, PRO, F.O. 50/351.

2. Russell to Wyke, F.O., No. 43, 10 Sep (r. 30 Oct) 1861, *ibid.,* F.O. 204/153.

3. Russell to Cowley, F.O., No. 1037, draft, 30 Sep 1861, marked seen by Palmerston, *ibid.,* F.O. 27/1380.

4. Russell Memorandum, 2 Oct (1861), *ibid.,* F.O. 50/358.

5. British Merchants Trading with Mexico and Owners of Mexican Bonds to Russell, 30 (r. 30) Sep 1861, *ibid.* There were 142 signatures, and the author of the petition was one J. D. Powles, who had been active in Mexican mining operations. See J. D. Powles to Russell, 10 Austin Friars, 17 (r. 18) Oct 1861, PRO, F.O. 50/358.

6. Draft to British Merchants Trading with Mexico and Owners of Mexican Bonds, F.O., 3 Oct. 1861, PRO, F.O. 50/358.

7. Palmerston Notation, dated 4 Oct. 1861, made on Russell Memorandum, 2 Oct (1861), *ibid.*

8. Hammond to Cowley, F.O., Pri., 5 Oct 1861, *ibid.,* F.O. 519/190.

9. Cowley to Russell, Paris, No. 1181, 2 (r. 3) Oct 1861, *ibid.,* F.O. 27/1397.

10. Cowley to Russell, Paris, Pri., 2 Oct 1861, *ibid.,* P.R.O. 30/22–56..

11. Crampton to Russell, Madrid, Telegram, 1:00 P.M. (r. 6:15 P.M.), 4 Oct 1861, marked copy to Lord Palmerston, *ibid.,* F.O. 72/1012.

12. Barrot to Thouvenel, Madrid, No. 103, 2 (r. 7) Oct 1861, MDAE: *CP, Espagne,* vol. 859.

13. Russell to Crampton, F.O., Telegram, 5 Oct 1861, cited by Russell to Crampton, F.O., No. 79, draft, 5 Oct 1861, PRO, F.O. 72/1002; Russell to Cowley, F.O., Telegram, 5 Oct 1861, cited by Russell to Cowley, F.O., No. 1049, draft, 5 Oct 1861, PRO, F.O. 27/1380.

14. Russell to Cowley, F.O., No. 1056, draft, 5 Oct 1861, PRO, F.O. 27/1380.

15. Russell to Crampton, F.O., No. 83, draft, 5 Oct 1861, *ibid.,* F.O. 72/1002.

16. Cowley to Russell, Paris, No. 1188, 4 (r. 5) Oct 1861, *ibid.,* F.O. 27/1397.

17. Draft to the Admiralty, F.O., 5 Oct 1861, *ibid.,* F.O. 50/358.

18. Cowley to Russell, Paris, No. 1206, 8 (r. 9) Oct 1861, *ibid.,* F.O. 27/1397.

19. Thouvenel to Cowley, Compiègne, 8 Oct 1861, referring to Cowley's letter of 7 Oct 1861, PRO, F.O. 519/207.

20. Cowley to Russell, Paris, No. 1217, 10 (r. 11) Oct 1861, ibid., F.O. 27/1397.

21. Crampton to Russell, Madrid, Telegram, 7 (r. 8) Oct 1861, *ibid.,* F.O. 72/1012.

22. Collantes-Crampton Conversation, 8 Oct 1861, sum. by Crampton to Russell, Madrid, No. 116, 19 (r. 24) Oct 1861, *ibid.,* F.O. 72/1010.

23. *Contemporaneo,* 10 Sep 1861, encl. (with translation) of Cramp-

ton to Russell, San Ildefonso, No. 76, 13 (r. 22) Sep 1861, *ibid.,* F.O. 72/1009.

24. See text of previous section of present investigation, footnoted by footnotes 174 and 176.

25. See text of previous section of present investigation, footnoted by footnote 182. See also text of present section of present investigation, footnoted by footnote 3.

26. Russell to Crampton, F.O., Telegram, 1: 15 P.M., 12 Oct 1861, cited by Russell to Crampton, F.O., No. 87, draft, 12 Oct 1861, PRO, F.O. 72/1002.

27. Russell to Crampton, F.O., Telegram, 2: 45 P.M., 10 Oct 1861, cited by Russell to Crampton, F.O., No. 84, draft, 10 Oct 1861, *ibid.*

28. Hammond to Cowley, F.O., Pri., 9 Oct 1861, ibid., F.O. 519/190.

29. Russell to Cowley, F.O., No. 1069, Con., 7 Oct 1861, and encl., *ibid.,* F.O. 146/979.

30. Romaine to Hammond, Admiralty, 7 (r. 8) Oca 1861, *ibid.,* F.O. 50/358.

31. Russell to Cowley, F.O., No. 1078, draft, 9 Oct 1861, marked seen by Palmerston, *ibid.,* F.O. 27/1380.

32. Romaine to Hammond, Admiralty, 10 (r. 10) Oct 1861, *ibid.,* F.O. 50/358.

33. Sir F. Grey to Hammond Admiralty, 10 (r. 10) Oct 1861, *ibid.*

34. This voluminous correspondence is contained in PRO, F.O. 50/358. These letters resulted from rumors of an impending intervention in Mexico and offered advice and demanded support of claims. Russell merely acknowledged these communications, sometimes saying the matter was under "serious consideration."

35. Extract of Mr. Farlane to Palmerston, n.d., for Russell's information, encl. of Barrington to Elliot, 28 Sep (r. 1 Oct) 1861, PRO, F.O. 50/358. Mr. Elliot was a minor official in the Foreign Office. The modern method was ". . . the use of opium, of Benzoin and of Alcoholic d⁻oughts . . ." in place of ". . . the old debilitating method . . ."

36. Romaine to Hammond, Admiralty, 10 (r. 10) Oct 1861, PRO, F.O. 50/358.

37. Cowley to Russell, Paris, No. 1217, 10 (r. 11) Oct 1861, *ibid.,* F.O. 27/1397.

38. Although the overtures to this effect were made by Eugenie and Estrada (see previous section of present investigation), the Austrian Government realized that ". . . this project originates entirely with the Emperor. . . ." See Metternich-Cowley Conversation, sum. by Cowley to Russell, Paris, No. 141, Con., 11 (r. 12) Feb 1862, *ibid.,* F.O. 17/1432.

39. Maximilian to Leopold I, Miramar, 10 Oct 1861, HHSA, AKM, sum. by DAWSON, p. 112; GAULOT, pp. 3–5.

40. Rechberg-Bloomfield Conversation, 26 Feb 1862, sum. by Bloomfield to Russell, Vienna, No. 94, 27 Feb 1862, PRO, F.O. 356/18. Bloomfield's report seems to have been overlooked hitherto. Dawson

claims that what passed at Rechberg's interview with Maximilian on 4 October remains unknown. See DAWSON, p. 112.

41. Maximilian to Leopold I, Miramar, 8 Oct 1861, HHSA, *AKM,* cited by DAWSON, p. 112.

42. Bloomfield to Russell, Vienna, Pri., 30 Jan 1862, PRO, F.O. 356/38.

43. Metternich-Cowley Conversation, sum. by Cowley to Russell, Paris, No. 141, Con., 11 (r. 12) Feb 1862, *ibid.,* F.O. 27/1432.

44. Maximilian to Leopold I, 1859, cited by CORTI, I, 86.

45. CORTI, I, 70–73, 84–86.

46. Bloomfield to Russell, Vienna, Pri., 16 Jan 1862, PRO, F.O. 356/38; Leopold I to Countess d'Hulst, Laeken, 27 Jan 1865, cited by Comtesse H. Reinach Foussemagne: *Charlotte de Belgique. Impératrice du Mexique* (Paris, 1925), p. 141. (Hereafter referred to as FOUSSEMAGNE).

47. Bloomfield to Russell, Vienna, Pri., 30 Jan 1862, PRO, F.O. 356/38.

48. Rechberg to Muelinen, Vienna, 7 Oct 1861 HHSA, Wrisungen nach Frankreich, cited by DAWSON, p. 114.

49. Metternich-Cowley Conversation, sum. by Cowley to Russell, Paris, No. 141, Con., 11 (r. 12) Feb 1862, PRO, F.O. 27/1432.

50. Rechberg to Muelinen, Vienna, 7 Oct 1861, HHSA, Weisungen nach Frankreich, cited in full by DAWSON, pp. 113–114.

51. Metternich-Cowley Conversation, sum. by Cowley to Russell, Paris, Pri., 6 Mar 1862, PRO, F.O. 519/229.

52. Rechberg to Metternich, Vienna, 28 Jul 1861, HHSA, Weisungen nach Frankreich, cited by DAWSON, p. 102.

53. Maximilian to Rechberg, Miramar, 8 Apr 1862, HHSA, Berufung, cited by DAWSON, p. 220.

54. Leopold I to Countess d'Hulst, Laeken, 27 Jan 1865, cited by FOUSSEMAGNE, p. 141.

55. John Lothrop Motley to Dr. O. W. Holmes, Vienna, 26 Feb 1862, cited by John Lothrop Motley: *The Correspondence of John Lothrop Motley,* ed. by George William Curtis (2 v., New York, 1889), II, 66. Motley was U.S. Minister to Vienna.

56. CORTI, I, 86.

57. Motley to Dr. O. W. Holmes, Vienna, 26 Feb 1862, cited by MOTLEY, II, 66–67.

58. Leopold I to Countess d'Hulst, Laeken, 27 Jan 1865, cited by FOUSSEMAGNE, p. 141.

59. HYDE, p. 117.

60. Chateaurenard to Thouvenel, London, No. 66, 19 (r. 20) Aug 1861, MDAE: CP, *Angleterre,* vol. 720. Chateaurenard was temporarily in charge of the French Embassy in London during Flahault's absence.

61. Franz Joseph to his Mother, Laxenburg, 30 Sep 1861, cited by Franz Schnürer, ed.: *Briefe Kaiser Franz Josephs I. an seine Mutter, 1838–1872* (Munich, 1930) pp. 306–307.

62. Charlotte to Countess d'Hulst, 18 Mar 1866, cited by FOUSSE-MAGNE, pp. 106–107.

63. Leopold I to Countess d'Hulst, 27 Jan 1865, cited by *ibid.*, p. 141.

64. Maximilian to Leopold I, Miramar, 8 Oct 1861, HHSA, *AKM,* cited by DAWSON, p. 144.

65. DAWSON, p. 148.

66. Muelinen—Estrada Conversation, 9 Oct 1861, sum. by Muelinen to Rechberg, 9 Oct 1861, HHSA, Berichte aus Paris, sum. & cited by DAWSON, p. 130.

67. Muelinen to Rechberg, 12 Oct 1861, HHSA, sum. by CORTI, I, 109.

68. Muelinen to Rechberg, Paris, 15 Oct 1861, HHSA, Berichte aus Paris, sum. & cited by DAWSON, p. 115.

69. Muelinen to Rechberg, 9 Oct 1861, HHSA, Berichte aus Paris, sum. and cited by *ibid.*, p. 130.

70. Muelinen to Rechberg, Paris, 15 Oct 1861, HHSA, Berichte aus Paris, sum. by *ibid.*, p. 115.

71. Estrada to Thouvenel, Paris, 21 Place de la Madeleine, Pri. & Con., 9 Oct 1861, MDAE: *CP, Mex.,* vol. 56.

72. See Appendix F of present investigation.

73. Thouvenel-Cowley Conversation, 18 Oct 1861, sum. by Cowley to Russell, Paris, No. 1243, Con., 18 (r. 19) Oct 1861, PRO, F.O. 27/1397.

74. Napoleon III to Leopold I, Compiègne, Pri., 9 Oct 1861, HHSA, sum. by CORTI, I, 111. Dawson dates the letter 11 Oct 1861. See DAWSON, p. 116. The discrepancy may be that Napoleon wrote the letter on 9 October and mailed it on 11 October.

75. Cowley to Russell, Paris, No. 1217, 10 (r. 11) Oct 1861, PRO, F.O. 27/1397.

76. Thouvenel to Flahault, Paris, No. 132, draft, 11 Oct 1861, MDAE: *CP, Angleterre,* vol. 720.

77. Cowley to Russell, Paris, No. 1217, 10 (r. 11) Oct 1861, PRO, F.O. 27/1397.

78. Thouvenel to Flahault, Paris, No. 132, draft, 11 Oct 1861, MDAE: *CP, Angleterre,* vol. 720.

79. Cowley to Russell, Paris, No. 1217, 10 (r. 11) Oct 1861, PRO, F.O. 27/1397.

80. Verbal Note on the measures to be pursued by the combined forces in Mexico, 10 Oct 1861, MDAE: CP, Mex., vol. 56. The measures outlined in the Verbal Note are identical with those proposed by Russell's despatch to Cowley of 9 October. See text footnoted by footnote 31 above.

81. Cowley to Russell, Paris, No. 1218, 10 (r. 11) Oct 1861, PRO, F.O. 27/1397.

82. Cowley to Russell, Paris, Pri., 10 Oct 1861, *ibid.*, P.R.O. 30/22–56.

83. Mon-Thouvenel Conversation, 10 Oct 1861, sum. by Mon to Col-

lantes, Paris, 10 Oct 1861, and Mon to Collantes, Con., 13 Oct 1861, cited respectively by DUVERNOIS, I, 36 and DOMENECH, II 385–386.

84. Barrot to Thouvenel, Madrid, No. 103, 2 (r. 7) Oct 1861, MDAE: *CP, Espagne,* vol. 859.

85. Mon to Collantes, Paris, 10 Oct 1861, cited by DUVERNOIS, I, 36.

86. Mon to Collantes, Con., 13 Oct 1861, cited by Domenech: *Histoire du Mexique,* II, 385.

87. Corti dates the letter 9 October 1861. See CORTI, I, 361–363. Dawson dates it 11 October 1861. See DAWSON, pp. 117–119. A copy of the letter in the archives of the Ministry of Foreign Affairs is only dated "October 1861." See MDAE: *CP, Angleterre,* vol. 720. Eugenie showed the letter to Hidalgo on 10 October 1861. See CORTI, I, 112. The discrepancy could be explained in that Napoleon wrote the letter on 9 October and dated it 11 October. The letter was forwarded to Flahault by Thouvenel on 12 October, the day after Thouvenel saw Napoleon. See below.

88. Thouvenel forwarded the letter the next day. See Thouvenel to Flahault, Paris, 12 Oct 1861, cited by THOUVENEL, II, 179.

89. Thouvenel-Cowley Conversation, 18 Oct 1861, sum. by Cowley to Russell, Paris, No. 1243, Con., 18 (r. 19) Oct 1861, PRO, F.O. 27/1397.

90. Thouvenel to Flahault, Paris, 12 Oct 1861, cited by THOUVENEL, II, 179.

91. Mon-Thouvenel Conversation, 12 Oct 1861, sum. by Mon to Collantes, Paris, 13 Oct 1861, cited by DOMENECH, II, 385–387.

92. Barrot to Thouvenel, Madrid, No. 107, 9 (r. 13) Oct 1861, MDAE: *CP, Espagne,* vol. 859.

93. Cowley-Thouvenel Conversation, 10 Oct 1861, sum. by Thouvenel to Flahault, Paris, No. 132, draft, 11 Oct 1861, MDAE: *CP, Angleterre,* vol. 720.

94. Cowley to Russell, Paris, Nos. 1217 & 1218, 10 (r. 11) Oct 1861, PRO, F.O. 27/1397; Cowley to Russell, Telegram, 2: 45 P.M. (r. 5: 40 P.M.), 10 Oct 1861, cited by Cowley to Russell, Paris, No. 1215, 10 (r. 11) Oct 1861, PRO, F.O. 27/1397; Cowley to Russell, Paris, Pri., 10 Oct 1861, PRO, P.R.O. 30/22–56.

95. Thouvenel-Mon Conversation, 13 Oct 1861, sum. by Thouvenel to Barrot, Paris, No. 38, 15 Oct 1861, MDAE: *CP, Espagne,* vol. 859.

96. OLLIVIER, V, 244–245. On 7 January 1863 Mon announced in the Cortes that he learned of Maximilian's candidacy on 13 October 1861. See DUVERNOIS, I, 48.

97. Cowley-Thouvenel Conversation, 10 Oct 1861, sum. by Thouvenel to Flahault, Paris, No. 132, draft, 11 Oct 1861, encl. of Thouvenel to Barrot, Paris, No. 38, draft, 15 Oct 1861, MDAE: *CP, Espagne,* vol. 859.

98. Thouvenel to Barrot, Paris, No. 38, draft, 15 Oct 1861, MDAE: *CP, Espagne,* vol. 859.

99. *Ibid.*

100. Russell to Cowley, F.O., No. 1096, draft, 12 Oct 1861, marked seen by Palmerston, PRO, F.O. 27/1380.

101. Russell to Cowley, Telegram, 12 Oct 1861, cited by Russell to Cowley, F.O., No. 1088, draft, 12 Oct 1861, *ibid.*

102. Russell to Crampton, F.O., No. 91, draft, 14 Oct 1861, PRO, F.O. 72/1002.

103. See Appendix G of present investigation.

104. Russell Memorandum, 31 Aug 1861, PRO, P.R.O. 30/22–21.

105. Palmerston notation, 11 Sep 1861, made on *Ibid.*

106. Russell to Cowley, F.O., No. 1078, draft, 9 Oct 1861, marked seen by Palmerston, PRO, F.O. 27/1380.

107. Russell to Cowley, F.O. No. 1096, draft, 9 Oct 1861, marked seen by Palmerston, *ibid.*

108. See Appendices A, B, and D of present investigation.

109. Russell to Cowley, F.O., No. 1078, draft, 9 Oct 1861, marked seen by Palmerston, PRO, F.O. 27/1380.

110. See Appendix H of present investigation.

111. See Appendix H of present investigation.

112. See Appendix H of present investigation.

113. Palmerston Note, 15 Oct 1861, sent to Russell, PRO, P.R.O. 30/22–56.

114. Cowley to Russell, Paris, Pri., 18 Oct 1861, *ibid.*

115. Flahault to Thouvenel, London, No. 74, 16 (r. 17) Oct 1861, MDAE: *CP, Angleterre,* vol. 720.

116. *Ibid.*

117. Hammond to Cowley, F.O., Pri., 19 Oct 1861, PRO, F.O. 519/190.

118. Cowley to Russell, Paris, No. 1234, 15 Oct 1861, PRO, F.O. 27/1397. The date of receipt is not marked on this despatch.

119. Cowley to Russell, Paris, No. 1237, 16 (r. 17) Oct 1861 *ibid.*

120. Cowley to Russell, Paris, Pri., 16 Oct 1861, PRO, P.R.O. 30/22–56.

121. Crampton to Russell, Madrid, Telegram, 15 (r. 15) Oct 1861, PRO, F.O. 72/1010. Owing to an interruption of telegraphic communication, Russell's telegram of 10 October, requesting the Spanish Ambassador to London be granted full powers to sign a convention, only reached Crampton on 14 October (Crampton to Russell, Madrid, No. 122, Con., 20 (r. 24) Oct 1861, PRO, F.O. 72/1010).

122. Flahault to Thouvenel, London, No. 74, 16 (r. 17) Oct 1861, MDAE, CP, Angleterre, vol. 720. Flahault's remarks to Russell were the same as Thouvenel's remarks to Cowley on 10 October, summarized in Thouvenel's instruction to Flahault of 11 October, which Flahault read Russell on 16 October. For the Thouvenel-Cowley conversation, see text of present section, between footnotes 76 and 81 above.

123. Flahault to Thouvenel, London, No. 74, 16 (r. 17) Oct 1861, MDAE: *CP, Angleterre,* vol. 720.

124. Cowley to Russell, Paris, Pri., 18 Oct 1861, PRO, P.R.O. 30/22–56.

125. Thouvenel to Flahault, Paris, No. 134, draft, 17 Oct 1861, MDAE: *CP, Angleterre,* vol. 720.

126. Thouvenel to Flahault, Paris, No. 132, draft, 11 Oct 1861, *ibid.* See text of present section, between footnotes 75 and 79.

127. Cowley to Russell, Paris, No. 1249, 18 (r. 19) Oct 1861, PRO, F.O. 27/1398.

128. Thouvenel to Flahault, Paris, No. 134, draft, 17 Oct 1861, MDAE: *CP, Angleterre,* vol. 720.

129. Thouvenel to Barrot, No. 41, draft, 17 Oct 1861, ibid., *Espagne,* vol. 859.

130. Flahault to Thouvenel, London, No. 75, 19 (r. 20) Oct 1861; Flahault to Thouvenel, London, Telegram, 6:50 P.M. (r. 10:00 P.M.), 18 Oct 1861, MDAE: *CP, Angleterre,* vol. 720.

131. See text of present section between footnotes 120 and 124 above.

132. Cited by Cowley to Russell, Paris, Pri., 18 Oct 1861, PRO, P.R.O., 30/22–56.

133. Thouvenel to Napoleon III at Palais de Compiègne, Paris, 1:10 P.M., 18 Oct 1861, MDAE: *CP, Angleterre,* vol. 720.

134. Cowley to Russell, Paris, No. 1243, Con., (r. 19) Oct 1861, PRO, F.O., 27/1397.

135. Cowley to Russell, Paris, No. 1249, 18 (r. 19) Oct 1861, *ibid.,* F.O. 27/1398.

136. Cowley to Russell, Paris, Pri., 18 Oct 1861, PRO, P.R.O. 30/22–56.

137. Cowley to Russell, Paris, No. 1249, 18 (r. 19) Oct 1861, PRO, F.O. 27/1398.

138. Flahault to Thouvenel, London, Telegram, 6:50 P.M. (r. 10:00 P.M.) 18 Oct 1861, MDAE: *CP, Angleterre,* vol. 720.

139. Thouvenel to Flahault, Paris, telegram, 19 Oct 1861, *ibid.*

140. Flahault to Thouvenel, London, No. 75, 19 (r. 20) Oct 1861, *ibid.* See also Appendix I of present investigation.

141. Flahault to Thouvenel, London, No. 75, 19 (r. 20) Oct 1861, MDAE: *CP, Angleterre,* vol. 720.

142. See Appendix I of present investigation. The words, "to seek," appear in the (first) British draft convention sent to Cowley. See Appendix G of present investigation. The copy Russell had before him when he made alterations contained "to ask" instead of "to seek." See Appendix I of present investigation. This alteration may have been the result of a copying mistake.

143. See Appendix I of present investigation. The word, "taken," was substituted for "enforced," and "into effect" replaced "out" (so that the sentence would not end with a preposition).

144. See Appendix G of present investigation.

145. See Russell marginal notation, Appendix H of present investigation.

146. See Appendix I of present investigation.

147. The words, "High Contracting Parties," immediately following what Russell crossed out, were converted from the object of a preposition of the crossed out words to the subject of the words following that were retained. See Appendix I of present investigation.

148. Russell only intend coastal operations against Mexico. In the original Article I it was stated that the allies would send forces "sufficient to capture, to occupy, and to hold the several fortresses, and military positions on the said (i.e. Atlantic) coasts, and to enforce a rigorous blockade of the Cities, Ports, and Harbours of the same." See Appendix G of present investigation. Thouvenel instructed Flahault to inform Russell of the possibility of operations in the interior of Mexico to "protect" the nationals of the allies. See footnote 125 above. Flahault claimed he made all Thouvenel's observations in this instruction known to Russell. See Flahault's No. 75, cited in footnote 130 above.

149. See Appendices H, I, and J of present investigation.

150. See Appendix I of present investigation.

151. Hammond and Palmerston Notes, Appendix I of present investigation.

152. Palmerston Note, Appendix I of present investigation.

153. See Appendix I of present investigation.

154. See Appendix J of present investigation.

155. Russell Note, Appendix I of present investigation.

156. See Appendix K of present investigation, an English translation of Thouvenel's translation.

157. In a document submitted to Napoleon III, dated "October 1861," the first British draft convention, in French, entitled "English Proposal," was written on the right hand side of eight pages (both sides). the left hand side of these pages was entitled "Counter Proposal," under which were comments on the "British Proposal" and the wording of the French "Counter Proposal" (French draft convention). There were no comments or a new rendering opposite the Preface of the first British draft convention. See MDAE: CP, Mex., vol. 56. In his despatch to Flahault, transmitting the French draft convention, Thouvenel stated that the Preamble was just a "repitition" of the British one. See Thouvenel to Flahault, No. 137, 21 Oct 1861, MDAE: *CP, Angleterre,* vol. 720.

158. See Appendix K of present investigation.

159. See Appendix G of present investigation.

160. See Appendix K of present investigation.

161. See Appendix G of present investigation.

162. On the French draft convention submitted to Russell by Flahault, an "x" was placed in the margin next to these words. See "Contre projet francais," PRO, F.O. 50/358.

163. See Appendix L of present investigation.

164. Flahault gave Russell the French draft convention on 22 October 1861. On that occasion Russell gave Flahault a copy of the second British draft convention, containing "to demand" in the Preface. See Flahault to Thouvenel, London, No. 77, 22 (r. 23) Oct 1861, MDAE:

*CP, Angleterre,* vol. 720. For the second British draft convention, see Appendix J of present investigation.

165. See Appendix L of present investigation. For the words "ask" and "seek", see footnote 142 above.

166. See Appendix F of present investigation.

167. See Appendix G of present investigation.

168. Thouvenel to Flahault, No. 137, draft, 21 Oct 1861, MDAE: *CP, Angleterre,* vol. 720.

169. See Appendix K of present investigation.

170. See Appendix G of present investigation.

171. See Appendix K of present investigation.

172. See Appendix K of present investigation.

173. See Appendix G of present investigation.

174. See Appendix K of present investigation.

175. Thouvenel to Flahault, No. 137, draft, 21 Oct 1861, MDAE: *CP, Angleterre,* vol. 720.

176. Thouvenel to Flahault, Paris, No. 139, 25 Oct 1861, *ibid.*

177. Flahault to Thouvenel, London, No. 75, 19 (r. 20) Oct 1861, *ibid.* Thouvenel specifically referred to the contents of this report in his instruction to Flahault to communicate the French draft convention to Russell. See Thouvenel to Flahault, No. 137, 21 Oct 1861, MDAE: *CP, Angleterre,* vol. 720.

178. Thouvenel to Flahault, Paris, 25 Oct 1861, THOUVENEL, II, 183.

179. Compare Article III of Appendix G of present investigation with Article II of Appendix K.

180. See Appendix G of present investigation.

181. See Appendix K of present investigation.

182. See Appendix G of present investigation.

183. Thouvenel to Flahault, No. 137, 21 Oct 1861, MDAE: *CP,* Angleterre, vol. 720.

184. See Appendix K of present investigation.

185. See Appendix G of present investigation.

186. See Appendix K of present investigation.

187. A comment to this effect was written opposite Article V of the (first) British draft convention submitted to Napoleon III. See MDAE: *CP, Mex.,* vol. 56. This is the same document cited in footnote 157 above.

188. See Appendix K of present investigation.

189. MDAE: *CP, Mex.,* vol. 56. This is the same document cited in footnote 157 above.

190. Thouvenel to Flahault, Paris, Pri., 25 Oct 1861, THOU-VENEL, II, 183.

191. Thouvenel to Flahault, No. 137, 21 Oct 1861, MDAE: *CP, Angleterre,* vol. 720.

192. Thouvenel to Barrot, No. 42, 22 Oct 1861, MDAE: *CP, Espagne,* vol. 859.

193. Reports arrived in London and Paris on the same day, 24 October 1861. See footnotes 196 and 197 below.

194. Russell to Crampton, F.O., No. 91, draft, 14 Oct 1861, PRO, F.O. 72/1002.

195. Thouvenel to Barrot, No. 41, draft, 17 Oct 1861, MDAE: *CP, Espagne,* vol. 859. The despatch was Thouvenel's No. 134 to Flahault. See footnote 125 above. The contents of this despatch are summarized in the text of this section above, between footnotes 125 and 128.

196. Crampton to Russell, Madrid, No. 118, 20 (r. 24) Oct 1861, PRO, F.O. 72/1010.

197. Barrot to Thouvenel, Madrid, No. 113, 21 (r. 24) Oct 1861, MDAE: *CP, Espagne,* vol. 859. A very edited version of this despatch appears in *DD, 1862,* p. 57.

198. Collantes to Mon, 22 Oct 1861, *AD,* 1862, III 315, cited by PERKINS, pp. 376–377.

199. Collantes to Spanish Ambassadors in Paris and London, 22 Oct 1861, cited by E. Lefêvre: *Documents Officiels Recuellis dans la Secretairerie Privée de Maximilien* (2 v., Paris, 1870), I, 91, cited by PERKINS, pp. 374–375.

200. Barrot to Thouvenel, Madrid, Telegram, noon (r. 2:00 P.M.), 24 Oct 1861, MDAE: *CP, Espagne,* vol. 859; Crampton to Russell, Telegram, 6:30 P.M. (r. 8:50 P.M.), 23 Oct 1861, PRO, F.O. 72/1010.

201. Owing to an interruption of telegraphic communication, Russell's telegram of 10 October only reached Crampton on 14 October. Collantes and O'Donnell, however, hesitated sending full powers, because Mon, the Spanish Ambassador to Paris, reported that the convention would be signed in Paris. Crampton saw Collantes on 18 October, and the Spanish Minister promised to send full powers to his Ambassador in London after the Spanish Government took the British draft convention into consideration. See Crampton to Russell, Madrid, No. 122, Con., 20 (r. 24) Oct 1861, PRO, F.O. 72/1010.

202. Flahault to Thouvenel, London, No. 77, 22 (r. 23) Oct 1861, MDAE: *CP, Angleterre,* vol. 720.

203. Flahault to Thouvenel, No. 78, 26 (r. 27) Oct 1861, *ibid.*

204. Thouvenel to Flahault, Paris, No. 139, 25 Oct 1861, *ibid.*

205. Flahault to Thouvenel, London, No. 77, 22 (r. 23) Oct 1861, *ibid.*

206. Barrot to Thouvenel, Madrid, Telegram, noon (r. 2:00 P.M.), *ibid., CP, Espagne,* vol. 859.

207. Flahault to Thouvenel, London, No. 77, 22 (r. 23) Oct 1861, *ibid., CP, Angleterre,* vol. 720.

208. Thouvenel to Flahault, Paris, No. 139, 25 Oct 1861, *ibid.*

209. Thouvenel to Flahault, Paris, Pri., 25 Oct 1861, THOUVENEL, II, 183.

210. Thouvenel to Flahault, Paris, No. 139, 24 Oct 1861, MDAE: *CP, Angleterre,* vol. 720.

211. Thouvenel to Flahault, Paris, Pri., 25 Oct 1861, THOUVENEL, II, 183.

212. Thouvenel to Flahault, Paris, No. 139, 25 Oct 1861, MDAE: *CP, Angleterre,* vol. 720.

213. Thouvenel to Barrot, No. 43, 26 Oct 1861, MDAE: *CP, Espagne,* vol. 859.

214. Thouvenel-Cowley Conversation, sum. by Cowley to Russell, Paris, No. 1267, 29 (r. 30) Oct 1861, PRO, F.O. 27/1398.

215. Napoleon III-Cowley Conversation, 8 Mar 1862, sum. & cited by Cowley to Russell, Paris, No. 299, Con., 10 (r. 11) Mar 1862, PRO, F.O. 27/1434.

216. Thouvenel-Cowley Conversation, sum. by Cowley to Russell, Paris, No. 1267, 29 (r. 30) Oct 1861, PRO, F.O. 27/1398.

217. Thouvenel to Flahault, Paris, No. 139, 25 Oct 1861, MDAE: *CP, Angleterre,* vol. 720.

218. *Ibid.*

219. Flahault to Thouvenel, London, Telegram, 4:00 P.M., 25 Oct 1861, *ibid.*

220. Contre projet français, PRO, F.O. 50/358.

221. Russell to Cowley, Pri., 28 Oct 1861, *ibid.,* F.O. 519/199.

222. See footnote 220 above. For this printed Article, see Appendix J of present investigation.

223. Flahault to Thouvenel, London, Telegram, 4:00 P.M., 25 Oct 1861, MDAE: *CP, Angleterre,* vol. 720.

224. Thouvenel to Flahault, Paris, No. 139, draft, 25 Oct 1861, *ibid.*

225. Thouvenel to Flahault, Paris, Pri., 25 Oct 1861, THOUVENEL, II, 183.

226. Thouvenel to Barrot, No. 43, draft, 26 Oct 1861, MDAE: *CP, Espagne,* vol. 859. Thouvenel enclosed the (second) British and French draft conventions, as well as a copy of the despatch to Flahault (see footnote 224 above) which outlined French objections to the (second) British draft convention.

227. Flahault to Thouvenel, No. 78, 26 (r. 27) Oct 1861, MDAE: *CP, Angleterre,* vol. 720.

228. Romaine to Hammond, Admiralty, Immediate and Confidential, 14 (r. 14) Oct 1861, PRO, F.O. 50/358.

229. Draft to Admiralty, F.O., Immediate and Confidential, 14 Oct 1861, *ibid.*

230. Flahault to Thouvenel, No. 78, 26 (r. 27) Oct 1861, MDAE: *CP, Angleterre,* vol. 720.

231. Draft to Admiralty, F.O., Immediate and Confidential, 14 Oct 1861, PRO, F.O. 50/358.

232. Palmerston to Russell, 94 Piccadilly, 9 Nov 1861, Palmerston Papers, British Museum MS. Room, letter book 48582.

233. Russell to Cowley, F.O., No. 713, draft, 19 Jun 1862, marked seen by Palmerston and the Queen, PRO, F.O. 27/1424.

234. See footnote 232 above.

235. Russell to Cowley, F.O., Pri., 27 Dec 1861, PRO, F.O. 519/199. On 5 October 1861 Russell received a report from Cowley that the French Government intended to send a force of about 1000. See foot-

note 16 above. The day after signing the convention, Russell sent a letter to the British Colonial Office, stating the French Government would send 1200 Marines. See Draft to Colonial Office, F.O., 1 Nov 1861, PRO, F.O. 50/358. From the estimates available to Russell before he signed the convention, therefore, his opinion of December 1861, could hardly have been different from that which he held in October 1861, for in December 1861 more than 1200 French troops were underway to Mexico then. See next section of present investigation.

236. Thouvenel to Flahault, Paris, No. 140, 28 Oct 1861, MDAE: *CP, Angleterre,* vol. 720.

237. Barrot to Thouvenel, Madrid, Telegram, 7:40 P.M., 28 Oct 1861, MDAE: *CP, Espagne,* vol. 859.

238. Cited by Flahault to Thouvenel, London, No. 80, 30 (r. 31) Oct, 1861, MDAE: *CP, Angleterre,* vol. 720.

239. This sentence referred to Article II of the (second) British draft convention. See Article IV of Appendix J of present investigation. Compare with Article III of Appendix L.

240. Flahault to Thouvenel, London, No. 80, 30 (r. 31) Oct 1861, MDAE: *CP, Angleterre,* vol. 720.

241. Flahault to Thouvenel, Telegram, 8:10 P.M., 30 Oct 1861, *ibid.*

242. Telegram to Crampton, F.O., 4:30 P.M., 30 Oct 1861, PRO, F.O. 72/1010.

243. Draft to Admiralty, 30 Oct 1861, PRO, F.O. 50/358. This was not sent until 31 Oct 1861. See same instruction, dated 31 Oct 1861, PRO, F.O. 50/358.

244. Thouvenel to Flahault, Paris, Telegram, 11:00 A.M., 31 Oct 1861, MDAE: *CP, Angleterre,* vol. 720.

245. See footnote 214 above.

246. See footnote 215 above.

247. See footnote 214 above.

248. Crampton to Russell, Telegram, 31 (r. "at night") Oct 1861, copy, PRO, F.O. 72/1010.

249. Flahault to Thouvenel, London, Telegram, 4:30 P.M., 31 Oct 1861, MDAE: *CP, Angleterre,* vol. 720. For the convention signed, see Appendix L of present convention.


Chapter IV


*1. The Instructions of the Allies to Their Diplomatic Representatives and Commanders-in-Chief*


1. Cowley to Russell, Paris, No. 1188, 4 (r. 5) Oct 1861, PRO, F.O 27/1397.

2. Romaine to Hammond, 7 (r. 8) Oct 1861, PRO, F.O. 50/358.

3. Romaine to Hammond, Admiralty, Immediate and Confidential, 14 (r. 14) Oct 1861, *ibid.*

4. Telegram to Crampton, F.O., 4:30 P.M., 30 Oct 1861, PRO, F.O. 72/1010.

5. Crampton to Russell, Telegram, 31 (r. "at night") Oct 1861, copy, *ibid.*

6. See footnote 23 of Section 1 of Chapter II of present investigation.

7. See footnote 23 of Section 1 of Chapter II of present investigation. The details of certain claims, such as the Legation Robbery and Laguna Seca, were known. See Section I of Chapter II and Appendix B of present investigation.

8. For an example, see footnote 206 of Section 1 of Chapter II of present investigation.

9. See below in text of this section. See also Sections 2 and 3 of Chapter III of present investigation.

10. See Appendices A, B, and D of present investigation.

11. The French claimants had been paid regularly in the past, and only $190,000 was required to liquidate their claims completely with the 8% of import duties assigned them. The Mexican Government had never completely complied with the terms of the Spanish and British conventions. The Juarez Government did not recognize the validity of Spanish conventions mortgaging 8% of Mexican custom duties to liquidate $9,000,000 in claims. Without the knowledge of the Spanish Government, no Mexican Government had ever applied the 12% mortgaged custom duties to liquidate Spanish claims recognized in 1851. These claims were in the process of liquidation by assigning to them part of the custom duties assigned British claims. British conventions recognized by the Juarez Government mortgaged 16% of Mexican import duties to liquidate British claims that amounted to $4,200,000 in 1861. Agreements made with Juarez by British naval commanders in 1859 and 1860 mortgaged 8% of all Mexican import duties and 5% of those of Vera Cruz and Tampico to pay arrears of over $1,000,000. Since these agreements stipulated that they would be converted into formal conventions if the Powers recognized the Juarez Government, Russell considered these agreements to have the force of conventions. Taking advantage of the technicality that these agreements were not conventions, Juarez refused to accept this view. While Russell refused to support officially the private loans made by British subjects to Mexico, these "London Bondholders" had made arrangements with Mexico in 1850 that 25% of all import duties be turned over to them to pay these debts. Including $12,000,000 in interest arrears, these debts amounted to $63,000,000 in 1861. The agreements of 1859 and 1860 guaranteed the London Bondholders their 25% of all Mexican import duties, in addition to 5% of the import duties collected in Vera Cruz and Tampico to make up arrears. Russell supported this lien, because it was provided for by agreements that he considered had the force of conventions. The liens against all Mexican import duties, therefore, were 77%: 20% (Spanish), 8% (French), 16% (British conventions), 8% (British "agreement" of 1859), 25% (London Bondholders). The British "agreement" of 1860

granted an additional 5% each to the London Bondholders and Con-
Tampico, making a total lien of 87% against import duties collected
vention Bondholders from import duties collected in Vera Cruz and
in these two ports. For British claims, see Appendices A and B of
present investigation. For Spanish claims, see Appendix D of present
investigation. For French claims, see footnote 129 of Section 3 of
Chapter I of present investigation. For $190,000 as the total Mexican
indebtedness recognized by conventions as of 1861, see Wyke to Russell,
Mexico City, No. 7, 25 Jun (r. 29 Jul) 1861, PRO, F.O. 50/353.

12. The chief revenue source of the Mexican Government was custom duties. There remained "additional" duties to be paid on goods
after passing through the Custom Houses. These duties amounted to
about 80% of the initial import duties. See footnote 143 of Section 1
of Chapter II of present investigation. The allies, however, wanted
reparation not only for claims already recognized by conventions but
for claims not yet officially recognized by the Mexican Government.

13. Russell to Admiralty, F.O., draft, 31 Oct 1861, marked seen by
Palmerston and the Queen, PRO, F.O. 50/358. Maitland was not to
seize Mazatlan without special orders.

14. Hammond to Flahault, F.O., Pri., copy, 31 Oct 1861, MDAE:
*CP, Angleterre,* vol. 720.

15. Russell to Wyke, F.O., No. 59, draft, 31 Oct 1861, marked seen
by Palmerston and the Queen, PRO, F.O. 50/351.

16. Russell to Wyke, F.O., No. 60, draft, 1 Nov 1861, marked seen
by Palmerston and the Queen, *ibid.*

17. Romaine to Hammond, Admiralty, 1 (r. 1) Nov 1861, PRO,
F.O. 50/358. The Admiralty reasoned that the Spanish expedition
would assemble at Havana. The French would probably go to Havana
or Port Royal, Jamaica. The British ships could go to Port Royal,
meet the French forces there, and then rendezvous with the Spanish at
the point suggested. It was 175 miles, or one day's sail from Havana,
and 540 miles, or three days' sail from Port Royal. When the date for
the departure from Port Royal were set, a despatch vessel might be
sent the day before from Port Royal to Port Jagna on the southern
coast of Cuba, from whence Havana could be telegraphed.

18. Russell to Cowley, F.O., No. 1178, draft, 1 Nov 1861, PRO,
F.O. 27/1381; Russell to Crampton, F.O., No. 114, draft, 1 Nov 1861,
PRO, F.O. 72/1002.

19. Russell to Cowley, F.O., No. 1176, 1 Nov. 1861, PRO, F.O.
146/982; Russell to Crampton, F.O., No. 112, draft, 1 Nov 1861, PRO,
F.O. 72/1002.

20. Russell to Crampton, F.O., Nos. 112 and 113, drafts, 1 Nov
1861, PRO, F.O. 72/1002; Russell to Cowley, F.O., No. 1176, 1
Nov. 1861, PRO, F.O. 146/982; Russell to Cowley, No. 1177, 1 Nov
1861, sum. by Cowley to Russell, Paris, No. 1298, 5 (r. 6) Nov 1861,
PRO, F.O. 27/1398.

21. Russell to Cowley, F.O., No. 1176, draft, 1 Nov 1861, PRO,
F.O. 27/1381.

22. Russell to Crampton, F.O., No. 112, draft, 1 Nov 1861, PRO, F.O. 72/1002.

23. Time Table for West India Mail Service for the year 1861, encl. of Post Office to Hammand, 30 Jan (r. 2 Feb) 1861, PRO, F.O. 50/357. Russell informed Crampton that the instruction in question would be sent to Wyke on 2 November. See Russell to Crampton, F.O., No. 112, draft, 1 Nov 1861, PRO, F.O. 72/1002. The actual instructions sent to Wyke in 1861 have been preserved, with dates of receipt marked on them, in the Public Record Office (F.O. 204/153). The only instruction in any way connected with the allied expedition that Wyke received in 1861 merely directed him to leave Vera Cruz and obtain instructions to be sent to Admiral Milne. See footnote 24 below.

24. Russell to Wyke, F.O., No. 56, 1 (r. 29) Nov 1861, PRO, F.O. 204/153. At the same time Russell directed the Admiralty to supply the necessary man-of-war to pick up Wyke at Vera Cruz. See Draft to Admiralty, F.O., 1 Nov 1861, PRO, F.O. 50/358.

25. These instructions, Nos 59 and 60 (see text footnoted by footnotes 15 and 16 above), only reached Wyke in January 1862. See PRO, F.O. 204/153.

26. Hammond to Cowley, F.O., Pri., 9 Nov 1861, PRO, F.O. 519/190. Hammond commented that ". . . the French are rather ticklish people to deal with."

27. Lyons to Russell, Washington, 3 Dec 1861, *BSP, 1862,* LXIV, 227.

28. Russell to Lyons, F.O., 6 Nov 1861, *ibid.,* LXIV, 217.

29. See below in text of this section.

30. Russell to Wyke, F.O., No. 64, draft, 15 Nov 1861, PRO, F.O. 50/351.

31. Draft to Colonial Office, 1 Nov 1861, PRO, F.O. 50/358.

32. The words following "Spain" were Palmerston's substitution for the following words of Russell's original draft: "to occupy with his Marines the island and fortress of San Juan de Ulloa." See Draft in Russell and Palmerston's handwritings and final version to Admiralty, F.O., 1 Nov 1861, PRO, F.O. 50/358.

33. These words were Palmerston's substitution for the following words of Russell's original draft: "If he (i.e., Admiral Milne) should be unable to obtain their (i.e., the French and Spanish Commanders') assent, he should at least obtain a separate fort or separate forts, and not form part of a Mixed garrison either with French or Spanish Forces." See Draft in Russell and Palmerston's handwritings and final version to Admiralty, F.O., 1 Nov 1861, PRO, F.O. 50/358.

34. Cowley to Russell, Paris, No. 1299, 5 (r. 6) Nov 1861, PRO, F.O. 27/1398.

35. Count Walewski-Count Muelinen Conversation, Etiolles, 2 Nov 1861, sum. & cited by Muelinen to Rechberg, Paris, 3 Nov 1861, *HHSA,* Berichte aus Paris, sum & cited by DAWSON, p. 125.

36. A telegram of 19 October 1861 to the French Ambassador to

Vienna authorized him confidentially to supply Rechberg with a copy. See SCHEFER, p. 139.

37. Muelinen to Rechberg, 3 Nov 1861, *HHSA,* Berichte aus Paris, sum. & cited by Philip Guedalla: *Palmerston* (London, 1926), pp. 432 and 491.

38. Muelinen to Rechberg, Paris, 3 Nov 1861, *HHSA,* Berichte aus Paris, cited by DAWSON, p. 125.

39. Barrot to Thouvenel, Madrid, Telegram, 2 (r. 2) Nov 1861, MDAE: *CP, Espagne,* vol. 859.

40. Flahault to Thouvenel, London, No. 82, 2 (r. 3) Nov 1861, MDAE: *Cp, Angleterre,* vol. 720.

41. Russell to Cowley, F.O., No. 1176, PRO, F.O. 146/982.

42. Cowley to Russell, Paris, No. 1299, 5 (r. 6) Nov 1861, PRO, F.O. 27/1398.

43. *Ibid.*

44. Flahault-Russell Conversation, 6 Nov 1861, sum. by Draft to Admiralty, F.O., 6 Nov 1861, PRO, F.O. 50/358.

45. Layard-Thouvenel Conversation, sum. by Layard to Russell, Pri., 31 Oct 1861, PRO, P.R.O. 30/22–28. Layard, a British Under-Secretary of State for Foreign Affairs, visited Cowley at the end of October at Chantilly, where Cowley often spent his weekends. Thouvenel also visited Cowley on Sunday, 27 October, and the Thouvenel-Layard Conversation resulted. See Cowley to Russell, Chantilly, Pri., 29 Oct 1861, PRO, F.O. 519/229. In his private letter to Russell, Layard, however, refers to "another conversation" with Thouvenel. Thouvenel's remarks to Layard, therefore, were made between 27 October and 31 October, when Layard wrote his letter.

46. See below.

47. Cowley to Russell, Paris, No. 1299, 5(r. 6) Nov 1861, PRO, F.O. 27/1398.

48. Colonel Claremont to Lord Cowley, Paris, No. 67, Con., 6 Nov 1861, encl. of Cowley to Russell, Paris, No. 1305, 7 (r. 8) Nov 1861, PRO, F.O. 27/1398. Claremont was a military attaché employed in the British Embassy in Paris.

49. See Appendix M of present investigation.

50. Jurien de La Gravière-Colonel Claremont conversation, 6 Nov 1861, sum. by Colonel Claremont to Lord Cowley, Paris, No. 67, Con., 6 Nov 1861, encl. of Cowley to Russell, Paris, No. 1305, 7 (r. 8) Nov 1861, PRO, F.O. 27/1398.

51. CORTI, I, 127.

52. Cowley to Russell, Paris, No. 1299, 5 (r. 6) Nov 1861, PRO, F.O. 27/1398.

53. Napoleon III to Maximilian, Paris, Pri., 14 Jan 1862, *HHSA,* cited by CORTI, I, 365.

54. Cowley to Russell, Paris, Nos. 1296-1299, 5 (r. 6) Nov 1861, PRO, F.O. 27/1398.

55. Thouvenel to Barrot, Telegram, 7.40 P.M., 5 Nov 1861, MDAE: *CP, Espagne,* vol. 859.

56. Barrot to Thouvenel, Madrid, Telegram, 2:29 P.M. (r. 5:20 P.M.), 6 Nov 1861, *ibid.*

57. Barrot to Thouvenel, Madrid, No. 123, 6 (r. 10) Nov 1861, *ibid.* This document was printed in the *DD, 1862* (p. 158), but all of Collantes' comments, except that he agreed with O'Donnell, were omitted.

58. Thouvenel to Flahault, Paris, No. 147, 11 Nov 1861, MDAE: *CP, Angleterre,* vol. 720.

59. Thouvenel to Barrot, No. 46, 12 Nov 1861, MDAE: *CP, Espagne,* vol. 859.

60. This observation has been made by Christian Schefer. See SCHEFER, p. 153.

61. Thouvenel to Jurien, draft, 11 Nov 1861, MDAE: *CP, Mex.,* vol. 57. This document was printed by the Ministry of Foreign Affairs in *DD, 1862* (pp. 123-125) and in *Le moniteur universel* of 20 May 1862. Dexter Perkins takes the document at face value and concludes that Napoleon III had ". . . no fixed intention to impose a government upon the Mexican people by force. . . ." See PERKINS, p. 361.

62. Thouvenel to Flahault, Paris, Pri., 11 Nov 1861, THOUVENEL, II, 186.

63. Thouvenel-Mon conversation, sum. by Chasseloup-Laubet to Jurien, 20 Nov 1861, sum & cited by SCHEFER, pp. 166-167. Chasseloup-Laubet was the French Minister of Marine and Colonies.

64. See Appendix M of present investigation. The head of the political affairs section of the French Ministry of Foreign Affairs noted that ". . . the formal desire of the Emperor has been to invest our admiral with powers which reserve to him, in the last resort, all decisions, and which, if an occasion arose, would subordinate Saligny's mission to his" (Marquis de Banneville to Flahault, Paris, Pri., 14 Nov 1861, THOUVENEL, II 189).

65. Thouvenel to Saligny, No. 15, draft, 11 Nov 1861, MDAE: *CP, Max.,* vol. 56.

66. See footnote 50 above. See also Madame Carette: *My Mistress, the Empress Eugénie; or, Court Life at the Tuileries* (2nd ed., London, 1889), p. 264.

67. Metternich* Napoleon III Conversation, Compiègne, 15 Nov 1861, sum. by Metternich to Rechberg, Compiègne, 16 Nov 1861, HHSA, cited by SALOMON (pp. 156-157), cited and sum. by CORTI (I, 128-129) and DAWSON (pp. 134-135).

68. Metternich to Rechberg, Compiègne, 16 Nov 1861, *HHSA,* Berichte aus Paris, sum. & cited by DAWSON, pp. 125-126.

69. Metternich to Rechberg, Compiègne, 16 Nov 1861, *HHSA, AKM,* sum. by DAWSON, p. 135.

70. Metternich-Napoleon III Conversation, 15 Nov 1861, cited, without source given, by DAWSON, p. 131.

71. Metternich-Napoleon III Conversation, Compiègne, 15 Nov 1861, sum. by Metternich to Rechberg, Compiègne, 16 Nov 1861, *HHSA,* cited by SALOMON, p. 156.

72. Metternich-Napoleon III Conversation, 15 Nov 1861, cited, without source given, by DAWSON, p. 131.

73. See Articles 5 and I of Appendices E and V respectively of present investigation for examples.

74. For further details of a "pretext" thesis, see Appendix C of present investigation.

75. Napoleon III revealed these secret instructions to Lord Cowley on 8 March 1862. For details of Napoleon's remarks, see Appendix C of present investigation. When Cowley told Thouvenel in March 1862 that the claims Saligny had wanted to press were merely an "excuse for remaining in Mexico," Thouvenel replied that ". . . no doubt such was the Emperor's wish. . . ." See Cowley-Thouvenel Conversation, 5 Mar 1862, sum. by Cowley to Russell, Paris, No. 267, Con., 6 (r. 7) Mar 1862, PRO, F.O. 27/1434. When Cowley informed Metternich of Saligny's demands, the Austrian replied that ". . . these demands were made purposely. . . ." See Cowley to Russell, Paris, Pri., 6 Mar 1862, PRO, F.O. 519/229.

76. Metternich to Rechberg, 15 Nov 1861, *HHSA, AKM,* sum. by DAWSON, p. 135.

77. The French expeditionary forces left Toulon between 12 and 29 November and arrived at Vera Cruz between 7 January and 16 February 1862. See Percy F. Martin: *Maximilian in Mexico: The Story of the French Intervention, 1861–1867* (New York, 1915), p. 94.

78. See below.

79. Admiral de la Roncière-Captain Hore Conversation, sum. by Captain Hore to Cowley, Paris, Pri., 18 Nov 1861, PRO, F.O. 519/241. Coal was ordered at Sidney, Cape Breton and Cardiff.

80. See Section 1 of Chapter V of present investigation.

81. Napoleon III-Cowley Conversation, 12 May 1862, sum. by Cowley to Russell, Paris, Pri., 13 May 1862, PRO, P.R.O. 30/22–57.

82. Napoleon III-Cowley Conversation, 8 Mar 1862, sum & cited by Cowley to Russell, Paris, No. 299, Con., 10 (r. 11) Mar 1862, PRO, F.O. 27/1434.

83. *Ibid.* Cowley reported: "His idea had been, that the expeditionary forces should have possessed themselves of Vera Cruz, and that the Commissioners should then have sent in their demands for redress, taking up with the troops such a forward position, as circumstances might have ordered necessary."

84. Napoleon III-Cowley Conversation, 8 Mar 1862, sum. & cited by Cowley to Russell, Paris, No. 299, Con., 10 (r. 11) Mar 1862, PRO, F.O. 27/1434.

85. Jurien to Thouvenel, at sea, 150 leagues from Martinique, 9 Dec 1861, MDAE: *CP, Mex.,* vol. 57. Jurien thanked Thouvenel for the 50,000 francs. A franc was approximately $0.20.

86. Santa Anna lost a leg while fighting the French during the "Pastry War." See 45 of Section 3 of Chapter I of present investigation. Santa Anna led the Mexican armies against the Americans during the Mexican War (1846–1848).

87. Santa Anna to Estrada, Con., 15 Feb 1862, encl. of Estrada to Thouvenel, Hotel Westminster, 13 Rue de la Paix, Paris, 5 Mar 1862, MDAE: *CP, Mex.,* vol. 58.

88. Serrano to Collantes, Havana, No. 89, 16 Dec 1861, *Diario de Las Sessiones de los Diputados, 2 Jun 1862, Apéndice Primero Num. 133,* (trans.) encl. of Crampton to Russell, Madrid, No. 255, 16 (r. 26) Jun 1862, PRO, F.O. 72/1035.

89. Santa Anna's letter reached the French Ministry of Foreign Affairs in 1862. See footnote 87 above. Serrano's report was published in 1862. See footnote 88 above.

90. Comte Fleury: *Souvenirs du Général Comte Fleury* (2 v., Paris, 1897–1898), II, 266–267.

91. See Section 2 of Chapter III of present investigation.

92. Section 1 of Chapter V of present investigation.

93. Conversations of Sebastion Schertzenlechner with Hidalgo and Almonte at Paris at the end of October 1861, sum. by Schertzenlechner to Maximilian, (Trieste, 6 Nov 1861), HHSA, sum. and cited by DAWSON, pp. 149–150. Corti gives the complete reference. See CORTI, I, 119.

94. Saligny to Thouvenel, Mexico City, No. 47, 29 Sep (r. 30 Oct) 1861, MDAE: *CP, Mex.,* vol. 55.

95. Napoleon answered, "They wear blue ones." He referred to the blue trousers of the French marines at first only intended to be sent to Mexico.

96. CORTI, I, 127.

97. See text above, footnoted by footnote 53.

98. CORTI, I, 127.

99. See text above, footnoted by footnote 50.

100. See Section 3 of Chapter III of present investigation.

101. See Section 1 of Chapter III of present investigation.

102. See Section 3 of Chapter III of present investigation. See also Palmerston-Flahault Conversation, (October 1861), sum. by Russell in Russell-Apponyi Conversation, February 1862, sum. by Apponyi to Rechberg, London, 15 Feb 1862, HHSA, Berichte aus London, sum. & cited by DAWSON, p. 127. Apponyi was Austrian Ambassador to London, and this report disillusioned the Austrian Government about British "approval."

103. See Section 3 of Chapter III of present investigation. See also Russell-Flahault Conversation, and Palmerston-Flahault Conversation, (October 1861), sum. by Flahault in Flahault-Apponyi Conversation, Feb 1862, sum. by Apponyi to Rechberg, London, 28 Feb 1862, sum. & cited by DAWSON, p. 127.

104. See Sections 2 and 3 of Chapter III of present investigation.

105. In his confidential instructions to Jurien, approved by Napoleon III, Thouvenel observed that the British Government "broached" the possibility of extending operations beyond Vera Cruz with "an extreme repugnance." The reason Thouvenel suggested was one that reconciled this attitude with what was told Flahault: "Parliamentary considera-

tions, without doubt, would have determined, theoretically, this negative response." See Appendix M of present investigation. Since these
instructions were communicated neither to the Austrian Government
nor to the Spanish Government, there was no reason to deceive Jurien.
He was trusted as having "prudence" enough not to "compromise
anything." See Thouvenel to Flahault, Paris, Pri., 21 Nov 1861,
THOUVENEL, II, 192.

106. Baron Beyens to Belgian Foreign Office, 30 Oct 1861, cited by
BEYENS, II, 239.

107. See footnote 74 of Section 3 of Chapter III of present investigation.

108. Leopold I to Napoleon III, Pri., 16 Oct 1861, HHSA, cited by
CORTI, I, 111.

109. Leopold I to Queen Victoria, Laeken, 17 Oct 1861, cited by
*Letters of Queen Victoria*, Series 1, III, 453.

110. See footnote 45 above.

111. Thouvenel-Layard Conversation, sum. by Layard to Russell, 31
Oct 1861, PRO, P.R.O. 30/22–28.

112. Thouvenel to Flahault, Paris, No. 147, draft, 11 Nov 1861,
MDAE: *CP, Angleterre,* vol. 720.

113. Collantes to Isturitz, Telegram, 7 Nov 1861, sum. by Isturitz to
Collantes, London, No. 219, 13 Nov 1861, *Diario de Las Sessiones de
Cortes. Congreso de los Diputados, 2 Jun 1862, Apéndice Primero
Num. 133,* (trans.) encl. of Crampton to Russell, Madrid, No. 255, 16
(r. 26) Jun 1862, PRO, F.O. 72/1035.

114. Flahault to Thouvenel, London, No. 86, 13 (r. 14) Nov 1861,
MDAE: *CP, Angleterre,* vol. 720.

115. Palmerston to Russell, 94 Piccadilly, Pri., 9 Nov 1861, PRO,
P.R.O. 30/22–21.

116. *Ibid.*

117. Hammond to Cowley, F.O., Pri., 9 Nov 1861, PRO, F.O. 519/
190.

118. Collantes to Isturitz, Telegram, (r. 10 Nov 1861), sum. by Isturitz to Collantes, London, No. 219, 13 Nov 1861, *Dinario de Las Sessiones de Cortes. Congreso de los Diputados, 2 Jun 1862, Apéndice
Primero Num. 133,* (trans.) encl. of Crampton to Russell, Madrid, No.
255, 16 (r. 26) Jun 1862, PRO, F.O. 72/1035.

119. Isturitz to Collantes, London, No. 219, 13 Nov 1861, *ibid.*

120. Flahault to Thouvenel, London, No. 86, 13 (r. 14) Nov 1861,
MDAE: *CP, Angleterre,* vol. 720.

121. Thouvenel to Flahault, Paris, No. 147, draft, 11 Nov 1861, *ibid.*

122. See Appendix L of present investigation.

123. Thouvenel to Flahault, Telegram, 11:30 A.M. (14 Nov 1861?),
MDAE: *CP, Angleterre,* vol. 720.

124. Russell to Wyke, F.O., No. 64, draft, 15 Nov 1861, marked
seen by Palmerston, the Cabinet and the Queen, PRO, F.O. 50/351.

125. Draft to Admiralty, 15 Nov 1861, marked seen by Palmerston,
the Cabinet and the Queen, PRO, F.O. 50/358. The only change was

that what Russell had written Wyke directly was to be communicated by the Admiralty to Admiral Milne.

126. Duke of Somerset to Russell, Admiralty, Pri., 14 Nov 1861, PRO, P.R.O. 30/22–24.

127. Draft to Admiralty, F.O., 15 Nov 1861, marked seen by Cabinet and Queen, PRO, F.O. 50/358.

128. Russell to Wyke, F.O., No. 65, draft, 15 Nov 1861, marked seen by Cabinet and Queen, PRO, F.O. 50/351.

129. Lord Clarendon claimed it was "Palmerstonian." For this comment and an example concerning Mexican affairs, see Lord Clarendon to Sir G. C. Lewis, Grosvenor Crescent, 4 Oct 1861, cited by Sir Herbert Maxwell, ed.: *The Life and Letters of George William Frederick, Fourth Earl of Clarendon, K.G., G.C.B.* (2 v., London, 1913), II, 240.

130. Palmerston to Russell, Pri., 7 Oct 1861, PRO, P.R.O. 30/22–21.

131. *Ibid.*

132. Sir George C. Lewis to Lord Clarendon, Harpton, 27 Oct 1861, cited by Sir Herbert Maxwell, ed.: *The Life and Letters of George William Frederick, Fourth Earl of Clarendon, K.G., G.C.B.* (2 v., London, 1913), II, 242.

133. See footnotes 13, 15, 16 above.

134. See footnotes 124, 125, 127, and 128 above.

135. See Appendix B of present investigation.

136. "The Case of the holders of Bonds of the National Debt contracted by Mexico in London," encl. of Committee of Mexican Bondholders, 10 Basinghall St., London, 23 (r, 26) Nov 1861, PRO, F.O. 97/280. This "Case" is one of the sources upon which Appendix B of the present investigation is based.

137. These negotiations were unofficial, because Wyke had suspended diplomatic relations in July 1861. See Section I of Chapter II of present investigation.

138. Wyke to Russell, Mexico City, No. 46, 28 Oct (r. 27 Nov) 1861, PRO, F.O. 50/354. For these negotiations, see Section 1 of Chapter II of present investigation.

139. Russell to Wyke, F.O., No. 69, draft, 28 Nov 1861, PRO, F.O. 50/351.

140. War Office to Hammond, 15 (r. 15) Nov 1861, PRO, F.O. 50/358. Since the Marines were not permitted to march inland, they would have to leave Vera Cruz in April 1862.

141. Russell to Crampton, F.O., No. 130, draft, 28 Nov 1861, PRO, F.O. 72/1002.

142. Russell to Cowley, F.O., No. 1324, draft, 2 Dec 1861, PRO, F.O. 27/1382.

143. For this convention, see Appendix E. of present investigation. For the negotiation of this convention, see Section 2 of Chapter II of present investigation.

144. Cowley to Russell, Paris, No. 1398, 3 (r. 4) Dec 1861, PRO, F.O. 27/1399.

145. Crampton to Russell, Madrid, No. 188, 15 (r. 22) Dec 1861, PRO, F.O. 72/1011.

146. Russell to Wyke, F.O., No. 82, draft, 26 Dec 1861, PRO, F.O. 50/351.

147. Prim's speech in Senate of the Cortes, 9 Dec 1862, translated into English from *Diario de las Sesiones de Cortes,* encl. 2 of Crampton to Russell, Madrid, No. 417, 27 (r. 31) Dec 1862, PRO, F.O. 72/1040. (Hereafter referred to as Prim-Senate-9 Dec 1862. Prim's speeches before the Senate on 10 and 11 December 1862, also translated and enclosed with Crampton's No. 417, hereafter will be referred to as Prim-Senate-10 Dec 1862, and Prim-Senate-11 Dec 1862).

148. Prim-Senate-9 Dec 1862. Prim was a leader of the "Progresistas" in O'Donnell's "Liberal Union."

149. Prim-Senate-9 Dec 1862. Prim was merely a Senator.

150. VERDUIN, p. 129. Prim especially distinguished himself in the Moroccan War (1859–1860).

151. Prim-Senate-9 Dec 1862.

152. *Ibid.*

153. Royal Decree, 13 Nov 1861, *Gazette,* Madrid, 19 Nov 1861, encl. of Crampton to Russell, Madrid, No. 155, 14 (r. 19) Nov 1861, PRO, F.O. 72/1011.

154. Royal Decree, 17 Nov 1861, *Gazette,* Madrid, 19 Nov 1861, encl. of *ibid.*

155. See Appendix N of present investigation.

156. See Section 2 of Chapter III of present investigation, between footnotes 17 and 19. See also Section 2 of Chapter IV of present investigation, footnote 78.

157. See Section 2 of Chapter IV of present investigation, between footnotes 90 and 91.

158. See Section 1 of Chapter III of present investigation, between footnotes 22 and 25.

159. *Contemporaneo,* 10 Sep 1861, encl. (with trans.) of Crampton to Russell, San Ildefonso, No. 76, 13 (r. 22) Sep 1861, PRO, F.O. 72/1009.

160. See Section 2 of Chapter III of present investigation, between footnotes 24 and 25. See also Section 2 of Chapter IV of present investigation, between footnotes 90 and 91.

161. See Appendices D and N of present investigation.

162. See Appendices D and N of present investigation.

163. See Appendix D of present investigation.

164. See Appendices D and N of present investigation.

165. See Appendix N of present investigation.

166. See Section 3 of Chapter I of present investigation, between footnotes 101 and 106.

167. See Appendix D of present investigation.

168. See Section 1 of Chapter III of present investigation, between footnotes 93 and 95. See also Appendix D of present investigation.

169. See Section 3 of Chapter V of present investigation, between footnotes 28 and 29.

170. See Section 3 of Chapter V of present investigation, between footnotes 28 and 29.

171. See Section 3 of Chapter V of present investigation, between footnotes 28 and 29.

172. See Section 3 of Chapter V of present investigation, between footnotes 164 and 165.

173. See Section 2 of Chapter IV of present investigation, between footnotes 88 and 89.

174. See Section 2 of Chapter III of present investigation, between footnotes 25 and 26.

175. Prim-Senate-9 Dec 1862.

176. VERDUIN, 6. 122. Other cults were permitted private rites.

177. Speech of Senor Rios Roasas in House of Deputies of Cortes, 14 Jun 1862, English summary of *Diario de las Sesiones de Cortes, No. 142,* encl. of Crampton to Russell, Madrid, No. 262, 18 Jun (r. 7 Jul) 1862, PRO, F.O. 72/1035.

178. VERDUIN, p. 131.

179. Schurz to Seward, 27 Sep 1861, Washington; Dept of State, Despatches, Spain, PERKINS, p. 376.

180. Beyens to Belgian F.O., 19 Oct 1861, BEYENS, I, 239.

181. ABBOTT, p. 630; H. Leonardon: "L'Espagne et La Question Du Mexique, 1861–1862, *"Annales des Sciences Politiques,* XVI (1901) 68; PERKINS, p. 377. See also footnote 97 of Section 1 of Chapter III of present investigation.

182. See Section 3 of Chapter V of present investigation, between footnotes 28 and 29.

183. See Section 3 of Chapter V of present investigation, between footnotes 28 and 29.

184. See Sections 2 and 3 of Chapter III of present investigation.

185. See Section 3 of Chapter III of present investigation, between footnotes 11 and 12.

186. See Section 3 of Chapter III of present investigation, between footnotes 84 and 85.

187. See Sections 2 and 3 of Chapter III of present investigation.

188. See Sections 2 and 3 of Chapter III of present investigation.

189. See Section 2 of Chapter V of present investigation, between footnotes 71 and 72.

190. See Section 3 of Chapter III of present investigation, between footnotes 197 and 198: Section 2 of Chapter V of present investigation, between footnotes 20 and 21; Section 2 of Chapter V of present investigation, between footnotes 136 and 137.

191. See Section 3 of Chapter V of present investigation, between footnotes 164 and 165.

192. See Section 2 of Chapter VI of present investigation, between footnotes 31 and 32.

193. See Section 2 of Chapter VI of present investigation, between footnotes 31 and 32.

194. See Appendix N of present investigation.

195. See Section 1 of Chapter IV of present investigation, between footnotes 54 and 55.

196. Prim-Senate-9 Dec 1862.

197. See Section 2 of Chapter V of present investigation, between footnotes 72 and 73 and between footnotes 140 and 142.

198. See below (Prim's remarks to Schurz).

199. See Sections 1 and 3 of Chapter I of present investigation.

200. Prim-Senate-9 Dec 1862.

201. Prim had married Mlle. Agüero, the niece of Gonzales Echeverria. See PRIM, p. 45. In November Gonzales Echeverria became Juarez' Minister of Finance. See Wyke to Russell, Mexico City, No. 51, 25 Nov 1861 (r. 1 Jan 1862), PRO, F.O. 50/354.

202. Prim-Senate-9 Dec 1862; Prim-Senate-10 Dec 1862; Prim-Senate-11 Dec 1862.

203. Schurz to Seward, 16 Nov 1861, Washington: Dept. of State, *Despatches, Spain,* PERKINS, pp. 380–381.

## 2. The Arrival of the European Expeditionary Forces in Mexico: European and American Reactions

1. Percy F. Martin: *Maximilian in Mexico: The Story of the French Intervention, 1861–1867* (N.Y., 1914), p. 94.

2. Cowley told Thouvenel that the British Marines would not go beyond Vera Cruz and Tampico (Thouvenel to Flahault, Paris, Pri., 21 Nov 1861, THOUVENEL, II, 192). A copy of Russell's instructions of 15 November 1861, containing comments on Jurien's instructions and giving reasons for not sending the Marines to Mexico City (see text footnoted by footnote 124 of Section 1 of Chapter IV of present investigation), was sent to the French Ministry of Foreign Affairs, and is filed in its archives (*CP, Mex.,* vol. 56).

3. Thouvenel to Flahault, Paris, Pri., 21 Nov 1861, THOUVENEL, II, 192–193.

4. Thouvenel to Jurien, draft, 29 Nov 1861, MDAE: *CP, Mex.,* vol. 57.

5. Jurien to Thouvenel, at sea, 250 leagues from Martinique, 7 Dec 1861, *ibid.*

6. When a reference was made to Mexico, it was only to state public apathy. See Lynn M. Case: *French opinion on the United and Mexico, 1860–1867: Extracts from the Reports of the Procureurs Generaux* (New York and London, 1936), p. 310, summarizing documents cited (pp. 309–435).

7. *Revue des Deux Mondes,* 1 Oct 1861, Eugene Forcade, sum. & cited by H. Reed West: *Contemporary French Opinion on the American Civil War* (Johns Hopkins University Studies in Historical and

Political Science, Series XLII, No. 1. Baltimore, 1924), p. 116 (Hereafter referred to as WEST). *Journal des Débats*, 11 Nov 1861, J.-J. Weiss, sum. by WEST, p. 116. Forcade lamented that the United States would not end its "vainglorious isolation" and join the expedition. Weiss believed the expedition would challenge the Monroe Doctrine.

8. *Revue Contemporaine*, 31 Oct 1861, cited by Frank Edward Lally: *French Opposition to the Mexican Policy of the Second Empire* (Johns Hopkins University Studies in Historical and Political Science, Series XLIX, No. 3. Baltimore, 1931), p. 5, f. 33. (Hereafter referred to as LALLY). The objection that the European Powers sought to violate the Monroe Doctrine "disappeared" owing to the ". . . design to invite the cooperation of the Washington government."

9. *Journal des Débats*, 26 Sep 1861, Louis Alloury, sum. by WEST, p. 116.

10. Journal des Débats, 4 Oct 1861, Louis Alloury, sum. by WEST, p. 116.

11. *Journal des Débats*, 9 Oct 1861, Prévost-Paradol, sum. & cited by Pierre Guiral: *Prévost-Paradol (1829–1830): Pensée et action d'un Libéral Sous le Second Empire* (Paris, 1955), pp. 297–298.

12. See footnote 7 above for Weiss' article of 11 November 1861. In November 1861 the *Correspondant* reported a rumor that the expedition would break Lincoln's blockade of the Confederacy (vol. LIX, 567, Nov 1861, P. Douhaire, sum. by WEST, p. 116).

13. Prince Napoleon's press organ foresaw that the expedition would cause Northern and Confederate "jealousy." See L'Opinion Nationale, 21 Dec 1861, cited by Lally, p. 33.

14. Grey, in Cowley's absence, reported to Russell: "Attached to the Ministry of the Interior there is a department for the supervision of the Press, at the head of which is a M. Gourdon. His office is a house immediately behind that now occupied by M. de Persigny, and in this office there is a large room in which the representatives of the Press daily meet to receive the latest news from M. Gourdon, which he in his turn has obtained from the Foreign Office" (Grey to Russell, Paris, No. 72, Con., 7 (r. 8) Jun 1862, PRO, F.O. 27/1392. See also Lynn M. Case: *French Opinion on War and Diplomacy during the Second Empire* (Philadelphia, 1954), pp. 3–6.

15. The two chief investigators of French press opinion on the Mexican expedition do not cite any comments. See LALLY and WEST.

16. For details, see Section 2 of Chapter II of present investigation.

17. *Le Constitutionnel*, 3 Oct 1861, sum. by De La Fuente to Thouvenel, Paris, Personnal, 9 Oct 1861, MDAE: *CP, Mex.*, vol. 56. De La Fuente protested that no attempt had been made against Saligny's life and enclosed the notes of the Mexican investigator of the affair. As Juarez' agent, De La Fuente apparently carefully read the French press. His letters, official and private, were filed in the French archives of the Ministry of Foreign Affairs in the volumes of *CP, Mex.* This protest was the only one of the kind that De la Fuente made in 1861.

18. Imperial Decree, Compiègne, 20 Nov 1861, cited by Le Moniteur, 22 Nov 1861.

19. Admiralty to F.O., 30 Sep 1861, sum. by Draft to Admiralty, F.O., 5 Oct 1861, PRO, 50/358.

20. Somerest to Russell, Admiralty, Pri., 27 Sep 1861, PRO, P.R.O. 30/22–24.

21. Draft to Admiralty, F.O., 1 Nov 1861, PRO, F.O. 50/358.

22. See Section 1 of Chapter IV of present investigation.

23. Draft to Colonial Office, F.O., 6 Nov 1861, PRO, F.O. 50/358.

24. Draft to Admiralty, F.O., 7 Nov 1861, *ibid.*

25. Romaine to Hammond, Admiralty, 25 (r. 25) Nov 1861, *ibid,* Von Donop to Wyke, HMS Jason off Sacrificios, 5 Dec 1861, encl. of Von Donop to Dunlop, HMS Jason, Vera Cruz, n.d., both encls. of Milne to Secretary of Admiralty, Terror at Bermuda, 13 Jan 1862, all encls. of Romaine to Hammond, Admiralty, 12 (r. 13) Feb 1862, PRO, F.O. 50/370.

26. Von Donop to Wyke, HMS Jason off Sacrificios, 5 Dec 1861. See footnote 25 above.

27. Wyke to Von Donop, Mexico City, 9 Dec 1861, encl. of Von Donop to Dunlop, HMS Jason, Vera Cruz, n.d., both encls. of Milne to Secretary of Admiralty, Terror at Bermuda, 13 Jan 1862, all encls. of Romaine to Hammond, Admiralty, 12 (r. 13) Feb 1862, PRO, F.O. 50/370.

28. Somerest to Russell, Admiralty, Pri., 7 Jan 1862, PRO, P.R.O. 30/22–24.

29. Milne to Senior Naval Officer in Jamaica, sum. by Milne to Dunlop, Bermuda, 20 Dec 1861, encl. of Milne to Secretary of Admiralty, Nile at Bermuda, 25 Dec 1861, all encls. of Romaine to Hammond, Admiralty, 20 (r. 21) Jan 1862, PRO, F.O. 50/370.

30. Draft to Admiralty, F.O., 16 Nov 1861, PRO, F.O. 50/358.

31. Draft to Admiralty, F.O., 18 Nov 1861, *ibid.*

32. Draft to Admiralty, F.O., 16 Nov 1861, *ibid.*

33. Draft to Admiralty, F.O., 8 Nov 1861, *ibid.*

34. See Section 1 of Chapter IV of present investigation.

35. Romaine to Hammond, Admiralty, 19 Nov 1861, PRO, F.O. 50/358.

36. Somerset to Russell, Admiralty, Pri., 16 Nov 1861, PRO, P.R.O. 30/22–24.

37. Wyke to Russell, Vera Cruz, No. 20, 15 Feb (r. 31 Mar) 1862, PRO, F.O. 50/364.

38. Palmerston Brunnow conversation, 8 Sep 1861, sum. by Palmerston to Russell, 94 Piccadilly, 9 Sep 1861, British Museum Additional MS. Room, Palmerston Papers, vol. 48582.

39. See Section 1 of Chapter III of present investigation.

40. Committee of Mexican Bondholders to Russell, 10 Basinghall St., London, 26 Aug (r. 2 Sep) 1861, with encl., sketch of instructions of Committee of Bondholders to Charles Whitehead, their agent in Mexico, PRO, F.O. 97/280.

41. Draft to Bondholders, 3 Sep 1861, initiated R(ussell), PRO, F.O. 97/280.

42. Brown, President of Liverpool Chamber of Commerce, to Russell, 10 (r. 11) Sep 1861; Memorial of Board of Directors of Manchester Chamber of Commerce to Russell, 11 (r. 12) Sep 1861, PRO, F.O. 50/358.

43. Draft to Liverpool Chamber of Commerce, F.O., 17 Sep 1861; Draft to Manchester Chamber of Commerce, F.O., 17 Sep, *ibid.*

44. Draft to Messrs. Bates Stokes & Co., F.O., 17 Sep 1861; Draft to William Orr, F.O., 11 Oct 1861; Draft to Mr. Bacon, 3 Oct 1861, *ibid.*

45. Bates Stokes & Co. to Russell, Liverpool, 7 (r. 17) Sep 1861, *ibid.*

46. William Orr to Russell, London, 1 (r. 7) Oct 1861, *ibid.*

47. John Bacon to Russell, 27 Sep 1861, *ibid.*

48. Tho. Green to Russell, 30 Cornhill, London, 16 (r. 20) Sep 1861, *ibid.*

49. J. D. Powles to Russell, 10 Austin Friars, 17 (r. 18) Oct 1861, *ibid.*

50. Mexican Merchants and Creditors to Russell, 30 (r. 30) Sep 1861, *ibid.* There were 45 signatures with London addresses attached, 38 representing Liverpool, 39 representing Manchester, and 20 of miscellaneous places or places not stated.

51. See footnote 50 above.

52. *The Times,* London, 18 Sep 1861.

53. See footnote 50 above.

54. D. Robertson to Russell, Berwick upon Tweed, 22 Sep 1861, PRO, P.R.O. 30/22–74.

55. *The Times,* London, 5 Jul 1861.

56. *The Times,* London, 27 Sep 1861.

57. See footnote 50 above.

58. Draft to British Merchants Trading with Mexico and owners of Mexican Bonds, F.O., 3 Oct 1861, PRO, F.O. 50/358.

59. Flahault to Thouvenel, London, No. 74, 16 (r. 17) Oct 1861, MDAE: *CP, Angleterre,* vol. 720. Russell's letter was published in the *AD, 1861* (IV, 399) without a reference to which British newspaper published it. Nor does Flahault give such a reference except that Russell's letter was made public.

60. *The Times,* London, 4 Oct 1861.

61. Palmerston to Russell, Pri., 7 Oct 1861, PRO, P.R.O. 30/22–21.

62. Letter of Whitehead, 6 Sep 1861, sum. by Committee of Mexican Bondholders to Russell, 10 Basinghall St., London, 17 (r. 22) Oct 1861, PRO, F.O. 97/280.

63. Committee of Mexican Bondholders to Russell, 10 Basinghall St., London, 17 (r. 22) Oct 1861, *ibid.* Russell sent Wyke a copy of this request for his comments (Russell to Wyke, F.O., No. 63, n.d. Nov 1861 (r. 6 Jan 1862), PRO, F.O. 204/153). Wyke replied that he did not see that the Bondholders had any stronger claim to Mexican wastelands than any other class of British creditors. The bondholders, in fact, did

not ". . . stand at the head of our very long list." See Wyke to Russell, Vera Cruz, No. 13, 31 Jan 1862, PRO, F.O. 204/160.

64. Messrs. McCalmont, Brothers & Co. to Russell, 7 (r. 8) Oct 1861, PRO, F.O. 50/358.

65. See footnote 73 below.

66. McCalmont, Brothers and Co. to Earl Russell, 3 Crown Court, London, 7 Oct 1861, cited by *The Daily News, The Morning Herald, The Evening Herald,* the *Morning Star,* and the *Dial,* in turn cited by David Robertson: *The "Mexican Bondholders." Letters of Messrs. Mc-Calmont, Brothers, & Co., and Reply thereto, by David Robertson, Esq., M.P., Honarary Chairman* (London, 1861), p. 3. (Hereafter referred to as ROBERTSON). A copy marked received 4 January 1862 is in the Public Record Office (F.O. 97/280).

67. David Robertson to Messrs. McCalmont, Brothers, & Co., 10 Basinghall St., London, 21 Oct 1861, cited by ROBERTSON, p. 8.

68. See footnote 70 below.

69. Richard Garde to Russell, 19 Grafton St., Marine Parade, Brighton, n.d., cited by *The Morning Herald,* 22 Oct 1861, in turn cited by ROBERTSON, p. 15.

70. Richard Garde: "A Letter to the Right Honourable Earl Russell on the *Absolute* right of the Mexican Bondholders, who are subjects of Her Most Gracious Majesty, by Richard Garde, Esq., A.M., Trin. Col. Dub., Barrister-at-Law of the Middle Temple." (London, 1861). Quotes from Phillimore, Vattel, and Locke were used in an attempt to substantiate the argument that British subjects had a "birthright," part of the "constitution and grounded in "natural right," that the British Government afford protection to foreign loans. Garde sent his work to Russell on 29 November 1861 (Richard Garde to Russell, 29 Nov (r. 3 Dec) 1861, PRO, F.O. 97/280).

71. "The Case of the holders of Bonds of the National Debt contracted by Mexico in London," encl. of Bondholders to Russell, 23 (r. 26) Nov 1861, PRO, F.O. 97/280. A week later the Bondholders wrote Russell to change the title to "The Case of *Her Majesty's subjects holding* Bonds of the National Debt contracted by Mexico in London." The Bondholders claimed they wanted protection only for *"British* property." The bulk of 10,241,650 of pounds sterling in bonds, it was asserted, were in British hands. There were only ". . . two or three holders of these bonds in Germany & Switzerland, as many in Mexico, and also a Traffic in low-priced public securities between the Stock-Exchanges of London and Amsterdam, which probably keeps one, and at times perhaps up to two, million of Mexican Bonds oscillating between England and Holland." See Committee of Mexican Bondholders to Russell, 10 Basinghall St., London, 30 Nov (r. 3 Dec) 1861, PRO, F.O. 97/280.

72. Bondholders to Russell, 23 (r. 26) Nov 1861, PRO, F.O. 97/280.

73. Hammond to Messrs McCalmont Bros & Co., 28 Oct 1861, encl. of Russell to Wyke, F.O., No. 53, 29 Oct (r. 29 Nov) 1861, PRO, F.O. 204/153.

74. Russell Drafts, 2 and 3 Dec 1861, PRO. F.O. 97/280. Russell refused to ". . . enter into detailed discussions . . .," because Wyke had a ". . . . large discretion on the subject . . .," and Russell did not want to ". . . fetter him by detailed instructions."

75. *The Times,* London, 8 Nov 1861.

76. *Gazette,* 15 Nov 1861, sum. by Committee of Mexican Bond-holders to Russell. 10 Basinghall St., London, 23 (r. 26) Nov 1861, PRO, F.O. 97/280.

77. *The Times,* London, 19 Nov 1861.

78. Serrano to Collantes, Havana, No. 89, 16 Dec 1861, *Diario de Las Sessiones de Cortes. Congreso de los Diputados, 2 Jun 1862, Apéndice Primero Num. 133,* (trans.) encl. of Crampton to Russell, Madrid, No. 255, 16 (r. 26) Jun 1862, PRO, F.O. 72/1035.

79. *Ibid;* Serrano to Collantes, Havana, No. 80, 26 Nov 1861, *ibid.*

80. Serrano to Collantes, Havana, No. 80, 26 Nov 1861, *ibid.*

81. Serrano to Collantes, Havana, No. 89, 16 Dec 1861, *ibid.*

82. Serrano to Collantes, Havana, No. 80, 26 Nov 1861, *ibid.*

83. *Ibid.*

84. Serrano to Collantes, Havana, No. 89, 16 Dec 1861, *ibid.*

85. Saligny to Thouvenel, Vera Cruz, No. 61, 31 Dec 1861 (r. 30 Jan 1862), MDAE: *CP, Mex.,* vol. 56; PRIM, p. 56. Prim left for Havana on 23 November 1861. See PRIM, p. 55.

86. See below in text of this section of present investigation.

87. Serrano to Collantes, Havana, No. 89, 16 Dec 1861, *Diario de Las Sessiones de Cortes. Congreso de los Diputados, 2 Jun 1862, Apéndice Primero Num. 133,* (trans.) encl. of Crampton to Russell, Madrid, No. 255, 16 (r. 26) Jun 1862, PRO, F.O. 72/1035.

88. Although it was probably impossible for the Spanish Government to send Serrano a copy of the Convention of London with the mail packet leaving at the very beginning of November, as Collantes said in the Cortes in January 1862, it is also true that on 1 November, at the very latest, the British Ambassador to Madrid communicated the substance of a telegram from Russell of 30 October that outlined the terms of the convention as they then stood and stated the convention would be signed shortly. The *Alva,* leaving Cadiz on 5 November, or the *San Quinitin,* leaving Malaga on 12 November, could have carried an outline of Russell's telegram, together with instructions to hold up the Spanish expedition at Havana. The mail steamer leaving early in November merely carried a British draft convention. In January 1862 Collantes explained in the Cortes that no orders could have been sent by that mail packet, because the allies had not at the time agreed on a rendezvous. There is some corroboration for this "rendezvous" argument. Don Antonio Lopez de Ceballos was sent as a Spanish diplomatic representative to accompany the Spanish expedition. Ceballos told Serrano that Collantes had said that it might be necessary to "search" for the British and French squadrons. Aside from this information, however, Ceballos knew nothing that could not be learned from a reading of the orders of 11 September and the British draft convention. On 10

November the Spanish Ambassador to London received a telegram from Collantes that there might be some "movement" undertaken by the Spanish forces at Havana before the arrival of Spain's allies. Whether this "movement" referred to Serrano's "search" for the French and British squadrons or whether Collantes' telegram was intended to serve to prepare the British Government for what did indeed happen, and perhaps was desired by Collantes, is not clear. No conclusive answer can be made on the basis of the explanatory documents presented to the Cortes in June 1862 and Collantes' speeches on the subject in the Cortes in January and June 1862. Commetning on these documents and Collantes' June speech, Crampton, the British Ambassador to Madrid, wrote to Russell: "I am far from attributing to the Spanish Government an intention to forestall the honours or advantages of the proposed operations in Mexico which were under discussion with its Allies; but it would certainly seem that it cannot be disculpated from a certain degree of mismanagement in neglecting to apprize the Captain General of Cuba officially of what was going forward." In a speech of January 1862 Collantes referred to an order to Serrano via the United States and that there was reason to believe that this order "miscarried" and never reached Serrano. In a report of 16 December 1861, Serrano mentions that he had just received a war department order mentioning an order sent via the United States and that he had not received it, probably owing to the disorders occasioned by the American Civil War. The existence and fate of the "lost" order still remain a puzzle. If such an order was indeed sent, it must have been sent after the departure of the mail packet leaving for Havana at the beginning of November. The French Ambassador to Madrid belived that the Spanish Government was surprised by Serrano's actions. Barrot believed Serrano acted out of jealousy when he heard Prim was to be Commander-in-Chief. But as O'Donnell remarked to Barrot, the nomination of Prim was made known too late for Serrano possibly to know of it before he ordered the Spanish expedition to Vera Cruz. The riddle, therefore, remains. Either the Spanish Government only "mismanaged" and waited to send complete orders stating a rendezvous and enclosing a copy of the Convention of London, or, orders were held up with a secret hope that Spanish forces alone would seize Vera Cruz. For Collantes' speech in January 1862, see translation of extract of *Diario de las Sessiones de Cortes,* 25 Jan 1862, encl. of Crampton to Russell, Madrid, No. 54, 1 (r. 9) Feb 1862, PRO, F.O. 72/1031. For debate in the Cortes, 10–14 June 1862, see Precise of Debate on the affairs of Mexico in House of Deputies of Cortes, an English summary of *Diario de las Sessiones de Cortes* Nos. 140–143 (1862), encl. of Crampton to Russell, Madrid, No. 262, 18 Jun (r. 7 Jul) 1862, PRO, F.O. 72/1035. For Russell's telegram of 30 October, see Telegram to Crampton, F.O., 4:30 P.M., 30 Oct 1861, PRO, F.O. 72/1010. For Crampton's reply, see Crampton to Russell, Madrid, No. 141, 1 (r. 5) Nov 1861, PRO, F.O. 72/1010. For telegram about "movement," see Isturitz to Collantes, London, No. 219, 13 Nov 1861, in documents submitted to Cortes in June 1862. For

Crampton's comments on these documents, see Crampton to Russell, Madrid, No. 262, 18 Jun (r. 7 Jul) 1862, PRO, F.O. 72/1035. For Barrot's theory about Serrano's "jealousy," see Crampton to Russell, Madrid, No. 7, Con., 4 (r. 14) Jan 1862, PRO, F.O. 72/1030. For O'Donnell's comments to Barrot in this connection, see Barrot to Thouvenel, Madrid, No. 139, 26 (r. 30) Dec 1861, MDAE: *CP, Espagne,* vol. 859. For all other matters mentioned above, see Serrano to Collantes, Havana, Nos. 80 and 89, 26 Nov & 16 Dec 1861, contained in *Diario . . .,* cited in full in footnote 78 above.

89. *Contemporaneo,* 10 Sep 1861, encl. (with trans.) of Crampton to Russell, San Ildefonso, No. 76, 13 (r. 22) Sep 1861, PRO, F.O. 72/1009. Crampton commented that ". . . a large portion of the Spanish Press has lately been advocating . . . the establishment of a monarchy in Mexico, and indulging in wild speculations as to the recovery by Spain of her ancient possessions in America and the 'Indies.'"

90. Speech of Queen of Spain at opening of Cortes, 8 Nov 1861, *Por S. M. La Reina en el acto solemne de abrirse las Cortés del reino ei 8 de Noviembre de 1861* (Imprenta Nacional, (1861)), encl. (with trans.) of Crampton to Russell, Madrid, No. 145, 8 (r. 13) Nov 1861, PRO, F.O. 72/1010.

91. Crampton to Russell, Madrid, No. 197, 17 (r. 22) Dec 1861, PRO, F.O. 72/1011.

92. Crampton to Russell, Madrid, No. 26, 9 (r. 14) Jan 1862, PRO, PRO, F.O. 72/1030.

93. Crampton to Russell, Madrid, No. 197, 17 (r. 22) Dec 1861, PRO, F.O. 72/1011.

94. VERDUIN, pp. 127–128.

95. Crampton to Russell, Madrid, No. 197, 17 (r. 22) Dec 1861, PRO, F.O. 72/1011.

96. *Ibid.*

97. Gortchakov to Olga Nicolaevna, 6 Jul 1861, Ch. Friese: Russland und Preussen vom Krimkrieg bis zum Polnischen Aufstand (Berlin, 1931), pp. 347 f., cited by W. E. Moss: *The European Powers and the German Question, 1848–71, With Special Reference to England and Russia* (Cambridge: Cambridge University Press, 1958), p. 99, f. 8.

98. Bismarck Bericht aus Petersberg, 11 Nov 1861, cited by L. von Raschdau, ed.: *Die Politischen Berichte des Fürsten Bismarck aus Petersberg und Paris, 1859–1862* (Berlin, 1920), Part II, p. 133.

99. Palmerston to Russell, 94 Piccadilly, 9 Sep 1861, British Museum Additional MS. Room, Palmerston Papers, vol. 48582.

100. Metternich to Pierre de Lano, Ch'ateau de Koenigswart, Pri., 23 Sep 1861, cited by Pierre de Lano: *The Secret of an Empire: The Empress Eugénie,* trans. from the French by Ethelred Taylor (London, 1895), p. 133.

101. Rechberg to Maximilian, 2 Dec 1861, cited by DAWSON, p. 215.

102. Speech of A. H. Layard, Under-Secretary for Foreign Affairs,

in House of Commons, 15 Jul 1862, *Hansard's Parliamentary Debates,* 3rd Series, CLXVIII (London, 1862), 370.

103. Marquis d'Azeglio to Russell, 23 Park Lane, London, 27 Nov 1861, with Russell notation, dtd 27 Nov 1861, PRO, F.O. 96/26.

104. Russell to Wyke, F.O., No. 78, 16 Dec 1861 (r. 14 Feb 1862), PRO, F.O. 204/153.

105. Russell to Marquis d'Azeglio, 4 Dec 1861, encl. of *Ibid.*

106. *Ibid.*

107. Speech of A. H. Layard, Under-Secretary for Foreign Affairs, in House of Commons, 15 Jul 1862, *Hansard's Parliamentary Debates,* 3rd Series, CLXVIII (London, 1862), 370; ABBOTT, pp. 627-628, f. 1.

108. Melgar Circular, 20 Nov 1861, *El peruano,* Lima, 17 Sep 1862, sum. by Robert W. Franzar: "Latin-American Projects to Aid Mexico During the French Intervention," *HAHR,* XXVIII (1948), 378.

109. Alcade to Melgar, 31 Jan 1862; Costa to Melgar, 14 May 1862; Salinas to Melgar, 28 Dec 1861, *El peruano,* Lima, 17 Sep 1862, sum. by Frazer: "Latin American Projects," p. 378.

110. For Romero's 16 conferences with Seward, from 23 September through 30 December 1861, see Mathias Romero, ed.: *Correspondencia de la Legacion Mexicana en Washington Durante La Intervencion Extranjera, 1860–1868: Collection de Documentos Para Formar La Historia de la Intervencion* (10 v., Mexico City, 1870–1892), I, 540– 669. (Hereafter referred to as ROMERO).

111. Romero to Seward, 23 Nov 1861, House Executive Document No. 100, 57 Congress, 2 Session, p. 134, cited by William S. Robertson: "The Tripartite Treaty of London," *HAHR,* XX (1940), 185.

112. Romero to Seward, 28 Nov 1861, House Executive Document No. 100, 57 Congress, 2 Session, p. 138, cited by Robertson: "The Tripartite Treaty of London," p. 185.

113. Romero to Fuente, 7 and 9 Jan 1862, ROMERO, II, 78, sum. by Frazer: "Latin American Projects," pp. 379–380.

114. Some Thoughts for the President's Consideration, 1 Apr 1861, cited in full by Carl Sandburg: *Abraham Lincoln: The War Years* (4 v., Rahway, N. J. 1939), I, 180–181.

115. Lincoln to Seward, Executive Mansion, 1 Apr 1861, cited in full by *Ibid,* I, 181.

116. Seward's original instructions to Charles Francis Adams, 21 May 1861, showing Lincoln's corrections, cited in full by John G. Nicolay and John Hay: *Abraham Lincoln: A History* (10 v., New York, 1890), IV, 270–275.

117. Thornton Kirkland Lothrop: *William Henry Seward* (Boston, 1909), p. 361, cited by MONAGHAN, p. 63.

118. Royal Decree Annexing Santo Domingo, 19 May 1861, *British Foreign and State Papers, 1861–1862,* LII (London, 1868), 1356.

119. See PERKINS, pp. 281–300; MOORE, VI, 515–516; Charles Callan Tansill: *The United States and Santo Domingo, 1798–1873: A Chapter in Caribbean Diplomacy* (Baltimore, 1938), pp. 212–215.

120. See OWSLEY, p. 116.

121. Seward to Corwin, No. 16, 24 Aug 1861, House Executive Document, No. 100, 37 Congress, 2 Session, p. 19, cited by J. Fred Rippy: *The United States and Mexico* (New York, 1926), p. 255.

122. Lord Lyons, Henri Mercier, and Gabriel J. Tassara to Seward, Washington, 30 Nov 1861, encl. of Lyons to Russell, No. 96, 3 Dec 1861, *BSP, 1862,* LXIV, 228.

123. Dayton to Seward, No. 51, 27 Sep 1861, Washington, Dept of State: *Despatches, France,* vol. 50, sum. by OWSLEY, pp. 116–117; Adams to Seward, 1 Nov 1861, House Executive Document No. 100, 37 Congress, 2 Session, p. 201, cited by John Holladay Latane: *The United States and Latin America* (Garden City, New York, 1920), p. 202. On 12 October 1861 Lord Lyons told Seward the objections Russell had made to Charles Francis Adams on 25 September 1861. See Lyons to Russell, Washington, No. 553, 14 (r. 28) Oct 1861, PRO, F.O. 5/772. For the details of the reactions of Russell, Palmerston, and Thouvenel to Seward's loan scheme, see Section 3 of Chapter III of present investigation.

124. For examples, see PERKINS, p. 427.

125. Seward to MM. Tassara, Mercier, and Lyons, Washington, 4 Dec 1861, encl. of Lyons to Russell, Washington, No. 102, 6 (r. 25) Dec 1861, *BSP, 1862,* LXIV, 231–232.

126. See Section 3 of Chapter II of present investigation.

127. Seward to Corwin, No. 32, 5 Dec 1861, Washington, Dept. of State: *Instructions, Mexico,* vol. 17, sum. by OWSLEY, p. 118.

128. Seward-Lyons Conversation, 21 Dec 1861, sum. by Lyons to Russell, Washington, No. 787, 21 Dec 1861 (r. 7 Jan 1862), PRO, F.O. 5/777.

129. Lyons to Russell, Washington, No. 553, 14 (r. 28) Oct 1861, PRO, F.O. 5/772.

130. Lyons to Russell, Washington, 23 Dec 1861, cited by Baron Thomas W. Legh Newton (Lord Newton): *Lord Lyons: A Record of British Diplomacy* (2 v., London, 1913), I, 69.

131. See MONAGHAN, p. 188.

132. See Elizabeth Haller: *Aspects of American Opinion Regarding Maximilian's Empire in Mexico* (Unpublished M.A. Thesis presented to the Faculty of the Graduate School of the University of Pennsylvania in 1940), p. 56, summarizing findings. (Hereafter referred to as HALLER). The first newspaper comments on the European intervention in Mexico cited by Haller were written in January 1862. See HALLER, pp. 30, 32.

133. Seward to Corwin, Washington, 15 Feb 1862, encl. 2 of Lyons to Russell, Washington, No. 129, 21 Feb (r. 7 Mar) 1862, PRO, F.O. 5/825.

134. For a brief, but documented, account, see BAILEY, pp. 351–357.

135. Palmerston to Duke of Somerset, 94 Piccadilly, 26 May 1861, British Museum Additional MS. Room, Palmerston Papers, vol. 48582.

136. Palmerston to Lord Herbert, 94 Piccadilly, 3 Jun 1861, *ibid.*

137. For what he terms "almost" a "war hysteria," see MONA-GHAN, pp. 148–150.

138. Palmerston to Duke of Newcastle, 1 Sep 1861, British Museum Additional MS. Room, Palmerston Papers, vol. 48582.

139. Palmerston to Russell, 94 Piccadilly, 9 Sep 1861, PRO, P.R.O. 30/22–21.

140. Arnold Whitridge: "The Trent Affair, 1861," *History Today,* IV, No. 6 (Jun 1954), p. 401.

141. Russell to Crampton, F.O., No. 134, draft, 4 Dec 1861, PRO, F.O. 72/1002.

142. Russell to Crampton, F.O., Telegram, 9 Dec 1861, cited by Russell to Crampton, F.O., No. 139, draft, 9 Dec 1861, *ibid.*

143. Milne's instructions, sum. by Milne to Dunlop, Bermuda, 20 Dec 1861, encl. of Milne to Secretary of Admiralty, *Nile* at Bermuda, No. 635, 25 Dec 1861, both encls. of Romaine to Hammond, Admiralty, 20 (r. 21) Jan 1862, PRO, F.O. 50/370.

144. Draft to Admiralty, F.O., 6 Dec 1861, PRO, F.O. 50/358.

145. Napoleon III-Slidell Conversation, Vichy, 16 Jul 1862, sum. by Slidell to Mason, 20 Jul 1862, cited by Louis Martin Sears: "A Confederate Diplomat at the Court of Napoleon III," *AHR,* XXVI (1921), 263. In a private letter Thouvenel stated: "The Emperor told me with sadness: 'Is this the thanks I get for my conduct in the *Trent* affair?'" See Thouvenel to Flahault, Paris, 12 Jun 1862, THOUVENEL, II, 319.

146. See *AD, 1861,* IV, 385–396.

147. Palmerston to Russell, Broadlands, 4 Nov 1859, British Museum Additional MS. Room, Palmerston Papers, vol. 48581. Palmerston stated he had not had any suspicions "Till lately."

148. Cowley to Russell, 7 Aug 1859, cited by Theodore Martin, ed.: *The Life of His Royal Highness, the Prince Consort* (5 v., London, 1875–1880), IV (3rd ed., 1879), 471.

149. Note by Baroche of meeting of Council of Ministers at Compiègne, 22 Nov 1861, Baroche Papers, 1035 f. 29–32, cited by Theodore Zeldin: *The Political System of Napoleon III* (London, 1958), pp. 105–106.

150. Thouvenel to Saligny, No. 17, draft, 30 Dec 1861, MDAE: *CP, Mex.,* vol. 56.

151. Dayton to Seward, No. 74, 6 Nov 1861, Washington, Dept. of State: Despatches, France, vol. 50, sum. by OWSLEY, p. 117.

152. Thouvenel to Flahault, Paris, 19 Sep 1861, THOUVENEL, II, 169.

153. Thouvenel to Saligny, No. 13, draft, 30 Sep 1861, MDAE: *CP, Mex.,* vol. 55.

154. Thouvenel to Flahault, Paris, 19 Sep 1861, THOUVENEL, II, 169.

155. Two excellent studies on the subject are OWSLEY and Ephraim Douglass Adams: *Great Britain and the American Civil War* (2 v., London, 1925).

156. Thouvenel to Jurien, draft, 30 Dec 1861, MDAE: *CP, Mex.,* vol. 57.

157. Comte Fleury: *Memories of the Empress Eugenie by Comte Fleury: Compiled from Statements, Private Documents and Personal Letters of the Empress Eugenie, From Conversations of the Emperor Napoleon III and From Family Letters and Papers of General Fleury, M. Franceschini Pietri, Prince Victor Napoleon and Other Members of the Court of the Second Empire* (2 v., New York and London, 1920), II, 107.

158. *Ibid.,* II, 108. Napoleon referred to Pedro I (1822–1831) and Pedro II (regency, 1831–1840; personal rule, 1840–1889), who ruled Brazil after independence from Portugal. Rouher, Minister without Portfolio, made remarks to the same effect before the French Legislature in May 1864. See *Le Moniteur,* 13 May 1864, sum. by PERKINS, p. 415.

159. See Section 2 of Chapter III of present investigation.

160. When the American Minister to Vienna tried to give Palmerston assurances, the Prime Minister sent Russell a note that Motley ". . . wishes us to believe they never speak, but he does not say they do not think of Canada. . . ." See Palmerston Note, 21 Sep 1861, PRO, F.R.O. 30/22–28.

161. Crampton to Russell, San Ildefonso, No. 92, 21 Sep (r. 11 Oct) 1861, PRO, F.O. 72/1009.

162. For Spanish anxiety of being isolated, see text of Section 2 of Chapter III of present investigation, between footnotes 16 and 26. For Spanish submission to British proposals, see text of Section 3 of Chapter III of present investigation, between footnotes 196 and 197.

163. See text of Section 2 of Chapter III of present investigation, between footnotes 23 and 26.

164. Crampton to Russell, San Ildefonso, No. 92, 21 Sep (r. 11 Oct) 1861, PRO, F.O. 72/1009.

165. See text of Section 2 of Chapter III of present investigation, between footnotes 25 and 26.

166. See text of Section 3 of Chapter III of present investigation, between footnotes 20 and 21.

167. See text of Section 3 of Chapter III of present investigation, between footnotes 196 and 197.

168. Dunlop to Milne, Challenger at Havana, No. 196, 5 Dec 1861, encl. of Admiralty to Hammond, 2 (r. 3) Jan 1862, PRO, F.O. 50/370.

169. In the afternoon of 10 December 1861.

170. Extract of a letter of Captain Von Donop of HMS Jason, encl. of Romaine to Hammond, Admiralty, 30 Jan (r. 4 Feb) 1862, PRO, F.O. 50/370. Admiral Rubalcava made his offer of cooperation on 11 December 1861.

171. Von Donop to Dunlop, HMS Jason, Vera Cruz, n.d., encl. of Romaine to Hammond, Admiralty, 12 (r. 13) Feb 1862, PRO, F.O. 50/370.

172. Extract of a letter of Captain Von Donop of HMS Jason, encl. of Romaine to Hammond, Admiralty, 30 Jan (r. 4 Feb) 1862, *ibid.*

173. General Order of General Gasset, 16 Dec 1861, *Diario Espanol,* Madrid, 23 Jan 1862, encl. 2 (translated) of Crampton to Russell, Madrid, No. 61, 3 (r. 9) Feb 1862, PRO, F.O. 72/1031.

174. Extract of a letter of Captain Von Donop of HMS Jason, encl. of Romaine to Hammond, Admiralty, 30 Jan (r. 4 Feb) 1862, PRO, F.O. 50/370.

175. See footnote 173 above.

176. Extract of a letter of Captain Von Donop of HMS Jason, encl. of Romaine to Hammond, Admiralty, 30 Jan (r. 4 Feb) 1862, PRO, F.O. 50/370.

177. Saligny to Thouvenel, Vera Cruz, No. 59, 22 Dec 1861 (r. 30 Jan 1862), MDAE: *CP, Mex.,* vol. 56.

178. Decree of General Gasset to Inhabitants of Vera Cruz, Vera Cruz, 17 Dec 1861, *Diario Espanol,* Madrid, 23 Jan 1862, encl. 2 (translated) of Crampton to Russell, Madrid, No. 61, 3 (r. 9) Feb 1862, PRO, F.O. 72/1031.

179. Proclamation of General Gasset to Inhabitants of Vera Cruz, Vera Cruz, 17 Dec 1861, *Diario Espanol,* Madrid, 23 Jan 1862, encl. 2 (translated) of *Ibid.*

180. See Sections 1 and 2 of Chapter II of present investigation.

181. Saligny to Serrano, Confidential, 22 Nov 1861, encl. of Serrano to Collantes, Havana, No. 89, 16 Dec 1861, *Diario de Las Sessiones de Cortes. Congreso de los Diputados, 2 Jun 1862, Apéndice Primero Num. 133.* (trans.) encl. of Crampton to Russell, Madrid, No. 255, 16 (r. 26) Jun 1862, PRO, F.O. 72/1035.

182. Saligny to Serrano, 24 Nov 1861, encl. of *Ibid.*

183. See Saligny to Serrano, 29 Nov 1861, encl. of *Ibid.*

184. See text of Section 1 of Chapter II of present investigation, footnoted by footnote 218.

185. Saligny to Thouvenel, Vera Cruz, No. 61, 31 Dec 1861 (r. 30 Jan 1862), MDAE: *CP, Mex.,* vol. 56; PRIM, p. 56.

186. See Section 3 of Chapter IV of present investigation.

187. For the Mexican Civil War, see Sections 2 and 3 of Chapter I of present investigation. For Miramon's motives on this occasion, see Section 3 of Chapter IV of present investigation.

188. For the doings of Zuloaga and Marquez, see Sections 1 and 2 of Chapter II of present investigation.

189. General Prim's speech before Senate of the Cortes, 9 Dec 1861, translated into English from the *Diario de las Sessiones de Cortes,* encl. 2 of Crampton to Russell, Madrid, No. 417, 27 (r. 31) Dec 1862, PRO, F.O. 72/1040.

190. Jurien to Thouvenel, Havana, No. 2, 29 Dec 1861, MDAE: *CP,* Mex., vol. 57.

191. Jurien to Thouvenel, Vera Cruz, No. 10, 28 Jan 1862, *ibid.*

192. Miranda to Estrada, Havana, 21 Dec 1861, encl. 1 of Estrada

to Thouvenel, Hotel Westminster, 13 Rue de la Paix, Paris, 17 Jan 1862, MDAE: *CP, Mex.*, vol. 58.

193. Jurien to Thouvenel, 30 Dec 1861, *ibid.*, vol. 57.

194. Milne to Dunlop, Bermuda, 20 Dec 1861, encl. of Romaine to Hammond, Admiralty, 20 (r. 21) Jan 1862, PRO, F.O. 50/370.

195. Milne to Secretary of Admiralty, No. 635, Nile at Bermuda, 25 Dec 1861, encl. of Romaine to Hammond, Admiralty, 20 (r. 21) Jan 1862, *ibid.*

196. Dunlop to Secretary of Admiralty, Challenger at Vera Cruz, No. 3, 15 Jan 1862, encl. of Admiralty to Hammond, Admiralty, Immediate, 3 (r. 3) Mar 1862, PRO, F.O. 50/370; Wyke to Russell, Vera Cruz, Nos. 1 & 2, 16 Jan (r. 2 Mar) 1862, PRO, F.O. 50/364; Prim to Minister of War, Vera Cruz, 15 Jan 1862, *Gazette,* Madrid, 17 Feb 1862, encl. 2 (trans.) of Crampton to Russell, Madrid, No. 91, 17 (r. 22) Feb 1862, PRO, F.O. 72/1031.

197. Saligny to Serrano, Con., 22 Nov 1861, encl. of Serrano to Collantes, Havana, No. 89, 16 Dec 1861, *Diario de Las Sessiones de Cortes. Congreso de los Diputados, 2 Jun 1862, Apéndice Primero Num. 133,* (trans.) encl of Crampton to Russell, Madrid, No. 255, 16 (r. 26) Jun 1862, PRO, F.O. 72/1035.

198. Wyke to Russell, Vera Cruz, No. 4, 16 Jan (r. 2 Mar) 1862, PRO, F.O. 50/364; BANCROFT, VI, 29–30.

199. Presidential Decree, Mexico City, 17 Dec 1861, *Le Trait d'Union, Journal Francais Universel,* Mexico City, 19 Dec 1861, encl. of Wyke to Russell, Vera Cruz, No. 60, 29 Dec 1861 (r. 29 Jan 1862) PRO, F.O. 50/354.

200. Presidential Manifesto to the Nation, Mexico City, 18 Dec 1861, *Le Trait d'Uunion, Journal Francais Universel,* Mexico City, 19 Dec 1861, encl. of *Ibid.*

201. Wyke to Russell, Vera Cruz, No. 2, 16 Jan (r. 2 May) 1862, PRO, F.O. 50/364.

202. See Section 1 of Chapter II of present investigation.

203. Wyke to Doblado, Vera Cruz, 3 Jan 1862, PRO, F.O. 204/163.

204. Wyke to Russell, Vera Cruz, No. 2, 16 Jan (r. 2 Mar) 1862, PRO, F.O. 50/364.

205. *Ibid.*

206. Prim to Minister of War, Vera Cruz, 15 Jan 1862, *Gazette,* Madrid, 17 Feb 1862, encl. 2 (trans.) of Crampton to Russell, Madrid, No. 91, 17 (r. 22) Feb 1862, PRO, F.O. 72/1031.

207. General Order of General Prim, Vera Cruz, 9 Jan 1862, *Gazette,* Madrid, 17 Feb 1862, encl. 2 (trans.) of *Ibid.*

209. See Section 1 of Chapter V of present investigation.

208. Prim to Minister of War, Vera Cruz, 15 Jan 1862, *Gazette,* Madrid, 17 Feb 1862, encl. 2 (trans.) of *Ibid.*

210. Maitland to Secretary of Admiralty, Bacchante at Callao, No. 24, 14 Jan 1862, encl. of Romaine to Hammond, Admiralty, 15 (r. 17) Feb 1862, PRO, F.O. 50/370.

### 3. The Intrigues of the Mexican Exiles,
### October–December 1861

1. Wyke to Russell, Vera Cruz, No. 32, 1 (r. 31) Mar 1862, PRO, F.O. 50/364.

2. A friend of Estrada wrote from Mexico City that the following classes could be counted on: "Property holders, peaceful people, the upper classes of good sense, and the clergy. . . ." See J.D. Ulibarri to Estrada, Mexico City, 29 Nov 1861, encl. 2 of Estrada to Thouvenel, Vienna, 6 Jan 1862, MDAE: *CP, Mex.*, vol. 58.

3. Mathew to Russell, Mexico City, No. 37, Confidential, 12 May (r. 27 Jun) 1861, PRO, F.O. 50/352.

4. See Sections 1 and 2 of Chapter II of present investigation.

5. Saligny to Serrano, 29 Nov 1861, encl. of Serrano to Collantes, Havana, No. 89, 16 Dec 1861, *Diario de Las Sessiones de Cortes. Congreso de los diputados, 2 Jun 1862, Apéndice Primero Num. 133,* (trans.) encl. of Crampton to Russell, Madrid, No. 255, 16 (r. 26) Jun 1862, PRO, F.O. 72/1035.

6. See Chapter I of present investigation.

7. Wyke to Russell, Vera Cruz, No. 32, 1 (r. 31) Mar 1862, PRO, F.O. 50/364.

8. See below.

9. On 9 October 1861. See text of Section 3 of Chapter III of present investigation, between footnotes 65 and 70.

10. Estrada to Maximilian, 21 Place de la Madeleine, Paris, 4 Oct 1861, *HHSA,* AKM, sum. & cited by DAWSON, p.. 109.

11. Estrada to Maximilian, 14 Oct 1861, HHSA, sum & cited by CORTI, I, 116.

12. CORTI, I, 116.

13. Schertzenlechner to Maximilian, (Trieste, 6 Nov 1861, HHSA), sum. & cited without source given by DAWSON, pp. 148–150, 152, Source is given by CORTI, I, 119.

14. Estrada's Address to Maximilian, Paris, 30 Oct 1861, cited in full by Frederick Hall: *Life of Maximilian I., Late Emperor of Mexico, with a Sketch of the Empress Carlota by Frederic Hall, One of His Majesty's Legal Advisers* (New York, 1868), pp. 26–27. This Address is briefly summarized by DAWSON (p. 150) and CORTI (I, 116).

15. DAWSON, p. 150. The three other Mexicans were Colonel Facio, Senor Andrade, and Senor Murphy.

16. Muelinen to Rechberg, Paris, 3 Nov 1861, HHSA, AKM, sum. & cited by DAWSON, pp. 154–155.

17. DAWSON, p. 187.

18. Mgr. Labastida to Miranda, Aug 1860, cited by Ralph Roeder: *Juarez and His Mexico: A Biographical History* (2 v., New York, 1947), I, 275.

19. DAWSON, p. 186.

20. Bach to Rechberg, Rome, 26 Nov 1861, *HHSA,* AKM, sum. & cited by *Ibid.,* pp. 186/187.

21. *Ibid.,* p. 187.

22. Metternich to Rechberg, Paris, 16 Nov 1861, *HHSA,* AKM, sum. and cited by *Ibid.,* p. 155.

23. Estrada to Thouvenel, Paris, Private and Confidential, 28 Nov 1861, MDAE: *CP, Mex.,* vol. 56. For details, see Section 1 of Chapter I of present investigation.

24. Estrada to Santa Anna, 31 Oct 1861, sum. by Santa Anna to Estrada, St. Thomas, (Virgin Islands), 30 Nov 1861, encl. of Estrada to Thouvenel, Vienna, Hotel Munsch, 19 Dec 1861, MDAE: CP, Mex., vol. 56. Santa Anna's Letter of 30 November, 1861, has been published. For a long quotation of it, see Colonel Auguste Charles Philippe Blanchot: *Mémoires: L'Intervention Francais au Mexique* (3 v., Paris, 1911), I 20–21.

25. Estrada to Thouvenel, Paris, Private and Confidential, 28 Nov 1861, MDAE: *CP, Mex.,* vol. 56.

26. Miranda to Estrada, New York City, 6 Nov 1861, encl. 1 of *Ibid.*

27. Estrada to Thouvenel, Paris, Private and Confidential, 28 Nov 1861, MDAE: *CP, Mex.,* vol. 56.

28. Metternich to Rechberg, Paris, 16 Nov 1861, *HHSA,* AKM, sum & cited by DAWSON, p. 156.

29. Metternich to Rechberg, 8 Nov 1861, *HHSA,* cited by SALO-MON, p. 150.

30. Metternich to Rechberg, Paris, 16 Nov 1861, *HHSA,* AKM, sum. & cited by DAWSON, p. 155.

31. Rechberg to Maximilian, Vienna, 6 Nov. 1861, *HHSA,* AKM, cited by DAWSON, p. 155. Rechberg enclosed Muelinen's report of 3 November 1861, summarizing Estrada's suggestion that Maximilian accept the Mexican throne from the Mexican exiles in Europe. See footnote 16 above.

32. Maximilian to Leopold I, Miramar, 18 Oct 1861, *HHSA,* cited by CORTI, I, 116–117.

33. Leopold I to Maximilian, 25 Oct 1861, *HHSA,* AKM, cited by DAWSON, p. 145.

34. Maximilian to Estrada, Miramar, 8 Dec 1861, cited by Frederic Hall: *Life of Maximilian I., Late Emperor of Mexico, with a Sketch of the Empress Carlota by Frederic Hall, One of His Majesty's Legal Advisers* (New York, 1868), pp. 27–28.

35. Maximilian to Rechberg, 9 Nov 1861, *HHSA,* AKM, cited by DAWSON, p. 152.

36. Maximilian to Rechberg, 11 Nov 1861, cited by *Ibid.,* p. 153.

37. Maximilian to Rechberg, 9 Nov. 1861, *HHSA,* AKM., cited by *Ibid.,* p. 152.

38. Maximilian to Rechberg, 11 Nov 1861, *HHSA,* AKM, cited by *Ibid., p.* 156.

39. Maximilian to Pius IX, Miramar, 13 Nov 1861, *HHSA,* AKM, cited by *Ibid.,* p. 151.

40. Pius IX to Maximilian, The Vatican, 29 Nov 1861, *HHSA,* AKM, cited by *Ibid.,* pp. 151–152.

41. See below.

42. Rechberg wrote Maximilian that, while Estrada was entitled to the "fullest confidence," a written authorization ". . . .may be lost or it may fall into the wrong hands. . . ." Furthermore an "indiscreet word" in such an authorization might "compromise" Maximilian ". . . in the event of the plan miscarrying." See Rechberg to Maximilian, 21 Nov 1861, *HHSA,* AKM, cited by DAWSON, p. 153. As an alternative Rechberg suggested he give Estrada his instructions verbally in Vienna, and Maximilian agreed. See DAWSON, pp. 153–154. At the beginning of December 1861 Rechberg instructed Metternich to invite Estrada to come to Vienna to talk over his plans with Rechberg. See DAWSON, p. 157.

43. Cowley to Russell, Paris, No. 1377, 29 (r. 30) Nov 1861, PRO, F.O. 27/1399.

44. See Section 3 of Chapter I of present investigation.

45. Consul General Crawford to Russell, Havana, No. 9, Separate, 5 Mar 1861, encl. of Hammond to Wyke, F.O., No. 5, 10 Apr (r. 29 May) 1861, PRO, F.O. 204/153.

46. BURKE, p. 167.

47. Doyle to Cowley, Hotel Bouillemont, Pri., 30 Nov 1861, PRO, F.O. 519/241. Doyle said he had his information from one of Miramon's "intimate friends."

48. Cowley to Russell, Paris, No. 1377, 29 (r. 30) Nov 1861, PRO, F.O. 27/1399.

49. CORTI, I, 122.

50. Metternich to Rechberg, Paris, 28 Nov 1861, *HHSA,* cited by *Ibid.*

51. Jurien to Thouvenel, Vera Cruz, No. 10, 28 Jan 1862, MDAE: *CP, Mex.,* vol. 57. When Miramon arrived in Havana, at first Serrano wanted to arrest him. See below.

52. Metternich to Rechberg, Paris, 28 Nov 1861, *HHSA,* cited by CORTI, I, 122.

53. Doyle to Cowley, Hotel Bouillemont, Pri., 30 Nov 1861, PRO, F.O. 519/241. See footnote 47 above for source of Doyle's information.

54. Cowley to Russell, Paris, No. 1377, 29 (r. 30) Nov 1861, PRO, F.O. 27/1399.

55. CORTI, I, 122.

56. Metternich to Rechberg, Paris, Pri., 2 Dec 1861, *HHSA,* cited by *Ibid.*

57. BURKE, p. 167.

58. See below.

59. DAWSON, p. 157.

60. Schertzenlechner to Maximilian, 11, 14, 16, 21 Dec 1861, *HHSA,* AKM, sum. & cited by *Ibid.,* pp. 184–185.

61. Rechberg to Metternich, 16 Dec 1861, *HHSA*, AKM, Berichte aus Paris, sum. by *Ibid.*, p. 185.

62. Rechberg to Metternich, 16 Dec 1861, *HHSA*, AKM, sum. & cited by *Ibid.*, p. 187.

63. Maximilian to Franz Joseph, 20 Feb 1862, *HHSA*, AKM, cited by *Ibid.*, p. 214.

64. Estrada to Maximilian, 30 Dec 1861, *HHSA*, AKM, sum. by *Ibid.*, p. 189. Estrada stayed at Miramar 24–29 December 1861.

65. Estrada-Senior Conversation, 27 Apr 1863, cited by SENIOR, II, 280–281.

66. DAWSON, p. 194.

67. Ibid., p. 188. Dawson does not cite these letters. Copies are located in the archives of the French Ministry of Foreign Affairs. See footnotes 68 and 69 below.

68. Santa Anna to Estrada, Private and Confidential, ?, encl. 2 of Estrada to Thouvenel, Private and Confidential, Paris, 28 Nov 1861, MDAE: *CP, Mex.*, vol. 56.

69. Santa Anna to Estrada, St. Thomas, (Virgin Islands), 30 Nov 1861, encl. of Estrada to Thouvenel, Vienna, Hotel Munsch, 19 Dec 1861, *ibid*.

70. DAWSON, p. 194.

71. Punkte mit Zeiner Majestat dem Kaiser stipulirt zu Venedig am 31 Dezember, 1861, MSS., *HHSA*, AKM, V. 1151, cited by DAWSON, p. 412.

72. *Ibid.*

73. Miranda to Estrada, New York City, 6 Nov 1861, encl. 1f of Estrada to Thouvenel, Paris, Private and Confidential, 28 Nov 1861, MDAE: *CP, Mex.*, vol. 56.

74. Punkte mit Zeiner Majestat dem Kaiser stipulirt zu Venedig am 31 Dezember, 1861, MSS., *HHSA*, AKM, V. 1151, cited by DAWSON, p. 413.

75. Rafael Rafael to Estrada, New York City, 15 Jan 1862, encl. of Estrada to Thouvenel, Hotel Westminster, 13 Rue de la Paix, Paris, 27 Jan 1862, MDAE: *CP, Mex.*, vol. 58.

76. DAWSON, p. 190.

77. Metternich-Napoleon III Conversation, sum. by Metternich to Rechberg, 22 Dec 1861, encl. of Rechberg to Maximilian, 25 Dec 1861, *HHSA*, sum. by CORTI, I 139. Corti does not give the date of Metternich's meeting with Napoleon, but it was 21 December 1861. See Metternich to Rechberg, 22 Dec 1861, *HHSA*, AKM, sum. & cited by DAWSON, pp. 189–190.

78. Metternich to Rechberg, 22 Dec 1861, *HHSA*, AKM, sum. & cited by DAWSON, pp. 189–190.

79. DAWSON, p. 187.

80. Maximilian to Rechberg, 27 Dec 1861, *HHSA*, cited by CORTI, I, 139.

81. Maximilian to Rechberg, telegram, 27 Dec 1861, sum. by DAWSON, p. 188.

82. Rechberg to Maximilian, telegram, 29 Dec 1861, sum. by *Ibid.,* p. 189.

83. Estrada to Rafael Rafael, Trieste, 29 Dec 1861, cited by Rafael Rafael to Estrada, New York City, 28 Jan 1861, MDAE: *CP, Mex.,* vol. 58.

84. Punkte mit Zeiner Majestat dem Kaiser stipulirt zu Venedig am 31 Dezember, 1861, MSS., *HHSA,* AKM, V. 1151, cited by DAWSON, p. 411.

85. Maximilian to Napoleon III, Miramar, 2 Jan 1862, *HHSA,* cited by CORTI, I, 364.

86. CORTI, I, 143.

87. *Ibid.;* DAWSON, p. 191.

88. Maximilian to Rechberg, 1 Jan 1862, *HHSA,* Berufung, sum. & cited by Dawson, pp. 191–192.

89. Punkte mit Zeiner Majestat dem Kaiser stipulirt zu Venedig am 31 Dezember, 1861, MSS., *HHSA,* AKM, V. 1151, cited by *Ibid.,* p. 412.

90. *Ibid.,* pp. 411–413.

91. Ibid., p. 412.

92. He sent a letter to Estrada from New York City on 6 November, another from Havana on 22 November. See Miranda to Estrada, New York City, 6 Nov 1861, encl. 1 of Estrada to Thouvenel, Private and Confidential, Paris, 28 Nov 1861, MDAE: *CP, Mex.,* vol. 56. See also Miranda to Estrada, Havana, 22 Nov 1861, encl. 1 of Estrada to Thouvenel, Vienna, 6 Jan 1862, MDAE: *CP, Mex.,* vol. 58.

93. Miranda to Estrada, Havana, 21 Dec 1861, encl. 1 of Estrada to Thouvenel, Hotel Westminster, 13 Rue de la Paix, 17 Jan 1862, MDAE: *CP, Mex.,* vol. 58.

94. *Ibid.*

95. Miranda to Estrada, Havana, 7 Dec 1861, *ibid.,* vol. 56.

96. Miranda to Estrada, Havana, 22 Nov 1861, encl. 1 of Estrada to Thouvenel, Vienna, 6 Jan 1862, *ibid.,* vol. 58.

97. Miranda to Estrada, 7 Dec 1861, *ibid.,* vol. 56.

98. Miranda to Estrada, 7 Dec. 1861, *HHSA,* sum. by CORTI, I, 133.

99. Miranda to Estrada, 21 Dec 1861, encl. 1 of Estrada to Thouvenel, Hotel Westminster, 13 Rue de la Paix, Paris, 17 Jan 1862, MDAE: *CP, Mex.,* vol. 58.

100. O'Donnell to Bishop of Havana, cited by Miranda to Rafael Rafael, in turn cited by Rafael Rafael to Estrada, New York City, 28 Jan 1862, *ibid.*

101. Wyke to Russell, Vera Cruz, No. 10, 30 Jan (r. 2 Mar) 1862, PRO. F.O. 50/364.

102. Jurien to Thouvenel, Vera Cruz, No. 10, 28 Jan 1862, MDAE: *CP, Mex.,* vol. 57.

103. See text of Section 2 of Chapter IV of present investigation, between footnotes 185 and 189.

104. Jurien to Thouvenel, Vera Cruz, No. 10, 28 Jan 1862, MDAE: *CP, Mex.,* vol. 57.

105. Rafael Rafael to Estrada, New York City, 15 Jan 1862, encl. of Estrada to Thouvenel, Hotel Westminster, 13 Rue de la Paix, Paris, 27 Jan 1862, *ibid.,* vol. 58.

106. Miranda to Estrada, Havana, 7 Dec 1861, *ibid.,* vol. 56.

107. Miranda to Estrada, 28 Dec 1861, *HHSA,* sum. & cited by CORTI, I, 152.

108. Lt. Charles Slaughter to Dunlop, Avon, 27 Jan 1862, encl. 2 of Romaine to Hammond, Admiralty, 4 (r. 5) Mar 1862, PRO, F.O. 50/370.

109. Wyke to Russell, Vera Cruz, No. 10, 30 Jan (r. 2 Mar) 1862, PRO, F.O. 50/364.

110. Miranda to Estrada, 28 Dec 1861, *HHSA,* sum. & cited by CORTI, I, 152.

111. Santa Anna to Estrada, St. Thomas, (Virgin Islands), 30 Nov. 1861, encl. of Estrada to Thouvenel, Vienna, Hotel Munsch, 19 Dec 1861, MDAE: *CP, Mex.,* vol. 56.

112. Santa Anna to Estrada, St. Thomas, (Virgin Islands), 31 Dec (1861), *HHSA,* sum. by CORTI, I, 152-153.

113. Santa Anna to Estrada, St. Thomas, (Virgin Islands), 31 Jan 1862, MDAE: *CP, Mex.,* vol. 58.

114. Santa Anna to Estrada, St. Thomas, (Virgin Islands), 15 Jan 1862, encl. of Estrada to Thouvenel, Hotel Westminster, 13 Rue de la Paix, 31 Jan 1862, *ibid.*

## Chapter V

### 1. The Negotiations of the European Representatives in Mexico, January-February 1862

1. Wyke to Russell, Vera Cruz, No. 3, 16 Jan (r. 2 Mar) 1862, PRO, F.O. 50/364.

2. Wyke to Russell, Vera Cruz, No. 19, 15 Feb (r. 31 Mar) 1862, *ibid.*

3. Wyke to Russell, Vera Cruz, No. 3, 16 Jan (r. 2 Mar) 1862, *ibid.*

4. Wyke claimed the proclamation was "slightly altered," but he did not consider the changes important enough to report them. See *Ibid.* Saligny left the reporting of this conference to Jurien, who merely forwarded the final version. See Saligny to Thouvenel, Vera Cruz, No. 62, 15 Jan (r. 21 Feb) 1862, MDAE: *CP, Mex.,* vol. 58. See also Jurien to Thouvenel, Vera Cruz, No. 5, 15 Jan 1862, MDAE: *CP, Mex.,* vol. 57. Dunlop reported military affairs to the British Admiralty and left the reporting of the details of the conferences to Wyke. For Dunlop's report of his first week in Mexico, see Dunlop to Secretary of Admiralty, Challenger at Vera Cruz, No. 3, 15 Jan 1862, encl. of

Admiralty to Hammond, Admiralty, Immediate, 3 (r. 3) Mar 1862, PRO, F.O. 50/370. Prim himself claimed that "no one" opposed the proclamation he had drawn up and that it was "generally considered good." See Prim-Senate-9 Dec 1862.

5. See Appendix P of present investigation.

6. Prim-Senate-9 Dec 1862.

7. Wyke to Russell, Vera Cruz, No. 3, 16 Jan (r. 2 Mar) 1862, PRO, F.O. 50/364.

8. Wyke to Russell, Orizaba, Pri., 30 Mar 1862, PRO, P.R.O. 30/22 –74. Wyke specifically justified the proclamation with these arguments.

9. Wyke to Russell, Vera Cruz, No. 60, 29 Dec 1861 (r. 29 Jan 1862), PRO, F.O. 50/354.

10. For the Mexican Civil War, see Sections 2 and 3 of Chapter I of present investigation.

11. Wyke to Russell, Vera Cruz, No. 32, (r. 31) Mar 1862, PRO, F.O. 50/364.

12. Wyke to Russell, Orizaba, No. 48, 13 Apr (r. 14 May) 1862, PRO, F.O. 50/365.

13. Wyke to Russell, Orizaba, Pri., 30 Mar 1862, PRO, P.R.O. 30/22–74.

14. Dunlop to Secretary of Admiralty, Orizaba, 17 Apr 1862, encl. of Paget to Hammond, Admiralty, 2 (r. 4) Jun 1862, PRO, F.O. 50/371.

15. Jurien to Thouvenel, Vera Cruz, No. 5, 15 Jan 1862, MDAE: *CP, Mex.*, vol. 57.

16. Saligny to Thouvenel, Vera Cruz, No. 62, 15 Jan (r. 21 Feb) 1862, *ibid.*, vol. 58.

17. Jurien to Thouvenel, Orizaba, No. 33, 10 Apr 1862, *ibid.*, vol. 57.

18. Jurien to Thouvenel, Cordova, 5 Mar 1862, *ibid.*

19. Wyke to Russell, Vera Cruz, No. 3, 16 Jan (r. 2 Mar) 1862, PRO, F.O. 50/364.

20. Wyke to Russell, Vera Cruz, No. 4, 16 Jan (r. 2 Mar) 1862, *ibid.*

21. John Elliot, Surgeon Marine Battalion, to Dunlop, Royal Marine Brigade, Vera Cruz, 3 Mar 1862, encl. 2 of Admiralty to Hammond, Admiralty, 31 Mar (r. 1 Apr) 1862, PRO, F.O. 50/370.

22. Dunlop to Secretary of Admiralty, Challenger at Vera Cruz, No. 3, 15 Jan 1862, encl. of Admiralty to Hammond, Admiralty, Immediate, 3 (r. 3) Mar 1862, *ibid.*

23. Wyke to Russell, Vera Cruz, Pri., 31 Dec 1861, PRO, P.R.O. 30/22–74.

24. Dunlop reported that there were 500 by 15 January 1862. See Dunlop to Secretary of Admiralty, Challenger at Vera Cruz, No. 3, 15 Jan 1862, encl. of Admiralty to Hammond, Admiralty, Immediate, 3 (r. 3) Mar 1862, PRO, F.O. 50/370.

25. Prim-Senate-9 Dec 1862.

26. Prim to Minister of War, Vera Cruz, 15 Jan 1862, *Gazette,*

Madrid, 17 Feb 1862, encl. 2 of Crampton to Russell, Madrid, No. 91, 17 (r. 22) Feb 1862, PRO, F.O. 72/1031.

27. Prim-Senate-9 Dec 1862.

28. Wyke to Russell, Vera Cruz, No. 3, 16 Jan (r. 2 Mar) 1862, PRO, F.O. 50/364.

29. Prim to Minister of War, Vera Cruz, 15 Jan 1862, *Gazette,* Madrid, 17 Feb 1862, encl. 2 of Crampton to Russell, Madrid. No. 91, 17 (r. 22) Feb 1862, PRO, F.O. 72/1031.

30. Wyke to Russell, Vera Cruz, No. 3, 16 Jan (r. 2 Mar) 1862, PRO, F.O. 50/364.

31. Dunlop to Secretary of Admiralty, Challenger at Vera Cruz, No. 3, 15 Jan 1862, encl. of Admiralty to Hammond, Admiralty, Immediate, 3 (r. 3) Mar 1862, PRO, F.O. 50/370.

32. Wyke to Russell, Vera Cruz, No. 3, 16 Jan (r. 2 Mar) 1862, PRO, F.O. 50/364.

33. Dunlop to Secretary of Admiralty, Challenger at Vera Cruz, No. 3, 15 Jan 1862, encl. of Admiralty to Hammond, Admiralty, Immediate, 3 (r. 3) Mar 1862, PRO, F.O. 50/370.

34. Wyke to Russell, Vera Cruz, No. 3, 16 Jan (r. 2 Mar) 1862, Immediate, 3 (r. 3) Mar 1862, PRO, F.O. 50/370.

35. *Ibid.*

36. Brigadier Vargas to British Consul, Vera Cruz, 10 (r. 10) Jan 1862, PRO, F.O. 204/162.

37. Wyke to Russell, Vera Cruz, No. 5, 17 Jan (r. 2 Mar) 1862, PRO, F.O. 50/364.

38. Dunlop to Secretary of Admiralty, Challenger at Vera Cruz, No. 3, 16 Jan (r. 2 Mar) 1862, PRO, F.O. 50/364.

40. Dunlop to Secretary of Admiralty, Challenger at Vera Cruz, No. 3, 15 Jan 1862, encl. of Admiralty to Hammond, Admiralty, Immediate, 3 (r. 3) Mar 1862, PRO, F.O. 50/370.

41. Dunlop to Milne, Challenger at Vera Cruz, No. 22, 30 Jan 1862, encl. 2 of Paget to Hammond, Admiralty, Immediate, 3 (r. 3) Mar 1862, *ibid.*

42. John Elliot, Surgeon Marine Battalion, to Dunlop, Royal Marine Brigade, Vera Cruz, 3 Mar 1862, encl. 2 of Admiralty to Hammond, Admiralty, 31 Mar (r. 1 Apr) 1862, *ibid.*

43. Jurien to Thouvenel, Vera Cruz, No. 5, 15 Jan 1862, MDAE: *CP, Mex.,* vol. 57.

44. Wyke to Russell, Vera Cruz, No. 6, 18 Jan (r. 2 Mar) 1862, PRO, F.O. 50/364.

45. Wyke to Russell, Vera Cruz, No. 8, Secret and Confidential, 19 Jan (r. 2 Mar) 1862, *ibid.*

46. Saligny to Thouvenel, Vera Cruz, No. 62, 15 Jan (r. 21 Feb) 1862, MDAE: *CP, Mex.,* vol. 58.

47. Wyke to Russell, Vera Cruz, No. 1, 16 Jan (r. 2 Mar) 1862, PRO, F.O. 50/364.

48. See Section 1 of Chapter IV of present investigation.

49. Russell to Wyke, F.O. No. 69, 28 Nov 1861, PRO, F.O. 50/351.

For details, see Section 1 of Chapter IV of present investigation, between footnotes 138 and 139.

50. Russell to Wyke, F.O., No. 81, 16 Dec 1861 (r. 14 Feb 1862 by Ariadne), PRO, F.O. 204/153. For details see Section 1 of Chapter IV of present investigation, between footnotes 140 and 146.

51. See Section 1 of Chapter IV of present investigation.

52. Russell had directed Wyke to take his legation to Jamaica, leave it there, then proceed himself to Bermuda or wherever Admiral Milne might be. See Russell to Wyke, F.O., No. 56, 1 (r. 29) Nov 1861, PRO, F.O. 204/153. Since Milne, Dunlop, and Wyke didn't go to Jamaica, the British Senior Naval Officer in Port Royal had no specific instructions of what to do with the bags of despatches sent to him from Russell for Wyke and did not take the initiative to forward them. See Wyke to Russell, Vera Cruz, No. 19, 15 Feb (r. 31 Mar) 1862, PRO, F.O. 50/364. When the British mail packet arrived at Vera Cruz on 27 January 1862 without any instructions for Wyke (Wyke to Russell, Vera Cruz, No. 12, 30 Jan (r. 2 Mar) 1862, PRO, F.O. 50/364), he had Commodore Dunlop send the Ariadne to Port Royal on the chance that Russell's instructions were there. On 14 February 1862 the Ariadne returned with four bags of Russell's instructions (Wyke to Russell, Vera Cruz, No. 19, 15 Feb (r. 31 Mar) 1862, PRO, F.O. 50/364), including Russell's two instructions about claims (see footnotes 49 and 50 above).

53. Proposed despatch from the Count of Reus to General Doblado, Vera Cruz, 14 Jan 1862, encl. 3 of Wyke to Russell, Vera Cruz, No. 8, 19 Jan (r. 2 Mar) 1862, PRO, F.O. 50/364.

54. Specifically and in accordance with instructions, Prim demanded the execution of the Mon-Almonte Treaty of 1859, which recognized previous arrangements. For Prim's instructions, see Appendix N of present investigation. For Spanish conventions recognized by the Mon-Almonte Treaty, see Appendix D of present investigation.

55. See Appendix D of present investigation.

56. See Appendix N of present investigation.

57. Specifically Prim named ". . . the injuries . . . inflicted . . .by the crimes committed in the Haciendas of San Vicente and Chicon-cuaque, and in the mine of San Dimas. . . ." For these claims, see Appendices D and N of present investigation.

58. See Appendix D of present investigation.

59. See Appendix N of present investigation.

60. Extract of letter of Captain VonDonop of HMS Jason, encl. of Dunlop to Secretary of Admiralty, Challenger off Cape St. Antonio, Cuba, 1 Jan 1862, encls. of Romaine to Hammond, Admiralty, 30 Jan (r. 4 Feb) 1862, PRO, F.O. 50/370.

61. Prim-Senate-9 Dec 1862.

62. Wyke to Russell, Vera Cruz, No. 8, Secret and Confidential, 19 Jan (r. 2 Mar) 1862, PRO, F.O. 50/364.

63. Dunlop to Secretary of Admiralty, Challenger at Vera Cruz, No.

3, 15 Jan 1862, encl. of Admiralty to Hammond, Admiralty, Immediate, 3 (r. 3) Mar 1862, PRO, F.O. 50/370.

64. Proposed Despatch from Sir C. Wyke to General Doblado, Vera Cruz, 12 Jan 1862, encl. 4 of Wyke to Russell, Vera Cruz, No. 8, Secret and Confidential, 19 Jan (r. 2 Mar) 1862, PRO, F.O. 50/364.

65. Wyke to Russell, Vera Cruz, No. 8, Secret and Confidential, 19 Jan (r. 2 Mar) 1862, PRO, F.O. 50/364.

66. See Appendix B of present investigation.

67. The exact figure, as of 1 January 1862, was $63,498,230: a debt of $51,208,250 plus $12,289,980 in arrears of interest on it. See Appendix B of present investigation.

68. Until 17 July 1861 proper interest payments had been made to the Convention Bondholders, and the original debt of $4,984,914.84 had been reduced to $4,174,280.00 with sinking fund payments of $810,634.84. See Appendix A of present investigation.

69. See Appendix D of present investigation.

70. For the details of Wyke's negotiations in 1861 on behalf of these claims, see Section 1 of Chapter II of present investigation.

71. Russell to Wyke, F.O., No. 38, draft, 21 Aug 1861, marked seen by Palmerston and Queen Victoria, PRO, F.O. 50/351. The Interventors were to be appointed in Vera Cruz and Tampico and have powers to reduce import duties up to one half, to appropriate to all Powers having conventions with Mexico that percentage of custom duties guaranteed by those conventions, and to assure that the Legation Robbery and the Laguna Seca claims be liquidated with Mexican custom duties. Russell specifically stated that he considered the "Aldham and Dunlop Compacts," recognizing the claims of the London Bondholders, as legitimately binding the Mexican Government.

72. Received 1 October 1861. See original Russell despatch in PRO, F.O. 204/153.

73. See footnote 71 above.

74. Wyke to Russell, Vera Cruz, No. 8, Secret and Confidential, 19 Jan (r. 2 Mar) 1862, PRO, F.O. 50/364.

75. Prim-Senate-9 Dec 1862.

76. See Appendix Q of present investigation.

77. The Convention of 1853. For details, see footnote 29 of Section 3 of Chapter I of present investigation.

78. For details of the Rieche claim, see footnote 51 of Section 2 of Chapter II of present investigation.

79. For the Jecker claim, see Appendix C of present investigation.

80. Saligny claimed the same right in connection with all criminal prosecution of French subjects.

81. See footnote 166 of Section 1 of Chapter II of present investigation.

82. Wyke to Russell, Vera Cruz, Pri., 31 Jan 1862, PRO, P.R.O. 30/22–74.

83. Jurien to Thouvenel, Vera Cruz, No. 5, 15 Jan 1862, MDAE: *CP, Mex.,* vol. 57.

84. Prim-Senate-9 Dec 1862.

85. *Ibid.* Actually Jecker received 75,000,000 (ca. $15,000,000) in bonds in return for 7,472,140 francs (ca. $1,494,428). See footnote 132 of Section 3 of Chapter I of present investigation.

86. Prim-Senate-9 Dec 1862.

87. Jurien to Thouvenel, Vera Cruz, No. 5, 15 Jan 1862, MDAE: *CP, Mex.,* vol. 57.

88. Wyke to Russell, Vera Cruz, No. 8, Secret and Confidential, 19 Jan (r. 2 Mar) 1862, PRO, F.O. 50/364.

89. Wyke to Russell, Mexico City, No. 80, 8 Jun (r. 18 Jul) 1862, PRO, F.O. 50/366.

90. Wyke to Russell, Vera Cruz, No. 7, 18 Jan (r. 2 Mar) 1862, *ibid.*

90. Wyke to Russell, Vera Cruz, No. 8, Secret and Confidential, 19 Jan (r. 2 Mar) 1862, PRO, *ibid.*

91. Wyke to Russell, Vera Cruz, No. 7, 18 Jan (r. 2 Mar) 1862, *ibid.*

92. Wyke to Russell, Vera Cruz, No. 8, Secret and Confidential, 19 Jan (r. 2 Mar) 1862, PRO, *ibid.*

93. Dunlop to Secretary of Admiralty, Challenger at Vera Cruz, No. 3, 15 Jan 1862, encl. of Admiralty to Hammond, Admiralty, Immediate, 3 (r. 3) Mar 1862, PRO, F.O. 50/370.

94. Jurien to Thouvenel, Vera Cruz, No. 5, 15 Jan 1862, MDAE: *CP, Mex.,* vol. 57.

95. See Section 1 of Chapter IV and Appendix C of present investigation.

96. Saligny to Thouvenel, Vera Cruz, No. 63, 20 Jan (r. 4 Mar) 1862, MDAE: *CP, Mex.,* vol. 58.

97. "Observations on the ultimatum that M. D. de Saligny prepared, Mexico, 1862," n.d., attached to Saligny to Thouvenel, Vera Cruz, No. 62, 15 Jan (r. 21 Feb) 1862, *ibid.* The ultimatum is enclosure 3 of Saligny's Number 62.

98. Prim-Saligny conversation, sum. by Wyke to Russell, Mexico City, No. 80, 8 Jun (r. 18 Jul) 1862, PRO, F.O. 50/366.

99. Second Conference of the Allied Commissioners, Vera Cruz, 10 Jan 1862, sum. by Wyke to Russell, Vera Cruz, No. 5, 17 Jan (r. 2 Mar) 1862, PRO, F.O. 50/364.

100. Jurien to Thouvenel, Vera Cruz, No. 5, 15 Jan 1862, MDAE. *CP, Mex.,* vol. 57.

101. *Ibid.*

102. Prim-Senate-9 Dec 1862.

103. Collective Note to the Mexican Government proposed by General Prim, encl. 2 of Jurien to Thouvenel, Vera Cruz, No. 5, 15 Jan 1862, MDAE: *CP, Mex.,* vol. 57.

104. Wyke to Russell, Vera Cruz, No. 8, Secret and Confidential, 19 Jan (r. 2 Mar) 1862, PRO, F.O. 50/364.

105. Wyke to Russell, Orizaba, No. 41, 30 Mar (r. 28 Apr) 1862, 1862, *ibid;* Dunlop to Secretary of Admiralty, Orizaba, 17 Apr 1862, encl. of Paget to Hammond, Admiralty, 2 (r. 4) Jun 1862, PRO, F.O. 50/371; Prim-Senate-11 Dec 1862.

106. Wyke to Russell, Vera Cruz, No. 8, Secret and Confidential, 19 Jan (r. 2 Mar) 1862, PRO, F.O. 50/364; Dunlop to Milne, Challenger at Vera Cruz, No. 23, 30 Jan 1862, encl. 3 of Admiralty to Hammond, Admiralty, Immediate, 3 (r. 3) Mar 1862, PRO, F.O. 50/370; Prim to Collantes, Orizaba, No. 24, 29 Mar 1862, *Diario de Las Sessiones de Cortes. Congreso de los Diputados, 2 Jun 1862, Apéndice Primero Num. 133*, (trans.) encl. of Crampton to Russell, Madrid, No. 255, 16 (r. 26) Jun 1862, PRO, F.O. 72/1035.

107. Wyke to Russell, Vera Cruz, No. 4, 16 Jan (r. 2 Mar) 1862, PRO, F.O. 50/364; Dunlop to Secretary of Admiralty, Challenger at Vera Cruz, No. 3, 15 Jan 1862, encl. of Admiralty to Hammond Admiralty, Immediate, 3 (r. 3) Mar 1862, PRO, F.O. 50/370; Prim-Senate-11 Dec 1862.

108. Wyke to Russell, Vera Cruz, No. 8, Secret and Confidential, 19 Jan (r. 2 Mar) 1862, PRO, F.O. 50/364. Wyke stated Prim agreed with him about the "formidable mountain-passes." Dunlop claimed he agreed with Prim's views. See Dunlop to Secretary of Admiralty, Challenger at Vera Cruz, No. 3, 15 Jan 1862, encl. of Admiralty to Hammond, Admiralty, Immediate, 3 (r. 3) Mar 1862, PRO, F.O. 50/370.

109. Jurien to Thouvenel, Vera Cruz, No. 5, 15 Jan 1862, MDAE: *CP, Mex.,* vol. 57.

110. Dunlop to Secretary of Admiralty, Challenger at Vera Cruz, No. 3, 15 Jan 1862, encl. of Admiralty to Hammond, Admiralty, Immediate, 3 (r. 3) Mar 1862, PRO, F.O. 50/370.

111. Jurien to Thouvenel, Vera Cruz, No. 5, 15 Jan 1862, MDAE: *CP, Mex.,* vol. 57.

112. Jurien to Thouvenel, Vera Cruz, No. 14, 15 Feb 1862, *ibid.*

113. Jurien to Thouvenel, Vera Cruz, No. 5, 15 Jan 1862, *ibid.*

114. Wyke to Russell, Vera Cruz, No. 8, Secret and Confidential, 19 Jan (r. 2 Mar) 1862, PRO, F.O. 50/364.

115. Jurien to Thouvenel, Vera Cruz, No. 5, 15 Jan 1862, MDAE: *C.P., Mex.,* vol. 57.

116. Collective Note sent to Mexico City by delegates of the Representatives, Vera Cruz, 14 Jan 1862, encl. 4 of *Ibid.*

117. Saligny to Thouvenel, Vera Cruz, No. 62, 15 Jan (r. 21 Feb) 1862, *ibid.,* vol. 58.

118. Prim-Senate-9 Dec 1862.

119. Wyke to Russell, Orizaba, No. 48, 13 Apr (r. 14 May) 1862, PRO, F.O. 50/365.

120. Wyke to Russell, Vera Cruz, No. 8, Secret and Confidential, 19 Jan (r. 2 Mar) 1862, PRO, F.O. 50/364.

121. Dunlop to Secretary of Admiralty, Orizaba, 17 Apr 1862, encl. of Paget to Hammond, Admiralty, 2 (r. 4) Jun 1862, PRO, F.O. 50/371.

122. Jurien to Thouvenel, Vera Cruz, No. 5, 15 Jan 1862, MDAE: *CP, Mex.,* vol. 57.

123. Wyke to Russell, Vera Cruz, No. 8, Secret and Confidential, 19 Jan (r. 2 Mar) 1862, PRO, F.O. 50/364.

124. Saligny to Thouvenel, Vera Cruz, No. 62, 15 Jan (r. 21 Feb) 1862, MDAE: *CP, Mex.,* vol. 58.

125. *Ibid.*

126. See below.

127. Saligny to Serrano, Confidential, 22 Nov 1861, encl. of Serrano to Collantes, Havana, No. 89, 16 Dec 1861, *Diario de las Sessiones de Cortes. Congreso de los Diputados, 2 Jun 1862, Apéndice Primero Num. 133,* (trans.) encl. of Crampton to Russell, Madrid, No. 255, 16 (r. 26) Jun 1862, PRO, F.O. 72/1035.

128. *Ibid.*

129. *Ibid;* Saligny to Serrano, 24 Nov 1861, encl. of Serrano to Collantes, Havana, No. 89, 16 Dec 1861, *ibid.*

130. Saligny to Serrano, Con., 22 Nov 1861, and Saligny to Serrano, 29 Nov 1861, encls. of Serrano to Collantes, Havana, No. 89, 16 Dec 1861, *ibid.*

131. Postscript, dated 31 Jan 1862, to Saligny to Thouvenel, Vera Cruz, No. 64, 29 Jan (r. 4 Mar) 1862, MDAE: *Cp, Mex.,* vol. 58.

132. See Section 2 of Chapter II of present investigation, between footnotes 123 and 124.

133. See Section 2 of Chapter II of present investigation, between footnotes 124 and 125.

134. Saligny to General Rollin, Vera Cruz, Pri., 1 Jan 1862, MDAE: *CP, Mex.,* vol. 58. General Rollin was a French General residing in France and a friend of Saligny. Rollin forwarded this letter to the French Ministry of Foreign Affairs, and it was filed in its archives.

135. Saligny to Serrano, Con., 22 Nov 1861, encl. of Serrano to Collantes, Havana, No. 89, 16 Dec 1861, *Diario de Las Sessiones de Cortes. Congreso de los Diputados, 2 Jun 1862, Apéndice Primero Num. 133,* (trans.) encl. of Crampton to Russell, Madrid, No. 255, 16 (r. 26) Jun 1862, PRO, F.O. 72/1035.

136. Jurien to Thouvenel, Tehuacan, No. 25, Con., 24 Mar 1862, MDAE: *CP, Mex.,* vol. 57.

137. Captain Thomasset, Jurien's Chef d'Etat Major, to Jurien, Tehuacan, 25 Mar 1862, encl. of Jurien to Thouvenel, Tehuacan, No. 26, 24 Mar 1862, *ibid.*

138. See footnote 125, and text it footnotes, of Section 2 of Chapter II of present investigation.

139. He wrote nothing of it to Thouvenel, and Wyke, who sent Russell Uraga's public letter to Saligny (see footnote 125 of Section 2 of Chapter II of present investigation), forwarded no correspondence between Saligny and Uraga, as the British Minister to Mexico would have been sure to do if it had been published.

140. Saligny to General Rollin, Vera Cruz, Pri., 1 Jan 1862, MDAE: *CP, Mex.,* vol. 58.

141. Thouvenel to Saligny, No. 1, draft, 31 Jan 1862, *ibid.*

142. See Section 1 of Chapter IV of present investigation.

143. Jurien to Thouvenel, Vera Cruz, No. 10, 28 Jan 1862, MDAE: *CP, Mex.,* vol. 57.

144. Jurien to Thouvenel, Vera Cruz, No. 6, 18 Jan 1862, *ibid.*

145. Prim-Senate-9 Dec 1862.

146. Jurien to Thouvenel, Vera Cruz, No. 8, 23 Jan 1862, MDAE: *CP, Mex.,* vol. 57.

147. Prim-Senate-11 Dec 1862.

148. Serrano to Minister of War, Havana, 24 Jan 1862, *Gazette,* Madrid, 17 Feb 1862, encl. 2 of Crampton to Russell, Madrid, No. 91, 17 (r. 22) Feb 1862, PRO, F.O. 72/1031.

149. Dunlop to Secretary of Admiralty, Challenger at Vera Cruz, No. 3, 15 Jan 1862, encl. of Admiralty to Hammond, Admiralty, Immediate, 3 (r. 3) Mar 1862, PRO, F.O. 50/370.

150. Dunlop to Milne, Challenger at Vera Cruz, No. 22, 30 Jan 1862, encl. 2 of Paget to Hammond, Admiralty, Immediate, 3 (r. 3) Mar 1862, *ibid.*

151. Wyke to Hammond, Vera Cruz, Pri., 14 Jan (r. 12 Mar) 1862, PRO, F.O. 50/364.

152. Wyke to Russell, Vera Cruz, No. 4, 16 Jan (r. 2 Mar) 1862, *ibid.*

153. Wyke to Russell, Vera Cruz, No. 7, 18 Jan (r. 2 Mar) 1862, *ibid.*

154. Saligny to Thouvenel, Vera Cruz, No. 63, 20 Jan (r. 4 Mar) 1862, MDAE: *CP, Mex.,* vol. 58.

155. Saligny left the reporting of the third conference of 13–14 January, involving the ultimatums, to Jurien on the excuse of being busy with the "correspondence with the interior." Saligny did not make a report of the final conference, of 9 April 1862, when it was decided to stop joint negotiations and action. Saligny claimed he had "fever" and had Jurien draw up the report. See Saligny to Thouvenel, Vera Cruz, No. 62, 15 Jan (r. 21 Feb) 1862, and Saligny to Thouvenel, Orizaba, Con., Pri., 12 Apr 1862, *ibid.* For the conference of 9 April, see Section 1 of Chapter VI of present investigation.

156. Wyke to Russell, Vera Cruz, No. 17, 6 Feb (r. 31 Mar) 1862, PRO, F.O. 50/364.

157. Wyke to Russell, Vera Cruz, No. 10, 30 Jan (r. 2 Mar) 1862, *ibid.*

158. Philip Baker to Russell, Pri., n.d. (r. 1 Oct 1861), PRO, F.O. 50/358.

159. Draft to Philip Baker, F.O., 7 Oct 1861, *ibid.*

160. See footnote 158 above. File F.O. 50/358 contains many other private letters.

161. Wyke to Russell, Vera Cruz, No. 9, 25 Jan (r. 2 Mar) 1862, PRO, F.O. 50/364.

162. Dunlop to Milne, Challenger at Vera Cruz, No. 23, 30 Jan 1862, encl. 3 of Admiralty to Hammond, Admiralty, Immediate, 3 (r. 3) Mar 1862, PRO, F.O. 50/370.

163. Wyke to Russell, Vera Cruz, No. 10, 30 Jan (r. 2 Mar) 1862, PRO, F.O. 50/364.

164. Dunlop to Milne, Challenger to Vera Cruz, No. 23, 30 Jan 1862, encl. 3 of Admiralty to Hammond, Admiralty, Immediate, 3 (r. 3) Mar 1862, PRO, F.O. 50/370. For the Legation Robbery, see Section 3 of Chapter I, Section 1 of Chapter II, and Appendix B of present investigation.

165. Wyke to Russell, Vera Cruz, No. 10, 30 Jan (r. 2 Mar) 1862, PRO, F.O. 50/364.

166. Jurien to Thouvenel, Vera Cruz, No. 9, 25 Jan 1862, MDAE: *CP, Mex.,* vol. 57.

167. Dunlop to Milne, Challenger at Vera Cruz, No. 23, 30 Jan 1862, encl. 3 of Admiralty to Hammond, Admiralty, Immediate, 3 (r. 3) Mar 1962, PRO, F.O. 50/370.

168. Jurien to Thouvenel, Vera Cruz, No. 9, 25 Jan 1862, MDAE: *CP, Mex.,* vol. 57.

169. Wyke to Russell, Vera Cruz, No. 10, 30 Jan (r. 2 Mar) 1862, PRO, F.O. 50/364.

170. *Ibid.*

171. Dunlop to Milne, Challenger at Vera Cruz, No. 23, 30 Jan 1862, encl. 3 of Admiralty to Hammond, Admiralty, Immediate, 3 (r. 3) Mar 1862, PRO, F.O. 50/370.

172. Wyke to Russell, Vera Cruz, No. 10, 30 Jan (r. 2 Mar) 1862, PRO, F.O. 50/364.

173. Wyke to Russell, Orizaba, No. 48, 13 Apr (r. 14 May) 1862, PRO, F.O. 50/365; Dunlop to Secretary of Admiralty, Orizaba, 17 Apr 1862, encl. of Paget to Hammond, Admiralty, 2 (r. 4) Jun 1862, PRO, F.O. 50/371.

174. Jurien to Thouvenel, Vera Cruz, No. 9, 25 Jan 1862, MDAE: *CP, Mex.,* vol. 57.

175. Wyke to Russell, Vera Cruz, No. 10, 30 Jan (r. 2 Mar) 1862, PRO, F.O. 50/364.

176. Jurien to Thouvenel, Vera Cruz, No. 9, 25 Jan 1862, MDAE: *CP, Mex.,* vol. 57.

177. *Ibid.*

178. Saligny to Thouvenel, 29 Jan 1862, cited by Saligny to Thouvenel, Vera Cruz, No. 69, 11 Mar (r. 9 Apr) 1862, *ibid.,* vol. 58.

179. Wyke to Russell, Vera Cruz, No. 10, 30 Jan (r. 2 Mar) 1862, PRO, F.O. 50/364.

180. Lt. Charles Slaughter to Capt. Paley, Supt. of Packets, Southampton, RMS Avon, Vera Cruz, 27 Jan 1862, and Lt. Charles Slaughter to Dunlop, Avon, 27 Jan 1862, encls. 1 and 2 of Romaine to Hammond, Admiralty, 4 (r. 5) Mar 1862, PRO, F.O. 50/370. Slaughter handed Dunlop the letter addressed to him on 27 January. In it was stated that Miramon boarded the Avon at Havana on 22 January 1862 with a passport giving his name as "M. Fernandez."

181. Captain Kennedy of the Challenger removed Miramon from the Avon to the Challenger. See Lt. Charles Slaughter to Capt. Paley,

Supt. of Packets, Southampton, RMS Avon, Vera Cruz, 27 Jan 1862, encl. I of Romaine to Hammond, Admiralty, 4 (r. 5) Mar 1862, *ibid.*

182. Dunlop to Secretary of Admiralty, Orizaba, 17 Apr 1862, encl. of Paget to Hammond, Admiralty, 2 (r. 4) Jun 1862, PRO, F.O. 50/371.

183. See footnote 181 above. On 28 January 1862 Miramon was shifted from the Challenger to the Jason and remained aboard it through 4 February 1862. See "List of Passengers Entertained on board H.M.S. Jason," encl. of Romaine to Hammond, Admiralty, 6 (r. 7) May 1862, *ibid.*

184. Wyke to Russell, Vera Cruz, Pri., 31 Jan 1862, PRO, P.R.O. 30/22–74.

185. Dunlop to Milne, Challenger at Vera Cruz, No. 23, 30 Jan 1862, encl. 3 of Paget to Hammond, Admiralty, Immediate, 3 (r. 3) Mar 1862, PRO, F.O. 50/370. Dunlop wrote Milne that Miramon would be sent to Havana on the Mersey, but Dunlop could not send the Mersey until the arrival of the Donegal as its replacement. Miramon apparently was sent to Havana on 4 or 5 February. See footnote 183 above.

186. *Ibid.*

187. Wyke to Russell, Vera Cruz, No. 10, 30 Jan (r. 2 Mar) 1862, PRO, F.O. 50/364.

188. Wyke to Russell, Vera Cruz, Pri., 31 Jan 1862, PRO, P.R.O. 30/22–74.

189. Wyke to Russell, Orizaba, No. 38, 27 Mar (r. 28 Apr) 1862, PRO, F.O. 50/364.

190. Wyke to Russell, Vera Cruz, No. 11, 30 Jan (r. 2 Mar) 1862, *ibid.*

191. Thomasset to Jurien, Vera Cruz, 31 Jan 1862, encl. of Jurien to Thouvenel, Vera Cruz, No. 7, Jan 1862, MDAE: *CP, Mex.,* vol. 57.

192. The allied officers waited three days. See *Ibid.*

193. Prim-Senate-9 Dec 1862.

194. *Ibid.* Prim said, "I could tell the Senate the origin of this gossip, as have already had the honour to tell it to the president of the Council and to the Minister of State; but unless the Senate orders it I shall not do so, from respect to the Spanish name which is borne by those who spread this report."

195. Prim-Senate-9 Dec 1862.

196. Napoleon III to Maximilian, 7 Mar 1862, HHSA, cited in full by CORTI, I, 370–371.

197. Doblado to Allied Commissioners, Mexico (City), 23 Jan 1862, encl. 3 of Wyke to Russell, Vera Cruz, No. 11, 30 Jan (r. 2 Mar) 1862, PRO, F.O. 50/364.

198. Felix, Prinz su Salm-Salm: *My Diary in Mexico in 1867, including the Last Days of the Emperor Maximilian; with leaves from the Diary of the Princess Salm-Salm* (2 v., London, 1868), I, 274.

199. Decree published by Juarez, 25 Jan 1862, encl. 7 of Saligny

to Thouvenel, Vera Cruz, No. 66, 16 Feb (r. 1 Apr) 1862, MDAE: *CP, Mex.,* vol. 58.

200. Jurien to Thouvenel, Vera Cruz, No. 10, 28 Jan 1862, *ibid.,* vol. 57.

201. Prim-Senate-9 Dec 1862.

202. Wyke to Russell, Vera Cruz, No. 11, 30 Jan (r. 2 Mar) 1862, PRO, F.O. 50/364. Wyke did not mention from whom he received these private letters.

203. John Elliot, Surgeon Marine Battalion, to Dunlop, Royal Marine Brigade, Vera Cruz, 3 Mar 1862, encl. 2 of Admiralty to Hammond, Admiralty, 31 Mar (r. 1 Apr) 1862, PRO, F.O. 50/370.

204. Dunlop to Milne, Challenger at Vera Cruz, No. 23, 30 Jan 1862, encl 3 of Paget to Hammond, Admiralty, Immediate, 3 (r. 3) Mar 1862, *ibid.*

205. Dunlop to Milne, Challenger at Vera Cruz, No. 22, 30 Jan 1862, encl. 2 of Paget to Hammond, Admiralty, Immediate, 3 (r. 3) Mar 1862, *ibid.*

206. Postscript, dated 31 Jan 1862, to Jurien to Thouvenel, Vera Cruz, No. 12, 29 Jan 1862, MDAE: *CP, Mex.,* vol. 57.

207. Jurien to Thouvenel, Vera Cruz, No. 12, 29 Jan 1862, *ibid.*

208. Postscript, dated 31 Jan 1862, of *Ibid.*

209. Wyke to Russell, Vera Cruz, Pri., 31 Jan 1862, PRO, P.R.O. 30/22–74.

210. Wyke to Russell, Vera Cruz, No. 32, 1 (r. 31) Mar 1862, PRO, F.O. 50/364.

211. Saligny to Thouvenel, Vera Cruz, No. 66, 16 Feb (r. 1 Apr) 1862, MDAE: *CP, Mex.,* vol. 58. Saligny did not give the date of the conference at which this discussion took place. For a reference to it, see Appendix S of present investigation.

212. Jurien to Thouvenel, Vera Cruz, No. 11, 29 Jan 1862, MDAE: *CP, Mex.,* vol. 57.

213. Dunlop to Milne, Challenger at Vera Cruz, No. 23, 30 Jan 1862, encl. 3 of Paget to Hammond, Admiralty, Immediate, 3 (r. 3) Mar 1862, PRO, F.O. 50/370.

214. Jurien to Thouvenel, Vera Cruz, No. 12, 29 Jan 1862, MDAE: *CP, Mex.,* vol. 57.

215. Saligny to Thouvenel, Vera Cruz, No. 64, 29 Jan (r. 4 Mar) 1862, *ibid.,* vol. 58. For Saligny's previous experience with Zamacona, see Section 2 of Chapter II of present investigation.

216. Postscript, dated 30 Jan 1862, of Jurien to Thouvenel, Vera Cruz, No. 12, 29 Jan 1862, MDAE: *CP, Mex.,* vol. 57.

217. John Elliot, Surgeon Marine Battalion, to Dunlop, Vera Cruz, 3 Mar 1862, encl. 2 of Admiralty to Hammond, Admiralty, 31 Mar (r. 1 Apr) 1862, PRO, F.O. 50/370. Elliot claimed only 12% died when the city was kept clean.

218. H. Mercier de Lacombe: *Le Mexique, L'Amérique du Nord et l'Europe, par H. Mercier de Lacombe* (Paris, 1863), p. 5.

219. Prim-Senate-9 Dec 1862.

220. Dunlop to Milne, Challenger at Vera Cruz, No. 23, 30 Jan 1862, encl. 3 of Paget to Hammond, Admiralty, Immediate, 3 (r. 3) Mar 1862, PRO, F.O. 50/370.

221. Wyke to Russell, Vera Cruz, No. 32, 1 (r. 31) Mar 1862, PRO, F.O. 50/364.

222. See Section 1 of Chapter II of present investigation, between footnotes 214 and 215. See also Ralph Roeder: *Juarez and His Mexico: A Biographical History* (2 v., New York, 1947), II, 383.

223. Wyke to Russell, Vera Cruz, No. 16, 31 Jan (r. 2 Mar) 1862, PRO, F.O. 50/364.

224. See Section 1 of Chapter II of present investigation.

225. Wyke to Russell, Vera Cruz, No. 16, 31 Jan (r. 2 Mar) 1862, PRO, F.O. 50/364.

226. Wyke to Russell, Vera Cruz, Pri., 31 Jan 1862, PRO, P.R.O. 30/22-74.

227. Prim-Senate-9 Dec 1862.

228. Wyke to Russell, Vera Cruz, Pri., 31 Jan 1862, PRO, P.R.O. 30/22-74.

229. Wyke to Russell, Vera Cruz, No. 32, 1 (r. 31) Mar 1862, PRO, F.O. 50/364. Wyke specifically stated that he was recalling Saligny's views shortly after Jurien's arrival in Mexico.

230. Prim-Senate-9 Dec 1862.

231. Wyke to Russell, Vera Cruz, Pri., 31 Jan 1862, PRO, P.R.O. 30/22-74.

232. Prim-Senate-9 Dec 1862.

233. See Section 1 of Chapter IV of present investigation.

234. Jurien to Thouvenel, Orizaba, 7 Mar 1862, MDAE: *CP, Mex.,* vol. 57.

235. See Section 1 of Chapter IV of present investigation.

236. Thomasset to Jurien, Vera Cruz, 31 Jan 1862, encl. of Jurien to Thouvenel, Vera Cruz, No. 7, Jan 1862, MDAE: *CP, Mex.,* vol. 57.

237. Maitland to Secretary of Admiralty, Bacchante to Callao, No. 24, 14 Jan 1862, encl. of Romaine to Hammond, Admiralty, 15 (r. 17) Feb 1862, PRO, F.O. 50/370.

238. Maitland to Wyke, Bacchante at Toboga Island, Panama, 22 Feb 1862, encl. 2 of Romaine to Hammond, Admiralty, 18 (r. 19) Mar 1862, *ibid.*

239. Maitland to Secretary of Admiralty, Bacchante at Toboga, No. 49, 6 Feb 1862, encl. of Admiralty to Hammond, Admiralty, 3 (r. 3) Mar 1862, *ibid.*

240. Maitland to Wyke, Bacchante at Toboga Island, Panama, 22 Feb 1862, encl. 2 of Romaine to Hammond, Admiralty, 18 (r. 19) Mar 1862, *ibid.*

241. Maitland to Secretary of Admiralty, Bacchante at Toboga, No. 72, 23 Feb 1862, encl. 1 of Romaine to Hammond, Admiralty, 18 (r. 19) Mar 1862, *ibid.* In this letter Hammond referred to Wyke's

directions, but in a letter written a day before Maitland stated he had not received any instructions from Wyke. See footnote 240 above.

242. Wyke to Maitland, Vera Cruz, 31 Jan 1862, PRO, F.O. 204/163.

243. At the conference of 18 January 1862. See above in text of this section of present investigation.

244. Maitland to Secretary of Admiralty, Bacchante at Acapulco, 18 Mar 1862, encl. of Romaine to Hammond, Admiralty, 30 (r. 30) Apr 1862, PRO, F.O. 50/370.

245. See footnote 52 above.

246. Wyke to Russell, Vera Cruz, No. 11, 30 Jan (r. 2 Mar) 1862, PRO, F.O. 50/364.

247. Wyke to Russell, Vera Cruz, No. 17, 6 Feb (r. 31 Mar) 1862, *ibid.*

248. Saligny to Thouvenel, Vera Cruz, No. 65, 17 Feb (r. 11 Mar) 1862, MDAE: *CP, Mex.,* vol. 58.

249. The Allied Commissioners to General Doblado, 2 Feb 1862, encl. 2 of Wyke to Russell, Vera Cruz, No. 17, 6 Feb (r. 31 Mar) 1862, PRO. F.O. 50/364.

250. Saligny to Thouvenel, Vera Cruz, No. 65, 17 Feb (r. 11 Mar) 1862, MDAE: *CP, Mex.,* vol. 58.

251. Jurien to Thouvenel, Vera Cruz, No. 13, 9 Feb 1862, *ibid.,* vol. 57.

252. Doblado to the Allied Commissioners, Mexico (City), 6 Feb 1862, encl. 2 of Wyke to Russell, Vera Cruz, No. 18, 12 Feb (r. 31 Mar) 1862, PRO, F.O. 50/364.

253. Jurien to Thouvenel, Vera Cruz, No. 13, 9 Feb 1862, MDAE: *CP, Mex.,* vol. 57.

254. Wyke's hopes for a pacific solution grew "fainter." See Wyke to Russell, Vera Cruz, No. 18, 12 Feb (r. 31 Mar) 1862, PRO, F.O. 50/364. Dunlop considered Doblado's note "ambiguous." See Dunlop to Milne, Challenger at Vera Cruz, No. 45, 26 Feb 1862, encl. 2 of Admiralty to Hammond, 31 Mar (r. 1 Apr) 1862, PRO, F.O. 50/370.

255. Dunlop to Milne, Challenger at Vera Cruz, No. 45, 26 Feb 1862, encl. 2 of Admiralty to Hammond, 31 Mar (r. 1 Apr) 1862, PRO, F.O. 50/370.

256. Wyke to Russell, Vera Cruz, No. 18, 12 Feb (r. 31 Mar) 1862, PRO, F.O. 50/364.

257. Jurien to Thouvenel, Vera Cruz, No. 13, 9 Feb 1862, MDAE: *CP, Mex.,* vol. 57.

258. The Allied Commissioners to General Doblado, 9 Feb 1862, encl. 3 of Wyke to Russell, Vera Cruz, No. 18, 12 Feb (r. 31 Mar) 1862, PRO, F.O. 50/364.

259. Prim-Senate-9 Dec 1862.

260. Jurien to Thouvenel, Vera Cruz, No. 13, 9 Feb 1862, MDAE: *CP, Mex.,* vol 57.

261. Major Digby left Vera Cruz on 11 February, arrived at Havana 16 February, made the purchases, paid by the British Consul in

Havana, left Havana 21 February with some of his purchases, having arranged that the remainder be sent to Vera Cruz by the next mail packet. See Dunlop to Milne, Challenger at Vera Cruz, Nos. 46 and 47, 27 Feb 1862, encls. of Admiralty to Hammond, 2 (r. 2) Apr 1862, PRO, F.O. 50/370. See also Dunlop to Milne, Challenger at Vera Cruz, 26 Feb 1862, encl. of Admiralty to Hammond, 31 Mar (r. 1 Apr) 1862, PRO, F.O. 50/370.

262. Dunlop to Milne, Challenger at Vera Cruz, 26 Feb 1862, encl. of Admiralty to Hammond, 31 Mar (r. 1 Apr.) 1862, PRO, F.O. 50/370.

263. *Ibid;* Prim-Senate-9 Dec 1862; Serrano to Minister of War, Havana, 24 Jan 1862, *Gazette,* Madrid, 17 Feb 1862, encl. 2 of Crampton to Russell, Madrid, No. 91, 17 (r. 22) Feb 1862, PRO, F.O. 72/1031.

264. Prim-Senate-9 Dec 1862; Appendix T of present investigation.

265. Wyke to Russell, Vera Cruz, No. 21, 16 Feb (r. 31 Mar) 1862, PRO, F.O. 50/364.

266. General Zaragoza to the General-in-Chief of the Allied Forces, Soledad, 10 Feb 1862; The Allied Commanders (Dunlop, Jurien, Prim) to General Zaragoza, Vera Cruz, 10 Feb 1862; The Allied Commissioners (all five) to General Doblado, Vera Cruz, 11 Feb 1862, encls. 2, 4, 5 of *Ibid.*

267. Wyke to Russell, Vera Cruz, No. 18, 12 Feb (r. 31 Mar) 1862, *ibid.*

268. Draft of a Proclamation to Mexicans, drawn up by Jurien, encl. of Jurien to Thouvenel, Vera Cruz, No. 14, 15 Feb 1862, MDAE: *CP, Mex.,* vol. 57. Compare with Appendix M of present investigation.

269. Wyke to Russell, Vera Cruz, No. 22, 17 Feb (r. 31 Mar) 1862, PRO, F.O. 50/364.

270. Jurien to Thouvenel, Vera Cruz, No. 14, 15 Feb 1862, MDAE: *CP, Mex.,* vol. 57.

271. Wyke to Russell, Vera Cruz, No. 23, 17 Feb (r. 31 Mar) 1862, and two enclosures thereto, Doblado to the Allied Commissioners, Mexico (City), both dated 13 Feb 1862. PRO, F.O. 50/364.

272. See Section 2 of Chapter V and Section 1 of Chapter VI of present investigation.

273. See footnote 52 above.

274. Russell to Wyke, F.O., No. 82, 16 Dec 1861 (r. 14 Feb 1862 by Ariadne), PRO, F.O. 204/153.

275. 11th Conference of the Allied Commissioners, Vera Cruz, 16 Feb 1862, sum. by Wyke to Russell, Vera Cruz, No. 24, 17 Feb (r. 31 Mar) 1862, PRO, F.O. 50/364.

276. For the Prim-Doblado negotiations, with the exception of Prim's reason for suggesting Article V of the Preliminaries of La Soledad, see Appendix S of present investigation. For the text of the Preliminaries, see Appendix R of present investigation. For Prim's motive for urging the insertion of Article V, see Prim.-Senate-9 Dec 1862.

277. See Appendix S of present investigation.

278. Wyke to Russell, Vera Cruz, No. 25, 22 Feb (r. 31 Mar) 1862, PRO, F.O. 50/364.

279. Jurien to Thouvenel, Vera Cruz, No. 17, 20 Feb 1862, MDAE: *CP, Mex.,* vol. 57.

280. Jurien to Thouvenel, Orizaba, 7 Mar 1862, *ibid.*

281. Jurien to Thouvenel, Cordova, 5 Mar 1862, *ibid.*

282. Saligny to Thouvenel, Vera Cruz, No. 73, 31 Mar (r. 29 Apr) 1862, *ibid.,* vol. 58.

283. Saligny to Thouvenel, Vera Cruz, No. 69, 11 Mar (r. 9 Apr) 1862, *ibid.*

284. Prim-Senate-9 Dec 1862.

285. John Elliot, Surgeon Marine Battalion, to Dunlop, Royal Marine Brigade, Vera Cruz, 3 Mar 1862, encl. 2 of Admiralty to Hammond, Admiralty, 31 Mar (r. 1 Apr) 1862, PRO, F.O. 50/370.

286. Wyke to Russell, Vera Cruz, No. 25, 22 Feb (r. 31 Mar) 1862, PRO, F.O. 50/364.

287. Dunlop to Milne, Challenger at Vera Cruz, 26 Feb 1862, encl. 2 of Admiralty to Hammond, 31 Mar (r. 1 Apr) 1862, PRO, F.O. 50/370.

288. *Ibid.*

289. Wyke to Russell, Vera Cruz, No. 25, 22 Feb (r. 31 Mar) 1862, PRO, F.O. 50/364.

290. Wyke to Russell, Vera Cruz, No. 26, 23 Feb 1862, PRO, F.O. 204/160.

291. 13th Conference of the Allied Commissioners, Vera Cruz, 24 Feb 1862, sum. by Wyke to Russell, Vera Cruz, No. 27, 26 Feb (r. 31 Mar) 1862, PRO, F.O. 50/364.

292. Unofficial conference of the Allied Commissioners, Vera Cruz, 25 Feb 1862, sum. by Dunlop to Milne, Challenger at Vera Cruz, 26 Feb 1862, encl. 2 of Admiralty to Hammond, 31 Mar (r. 1 Apr) 1862, PRO, F.O. 50/370.

293. Wyke to Russell, Vera Cruz, No. 29, 28 Feb (r. 31 Mar) 1862, PRO, F.O. 50/364.

294. Wyke to Russell, Vera Cruz, No. 34, 5 Mar (r. 28 Apr) 1862, *ibid.* Wyke specifically mentioned 59% as due British creditors. For the details, see footnote 11 of Section 1 of Chapter IV of present investigation.

295. Saligny to Thouvenel, Vera Cruz, No. 68, 3 Mar (r. 3 Apr) 1862, MDAE: *CP Mex.,* vol. 58.

296. Prim to Doblado, Vera Cruz, 26 Feb 1862, PRO, F.O. 204/163.

297. Wyke to Russell, Vera Cruz, No. 28, 26 Feb (r. 31 Mar) 1862, PRO, F.O. 50/364.

298. Wyke to Russell, Orizaba, No. 36, 10 Mar (r. 28 Apr) 1862, *ibid.*

299. Wyke to Russell, Vera Cruz, No. 29, 28 Feb (r. 31 Mar) 1862, *ibid.*

## 2. Maximilian and Negotiations Among the European Powers, December 1861—February 1862

1. Crampton to Russell, Madrid, Telegrams, 3:00 P.M. (r. 6:5 P.M.) 27 Dec 1861 and 11:10 P.M. 28 (r. 1:35 P.M. 29) Dec 1861, PRO, F.O. 72/1012; The First Secretary of State to the Spanish Ambassador to Paris, Madrid, 21 Dec 1861, Telegram communicated by the Spanish Ambassador to Paris to the French Ministry of Foreign Affairs, MDAE: *CP, Espagne,* vol. 859; Barrot to Thouvenel, Madrid, No. 139, 26 (r. 30) Dec 1861, MDAE: *CP, Espagne,* vol. 859.

2. Russell to Crampton, F.O., Telegram, 12:5 P.M., 28 Dec 1861, cited by Russell to Crampton, F.O., No. 157, draft, 28 Dec 1861, PRO, F.O. 72/1002.

3. Crampton to Russell, Madrid, Telegram, 11:10 P.M. 28 (r. 1:35 P.M. 29) Dec 1861, PRO, F.O. 72/1012.

4. For Russell's fears of Spanish designs to establish religious intolerance in Mexico, see Section 2 of Chapter III of present investigation.

5. Russell to Cowley, F.O., Pri., 27 Dec 1861, PRO, F.O. 519/199.

6. Isturiz to Russell, Spanish Legation, London, 13 (r. 14) Jan 1862, *B.S.P.,* 1862, LXIV, 250–251. Isturiz enclosed Serrano's instructions to the Head of the Spanish Expedition to Mexico, dated 13 December 1861, wherein Serrano dirceted that the *status quo* be maintained in Vera Cruz until the arrival of Spain's allies.

7. Russell to Isturiz, 16 Jan 1862, sum. by Collantes in conversation with Crampton, sum. by Crampton to Russell, Madrid, No. 50, 30 Jan (r. 9 Feb) 1862, PRO, F.O. 72/1030. See also E. Lefêvre: *Le Mexique et L'Intervention Europeene, par le citoyen E. Lefêvre* (Mexico City, 1862), p. 350.

8. E. Lefêvre: *Le Mexique et L'Intervention Europeene, par le citoyen E. Lefêvre* (Mexico City, 1862), p. 350.

9. Russell to Isturiz, F.O., 23 Jan 1862, *ibid.,* p. 352.

10. Thouvenel to Barrot, No. 54, draft, 24 Dec 1861, MDAE: *CP, Espagne,* vol. 859.

11. Barrot-Collantes Conversation, 28 Dec 1861, sum. by Barrot to Thouvenel, Madrid, No. 143, 29 Dec 1861 (r. 2 Jan 1862), *ibid.*

12. Barrot-Crampton Conversation, sum. by Crampton to Russell, Madrid, No. 7, Con., 4 (r. 14) Jan 1862, PRO, F.O. 72/1030.

13. *Ibid;* Barrot to Thouvenel, Madrid, No. 139, 26 (r. 30) Dec 1862, MDAE: *CP, Espagne,* vol. 859.

14. O'Donnell-Barrot Conversation, sum. by Barrot to Thouvenel, Madrid, No. 139, 26 (r. 30) Dec 1862, *ibid.* O'Donnell commented that Prim's appointment wasn't made known until 14 or 15 November, and Serrano's letter reporting his decision was dated 26 November.

15. Thouvenel-Cowley Conversation, sum. by Cowley to Russell, Paris, No. 1492, Con., 31 Dec 1861, PRO, F.O. 27/1400.

16. Cowley to Crampton, Chantilly, Pri., 28 Dec 1861, PRO, F.O. 519/229.

17. Jurien-Prim Conversation, Vera Cruz, 17 Jan 1862, sum. by

Jurien to Thouvenel, Vera Cruz, No. 6, 18 Jan 1862, MDAE: *CP, Mex.,* vol. 57.

18. Metternich to Rechberg, Pri., accompanying despatch of 4 Jan 1862, HHSA, sum. & cited by CORTI, I, 130–131.

19. Napoleon III-Thouvenel Conversation, sum. by Thouvenel-Cowley Conversation, sum. by Cowley to Russell, Paris, No. 44, 17 (r. 18) Jan 1862, PRO, F.O. 27/1431.

20. Thouvenel to Flahault, Paris, Pri., 17 Jan 1862, THOUVENEL, II, 225–226.

21. Collantes to Mon, Madrid, 9 Dec 1861, *Diario de Las Sessiones de Cortes. Congreso de los Diputados, 2 Jun 1862, Apéndice Primero Num. 133,* (trans.) encl. of Crampton to Russell, Madrid, No. 255, 16 (r. 26) Jun 1862, PRO, F.O. 72/1035. Collantes specifically referred to Mon's despatch of 13 October 1861. For its contents, see Section 3 of Chapter II of present investigation, between footnotes 90 and 91. Leonardon claims that Collantes waited two months before answering Mon's report, because at first Collantes took Thouvenel's suggestion unimportant. See PRIM, pp. 52–53. Schefer claims Collantes' instruction of 9 December 1861 led directly to Napoleon's decision to send reinforcements to Mexico. See SCHEFER, p. 174.

22. Saligny to Thouvenel, Mexico City, No. 52, 15 Nov 1861 (r. 6 Jan 1862); Saligny to Thouvenel, Mexico City, No. 59 *(bis),* 15 Nov 1861 (r. 2 Jan 1862), MDAE: *CP, Mex.,* vol. 56. For more details, see Sections 1 and 2 of Chapter II of present investigation.

23. Saligny to Thouvenel, Mexico City, No. 55, 25 Nov 1861 (r. 2 Jan 1862), MDAE: *CP, Mex.,* vol. 56.

24. See Section 1 of Chapter IV of present investigation, between footnotes 94 and 95.

25. Miranda to Estrada, Havana, 22 Nov 1861, and J. D. Ulibarri to Estrada, Mexico City, 29 Nov 1861, encls. 1 and 2 of Estrada to Thouvenel, Vienna, 6 Jan 1862, MDAE: *CP, Mex.,* vol. 58.

26. See below.

27. For Maximilian's meeting with Franz Joseph, see Section 3 of Chapter IV of present investigation. On 8 January 1862 Napoleon III saw Metternich and told him Maximilian and Franz Joseph's decision were approved. See Metternich to Rechberg, 8 Jan 1862, HHSA, sum. by CORTI, I, 143–144. For the date of the meeting, see Metternich to Rechberg, 8 Jan 1862, HHSA, AKM, sum. by DAWSON, p. 193. For Thouvenel's confidance given Cowley that Napoleon III decided to send reinforcements on Maximilian's account, see below.

28. Thouvenel-Cowley conversation, sum. by Cowley to Russell, Chantilly, Pri., 21 Jan 1862, PRO, P.R.O. 30/22–57.

29. Napoleon III to Randon, Paris, 9 Jan 1862, cited by Maréchal Jacques L. Randon: *Mémoires du Maréchal Randon* (2 v., Paris, 1875–1877), II, 60–61.

30. Cowley to Russell, Paris, No. 141, Con., 11 (r. 12) Feb 1862, PRO, F.O. 27/1432.

31. Metternich to Rechberg, 8 Jan 1862, HHSA, sum. by CORTI, I, 143–144 and DAWSON, p. 193.

32. DAWSON, p. 195.

33. See Section 3 of Chapter IV of present investigation, between footnotes 90 and 91.

34. DAWSON, p. 207.

35. Napoleon III to Maximilian, Paris, 14 Jan 1862, HHSA, cited in full by CORTI, I, 365–366.

36. DAWSON, p. 207.

37. Estrada to Maximilian, 8 Jan 1862, HHSA, AKM, cited by ibid., p. 195.

38. Estrada to Baron de Pont, 10 Jan 1862, HHSA, AKM, ibid.

39. Estrada to Maximilian, 15 Jan 1862, HHSA, AKM, ibid., p. 196.

40. Estrada to Baron de Pont, 10 Jan 1862, HHSA, AKM, ibid., p. 195.

41. Estrada to Maximilian, 15/17 Jan 1862, HHSA, cited by CORTI, I, 146.

42. Estrada to Maximilian, Paris, 18 Jan 1862, HHSA, sum. & cited by ibid., I, 150.

43. Estrada to Maximilian, 9 Feb 1862, HHSA, AKM, DAWSON, p. 230.

44. Ibid.

45. Cowley to Russell, Paris, No. 44, 17 (r. 18) Jan 1862, PRO, F.O. 27/1431.

46. Cowley to Russell, Paris, Pri., 17 Jan 1862, PRO, F.O. 519/229.

47. Thouvenel to Flahault, No. 3, draft, 17 Jan 1862, MDAE: CP, Angleterre, vol. 721.

48. Thouvenel to Flahault, Paris, Pri., 17 Jan 1862, THOUVENEL, II, 226.

49. Coded telegram to Barrot, Paris 5:5 P.M., 17 Jan 1862, MDAE: CP, Espagne, vol. 860.

50. Thouvenel to Barrot, No. 2, draft, 21 Jan 1862, ibid.

51. Mon to Collantes, Paris, No. 31, 18 Jan 1862, Diario de Las Sessiones de Cortes. Congreso de los Diputados, 2 Jun 1862, Apéndice Primero Num. 133, (trans.) encl. of Crampton to Russell, Madrid, No. 255, 16 (r. 26) Jun 1862, PRO, F.O. 72/1035.

52. Miranda to Estrada, Havana, 21 Dec 1861, encl. 1 of Estrada to Thouvenel, Hotel Westminster, 13 Rue de la Paix, Paris, 17 Jan 1862, MDAE: CP, Mex., vol. 58. The Minister was Gonzales Echeverria, Juarez' Minister of Finance.

53. See Section of Chapter III of present investigation, between footnotes 78 and 80.

54. Napoleon III to Prim, 24 Jan 1862, cited by Emile de la Bèdollière: Histoire de la Guerre du Mexique, Illustrée par Janet-Lange et Gustave Dore (Paris, 1866), p. 5. Schefer claims Napoleon's letter was an attempt to seduce the Spaniard by flattery. See SCHEFER, p. 177.

55. See footnotes 45 and 46 above.

56. Russell to Cowley, Telegram, 18 Jan 1862, cited by Russell to Cowley, F.O., No. 69, draft, 18 Jan 1862, PRO, F.O. 27/1419.

57. Russell to Cowley, Pembroke Lodge, Richmond Park, Pri., 18 Jan 1862, PRO, F.O. 519/199.

58. Palmerston to Russell, Pri., 19 Jan 1862, PRO, Gifts and Deposits 22 (Russell Papers): 22, cited by Herbert C. F. Bell: *Lord Palmerston* (2 v., London, 1936), II, 313–314. Also cited by Harold Temperley and Lillian M. Penson, eds.: *Foundations of British Foreign Policy, from Pitt (1792) to Salisbury (1902), or, Documents, Old and New* (Cambridge 1938), p. 295. The Russell Papers are now designated P.R.O. 30/22.

59. Herbert C. F. Bell: *Lord Palmerston* (2 v., London, 1936), II, 313.

60. See Sections 2 and 3 of Chapter III of present investigation.

61. See below.

62. Russell to Wyke, F.O., No. 7, draft, 27 Jan 1862, marked seen by Palmerston, PRO, F.O. 50/363.

63. A copy is located in MDAE: *CP, Mex.,* vol. 58.

64. Herbert C. F. Bell: *Lord Palmerston* (2 v., London, 1936), II, 313.

65. Russell to Wyke, F.O., No. 7, draft, 27 Jan 1862, marked seen by Palmerston, PRO, F.O. 50/363.

66. "It would never do for us to set up a monarchy in Mexico, though if they did it for themselves, I should think they took the wisest course." See Russell to Cowley, Pri., 9 Sep 1861, PRO, F.O. 519/199.

67. "It would be a good thing for Europe that a regular and orderly government should be established in Mexico and that probably could be done only by a monarchy." See Palmerston to Russell, 13 Aug 1863, cited by Sir Victor Wellesley and Robert Sencourt, eds.: *Conversations with Napoleon III: A Collection of Documents, mostly unpublished and almost entirely Diplomatic, Selected and arranged with Introductions* (London, 1934), p. 223. Palmerston believed monarchies were inherently better than republics: ". . . Republica where the Masses govern, are far more quarrelsome, and more addicted to fighting than Monarchies which are governed by comparatively few Persons." See Palmerston to Cobden, 94 Piccadilly, Priv., 8 Jan 1862, British Museum Additional MS. Room, Palmerston Papers, vol. 48582.

68. Collantes-Crampton conversation, 31 Jan 1862 (evening), sum. by Crampton to Russell, Madrid, No. 52, Con., 31 Jan (r. 9 Feb) 1862, PRO, F.O. 72/1030.

69. Barrot to Thouvenel, Madrid, No. 7, 25 (r. 28) Jan 1862, MDAE: *CP, Espagne,* vol. 860.

70. Collantes-Crampton conversation, 31 Jan 1862 (evening), sum. by Crampton to Russell, Madrid, No. 52, Con, 31 Jan (r. 9 Feb) 1862, PRO, F.O. 72/1030.

71. Barrot to Thouvenel, Madrid, No. 7, 25 (r. 28) Jan 1862, MDAE: *CP, Espagne,* vol. 860.

72. Collantes-Crampton conversation, 31 Jan 1862 (evening), sum. by Crampton to Russell, Madrid, No. 52, Con., 31 Jan (r. 9 Feb) 1862, PRO, F.O. 72/1030.

73. Collantes to Prim, cited without date given by Prim-Senate-10 Dec 1862, and dated 22 Jan 1862 by Collantes' speech in Cortes, *Gazette*, Madrid, 13 Jun 1862, cited by H. Leonardon: "L'Espagne et La question du Mexique, 1861–1862," *Annales des Sciences Politiques*, XVI (1901), 80.

74. Speech of Collantes before Chamber of Deputies, 25 Jan 1862, trans. of extract of Diario de las Sessiones de Cortes, 25 Jan 1862, encl. of Crampton to Russell, No. 54, 1 (r. 9) Feb 1862, PRO, F.O. 72/1031. Barrot also sent a summary of the speech to Thouvenel. See encl. of Barrot to Thouvenel, Madrid, No.—, 29 Jan (r. 3 Feb) 1862, MDAE: *CP, Espagne,* vol. 860.

75. Russell to Cowley, F.O., No. 74, draft, 20 Jan 1862, marked seen by Palmerston and the Queen, PRO, F.O. 72/1419.

76. Flahault to Thouvenel, London, No. 3, 20 (r. 21) Jan 1862, MDAE: *CP, Angleterre,* vol. 721.

77. Russell to Cowley, F.O., No. 74, draft, 20 Jan 1862, marked seen by Palmerston and the Queen, PRO, F.O. 27/1419.

78. Cowley to Russell, Paris, No. 56, 21 (r. 22) Jan 1862, PRO, F.O. 27/1431.

79. Colonel Claremont to Cowley, Paris, No. 5, Con, 21 Jan 1862, encl. of Cowley to Russell, Paris, No. 64, 21 (r. 25) Jan 1862, *ibid.*

80. Cowley to Russell, Paris, No. 75, 24 (r. 25) Jan 1862, *ibid.*

81. Cowley to Russell, Telegram, 22 Jan 1862, cited by Cowley to Russell, Paris, No. 65, Con., 22 (r. 25) Jan 1862, *ibid.*

82. See footnotes 79 and 80 above.

83. Moniteur, 20 Jan 1862, encl. of Cowley to Russell, Paris, No. 49, 20 (r. 22) Jan 1862, PRO, F.O. 27/1431.

84. Draft to Admiralty, F.O., 23 Jan 1862, PRO, F.O. 50/370.

85. Russell to Bloomfield, F.O., No. 27, draft, 29 Jan 1862, PRO, F.O. 7/625.

86. Russell to Crampton, F.O., No. 19, draft, 23 Jan 1862, PRO, F.O. 72/1028.

87. Russell to Wyke, F.O., No. 7, draft, 27 Jan 1862, marked seen by Palmerston, PRO, F.O. 50/363.

88. Draft to Admiralty, F.O., Immediate, 31 Jan 1862, PRO, F.O. 50/370.

89. A copy is filed in MDAE: *CP, Mex.,* vol. 58.

90. DAWSON, p. 207.

91. Maximilian to Napoleon III, Miramar, 22 Jan 1862, HHSA, cited in full by CORTI, I, 367–368.

92. DAWSON, p. 207.

93. Protokoll mit General Almonte unterzeichnet zu Miramar am 22 Januar, 1862, *HHSA,* AKM, cited in full by DAWSON, pp. 197–198.

94. Maximilian to Napleon III, Miramar, 22 Jan 1862, *HHSA,* cited in full by CORTI, I, 367–368.

95. Maximilian to Metternich, 23 Jan 1862, *HHSA,* AKM, cited by DAWSON, p. 199.

96. Article VIII of Protokoll mit General Almonte unterzeichnet zu Miramar am 22 Januar, 1862, *HHSA,* AKM, DAWSON, p. 198.

97. Article XII, *ibid.*

98. Maximilian to Metternich, 23 Jan 1862, *ibid.,* p. 199.

99. See Section 3 of Chapter IV of present investigation.

100. Maximilian to Napoleon III, Miramar, 22 Jan 1862, *HHSA,* CORTI, I, 368.

101. *Ibid.,* I, 367.

102. Article XI of Protokoll mit General Almonte Unterzeichnet zu Miramar am 22 Januar, 1862, *HHSA,* AKM, DAWSON, p. 198.

103. Article X, *ibid.*

104. Article IX, *ibid.* For Maximilian's original proposal, see Section 3 of Chapter IV of present investigation, between footnotes 87 and 88.

105. Maximilian to Napoleon III, Miramar, 22 Jan 1862, *HHSA,* CORTI, I, 367–368.

106. Articles I, II, III of Protokoll mit General Almonte Unterzeichnet zu Miramar am 22 Januar, 1862, *HHSA,* AKM, DAWSON, p. 197.

107. Maximilian to Napoleon III, Miramar, 22 Jan 1862, *HHSA,* CORTI, I, 368.

108. Articles IV (loan), V (machinery of government), VI (titles), VII ($200,000) of Protokoll mit General Almonte Unterzeichnet zu Miramar am 22 Januar, 1862, *HHSA,* AKM, DAWSON, pp. 197–198.

109. Pius IX to Maximilian, 9 Feb 1862, *HHSA,* AKM, *ibid.,* pp. 210–211.

110. Estrada to Maximilian, 19 Feb 1862, *HHSA,* Berufung, *ibid.,* p. 223.

111. Santa Anna to Estrada, St. Thomas, 15 Jan 1862, encl. of Estrada to Thouvenel, Hotel Westminster, 13 Rue de la Paix, Paris, 31 Jan 1862, MDAE: *CP, Mex.,* vol. 58.

112. Estrada to Baron de Pont, 4 Feb 1862, *HHSA,* AKM, DAWSON, p. 232. Estrada enclosed Santa Anna's letter, but Dawson misdates it 5 January 1862. See footnote 111 above.

113. Estrada to Maximilian, 25 Feb 1862, *HHSA,* Berufung, DAWSON, p. 222.

114. Pius IX to Maximilian, 9 Feb 1862, *HHSA,* AKM, *ibid.,* p. 211.

115. *Ibid.,* p. 210.

116. Labastida to Maximilian, 7, 10, 17 Feb 1862, *HHSA,* CORTI, I, 147.

117. Leopold I to Maximilian, Osborne, 7 Feb 1862, *HHSA, ibid.,* I, 155.

118. Almonte to Maximilian, Paris, 30 Jan 1862, *HHSA, ibid.,* I 147.

119. Napoleon III-Metternich conversation, 30 Jan 1862, sum by Rechberg to Maximilian, 2 Feb 1862, *HHSA,* AKM, DAWSON, p. 201.

120. Maximilian to Rechberg, 6 Feb 1862, *HHSA,* AKM, *ibid.,* pp. 201–202.

121. Rechberg to Metternich, 8 Feb 1862, *HHSA,* Weisungen nach Frankreich, *ibid,* p. 202.

122. Russell to Bloomfield, F.O., No. 27, draft, 29 Jan 1862, PRO, F.O. 7/625.

123. Bloomfield to Russell, Vienna, Pri., 16 Jan 1862, PRO, F.O. 356/38.

124. Bloomfield to Russell, Vienna, No. 47, 30 Jan 1862, PRO, F.O. 356/18.

125. Bloomfield to Russell, Vienna, No. 64, Con., 6 Feb 1862, *ibid.*

126. Bloomfield to Russell, Vienna, Pri., 8 Feb 1862, PRO, F.O. 356/38.

127. Cowley to Russell, Paris, No. 113, Con., 5 (r. 8) Feb 1862, PRO, F.O. 27/1432.

128. Cowley to Russell, Paris, No. 141, Con., 11 (r. 12) Feb 1862, *ibid.*

129. See footnote 86 above.

130. Crampton to Russell, Madrid, No. 50, 30 Jan (r. 9 Feb) 1862, PRO, F.O. 72/1030.

131. Crampton to Russell, Telegram, 29 Jan 1862, cited by Crampton to Russell, Madrid, No. 49, 29 Jan (r. 9 Feb) 1862, *ibid.*

132. Russell to Crampton, F.O., Telegram, 6.50 P.M., 30 Jan 1862, cited by Russell to Crampton, F.O. No. 26, 30 Jan 1862, PRO, F.O. 72/1028.

133. Crampton to Russell, Madrid, No. 51, 31 Jan (r. 9 Feb) 1862, PRO, F.O. 72/1030.

134. Crampton to Russell, Madrid, No. 52, Con., 31 Jan (r. 9 Feb) 1862, *ibid;* Crampton to Russell, Telegram, 31 Jan 1862, cited by Crampton to Russell, Madrid, No. 52, 1 (r. 9) Feb 1862, PRO, F.O. 72/1031.

135. Collantes to Isturiz, 1 Feb 1862, cited by Prim-Senate,-10 Dec 1861.

136. Russell to Crampton, F.O., Telegram, 3:30 P.M., 1 Feb 1862, cited by Russell to Crampton, F.O., No. 28, draft, 1 Feb 1862, PRO, F.O. 72/1031.

137. Crampton to Russell, Madrid, No. 59, Con., 2 (r. 9) Feb 1862; Crampton to Russell, Telegram, 2 Feb 1862, cited by Crampton to Russell, Madrid, No. 58, 2 (r. 9) Feb 1862, PRO, F.O. 72/1031. The quotation is from Crampton's No. 59.

138. Russell to Crampton, F.O., Telegram, 9:45 P.M., 2 Feb 1862, cited by Russell to Crampton, F.O., No. 30, draft, 2 Feb 1862, PRO, F.O. 72/1028.

139. Crampton to Russell, Madrid, No. 64, 4 (r. 9) Feb 1862; Crampton to Russell, Telegram, 3 Feb 1862, cited by Crampton to Russell, Madrid, No. 60, 3 (r. 9) Feb 1862, PRO, F.O. 72/1031. Quotations are from Crampton's No. 64.

140. Count Crivelli to Rechberg, 3 Feb 1862, HHSA, CORTI, I, 154.

141. O'Donnell to Prim, 6 Feb 1862, cited by Prim-Senate-10 Dec 1862.

142. Collantes to Prim, 7 Feb 1862, cited by Prim-Senate-10 Dec 1862.

143. Almonte-Prim Conversation, Vera Cruz, end of Feb 1862, cited by Prim-Senate-10 Dec 1862.

144. O'Donnell to Prim, Pri., 7 Apr 1862, cited by Prim-Senate-10 Dec 1862.

145. Castro-Collantes debate in Chamber of Deputies of Cortes, 5 Feb 1862, (trans.) extract of *Gazette,* encl. 2 of Crampton to Russell, Madrid, No. 69, 6 (r. 12) Feb 1862, PRO, F.O. 72/1031.

146. Leading article in *Morning Post,* 4 Feb 1862, cited in full by DAWSON, pp. 415–418.

147. Castro-Collantes debate in Chamber of Deputies of Cortes, 5 Feb 1862, (trans.) extract of *Gazette,* encl. 2 of Crampton to Russell, Madrid, No. 69, 6 (r. 12) Feb 1862, PRO, F.O. 72/1031.

148. Leopold I to Maximilian, Osborne, 7 Feb 1862, *HHSA,* CORTI, I, 155.

149. Metternich to Rechberg, 9 Feb 1862, DAWSON, p. 217.

150. *Ibid.*

151. Eugenie to Metternich, 7 Feb 1862, *HHSA,* AKM, cited in full, *ibid.,* pp. 216–217. Also cited in full by Robert Sencourt: *The Life of the Empress Eugénie* (London, 1931), p. 164.

152. Metternich to Rechberg, 9 Feb 1862, DAWSON, p. 217.

153. Leopold I to Maximilian, Osborne, 7 Feb 1862, *HHSA,* CORTI, I, 155.

154. Napoleon commented that an "unscrupulous government" had obliged France, Spain, and Great Britain to protect "our nationals" and to obtain redress of grievances in accordance with international law. See *Moniteur,* 28 Jan 1862. Cowley sent a copy of the speech printed by the French Government in pamphlet form to Russell. See encl. of Cowley to Russell, Paris, No. 83, 27 (r. 28) Jan 1862, PRO, F.O. 27/1431.

155. *Moniteur,* 30 Jan 1862.

156. *Patrie,* sum. by *Siècle,* 1 Feb 1862, Taxile Delord, sum. by WEST, p. 117.

157. Metternich to Rechberg, 30 Jan 1862, *HHSA,* Berichte aus Paris, DAWSON, pp. 215–216.

158. *Moniteur,* 1 Feb 1862.

159. Journal des Débats, 29 Jan 1862, J.-J. Weiss, sum. by WEST, p. 116.

160. Cowley to Russell, Paris, No. 75, 24 (r. 25) Jan 1862, PRO F.O. 27/1431.

161. Colonel Claremont to Cowley, Paris, No. 9, 27 Jan 1862, encl. of Cowley to Russell, Paris, No. 85, 27 (r. 29) Jan 1862, *ibid.*

162. Encl. of Cowley to Russell, Paris, No. 109, 4 (r. 5) Feb 1862, PRO, F.O. 27/1432.

163. Cowley to Russell, Paris, No. 110, Con., 4 (r. 5) Feb 1862, *ibid.*

164. Cowley to Russell, Paris, Pri., 11 Feb 1862, PRO, F.O. 519/229.

165. Russell to Bloomfield, F.O., No. 38, draft, 5 Feb 1862, PRO, F.O. 7/625. This was Russell's reply to Bloomfield's report No. 47 of 30 January 1862. See footnote 124 above.

166. Russell to Bloomfield, F.O., No. 57, draft, 13 Feb 1862, PRO, F.O. 7/625. This was in answer to Bloomfield's report No. 64 of 6 Feb 1862. See footnote 125 above.

167. See Section 3 of Chapter III of present investigation.

168. Apponyi to Rechberg, London, 15 Feb 1862, *HHSA,* Berichte aus London, DAWSON, p. 127.

169. Bloomfield to Russell, Vienna, No. 79, 13 Feb 1862, PRO, F.O. 356/18.

170. Rechberg to Metternich, 21 Feb 1862, *HHSA,* Weisungen nach Frankreich, DAWSON, pp. 217–218.

171. Bloomfield to Russell, Vienna, No. 94, 27 Feb 1862, PRO, F.O. 356/18.

172. See Section 3 of Chapter III of present investigation, between footnotes 49 and 50.

173. See Section 3 of Chapter IV of present investigation.

174. Rechberg to Maximilian, 4 Jan 1862, *HHSA,* AKM, DAWSON, p. 193.

175. Maximilian to Rechberg, 9 Nov 1861, *HHSA,* AKM, *ibid.,* p. 152.

176. Rechberg to Maximilian, 4 Jan 1862, *HHSA,* AKM, *ibid.,* p. 193.

177. Metternich-Cowley Conversation, sum. by Cowley to Russell, Paris, No. 141, Con., 11 (r. 12) Feb 1862, PRO, F.O. 72/1432.

178. Metternich to Rechberg, 30 Jan 1862, *HHSA,* Berichte aus Paris, DAWSON, p. 216.

179. Rechberg to Maximilian, Vienna, 1 Feb 1862, *HHSA,* CORTI, I, 151. Maximilian replied that he would give Estrada only occasional missions. See Maximilian to Rechberg, Miramar, 4 Feb 1862, *HHSA,* CORTI, I, 151.

180. Rechberg-Bloomfield Conversation, 26 Feb 1862, sum. by Bloomfield to Russell, Vienna, No. 94, PRO, F.O. 356/18. Bloomfield reported that Rechberg said ". . . that he had sent to Ct. Apponyi for Your Lordship's information the copy of a letter which he had addressed last October to Ct. Muelinen, the Austrian Chargé d'Affaires at Paris on the first intimation received here on the subject." For this

document, see Section 3 of Chapter III of present investigation, between footnotes 49 and 50.

181. Maximilian to Rechberg, Miramar, 8 Apr 1862, *HHSA,* Berufung, DAWSON, p. 219.

### 3. The Reactions of the European Powers to the Initial Negotiations of their Representatives in Mexico

1. Prim to Minister of War, Vera Cruz, 15 Jan 1862, *Gazette,* Madrid, 17 Feb 1862, encl. 2 of Crampton to Russell, Madrid, No. 91, 17 (r. 22) Feb 1862, PRO, F.O. 72/1031.

2. *Ibid.*

3. Collantes to Chargé D'Affaires of Spain in Paris, Madrid, Telegram, 18 Feb 1862; Barrot to Thouvenel, Madrid, Telegram, 8:30 P.M., 19 Feb 1862, MDAE: *CP, Espagne,* vol. 860.

4. Saligny to Thouvenel, Vera Cruz, No. 62, 15 Jan (r. 21 Feb) 1862, MDAE: *CP, Mex.,* vol. 58. Although this report is stamped as received 21 February, it was received on 20 February. See Cowley to Russell, Paris, No. 194, 21 (r. 22) Feb 1862, PRO, F.O. 27/1433. That no reports were received from Jurien is stated by Thouvenel's telegram of 21 February, cited in full in footnote 9 below. Unfortunately Jurien's reports were not marked when received.

5. Thouvenel to Barrot, Paris, Telegram, 2:00 P.M., 20 Feb 1862, MDAE: *CP, Espagne,* vol. 860.

6. Thouvenel to Barrot, No. 7, draft, 20 Feb 1862, *ibid.*

7. Cowley to Russell, Paris, No. 194, 21 (r. 22) Feb 1862, PRO, F.O. 27/1433.

8. Cowley to Crampton, Paris, Pri., 21 Feb 1862, PRO, F.O. 519/229.

9. Telegram of 21 Feb 1862 to MM. Admiral Jurien de La Graviére and Dubois de Saligny, sent to French Consul at Cadiz, MDAE: *CP, Mex.,* vol. 57. Parts of this telegram have been summarized by: SCHEFER, pp. 184–185; Robert Sencourt: *Napoleon III: The Modern Emperor* (London, 1933), p. 274; William S. Robertson: "The Tripartite Treaty of London," *HAHR,* XX (1940), 186.

10. See Section 1 of Chapter IV of present investigation.

11. See Section 1 of Chapter IV of present investigation.

12. See footnote 7 above.

13. Thouvenel to Flahault, Paris, No. 12, draft, 22 Feb 1862, MDAE: *CP, Angleterre,* vol. 721.

14. Flahault to Thouvenel, London, No. 8, 24 (r. 25) Feb 1862, *ibid.*

15. See below.

16. See footnote 1 above.

17. Russell to Wyke, F.O., No. 19, draft, 24 Feb 1862, marked seen by Palmerston, PRO, F.O. 50/363.

18. Russell to Wyke, F.O., No. 20, draft, 25 Feb 1862, marked seen by Palmerston and the Queen, *ibid.*

19. See footnotes 17 and 18 above.

20. Encls. of Russell to Cowley, F.O., No. 222, draft, 26 Feb 1862, PRO, F.O. 27/1420.

21. Draft to Admiralty, 26 Feb 1862, PRO, F.O. 50/370.

22. Draft to Admiralty, F.O., 23 Jan 1862; Draft to Admiralty, F.O., Immediate, 31 Jan 1862, PRO, F.O. 50/370. The draft of 23 January specifically stated that French reinforcements had orders to march to Puebla within twenty-four hours after landing at Vera Cruz. Compare with Valazé's remarks, cited in Section 2 of Chapter V of present investigation, between footnotes 78 and 79.

23. Admiralty to Milne, No. 93, 1 Feb 1862, sum. by Romaine to Milne, Admiralty, 11 March 1862, encl. of Romaine to Hammond, Admiralty, 12 (r. 13) Mar 1862, PRO, F.O. 50/370.

24. Romaine to Hammond, Admiralty, 27 Feb 1862, *ibid.*

25. Admiralty to Milne, No. 154, 28 Feb 1862, sum. by Romaine to Milne, Admiralty, 11 Mar 1862, encl. of Romaine to Hammond, Admiralty, 12 (r. 13) Mar 1862, *ibid.*

26. See footnote 5 above.

27. Barrot to Thouvenel, Madrid, No. 15, 21 (r. 24) Feb 1862, MDAE: *CP, Espagne,* vol. 860.

28. See footnote 5 above.

29. Barrot to Thouvenel, Madrid, No. 15, 21 (r. 2 Mar) 1862, MDAE: *CP, Espagne,* vol. 860. This report, stating such hostility of Juarez, was published, with no important changes, in 1863 by the French Government, no doubt to justify French policy by making it seem that the Spanish Government agreed about the desirability of upsetting the Juarez Government. See *DD, 1862,* pp. 175–177.

30. Cowley to Russell, Paris, No. 228, 28 Feb (r. 1 Mar) 1862, PRO, F.O. 27/1434.

31. *Ibid.*

32. Cowley to Russell, Paris, No. 229, Con., 28 Feb (r. 1 Mar) 1862, *ibid.*

33. Cowley to Russell, Paris, No. 230, 28 Feb (r. 1 Mar) 1862, *ibid.*

34. *Ibid.*

35. Transcript of various letters between Saligny and Wyke, encl. 2 of Saligny to Thouvenel, Mexico City, No. 55 *(bis),* Con., 26 Nov 1861 (r. 6 Jan 1862), MDAE: *CP, Mex.* vol. 56.

36. For details, see Section 1 of Chapter II of present investigation.

37. See footnote 4 above.

38. See Section 2 of Chapter IV, between footnotes 189 and 190, of present investigation.

39. See Section 1 of Chapter IV, between footnotes 94 and 95, of present investigation.

40. Miranda to Estrada, Havana, 21 Dec 1861, encl. 1 of Estrada to Thouvenel, Hotel Westminster, 13 Rue de la Paix, Paris, 17 Jan 1862, MDAE: *CP, Mex.,* vol. 58.

41. See Appendix X (1) of present investigation.

42. See below.

43. See footnotes 30, 32, and 33 above.

44. Russell to Cowley, F.O., No. 236, draft, 1 Mar 1862, marked seen by Palmerston and the Queen, PRO, F.O. 27/1421.

45. Wyke to Russell, Vera Cruz, Nos. 1–16, 16–31 Jan (r. 2 Mar) 1862, PRO, F.O. 50/364.

46. Russell to Cowley, F.O., No. 240, Con., draft, 3 Mar 1862, PRO, F.O. 27/1421. The enclosure was Wyke's No. 8. See Wyke to Russell, Vera Cruz, No. 8, Secret and Confidential, 19 Jan (r. 2 Mar) 1862, PRO, F.O. 50/364. Wyke's report summarized the 3rd conference of the Allied Commissioners of 13–14 January 1862. For it, see Section 1 of Chapter V of present investigation.

47. Cowley to Russell, Paris, No. 260, 4 (r. 5) Mar 1862, PRO, F.O. 27/1434.

48. *Ibid.*

49. Cowley to Russell, Pri., 4 Mar 1862, PRO, P.R.O. 30/22–57.

50. Saligny to Thouvenel, Vera Cruz, Nos. 63 and 64, 20 and 29 Jan (r. 4 Mar) 1862, MDAE: *CP, Mex.,* vol. 58. Saligny's No. 65 of 17 February arrived in Paris on 11 March. See Saligny to Thouvenel, No. 65, 17 Feb (r. 11 Mar) 1862, MDAE: *CP, Mex.,* vol. 58.

51. The date of receipt was not marked on Jurien's reports, but see below for Napoleon's letter to Maximilian stating a knowledge of a report of Jurien's of 9 February. Jurien's reports through 9 February contain more than one hundred pages. See MDAE: *CP, Mex.,* vol. 57.

52. See Appendix X (1) of present investigation (Napoleon read everything about Mexico that arrived at the Ministry of Foreign Affairs). See also Napoleon's letter to Maximilian, cited below. This letter clearly indicates Napoleon's knowledge of the reports from Mexico.

53. Napoleon III to Maximilian, 7 Mar 1862, *HHSA,* CORTI, I 370.

54. Thouvenel to Flahault, No. 14, draft, 7 Mar 1862, MDAE: *CP, Angleterre,* vol. 721.

55. See footnote 8 above.

56. Thomasset to Jurien, Vera Cruz, 31 Jan 1862, encl. of Jurien to Thouvenel, Vera Cruz, No. 7, Jan 1862, MDAE: *CP, Mex.,* vol. 57.

57. Santa Anna to Estrada, Con., 15 Feb 1862, encl. of Estrada to Thouvenel, Hotel Westminster, 13 Rue de la Paix, Paris, 5 Mar 1862, *ibid.,* vol. 58.

58. The report was from the captain of the *Foudre.* See Eugenie to Charlotte, 3 Feb 1862, *HHSA,* CORTI, I, 144. That the captain was in Vera Cruz harbor at arrival is stated in a report from the captain of a British ship there at the same time. See Extract of a letter of Captain Von Donop of HMS *Jason,* encl. of Romaine to Hammond, Admiralty, 30 Jan (r. 4 Feb) 1862, PRO, F.O. 50/370.

59. Eugenie to Charlotte, Paris, 3 Feb 1862, *HHSA,* CORTI, I, 369.

60. For Saligny's report, see footnote 4 above. For Jurien's report,

see Jurien to Thouvenel, Vera Cruz, No. 10, 28 Jan 1862, MDAE: *CP, Mex.,* vol. 57.

61. Jurien to Thouvenel, Vera Cruz, No. 13, 9 Feb 1862, MDAE: *CP, Mex.,* vol. 57.

62. Postscript, dated 31 Jan 1862, to Saligny to Thouvenel, Vera Cruz, No. 64, 29 Jan (r. 4 Mar) 1862, *ibid.,* vol. 58.

63. For this intrigue, see Section 1 of Chapter V, between footnotes 124 and 141 of present investigation.

64. For Thouvenel's hopes that Wyke could be induced to support this scheme, see below in text of this section, between footnotes 99 and 103.

65. Beyens to Belgian F.O., 16 Mar 1862, BEYENS, I, 245.

66. See above in text of this section, between footnotes 28 and 29.

67. Comte Fleury: *Souvenirs du Général Comte Fleury* (2 v., Paris, 1897–1898), II, 260.

68. Napoleon III to Maximilian, 7 Mar 1862, *HHSA,* CORTI, I, 370–371. The remark about Prim's aide-de-camp referred to Brigadier Milans, who rumor had it, toasted the "Universal Republic" while in Mexico City awaiting an answer to the Collective note sent Juarez. For details, see Section 1 of Chapter V, between footnotes 191 and 196 of present investigation.

69. Metternich to Rechberg, 9 Mar 1862, *HHSA,* DAWSON, pp. 223–224, and CORTI, I, 162.

70. Madame Carette: *My Mistress, the Empress Eugénie; or, Court Life at the Tuileries* (London, 2nd ed., 1889), pp. 265–267.

71. *Moniteur,* 7 Mar 1862.

72. Russell to Crampton, F.O., Telegram, 11:00 A.M., 6 Mar 1862, cited by Russell to Crampton, F.O., No. 51, draft, 6 Mar 1862, PRO, F.O. 72/1028.

73. Russell to Wyke, F.O., No. 25, draft, 4 Mar 1862, marked seen by Palmerston and the Queen, PRO, F.O. 50/363.

74. See Section 1 of Chapter V of present investigation for these suggestions of Wyke.

75. Russell to Cowley, Pri., 5 Mar 1862, PRO, F.O. 519/199.

76. Russell to Wyke, F.O., No. 26, draft, 4 Mar 1862, marked seen by Palmerston, PRO, F.O. 50/363.

77. Russell to Wyke, F.O., No. 29, draft, 11 Mar 1862, marked seen by Palmerston and the Queen, PRO, F.O. 50/3, *ibid.*

78. F.O. to Admiralty, 10 Mar 1862, encl. of Russell to Wyke, F.O., No. 28, draft, 11 Mar 1862, marked seen by Palmerston and the Queen, *ibid.*

79. Draft to Admiralty, F.O., 10 Mar 1862, initialled (R(ussell) and marked seen by Palmerston, PRO, F.O. 50/370.

80. Hammond to Wyke, F.O., Pri., 14 Mar 1862, PRO, F.O. 50/363.

81. Russell to Wyke, F.O., No. 26, draft, 4 Mar 1862, marked seen by Palmerston, *ibid.*

82. Cowley to Russell, Paris, No. 267, Con., 6 (r. 7) Mar 1862, PRO, F.O. 27/1434.

83. Cowley to Russell, Paris, No. 299, Con., 10 (r. 11) Mar 1862, *ibid.*

84. See Section 1 of Chapter VI of present investigation.

85. See footnote 82 above.

86. Russell to Cowley, F.O., No. 260, Con., draft, 8 Mar 1862, PRO, F.O. 27/1421.

87. Layard to Cowley, F.O., Pri., 8 Mar 1862, PRO, F.O. 519/195.

88. Draft to Admiralty, F.O., 8 Mar 1862, marked settled in the cabinet, PRO, F.O. 50/370.

89. *Ibid.*

90. For Dunlop's report, see Dunlop to Milne, Challenger at Vera Cruz, No. 23, 30 Jan 1862, encl. of Paget to Hammond, Admiralty, Immediate, 3 (r. 3) Mar 1862, *ibid.* For Russell's instructions to the Admiralty, see Draft to Admiralty, F.O., 10 Mar 1862, initialed R(ussell), marked seen by Palmerston, PRO, F.O. 50/370. Russell's reference to Dunlop's use of "regeneration" referred to Dunlop to Secretary of Admiralty, Challenger at Vera Cruz, No. 3, 15 Jan 1862, encl. of Paget to Hammond, Admiralty, Immediate, 3 (r. 3) Mar 1862, PRO, F.O. 50/370.

91. This suggestion was made by Dunlop in his report number 3 of 15 January to the Secretary of the Admiralty, cited in footnote 90 above.

92. Draft to Admiralty, F.O., 10 Mar 1862, PRO, F.O. 50/370. Russell probably remembered a report from the War Office to this effect. See War Office to Hammond, 15 (r. 15) Nov 1861, PRO, F.O. 50/358.

93. Romaine to Hammond, Admiralty, 12 (r. 13) Mar 1862, and encl., Romaine to Milne, Admiralty, 11 Mar 1862, PRO, F.O. 50/370.

94. Draft to Admiralty, F.O. 25 Mar 1862, *ibid.*

95. Thouvenel to Flahault, Paris, No. 15, draft, 7 Mar 1862, MDAE: *CP, Angleterre,* vol. 721.

96. Thouvenel to Saligny, No. 3, draft, 28 Feb 1862, marked copy communicated to London, MDAE: *CP, Mex.,* vol. 58.

97. Thouvenel to Jurien, draft, 28 Feb 1862, *ibid.,* vol. 57.

98. Thouvenel to Flahault, Paris, No. 15, draft, 7 Mar 1862, MDAE: *CP, Angleterre,* vol. 721.

99. Thouvenel to Flahault, Paris, No. 14, draft, 7 Mar 1862, *ibid.*

100. Thouvenel to Flahault, Paris, Pri., 7 Mar 1862, THOUVENEL, II, 242.

101. For details, see Section 1 of Chapter III, between footnotes 36 and 37 of present investigation.

102. See footnote 62 above.

103. Thouvenel to Flahault, Paris, Pri., 7 Mar 1862, THOUVENEL, II, 241–242.

104. Russell to Cowley, F.O., No. 267, draft, 11 Mar 1862, marked seen by Palmerston and the Queen, PRO, F.O. 27/1421.

105. Flahault to Thouvenel, London, No. 10 *(bis),* 11 (r. 12) Mar 1862, MDAE: *CP, Angleterre,* vol. 721.

106. *Ibid.*

107. Russell to Cowley, F.O., No. 267, draft, 11 Mar 1862, marked seen by Palmerston and the Queen, PRO, F.O. 27/1421.

108. *Ibid;* Flahault to Thouvenel, London, No. 10 *(bis)*, 11 (r. 12) Mar 1862, MDAE: *CP, Angleterre,* vol. 721.

109. Flahault to Thouvenel, London, No. 10 *(bis)*, 11 (r. 12) Mar 1862, MDAE: *CP, Angleterre,* vol. 721.

110. Russell to Cowley, F.O., No. 267, draft, 11 Mar 1862, marked seen by Palmerston and the Queen, PRO, F.O. 27/1421.

111. *Ibid;* Flahault to Thouvenel, London, No. 10 *(bis)*, 11 (r. 12) Mar 1862, MDAE: *CP, Angleterre,* vol. 721.

112. Flahault to Thouvenel, London, No. 10 *(bis)* 11 (r. 12) Mar 1862, MDAE: *CP, Angleterre,* vol. 721.

113. Russell to Wyke, F.O., No. 32, original draft, later revised and dated 15 Mar 1862, marked seen by Palmerston and the Queen, PRO, F.O. 50/363.

114. Russell to Cowley, F.O., No. 267, draft, 11 Mar 1862, marked seen by Palmerston and the Queen, PRO, F.O. 27/1421.

115. Russell to Wyke, No. 32, encl. of Russell to Cowley, No. 268, 12 Mar 1862, sum. by Russell to Cowley, F.O., No. 286, draft, 15 Mar 1862, *ibid.*

116. Cowley to Russell, Paris, No. 335, 14 (r. 15) Mar 1862, PRO, F.O. 27/1435.

117. Cowley-Thouvenel Conversation, 13 Mar 1862, sum. by Cowley to Russell, Paris, No. 336, 14 (r. 14) Mar 1862, *ibid.*

118. Russell to Cowley, F.O., Pri., 15 Mar 1862, PRO, F.O. 519/199.

119. Russell to Wyke, F.O., No. 32, draft, with alterations, 15 Mar 1862, marked seen by Palmerston and the Queen, PRO, F.O. 50/363.

120. See Section 1 of Chapter V, between footnotes 63 and 75 of present investigation.

121. Russell to Wyke, F.O., No. 33, draft, 15 Mar 1862, PRO, F.O. 50/363.

122. Thouvenel to Saligny, Paris, 14 Mar 1862, *DD, 1862,* pp. 170–171. All quotations are from the original draft, cited in footnote 123 below.

123. Thouvenel to Saligny, Paris, No. 4, draft, 14 Mar 1862, MDAE: *CP, Mex.,* vol. 58.

124. Thouvenel to Jurien, draft, 14 Mar 1862, *ibid.,* vol. 57.

125. See Section 2 of Chapter V of present investigation.

126. Russell to Crampton, F.O., Telegram, 11:00 A.M., 6 Mar 1862, cited by Russell to Crampton, F.O., No. 51, draft, 6 Mar 1862, PRO, F.O. 72/1028.

127. Crampton to Russell, Madrid, No. 103, 7 (r. 12) Mar 1862, PRO, F.O. 72/1032.

128. Russell to Crampton, F.O., No. 71, draft, 26 Mar 1862, PRO, F.O. 72/1028.

129. See footnote 29 above, and text it footnotes.

130. Thouvenel to Barrot, No. 9, draft, 8 Mar 1862, MDAE: *CP, Espagne,* vol. 860.

131. Sum. by Barrot to Thouvenel, Madrid, No. 18, 16 (r. 21) Mar 1862, *ibid.*

132. Barrot to Thouvenel, Madrid, No. 18, 16 (r. 21) Mar 1862, *ibid.* Barrot reported that Collantes did not believe Prim had entered a coalition with the British against the French Commissioners. Prim acted as an "arbitrator."

133. Beyens to Belgian F.O., 16 Mar 1862, BEYENS, I, 245.

134. *Ibid.*

135. Thouvenel to Barrot, No. 10, draft, 20 Mar 1862, MDAE: *CP, Espagne,* vol. 860.

136. Cowley-Thouvenel conversation, 20 Mar 1862, sum. by Cowley to Russell, Paris, No. 372, 20 (r. 21) Mar 1862, PRO, F.O. 27/1435.

137. Thouvenel to Flahault, Paris, Pri., 21 Mar 1862, THOUVENEL, II, 259.

138. Cowley to Crampton, Paris, Pri., 21 Mar 1862, PRO, F.O. 519/229.

139. Telegraphic Despatch to French Consul at Cadiz, for transmittal to Jurien, 20 Mar 1862, signed Chasseloup-Laubet, 5:30 P.M., MDAE: *CP, Mex.,* vol. 57.

140. Telegraphic Despatch to French Consul at Cadiz, for transmittal by the packet to Saligny to transmit to Lorencez, 3:30 P.M., 20 Mar 1862, coded, *ibid.,* vol. 58.

141. Coded telegram from Thouvenel to Saligny, Paris, 20 Mar 1862, *ibid.*

142. See Section 1 of Chapter VI of present investigation.

143. Cowley to Russell, Paris, No. 372, 20 (r. 21) Mar 1862 (disapproval), PRO, F.O. 27/1435; Cowley to Russell, Paris, No. 404, 25 (r. 26) Mar 1862 (Jurien's recall), PRO, F.O. 27/1436.

144. Thouvenel to Barrot, No. 10, draft, 20 Mar 1862; Thouvenel to Barrot, Paris, coded telegram, 2:30 P.M., 20 Mar 1862, MDAE: *CP, Espagne,* vol. 860.

145. Prim's reports arrived in Madrid on 21 March 1862. See Collantes to Prim, Madrid, 22 Mar 1862, *DD, 1862,* p. 181.

146. Collantes to Prim, Madrid, 22 Mar 1862, DD, 1862, pp. 180–181.

147. *Ibid.* For details, see below.

148. Barrot to Thouvenel, Madrid, No. 24, 23 (r. 26) Mar 1862, MDAE: *CP, Espagne,* vol. 860.

149. *Ibid.*

150. *Ibid.,* and enclosure thereof, dated 23 Mar 1862.

151. Encl. of Thouvenel to Flahault, No. 28 draft, 27 Mar 1862, MDAE: *CP, Angleterre,* vol. 721.

152. Flahault to Thouvenel, London, No. 18, 28 (r. 30) Mar 1862, *ibid.*

153. Thouvenel to Saligny, Paris, No. 5, draft, 31 Mar 1862, MDAE: *CP, Mex.,* vol. 58.

154. See Appendix R of present investigation.

155. Thouvenel to Saligny, Paris, No. 5, draft, 31 Mar 1862, MDAE: *CP, Mex.,* vol. 58.

156. *Moniteur,* 2 Apr 1862.

157. Russell to Wyke, F.O., Nos. 39, 40, 41, 48, 49; 31, 31, 31 Mar; 1, 1 Apr 1862, drafts, PRO, F.O. 50/363.

158. Russell to Cowley, F.O., No. 350, draft, 2 Apr 1862, PRO, F.O. 27/1422.

159. Russell to Crampton, F.O., Telegram, 3:55 P.M., 2 Apr 1862, cited by Russell to Crampton, F.O., No. 74, draft, 2 Apr 1862, PRO, F.O. 72/1028.

160. Collantes to Prim, Madrid, 22 Mar 1862, *DD, 1862,* pp. 180–181.

161. Barrot to Thouvenel, Madrid, No. 24, 23 (r. 26) Mar 1862, MDAE: *CP, Espagne,* vol. 860.

162. *Ibid.*

163. Encl., dtd 23 Mar 1862, of *ibid.*

164. Collantes to Prim, Madrid, 22 Mar 1862, *DD, 1862,* p. 181.

165. Barrot to Thouvenel, Madrid, No. 24, 23 (r. 26) Mar 1862, MDAE: *CP, Espagne,* vol. 860. All of the remarks of Collantes and O'Donnell cited were deleted from Barrot's report that was published by the French Government in 1863. See *DD, 1862,* pp. 177–179.

166. Thouvenel received Barrot's report on 26 March and answered it on 1 April. See footnote 165 above and 167 below.

167. Thouvenel to Barrot, Paris, No. 12, draft, 1 Apr 1862, MDAE: *CP, Espagne,* vol. 860.

168. Barrot told Crampton of the receipt of such a report from Flahault. See Barrot-Crampton Conversation, 8 Apr 1862, sum. by Crampton to Russell, Madrid, No. 167, 9 (r. 16) Apr 1862, PRO, F.O. 72/1033. Unfortunately enclosures of instructions sent by Thouvenel are usually not marked on those instructions. For Flahault's report, see footnote 152 above.

169. Cowley to Russell, Paris, No. 453, 4 (r. 5) Apr 1862, PRO, F.O. 27/1436.

170. Cowley to Russell, Paris, Pri., 4 Apr 1862, PRO, P.R.O. 30/22–57.

171. Cowley to Russell, Paris, No. 453, 4 (r. 5) Apr 1862, PRO, F.O. 27/1436.

172. Russell to Cowley, F.O., Pri., 5 Apr 1862, PRO, F.O. 519/199.

173. Barrot to Thouvenel, Madrid, No. 20, 20 (r. 24) Mar 1862, MDAE: *CP, Espagne,* vol. 860.

174. Thouvenel did not learn that he was wrong until the receipt of two reports from Marrot that arrived in Paris on 13 and 15 April. See footnote 186 below. On 15 April Thouvenel replied to these reports and stated "our surprise." See footnote 192 below.

175. Russell to Crampton, F.O., Telegram, 3:55 P.M., 2 Apr 1862, cited by Russell to Crampton, F.O., No. 74, draft, 2 Apr 1862, PRO, F.O. 72/1028.

176. Crampton to Russell, Madrid, No. 163, Con., 3 (r. 16) Apr 1862, PRO, F.O. 72/1033. The contents of this report were summarized by Crampton to Russell, Telegram, 4 Apr 1862, cited by Crampton to Russell, Madrid, No. 172, 11 (r. 16) Apr 1862, PRO, F.O. 72/1033.

177. Barrot to Thouvenel, Madrid, Telegram, 4 Apr 1862, MDAE: *CP, Espagne,* vol. 860.

178. Russell to Cowley, F.O., Pri., 5 Apr 1862, PRO, F.O. 519/199.

179. Thouvenel to Barrot, Telegram, 2:30 P.M., 5 Apr 1862, MDAE: *CP, Espagne,* vol. 860.

180. See footnote 174 above.

181. See Barrot-Crampton Conversation, 8 Apr 1862, sum. by Crampton to Russell, Madrid, No. 167, 9 (r. 16) Apr 1862, PRO, F.O. 72/1033.

182. Crampton-O'Donnell Conversation, 3 Apr 1862, sum. by Crampton to Russell, Madrid, No. 163, Con., 3 (r. 16) Apr 1862, PRO, F.O. 72/1033. The Contents of this report were summarized by Crampton to Russell, Telegram, 4 Apr 1862, cited by Crampton to Russell, Madrid, No. 172, 11 (r. 16) Apr 1862, PRO, F.O. 72/1033.

183. See footnote 182 above.

184. Crampton to Russell, Madrid, No. 168, 10 (r. 16) Apr 1862, PRO, F.O. 72/1033.

185. Extract of *Gazette* of 10 Apr 1862, encl. of *ibid.*

186. Barrot to Thouvenel, Madrid, No. 29, 11 (r. 15) Apr 1862, MDAE: *CP, Espagne,* vol. 860. The speech appeared in the *Gazette* of 10 April. See footnote 185 above. On the same day Barrot sent Thouvenel a translation of the crucial sentence, without a comma after "General Prim." Barrot commented Collantes took a position ". . . in complete contradiction . . . with the declarations that he made to me. . . ." See Barrot to Thouvenel, Madrid, No. 27, 10 (r. 13) Apr 1862, MDAE: *CP, Espagne,* vol. 860. For the comma, see below.

187. Barrot to Thouvenel, Madrid, No. 29, 11 (r. 15) Apr 1862, MDAE, *CP, Espagne,* vol. 860.

188. *Ibid.*

189. Barrot to Thouvenel, Madrid, No. 30, 14 (r. 20) Apr 1862, *ibid.*

190. Summary, dtd 23 Mar 1862, encl. of Crampton to Russell, Madrid, No. 181, 13 (r. 18) Apr 1862, PRO, F.O. 72/1033. In his letter of transmittal, Crampton stated he received the summary from Collantes in the evening of 12 April 1862. The summary given Crampton is identical to the one given Barrot.

191. Russell to Crampton, F.O., Telegram, 1.00 P.M., 10 Apr 1862, cited by Russell to Crampton, F.O., No. 80, draft, 10 Apr 1862, PRO, F.O. 72/1028.

192. Thouvenel to Barrot, Paris, No. 14, draft, 15 Apr 1862, MDAE: *CP, Espagne,* vol. 860.

193. See footnotes 185 and 184 above.

194. See footnote 190 above.

195. Russell to Cowley, F.O., No. 441, draft, 21 Apr 1862, PRO, F.O. 27/1422.

196. Cowley to Russell, Telegram, 2:25 P.M., 24 Apr 1862, cited by Cowley to Russell, Paris, No. 524, 24 (r. 26) Apr 1862, PRO, F.O. 1437.

197. "Note for the Emperor," 11 Nov 1867 (written by Persigny), Duc de Persigny: *Mémoires du Duc de Persigny Publiés Avec Des Documents Inédits, un avant-propos et un épilogue par M. H. De Laire Cte D'Espagny, Ancien Sécretaire Intime Du Duc* (2nd ed., Paris, 1896), p. 393.

198. Cowley to Russell, Paris, No. 532, 25 (r. 26) Apr 1862, *ibid.*


## Chapter VI

### *1. The Breakdown of the Convention of London in Mexico*

1. Dunlop to Secretary of Admiralty, Orizaba, No. 26, 11 Apr 1862, encl. 2 of Admiralty to Hammond, Admiralty, 14 May 1862, PRO, F.O. 50/371.

2. Miranda to Estrada, Vera Cruz, 6 Mar 1862, encl. of Estrada to Thouvenel, Paris, Hotel Westminster, 13 Rue de la Paix, 9 Apr 1862, MDAE: *CP, Mex.,* vol. 58.

3. See Appendix T of present investigation.

4. Wyke to Russell, Orizaba, No. 38, 27 Mar (r. 28 Apr) 1862, PRO, F.O. 50/364.

5. Jurien to Thouvenel, Cordova, 5 Mar 1862, MDAE: *CP, Mex.,* vol. 58.

6. Prim-Senate-10 Dec 1862. See also Appendix T of present investigation.

7. Prim-Senate-10 Dec 1862. Te instructions Prim received were from Collantes and dated 22 January 1862. For the details of the contents of these instructions, see Section 2 of Chapter V of present investigation, between footnotes 72 and 73.

8. Prim-Senate-10 Dec 1862.

9. See Appendix T of present investigation.

10. See Appendix T of present investigation.

11. Secretary of Admiralty to Milne, Nos. 55, 70, 93, dtd. 21 and 24 Jan, 1 Feb 1862, sum. and stated as received by Dunlop to Milne, Challenger at Vera Cruz, No. 49, 2 Mar 1862, encl. 1 of Admiralty to Hammond, Admiralty, 31 Mar (r. 1 Apr) 1862, PRO, F.O..50/370.

12. Russell to Wyke, F.O., No. 7, 27 Jan (r. 1 Mar) 1862, PRO, F.O. 204/159.

13. Prim to Napoleon III, Orizaba, 17 Mar 1862, Sara Yorke Stevenson: *Maximilian in Mexico: A Woman's Reminiscences of the French Intervention, 1862–1867* (New York, 1891), pp. 25–27.

14. Dunlop to Milne, Challenger at Vera Cruz, 4 Mar 1862, encl.

of Romaine to Hammond, Admiralty, 1 (r. 2) Apr 1862, PRO, F.O. 50/370.

15. Wyke to Russell, Vera Cruz, No. 32, 1 (r. 31) Mar 1862, PRO, F.O. 50/364.

16. Jurien to Thouvenel, Vera Cruz, No. 16, 20 Feb 1862, MDAE: *CP, Mex.*, vol. 57.

17. See Appendix T of present investigation.

18. Dunlop to Milne, Challenger at Vera Cruz, No. 49, 2 Mar 1862, encl. 1 of Admiralty to Hammond, Admiralty, 31 Mar (r. 1 Apr) 1862, PRO, F.O. 50/370.

19. Admiralty to Hammond, 2 (r. 2) Apr 1862, *ibid.*

20. Wyke's statement made during conference of 2 Mar 1862, reported by Saligny to Thouvenel, Vera Cruz, No. 69, 11 Mar (r. 9 Apr) 1862, MDAE: *CP, Mex.*, vol. 58.

21. Saligny to Thouvenel, Vera Cruz, No. 69, 11 Mar (r. 9 Apr) 1862, *Ibid.*

22. Saligny to Thouvenel, Vera Cruz, No. 68, 3 Mar (r. 3 Apr) 1862, *ibid.*

23. Wyke to Russell, Pri., 3 Mar 1862, Vera Cruz, PRO, P.R.O. 30/22–74.

24. Wyke to Russell, Orizaba, No. 37, 27 Mar (r. 28 Apr) 1862, PRO, F.O. 50/364.

25. See Section 1 of Chapter V of present investigation, between footnotes 275 and 277 and between footnotes 290 and 297.

26. Wyke to Russell, Vera Cruz, No. 35, 6 Mar (r. 28 Apr) 1862, PRO, F.O. 50/364.

27. Wyke to Russell, Orizaba, No. 37, 27 Mar (r. 28 Apr) 1862, *ibid.*

28. Corwin to Doblado, Mexico City, 10 Mar 1862, *Papers relating to Foreign Affairs, 1862* (Washington, 1863) pp. 736–737.

29. Wyke to Russell, Orizaba, No. 36, 10 Mar (r. 28 Apr) 1862, PRO, F.O. 50/364.

30. Saligny to Thouvenel, Vera Cruz, No. 69, 11 Mar (r. 9 Apr) 1862, MDAE: *CP, Mex.*, vol. 58.

31. Prim to Jurien, Orizaba, 15 Mar 1862, encl. 4 of Jurien to Thouvenel, Tehuacan, No. 25, Con., 24 Mar 1862, *ibid.*, vol. 57. ...

32. Saligny to Thouvenel, Vera Cruz, No. 69, 11 Mar (r. 9 Apr) 1862, *ibid.*, vol. 58.

33. Quoted by Jurien to Lorencez, Tehuacan, 24 Mar 1862, encl. 18 of Jurien to Thouvenel, Tehuacan, No. 25, Con., 24 Mar 1862, *ibid.*, vol. 57.

34. Napoleon to Jurien, 30 Jan 1862, quoted by Jurien to Lorencez, Tehuacan, 24 Mar 1862, encl. 18 of Jurien to Thouvenel, Tehuacan, No. 25, Con., 24 Mar 1862, *ibid.*

35. Thouvenel to Jurien, draft, 30 Jan 1862, *ibid.*

36. Jurien to Prim, 17 Mar 1862, Prim-Senate 10 Dec 1862.

37. Jurien to Thouvenel, Cordova, 5 Mar 1862, MDAE: *CP, Mex.*, vol. 57.

38. Jurien to Thouvenel, Cordova, 5 Mar 1862, *ibid.*

39. Jurien to Thouvenel, Orizaba, 7 Mar 1862, *ibid.*

40. Jurien to Thouvenel, Cordova, 5 Mar 1862, *ibid.*

41. Saligny to Thouvenel, Vera Cruz, No. 68, 3 Mar (r. 3 Apr) 1862, *ibid., vol. 58.*

42. Thouvenel to Saligny, No. 1, draft, 31 Jan 1862, *ibid.*

43. Saligny to Thouvenel, Vera Cruz, No. 69, 11 Mar (r. 9 Apr) 1862, *ibid.*

44. Maréchal Jacques L. Randon: *Mémoires du Maréchal Randon* (2 v., Paris, 1875–1877), II, 62.

45. Saligny to Thouvenel, Vera Cruz, No. 69, 11 Mar (r. 9 Apr) 1862, MDAE: *CP, Mex., vol. 58.*

46. Jurien to Prim and Wyke, Tehuacan, 24 Mar 1862, encl. 3 of Wyke to Russell, Orizaba, No. 38, 27 Mar (r. 28 Apr) 1862, PRO, F.O. 50/364.

47. Saligny to Thouvenel, Vera Cruz, No. 69, 11 Mar (r. 9 Apr) 1862, MDAE: *CP, Mex., vol. 58.*

48. Saligny to Thouvenel, Orizaba, No. 76, 26 May (r. 29 Jun) 1862, *ibid.*

49. Order of the Day, issued by Lorencez to his troops, 21 May 1862, encl. 3 of *ibid.*

50. Saligny to Thouvenel, Vera Cruz, No. 69, 11 Mar (r. 9 Apr) 1862, *ibid.*

51. Doblado to Allied Commissioners, Mexico City, 10 Mar 1862, encl. 2 of Saligny to Thouvenel, Vera Cruz, No. 70, 22 Mar (r. 25 Apr) 1862, *ibid.*

52. Prim to Jurien, Orizaba, 12 Mar 1862, encl. 3 of Jurien to Thouvenel, Tehuacan, No. 21, 15 Mar 1862, *ibid., vol. 57.*

53. *Ibid.*

54. Jurien to Saligny, Tehuacan, Con., 13 Mar 1862, encl. 3 of Jurien to Thouvenel, Tehuacan, No. 25, Con., 24 Mar 1862, *ibid.*

55. Jurien to Prim, Tehuacan, 13 Mar 1862, encl. 4 of Saligny to Thouvenel, Vera Cruz, No. 70, 22 Mar (r. 25 Apr) 1862, *ibid., vol. 58.*

56. Saligny to Prim, Vera Cruz, 15 Mar 1862, encl. 5 of Saligny to Thouvenel, Vera Cruz, No. 70, 22 Mar (r. 25 Apr) 1862, *ibid.*

57. Jurien to Saligny, Tehuacan, 24 Mar 1862, encl. 17 of Jurien to Thouvenel, Tehuacan, No. 25, Con, 24 Mar 1862, *ibid., vol. 57.*

58. Almonte to Napoleon III, Vera Cruz, 18 Mar 1862, *HHSA,* CORTI, I, 165–166.

59. Miranda to Estrada, Vera Cruz, 6 Mar 1862, encl. of Estrada to Thouvenel, Hotel Westminster, 13 Rue de la Paix, Paris, 9 Apr 1862, MDAE: *CP, Mex., vol. 58.*

60. Miranda to Estrada, Cordova, 27 Mar 1862, encl. of Estrada to Thouvenel, Hotel Westminster, Paris, 30 Apr 1862, *ibid.*

61. Saligny to Thouvenel, Vera Cruz, No. 70, 22 Mar (r. 25 Apr) 1862, *ibid.*

62. Wagner to Saligny, Mexico City, 22 Feb 1862, encl. 1 of Saligny to Thouvenel, Vera Cruz, No. 68, 3 Mar (r. 3 Apr) 1862, *ibid.*

63. See text above, footnoted by footnotes 45 and 46.

64. Saligny to Thouvenel, Vera Cruz, No. 70, 22 Mar (r. 25 Apr) 1862, MDAE: *CP, Mex.*, vol. 58.

65. Dunlop to Secretary of Admiralty, Orizaba, No. 26, 11 Apr 1862, encl. 2 of Admiralty to Hammond, Admiralty, 14 May 1862, PRO, F.O. 50/371.

66. Saligny to Thouvenel, Vera Cruz, No. 70, 22 Mar (r. 25 Apr) 1862, MDAE: *CP, Mex.*, vol. 58.

67. *Ibid.*

68. Saligny to Thouvenel, Vera Cruz, No. 73, 31 Mar (r. 29 Apr) 1862, *ibid.*

69. Wyke to Russell, Orizaba, No. 38, 27 Mar (r. 28 Apr) 1862, PRO, F.O. 50/364.

70. Dunlop to Secretary of Admiralty, Orizaba, No. 26, 11 Apr 1862, encl. 2 of Admiralty to Hammond, Admiralty, 14 May 1862, PRO, F.O. 50/371.

71. Jurien to Thouvenel, Tehuacan, 17 Mar 1862, MDAE: *CP, Mex.*, vol. 57.

72. Jurien to Prim, 17 Mar 1862, Prim-Senate-10 Dec 1862.

73. Prim to Jurien, Orizaba, 21 Mar 1862, encl. 9 of Jurien to Thouvenel, Tehuacan, No. 25, 24 Mar 1862, MDAE: *CP, Mex.*, vol. 57.

74. Saligny to Thouvenel, Vera Cruz, No. 72, 28 Mar (r. 29 Apr) 1862, *ibid.*, vol. 58; Prim-Senate-10 Dec 1862.

75. Wyke to Russell, Orizaba, No. 37, 27 Mar (r. 28 Apr) 1862, PRO, F.O. 50/364; Prim-Senate-10 Dec 1862; Prim to Jurien, 20 Mar 1862, PRIM, pp. 77–78; Prim to Jurien, Orizaba, 20 Mar 1862, H. Leonardon: "L'Espagne et La Question Du Mexique, 1861–1862," *Annales des Sciences Politiques,* XVI (1901), 85–85.

78. *Ibid.*

79. Jurien to Prim, Tehuacan, 20 Mar 1862, encl. 6 of Jurien to Thouvenel, Tehuacan, No. 25, Con., 24 Mar 1862, MDAE: *CP, Mex.*, vol. 57. See also Prim-Senate-10 Dec 1862.

80. Prim-Senate-10 Dec 1862.

81. Prim-Senate-10 Dec 1862.

82. Prim to Jurien, Orizaba, 21 Mar 1862, encl. 9 of Jurien to Thouvenel, Tehuacan, No. 25, Con., 24 Mar 1862, MDAE: *CP, Mex.*, vol. 57. See also Prim-Senate-10 Dec 1862.

83. Wyke to Russell, Orizaba, No. 37, 27 Mar (r. 28 Apr) 1862, PRO, F.O. 50/364; Prim-Senate-11 Dec 1862; Appendix T of present investigation.

84. Jurien to Prim, Tehuacan, 22 Mar 1862, encl. 10 of Jurien to Thouvenel, Tehuacan, No. 25, Con. 24 Mar 1862, MDAE: *CP, Mex.*, vol. 57. See also Prim-Senate-10 Dec 1862.

85. Jurien to Prim. Tehuacan, 11:00 P.M., 22 Mar 1862, encl. 12 of Jurien to Thouvenel, Tehuacan, No. 25, Con., 24 Mar 1862, MDAE: *CP, Mex.*, vol. 57. See also Prim-Senate-11 Dec 1862.

86. Jurien to Lorencez, Tehuacan, 23 Mar 1862, encl. 12 *(bis)* of

Jurien to Thouvenel, Tehuacan, No. 25, Con., 24 Mar 1862, MDAE: *CP, Mex.,* vol. 57.

87. Prim to Jurien, Orizaba, 23 Mar 1862, encl. 1 of Wyke to Russell, Orizaba, No. 38, 27 Mar (r. 28 Apr) 1862, PRO, F.O. 50/364. See also encl. 13 of Jurien to Thouvenel, Tehuacan, No. 25, Con., 24 Mar 1862, MDAE: *CP, Mex.,* vol. 57. See also Prim-Senate-11 Dec 1862.

88. Wyke and Prim to Jurien, Orizaba, 23 Mar 1862, encl. 2 of Wyke to Russell, Orizaba, No. 38, 27 Mar (r. 28 Apr) 1862, PRO, F.O. 50/364. In Wyke's No. 38 to Russell. Wyke states that a similar communication was sent to Saligny. Dunlop was also sent a summons. See Dunlop to Milne, Challenger at Vera Cruz, No. 75, 27 Mar 1862, encl. of Romaine to Hammond, Admiralty, 29 Apr (r. 1 May) 1862, PRO, F.O. 50/370.

89. Wyke to Russell, Orizaba, No. 38, 27 Mar (r. 28 Apr) 1862, PRO, F.O. 50/364.

90. *Ibid:* Prim-Senate-10 Dec 1862.

91. Lorencez to Mangin, 24 Mar 1862, sum. by Saligny to Thouvenel, Vera Cruz, No. 73, 31 Mar (r. 29 Apr) 1862, MDAE: *CP, Mex.,* vol. 58.

92. Prim-Senate-11 Dec 1862; Saligny to Thouvenel, Vera Cruz, No. 71, 26 Mar (r. 29 Apr) 1862, MDAE: *CP, Mex.,* vol. 58; Wyke to Russell, Orizaba, No. 39, 29 Mar (r. 28 Apr) 1862, PRO, F.O. 50/364.

93. Jurien to Thouvenel, Tehuacan, No. 25, Con., 24 Mar 1862, MDAE: *CP, Mex.,* vol. 57.

94. Captain Thomasset to Jurien, 24 Mar 1862, encl. of Jurien to Thouvenel, Tehuacan, No. 26, 24 Mar 1862, *ibid.*

95. Jurien to Wyke and Prim, Tehuacan, 24 Mar 1862, encl. 3 of Wyke to Russell, Orizaba, No. 38, 27 Mar (r. 28 Apr) 1862, PRO, F.O. 50/364.

96. Jurien to Prim, Tehuacan, 24 Mar 1862, encl. 20 of Jurien to Thouvenel, Tehuacan, No. 25, Con., 24 Mar 1862, MDAE: *CP, Mex.,* vol. 57.

97. Jurien to Lorencez, Tehuacan, 24 Mar 1862, 11:00 P.M., encl. 19 of Jurien to Thouvenel, Tehuacan, No. 25, Con., 24 Mar 1862, *ibid.*

98. See Appendix R of present investigation.

99. Jurien to Prim, Tehuacan, Con., 25 Mar 1862, encl. 22 of Jurien to Thouvenel, Tehuacan, No. 25, Con., 24 Mar 1862, MDAE: *CP, Mex.,* vol. 57.

100. Jurien to Doblado, Tehuacan, 26 Mar 1862, encl. 23 of Jurien to Thouvenel, Tehuacan, No. 25, Con., 24 Mar 1862, *ibid.*

101. Jurien to Wyke, Tehuacan, 29 Mar 1862, encl. 1 of Wyke to Russell, Orizaba, No. 40, 30 Mar (r. 28 Apr) 1862, PRO, F.O. 50/364. See also Appendix T of present investigation.

102. General Zaragoza to Jurien, San Andrez Chalchicomula, 26 Mar 1862, encl. 1 of Jurien to Thouvenel, Tehuacan, No. 28, 27 Mar 1862, MDAE: *CP, Mex.,* vol. 57.

103. Jurien to Zaragoza, Tehuacan, 27 Mar 1862, encl. 2 of Jurien to Thouvenel, Tehuacan, No. 28, 27 Mar 1862, *ibid.*

104. For Jurien's statement that this letter was sent, see Appendix T of present investigation.

105. Jurien to Prim, Tehuacan, 27 Mar 1862, encl. 5 of Jurien to Thouvenel, Tehuacan, No. 28, 27 Mar 1862, MDAE: *CP, Mex.,* vol. 57.

106. Wyke to Russell, Orizaba, No. 39, 29 Mar (r. 28 Apr) 1862, PRO, F.O. 50/364.

107. Prim-Senate-10 Dec 1862.

108. Prim to Collantes, Orizaba, No. 24, 29 Mar 1862, *Diario de Las Sessiones de Cortes. Congreso de los Diputados, 2 Jun 1862, Apéndice Primero Num. 133,* (trans.) encl. of Crampton to Russell Madrid, No. 255, 16 (r. 26) Jun 1862, PRO, F.O. 72/1035.

109. *Ibid.*

110. Jurien to Thouvenel, Tehuacan, 28 Mar 1862, 1:00 A.M., MDAE: *CP, Mex.,* vol. 57.

111. Russell to Wyke, F.O., No. 19, 24 Feb (r. 29 Mar) 1862, PRO, F.O. 204/159; Russell to Wyke, F.O., No. 20, 25 Feb (r. 29 Mar) 1862, PRO, F.O. 204/159. For the details of these instructions, see Section 3 of Chapter V of present investigation, between footnotes 16 and 18. On 29 March 1862, Prim acknowledged receipt of instructions from Collantes, dated 7 February 1862 and enclosing instructions, dated 1 February 1862, to the Spanish Ambassador to London. See Prim to Collantes, Orizaba, No. 24, 29 Mar 1862, *Diaria de Las Sessiones de Cortes, Congreso de los Diputados, 2 Jun 1862, Apéndice Primero Num. 133,* (trans.) encl. of Crampton to Russell, Madrid, No. 255, 16 (r. 26) Jun 1862, PRO, F.O. 72/1035. For Collantes' instructions of 7 February, see Section 2 of Chapter V of present investigation, between footnotes 141 and 142. For Collantes' instructions of 1 February to the Spanish Ambassador to London, see Section 2 of Chapter V of present investigation, between footnotes 134 and 135.

112. Prim to Collantes, Orizaba, No. 24, 29 Mar 1862, *Diario de Las Sessiones de Cortes. Congreso de los Diputados, 2 Jun 1862, Apéndice Primero Num. 133,* (trans.) encl. of Crampton to Russell, Madrid, No. 255, 16 (r. 26) Jun 1862, PRO, F.O. 72/1035; Wyke to Russell, Orizaba, No. 38, 27 Mar (r. 28 Apr) 1862, PRO, F.O. 50/364.

113. See Appendix T of present investigation.

114. Milne to Secretary of Admiralty, Nile at Bermuda, No. 288, 9 Apr 1862, encl. of Romaine to Hammond, Admiralty, 29 (r. 30) Apr 1862, PRO, F.O. 50/370.

115. On 31 March 1862 Saligny acknowledged receipt of Thouvenel's instructions of 28 February 1862 and the "telegram" of 21 February 1862. See Saligny to Thouvenel, Vera Cruz, No. 73, 31 Mar (r. 29 Apr) 1862, MDAE: *CP, Mex.,* vol. 58. For Thouvenel's instructions of 28 February to Saligny, see Section 3 of Chapter V of present investigation, between footnotes 95 and 96. For Thouvenel's "telegram" of 21 February for Jurien and Saligny, see Section 3 of Chapter V of present investigation between footnotes 8 and 9. On 10 April

1862 Jurien acknowledged Thouvenel's instructions of 28 February. See Jurien to Thouvenel, Orizaba, No. 33, 10 Apr 1862, MDAE: *CP, Mex.,* vol. 57. For Thouvenel's instructions of 28 February to Jurien, see Section 3 of Chapter V of present investigation, between footnotes 96 and 97. Jurien probably received Thouvenel's instructions of 28 February before 9 April, when the last conference of the Allied Commissioners was held. On 3 April Jurien referred to having just received instructions "from Europe." See Jurien to Wyke, Bivac of Puente Colorado, 3 Apr 1862, encl. 3 of Wyke to Russell, Orizaba, No. 42, 3 Apr (r. 14 May) 1862, PRO, F.O. 50/365. The question of when Jurien received Thouvenel's instructions of 28 February is of little importance, because these instructions merely summarized Thouvenel's "telegram" of 21 February to Jurien and Saligny. Saligny acknowledged this telegram on 31 March, and thefore both Saligny and Jurien knew its contents before the last meeting of the Allied Commissioners on 9 April.

116. Saligny received Thouvenel's instructions of 14 March 1862 on 13 April 1862. See Saligny to Thouvenel, Orizaba, No. 74, 25 Apr 1862, MDAE: *CP, Mex.,* vol. 58. For Thouvenel's instructions of 14 March to Saligny, see Section 3 of Chapter V of present investigation, between footnotes 121 and 123. Jurien received Thouvenel's instructions of 14 March on 14 April. See Jurien to Thouvenel, Cordova, No. 36, 18 Apr 1862, MDAE: *CP, Mex.,* vol. 57. For Thouvenel's instructions of 14 March to Jurien, see Section 3 of Chapter V of present investigation, between footnotes 123 and 124. The "telegrams" of 20 March 1862 (see Section 3 of Chapter 5 of present investigation, between footnotes 138 and 141) which relieved Jurien arrived at the end of April 1862, when Saligny acknowledged that he had "just" received them. See P.S. of Saligny to Thouvenel, Orizaba, No. 74, 25 Apr 1862, MDAE: *CP, Mex.,* vol. 58.

117. Russell to Wyke, F.O., No. 32, 15 Mar (r. 13 Apr) 1862, PRO, F.O. 204/159.

118. Russell to Wyke, F.O., Nos. 40, 48, 49; 31 Mar, 1 Apr, 1 Apr, (r. 29 Apr) 1862, *ibid.*

119. Saligny to Thouvenel, Vera Cruz, No. 73, 31 Mar (r. 29 Apr) 1862, MDAE: *CP, Mex.,* vol. 58.

120. Jurien to Thouvenel, Orizaba, No. 33, 10 Apr 1862, *ibid.,* vol. 57.

121. Jurien to Napoleon III, Orizaba, 10 Apr 1862, *ibid.*

122. See Appendix T of present investigation.

123. See Appendix T of present investigation.

124. *El Eco de Europa,* Orizaba, 9, 19 Mar 1862, encl. 2 of Saligny to Thouvenel, Vera Cruz, No. 70, 22 Mar (r. 25 Apr) 1862, MDAE: *CP, Mex.,* vol. 58.

125. See Appendix T of present investigation.

126. Doblado to the Allied Commissioners, Mexico City, 3 Apr 1862, E. Lefévre: *Le Mexique et L'Intervention Europeenne, par le citoyen E. Lefévre* (Mexico City, 1862), pp. 383–384.

127. See Appendix T of present investigation.

128. Saligny and Jurien to Doblado, Orizaba, No. 33, 10 Apr 1862, encl. 1 of Jurien to Thouvenel, Orizaba, No. 33, 10 Apr 1862, MDAE: *CP, Mex.,* vol. 57.

129. Telegraphic Despatch of 21 Feb 1862 to MM. Admiral Jurien de La Gravière and Dubois de Saligny, *ibid.*

130. Saligny and Jurien to Doblado, Orizaba, 9 Apr 1862, encl. 1 of Jurien to Thouvenel, Orizaba, No. 33, 10 Apr 1862, *ibid.*

131. See Appendix T of present investigation.

132. Allied Plenipotentiaries to Doblado, Orizaba, 9 Apr 1862, encl. 1 of Wyke to Russell, Orizaba, No. 56, 17 Apr (r. 2 Jun) 1862, PRO, F.O. 50/365.

133. See Appendix T of present investigation.

134. See Appendix T of present investigation.

135. Encl. of Wyke to Russell, Orizaba, No. 45, 11 Apr (r. 14 May) 1862, PRO, F.O. 50/365.

136. Encl. of Jurien to Thouvenel, Orizaba, No. 33, 10 Apr 1862, MDAE: *CP, Mex.,* vol. 57.

137. Prim-Senate-10 Dec 1862.

138. See Appendix V of present investigation.

139. Wyke to Russell, Orizaba, Pri., 12 Apr 1862, PRO, P.R.O. 30/22-74.

140. PRIM, pp. 89-91.


## 2. The Breakdown of the Convention of London in Europe

1. Russell to Wyke, F.O., Nos. 52-54, drafts dated 30 Apr 1862; Russell to Wyke, F.O., Nos, 63, 67, 69; 17 May, 22 May, 27 Jun 1862, drafts, PRO, F.O. 50/363.

2. Draft to Admiralty, F.O., 30 Apr 1862, PRO, F.O. 50/370.

3. Draft to Admiralty, F.O., 5 Jun 1862, PRO, F.O. 50/371.

4. Draft to Admiralty, 6 Jun 1862, marked seen by Palmerston, *ibid.*

5. Russell to Grey (in Cowley's absence), F.O., No. 37, draft, 23 Jul 1862, PRO, F.O. 27/1425.

6. Speech of A. H. Layard in House of Commons, 15 July 1862, *Hansard's Parliamentary Debates,* 3rd series, CLXVIII (London, 1862), 367.

7. Russell to Wyke, F.O., No. 54, draft, 30 Apr 1862, PRO, F.O. 50/363.

8. Russell to Wyke, F.O., No. 63, draft, 24 May 1862, marked "substituted for that of yesterday," *ibid.*

9. Russell to Cowley, Telegram, 6:00 P.M., 29 Apr 1862, cited by Russell to Cowley, F.O., No. 467, draft, 29 Apr 1862, PRO, F.O. 27/1422.

10. Russell to Crampton, F.O., Telegram, 6:00 P.M., 29 Apr 1862, cited by Russell to Crampton, F.O., No. 99, draft, 29 Apr 1862, PRO, F.O. 72/1028.

11. Encl. of Wyke to Russell, Orizaba, No. 45, 11 Apr (r. 14 May) 1862, PRO, F.O. 50/365.

12. Russell to Cowley, F.O., Pri., 17 May 1862, PRO, F.O. 519/199.

13. Draft to Admiralty, F.O., 17 May 1862, PRO, F.O. 50/371.

14. Entry, dated 17 May 1862, "The Queen's Letters 1862," PRO, 30/22–14.

15. Russell to Cowley, Pri., 28 May 1862, PRO, F.O. 519/199.

16. Russell to Cowley, F.O., Pri., 18 Jun 1862, ibid.

17. Crampton to Russell, Telegram, 23 May 1862, cited by Crampton to Russell, Madrid, No. 261, 18 Jun (r. 7 Jul) 1862, PRO, F.O. 72/1035.

18. Russell to Crampton, F.O., Telegram, 24 May 1862, cited by Russell to Crampton, F.O., No. 109, draft, 26 May 1862, PRO, F.O. 72/1029.

19. See below.

20. Speech of the Queen opening Cortes, 1 Dec 1862, encl. 2 of Crampton to Russell, Madrid, No. 387, 1 (r. 5) Dec 1862, PRO, F.O. 72/1038.

21. Crampton to Russell, Madrid, No. 389, 2 (r. 6) Dec 1862, PRO, F.O. 72/1038.

22. Russell to Crampton, F.O., No. 215, draft, 9 Dec 1862, PRO, F.O. 72/1029.

23. Russell to Cowley, Pri., 21 Jun 1862, PRO, F.O. 519/199.

24. "Correspondence Respecting the Affairs of Mexico: Presented to both Houses of Parliament by Command of Her Majesty, 1862," British Sessional Papers, 1862, LXIV, 101–444. (University of Pennsylvania microfilms). The bulk of this correspondence is again reproduced, with some minor changes, in the "blue books." See British and Foreign State Papers, LII–LIII.

25. Hammond to Cowley, F.O., Pri., 17 May 1862, PRO, F.O. 519/190.

26. Crampton to Russell, Madrid, No. 194, Con., 30 Apr (r. 19) May 3; 1862, PRO, F.O. 72/103. Crampton to Russell, Madrid, No. 195, 1 (r. 19) May 1862, PRO, F.O. 72/1034.

27. PRIM, pp. 89–91.

28. Barrot to Thouvenel, Madrid, Telegram, 11:12 A.M. (r. 5:10 P.M.) 19 May 1862, MDAE: CP, Espagne, vol. 860.

29. Barrot to Thouvenel, Telegram, 1:25 P.M., 20 May 1862, ibid.

30. Barrot to Thouvenel, Madrid, No. 40, 14 (r. 18) May 1862, ibid.

31. See Section 2 and 3 of Chapter III of present investigation.

32. Barrot to Thouvenel, Madrid, No. 40, 14 (r. 18) May 1862, MDAE: CP, Espagne, vol. 860.

33. Crampton to Russell, Madrid, No. 246, 22 (r. 27) May 1862, PRO, F.O. 72/1034.

34. Collantes to Ceballos, Madrid, 7 Jul 1862, "Documents relative to the Mexican question, since the withdrawal of the Spanish Expeditionary Force Until Date," English trans. of Diario de las Sessiones de

*Cortes,* 5 Dec 1862, encl. of Crampton to Russell, Madrid, No. 413, 27 (r. 31) Dec 1862, PRO, F.O. 72/1039.

35. Precis of the sessions of the Chamber of Deputies of the Cortes, 10–14 Jun 1862, encl. of Crampton to Russell, Madrid, No. 262, 18 Jun (r. 7 Jul) 1862, PRO, F.O. 72/1035.

36. Speech of Collantes in Cortes, 19 May 1862, sum. by Barrot to Thouvenel, Madrid, No. 42, 19 (r. 22) May 1862, MDAE: *CP, Espagne,* vol. 860.

37. Collantes to Spanish Chargé d'Affaires in Paris, Madrid, 21 May 1862, "Documents relative to the Mexican question, since the withdrawal of the Spanish Expeditionary Force Until Date," Engl. trans. of *Diario de las Sessiones de Cortes,* 5 Dec 1862, encl. of Crampton to Russell, Madrid, No. 413, 27 (r. 31) Dec 1862, PRO, F.O. 72/1039.

38. *Ibid.*

39. Thouvenel to Barrot, Paris, No. 28, 10 Jun 1862, MDAE: *CP, Espagne,* vol. 861.

40. Collantes to Ceballos, Madrid, 7 Jul 1862, with notations, forwarded to London on 11 Jul and to Paris on 17 Jul, "Documents relative to the Mexican question, since the withdrawal of the Spanish Expeditionary Force Until Date," Engl. trans. of *Diario de las Sessiones de Cortes,* 5 Dec 1862, encl. of Crampton to Russell, Madrid, No. 413, 27 (r. 31) Dec 1862, PRO, F.O. 72/1039.

41. Royal Decree, 27 Jul 1862, extract from *Gazette,* encl. of Crampton to Russell, San Ildefonso, No. 311, 3 (r. 8) Aug 1862, PRO, F.O. 72/1036.

42. Crampton to Russell, San Ildefonso, No. 310, 28 Jul (r. 3 Aug) 1862, PRO, F.O. 72/1035.

43. Collantes to Concha, Madrid, 29 Jul 1862, "Documents relative to the Mexican question, since the withdrawal of the Spanish Expeditionary Force Until Date," Engl. trans of *Diario de las. Sessiones de Cortes,* 5 Dec 1862, encl. of Crampton to Russell, Madrid, No. 413, 27 (r. 31) Dec 1862, PRO, F.O. 72/1039.

44. Note Verbale sent to the Marquis de la Havane (i.e., General Concha) by Drouyn de Lhuys (i.e., Thouvenel's successor), 29 Oct 1862, encl. 2 of Drouyn de Lhuys to Barrot, Paris, 22 Dec 1862, *DD, 1862,* p. 203.

45. Cowley to Russell, Paris, No. 572, 2 (r. 3) May 1862, PRO, F.O. 27/1438.

46. Cowley-Napoleon III Conversation, 12 May 1862, sum. by Cowley to Russell, Paris, Pri., 13 May 1862, PRO, P.R.O. 30/22–57.

47. Eugenie-Metternich Conversation, sum. by Rechberg to Maximilian, 3 May 1862, *HHSA,* CORTI, I, 164.

48. Barrot to Thouvenel, Madrid, Telegram, 11:12 A.M. (r. 5:10 P.M.) 19 May 1862, MDAE: *CP, Espagne,* vol. 860.

49. See Appendix U of present investigation.

50. Barrot to Thouvenel, Madrid, Telegram, 4:30 P.M., 10 May 1862, MDAE: *CP, Espagne,* vol. 860.

51. Cowley to Russell, Telegram, 1:45 P.M., 17 May 1862, cited by

Cowley to Russell, Paris, No. 640, 17 (r. 19) May 1862, PRO, F.O. 27/1438.

52. Cowley to Russell, Paris, Pri., 20 May 1862, PRO, P.R.O. 30/22–57.

53. Cowley to Russell, Paris, No. 663, 20 (r. 21) May 1862, PRO, F.O. 27/1439.

54. See above.

55. Cowley to Russell, Paris, Pri., 29 May 1862, PRO, F.O. 519/229.

56. Napoleon III to Maximilian, Paris, 7 Jun 1862, *HHSA,* CORTI, I, 373.

57. Eugenie to Charlotte, Tuileries, 7 Jul 1862, *HHSA,* CORTI, I. 374.

58. Bismarck Bericht aus Paris, 15 Jun 1862, L. von Raschdau, ed.: *Die Politischen Berichte des Fürsten Bismarck aus Petersburg und Paris, 1859–1862* (Berlin, 1920, part II, p. 206.

59. See Section 3 of Chapter V. *Die Politischen Berichte des Fürsten Bismarck aus Petersburg.*

60. Bismarck Bericht aus Paris, 15 Jun 1862, L. von Raschdau, ed.:

61. Napoleon to Lorencez, Fontainebleau, 15 Jun 1862, MDAE: *CP, Mex.,* vol. 59.

62. Encl. 3 of Saligny to Thouvenel, Orizaba, No. 76, 26 May (r. 29 Jun) 1862, MDAE: *CP, Mex.,* vol. 58. I have used the translation made by Abbot. See ABBOT, p. 632.

63. Saligny to Thouvenel, Orizaba, No. 76, 26 May (r. 29 Jun) 1862, MDAE: *CP, Mex.,* vol. 58.

64. Napoleon III to Randon, Fontainebleau, 29 Jan 1862, Maréchal Jacques L. Randon: *Mémoires du Maréchal Randon* (2 v., Paris, 1875–1877), II, 66.

65. Randon to Napoleon III, Paris, 2 Jul 1862, *ibid.,* II, 68. Cowley to Russell, Paris, Pri., 4 Nov 1862, PRO, PRO, P.R.O.

66. Cowley-Drouyn de Lhuys conversation, 4 Nov 1862, sum. by Cowley to Russell, Paris, Pri., 4 Nov 1862, PRO, PRO, P.R.O. 30/22–58.

67. Mettternich to Rechberg, Fontainebleau, 30 Jun 1862, *HHSA,* AKM, DAWSON, p. 248.

68. See Appendix V of present investigation.

69. Seward's Diary or Notes on the War, entry for 10 Mar 1862, George E. Baker: *The Works of William H. Seward* (5 v., Boston, 1883), V, 49.

70. Robert W. Frazer: "Latin American Projects to Aid Mexico During the French Intervention," *HAHR,* XXI (1941), 51–78.

71. Cowley to Russell, Paris, Pri., 1 Jul 1862, PRO, P.R.O. 30/22–58.

72. Comte Fleury: *Memoiren der Kaiseren Eugenie von Graf Fleury: Nach Mitteilungen, privaten Urkunden, persoenlichen Briefen der Kaiserin, Gespraechen des Kaisers Napoleon III, nach Familien-briefen und hinterlassenen Papieren von General Fleury, Franceschini*

*Pietri, Prinz Viktor Napoleon und anderen Gliedern der Hofgesell-schaft des zweiten Kaiserreiches* (2 vol., Leipzig, 1921), II. 110.


## Chapter VII

1. Metternich-Cowley Conversation, sum. by Cowley to Russell, Paris, Pri., 6 May 1862, PRO, F.O. 519/229.


## Appendix A

1. Memorandum on British Convention, Pakenham Convention, 15 Oct 1842, encls. 1 and 2 of Wyke to Russell, Mexico City, No. 32, Confidential, 26 Aug (r. 29 Sep) 1861, PRO, F.O. 50/354.

2. Memorandum on British Convention, Doyle Convention, 4 Dec 1851, encls. 1 and 7 of Wyke to Russell, Mexico City, No. 32, Confidential, 26 Aug (r. 29 Sep) 1861, *ibid.*

3. Memorandum on British Convention, Padre Moran Convention, 6 Dec 1851, encls. 1 and 7 of Wyke to Russell, Mexico City, No. 32, Confidential, 26 Aug (r. 29 Sep) 1861, *ibid.*

5. Wyke to Russell, Mexico City, No. 42, Confidential, 26 Aug (r. 29 Sep) 1861, *ibid.*

4. Order of 7 Feb 1852, encl. 8 of Wyke to Russell, Mexico City, No. 32, Confidential, 26 Aug (r. 29 Sept.) 1861, *ibid.*

6. Martinez del Rio to Mathew, Mexico City, 24 May 1861, encl. 9 of *Ibid.*

7. Wyke to Russell, Mexico City, No. 32, Confidential, 26 Aug (r. 29 Sep) 1861, *ibid.*

8. Memorandum on British Convention, Doyle's Sub-convention, 27 Nov 1852, encls. 1 and 3 of *Ibid.*

9. Memorandum on British Convention, encl. 1 of Wyke to Russell, Mexico City, No. 32, Confidential, 26 Aug (r. 29 Sep) 1861, *ibid.* Statistical tables of just what Mexico was supposed to pay and what actually was paid, 1852 through 1861, are given.

10. Otway Convention, 10 Aug 1858, encl. 4 of Wyke to Russell, Mexico City, No. 32, Confidential, 26 Aug (r. 29 Sep) 1861, *ibid.* Wyke was unable to explain why the mortgage on Mexican customs was increased by 1 per cent and thought it might have been done by Mexico voluntarily (Memorandum on British Convention, encl. 1 of *Ibid.*).

11. Memorandum on British Convention, encl. 1 of Wyke to Russell, Mexico City, No. 32, Confidential, 26 Aug (r. 29 Sep) 1861, *ibid.*

12. A French convention already mortgaged Mexican custom duties on French cargoes. See footnote 129 of Section III of Chapter I of the present investigation.

13. Memorandum on British Convention, encl. 1 of Wyke to Russell, Mexico City, No. 32, Confidential, 26 Aug (r. 29 Sep) 1861, PRO, F.O. 50/354. Wyke states "$350,000" were "occupied." Actually Mexico did not meet two semi-annual payments (4 June and 4 December) of $149,547.45 each, due the British Convention Bondholders, and two payments of $29,490 each, due the Padre Moran claimants.

14. *Ibid*. See also Appendix B of present investigation.

15. Memorandum on British Convention, encl. 1 of Wyke to Russell, Mexico City, No. 32, Confidential, 26 Aug (r. 29 Sep) 1861, PRO, F.O. 50/354. The most Mexico ever paid in a single year was $443,306.35, in 1854 *(Ibid.)*.

16. Wyke to Russell, Mexico City, No. 32, Confidential, 26 Aug (r. 29 Sep) 1861, *ibid*.

17. Wyke to Russell, Mexico City, No. 44, Confidential, 27 Oct (r. 27 Nov) 1861, *ibid*.

18. *Ibid*.

19. Davidson, Secretary, to Perry, Mexico City, 15 Oct 1861, encl. of Buckmaster to Layard, 10 (r. 11) Dec 1861, *ibid.*, F.O. 50/358. Voting was by shares. Perry obtained a vote of $1,522,000, against $35,000 for Glennie.

20. Wyke to Russell, Mexico City, No. 44, Confidential, 27 Oct (r. 27 Nov) 1861, *ibid.*, F.O. 50/354.

21. Perry to Davidson, Secretary, Mexico City, 21 Oct 1861, encl. of Buckmaster to Layard, 10 (r. 11) Dec 1861, *ibid.*, F.O. 50/358.

22. Wyke to Russell, Mexico City, No. 49, 19 Nov 1861 (r. 1 Jan 1862), *ibid.*, F.O. 50/354. Wyke wrote to Russell that there were three objections to Perry's election: (1) it would be tacit recognition of the old agency under a new name, as Perry was a mere creature of Martinez del Rio, (2) the Mexican Government was also against Perry, as it wished to separate the British and Spanish Conventions and Perry's election would be regarded as a subterfuge for carrying on the old system that produced only difficulties, (3) her Majesty's Minister, to whom the Bondholders looked for protection, ought to have the right to approve or disapprove a nominee (Wyke to Russell, Mexico City, No. 44, Confidential, 27 Oct (r. 27 Nov) 1861, *ibid.*).

23. Perry to Bondholders of the British Convention, Mexico City, 1 Nov 1861, encl. of Buckmaster to Russell, 10 (r. 12) Jan 1862, *ibid.*, F.O. 50/370.

24. Wyke to Russell, Mexico City, No. 49, 19 Nov 1861 (r. 1 Jan 1862), *ibid.*, F.O. 50/354.

25. Russell's despatch was dated 30 October, when he was busy with negotiations to complete the Tripartite Treaty of London. He seems not to have read Wyke's explanation of the "negligence" of Martinez del Rio very carefully. At any rate, Russell was more impressed with a letter from Mr. Grant, a British subject resident in Mexico, received at the same time as Wyke's despatch. Mr. Grant charged that many of the Convention Bonds had been purchased by Mexicans whose claims the British Government was supporting. Russell, however, be-

lieved that "... those Mexicans ... who have purchased Bonds from the British Creditors, have acquired a right to the original conditions stipulated in the Convention, and consequently even if the Agency were changed, it is by no means certain that Mr. Grant would be satisfied ..." There might be, Russell admitted, other grounds for a change of agents, which might "... ultimately (be) carried into effect." Wyke, therefore, was authorized, when "... any new arrangements are made ...," to transfer the agency of the fund to Glennie (Russell to Wyke, F.O., No. 54, 30 Oct (r. 29 Nov) 1861, PRO, F.O. 204/153; Grant to Russell, 24 Aug 1861, encl. of Russell to Wyke, F.O. No. 54, draft, 30 Oct 1861, *ibid.*, F.O. 50/351).

26. Summary of Wyke to Russell, No. 44, Confidential, 27 Oct 1861, F.O., 13 Dec 1861, with Hammond notation, dated 13 Dec 1861, and undated note by Russell, PRO, F.O. 50/358.

27. "... I do not think it advisable to interfere with the choice of the Bondholders as matters now stand, but it will be proper that you should be guarded in your communications with Mr. Perry, and that close attention should be paid to prevent any irregularities such as those to which you have alluded in a former despatch, taking place in carrying on the Agency" (Russell to Wyke, F.O., No. 81, 16 Dec 1861 (r. 14 Feb 1862 by *Ariadne*), PRO, F.O. 204/153).

## Appendix B

1. *Report of the Committee of Public Credit of the Mexican Chamber of Deputies on the Adjustment of the English Debt. Dated April 1st, 1850.* Translated from the Spanish (London, 1850), p. 5, PRO, F.O. 97/273. (Hereafter referred to as REPORT). "The Case of the Holders of Bonds of the National Debt contracted by Mexico in London," 22 Nov 1861, encl. of Committee of Mexican Bondholders to Russell, 10 Basinghall St., London, 23 (r. 26) Nov 1861, PRO, F.O. 97/289. (Hereafter referred to as CASE). The REPORT is the Mexican version of the history of the London Bondholders, the CASE the version of the Bondholders.

2. The loan was negotiated by Manning and Marshall, established at Mexico City, as representatives of Barclay, Richardson & Co. of London. See REPORT, p. 5.

3. *Ibid.*

4. *Ibid.*

5. The Goldschmidt loan of $16,000,000 was floated through 24,000 bonds, to that amount, sold at 55%, producing only $8,000,000 for Mexico (since 5% was retained by Goldschmidt as a commission) Barclay, Richardson & Co. also issued 24,000 bonds for $16,000,000, sold at 86¾, producing $13,880,000. The two loans, therefore, only produced $21,880,000 for Mexico. See REPORT, pp. 67–68. From this commission and other charges were also subtracted. See footnote 8 below.

6. REPORT, p. 73.

7. See footnote 5 above. Mexico lost $8,000,000 by the Goldschmidt loan and $2,120,000 by the Barclay, Richardson & Co. loan, because the bonds issued sold below par.

8. These charges were $8,130, 685. See REPORT, p. 69.

9. In 1823, without any authority from the Mexican Government, Sr. D. Vicente Rocafuerte made a loan to the Republic of Columbia of $315,000, on condition that it be repaid within eighteen months. Only $8,500 was ever repaid. See REPORT, p. 70.

10. When Goldschmidt failed, the company owed Mexico eleven thousand and some odd hundred pounds sterling, but assets to cover this were recovered in Mexico City. See REPORT, p. 8. When Barclay, Richardson & Co. failed, the house owed $2,244, 542, but enough paper, tobacco and debts were attached so that Mexico only lost $1,519, 644. See REPORT, p. 70

11. REPORT, p. 8.

12. The principal and arrears of interest on the 5% loan were $17,219,931.46. Principal and arrears of interest on the 6% loan, together with a 12½% premium given at the time of the 1837 conversion, was $29,019,789. See REPORT, p. 10. Subtracting the 12½% compensation, amounting to $2,560,100 (see REPORT, p. 73) from the above $29,019,789, the figure $26,459,689 is arrived at, the principal and arrears of interest of the 6% loan in 1837. Consequently Mexican indebtedness in 1837 was $43,679,620, the sum of $26,459,689 and $17,219,931.46. Burke gives Mexican indebtedness, as of 1 October 1837, the date of the conversion, as $46, 235,000. See BURKE, p. 132. This figure includes the $2,560,100. Likewise a Memorandum prepared by Mr. White, the agent in Mexico of Baring Brothers, then agents of the London Bondholders, gives the total debt at the time of the 1837 conversion as $46,240,000. See Memorandum, Mexico City, 22 May 1862, prepared by Mr. White, encl. of Wyke to Russell, Mexico City, No. 71, 22 May (r. 28 Jul) 1862, PRO, F.O. 97/280. "Hereafter referred to as WHITE MEMORANDUM). For the exact figures of the conversion, see below.

13. REPORT, p. 9.

14. Ibid., p. 11.

15. After the resignation of Baring, Brothers & Co., the successors of Barclay, Richardson & Co., which failed, the Mexican Chargé d'Affaires, Don Augustine Iturbide, appointed Messrs. F. de Lizardi & Co. as financial agents of Mexico, and this appointment was afterwards confirmed by Mexico. See REPORT, p. 9.

16. REPORT, pp. 10, 73.

17. The reduction of the interest rate from 6% to 5% from 1837 to 1849 saved Mexico $2,457,540, and the 10 year suspension of interest on the deferred bonds saved Mexico $10,114,930. From this total of $12,572, 470 saved must be subtracted the $2,560, 100 granted the Bondholders as compensation for the interest reduction of 1%

on the 6% loan. This compensation was granted by accepting the old
6% bonds at 12½% above par.

18. REPORT, p. 11.

19. *Ibid.*, pp. 11–12, 74; CASE.

20. REPORT, p. 10.

21. *Ibid.*, p. 19.

22. Burke gives the total as $46,235,000. See BURKE, p. 132. Ala-
man gives the total as $46,236,892. See REPORT, p. 119. The Bond-
holders give the total as $46,239, 685. See REPORT, p. 119. Mr.
White gives the total as $46,240,000. See WHITE MEMORANDUM.

23. Lizardi & Co. had issued $27,500,000 in deferred bonds, and
when Lizardi & Co. were relieved as financial agents of Mexico in
1845 by Messrs. Schneider & Co., the new agents stated that
$23,120,000 should have been issued in deferred bonds originally plus
$458,250 to pay part of the April 1843 dividend, as authorized by
Mexico. Therefore the $3,921,750 in "excess" deferred bonds was
demanded of Lizardi & Co., and an order of 27 June 1846 of the
Minister of Finance called on Lizardi & Co to hand over the said
$3,921, 750 in deferred bonds. See REPORT, p. 20. Since the Mexican
Government acquiesced in the excess issue of active bonds, these were
recognized as valid, although the deferred and active bonds were supposed to be equal in amount, and so $23,120,000 may be taken as
the amount of bonds Lizardi & Co. should have issued in active as well
as deferred bonds, making a total issue of bonds to the amount of
$46,240,000.

24. REPORT, p. 13.

25. *Ibid.*, p. 119.

26. *Ibid.*, p. 14.

27. *Ibid.*, pp. 12–13.

28. *Ibid.*, pp. 14, 18.

29. *Ibid.*, p. 14.

30. *Ibid.*, p. 19.

31. *Ibid.*, p. 20; WHITE MEMORANDUM.

32. REPORT, p. 15.

33. *Ibid.*, p. 121.

34. So the authors of the REPORT believe. See *ibid.*

35. *Ibid.*, pp. 14, 121.

36. *Ibid.*, p. 120.

37. *Ibid.*, p. 15.

38. *Ibid.*, pp. 16–17.

39. *Ibid.*, p. 17.

40. For the conversion of 1846, see below.

41. REPORT, p. 36.

42. *Ibid.*

43. *Ibid.*, pp. 15, 18.

44. *Ibid.*, p. 16.

45. *Ibid.*, p. 20.

46. *Ibid.*

47. WHITE MEMORANDUM.

48. Ibid; REPORT, pp. 28, 113–114.

49. REPORT, pp. 28, –114; CASE. The $27,958,250 was the sum of the $27,500,000 active bonds issued by Lizardi and the $458,250 of deferred bonds rendered active to meet ⅔ of the dividend payment of April 1843. The $1,000,000 in active bonds in virtue of the law of 28 Jul 1843 was not included in the conversion of 1846, and what happened to these bonds is a mystery.

50. REPORT, pp. 28, 113–114; CASE. The $3,921,750 of "excess" deferred bonds issued by Lizardi was not recognized.

51. REPORT, pp. 28, 113–114.

52. CASE.

53. Ibid: REPORT, pp. 28, 113–114.

54. 90% of the active bonds amounted to $25,162,425 (loss of $2,795,825), 60% of the deferred bonds to $13,872,000 (loss of $9,248,000), 60% of $2,495,480 in debentures to $1,497,288 (loss of $998,192). The Bondholders, in summarizing their losses in their CASE, stated they obtained, in new bonds, $25,162,425 for their $27,958,250 in old active bonds. This agrees with the above figures. But the Bondholders gave $15,372,000 as the amount of bonds received for $25,615,480 in deferred bonds ($23,120,000) and debentures ($2,495,480), whereas 60% of $25,615,480 is not $15,372,000, but $15,369,288. This difference of $2,712 accounts for the difference between the $40,534,425, given by the Bondholders as the amount of bonds they received by the conversion, and the $40,531,713 arrived at by a mathematical calculation of the conversion, based on figures upon which the Mexicans and the Bondholders were agreed (with the exception of the sum of the debentures, where there is only a difference of $480).

55. CASE. Adding this $5,500,000 to the losses they sustained by the conversion, the Bondholders arrived at a total loss of $18,539,305 (CASE). In a booklet published in 1860, the Bondholders claimed that they lost in connection with the 1846 conversion "about" $18,539,300. See Mexican National Debt, Contracted in London. Decrees and Regulations Since the Adjustment of October 14th/December 23rd 1860 (London, 1860), p. 6, PRO, F.O. 50/359. (Hereafter referred to as MEXICAN NATIONAL DEBT).

56. REPORT, p. 28.

57. Mexico issued Manning & Makintosh $10,906,535 in bonds and $1,599,999 in cash, and in return received $5,800,000 in various bonds and paper and $1,756,903 in cash, so that the net transaction was that Mackintosh got for $156,904 in cash, bonds to the amount of $5,106,535. See REPORT, pp. 31–32.

58. Dover to Russell, London, 22 (r. 25) Feb 1862, PRO, F.O. 97/280.

59. REPORT, p. 113.

60. Ibid., p. 37.

61. Ibid., p. 38.

62. *Ibid.*

63. MEXICAN NATIONAL DEBT, pp. 3–5.

64. The bonds of the conversion of 1846 were to be exchanged for others to be issued by the Mexican treasury. No bond of new stock was to be issued, except for one of the old stock of the same value and number, and old stocks were to be cancelled by punching a hole in the center of them.

65. MEXICAN NATIONAL DEBT, p. 6; CASE.

66. CASE.

67. The bonds were to be bought up at the current price of the day, provided it was not above par.

68. CASE.

69. $20,483,300 by the lowering of the interest rate to 3% plus $6,452,240 in arrears of interest lost. See CASE.

70. MEXICAN NATIONAL DEBT, p. 6.

71. CASE.

72. The 1 July 1851 dividend was paid on 15 February 1851; the 1 January 1852 dividend on 8 March 1852; the 1 July dividend on 15 November 1852; the 1 January 1853 dividend on 16 October 1854; the 1 July 1853 dividend on 15 October 1855; the 1 January 1854 dividend in two parts, on 7 October 1858 and 10 October 1861. See CASE.

73. The 15 dividend payments of $768,123.75 each for 1 July 1854 through 1 July 1861, to which $307,249.50 still owed the 1 January 1854 dividend (paid 10 October 1861) must be added.

74. Sinking fund payments of $250,000 annually for the four years, 1857–1860.

75. Adding $768,123.75 (1 January 1862 dividend) to the $11,829,105.75 in arrears in 1 July 1861 and subtracting the $307,249.50 owed the 1 January 1854 dividend paid 10 October 1861. This figure agrees with the calculation of the London Bondholders. See CASE.

76. Sinking fund payments of $250,000 annually for the 5 years, 1857–1861.

77. REPORT, pp. 47–48.

78. *Report of the Committee of Mexican Bondholders, Presented to the General Meeting of Bondholders at the London Tavern, 15th May, 1854* (London, 1854), p. 13, PRO, F.O. 97/273.

79. *Report of the Committee of Mexican Bondholders, Presented to the General Meeting of Bondholders at the London Tavern, 6th August, 1856* (London, 1856), Appendix I, No. 2, PRO, F.O. 97/274.

80. Such as the one enclosed by the Committee of Mexican Bondholders to Hammond, 10 Basinghall St., London, 22 (r. 23) Apr 1857, PRO, F.O. 97/275. This stated interest in arrears as of 1 January 1857 was $5,371,866.25.

81. Memorandum, F.O., 15 May 1854, signed M(almesbury), PRO, F.O. 97/273.

82. A. H. Layard in House of Commons, 15 Jul 1862, *Hansard's Parliamentary Debates*, 3rd Series, CLXVIII (London, 1862), 365.

83. "Steps taken in 1857–1858 in respect to the claims of the Mexican Bondholders," F.O. Memorandum, 31 May 1858, PRO, F.O. 97/275.

84. Otway to Malmesbury, Mexico City, No. 135, 27 Sep (r. 1 Nov) 1858, PRO, F.O. 97/275.

85. Circular order of 27 Aug 1852, MEXICAN NATIONAL DEBT, pp. 8–10.

86. *Report of the Committee of Mexican Bondholders, Presented to the General Meeting of Bondholders at the London Tavern, 15th May, 1854* (London, 1854), p. 9, PRO, F.O. 97/273.

87. MEXICAN NATIONAL DEBT, p. 19.

88. Supreme Order, 15 Mar 1857, ibid., p. 20.

89. F.O. to Lettsom, No. 20, 12 Jun 1858, PRO, F.O. 97/275.

90. Robertson to F.O., 20 Feb 1858, sum. by "Steps taken in 1857–1858 in respect to the claims of the Mexican Bondholders," F.O. Memorandum, 31 May 1858, PRO, F.O. 97/275.

91. F.O. to Robertson, 24 Feb 1858, sum. by *ibid*.

92. Malmesbury to Otway, F.O., No. 3, draft, 1 Jul 1858, PRO, F.O. 97/275.

93. Unless the monastic property were nationalized. See Otway to Malmesbury, Mexico City, No. 135, 27 Sep (r. 1 Nov) 1858, PRO, F.O. 97/275.

94. See footnote 70 of Section 1 of Chapter II of present investigation.

95. F.O. Memorandum, 6 Jun 1862, PRO, F.O. 97/280.

96. Resolutions passed at General Meeting of Mexican Bondholders, London Tavern, 4 Jul 1861 (r. 26 Jul 1861), PRO, F.O. 97/280.

97. Russell to Wyke, F.O., No. 3, draft, 30 Mar 1861, PRO, F.O. 50/351.

98. See footnote 69 of Section 1 of Chapter II of present investigation.

99. See footnote 96 above.

100. See footnote 141 of Section 3 of Chapter I of present investigation.

101. Committee of Mexican Bondholders to Russell, 10 Basinghall St., London, 14 Des 1860, PRO, F.O. 50/359.

102. Russell to Wyke, F.O., No. 3, draft, 30 Mar 1861, PRO, F.O. 50/351.

## Appendix C

1. J. B. Jecker to Conti, Paris, 8 Dec 1869, cited by A. Poulet-Malassis (ed.): *Papiers Secrets et Correspondance du Second Empire. Réimpression complète de l'édition de l'Imprimerie Nationale, annotée*

*et augmentée de nombreuses pièces publiée à l'étranger, et recueillies par A. Poulet-Malassis* (3rd ed., Paris, 1873), pp. 1–3.

2. Ernest Hamel: *Histoire Illustrée du Second Empire, pécédée des événements de 1848 A 1852* (3 v. in 1, Paris, 1873–1874), III, 76–78; Viscomte de Beaumont-Vassy: *Histoire Intime du Second Empire* (Paris, 1874), pp. 311–315; Pierre de Lano: *Le Secret d'Un Empire: La Cour de Napoleon III* (5th ed., Paris, 1892), pp. 338–339; Alfred Stern: *Geschichte Europas von 1848 bis 1871* (10 v., Stuttgart and Berlin, 1894–1924), IX, 18–19; Frédéric Loliée: *Le Duc de Morny: The Brother of an Emperor and the Maker of an Empire,* adapted by Bryan O'Donnell (London, 1910), p. 286; Percy F. Martin: *Maximilian in Mexico: The Story of the French Intervention, 1861–1867* (New York, 1914), pp. 48–49; Oskar Von Wertheimer: *Napoleon III. Abenteurer, Frauenheld, Cäsar* (Berlin, 1928), p. 294; Philip Guedalla: *The Second Empire* (Rev. ed., London, 1932), p. 251; Dexter Perkins: *The Monroe Doctrine, 1826–1867* (Baltimore, 1933), p. 382; Jesse Burton Hendrick: *Statesmen of the Lost Cause: Jefferson Davis and His Cabinet* (Boston, 1939), p. 306; Christian Schefer: *La Grande Pensée de Napoleon III: Les Origines de l'Expedition Du Mexique (1858–1862)* (Paris, 1939), p. 78; Ralph Roeder: *Juarez and His Mexico: A Biographical History* (2 v., New York, 1947), I, 283; Thomas A. Bailey: *A Diplomatic History of the American People* (4th ed:. New York, 1950), p. 378.

3. A. Poulet-Malassis (ed.): *Papiers Secrets et Correspondance du Second Empire. Réimpression complète de l'édition de l'Imprimerie Nationale, annotée et augmentée de nombreuses pièces publiée à l'étranger, et recueillies par A. Poulet-Malassis* (3rd ed., Paris, 1873), pp. 3–4.

4. Jerrold Blanchard: The Life of Napoleon III, *Derived from State Records, From Unpublished Family Correspondence, and From Personal Testimony* (4 v., London, 1874–1882), IV, 339.

5. In his "Journal olographe" under the date of 10 June 1861, Armand de Montluc noted: "M. de Marpon is a man of affairs, the agent of M. de Morny, and M. de Pierres is leaving for Chihuahua to reach an agreement with M. Roger Dubos, with respect to the affair of Martinez del Rio (200 leagues of ground)." See Armand de Montluc: *Correspondance de Juarez et de Montluc, Ancien Consul Général de Mexique, Accompagnée de Nombreuses Lettres de Personnages Politiques Relative A L'Expédition Du Mexique,* ed. Léon de Montluc (Paris, 1885), p. 51. Montluc's journal seems to have been overlooked by historians of Napoleon's Mexican policy.

6. See Section II of Chapter II of the present investigation.

7. The ultimatum is given in full in Appendix Q of the present investigation.

8. Under the date of 25 June 1861, Montluc wrote in his journal: "The affair of the purchase of 200 leagues of ground of Martinez del Rio will be terminated; the affair will be carried out under the protection of the government in order to stimulate emigration. . . . The

Marquis de Pierres, or rather his son, has left to make a report." Under the date of 15 August 1862, Montluc noted: "M. the Duc de Morny has bought the hacienda Encinillas, and they want to know whether Nafarrondo de Bilbao thinks that Madame Cursier would buy the hacienda of Saucillo, State of Chihuahua, and at what price?" See MONTLUC, pp. 51, 118.

9. Marcel Boulenger: *Le Duc De Morny: Prince Francais* (Paris, 1925), pp. 130–131.

10. Frédéric Loliée: *Le Duc de Morny: The Brother of an Emperor and the Maker of an Empire,* adapted by Bryan O'Donnell (London, 1910), p. 286.

11. Eugenie-Paléologue Conversation, 27 Dec 1903, cited by Maurice Paléologue: *The Tragic Empress: Intimate Conversations with the Empress Eugénie, 1901 to 1911,* trans. Hamish Miles (London, n.d., ca. 1928), p. 84.

12. Maximilian to Napoleon III, 27 Dec 1865, Emile Ollivier: *L'Empire Liberal: Etudes, Récits, Souvenirs* (18 v., Paris, 1895–1912), VII, 537, cited by Lynn M. Case: *French Opinion on the United States and Mexico, 1860–1867: Extracts from the Reports of the Procureurs Généraux* (New York and London, 1936), p. 335, n. 78.

13. *Ibid.*

14. See Appendix V of the present investigation.

15. Taxile DeLord: *Histoire du Second Empire* (6 v., Paris, 1869–1875), III, 291–292; John Musser: *The Establishment of Maximilian's Empire in Mexico: A Thesis Presented to the Faculty of the Graduate School of the University of Pennsylvania in Partial fulfilment of the Degree of Doctor of Philosophy* (Menasha, Wisconsin, 1918), p. 12.

16. The "new duke" referred to in an intercepted letter of 24 August 1862 might be a reference to Morny. An Imperial Decree, dated 8 July 1862, conferred the title of Duke to the then Count Morny. See *Le Moniteur Universel: Journal officiel de L'Empire Francais,* 18 July 1862. An intercepted letter dated 14 September 1862 outlines a scheme of "these gentlemen." When Mexico City would be occupied, they foresaw that there would be a movement of convoyed wagons between Vera Cruz and Mexico City. Persons "sustained by Powerful influence" could ship dollars in the empty wagons going from Mexico City to Vera Cruz, and the money paid to convoy conductas could be saved. The scheme was very similar with one Morny carried out when he was Special French Envoy to St. Petersburg. Then he took 43 carriages of laces, silks, and feminine finery with him and used his diplomatic immunity to avoid Russian custom duties. Once in Russia, Morny auctioned the duty-free goods off at an estimated profit of 800,000 roubles. See Percy F. Martin: *Maximilian in Mexico: The Story of the French Intervention, 1861–1867* (New York, 1914), p. 49, and Jay Monaghan: *Diplomat in Carpet Slippers: Abraham Lincoln Deals with Foreign Affairs* (Indianapolis and New York, 1945), p. 66. For the intercepted letters, see Appendix V of the present investigation.

17. Albert Guerard: *Napoleon III* (Cambridge, Mass., 1943), pp.

225–226; Frédéric Loliée: Le Duc de Morny: *The Brother of an Emperor and the Maker of an Empire,* adapted by Bryan O'Donnell (London, 1910), p. 285; Count Egon Caesar Corti: *Maximilian and Charlotte of Mexico,* trans. Catherine Alison Philips (2 v., New York, 1928), I, 103; Paul Gaulot: *La Vérité sur l'Expédition du Mexique d'après les Documents Inédits de Ernest Louet, Payeur en Chef du Corps Expeditionnaire: Réve d'Empire* (Paris, 1889), p. 23.

18. There could not have been many candidates for a temporary post to a Mexico in turmoil. Saligny had experience in American affairs and most probably knew Spanish. See Christian Schefer: *La Grande Pensée de Napoleon III: Les Origines de l'Expédition Du Mexique (1858–1862)* (Paris, 1939), p. 64.

19. *Ibid.*

20. Xavier Elsesser to Montluc, Porentruy, 1 Oct 1860, cited by MONTLUC, pp. 47–49.

21. A. de Morineau to Du Camp, Paris, Aug 1877, cited by Maxime du Camp: *Les Convulsions de Paris* (4 v., Paris, 1878–1880), I, 512–516. Morineau was a pensioned Consul of France, former manager of the General Consulates of Switzerland and Spain in Mexico. He answered Du Camp's request for information about Jecker in connection with the book being prepared about the Commune, at which time Jecker was shot.

22. See Section II of Chapter II of the present investigation.

23. Albert Guerard: *Napoleon III* (Cambridge, Mass., 1943), pp. 225–226.

24. Xavier Elsesser to Montluc, Porentruy, 1 Oct 1860, cited by MONTLUC, pp. 47–49.

25. Paul Gaulot: *La Vérité sur L'Expédition du Mexique d'après les Documents Inédits de Ernest Louet, Payeur en Chef du Corps Expéditionnaire: Réve d'Empire* (Paris, 1889), p. 23. Saligny supposedly made this statement to Ernest Louet, whose papers Gaulot used.

26. Sara Yorke Stevenson: *Maximilian in Mexico: A Woman's Reminiscences of the French Intervention, 1862–1867* (New York, 1891), p. 21. Sara Yorke Stevenson was an American studying in Paris at the beginning of the French intervention in Mexico. She knew many persons at court and went to Mexico in 1862, because a relative was murdered there.

27. Christian Schefer: *La Grande Pensée de Napoleon III: Les Origines de l'Expédition Du Mexique (1858–1862)* (Paris, 1939, pp. 63–66.

28. See footnote 59 of Section I of Chapter II of the present investigation.

29. Thouvenel to Saligny, Paris, No 11, draft, 29 Jul 1861, MDAE: *CP, Mex.,* LV.

30. Russell to Wyke, F.O., No. 35, 31 Jul (r. 4 Sep) 1861, PRO, F.O. 204/153.

31. See footnote 104 of Section II of Chapter II of the present investigation.

32. See footnote 114 of Section II of Chapter II of the present investigation.

33. See text of Section II of Chapter II of the present investigation between footnotes 110 and 118.

34. See footnote 24 of Section II of Chapter II of the present investigation and text referred to by it.

35. Bertita Harding: Phantom Crown: *The Story of Maximilian and Carlota of Mexico* (London, 1935), pp. 71–72.

36. See footnote 29 of Section II of Chapter II of the present investigation.

37. See Section I of Chapter III of the present investigation.

38. See Section 2 of Chapter III of the present investigation.

39. See Sections 2 & 3 of Chapter III of the present investigation.

40. See Appendix F of the present investigation.

41. See footnote 43 below.

42. Daniel Dawson viewed the records of the Public Record Office, but primarily for the period before 1861. See *The Mexican Adventure* (London, 1935). William Spence Robertson was chiefly interested in the negotiation of the Tripartite Treaty of London of 31 October 1861 and only briefly touches its breakdown in 1862. For the most part, he viewed the instructions from Russell to Cowley in the Public Record Office. See "The Tripartite Treaty of London," *Hispanic American Historical Review,* XX (1940), 167–189.

43. Cowley-Napoleon III Conversation, 8 Mar 1862, sum. by Cowley to Russell, Paris, No. 299, Confidential, 10 (r. 11) Mar 1862, PRO, F.O. 27/1434.

44. Maxime Du Camp: *Souvenirs d'un Demi-Siècle* (2 v., Paris, 1949), I, 233.

45. Albert D. Vandam: *An Englishman in Paris (Notes and Recollections)* (2 v., London, 1892), I, 66–68.

46. Slidell to a correspondent, (early) 1863, cited by Beckles Willson: *John Slidell and the Confederates in Paris, 1862–1865* (New York, 1932), p. 205.

47. Robert Christophe: *Le Duc de Morny: "Empereur" Des Francais Sous Napoleon III* (Paris, 1951), p. 203.

48. Comte Emile de Keraltry: *La Créance Jecker, Les Indemnités Francaises et Les Emprunts Mexicains* (Paris, 1868), pp. 18–19.

49. E. Lefêvre popularized the idea that the Jecker bonds were the chief cause of the French intervention in Mexico. He was a French journalist, the editor of the *Tribune de Mexique.* His sympathies were republican, and he was permitted to view the papers left behind in Mexico by Maximilian. The resulting *Documents Officiels* bristled with statistical matter concerning the Jecker bonds, implied to be the chief cause of the expedition. Keraltry also wrote works that became classics of statistical detail on the Jecker bonds. These works were referred to again and again by later historians. Aside from historians who have quoted Jecker's letter to Conti of 1869 or stated their belief in a Jecker-Morny deal (see footnote 2 above), Aubry, Bratianu, and

Lord Acton have given the Jecker bonds as an important cause of the Mexican Expedition of Napoleon III. Rheinhardt blames the expedition on Morny and Eugenie. See E. Lefêvre: *Le Mexique et L'Intervention Europeene* (Mexico City, 1862); E. Lefêvre: *Documents Officiels Recueillis Dans La Sécretairie Privée de Maximilien: Histoire de l'Intervention Francaise Au Mexique* (2 v., Brussells and London, 1869); Comte Emile de Keraltry: *La Créance Jecker, Les Indemnités Francaises et Les Emprunts Mexicains* (Paris, 1868); Comte Emile de Keraltry: *L'Empereur Maximilien: Son Elevation et Sa Chute* (Leipzig, Brussells, Turin, Florence, London, Edinborough, Amsterdam, Basel, Geneva, and Ghent, 1867); Octave Aubry: *Le Second Empire* (7th ed., Paris, 1938), p. 321; G. I. Bratianu: *Napoléon III et Les Nationalités* (Paris, 1934), p. 21; Lord Acton: *Historical Essays and Studies by John Emerich Edward Dalberg-Acton, First Baron Acton,* eds. John Neville Figgis and Reginald Vere Laurence (London, 1907), p. 147; Emile Alphons Rheinhardt: *Napoleon and Eugenie: The Tragicomedy of an Empire,* trans. Hannah Waller (New York, 1931), p. 241. Taxile Delord and John Musser were "convinced" by the intercepted correspondence of 1862. See footnote 15 above.

50. Albert Guerard: *Napoleon III* (Cambridge, Mass., 1943), pp. 225–226.

51. Daniel Dawson: *The Mexican Adventure* (London, 1935), p. 97.

52. *Ibid.,* p. 96.

53. *Ibid.,* p. 97.

54. Marcel Boulenger: *Le Duc de Morny: Prince Francais* (Paris, 1925), p. 132.

55. Robert Christophe: *Le Duc de Morny: "Empereur" Des Francais Sous Napoleon III* (Paris, 1951), pp. 218–219.

56. Maristan Chapman (pseud. of Mary Ilsley Chapman and John Stanton Higham Chapman): *Imperial Brother: A Life of The Duc de Morny* (London, 1921), pp. 229–301.


## Appendix D

1. Richard A. Johnson: "Spanish-Mexican Diplomatic Relations, 1853–1855," *HAHR,* XXI (1941), 562.

2. PRIM, p. 42.

3. Hubert Herring: *A History of Latin America from the Beginnings to the Present* (London, 1954), pp. 311–312. The few survivors of yellow fever were attacked and defeated by Santa Anna.

4. Richard A. Johnson: "Spanish-Mexican Diplomatic Relations, 1853–1855," *HAHR,* XXI (1941), 562. These titles were vaguely referred to as the "appropriate and national" debt. See PRIM, p. 45.

5. BURKE, p. 134.

6. Richard A. Johnson: "Spanish-Mexican Diplomatic Relations, 1853–1855," *HAHR,* XXI (1941), 563.

7. *Ibid.,* pp. 563–564.

8. *Ibid.,* pp. 564–565.

9. *Ibid.,* p. 565; H. Leonardon: "L'Espagne et La Question du Mexique," *Annales des Sciences Politiques,* XVI (1901), 59.

10. Richard A. Johnson: "Spanish-Mexican Diplomatic Relations, 1853–1855," *HAHR,* XXI (1941), 571. This issue came up in December 1854, when several claims hinged on how the treaty would be interpreted.

11. PRIM, p. 43. Mexico even confiscated the property of some claimants suspected of fraud.

12. DAWSON, p. 36.

13. PRIM, p. 43. In July 1856 the Spanish Minister made an agreement with Mexico, whereby the Treaty of 1853 would be recognized, with the stipulation that debts might be revised. The Spanish Government, however, did not approve this agreement.

14. PRIM, p. 43, DAWSON, p. 37.

15. PRIM, p. 43.

16. *Ibid.,* pp. 43–44.

17. BANCROFT, V, 775–776; H. Leonardon: "L'Espagne et La Question du Mexique," *Annales des Sciences Politiques,* XVI (1901), 61; PRIM, p. 45.

18. BURKE, p. 101.

19. Cte. A. de La Londe, Interim Chargé, to Thouvenel, Mexico City, No. 459, 28 Aug (r. 28 Sep) 1860, MDAE: *CP, Mex.,* vol. 53. Recognition proceedings took place on 22 August 1860.

20. Pacheco-Mathew Conversation, sum. by Mathew to Russell, 28 Sep 1860, DAWSON, pp. 39–40.

21. Pacheco to Collantes, 24 Sep 1860, Clement Duvernois: *L'Intervention Francais au Mexique, Accompagnée de Documents Inédits et d'un long Mémoire addressé par L'Empereur Maximulian á L'Empereur Napoléon et rémis á Paris par L'Impératrice Charlotte: Précedée d'une Preface de Clement Duvernois* (2 v., Paris, 1868), I, 10–11.

22. *Gazette* de Madrid, 23 and 24 Nov 1861, H. Mercier de Lacombe: *Le Mexique, L'Amerique de Nord et L'Europe* (Paris, 1863), p. 31.

23. Ocampo to Pacheco, 12 Jan 1861, *L'Estafette des Deux Mondes,* Mexico City, 17 Jan 1861, encl. of Mathew to Russell, Jalapa, No. 2, 28 Jan (r. 28 Feb) 1861, PRO, F.O. 50/352.

24. Saligny to Thouvenel, Mexico City, 26 Jan 1861, encl. I of Saligny to Thouvenel, Mexico City, No. 6, 28 Jan (r. 1 Mar) 1861, MDAE: *CP, Mex.,* vol. 54.

25. BANCROFT, V, 776. Some Spanish subjects had bought up some of the bonds of the internal debt of Mexico at 12% of par and wanted to redeem them at 100%. See BURKE, p. 100.

26. BANCROFT, V, 776.

27. Camyn-De La Fuente meeting, 20 Aug 1861, sum. by De La Fuente to Mexican Minister of Foreign Relations, 24 Aug 1861, E. Lefêvre: *Documents Officiels Recueillis Dans La Secrétairerie Privée de Meximilien: Histoire de L'Intervention Francaise au Mexique, par*

*E. Lefèvre, Rédacteur en chef de la Tribune de Mexique* (2 v., Brussels and London, 1869), I, 100–101. Camyn was Under Secretary to the Spanish Minister of State. De La Fuente was an agent of Juarez sent to Europe to settle differences between Spain and Mexico.

28. See Appendix N of present investigation.

29. 96 reals (or réaux) were equivalent to $4.87 in 1862, and so 10,000,000 reals would be $406,356.31. See "Table of Pars of Exchange," 28 May 1862, F.O. Circular, PRO, F.O. 27/1423.

30. See Appendix A of present investigation.

31. "Memorandum on British Convention," encl. 1 of Wyke to Russell, Mexico City, No. 32, Con., 26 Aug (r. 29 Sep) 1861, PRO, F.O. 50/354.

32. BANCROFT, VI, 38; E. Lefèvre: *Le Mexique et L'Intervention Europeenne, par le citoyen E. Lefèvre* (Mexico City, 1862), p. 295; John Musser: *The Establishment of Maximilian's Empire in Mexico: A Thesis Presented to the Faculty of the Graduate School of the University of Pennsylvania in Partial Fulfilment of the Requirements for the Degree of Doctor of Philosophy* (Menasha, 1918), p. 11. All three sources agree on the same figure (but Bancroft leaves out the 29 cents).

33. $825,720.00 (on 4 June 1861) plus two interest payments (4 December 1861 and 4 June 1862) of $24,771.60 each. See "Memorandum on British Convention," encl. 1 of Wyke to Russell, Mexico City, No. 32, Con., 26 Aug (r. 29 Sep) 1861, PRO, F.O. 50/354.

34. Proposed ultimatum of Prim (to be sent to Doblado), Vera Cruz, 14 Jan 1862, encl. 3 of Wyke to Russell, Vera Cruz, No. 8, 19 Jan (r. 2 Mar) 1862, PRO, F.O. 50/364.

35. *Ibid.*

36. See Appendix N of present investigation.

37. Proposed ultimatum of Prim (to be sent to Doblado), Vera Cruz, 14 Jan 1862, encl. 3 of Wyke to Russell, Vera Cruz, No. 8, 19 Jan (r. 2 Mar) 1862, PRO, F.O. 50/364.

38. Prim-Senate-9 Dec 1862.

39. BURKE, pp. 137–138.

40. See Section 2 of Chapter VI of present investigation for the final breakdown of negotiations in 1862.


### Sources of Appendices of Documents
(Appendices E through V)

E. Encl. 3 of Saligny to Thouvenel, Mexico City, No. 14, 28 Mar (r. 30 Apr) 1861, MDAE: *CP, Mex.,* vol. 54.

F. A copy is filed in MDAE: *CP, Angleterre,* vol. 720. Corti found another copy in the HHSA. See CORTI, I, 361–363.

G. Encl. of Russell to Cowley, F.O., No. 1069, Con., 7 Oct 1861, PRO, F.O. 146/979.

H. PRO, F.O. 50/358.

I. *Ibid.*

J. *Ibid.*

K. *Ibid.* Another copy is located in MDAE: *CP, Mex.*, vol. 56.

L. PRO, F.O. 93/78 (original). See also *B.S.P., 1862*, LXIV, 80–82.

M. MDAE: *CP, Mex.*, vol. 57.

N. Encl. of Collantes to Spanish Ambassador to Paris, Madrid, 14 Nov 1861, *ibid.*, vol. 56.

O. Encl. 3 of Wyke to Russell, Mexico City, No. 51, 25 Nov 1861 (r. 1 Jan 1862), PRO, F.O. 50/354.

P. Encl. 1 of Jurien de la Gravière to Thouvenel, Vera Cruz, No. 5, 15 Jan 1862, MDAE: *CP, Mex.*, vol. 57. Wyke sent Russell an undated copy. See Encl. 3 of Wyke to Russell, Vera Cruz, No. 3, 16 Jan (r. 2 Mar) 1862, PRO, F.O. 50/364.

Q. Encl. 3 of Jurien de La Gravière to Thouvenel, Vera Cruz, No. 5, 15 Jan 1862, MDAE: *CP, Mex.*, vol. 57. The copy Saligny sent Thouvenel was advance dated to 15 January 1862. See encl. 3 of Saligny to Thouvenel, Vera Cruz, No. 62, 15 Jan 1862, MDAE: *CP, Mex.*, vol. 58. The copy Wyke sent Russell was undated. See encl. 4 of Wyke to Russell, Vera Cruz, No. 8, Secret and Confidential, 19 Jan (r. 2 Mar) 1862, PRO, F.O. 50/364.

R. Encl. 2 of Wyke to Russell, Vera Cruz, No. 25, 22 Feb (r. 31 Mar) 1862, PRO, F.O. 50/364.

S. Encl. 4 of Wyke to Russell, Vera Cruz, No. 25, 22 Feb (r. 31 Mar) 1862, PRO, F.O. 50/364.

T. Encl. of Wyke to Russell, Orizaba, No. 45, 11 Apr (r. 14 May) 1862, PRO, F.O. 50/365.

U. *Epoca,* 25 Apr 1862, encl. 2 of Crampton to Russell, Madrid, No. 203, Secret and Confidential, No. 203, 6 (r. 19) May 1862, PRO, F.O. 72/1034.

V. House Executive Document, 37th Congress, 3rd Session, No. 23.


## Sources Consulted

### Archive Sources

Archives du ministère des affaires étrangères. Paris.
  Correspondence Politique.
    Angleterre.
        720. Flahault, Jun-Dec 1861.
        721. Flahault, Jan-Jul 1862.
    Espagne.
        859. Barrot, Jul-Dec 1861.
            860. Barrot, Jan-May 1862
    Mexique.
        53. Gabriac/Saligny, Mar- Dec 1860.
        54. Saligny, Jan-May 1861.
        55. Saligny, Jun-Sep 1861.

56. Saligny, Oct-Dec 1861.
57. Jurien de la Gravière.
58. Saligny, Jan-May 1862.
   Reports, instructions, memoranda, telegrams, verbal notes,
   even private letters are filed chronologically. The Correspondence between Thouvenel and Flahault and between
   Thouvenel and Barrot is invaluable for the negotiation of the
   Convention of London and for French, British, and Spanish
   attitudes toward that convention after its negotiation. Saligny's reports and Thouvenel's instructions to Saligny in no
   way link the Duke of Morny with the Jecker bonds. The
   first reference made by Saligny to Maximilian was in a private letter written in January 1862. Saligny's reports of 1861
   concern his negotiations with the Juarez Government. Most
   reports summarizing the conferences of the Allied Commissioners in Mexico in 1862 were written by Admiral Jurien.
   Unfortunately the date of receipt was not marked on Jurien's
   reports. Throughout the volumes of Saligny's reports are filed
   private letters from Mexican exiles, forwarded to Thouvenel
   by Estrada. There is little to indicate Napoleon's orders to
   Thouvenel, the Minister of Foreign Affairs. Only sometimes
   did Thouvenel specifically state that he was acting under
   instructions. Napoleon seldom wrote remarks on documents
   and only a few copies of letters the Emperor wrote are on file.
   It is impossible to determine just who made the frequent
   underlinings on reports received from Mexico. These underlinings, however, show what type of information was received
   with interest.
Papiers Thouvenel.
   Thouvenel's private papers. Some private letters from Jurien,
   but others are filed in volume 57 of Correspondance Politique,
   Mexique.
British Museum Additional MSS Room. London.
   Palmerston Papers. Volumes CLXII–CLXVII.
   Entry books of out letters, 1853–1862, 1865. Reveal Palmerston's
   fears of French aggression and American seizure of Canada. A
   few references to Mexico.
Broadlands Archive.
   Palmerston Papers.
   Private collection of Palmerston Papers in the possession of the
   Montbatten family, by whose kind permission letters pertaining
   to Mexico were made available. In his private letters to Lord
   Palmerston, Lord Russell gave his opinion that Maximilian
   would be a fool to go to Mexico.
Public Record Office. London.
   Bloomfield Papers. F.O. 356.
   17. From Vienna, 1961.
   18. From Vienna, 1862.

32. Letters Received, 1857–1864.
38. Entry book of out letters, 1861–1864.
   Drafts of Bloomfield's reports to Russell, 1861–1862. Private correspondence between Bloomfield and Russell. Bloomfield was unable to unearth much information about Maximilian's candidacy.

Cowley Papers. F.O. 519.

178. From Earl of Clarendon, 1859–1862.
184. From Earl Granville, 1852–1871.
189. From Edmund Hammond, 1860.
190. From Edmund Hammond, 1861–1862.
195. From Austen Henry Layard.
197. From Lord Russell, 1852–1859.
198. From Lord Russell, 1860.
199. From Lord Russell, 1861–1862.
207. From Ministers of the French Government, 1852–1867.
226. Entry Book of out letters to Russell and others, 1859–1860.
227. Entry Book of out letters to Russell, 1860.
228. Entry Book of out letters to Russell, 1860–1861.
229. Entry Book of out letters to Russell, 1861–1862.
230. Entry Book of out letters to Russell, 1862–1863.
241. From various persons, 1859–1861.
242. From various persons, 1862–1864.
   Clarendon believed the Mexican policy of Napoleon III was a chimera. Granville's letters make no reference to Mexico. Edmund Hammond was Permanent Under-Secretary of State for Foreign Affairs. Many of his letters concern the negotiation of the Tripartite Treaty of London. He also reported Russell's private views on Mexico. Henry Layard was Under-Secretary of State for Foreign Affairs, and his private letters to Cowley make passing references to Mexico. Lord Russell's private letters to Lord Cowley are important for details of the negotiation of the Tripartite Treaty of London, and for Russell's frank exposure of the motives for his Mexican policy. F.O. 519/207 contains some notes from Thouvenel to Cowley about Anglo-French negotiations with a view to an intervention in Mexico in 1861. Cowley's entry books of letters to Russell are easy to read, because Cowley did not copy his letters himself. The originals are in the Russell Papers and are very hard to decipher. In these letters Cowley reported many conversations with Napoleon III and Thouvenel about Mexico. French motives. Cowley himself believed the Mexican These conversations are invaluable for an understanding of policy of France was unrealistic. F.O. 519/241–242 contain a few letters to Cowley mentioning Mexican affairs, but they are relatively unimportant.

Foreign Office Correspondence.

Austria. F.O. 7.

605. Lord Russell's drafts of instructions to Lord Bloomfield, May-Dec 1861.

625–626. Lord Russell's drafts of instructions to Lord Bloomfield, 1862.

611–615. Lord Bloomfield's reports, Jun-Dec 1861.

627–640. Lord Bloomfield's reports, 1862.

When instructed to find out what he could about the candidacy of Maximilian, Lord Bloomfield was unable to obtain much information that was not just current gossip.

Belgium. F.O. 123.

105. F.O. instructions to Lord Howard de Walden, 1861.

106. Reports of Lord Howard de Walden, 1861.

107. Miscellaneous received by Lord Howard de Walden, 1861.

108. Miscellaneous sent by Lord Howard de Walden, 1861.

109. F.O. Instructions to Lord Howard de Walden, 1861.

110. Reports of Lord Howard de Walden, 1862.

111. Miscellaneous sent and received, 1862.

Not one reference to Mexico.

France.

F.O. 27/1372–1382. Lord Russell's drafts of instructions to Lord Cowley, 1861.

F.O. 27/1419–1430. Lord Russell's drafts of instructions to Lord Cowley, 1862.

F.O. 27/1383–1400. Lord Cowley's reports, 1861.

F.O. 27/1431–1448. Lord Cowley's reports, 1862.

F.O. 146/979–983. Archives of Her Majesty's Embassy at Paris. Oct-Nov 1861.

Throughout September and the first three weeks of October 1861 Lord Cowley carried on the negotiations that resulted in the signing of the Tripartite Treaty of London on 31 October 1861. The F.O. 146 series contains the originals of Russell's instructions to Cowley, including the enclosures. One of these enclosures was Russell's original draft treaty sent to Cowley at the beginning of October. It is not found in the F.O. 27 series of Russell's drafts of instructions to Cowley. Parts of this draft treaty have been published by William Spence Robertson ("The Tripartite Treaty of London," *Hispanic American Historical Review,* XXI (1941), 174–175). Russell's instructions to Cowley set forth the official Mexican policy of Great Britain, but Cowley's reports, in addition to reporting the official French position toward Mexico for British consumption, often contain summaries of conversations with Napoleon III and Thouvenel in which they made confidential statements about Mexican affairs.

Italy.

F.O. 45.
2. Lord Russell's drafts of instructions to Sir J. Hudson, Jul-Dec 1861.
9. Hudson's reports, Sep-Dec 1861.
21–25. Hudson's reports, 1862.
No references to Mexico. Italy's Mexican policy was made known to Great Britain unofficially through the Italian representative to Great Britain.

Mexico.

| | |
|---|---|
| F.O. 50/351. | Lord Russell's drafts of instructions to Mr. Mathew and Sir Charles Wyke, 1861. |
| F.O. 50/363. | Lord Russell's drafts of instructions to Wyke, 1862. |
| F.O. 204/153. | From F.O., 1861 (original instructions). |
| F.O. 204/159. | From F.O., 1862 (original instructions). |
| F.O. 50/351–354. | Mathew and Wyke's reports, 1861. |
| F.O. 50/364–367. | Wyke's reports, 1862. |
| F.O. 204/154. | Mathew and Wyke's reports, 1861 (drafts). |
| F.O. 204/160. | Wyke's reports 1862 (drafts). |
| F.O. 50/356–358. | Domestic. Various domestic, 1861. |
| F.O. 50/370–372. | Various domestic, 1862. |
| F.O. 97/273. | London Bondholders, 1847–1854. |
| F.O. 97/274. | London Bondholders, 1854–1857. |
| F.O. 97/275. | London Bondholders, 1857–1859. |
| F.O. 50/359. | London Bondholders, 1860–1861. |
| F.O. 97/280. | London Bondholders, 1861–1863. |
| F.O. 97/278. | French Expedition, Jun 1862–Jun 1863. |
| F.O. 97/279. | French Expedition, Jul 1863–Dec 1864. |
| F.O. 204/157–158. | Miscellaneous, 1861. |
| F.O. 204/162–163. | Miscellaneous, 1862. |

The F.O. 50 series contains the official correspondence between Wyke (originals) and Russell (drafts), but some reports and instructions are missing documents are readily available in the F.O. 204 series (Russell's originals, with dates received by Wyke; Wyke's drafts), but the files of this series have only some of Wyke's drafts of reports. When it has to do with claims, the Russell-Wyke correspondence is often filed in the F.O. 50 and 97 series of volumes having to do with the London Bondholders and other claims. The five volumes of materials about the London Bondholders (1847–1863) contain minutes of meetings of the London Bondholders, pamphlets on the history of decrees of and agreements with Mexico, and correspondence between the Bondholders and the Foreign Office. These volumes are the sources of Appendix B of the present investigation ("The London Bondholders, 1823–1861"). The volumes titled "Domestic" and "Various Domestic" (F.O. 50/356–358; F.O. 50/370–372) are very important and apparently have been overlooked hitherto. They contain letters of persons who had claims against Mexico, correspondence between the Foreign Office and the Colonial Office and between the Foreign Office and the Admiralty about Mexican affairs. The Admiralty correspondence of 1862 encloses the reports of Commodore Dunlop, who was in military command of the British expeditionary force to Mexico in 1862. F.O. 50/358 contains draft treaties, memoranda, marginal comments of Russell and Palmerston that relate to the negotiations that led to the signing of the Tripartite Treaty of London of 31 October 1861. The volumes on the French Expedition contain materials for the most part duplicated from the F.O. 27 and 50 series. The F.O. 204 series for 1861 and 1862 titled "Miscellaneous" contain private letters of Wyke to Lord Lyons, correspondence between Wyke and persons having claims against Mexico, and correspondence between Wyke and Admiral Maitland, the British Senior Naval Officer off the west coast of Mexico in 1862.

Spain. F.O. 72.

1001–1002. Lord Russell's drafts of instructions to Buchanon, Edwardes, Crampton, 1861.

1028–1029. Lord Russell's drafts of instructions to Crampton, 1862.

1003–1011. Buchanon, Edwardes, Crampton's reports, 1861.

1012. Telegrams from Spain, 1861.

1030–1040. Crampton's reports, 1862.

Crampton played a similar role to that of Cowley in September and October 1861 in carrying out the initial negotiations that led to the Tripartite Treaty of London. Many conversations with Collantes and O'Donnell are reported Almost word for word Crampton sent the papers pertaining to Mexican affairs presented to the Cortes as enclosures of his reports, almost invariably with English translations.

U.S.A. F.O. 5.

754–758. Lord Russell's drafts of instructions to Lord Lyons, 1861.

817–822. Lord Russell's drafts of instructions to Lord Lyons, 1862.

759–777. Lord Lyons' reports, 1861.

823–840. Lord Lyons' reports, 1862.

Russell's instructions to Lyons on Mexican affairs include

the British refusal to accept Seward's proposal of a loan to Mexico as an alternative to a European intervention in Mexico, the British offer to include the United States in the intervention in Mexico, and British disavowals of ulterior motives. Lyons' reports contain summaries of conversations with Seward on these matters.

Miscellaneous.

F.O. 96/26. Minutes, Memoranda of Lords Malmesbury and Russell.

F.O. 96/27. Minutes, Memoranda of Lords Russell, Clarendon, Stanley.

F.O. 96/27 contains nothing on Mexican affairs, and F.O. 96/26 just a few minutes and memoranda of Russell on Mexican affairs.

Russell Papers. P.R.O. 30/22.

14. 1860–1863.
19. Gladstone, 1859–1862.
21. Palmerston, 1860–1861.
24. Duke of Somerset, 1859–1862.
25. Remaining members of Cabinet, 1859–1862.
27. Memorandum. Cabinet opinions, 1859–1865.
28. Official Correspondence (Not Cabinet), 1859–1865.
29. Miscellaneous Correspondence (Not official), 1859–1865.
30. To the Queen and Palmerston, 1859–1865.
31. Drafts to remaining members, 1859–1865.
56. French Embassy, 1861.
57. French Embassy, Jan–Jun 1862.
58. French Embassy, Jul–Dec 1862.
74. Mexico, 1859–1865.

The files "1860–1863," "Palmerston, 1869–1861," "French Embassy, 1861," and "Mexico, 1859–1865" contain memoranda, notes and private letters to Lord Russell from Lord Palmerston that reveal his motives for intervening in Mexico. The files titled "French Embassy" contain the original private letters of Lord Cowley to Lord Russell. Some of these letters have to do with the negotiation of the Tripartite Treaty of London. Especially valuable are Cowley's reports on conversations with Napoleon III, Thouvenel, and Prince Metternich about Mexican affairs. The file "Mexico, 1859–1865" contains the private letters to Lord Russell from Mathew and Wyke, in which they are more frank than in their official correspondence. The Duke of Somerset was the High Lord of the Admiralty, and his private letters to Lord Russell reveal the position of the Admiralty toward an intervention in Mexico. "To the Queen and Palmerston, 1859–1865" contains nothing on Mexico, but "1860–1863" contains Russell's correspondence with Queen Victoria in 1861 about the intervention in

Mexico and extracts of letters to Russell from the Queen in 1862. P.R.O. 30/22–28 contains a few letters of Hammond to Russell about Mexican affairs. A letter from Layard to Russell relates an important conversation with Thouvenel just before the signature of the Tripartite Treaty of London. The remaining files consulted (P.R.O. 30/22–19; P.R.O. 30/22–25; P.R.O. 30/22–27; P.R.O. 30/22–31) contain no references to Mexico.

## Printed Sources

Albe, Duc d.', ed.: *Lettres Familières de L'Impératrice Eugénie Conservées dans Les Archives du Palais de Liria*. 2 v., Paris, 1935.
Private letters of Eugenie to her sister and brother-in-law, the Duc D'Albe. Reveals Eugenie's sympathies with Spain. Passing references to Hidalgo.

Ambès, Baron D.': *Memoires Inédits sur Napoléon III par le Baron d'Ambès, recueillis et annotés par Charles Sismond et M.-C. Poinsot*. 2 v., Paris, 1909–1910.
Annecdotes and current events related in a running journal. Anti-Eugenie.

*Archives Diplomatiques: Recueil De Diplomatie et D'Histoire*.
Published under the auspices of the French Ministry of Foreign Affairs. Paris, 1861 ff.
Official documents issued by the Powers. The French documents are largely from the French Yellow Books. The volumes for 1861 have documents relating to French and Spanish attitudes toward the McLane-Ocampo Treaties.

Baker, George E., ed.: *The Life and Works of William H. Seward*. 5 v., Boston, 1884.
Seward's motives for his Mexican policy are revealed in his private letters and diary.

Barante, Claude de, ed.: *Souvenirs du Baron De Barante De l'Académie Francaise, 1782–1866, Publiés par son petit-fils, Claude De Barante*. 8 v., Paris, 1890–1901.
Letters among royalists. A letter of Guizot is cited that gives his opinion on the Mexican expedition.

Bédollière, Emile de la, ed.: *Histoire de la Guerre du Mexique, Illustrée par Janet-Lange et Gustave Dore*. Paris, 1866.
Contains a letter from Napoleon to Prim. Otherwise most of the documents are merely copied from the "yellow books."

Belleyme, Adolphe de: *La France et Le Mexique, par Adolphe de Belleyme, Député au Corps législatif*. Paris, 1863.
A polemic in favor of withdrawing the French expedition from Mexico.

Beyens, Baron Napoléon: *Le Second Empire vu par un Diplomate Belge*. 2 v., Paris, 1925.

Based on diplomatic correspondence of Baron Eugène Beyens, his Private letters, Baron Napoléon's reminiscences and talks with his father, Baron Eugène, who was the representative of Belgium to Paris during the Second Empire. Beyens was amazingly well informed of diplomatic maneuvres, including the Mexican policy of France. Beyens believed the chief causes of the Mexican expedition were to divert attention from the Italian Question and from possible liberalism in France. The attitudes and frame of mind of Thouvenel and Napoleon III at crucial times are sketched.

Bicknell, Anna L.: *Life in the Tuileries Under the Second Empire, by Anna L. Bicknell, an Inmate of the Palace.* London, 1895.
The author was governess of the children of Duchesse de Tascher de la Pagerie and has some comments on Eugenie's personality.

Bigelow, John: *Retrospections of an Active Life.* 5 v., I-III, New York, 1909; IV-V, Garden City, 1913.
Bigelow was United States Consul General in Paris at the beginning of the American Civil War, when he was more concerned about Confederate influence in Europe than with the European intervention in Mexico.

Billault, A.: *Oeuvres de M. Billault, précédées d'une notice biographique.* 2 v. in I, Paris, 1865.
Billault was Minister without Portfolio, who defended imperial policies before the *Corps legislatif.* His entire speech to that body on 26 June 1862, concerning Mexican affairs, is included in this collection.

Blanchot, Colonel Auguste Charles Philippe: *Mémoirs: L'Intervention Francaise au Mexique.* 3 v., Paris, 1911.
Blanchot went to Mexico in 1862 as a member of the French expeditionary force. An apologist for the French view, with a strong bias against Juarez and Prim.

*British and Foreign State Papers.* Compiled by the librarian and keeper of papers of the Foreign Office. London, 1836 ff.
Volumes LII and LIII reproduce the bulk of the "Correspondence Respecting the Affairs of Mexico. . . ." printed in the *British Sessional Papers,* 1862, LXIV, 101–444, but sometimes omissions of text are not indicated. There are some stylistic changes from the texts printed in the "Correspondence. . . ."

Carette, Madame: *My Mistress, the Empress Eugénie; or, Court Life at the Tuileries.* 2nd ed., London, 1889.
The author was Eugenie's "Private Reader" and appears to reflect the ideas of the imperial couple about Mexican affairs.

Case, Lynn M.: *French Opinion on the United States and Mexico, 1860–1867; Extracts from the Reports of the Procureurs Généraux.,* New York, 1936.
Part III (pp. 309–435) contains extracts of the secret administrative reports of the *Procureurs Généraux* on French public opinion on Mexico. Professor Case believes that the reports of the *Procureurs* are a much more accurate index of French public opinion during

the Second Empire than newspapers. Opinion was apathetic until July 1862, when a mounting opposition began, and consequently it was not the pressure of public opinion that initiated the French expedition to Mexico.

"Correspondence Respecting the Affairs of Mexico: Presented to both Houses of Parliament by Command of Her Majesty, 1862," *British Sessional Papers, 1862,* LXIV, 101–444. (University of Pennsylvania microfilms).

A large portion of the correspondence between Lord John Russell and his diplomatic representatives to Mexico, the United States, France, and Spain was published in order to justify British policy before Parliament. A comparison with the original documents reveals that the published documents were edited and altered slightly, sometimes with a view to improving style, at other times to spare the susceptibilities of persons mentioned. Private letters, of course, are not printed.

D'Espagny, M. H. de Laire Cte., ed.: *Mémoires du Duc de Persigny Publiés Avec Des Documents Inédits, un avant-propos et un epilogue par M. H. De Laire Cte D'Espagny, Ancien Secretaire Intime Du Duc.* 2nd ed., Paris, 1896.

In a "Note" of 1869 for Napoleon III, Persigny recalls that Eugenie wanted to disavow the Preliminaries of La Soledad in 1862.

*Documents diplomatiques (livres jaunes).* Published by the French Ministry of Foreign Affairs. Paris, 1861 ff.

The documents on Mexico for 1861 and 1862 were carefully edited to make it appear that the expedition to Mexico was occasioned by French claims, but the Jecker bonds are never mentioned.

Du Campt, Maxime: *Souvenirs d'un Demi-Siècle.* 2 v., Paris, 1949.

Contains an annecdote about the Jecker bonds.

Emerit, Marcel; ed.: *Lettres de Napoléon à Madame Cornu, en Grande Partie Inédites, Texte Integral Publié et commenté par Marcel Emerit, Docteur ès Lettres.* 2 v., Paris, 1937.

Madame Cornu was Napoleon III's foster sister. Unfortunately there are no letters for 1861, only two for 1862, and very few for the period thereafter, and no references to Mexico.

Ernest, Otto, ed.: *Franz Joseph as Revealed by His Letters,* trans. Agnes Blake. London, 1927.

Letters from the *Haus-Hof-und Staatsarchiv* in Vienna. The editor inclines to the view that Franz Joseph was glad to get rid of Maximilian by sending him to Mexico.

Ernst II, Herzog von Saxe-Coburg-Gotha: *Aus Meinem Leben und Meiner Zeit.* 3 v., Berlin, 1887–1889.

Concerned primarily with German affairs. Comments on Napoleon III's character, based on conversations with him.

Evans, Dr. Thomas W.: *The Memoirs of Dr. Thomas W. Evans: Recollections of the Second Empire,* ed. Edward A. Crame. 2 v., London, 1905.

Dr. Evans was the American dentist to the French Imperial Family.

He was kept busy supplying Napoleon III with information about the American Civil War and apparently had little interest in Mexican affairs. Very biased in favor of Napoleon III, with interesting remarks about his character.

Fleury, Comte: *Memoirs of the Empress Eugenie by Comte Fleury: Compiled from Statements, Private Documents and Personal Letters of the Empress Eugenie, From Conversations of the Emperor Napoleon III and From Family Letters and Papers of General Fleury, M. Franceschini Pietri, Prince Victor Napoleon and Other Members of the Court of the Second Empire.* 2 v., New York and London, 1920.

Important for Eugenie's motives for the Mexican Expedition, but unfortunately references are not given. Fleury was Napoleon III's aide-de-camp. Very important for the motives of the Emperor.

Guedalla, Phillip, ed.: *The Palmerston Papers: Gladstone and Palmerston, being the Correspondence of Lord Palmerston with Mr. Gladstone, 1851–1865.* London, 1928.

Primarily financial matters, but some letters reveal Palmerston's distrust of France and his desire to enlarge the British army and navy.

Hall, Frederic: *Life of Maximilian I., Late Emperor of Mexico, with a Sketch of the Empress Carlota, by Frederic Hall, One of His Majesty's Legal Advisers.* New York, 1868.

Hall was an American lawyer who aided in Maximilian's defense in his court martial. Valuable for personal sketches of Maximilian and Charlotte and some Estra-Maximilian correspondence cited. Favorable to Maximilian.

*Hansard's Parliamentary Debates,* 3rd series.

Volumes CLXVII and CLXVIII contain debates on British Mexican policy in the Houses of Lords and Commons.

Harris, James Howard, 3rd Earl of Malmesbury: *Memoirs of an Ex-Minister: An Autobiography.* 2 v., London, 1884.

Valuable for Malmesbury's Mexican policy as Foreign Secretary.

Haswell, James M.: *The Man of His Time: Part I, The Story of the Life of Napoleon III; Part II, The Same Story as Told by Popular Caricaturists of the Last Thirty Years.* London, 1871.

Part II is a collection of caricatures, including one on Napoleon III's Mexican policy.

Hauterive, Ernest d.', ed.: "Correspondence Inédite de Napoléon III et du Prince Napoléon," I–V, *Revue des Deux Mondes,* 15 Dec 1923, pp. 763–796; 1 Jan 1924, pp. 51–84; 1 Feb 1924, pp. 519–545; 1 Mar 1924, p. 79–114; 15 Mar 1924, pp. 319–352.

Letters from the archives of the Villa Prangins, where Prince Napoleon had already classified the letters. The period from 1837 to 1872 is spanned. Interesting for Prince Napoleon's criticism of Napoleon III.

————: *Napoléon III et Le Prince Napoléon. Correspondance Inédite.* Paris, 1925.

What had already appeared in the *Revue des Deux Mondes* in book form, with some difference in editing.

*House Executive Document,* 37 Congress, 3 session, no. 23.

Contains, in English translation, the ten letters addressed to J. B. Jecker in 1862 by his relatives and friends in Europe. These letters were intercepted and originally published by the Mexican Government in Mexican newspapers.

Hübner, Graf Joseph Alexander Von: *Neuf Ans de Souvenirs D'Un Ambassadeur D'Autriche A Paris Sous Le Second Empire 1851–1859, Publiés Par Son Fils, Le Comte Alexandre de Hübner.* 2 v., Paris, 1904.

The journal of the Austrian Ambassador to Paris from 1851 to 1859. Extracts of letters to Buol, Austrian Minister of Foreign Affairs. Important for conversations with Napoleon III and Eugenie that are summarized and cited by a keen observer.

Johnson, A. H., ed.: *The Letters of Charles Greville and Henry Reeve, 1836–1865.* London, 1924.

No mention of Mexico, but an interesting estimate of Napoleon III by Greville.

*Le Moniteur Universal: Journal Officiel de L'Empire Francais.*

Official journal of the Second Empire until 1869. Diplomatic documents, official statements, and the debates in the legislature are given. Copies for the years 1861 and 1862 were examined. Invaluable for the way the French Government tried to prepare French public opinion for the Maximilian candidature.

Manning, William R., ed.: *Diplomatic Correspondence of the United States: Inter-American Affairs, 1831–1860.* 12 v., Washington, 1932–1939.

Volume IX is an extensive collection of correspondence, selected from the archives of the Department of State of the United States, between the Secretaries of State and their Ministers to Mexico, 1848–1860. The McLane-Ocampo Treaties are given in full.

Martin, Theodore, ed.: *The Life of His Royal Highness, the Prince Consort.* 5 v., London, 1875–1880.

Letters and extracts of diaries of Albert and Victoria. Many references to Napoleon III.

Maxwell, Sir Herbert, ed.: *The Life and Letters of George William Frederick, Fourth Earl of Clarendon, K.G., G.C.B.* 2 v. London, 1913.

Extremely important for a letter of Sir George Lewis, the Secretary of State for War, about the British cabinet meeting before the signing of the Tripartite Treaty of London of 31 October 1861.

Mérimée, Prosper: *Lettres de Prosper Mérimée A La Comtesse de Montijo, Mère de l'Impératrice Eugénie.* Private edition, published under the direction of the Duc D'Albe, 2 v., Paris, 1930.

————: *Letters to an Unknown* (Jenny Dacquin), trans. Henri Pene Du Bois. London, 1903.

————: *Lettres à M. Panizzi, 1850–1870, publiées par M. Louis*

*Fagan du Cabinet des Estampes au British Museum.* 3rd ed., 2 v., Paris, 1881.
Mérimée often accompanied Napoleon III and Eugenie, but did not appear to have known any more about the Mexican expedition than was current in court circles.

Metternich-Sandor, Princess Pauline Maria Wulpurga Von: *Eclairs du Passé* (1859-1870). Zurich, Leipzig, Vienna, 1922.
Reminiscences of court life by the wife of Richard de Metternich, Austrian Ambassador to Paris, 1859–1871.

Montluc, Armand de: *Correspondance de Juarez et de Montluc, Ancien Consul Général du Mexique, Accompagnée de Nombreuses Lettres de Personnages Politiques Relative A L'Expédition du Mexique,* ed. *Léon de Montluc.* Paris, 1885.
Armand de Montluc was a Frenchman who sympathized with the Juarez Regime, which named him Consul General in Paris in 1861. Valuable correspondence between Montluc and the Mexican Government. Contains some letters and extracts from Montluc's journal that pertain to Jecker. Generally overlooked by students of Napoleon III's Mexican policy.

Moore, John Bassett, ed.: *A Digest of International Law, as embodied in Diplomatic Discussions, Treaties and Other International Agreements, International Awards, The Decisions of Municipal Courts, and the Writings of Jurists, and especially in Documents, Published and Unpublished, Issues of Presidents and Secretaries of State of the United States, the Opinions of the Attorneys-General, and the Decisions of Courts, Federal and State.* 8 v., Washington, 1906.
A classic on International Law. Contains some documents relative to the Mexican policy of the United States.

Motley, John Lothrop: *The Correspondence of John Lothrop Motley,* ed. George William Curtis, 2 v., New York, 1889.
Pasing references to Maximilian by the American Minister to Austria during the American Civil War.

Ollivier, Emile: *L'Empire Libéral: Etudes, Récits, Souvenirs.* 18 v., Paris, 1895–1912. Detailed history of the Second Empire, based on Ollivier's reminiscences, printed documents, and some sources that are not readily apparent. Slight on the Mexican expedition.

Paléologue, Maurice, ed.: *The Tragic Empress: Intimate Conversations with the Empress Eugénie, 1901 to 1911,* trans. Hamish Miles. London, n.d., ca. 1928.
In a conversation of 10 January 1904 Eugenie related her and Napoleon III's motives for their Mexican policy.

*Papers relating to Foreign affairs (1861–1870).* Washington, 1862–1871.
Documents submitted to Congress. The volume for 1861–1862 was consulted for Seward's Mexican policy.

Poulet-Malassis, A., ed.: *Papiers Secret et Correspondance du Second Empire. Réimpression complète de l'édition de l'Imprimerie Nationale, annotée et augmentée de nombreuses pièces publiée à l'étranger, et recueillies par A. Poulet-Malassis.* 3rd ed., Paris, 1873.

Contains the complete text of the famous letter of J. B. Jecker to Conti, of 8 December 1869.

Quinet, Edgar: *L'Expedition du Mexique*. London, 1862.
Propaganda pamphlet against the Mexican expedition by an opponent of Napoleon III's regime.

Randon, Maréchal Jacques L.: *Mémoires du Maréchal Randon.* 2 v., Paris, 1875–1877.
Contains very important letters between Napoleon III and his Minister of War concerning Mexico.

Raschdau, L. von, ed.: *Die Politischen Berichte des Fürsten Bismarck aus Petersberg und Paris, 1859–1862.* Berlin, 1920.
Two reports of Bismarck touch on his minor connections with the Mexican expedition.

Richardson, James D., ed.: *A Compilation of the Messages and Papers of the Confederacy, including the Diplomatic Correspondence, 1861–1862.* 2 v., Nashville, 1904–1906.
Useful for the activities of Confederate agents abroad.

————: *The Messages and Papers of the Presidents.* 10 v., Washington, 1896–1899.
Volume V contains President Buchanon's messages to Congress concerning Mexico.

Romero, Mathias, ed.: *Correspondencia de la Legacion Mexicana en Washington Durante La Intervencion Extranjera, 1860–1868: Collection de Documentos Para Formar La Historia de la Intervencion.* 10 v., Mexico City, 1870–1892.
The diplomatic correspondence of Mathias Romero, who represented Juarez in Washington. Valuable summaries of Romero's attempts to push Seward into effective action against the European intervention in Mexico. Volume I covers 1860–1861, volume II, 1862.

————: *Dinner to Senor Matias Romero, Envoy Extraordinary and Minister Plenipotentiary from Mexico, on the 29th of March, 1864.* New York, 1864.
Contains a speech by Romero on behalf of Juarez and against Maximilian.

Salviac de Viel-Castel, Comte Horace: *Mémoires du Comte Horace de Viel Castel sur Le Règne de Napoléon III (1851–1864), Publiés D'Après Le Manuscrit Original et Ornés d'um Portrait de l'Auteur.* 2nd ed., 6 v., Paris, 1883–1884.
A few passing references to Mexico.

Schnürer, Franz, ed.: *Briefe Kaiser Franz Josephs I. an seine Mutter, 1838–1872.* Munich, 1930.
Contains references to Maximilian and Charlotte.

Sencourt, Robert, ed. (?): "Les Fiancailles de l'Impératrice: Lettres à La Duchesse D'Albe," *Revue des Deux Mondes,* 15 Jul 1932, pp. 295–301.
A few letters of Eugenie to her sister.

Senior, Nassau William: *Conversations with Distinguished Persons*

*During the Second Empire from 1860 to 1863 by the Late Nassau William Senior,* ed. M.C.M. Simpson. 2 v., London, 1880.
Senior's conversations, edited by his daughter. Especially important conversations with Estrada and Drouyn de Lhuys, Thouvenel's successor as Minister of Foreign Affairs, concerning Mexican affairs.

————: *Conversations with M. Thiers, M. Guizot, and Other Distinguished Persons, During the Second Empire, by the Late Nassau William Senior,* ed. M.C.M. Simpson. 2 v., London, 1878.
More important for characterizations of Napoleon III than for his Mexican policy.

Seward, Frederick W., ed.: *Seward at Washington as Senator and Secretary of State: A Memoir of His Life with Selections from His Letters.* 2 v., New York, 1891.
Seward's Mexican policy is scarcely touched.

Stevenson, Sara Yorke: *Maximilian in Mexico: A Woman's Reminiscences of the French Intervention, 1862–1867.* New York, 1891.
Memoirs of the American archaeologist, who studied in Paris and went to Mexico in 1862, owing to the murder of a relative there. Generally hostile to Napoleon III.

Tascher de la Pagerie, Comtesse Stéphanie de: *Mon Séjour aux Tuileries, 1852–1858.* Paris, 1893.

————: *Mon Séjour aux Tuileries, 1859–1865.* Paris, 1894.

————: *Mon Séjour aux Tuileries, 1866–1871.* Paris, 1895.
Very pro-Napoleon III. Important for characterizations of him, rather than for political events.

Temperley, Harold and Penson, Lillian M., eds.: *Foundations of British Foreign Policy, From Pitt (1792) to Salibury (1902), or, Documents, Old and New.* Cambridge, 1938.
Contains a few letters of Palmerston about Mexican affairs.

*The Annual Register or a View of the History and Politics of the Year 1861.* London, 1862.
Contains a few hints of events otherwise perhaps overlooked.

*The Political and Historical Works of Louis Napoleon Bonaparte, President of the French Republic, Now First Collected, with An Original Memoir of His Life, Brought Down to the Promulgation of the Constitution of 1852, and Occasional Notes.* 2 v., London, 1852.
An English edition of *Oeuvres de Louis-Napoléon Bonaparte* (3 v., Paris, 1848), edited by Charles-Edouard Temblaire. Contains a note on the French Pastry War of 1838–1839 that may possibly be Napoleon's first written reference to Mexico.

Thouvenel, L., ed.: *Le secret de l'Empereur. Correspondance confidentielle et inédite exchangée entre M. Thouvenel, Le Duc de Gramont et le General Comte de Flahault, 1860–1862.* 2 v., Paris, 1889.
The private letters of Thouvenel to Flahault, the French Ambassador to London, throw much light on French motives for intervening in Mexico.

*Times* (London).
Copies for the years 1861 and 1862 were examined.

Vandam, Albert D.: *An Englishman in Paris (Notes and Recollections).* 2 v., London, 1892.
Contains an anecdote on Morny and the Mexican expedition.

Victoria, Queen: *The Letters of Queen Victoria.* 1st ser., 1837–1861. ed. Arthur Christopher Benson and Viscount Esher. 2nd ser., 1861–1885, ed. George Earle Buckle. 6 v., London, 1908, 1926.
Passing references to Mexico and Maximilian.

Wellesley, Col. the Hon. F. A. ed.: Secrets of the Second Empire: *Private Letters from the Paris Embassy: Selections from the papers of Henry Richard Charles Wellesley 1st Earl Cowley, Ambassador at Paris, 1852–1867, Edited by his Son, Colonel The Hon. F. A. Wellesley.* New York and London, 1929.
Important for Napoleon III's Confederate policy.

Wellesley, Sir Victor and Sencourt, Robert, eds.: *Conversations With Napoleon III: A Collection of Documents, mostly unpublished and almost entirely Diplomatic, Selected and arranged with Introductions.* London, 1934.
Important for Cowley's private letters to Russell on Mexican affairs Limitations of space, however, did not permit more than a selection

## Historical Works Cited

Abbott, James S. C.: *The History of Napoleon III, Emperor of the French, Including a brief narrative of all the most important events which have occurred in Europe Since the fall of Napoleon I Until the present time.* Boston, 1869.
Chapter XXXVII is an account of the European expedition to Mexico that is surprisingly circumspect for a contemporary historian

Acton, Lord: *Historical Essays and Studies by John Emerich Edward Dalberg-Acton, First Baron Acton,* eds. John Neville Figgis and Reginald Vera Laurence. London, 1907.
Includes "The Rise and Fall of the Mexican Empire," a lecture delivered in 1868. Sympathetic toward Mexico. Apparently based on Blue Books and Yellow Books.

Aubry, Octave: *Le Second Empire.* 7th ed., Paris, 1938.
More concerned with court and internal affairs than with foreign policy. Includes the Jecker bonds and Eugenie's ideas of regenerating Mexico as chief causes of the Mexican expedition.

————: *L'Impératrice Eugénie.* Paris, 1933.
Popular and chatty. Gives Eugenie credit for the Mexican expedition.

Bailey, Thomas A.: *A Diplomatic History of the American People* (Crofts American History Series, ed. Dixon Ryan Fox). 4th ed., New York, 1950.

Chapter XXIII is a brief summary of American attitudes towards Maximilian, based on printed works.

Bancroft, Frederic: *The Life of William H. Seward.* 2 v., New York and London, 1900.
Probably the best biography of Seward.

Bancroft, Hubert Howe: *History of Mexico.* 6 v., San Francisco, 1883–1888.
Excellent study of Mexican History in the nineteenth century. Based largely on Spanish and Mexican printed works. Volume VI contains an account of the French intervention that is very fair.

————: *Resources and Development of Mexico. San Francisco,* 1893.
Valuable for economic conditions in Mexico.

Beaumont-Vassey, Viscomte de: *Histoire Intime du Second Empire* Paris, 1874.
Gives Eugenie's urgings and the Jecker bonds as the chief reasons for the Mexican expedition.

Bell, Herbert C. F.: *Lord Palmerston.* 2 v., London, 1936.
Bell used the Russell Papers. Cites a few important letters from Palmerston to Russell about Mexico.

Billington, Ray Allen: *The Far Western Frontier, 1830–1860.* (New American Nation Series, eds. Henry Steele Commager and Richard B. Morris). London, 1956.
Chapter VII is a good brief summary of Manifest Destiny.

Blanchard, Jerrold: *The Life of Napoleon III, Derived from State Records, From Unpublished Family Correspondence, and From Personal Testimony.* 4 v., London, 1874–1882.
As an apologist for Napoleon III, Blanchard had the benefit of being permitted to view some private papers. The attempt to vindicate Napoleon's Mexican policy is unconvincing. Excellent for Napoleon's Nicaragua Canal plan.

Boon, Hendrick N.: *Rêve et Réalité dans l'oeuvre économique et sociale de Napoleon III.* The Hague, 1936.
Hardly touches the Mexican policy of Napoleon.

Boulenger, Marcel: *Le Duc De Morny: Prince Francais.* Paris, 1925.
Attempts to discredit Jecker's letter to Conti of 8 December 1869, the basis of the assertion that Morny promised to support the Jecker bonds, but adds nothing new.

Bratianu, G. I.: *Napoléon III et Les Nationalités.* Paris, 1934.
Attributes the Mexican expedition to Eugenie and her "Austrian sympathies" and asserts that the Jecker bonds played a considerable role.

Burke, Ulick Ralph *A Life of Benito Juarez, Constitutional President of Mexico.* London and Sydney, 1894.
Eulogistic biography of Juarcz, based on secondary works, printed documents, especially the British Blue Books. Excellent summary of British, French, and Spanish claims on Mexico in 1861, though misleading in some particulars. Chapter VII summarizes Wyke's

reports to Russell in 1861, from the Blue Books, but has a caustic anti-Wyke bias.

Callahan, James Morton: *American Policy in Mexican Relations.* New York, 1932.

Brilliant brief history of the diplomatic relations of the United States with Mexico by an outstanding scholar.

Case, Lynn M.: *French Opinion on War and Diplomacy during the Second Empire.* Philadelphia, 1954.

Excellent study, based primarily on the reports of the *Procureurs génèraux,* but also on the archives of Brussells, Paris, Bern, Washington, and London, as well as newspapers and numerous other printed sources. A complement to the author's *French opinion on the United States and Mexico, 1860–1867; extracts from the report: of the procureurs généraux* (New York, 1936).

Chapman, Maristan (pseud. of Mary Ilsley Chapman and John Stanton Higham Chapman): *Imperial Brother: A Life of the Duc de Morny.* London, 1932.

Over emphasizes the role of Morny during the Second Empire. Does not footnote "conversations." Asserts Eugenie and the Jecker bonds decided Morny to back the Mexican expedition.

Christophe, Robert: Le Duc de Morny: *"Empereur" Des Francais Sous Napoleon III.* Paris, 1951.

Reviews the literature on the Jecker affair and concludes that Morny urged intervention in Mexico to make a profit for himself.

Conti, Count Egon Caesar: *Maximilian and Charlotte of Mexico,* trans. Catherine Alison Phillips. 2 v., New York, 1928.

A pioneer study, based on the author's thorough examination of the *Archiv des Kaisers Maximilian von Mexiko* in the *Haus-Hof-und Staatsarchiv* of Vienna that was opened to the public after World War I. The "Maximilianarchiv" contains the documents and letters preserved by Maximilian about the preliminaries to the establishment of the Empire in Mexico. Of paramount importance are the letters between Maximilian and Napoleon III, Charlotte and Eugenie, Maximilian and the Mexican exiles, especially Estrada. These letters. together with Richard de Metternich's reports from Paris, represent the most important sources for the negotiations of Napoleon III and Maximilian with a view to establishing an Empire in Mexico. Many of these letters are contained in full in appendices. Corti's approach was chiefly biographical, and consequently the official negotiations of France, Spain, Great Britain, and the United States for an intervention in Mexico are not covered in detail. Corti's scholarly account, however, is a must for any student of the Mexican Policy of the Powers in the 1860's. The translation from the original German work of Corti *(Maximilian und Charlotte von Mexiko.* 2 v., Vienna, Zurich, Leipzig, 1924) is an accurate one by a professional translator.

Dawson, Daniel: *The Mexican Adventure.* London, 1935.

The author utilized the same primary sources as Count Corti and cites many of the same documents, some at greater length. In some respects Dawson's evaluation of these documents is more critical than that of Corti. Dawson was interested in placing Maximilian in the setting of the Mexican policies of the Powers. Although the records of the British Public Record Office were used for the introductory chapters on the Mexican policies of the Powers before 1861, only the printed documents laid before Parliament were utilized for 1861 and after. Dawson did his research in the early 1920's and therefore was unable to consult the Russell Papers and the Cowley Papers. Nor did he look at the archives of the French Ministry of Foreign Affairs, upon which the other study of the background of the European intervention in Mexico in 1861 (by Christian Schofer) is almost exclusively based. Dawson and Schefer's studies, therefore, complement each other.

Debidour, Antonin: *Histoire Diplomatique de L'Europe depuis L'- Ouverture Du Congrès de Vienne Jusqu'a La Cloture Du Congrès de Vienne Jusqu'a La Cloture Du Congrès de Berlin (1814–1878).* 2 v., Paris, 1891.
General. Useful for thumbnail biographies in footnotes.

Delord, Taxile: *Histoire du Second Empire.* 6 v., Paris, 1869–1875.
Generally hostile to Napoleon III's Mexican policy. Good summaries of the sessions of the *Corps legislatif.* Most documents quoted are from the British Blue Books and the French Yellow Books.

Domenech, Emmanuel: *Histoire du Mexique, Juarez et Maximilien: Correspondances Inédites des Présidents, Ministres et Généraux Almonte, Santa-Anna, Gutierrez, Miramon Marquez, Mejia, Woll, etc., etc. de Juarez, de l'Empereur Maximilien et de L'Impératrice Charlotte, par Emmanuel Domenech, Ancien Directeur de la Presse du Cabinet de l'Empereur Maximilien, ex-aumônier de l'Armée Francaise du Mexique.* 3 v., Paris, 1868.
Abbé Domenech was chaplain to the French expeditionary corps in Mexico and later press secretary for Maximilian. Domenech went to Mexico in 1864 and had a reactionary bias. This work contains important documents on the doings of the Mexican exiles.

————: *La Mexique Tel Qu'il Est: La Vérité sur son climat, ses habitants et son Gouvernement par Emmanuel Domenech, Ancien Directeur de la presse du Cabinet de S. M. L'Empereur Maximilien, ex-aumônier du corps expéditionnaire.* Paris, 1867.
Valuable for population statistics.

Du Camp, Maxime: *Les Convulsions de Paris,* 4 v., Paris, 1878–1880.
A letter of 1877 of A. de Morineau, then pensioned Consul and former manager of the General Consulates of Switzerland and Spain in Mexico, is given as Appendix 8 of volume I. This letter contains information on Jecker in answer to Du Camp's request for it in connection with his work on the Commune, when Jecker was shot.

Dunham, Arthur Louis: *The Anglo-French Treaty of Commerce of 1860 and the Progress of the Industrial Revolution in France.*

(Volume IX of University of Michigan Publications in History and Political Science). Ann Arbor, 1930.

The first seven chapters are Dunham's doctoral dissertation on the Treaty of Commerce between England and France. The remaining chapters deal with the development of French industries. Excellent for the French economic situation in the 1860's. Based on the archives of the French Ministry of Foreign Affairs, the British Public Record Office and private letter collections.

Dunn, Frederick Sherwood: *The Diplomatic Protection of Americans in Mexico*. New York, 1933.

Excellent on the claims of the United States on Mexico. The author used the archives of the United States State Department.

Duvernois, Clement: *L'Intervention Francaise au Mexique, Accompagnée de Documents Inédits et d'un long Mémoire addressé par L'Empereur Maximilien à L'Empereur Napoléon et rémis à Paris par L'Impératrice Charlotte: Précedée d'une Preface de Clement Duvernois*. 2 v., Paris, 1868.

Contains extracts of Spanish documents.

Esslinger, Elisabet: *Kaiserin Eugenie Und Die Politik Des zweiten Kaiserreichs*. Stuttgart, 1932.

Credits Eugenie with being the prime mover of the Mexican expedition. Based especially on Fleury's memoirs and Paléologue's conversations with Eugenie.

Flint, Henry M.: *Mexico Under Maximilian*. Philadelphia, 1867. Important for population statistics. Main emphasis is on the period after 1863. Decidedly slanted in favor of Maximilian.

Fuller, John D. P.: *The Movement for the Acquisition of All Mexico, 1846-1848*. (No. 1 of Series LIV of The Johns Hopkins University Studies in Historical and Political Science). Baltimore, 1936.

Concludes that the most important reason for the failure of this movement in the United States to annex all Mexico was lack of time for expansionist sentiment to develop.

Gaulot, Paul: *La Vérité sur L'Expédition du Mexique d'après les Documents Inédits de Ernest Louet, Payeur en Chef du Corps Expeditionnaire: Réve d'Empire, par Paul Gaulot*. Paris, 1889.

Contains important documents collected by Ernest Louet, especially about Estrada's doings in 1861, but more concerned with events after the arrival of the allied expeditionary corps in Mexico than with the background of that intervention.

Guedalla, Philip: *The Second Empire*. Rev. ed., London, 1932.

Spirited, general account, based on secondary sources. Gives the Jecker bonds as a reason for the French expedition to Mexico.

Guerard, Albert: *Napoleon III*. Cambridge, Mass., 1943.

General. Depreciates the Jecker bonds and the resources of Sonora as causes of the French expedition to Mexico. Stresses Eugenie's influence on Napoleon III.

Guiral, Pierre: *Prévost- Paradol (1829-1870): Pensée et Action D'Un Libéral Sous Le Second Empire*. Paris, 1955.

A biography and an appraisal of the influence of the liberal journalist. Quotes or summarizes his articles, including some on Mexico.

Haller, Elizabeth: *Aspects of American Opinion Regarding Maximilian's Empire in Mexico*. M. A. Thesis presented to the Faculty of the Graduate School of the University of Pennsylvania in 1940.
Useful for United States newspaper comment on the European intervention in Mexico in early 1862. The thesis is defended that American public opinion was more focused on the Civil War.

Hamel, Ernest: *Histoire Illustrée du Second Empire précédée des événevents de 1848 A 1852*. 3 v. in 1, Paris, 1873–1874.
Approvingly quotes Jecker's letter to Conti of 8 December 1869.

Harding, Bertita: *Phantom Crown: The Story of Maximilian and Carlota of Mexico*. London, 1935.
Historical romance purporting to be genuine history. Based on secondary works. Napoleon III is made to seem a wicked intriguer, Maximilian a dupe, Juarez a hero.

Hendrick, Burton Jesse: *Statesmen of the Lost Cause: Jefferson Davis and His Cabinet*. Boston, 1939.
Chapter IV is a colorful account of Pickett's mission to Mexico in 1861 and is based on the Pickett Papers.

Herring, Hubert: *A History of Latin America from the Beginnings to the Present*. London, 1954.
Readable general history.

Holt, W. Stull: *Treaties Defeated by the Senate: A Study of the Struggle between President and Senate over the Conduct of Foreign Relations*. Baltimore, 1933.
Contains a general account of the McLane-Ocampo Treaties.

Hyde, H. Montgomery: *Mexican Empire: The History of Maximilian and Carlota of Mexico*. London, 1946.
A colorful account, based on the National Archives of Mexico and the United States, and the *Haus-Hof-und Staatsarchiv*.
Contains an excellent critical bibliography.

Indeville, Henry D.': *Journal d'un Diplomat en Italie: Notes Intimes Pour Servir à l'Histoire du Second Empire: Turin, 1859–1862*. Paris, 1872.
A rambling account.

Jordan, Donaldson, and Pratt, Edwin J.: *Europe and the American Civil War*. Boston and New York, 1931.
European opinion on the American Civil War. Based on newspapers, public addresses, diplomatic correspondence. The archives of the French Ministry of Foreign Affairs were closed to the authors. Unfortunately there are no footnotes, to cut publishing costs.

Kéralty, Comte Emile de: *La Créance Jecker, Les Indemnités Francaises et Les Emprunts Mexicains*. Paris, 1868.
Statistical work on European claims on Mexico. Yellow and Blue Books are the main sources.

—————: *L'Empereur Maximilien: Son Elevation et Sa Chute*. Leipzig, Brussels, Turin, Florence, London, Edinborough, Amsterdam,

Basel, Geneva, and Ghent, 1867.
A pro-French account.

La Gorce, Pierre de: *Historie du Second Empire*. 7 v., Paris, 1894–1905.
Excellent study. The Mexican expedition is treated at length. Based on printed materials.

——————: *Napoleon III et Sa Politique*. 7th ed., Paris, 1933.
Urbane and general. The Mexican policy of Napoleon III is seen as essentially idealistic.

Lally, Frank Edward: *French Opposition to the Mexican Policy of the Second Empire*. (Johns Hopkins University Studies in Historical and Political Science, Series XLIX, No. 3). Baltimore, 1931.
Based almost entirely on newspapers and should be read in the light of Professor Case's *French Opinion on the United States and Mexico*. . . . Lally's thesis is that the Imperial Government hedged and whitewashed the expedition and inadequately answered the doubts of the Independent Press and played up military successes.

Lano, Pierre de: *Le Secret d'Un Empire: La Cour de Napoleon III*, 5th ed., Paris, 1892.
Quotes Jecker's letter to Conti of 1869 and claims it leaves no doubt about Morny's role in the Mexican expedition.

——————: *The Secret of an Empire: The Empress Eugénie*, trans. Ethelred Taylor. London, 1895.
Claims Eugenie and Princess Pauline de Metternich, the wife of the Austrian Ambassador to Paris, planned the candidacy of Maximilian.

Latane, John Holladay: *The United States and Latin America*. Garden City, 1920.
Contains a chapter on the European intervention in Mexico, based on the "blue books."

Lefêvre, E.: *Documents Officiels Recueillis Dans La Secrétairerie Privée de Maximilien: Historie de l'Intervention Francaise au Mexique, par. E. Lefêvre, Rédacteur en chef de la Tribune de Mexique*. 2 v., Brussels and London, 1869.
Lefêvre was a French journalist, who sympathized with the Juarez Regime. He was permitted to view some of Maximilian's papers seized by the Mexican Government. The correspondence of De La Fuente, an agent sent to Europe by Juarez, is very important, but Lefêvre's narrative is extremely biased in favor of Mexico.

——————: *Le Mexique et L'Intervention Europeene, par le citoyen E. Lefêvre*. Mexico City, 1862.
Statistical work on French claims. By implication the Jecker bonds are given as the main cause of the French intervention in Mexico.

Leonardon, H.: *Prim*. Paris, 1901.
The description of Prim's role in Mexico is based primarily on the papers and documents presented to the Cortes. A good background of Spanish-Mexican relations before the intervention in 1861. A generally sound but brief summary of Prim's part in the breakdown of the Tripartite Treaty of London of 31 October 1861.

Loliée, Frédéric: *Le Duc de Morny: The Brother of an Emperor and the Maker of an Empire,* adapted by Bryan O'Donnell. London,1910.
Accepts the truth of Jecker's assertion of a deal with Morny.

Martin, Lieutenant-Colonel Charles: *Précis des Evénements de la Campagne du Mexique en 1862, par Ch. Martin, Précéde d'une Notice Géographique et Statistique sur le Mexique par Léon Deluzy.* Paris, 1863.
Apologist for France's Mexican policy. Valuable population statistics.

Martin, Percy F.: *Maximilian in Mexico: The Story of the French Intervention,* 1861–1867. New York, 1914.
One of the better biographies of Maximilian based on printed works only.

Monaghan, Jay: *Diplomat in Carpet Slippers: Abraham Lincoln Deals with Foreign Affairs.* Indianapolis, and New York, 1945.
Based on printed materials. Adds nothing new. Overemphasis on the role of Lincoln.

Mosse, W. E.: *The European Powers and the German Question, 1848–1871, With Special Reference to England and Russia.* Cambridge, 1958.
Mosse used materials in the British Public Record Office. Useful for British Policy toward continental Europe.

Musser, John: *The Establishment of Maximilian's Empire in Mexico: A Thesis Presented to the Faculty of the Graduate School of the University of Pennsylvania in Partial Fulfillment of the Requirements for the Degree of Doctor of Philosophy.* Menasha, 1918.
Based exclusively on printed works. Relies on Bancroft's *History of Mexico* to a large extent. The Tripartite Treaty of London of 31 October 1861 is covered in a few pages, and French motives are not documented. Brief summary of Seward's Mexican policy.

Newton, Baron Thomas W. Legh (Lord Newton): *Lord Lyons: A Record of British Diplomacy.* 2 v., London, 1913.
Biography of the British Minister to the United States during the American Civil War. Official and private correspondence is cited, including occasional references to Seward's Mexican policy.

Nicolay, John G., and Hay, John: *Abraham Lincoln: A History.* 10 v., New York, 1890.
Detailed history by Lincoln's secretaries.

Owsley, Frank Lawrence: *King Cotton Diplomacy: Foreign Relations of the Confederate States of America.* Chicago, 1931.
Contains a brief summary of Seward's Mexican policy, based on the archives of the United States State Department.

Perkins, Dexter: *Hands Off: A History of the Monroe Doctrine.* Boston, 1941.
The Historian of the Monroe Doctrine summarizes his life's research.
————: *The Monroe Doctrine, 1826–1867.* Baltimore, 1933.
Contains many summaries of documents from the archives of the French Ministry of Foreign Affairs on the background of the Mexican

expedition. The main emphasis, however, is on the growth of the importance of the Monroe Doctrine.

Priestley, Herbert Ingram: *The Mexican Nation, a History.* London, 1923.
Contains a short chapter on the European intervention in Mexico.

Reinach Foussemagne, Comtesse H. de: *Charlotte de Belgique, Impératrice du Mexique.* Paris, 1925.
An excellent biography of Charlotte that complements Corti's study in that the author made use of the Belgian archives and private letter collections.

Rheinhardt, Emile Alphons: *Napoleon and Eugenie: The Tragicomedy of an Empire,* trans. Hannah Waller. New York, 1931.
Covers the Mexican expedition in a dozen pages and blames it on Eugenie and Morny.

Rippy, J. Fred: *Latin America: A Modern History.* Ann Arbor, Mayflower, and London, 1958.
Takes Napoleon III's letter to General Forey of 3 July 1862 as the measure of French purposes in Mexico. Contains statistics on French trade in Latin America.

——: *The United States and Mexico.* New York, 1926.
Well-documented brief summary of relations between the United States and Mexico.

Roeder, Ralph: *Juarez and His Mexico: A Biographical History.* 2 v., New York, 1947.
Popular and general. Based on secondary sources, Mexican newspapers and the archives of the Museo Nacional de Historia y Antropologéa in Mexico.

Russell. Addison Peale: *Thomas Corwin: A Sketch.* Cincinnati, 1881.
Brief biography of Seward's Minister to Mexico during the Civil War by a personal friend.

Salm-Salm, Felix, Prinz zu: *My Diary in Mexico in 1867, including the Last Days of the Emperor Maximilian; with leaves from the Diary of the Princess Salm-Salm.* 2 v., London, 1868.
More important for the last days of Maximilian's reign than for the establishment of the monarchy.

Salomon, Henry: *L'Ambassade de Richard De Metternich A Paris.* Paris, 1931.
The first few pages of Chapter IX cite a few passages of the correspondence of Metternich, Rechberg, Napoleon III, and Eugenie, found in the Haus-Hof-und Staatsarchiv in Vienna. Salomon's emphasis is on the "clairvoyance" of Metternich and the "blindness" of Eugenie, Maximilian, and Charlotte.

Sandburg, Carl: *Abraham Lincoln: The War Years.* 4 v., New York, 1939.
Colorful general account.

Schefer, Christian: *La Grande Pensée de Napoleon III: Les Origines de l'Expedition du Mexique (1858-1862).* Paris, 1939.
Based on the archives of the Ministry of Foreign Affairs in Paris.

Contains a general summary of the background of the French expedition to Mexico. The description of the negotiation of the Tripartite Treaty of London of 31 October 1861 complements the article by Robertson, based almost entirely on the archives of the British Public Record Office. Unfortunately Schefer's study is almost devoid of footnotes.

Scroggs, William O.: *Filibusters and Financiers: The Story of William Walker and His Associates.* New York, 1916.
The classic account.

Sencourt, Robert: *The Life of the Empress Eugénie.* London, 1931.
Based on the *Haus-Hof-und Staatsarchiv* and the archives of the Duc D'Albe. The Mexican affair is briefly covered.

————: *Napoleon III: The Modern Emperor.* London, 1933.
Based on the archives of London, Vienna, Paris, and the Duc D'Albe. Skimpy on the Mexican expedition, but a few important documents are cited and summarized.

Stern, Alfred: *Geschichte Europas von 1848 bis 1871.* 10 v., Stuttgart and Berlin, 1894–1924.
Volume IX briefly summarizes Napoleon III's motives for the Mexican expedition.

Tansill, Charles Callan: *The United States and Santo Domingo, 1798–1873: A Chapter in Caribbean Diplomacy.* Baltimore, 1938.
Contains a brief account of Seward's Santo Domingo policy.

Thompson, J. M.: *Louis Napoleon and The Second Empire.* Oxford, 1956.
Contains a very brief summary of Napoleon's Mexican policy.

Verduin, Arnold Robert: *Modern Spanish Constitutions (1808–1931): A dissertation submitted in partial fulfillment of the requirements for the degree of Doctor of Philosophy in the University of Michigan.* Typescript, University of Michigan, 1934.
Contains a running survey of Spanish internal and foreign affairs. Based largely on Spanish published materials.

Weinberg, Albert K.: *Manifest Destiny: A Study of Nationalist Expansion in American History.* Baltimore, 1935.
The classic on the idea.

Wertheimer, Oskar Von: *Napoleon III. Abenteurer, Frauenheld, Cäsar.* Berlin, 1928.
Very skimpy on Mexico. Approvingly quotes from Jecker's letter to Conti of 1869.

West, W. Reed: *Contemporary French Opinion on the American Civil War.* (Johns Hopkins University Studies in Historical and Political Science XLII, No. 1). Baltimore, 1924.
The first part of Chapter VII briefly summarizes French newspaper opinion on Mexico in 1861–1862.

Willson, Beckles: *John Slidell and the Confederates in Paris, 1862–1865.* New York, 1932.
Popular. Chapter VIII contains background information on the Mexican expedition.

Zeldin, Theodore: *The Political System of Napoleon III*. London, 1958.
Mainly concerned with French internal politics. Based on prefect reports and private letter collections.

## Historical Articles

Callahan, J. M.: "The Mexican Policy of Southern Leaders Under Buchanan's Administration," *American Historical Association Annual Report, 1910*.
Gives a general account of the McLane-Ocampo treaties.

Corti, Count Caesar Egon: "Les Idées de l'Impératrice Eugénie sur le Redressement de la Carte de l'Europe, d'après des rapports du Prince Richard de Metternich," *Révue des Etudes Napoléoniennes: Les Origines de l'Europe Nouvelle*, IIe Année, II (1921), 147–155.
Eugenie's conversation with Metternich in 1863, when she told him how she would like to change the map of Europe.

Crenshaw, Ollinger: "The Knights of the Golden Circle. The Career of George Bickley," *American Historical Review*, XLVII (1941), 23–50.
The filibustering activities of Bickley, who founded the secret and military organization known as the Knights of the Golden Circle, that he wanted to use to Americanize and ultimately annex Mexico for the creation of more slave states.

Ferris, Nathan L.: "The Relations of the United States with South America during the American Civil War," *Hispanic American Historical Review*, XXI (1941), 51–78.
Finds that the propaganda of the Ministers from Washington to South America included the idea that the preservation of the Union was necessary for protection against foreign intervention in the New World.

Frazer, Robert W.: "Latin-American Projects to Aid Mexico During the French Intervention," *Hispanic American Historical Review*, XXVIII (1948), 377–388.
Based almost entirely on Romero's *Correspondencia de la Legacion Mexicana en Washington*. . . . Perus was the leader in formulating such projects, which failed, partly through the refusal of the United States to participate.

Golder, Frank A.: "The American Civil War through the Eyes of a Russian Diplomat," *American Historical Review*, XXVI (1921), 454–463.
In 1917 Golder was permitted to view the materials in the Russian archives up to 1870. He based this article on the correspondence of Edouard de Stoeckl, Russian Minister to Washington during the Civil War. Stoeckl's estimate of Lincoln and Seward was uncomplementary and unfair.

————: "The Russian Fleet and the Civil War," *American Historical Review*, XX (1915), 801–812.

Deflates the theory that the coming of the Russian fleet to the shores of the United States in 1863 was solely owing to Russian sympathy to the North during the Civil War. Shows that the Russian fleet was sseking safe harbors in case of a European war over the Polish question.

Johnson, Richard A.: "Spanish-Mexican Diplomatic Relations, 1853–1855," *Hispanic American Historical Review*, XXI (1941), 559–576.

Based on Spanish and Mexican printed works. An excellent study of the causes of Mexican-Spanish friction.

Jones, Wilbur Devereux: "The British Conservatives and the American Civil War," *American Historical Review*, LVIII (1953).

Challenges the theory that the British Conservatives had bonds of sympathy with the South and concludes their policy was based on party tradition and political expediency. Based largely on the Disraeli Papers.

Knapp, Jr., Frank A.: "Parliamentary Government and the Mexican Constitution of 1857: A Forgotten Phase of Mexican Political History," *Hispanic American Historical* Review, XXXIII (1953), 65–87.

Based on Spanish printed works. Good description of the development of cabinet government in Mexico in 1861. Interesting account of the rejection of the Wyke-Zamacona Treaty by the Mexican Congress.

Leonardon, H.: "L'Espagne et La Question Du Mexique, 1861–1867," *Annales des Sciences Politiques*, XVI (1901), 59–95.

Excellent study of Spanish policy toward Mexico, but the main emphasis is on General Prim. Based largely on papers presented to the Cortes.

Leroy-Bealieu, Anatole: "La Politique du Second Empire," *Revue des Deux Mondes*, 1 Apr 1872, pp. 536–572.

Concerned chiefly with Europe. Accuses Napoleon III of irresolution and lack of planning.

Mazade, Charles de: "La Question du Mexique dans le Parlement espagnol," *Revue des deux Mondes*, 15 Jan 1863, pp. 505–512.

Condemns the Spanish withdrawal from Mexico from the French viewpoint.

Pingaud, Albert: "La Politique Extérieure du Second Empire," *Revue Historique*, CLVI (1927), 41–68.

Circumspect on Napoleon III's foreign policy, based on secondary sources.

Robertson, William Spence: "Metternich's Attitude Towards Revolutions in Latin America," *Hispanic American Historical Review*, XXI 1941), 538–558.

Based on the *Haus-Hof-und Staatsarchiv* and the archives of the Ministry of Foreign Affairs in Paris. Concludes Metternich's attitude was in harmony with the principle of Legitimacy.

————: "The Tripartite Treaty of London," *Hispanic American Historical Review,* XX (1940), 167–189.

Attributes the breakdown of the treaty to the failure of the contracting parties to specify just how the intervention in Mexico would be carried out and French mental reservations. The author used the archives of the Public Record Office, particularly the series F.O. 146, the Embassy Archives of correspondence, including enclosures, of Lord Cowley, the British Ambassador to Paris. A week before the signing of the treaty, however, negotiations were shifted to London, and Robertson overlooked F.O. 50/358 ("Mexico. Domestic Various."), which contains draft treaties by Russell and Palmerston and their marginal comments. Although the Russell Papers and part of the Cowley Papers were available at the time Robertson did his research in 1931, he did not utilize these important sources. The author viewed the records of the French Ministry of Foreign Affairs, but overlooked or disregarded the French "Contre-Projet." Robertson was chiefly interested in the negotiation of the Tripartite Treaty of London and scarcely touches its breakdown. Complementary to Christian Schefer's study of the negotiation of the treaty, based solely on the archives of the French Ministry of Foreign Affairs.

Sears, Louis Martin: "A Confederate Diplomat at the Court of Napoleon III," *American Historical Review,* XXVI (1921), 255–281.

Slidell is the Confederate Diplomat. He tried to use Southern tolerance of Napoleon III's Mexican policy as an argument for French recognition of the Confederacy. Based on the Mason Papers, acquired by the Library of Congress in 1912. (The Slidell Papers have been destroyed).

Whitridge, Arnold: "The Trent Affair, 1861," *History Today,* IV (1954), 394–402.

A general account based on secondary sources.

Williams, Roger L.: "Louis Napoleon: A Tragedy of Good Intentions," *History Today,* IV (1954), 219–226.

Overemphasis on similarities between Louis Napoleon's early works and later policies of the Eecond Empire lead the author to the strained thesis that Napoleon III followed a preconceived plan.

Wilson, Howard L.: "President Buchanan's Proposed Intervention in Mexico," *American Historical Review,* V (1899–1900), 687–701.

Good general account based, however, on readily accessible sources.

Printed Materials Consulted

(Not Cited)

Adams, Ephriam Douglass: *Great Britain and the American Civil War.* 2 v., London, 1925.

Alvensleben, Baron Max. von: *With Maximilian in Mexico: From the Note-Book of a Mexican Officer, by Max., Baron Von Alvensleben, Late Lieutenant in the Imperial Mexican Army.* London, 1867.

Arnaud, René: *La Deuxième République et le Second Empire.* 3rd ed., Paris, 1929.

Arvin, Newton, ed.: *The Selected Letters of Henry Adams.* New York, 1951.

Auvergne, Edmund B. D.: *Napoleon The Third: A Biography.* London, 1929.

————: *The Coburgs: The Story of the Rise of a Great Royal House.* London, n.d.

Bac, Ferdinard: *Napoléon III Inconnu.* Paris, 1932

Bagger, Eugene: *Francis Joseph: Emperor of Austria—King of Hungary.* New York, 1927.

Bancroft, Hubert Howe: *A Popular History of the Mexican People.* London, 1888.

Bapst, Germain: Le Maréchal Canrobert. *Souvenirs d'un siècle.* 6 v., Paris, 1898–1899.

Barthez, Altoine Charles Ernest: *La Famille Impériale A Saint-Cloud et a Biarritz.* Paris, 1913.

Beard, Charles A. and Smith, G. H. E.: *The Idea of National Interest: An Analytical Study in American Foreign Policy.* New York, 1934.

Beauregard, Cte. D. De: *Etude et Revue de l'Histoire de Napoléon III: Jadis et Maintenant: D'Après les matériaux et les documents les plus authentiques.* Nice, 1903.

Bemis, S. F.: *The Latin American Policy of the United States: An Historical Interpretation.* New York, 1943.

Benoist, Charles: *L'Espagne, Cuba et les Etats-Unis.* Paris, 1898.

Bertaut, Jules: *Napoléon III Secret.* Paris, 1939.

Blanchard, Marcel: *Le Second Empire.* Paris, 1950.

Bloomfield, Baroness Georgiana: *Reminescences of Court and Diplomatic Life, by Georgiana Baroness Bloomfield.* 2 v., London, 1883.

Bulle, C.: *Geschichte Des Zweiten Kaiserreiches und des Königreiches Italien,* (Theil 3 of Haupt Abtheilung IV of Wilhelm Oncken: *Allgemeine Geschichte in Einzeldarstellungen).* Berlin, 1890.

Brooks, Graham: *Napoleon III.* London, 1936.

Bulloch, James D.: *The Secret Service of the Confederate States in Europe, or, How the Confederate Cruisers were Equipped.* 2 v., London, 1883.

Bulwer, Sir Henry Lytton (Lord Dalling): *The Life of Henry John Temple, Viscount Palmerston: with Selections from his Diaries and Correspondence.* 3 v., London, 1870–1874.

Cadogan, Edward: *Makers of Modern History: Three Types: Louis Napoleon—Cavour—Bismarck.* London, 1905.

Callahan, James Morton: *The Diplomatic History of the Southern Confederacy.* Baltimore, 1901.

Cecil, Algernon: *Queen Victoria and Her Prime Ministers.* London, 1953.

Chadwick, French Ensor: *The Relations of the United States and Spain: Diplomacy.* New York, 1909.

Chapman, J. M. and Brian, *The Life and Times of Baron Haussmann: Paris in the Second Empire.* London, 1957.

Charles-Roux, Francois: *Alexandre II, Gortchakoff et Napoléon III.* Paris, 1913.

Clapp, Margaret: *Forgotten First Citizen: John Bigelow.* Boston, 1947.

Dansette, Adrien: *Les Amours de Napoléon III.* Paris, 1938.

Daudet, Alphonse: *Trente ans de Paris: A Traverse Ma Vie et Mes Livres.* Paris, 1888.

Daudet, Ernest: *Une Vie D'Ambassadrice Au Siècle Dernier: La Princesse de Lieven.* New ed., Paris, 1933.

Daudet, Lucien: *Dans L'Ombre de l'Impératrice Eugénie: Lettres Intime Adressé à Madame Alphonse Daudet.* 4th ed., Paris, 1935.

Dennet, Tyer, ed.: *Lincoln and the Civil War in the Diaries and Letters of John Hay.* New York, 1939.

Dubose, John Witherspoon: *The Life and Times of William Lowndes Yancey: A History of Political Parties in the United States, from 1834 to 1864. Especially as to the Origin of the Confederate States.* Birmingham, 1892.

Du Camp, Maxime: *Maxime Du Camp's Literary Recollections.* 2 v., London, 1893.

Dulles, Foster Rhea: *The Road to Teheran: The Story of Russia and America, 1781–1943.* Princeton, 1945.

Ebeling, Adolph: *Napoleon III und sein Hof: Denkwürdigkeiten, Erlebnisse und Erinnerungen aus der Zeit des Zweiten französischen Kaiserreichs, 1851–1870 von Adolph Ebeling.* 2 v., Cologne and Leipzig, 1891–1894.

Einstein, Lewis: *Napoleon III and American Diplomacy at the Outbreak of the Civil War: An Address read in French before the Société d'Histoire Diplomatique at Paris on the Ninth of June, 1905.* London, 1905.

Engel-Jánosi, F.: *Graf Rechberg: Vier Kapitel zu Seinen Und Osterreichs Geschichte.* Munich and Berlin, 1927.

Filon, Augustin: *Souvenirs sur l'Impératrice Eugénie.* Paris, 1920.

Fleury, Comte and Sonolet, Louis: *La Société du Second Empire.* 4 v., Paris, 1911–1924.

Forbes, Archibald: *The Life of Napoleon The Third.* London, 1898.

Friedjung, Henrich: *The Struggle for Supremacy in Germany, 1859–1866.* New York, 1935.

Friese, Christian: *Russland und Preussen vom Krimkrieg bis zum Polnischen Aufstand.* Berlin, 1931.

Gooch, G. P. and Ward, Sir A. W., eds.: *The Cambridge History of British Foreign Policy, 1783–1919.* 3 v., London, 1922–1923.

Grabinski, Comte Joseph: *Un Ami de Napoleon III: Le Comte Arese et La Politique Italienne Sous le Second Empire.* Paris, 1897.

Granier de Cassagnac, A.: *Souvenirs du Second Empire.* 3 v., Paris, 1879–1882.

Guedalla, Philip: *Palmerston*. London, 1926.

Guériot, Paul: *Napoleon III*. 2 v., Paris, 1933–1934.

Hallberg, Charles W.: *Franz Joseph and Napoleon III, 1852–1864. A Study of Austro-French Relations*. New York, 1955.

Halt, Robert, ed.: *Papiers sauvées Des Tuileries Suite A La Correspondance de La Famille Imperiale*. Paris, 1871.

Hanna, Alfred J. and Kathryn Abbey: "The Immigration Movement of the Intervention and Empire as Seen Through the Mexican Press," *Hispanic American Historical Review*, XXVII (1947), 247–268.

Harcourt, Comte Bernard D.': *Les Quatres Ministères de M. Drouyn de Lhuys*. Paris, 1882.

Hellwald, Friedrich von: *Maximilian I. Kaiser von Mexico. Sein Leben, Wirken und sein tod, nebst einem Abriss der Geschichte Mexico's*. 2 v., Vienna, 1869.

Hoetzsch, Otto, ed.: *Peter von Meyendorff: Ein russischer Diplomat An den Höfen von Berlin und Wien: Politischer und Privater Briefwechsel, 1826–1863*. 3 v., Berlin and Leipzig, 1923.

Kirwan, A. V.: *Modern France: Its Journalism, Literature and Society*. London, 1863.

La Gorce, Pierre de: *Au Temps du Second Empire*. Paris, 1935.

————: *Napoleon III et Sa Politique*. 7th ed., Paris, 1933.

Lano, Pierre de: *Le Secret d'Un Empire: L'Empereur Napoleon III*, Paris, 1893.

Legge, Edward: *The Comedy and Tragedy of the Second Empire: Paris Society in the Sixties, including letters of Napoleon III, M. Pietri, and Comte de La Chapelle, and Portraits of the Period*. London and New York, 1911.

Lesseps, Ferdinand de: *Recollections of Forty Years*, trans. C. B. Pitman. 2 v., London 1887.

Lesueur, Emile: *Le Prince de la Tour d'Auvergne et le Secret de l'Imperatrice: Contribution a l'histoire diplomatique du Second Empire*. Paris, 1930.

Loftus, Lord Augustus: *The Diplomatic Reminiscences of Lord Augustus Loftus, 1837–1862*. 2 v., Leipzig, 1892.

Loliée, Frédéric: *Women of the Second Empire: Chronicles of the Court of Napoleon III, compiled from unpublished documents*, trans. Alice M. Ivimy. London, 1907.

Malo, Henri: *Thiers 1797–1877*. Paris, 1932.

Margutti, Albert Lieutenant-General Baron Von: *The Emperor Francis Joseph and His Times*. London, 1921.

Martin, Henri: *Histoire de France Depis 1789 Jusqu'a Nos Jours*. 8 v., Paris, 1878–1885.

Masseras, E.: *Un Essai d'Empire au Mexique*. Paris, 1879.

Maupas, M. de: *Mémoires sur Le Second Empire*. 2 v., Paris, 1884–1885.

Maurain Jean: *La Politique Ecclesiasticue du Second Empire de 1852 A 1869*. Paris, 1930.

Maurain, Jean: *Un Bourgeois Francais Au XIXe Siècle: Baroche, Ministre de Napoléon III, daprès ses papiers inédits.* Paris, 1936.

Muraour, Emile: *Le Mexique: Conqûête du Mexique par Fernand Cortez; Guerre de l'Indépendence et Republique; Expédition francaise au Mexique, 1861–1863.* Paris, 1863.

Murray, Robert Hammond, ed.: *Maximilian, Emperor of Mexico: Memoirs of his Private Secretary, José Luis Blasio.* New Haven, 1934.

Oliphant, M. O. W., Mrs.: *Memoir of Count De Montalembert, Peer of France, Deputy for the Department of Doubs: A Chapter of Recent French History.* 2 v., Leipzig, 1872.

Ollendorff, Paul, ed.: *Extrait Des Mémoires du Duc De Morny: Une Ambassade en Russie, 1856.* Paris, 1892.

Paléologue, Maurice: *Tragic Empress: The Story of Elizabeth of Austria,* trans. H. J. Stenning. London, 1950.

Palm, Franklin Charles: *England and Napoleon III: A Study of the Rise of a Utopian Dictator.* Durham, N.C., 1948.

Raindre, Gaston: "Les Papiers inédits du Comte Walewski: Souvenirs et Correspondance. 1855–1868," *La Revue de France,* 1 Jan 1925, pp. 74–104; 1 Feb 1925, pp. 485–511; 1 Mar 1925, pp. 39–56; 15 May 1925, pp. 281–305; 1 Jul 1925, pp. 82–96; 15 Jul 1925, pp. 311–326.

Reclus, Maurice: *Ernest Picard, 1821–1877. Essai de Contribution à L'Histoire du Parti Républicain d'après des documents inédits. Thèse Complèmentaire Présentée à la Faculté des Lettres de Toulouse.* Paris, 1912.

Redlich, Joseph: *Emperor Francis Joseph of Austria: A Biography.* New York, 1929.

Reeve, Henry, ed.: *The Greville Memoirs (Third Part): A Journal of the Reign of Queen Victoria from 1852 to 1860 by the Late Charles C. F. Greville, Esq., Clerk of the Council.* 2 v., London.

Reid, Stuart J., ed.: *The Prime Ministers of Queen Victoria.* New ed., 9 v., London, 1905–1906.

Rippy, J. Fred: *Latin America in World Politics: An Outline Survey.* New York, 1926.

Robertson, C. G.: *Bismarck.* New York, 1919.

Robertson, William Spence: *France and Latin-American Independence.* Baltimore, 1939.

Russell, John Earl: *Recollections and Suggestions, 1813–1873.* London, 1875.

Salm-Salm, Agnes, Prinzessin zu: *Ten Years of My Life.* 2 v., London, 1875–1876.

Saunders, Edith: *The Age of Worth: Courturier to the Empress Eugénie.* London, New York, Toronto, 1954.

Schnerb, Robert: *Rouher et le Second Empire.* Paris, 1949.

Seignobos, Ch.: *La Révolution de 1884—Le Second Empire (1848–1859).* (Vol. VI of Ernest Lavisse, ed.: *L'Histoire de France Contemporaine depuis La Révolution jusqu'à La Paix de 1919).* Paris, 1921.

————: *Le Déclin de L'Empire et L'Establissement de La Troisième Republique (1859–1875)*. (Vol. VII of Ernest Lavisse, ed.: *L'Histoire de France Contemporaine*. . . .)

Simpson, F. A.: *Louis Napoleon and the Recovery of France*. 3rd ed., London, 1951.

Simpson, M. C. M., Mrs.: *Many Memories of Many People*. London, 1898.

Smith, Monroe: *Bismarck and German Unity*. New York, 1923.

Stockmar, Baron: *Memoirs of Baron Stockmar by His Son, Baron E. Von Stockmar*, ed. F. Max. Muller, 2 v., London, 1873.

Stoddart, Jane T.: *The Life of the Empress Eugenie*. London, 1906.

Sybel, Heinrich von: *The Founding of the German Empire by William I, based Chiefly upon Prussian State Documents*, trans. Marshall Livingstone Perrin. 7 v., New York, 1890–1898.

Sybik, Heinrich; Ritter von: *Deutsche Einheit: Idee und Wirklichkeit von Heiligen Reich bis Königgratz*. 4 v., Munich, 1935–1942.

Taylor, A. J. P.: *The Struggle for Mastery in Europe, 1848–1918*. (Oxford History of Modern Europe). Oxford, 1954.

Thouvenel, L., ed.: *Pages de l'Histoire du Second Empire D'Après les Papiers de M. Thouvenel, Ancien Ministre des Affaires Etrangères (1854–1866)*. Paris, 1903.

Tschuppik, Karl: *The Reign of the Emperor Francis Joseph, 1848–1916*, trans. C. J. S. Sprigge. London, 1930.

Vanel, Gabriel: *Le Second Empire, Souvenirs d'Un Contemporain*. Caen, 1936.

Walpole, Spencer: *The Life of Lord John Russell*. 2v., London, 1889.

Weil, Georges: "Les Saint-Simoniens Sous Napoleon III," *Révue des Etudes Napoléoniennes*, 2e Année, III (1913), 391–406.

Wencker-Wildberg, Friedrich: *Eugenie: Die letzte Kaiserin der Franzosen*. Hamburg, 1937.

Whitaker, Arthur Preston: *The United States and the Independence of Latin America, 1800–1830*. Baltimore, 1941.

# Index

## A

Aberdeen, Lord, 26
Adams, Charles Francis, 164, 165, 168, 170, 174, 268
Aláman, Louis, 486
Albert, Prince, 360
Aldham, Captain, 62, 63, 69, 75, 78, 89, 107, 169, 456, 473
Almonte, Juan Nepomucene, 41, 42, 46, 47, 50, 125, 127, 236, 237, 281–286, 290, 340, 348–354, 358, 359, 386, 395, 396, 404–427, 431, 436–440, 449, 451, 487–490, 528, 558–562
Alvarez, 591
Andrade, 352
Antonelli, Cardinal, 282, 283
Apponyi, 362, 363, 365
Arrangiz, Francisco de, 571

## B

Bach, Baron, 283
Baker, Philip, 311, 312
Barclay, Richardson & Co., 458
Barrot, 146, 175, 190, 191, 208, 210, 224, 225, 337, 342, 366, 371, 373, 378, 383, 394–401, 523
Baudin, Admiral, 142
Bazancount, 589
Beale, 79, 80, 138
Bell, 344
Beyens, Baron Napoléon, 157, 239, 251, 360, 378, 395

Bismarck, 438
Bloomfield, Lord, 181, 353, 354, 360, 362–365
Bodmer, 66
Boulenger, Marcel, 483
Buchanan, President, 35–37, 46, 56, 444
Burke, Ulick Ralph, 490
Bustamente, 25

## C

Callahan, 8
Cambridge, Duke of, 27
Camyn, 136
Casanova, General, 95, 100
Casanova, Mrs., 103
Case, Lynn M., 9, 477
Cass, 34, 35, 37, 72
Castillon, M., 595
Castro, 359
Catholic Church, 280, 285, 290, 350–352, 446, 576, 577
Cautelenne, Colonel, 412, 413, 417
Cavour, Camillo, 160
Ceballos, Juan A. L. de, 570
Cenobio, General, 567
Chapman, Maristan, 483
Charles, Archduke of Austrian, 25
Charlotte, Archduchess, 6, 156, 181, 184, 290, 438
Chasseloup-Laubat, 128
Christophe, Robert, 483
Claremont, Colonel, 346, 347

793

Clarendon, Lord, 27, 30, 31, 38, 39, 157
Collantes, Calderon, 35, 42, 43, 55, 56, 124, 125, 143–147, 177–190, 208, 209, 224, 225, 241, 246–253, 265, 338, 345–348, 355–359, 371–373, 378, 383, 393–395, 398–405, 449, 488–490, 525–531
Conti, 476, 483
Corpancho, Manuel Nicolas, 267
Cortes, Hernan, 178
Cortez, Ferdinand, 250, 338, 485
Corti, Egon Caesar, 6, 8
Corwin, Thomas, 78, 84, 87, 104, 115–121, 162, 269, 270, 408
Cowley, Lord, 7, 30, 45, 122, 123, 128, 132, 133, 137, 141–157, 161–168, 170–189, 191–199, 214, 222–227, 240, 246, 272, 286, 337–347, 354, 360–362, 366–368, 374–376, 382–386, 391, 392, 399, 402, 430–437, 442, 449–451, 480, 498–500
Crampton, 144–149, 151–154, 166, 167, 175–178, 192, 214–217, 245, 246, 348, 355–357, 399, 400, 430, 432

D

Dacres, Admiral, 387
D'Albe, Duchesse, 44, 126
D'Aumale, Duc, 29–31, 40, 45, 158
Dawson, Daniel, 68, 131, 132, 482, 483
Dayton, 168
De Chevardier, 589, 593–595, 597
Degollado, General, 60, 69, 76, 82
de la Gravière (see Jurien)
del Bosch, Milans, 315
de Lhuys, Drouyn, 440, 441
de Lorencez, General, 341, 343, 347, 379, 395, 396, 405, 408, 410, 412–420, 424, 439–441, 579, 580, 586
del Rio, Martinez, 454–457
Doazan, 584
Doblado, General Manuel, 93, 113–

115, 279, 307–320, 324–333, 378, 381, 382, 389–390, 406–414, 427, 428, 544–554, 566
Don Juan, Enfant, 28, 572
Douay, General, 589
Doyle, Convention, 453–456
Du Camp, Maxine, 480
Dunlop, Hugh, 53, 62, 69, 75, 89, 278, 280, 293, 295–299, 301, 303–309, 312–314, 317–319, 324–327, 334, 348, 382, 386–389, 394, 405–412, 423, 426, 428, 430, 449, 455, 456, 473, 474, 538, 544, 570

E

Echeverria, Gonzales, 325, 326, 334, 416, 417, 419, 564
Elio, General, 126
Elsesser, 60, 477, 478, 579
Escaudon, Don Manuel, 85
Estrada, Don Jose Maria Gutierrez de, 25–31, 125, 126, 130–132, 159, 161, 182–185, 236, 276, 278, 281–292, 340, 341, 349–353, 364, 375, 377, 411, 572
Estrada, Fernando, 282
Eugenie, Empress, 9, 28, 43–46, 126, 127, 154–159, 185, 223, 236, 237, 282, 284, 338, 341, 352, 360, 376–379, 399, 402, 436, 438, 445, 446, 451, 452, 476, 480, 483

F

Farlane, 180
Fernandez, M. (Miramon), 292, 313
Filibustering, 38, 116
Fillmore, President, 115
Flahault, Count, 145–149, 160, 161, 168, 185–189, 196–201, 209–214, 222, 228, 238, 241, 242, 254, 342, 346, 354, 363, 369, 387–391, 396, 431, 446, 495–497, 509, 510, 514, 518–520
Flandres, Duc de, 356

Fleury, Comte, 45, 157, 236, 378, 452

Forey, General, 440, 579, 584, 588, 597

Forsyth, John, 32–34, 46

Fossey, 587, 590, 595

Fould, Achille, 271

Foussemagne, Countess Reinach, 6

Franz Joseph, Emperor, 154, 180–182, 184, 286, 288, 289, 339, 352, 353, 364

Frederick, Archduke, 27

Fuente, De La, 129, 130, 135, 136, 139, 140


G

Gabriac, Comte de, 29, 30, 40, 41, 43, 46, 47, 49, 50, 59, 60, 98

Gadsden, James, 33

Garde, Richard, 261, 262

Garruste-Labadie & Co., 492

Gasset, General, 114, 274, 275, 355

Glennie, 61, 66, 456, 457

Goldschmidt, B. A. & Co., 458

Gortchakov, 265

Gramont, Duc de, 353

Gravière (see Jurien)

Guerard, Albert, 482, 483

Gutierrez (see Estrada)

Guzman, Don Leon, 73, 75, 102–105


H

Hammond, 138, 140, 150, 179, 197, 213, 214, 241, 309, 382, 457, 505–509

Harding, Mrs., 479

Hendrick, Burton Jesse, 8

Hidalgo y Esnaurrizar, Jose Manuel, 27, 28, 31, 43–47, 56, 125, 126, 154–159, 185, 223, 236, 237, 281–286, 290, 339–343, 351, 352, 375, 437, 443, 449, 451, 571–578

Hottinguer, 478

House of Commons, 470

Hübner, Baron, 157

Humboldt, 595

I

Isabella II, 251, 264, 429, 432, 498, 505, 510, 514, 517

Isturiz, Xavier de, 178, 209, 211, 213, 241, 242, 337, 356, 357, 517–520

Iturbide, D. Augustin, 461


J

Jecker bonds, 60, 67, 78, 97–104, 123, 128–133, 300–302, 384, 388–393, 423, 436, 445, 475–484

Jecker correspondence, 579–597

Joinville, Prince de, 142

Juarez, Benito, 33, 35–38, 41, 42, 46, 54, 58, 61, 62, 72, 83, 93–95, 104, 106, 110–113, 118, 122–126, 226–229, 250–252, 260, 278–280, 285, 312, 315, 372, 373, 389, 394–396, 403, 406, 408, 416, 421, 426, 428, 438, 444, 445, 451, 455, 456, 488, 526, 567, 579, 580, 592

Jurien, de la Gravière, 223–237, 241–244, 254, 255, 277–280, 288–309, 312, 313, 317–319, 324–328, 332, 333, 336, 366–368, 375–380, 388, 389, 393–396, 407–421, 425–431, 442, 448–451, 521, 528, 538, 544, 560–562, 584, 593


K

Keraltry, Comte Emile de, 481, 482

"King Cotton Diplomacy," 273

King of Prussia, 177, 265


L

Labastida, Mgr. de, 282, 283, 286–288, 290, 340, 349–352

Lacroix, 584

La Gorce, 6

Lapierre, 581, 583

Larrien, Admiral, 280, 323

Layard, 241, 242

Leon, Porfirio, 111

Leonardon, H., 5, 8

Leopold, King, 184, 186, 187, 239,

284, 290, 352, 356, 359, 360, 446, 449, 497

Lerdo de Tejada, Sebastian, 89, 90

Lettsom, 29, 30, 49

Lewis, Sir George, 244

Lincoln, Abraham, 149, 156, 259, 263, 267, 268, 271, 273

Lizardi, F. de & Co., 459, 460–467

Londe, Comte A. De La, 570

Lorencez, General (see de Lorencez)

Louet, Ernest, 478

Louis Philippe, 27, 30, 595

Lyons, Lord, 39, 77, 81, 121, 162, 220, 270

M

McCalmont, Brothers, & Co., 261, 262

McLane, Robert M., 35–37, 47

McLane–Ocampo Treaty, 39, 46, 54–57, 444

Maitland, Admiral, 218, 243, 244, 280, 322–324

Malmesbury, Lord, 41, 43, 50–53, 62, 134, 470–472

Mangin, Commandant, 412, 418

"Manifest Destiny," 32, 33, 38, 118, 119

Manning & Mackintosh & Co., 466

Marie Louise, 155

Marpon, M. de, 475, 476

Marquez, General, 61, 73, 76, 77, 79, 80, 82, 103, 108, 113, 148, 276, 277, 409, 567

Mason, 270, 271

Mata, 101

Mathew, 53–58, 61–94, 103, 104, 123, 128, 280

Maury, 48

Maximilian, Archduke, 5, 69, 113, 127, 154, 159, 175, 180–184, 190, 235, 266, 281–284, 287–289, 339, 340, 349–354, 364, 379, 386, 403, 427, 437, 438, 441, 443, 445, 446, 448, 449, 452, 477, 495

Maximilian and Carlota of Mexico, The Story of, 479

Menduinas, Colonel, 297

Metternich, 6, 25, 26, 130, 132, 158, 160, 161, 182, 183, 231–234, 238, 283, 286–290, 340, 352, 354, 360, 361, 364, 379, 441, 449, 450

Milne, Admiral, 139, 220–222, 242, 243, 271, 274, 278, 293, 298, 314, 387, 406, 423, 430

Miramon, 35, 36, 54, 57–59, 79, 94, 99, 122, 124, 129, 245, 249, 276, 285, 286, 291–301, 312–314, 324, 386, 387, 394, 404, 488, 567

Miranda, Padre, 276, 278, 283, 287, 288, 290, 291, 343, 375, 404, 411, 427, 567

Mirandoi, General, 591

Modena, Duke of, 126, 132, 158

Mon, 145–147, 150, 188–191, 488, 489, 528

Monroe Doctrine, 27, 29, 32–36, 47, 167, 171, 255, 259, 269, 443, 577

Montijo, Countess of, 28

Montluc, Armand de, 47

Montpensier, Duke of, 158

Mora, Jose Luis, 463

Moran, William, 92

Morny, Duc de, 99, 475–478, 480–484

Muelinen, Count, 161, 182, 183, 185, 222, 282

Murat, Prince Lucien, 595

Murphy, Tomas, 29, 125, 136, 463

N

Napoleon III, 6, 9, 29–31, 43–47, 69, 99, 100, 112, 113, 126–135, 154–162, 177, 182–187, 197–199, 203, 204, 210, 213, 222–226, 228, 231–239, 255, 271–273, 285, 288, 289, 303, 315, 321, 338–343, 347, 348, 352, 354, 360, 364, 367, 375–380, 384–386, 395, 399, 402, 404, 408–410, 416, 419, 431, 432, 436–443, 445–452, 477, 480, 495–497, 575

O

Ocampo, 36, 37, 76, 103
O'Donnell, Marshal, 144, 151, 152, 165, 166, 175, 176, **188**, **214**, 217, 224, 225, 230, 250–253, 274, 291, 337, 348, 355–358, 362, 371, 398–401, 405, 432, 446, 449
Ollivier, Emile, 5
Ortega, General, 108
Osegura, Andres, 136
Otway, 48–53, 68, 77, 81, 89, 455, 456, 471, 472
Owsley, Frank L., 8

P

Pacheco, 94–96, 124, 125, 136, 248, 249, 265, 285, 487, 488
Padre Moran Convention, 453–455, 488
Pakenham, 453
Palacio, 73, 106
Palmerston, 7, 9, 27, 45, 68, 69, 126–129, 138, 140, 146–149, 152–154, 162–173, 180, 185, 189, 192, 196, 202, 212, **221**– 222, 232, 238–241, 244, 261, 265, 270–273, 290, 341–344, 363, 370, 445, 446, 448, 449, 470, 495, 505–509
Parma, Duke of, 158
Payno, 468
Penaud, Admiral, 141
Pereire, Emile and Isaac, 480
Perkins, Dexter, 8
Perry, Edward, 456, 457
Persigny, 157
Philip II, 341
Pickett, John, 115–121
Polk, President, 33
Pope Pius IX, 285, 352
Powles' petition, 259–261
Prévost-Paradol, 255
Prim, General Juan, 9, 42, 133, 136, 237, 242, 246–254, 263, 276–280, 291–334, 343, 345, 358, 365, 366, 369–380, 383, 384, 388, 394–419, 422–429,
437, 448, 449, 451, 452, 488– 490, 525–531, 588

Q

Queen Isabella II, 251, 264, 429, 432
Queen Victoria, 51, 52, 127, 159, 167, 168, 187, 240, 244, 352, 360, 429, 431, 446, 498, 505, 510, 514, 517, 525

R

Radepont, Marquis de, 29–31
Rafael Rafael, 288–290
Rainer, Archduke, 159
Raiss, 587, 590, 595
Ramirez, Fernando, 486
Randon, 440, 452
Receveur, M. Le, 592, 594, 595
Rechberg, Count, 130–132, 161, 180–187, 222, 266, 283–289, 352, 353, 360, 363–365
Reichtoffen, 595
Reus, El Sonde de (see Prim), 358, 538, 544–553, 555–570
Revolutions of 1848, 27
Ribera, Marques de la, 486
Riddle, Dr., 120
Rieche, M., 103, 105
Rippy, 8
Robertson, David, 7, 134, 261
Robertson, William P., 469, 472
Robinson, 461
Robles, General, 113, 114, 307, 308, 378, 389, 409, 418–420
Romero, Mathias, 267
Rothschild, 289
Roze, 584
Rubalcava, Admiral, 274
Russell, Lord John, 7, 9, 43, 53– 57, 61–78, 80–86, 110, 122– 128, 132–154, 161–180, 187– 203, 209, 211–224, 227, 238–246, 252, 254, 260–262, 266, 271– 276, 296, 298–302, 309, 312, 320, 328, 336–338, 342–348, 353–367, 360–365, 368, 369– 376, 381–383, 386–394, 397, 399–405, 423, 429–431, 436,

445–450, 456, 457, 473, 474, 502–510, 514, 517–520, 584

**S**

Santa Anna, 28, 29, 32, 236, 281, 283, 287–290, 292, 340, 349–353, 377, 572

Saligny, Dubois de, 46, 59–62, 74, 78, 79, 83–115, 122–125, 128–135, 139, 141–145, 158, 224, 225, 229–237, 276, 279, 280, 293, 295, 297, 300–303, 306–313, 317–325, 332–339, 366–368, 371, 375–379, 383–385, 388–396, 407–412, 419, 424–431, 439–441, 448–451, 476–480, 483, 484, 491, 528, 538, 544, 579–584, 592, 597

Schefer, Christian, 8, 478

Schertzenlechner, Sebastian, 281, 285, 286, 290

Schneider & Co., 465

Schurz, Carl, 251–254

Sears, 8

Sebastian, Don, 251

Serrano, General Francisco, 236, 263, 276, 285, 291, 292, 337, 527

Seward, William H., 116, 119–121, 149, 162, 164, 267–273, 441, 448

Sisters of Charity, 79, 95, 96, 105, 123

Slaughter, Lt. Charles, 313

Slidell, John, 270, 271, 481

Somerset, Duke of, 166, 243

Sprague, Thomas, 116

Stevenson, Sara Yorke, 478

**T**

Tapia, Don Santiago, 117

Teba family, 28

Teran, Don Jesus, 417, 419, 564

Tetuan, Marechal Duc de, 523

Thomasset, Captain, 315, 321, 322, 377, 419

Thouvenel, 9, 46, 56, 58, 59, 86, 94, 98, 99, 106, 110–112, 122, 123, 128–130, 133–154, 160–

177, 179, 187–191, 197–202, 211–215, 222–233, 239–246, 252–254, 272, 273, 303, 308, 318, 337–343, 346, 347, 354, 361, 364–369, 374–377, 382–384, 387–396, 399–402, 408, 409, 412, 413, 424, 427, 436–438, 446, 449, 451, 478, 479, 521

Toombs, 117

Trent Affair, 270, 271, 278

**U**

Uraga, José, 113, 114, 278, 307, 308, 314, 378, 409, 567

**V**

Valazé, Colonel, 347, 370, 586

Valle, General, 76

Vandam, Albert, 481

Victoria (see Queen Victoria)

Von Donop, Captain, 274

**W**

Wagner, Baron, 104, 108, 109, 377, 412, 438

Wagner, Fritz, 10

Walewski, Count, 30, 31, 39, 160, 161, 222, 481

Walker, William, 38, 116

Walsham, John, 570

Washington's Farewell Address, 269

Whitehead, 61, 75, 88, 134, 135

Wilkes, Captain, 270

William I, 177, 265

Woll, General, 591

Worrall, Thomas, 92, 93

Wyke, Sir Charles, 63–94, 102–111, 114, 115, 120, 123–127, 129–139, 141–145, 159, 169, 172, 196, 211, 218–224, 227, 232, 242–245, 261, 266, 274, 276–281, 293–310, 312–314, 317–325, 328, 332, 334, 339, 344, 348, 366, 369–376, 381, 382, 388–394, 397, 406–410, 414, 417–419, 422, 423, 425, 428–430, 445, 449, 454, 456,

457, 473, 504, 528, 532, 536, 538, 544, 561–569, 586, 591

**Z**

Zamaconia, Manuel Maria de, 79, 83–91, 93, 106–112, 318, 319, 532, 536

Zaragoza, General, 327, 328, 419, 421, 545, 559, 570

Zarco, Francisco, 64–66, 72, 73, 95–102, 104, 105, 128, 129, 491

Zuloaga, President, 33–35, 40–43, 51, 54, 76, 113, 276, 409, 478, 567